THE RADICAL RIGHT

THE RADICAL RIGHT

Third Edition

Daniel Bell, editor

With a new introduction by **David Plotke**

Afterword by **Daniel Bell**

Transaction Publishers
New Brunswick (U.S.A.) and London (U.K.)

Second printing 2008

New material this edition copyright © 2002 by Transaction Publishers, New Brunswick, New Jersey. Originally published in 1955 by Criterion Books.

This book is printed on acid-free paper that meets the American National Standard for Permanence of Paper for Printed Library Materials.

Library of Congress Catalog Number: 00-062927
ISBN: 978-0-7658-0749-6
Printed in the United States of America

Library of Congress Cataloging-in-Publication Data

New American right.
    The radical right / Daniel Bell, editor ; with a new introduction by David Plotke, and an afterword by Daniel Bell.—3rd ed.
        p. cm.
    Original title: The new American right.
    Includes bibliographical references and index.
    ISBN: 978-0-7658-0749-6 (pbk : alk. paper)
        1. United States—Politics and government—1953-1961.
    2. United States—Politics and government—1961-1963. 3. Conservatism—United States. 4. Right and left (Political science)
    I. Bell, Daniel. II. Title.

E835 .B4 2000
320.973'09'045—dc21   00-062927

Interpretations of American Politics, by Daniel Bell; *The Pseudo-Conservative Revolt,* by Richard Hofstadter; *The Intellectuals and the Discontented Classes,* by David Riesman and Nathan Glazer; *The Revolt Against the Elite,* by Peter Viereck; *Social Strains in America,* by Talcott Parsons; and *The Sources of the "Radical Right,"* by Seymour Martin Lipset, originally appeared in a hardcover edition under the title *The New American Right,* which was published in 1955 by Criterion Books. *The Radical Right,* an expanded and updated version of *The New American Right,* was originally published in hardcover by Doubleday & Company, Inc., in 1963, by arrangement with Criterion Books.

CONTENTS

THE CONTRIBUTORS

DANIEL BELL is Henry Ford II Professor of Social Science Emeritus at Harvard University and currently Scholar-in-Residence at the American Academy of Arts and Sciences. He is the author/editor of eighteen books. Among these are *The Coming of Post-Industrial Society*, *The End of Ideology*, and *The Cultural Contradictions of Capitalism*, the latter two being named by the *Times Literary Supplement* (London) in 1995 as among the one hundred most influential books published since the end of World War II.

RICHARD HOFSTADTER (1916-1970) was De Witt Clinton Professor of American History at Columbia University and Pitt Professor in American History at Cambridge University. He was the author of the Pulitzer Prize-winning *The Age of Reform*, and, among other books, *The American Political Tradition* and *Anti-Intellectualism in American Life*.

DAVID RIESMAN is Henry Ford II Professor of Social Science Emeritus at Harvard University. He was Professor of Social Science at the University of Chicago, and a visiting professor at Yale. His books include *The Lonely Crowd*, *Individualism Reconsidered*, *Thorstein Veblen*, and *Constraint and Variety in American Education*.

NATHAN GLAZER is Professor Emeritus at the Graduate School of Education, Harvard University, and co-editor of *The Public Interest*. He has taught at the University of California at Berkeley and Columbia University. His books include *The Lonely Crowd*, *Beyond the Melting Pot*, *The Social Basis of American Communism*, and *We Are All Multiculturalists Now*.

PETER VIERECK is Professor of Modern History Emeritus at Mount Holyoke College. Among his writings in the history of ideas are *Metapolitics: From the Romantics to Hitler*, *Conservatism Revisited*, *The Shame and Glory of the Intellectuals*, *The Unadjusted Man*, and

Conservatism. He is the author of numerous books of poetry, including *Terror and Decorum* and *Tide and Continuities: Last and First Poems, 1995-1938.*

TALCOTT PARSONS (1907-1979) was Professor of Sociology at Harvard University, and a member of that department from its inception in 1931. He was a past president of the American Sociological Association. His major works include *The Structure of Social Action, The Social System,* and *Toward a General Theory of Action* (with Edward Shils).

ALAN F. WESTIN is Professor of Public Law and Government (retired) at Columbia University. His books include *The Changing Workplace, Individual Rights in the Corporation, The Anatomy of a Constitutional Law Case, The Supreme Court: Views from the Inside,* and *The Uses of Power.*

HERBERT H. HYMAN (1918-1985) was Professor of Sociology at Wesleyan University and Columbia University (1951-1969). He was President of the American Association for Public Opinion Research and recipient of its Julian Woodward Memorial Award for Distinguished Achievement. He was visiting professor at the University of Oslo and the University of Ankara. His books include *Survey Design and Analysis, Interviewing in Social Research,* and *Political Socialization.*

SEYMOUR MARTIN LIPSET is a senior fellow at the Hoover Institution and Hazel Professor of Public Policy at George Mason University. Previously he was the Caroline S.G. Munro Professor of Political Science and Sociology at Stanford University (1975-90) and the George D. Markham Professor of Government and Sociology at Harvard University. He is the author of *Political Man, Agrarian Socialism, Union Democracy* (with James Coleman and Martin Trow), *Social Mobility in Industrial Society* (with Reinhard Bendix), *American Exceptionalism,* and numerous other books.

DAVID PLOTKE is Associate Professor of Political Science at the Graduate Faculty of New School University. He is the author of *Building a Democratic Political Order: Reshaping American Liberalism in the 1930s and 1940s.*

Introduction to the Transaction Edition (2001)

THE SUCCESS AND ANGER OF THE MODERN AMERICAN RIGHT[1]

David Plotke

Two sets of vivid images capture the dramatic course of the American right over the last quarter century. A triumphant President Ronald Reagan provides the primary images. In the 1980s he often seemed to beam with the confidence of having achieved great success. His position as the most effective and influential president of recent decades seems secure, even among those who remain strongly opposed to most of his policies. His administrations receive substantial credit for ending the Cold War on American terms, even as debate continues about the sources and meaning of this momentous result.

The horrible bombing of a major government building in Oklahoma City provides a second set of enduring images, full of death and destruction. Timothy McVeigh, the author of this act, was linked to shadowy parts of the contemporary ultraright. Facing his execution in 2001, McVeigh affirmed the political rage and bitterness that led him to engage in spectacular terrorism against the American state.

Reaganism, the dominant outlook of the modern American right, has roots that go back to conservative intellectual and political movements of the 1950s and 1960s, including currents which in those years were deemed marginal and extremist. The roots of the ultraright of the 1990s have intersecting, though by no means identical, sources. Thus, one route from the conservative milieus of 1950–64 led toward national power and redefining the terms of American political argument. Another led toward a furtive and conspiratorial network of ultraright militants and terrorists.

To understand these developments it makes sense to look at analyses of the American right in the first two decades after World War II. A serious evaluation of the American right of those years might well begin with *The Radical Right*, which was first published in 1963. The book is an expanded and updated version of *The New American Right*, published in 1955. The 1963 edition remains one of the best books about the modern American right. *The New American Right* focused on McCarthyism as a political and a social phenomenon. *The Radical Right* reprinted the main essays from that volume. It also examined the new right of the early 1960s and included the authors' reflections on their prior evaluations of McCarthyism.[2]

I

The Radical Right's Argument

In the United States, McCarthyism is part of history rather than a fact of daily political life. Yet if Joseph McCarthy's efforts partly expressed frustration and anger at modernizing forces that proved hard to resist, they also helped chart a political course that has been expanded and reshaped by notable figures. The list of those who were influenced by McCarthy, and who were willing to defend at least parts of his project, includes Goldwater, Nixon, Reagan, and Gingrich. This list signals the enduring political influence of elements of the far right of the first two decades after World War II.

What were the main positions and the composition of these distinctive forces on the right in the 1950s and the first half of the 1960s? What warranted calling them radical? *TRR*'s authors recognized the vehement opposition of these currents to domestic and international Communism, their sharp rejection of the New Deal, and their difficulty in distinguishing between the two. *TRR*'s controversial point of departure was to regard the basic positions of what it termed the radical right as so excessive in their estimation of the Communist threat and so unrealistic in their rejection of New Deal reforms as to be unreasonable. Thus Richard Hofstadter cited the "dense and massive irrationality" of the radical right (Richard Hofstadter, "The Pseudo-Conservative Revolt," 81). From this starting point the authors sought to understand the radical right in ways that went beyond the programs and self-descriptions of its leaders and organizers (Daniel Bell, "The Dispossessed," 8, 13; Seymour Martin Lipset, "The Sources of the 'Radical Right,'" 360–65; Talcott Parsons, "Social Strains in America," 209). In this context "radical" was intended not merely as a way to underline that these groups were very conservative in conventional left-right terms, but to stress that these currents aimed at a real break with prevailing institutions and practices, though they disagreed among themselves about just how profound a break was required.

The key argument of *The Radical Right* explained the phenomenon of McCarthyism and its political successors in terms of conflicts over social status and the shape of American culture. The introductory essay by Daniel Bell focused on the social dislocation of significant groups in the post-New Deal decades. Many members of these groups perceived themselves as dispossessed and victimized by recent changes, even if it was not possible to regard them as having undergone any great suffering. Richard Hofstadter's essay focused on his concept of status politics. Hofstadter linked McCarthyism to prior forms of American radicalism that blamed opaque processes and concealed forces for creating disorder and uncertainty. Thus McCarthyism echoed pre-New Deal modes of political and social radicalism in its hyperbole and inclination toward conspiratorial views of political life. Seymour Martin Lipset elaborated the status politics view. He also traced the recent history of radicalism on the right, linking McCarthyism to populist anti-Communism in the 1930s. Nathan Glazer and David Riesman emphasized the resentful anti-elitism that suffused the radical right in the 1950s, and considered why intellectuals had trouble responding effectively. For Peter Viereck, this populist radicalism and anti-elitism were notably distant from any genuine conservatism. The wide support for such positions marked the failure of the American right to police its own precincts. Talcott Parsons emphasized the inability of the radical right to reconcile itself to modernizing imperatives.

The authors of *The Radical Right* converged in regarding McCarthyism and the radical right of the early 1960s as a distorted and unrealistic response to Communism. A major source of this distortion was the inability of relevant social groups to recognize or cope with status changes that had been generated by postwar prosperity. There was a Communist threat, at least internationally, and there were deep social changes in the United States. McCarthyism was distinguished by its unreflective linking of these realities, which resulted in an outpouring of anger and resentment at allegedly disloyal elites.

McCarthyism was anti-elitist, conspiratorial, and fevered. For the authors of *The Radical Right*, this linked McCarthyism both to American traditions of populist radicalism and to previous expressions of authoritarian radicalism on the right. Here the authors were easily misinterpreted to mean either that McCarthyism was literally continuous in social and organizational terms with prior populist movements; or that McCarthyism was wholly a popular movement of the intolerant and fanatical. In part, this reading was fostered by the authors' attempts to distance themselves from Marxist and Progressive readings of the political right in which its popular forms merely reflect the schemes of reactionary elites. The authors' main point is now familiar. Once a movement introduces durable themes into a national political culture or tradition, those themes (or discourses) become widely available to later forces who may not be identical in aims or composition to those who came before them.

The Radical Right viewed its subject as historically rooted rather than episodic or spontaneous. It considered these forces to have a mass character and a real popular following. They did not simply express the strategies of other political agents, notably conservative Republican elites or business groups. In the large literature on the American right it remains distinctive to consider the radical right as historically rooted, mass, and popular. By historically rooted I mean that *The Radical Right* linked the upsurge of radical right activity and thought in the 1950s and early 1960s to aspects of prior political efforts and discourses, from Populism in the 1890s through Coughlin in the 1930s.[3] Each of these links can be debated. The point is that the postwar radical right did not emerge simply as a response to special Cold War circumstances. By mass and popular, I mean that the authors consider the radical right to have gained significant support and widespread sympathy. If these currents were almost certain to remain a minority, especially in such variants as the John Birch society, they were by no means inconsequential. The diversity of their support indicates that we are talking about more than a narrow sectarian outburst. The authors of *TRR* argued that the political initiatives of the radical right expressed and partly articulated general social tensions. Its leaders and main organizations developed political views, rather than taking isolated positions for narrow or purely instrumental reasons.

The New American Right and *The Radical Right* occasioned debate in academic circles and beyond.[4] Among the criticisms of the book's arguments, four stand out for their enduring interest.

From the right—and not only the radical right—there was general hostility to the basic project of *The Radical Right*. Its starting point was rejected in favor of the view that McCarthyism was a reasonable, if sometimes excessive, reaction to the genuine threat of Communism. If McCarthy's methods were dubious, and his claims about the extent of domestic Communist influence were inflated, these were partial errors rather than grave misjudgments that could warrant defining his project as unreasonable. Critics on the right thus took issue with the basic effort to find status or other dynamics to explain McCarthyism. In their view, there was no need to search for latent sources of a political effort whose manifest self-description was close enough to the truth to require that it be treated with the same respect accorded other reasonable political forces.[5]

From a different political direction several analysts, notably Nelson Polsby (and later Michael Rogin), charged *TRR* with missing the obvious—that McCarthyism was a political force primarily among Republicans. Its dynamic, in this view, had more to do with political and strategic maneuvers in and around that party than with any allegedly deeper social and cultural forces.[6] For some proponents of this view, *TRR*'s judgment of McCarthyism as unreasonable missed its strategic rationality for parts of the Republican right. McCarthy was a useful club, for a time, with which to beat Democratic leaders and elites.

It was consistent with this view, though not logically required by it, for critics on the left to argue that *TRR* went wrong whenever and to whatever extent it sought to depict McCarthyism as having a popular and mass dimension. At the political level, this critique meant emphasizing the links between McCarthyism and conservative Republican forces. At the social level, this meant trying to refute claims about the popular and multiclass character of McCarthy's supporters. At the cultural level, the aim was to reject any association of the authoritarian elements of the radical right with working class and other nonelite social groups. In historical terms, the idea was to mark off the radical right of the postwar decades as sharply as possible from the populism of the late 19th and early 20th centuries, so the latter might remain as a source of democratic inspiration for contemporary reformers and radicals.

Finally, several commentators on *TRR* argued that the central concepts of status politics, dispossession, and related concepts were not specified clearly and were therefore hard to assess accurately.[7]

In the decades since the publication of *TRR*, these critiques have remained alive in debates about how to understand radical right politics. Whenever the radical right is analyzed in terms of status and cultural conflicts, critics counter that its significance lies mainly in political conflicts among party factions. Others point out that the radical right's initiatives are in some sense functional for the projects of the right as a whole. And analysts debate whether and in what sense the radical right has gained a genuinely popular character.

These debates are most pertinent at times when the broader right has made its largest advances. One notable moment was the late 1960s and early 1970s. A second important moment was the early 1980s, when making sense of Reaganism and the "new right" was obviously necessary. A third important moment was marked by the conservative electoral shift in the mid-1990s associated with Newt Gingrich and the "Contract with America."

While the arguments of *TRR* have been vigorously criticized, its framework has not been replaced by a better way of understanding its subject. Arguments about how to interpret the presence and intermittent growth of a radical right have most often counterposed views like those in *TRR* to theories in which the radical right acts as a commando force on behalf of more respectable rightist forces. The latter accounts are at times partly true, but rarely do much explanatory work because they do not illuminate why such initiatives sometimes gain substantial popularity and at other points fail badly.

Three questions arise in reconsidering *TRR*'s account of the radical right in the 1950s and 1960s:

First, how should one assess *TRR*'s evaluation of McCarthyism and the Birch Society?

Second, what does this analysis suggest about the course of the American right after the early 1960s?

Third, how should one assess the theoretical and conceptual efforts of *TRR*? I will consider this question mainly in terms of *TRR*'s account of the radical right and the implications of that account for analyzing the subsequent development of the right in American politics. Given the broad theoretical interests of the authors, this question raises general issues. One concerns the role of psychological categories and evaluations in evaluating political protest. Another concerns the theoretical implications of the concept of status politics.

II

McCarthyism and American Politics

I begin with the book's judgments of McCarthyism and the radical right of the early 1960s. How should we evaluate the authors' analyses? We can gauge their efforts partly by weigh-ing *TRR*'s arguments against those of its critics.

Was McCarthyism Reasonable?

The question is not whether McCarthy's judgments and tac-tics were valid. The issue is whether they were sufficiently defective to be regarded as unreasonable. Was it legitimate for the authors to consider McCarthyism and its successors in the 1960s to be lacking in basic judgment to such an extent that no account with explanatory aims could simply take these forces on their own terms? Conservative critics of *TRR* rec-ognized the importance of *TRR*'s depiction of McCarthyism as essentially unreasonable. On that basis alone they rejected the book.

Here the substance of *TRR*'s position remains valid. To consider a political position or project as unreasonable entails claims about both its validity and its forms of expression. The basic point of McCarthyism was that American society was at grave risk of internal subversion from Communists and their sympathizers. Yet no such large and grave risk of internal Communist subversion existed by the early 1950s. Commu-nists had been present in the government in the 1930s and 1940s. They had gained prominence in cultural life, and sub-stantial influence in the mass movements affiliated with the New Deal, primarily the trade unions. By the time of McCarthy's initial prominence in 1950, however, loyalty in-vestigations and purges had been underway for years in all these areas. The Communist Party was politically marginal, on its own and in the broader Popular Front milieus that had withered in the first years of the Cold War.[8]

Democratic foreign policies were more consistently anti-Communist in an active, internationalist form than the poli-cies proposed by most conservative Republicans. McCarthyism might be depicted as a reasonable but excessive response to Communism if its domestic hyperbole were com-pensated for by advocacy of a coherent and plausible foreign policy. No such policy was proposed. Among the reasons for this absence, lingering divisions about internationalism among conservative Republicans certainly figured.[9]

TRR's depiction of McCarthyism as basically unreasonable is more accurate than considering the latter as a reasonable if excessive response to a dire internal threat. This does not grant a license to deny any forms of rationality to the proponents of McCarthyism. It does justify widening the explanatory lens in something like the manner that the authors of *TRR* recommend. This means looking at social and cultural forces that might be implicated in generating support for McCarthy's project.

TRR's position also means that McCarthy's wild speeches and statements signified something, and that it is worth considering what they meant. Unless one takes the position that political discourses don't matter at all (as against behavior or some other factor) one only needs to read a few of McCarthy's speeches to see that he was distinctive. He was unusual and at times innovative in his fury, his willingness to name and attack individuals, his disrespect for liberal norms, and his intensely resentful criticism of elites. He often laced his arguments with strong claims of conspiracy, as in 1951 when he grouped George Marshall and Dean Acheson as members of "a conspiracy on a scale so immense as to dwarf any previous such venture in the history of man."[10]

McCarthyism as a Republican Strategy?

Several commentators criticized *TRR* for failing to appreciate the obvious: McCarthy's supporters were largely Republican, and his efforts aided Republicans who wanted to reduce Democratic power. Taken too narrowly this claim would not make sense, however, because *TRR*'s authors clearly recognized both points. The force of the argument is that McCarthyism can best be explained as a conservative Republican initiative.

This criticism is limited by an apparent misunderstanding of what *TRR* was trying to explain. The aim was not to explain the existence of conservative Republicans. Nor was the aim to explain the attraction of McCarthyism for some of them, although this attraction was noted (Lipset, "The Sources of the 'Radical Right,'" 345).

What needed explanation was the emergence of McCarthyism as a relatively broad and occasionally success-ful effort to reshape national political discourse and to influ-ence the results of elections. The presence of conservative Re-publicans who generally agreed with McCarthy cannot explain these results, as such currents had existed from the early New Deal to the 1950s. Numerous attempts had been made to un-dermine the New Deal and Democratic power by denouncing Communist influence and assailing the radicalism of the new state agencies and programs. Most such efforts failed to pro-duce major political results.

Why did McCarthyism get so much further, even if its sup-porters (and some opponents) overstated its successes? The main relevant factors cited by Polsby were linked to a chang-ing international situation in which Communism loomed large and American power was newly challenged. But such factors would be much more salient in explaining a McCarthyism that did not exist. This McCarthyism would have focused clearly on the Soviet Union and its allies and would have posed a compelling alternative to the containment strategy developed by the Truman administration.

Several critics suggested a similar but subtler explanation for the rise of McCarthyism. In this view, McCarthyism's brief ascent as a significant political force was due to the fact that conservative and even centrist Republicans regarded it as a valuable device for damaging Democrats. The idea is that Re-publican leaders were happy to see someone attack the Demo-cratic leadership in an unqualified and even brutal way. They were also pleased that the critic and his main associates were far enough away from them so that they did not have to bear much responsibility for the attacks.

This might have been a provocative explanation: Mc-Carthyism grew from a minor current to a substantial politi-cal force because Republican elites encouraged and benefited from it. We would not need to refer to status politics or to make any other social and cultural argument to account for something that could be explained by the adroit maneuvering of Republican leaders.

Yet the proponents of this argument did not develop or support it seriously. They did not show that Republican elites actually did manage events to produce such a result; in fact, no one has shown that this occurred. A more likely story is that McCarthyism emerged mainly apart from any explicit strategic intervention or calculation by Republican national leaders. Center and center-right Republicans were ambivalent about McCarthy even while Truman was in power. They appreciated his strident anti-Democratic attacks, but not his evident disrespect for authority. Ambivalence became opposition for many leading Republicans when Eisenhower's victory was not matched by any new restraint from McCarthy. Instead, he continued and even expanded his attacks on national elites.

If this account is basically accurate, we cannot explain McCarthyism primarily in terms of elite Republican maneuvers. (And we are therefore not forced onto the shaky ground of "who benefits?" arguments.) Instead, we return to the problem of understanding how political currents that had been marginal in the 1930s and 1940s gained so much attention and achieved at least a few notable political victories in the 1950s, even while taking more extreme and extravagant forms.

Yet another strategic and political account of McCarthyism might start by emphasizing not the unsurprising elements of McCarthy's support but its more distinctive features. Public opinion data available on McCarthyism do show that the strongest support for McCarthy came from conservative Republicans and the strongest supporters of the Republican Party (analytically distinct categories that were often identified). But it is misleading to leave the characterization of McCarthyism's support at that point. First, if one brackets "strong Republicans," support for McCarthy was similar among all other groups defined by their party identification. Roughly 10 percent of weak Republicans and of Democrats of all types avowed their support for McCarthy. Second, support for McCarthy was relatively strong among a number of primarily Democratic social groups.[11]

These factors suggest a significant strategic dimension to McCarthyism. McCarthy did not simply rally the troops, assembling the most conservative parts of the Republican Party to reenact their routine defeats by supporters of the New Deal. While McCarthy certainly mobilized conservative Republicans, what made his effort distinctive was its ability to cut into the Democratic coalition and gain support from among pro-Democratic social forces. Seen in this light, McCarthyism appears as an early effort to break apart the national Democratic coalition "from below." It is less the predecessor of the exotic radical right currents of the early 1960s than of parts of the Goldwater campaign and of the Wallace movement of the second half of the 1960s. *To appreciate this strategic dimension of McCarthyism would mean emphasizing what was unusual in its approach, rather than focusing on its continuity with traditional conservative Republicanism.*

The critique of *TRR* for not recognizing the obvious is unsatisfactory. It misunderstands what needs to be explained, which was not the presence of Republican conservatism, but its vitality and intermittent success after years of failure. The more interesting strategic elements of McCarthyism were linked to its political and social novelty.

McCarthyism and Populism

An important criticism of *TRR* charged it with failing to understand American Populism and wrongly identifying McCarthy and his supporters as heirs to that movement. This charge was developed in Michael Rogin's 1967 book, *McCarthy and the Intellectuals*. Partly following Polsby's critique, Rogin emphasized the conservative and Republican sources of McCarthy's support. His argument was based on analyzing electoral data in Wisconsin and the Dakotas. These data showed considerable discontinuities between the geographic (and thus social) sources of McCarthy's support and support for earlier Populist and Progressive campaigns.[12]

TRR's claims about the populist dimension of McCarthyism are often loosely formulated (Lipset, "Sources of the 'Radical Right,'" 335). Yet they are not really refuted by Rogin's analysis. He showed that there was not a high degree of continuity between the organizations and constituencies of post-

World War I populism and progressivism in the upper Midwest and McCarthyism. *TRR*'s authors sometimes made claims that are vulnerable to this rejoinder. However, their main argument regarding populism was not about specific organizations or even constituencies. Hofstadter, Bell, and others proposed that McCarthy's popularity derived partly from his ability to link up with elements of a durable populist tradition that had resonance in numerous political and social locations.

This difference registers a familiar disagreement among analysts of American Populism of the late 19th century and its successors. Defenders of the earlier movement generally stay close to its original and primary organizations, and then focus on successor political forms that were located clearly on the left. Those who are less convinced of the virtues of Populism define the phenomenon more broadly to include a variety of political figures and movements. Rogin's book strongly advanced the first conception. He vigorously criticized what he took to be an underlying fear of popular movements and mass democratic politics in *TRR*. McCarthyism, in his view, was not populism at all, but a mobilization of familiar strands of extreme conservatism. Thus imputing the authoritarian and sinister elements of McCarthyism to populism is not only wrong but also a clear expression of a fearful and distrustful stance toward popular politics.

For historians of American politics in the 19th century, this continues to be an interesting controversy. As regards the American right in the second half of the twentieth century, this debate was settled soon after Rogin's book appeared, insofar as such debates can ever be settled by actual political events. With the national prominence of George Wallace in the late 1960s and early 1970s it was obvious that populist motifs in American political culture were available to a wide array of political forces.[13] American populism is varied and complex in its meanings. There is no way to expel McCarthy from a diverse tradition that includes several versions of Tom Watson and William Jennings Bryan, Robert La Follette and Father Coughlin, and Huey Long and George Wallace. Innumerable Southern racists have relied on populist themes, while in the

1980s Jesse Jackson used populist arguments to try to expand his electoral base to include more white voters. In the 1990s, Patrick Buchanan deployed populist motifs as part of his attack on the Republican national leadership. Part of the novelty and dynamism of McCarthyism derived from McCarthy's willingness to experiment with populist themes, a course that much of the Republican leadership regarded with skepticism or disdain.

Status Politics?

What does one make of the core argument that McCarthyism was driven by the status concerns of groups whose positions had been disrupted by economic and social growth?

I will discuss this argument at length later. In my view, this conception was (and remains) provocative and fruitful, despite being loosely formulated. It was a more promising route toward explaining McCarthyism than the two main alternatives on the table in the 1950s and 1960s. One of these was to identify McCarthyism as a conservative Republican mobilization. The other was to claim that this mobilization served the interests of reactionary elites and was thereby caused by them. In this context, *TRR*'s argument about status politics opened important questions that otherwise would not have been addressed.

Diagnosis and Criticism

If McCarthyism was unreasonable, does that imply that psychological categories are needed to understand its proponents? One current of argument, though not primary in *TRR*, suggests an affirmative answer. This might be the weakest part of the book (Hofstadter, "Pseudo-Conservatism Revisited: A Postscript," 99–100; David Riesman and Nathan Glazer, "The Intellectuals and the Discontented Classes," 118).

In the 1950s and later, analysts of political and social life often used psychological categories to explain the choices and views of those with whom they strongly disagreed. This approach substitutes psychological for political categories in a way that is often problematic. It tends to presume rather than show that a political position is unreasonable and further presumes that the problem is psychological. Such an approach might have been valid for some of the cases with which *TRR*'s authors were concerned. There were notably disturbed people among those involved in the McCarthy effort, and that was clearly the case with the Birchers and the radical right of the early 1960s.

Yet even here the clinical approach does not do much explanatory work. It is difficult to explain a political position or action as a function of psychic conflict and disturbance. To do so requires knowing more about the subject (and about the clinical theory used to make such a judgment) than social scientists and historians usually know.

The history of the right after *TRR* poses further problems. If the positions of the 1950–63 radical right expressed psychological disturbance, then today such problems appear at the center of the Republican Party, in the Speaker's office, and on the Supreme Court. If it is disturbed to be angry and on the fringe, how can we explain the capacity of such forces to enter and transform mainstream American politics?

The clinical approach also threatens a key argument of *TRR*. The concept of status politics implies that rightist activism is a plausible form of politics, not one distinctly in need of psychological explanation. If status politics is a relatively common political mode, why shouldn't individuals who experience a decline in status try to recoup their losses? Moreover, it is in the nature of losing status that recovering it is an uncertain and risky process, one apt to be full of passion.

Such difficulties have led to problems for those whose political view of the right is mainly critical. Beginning with *TRR*, critics use psychoanalysis in discussing McCarthy, Nixon, Reagan, and others on the right, and use political interpretation and argument in assessing the right's critics and opponents. The tendency to treat one's friends as healthy (even if misguided) and one's enemies as disordered seems hard to resist.

We are probably better off starting with social and political causes and addressing the issues raised by substantive arguments. Since *TRR* was published, political ideas that were then widely regarded as crazy have become a major part of national discourse. Such ideas include the following: government is generally terrible, taxes are close to theft, and evolution is no more legitimate a view than the Bible's account of creation.

As these examples suggest, in considering political discourses and arguments it is no easy matter to distinguish the politically unreasonable from the clinically irrational. Both concepts are valid, yet both are very difficult to define and employ precisely, and both are vulnerable to partisan misuse.[14] Here *TRR*'s difficulties designate a zone of problems that largely remain unsettled and unsettling.

The Problem of Pseudoconservatism

One strand of *The Radical Right* still merits attention although it was not often debated when the book's merits were first assessed. The authors identify and reject a politics that claims to be conservative but strives with vigor and passion to change political and social life. This conservatism wants to undermine conventional practices. When its proponents urge overturning corrupt forms and punishing betrayers, the impulse is disruptive and even rageful.

This critique accompanies complaints about the lack of a proper conservatism. As against the bully Joseph McCarthy and the paranoid Robert Welch (head of the John Birch Society in the early 1960s), where is the responsible right? Such a right would respect authority. It would be resolutely committed to liberal procedures. It would accept at least limited state action, with the aim of maintaining political and social decency. Such a right might even hesitate before giving unqualified support to the market (Viereck, "The Philosophical 'New Conservatism,'" 197–201).[15]

The Radical Right contrasts the actual radical right with this conception of a responsible right. Yet something like this latter, more reasonable right had a major national presence in the Eisenhower administration and the Republican Party's center. Should the radical right have emulated this moderate right? That would have undermined its rationale. Eisenhower, after all, appeared to the radical right as a moderate conservative who changed nothing.

Perhaps the aim is subtler—the authors mean to indict the right edge of respectable opinion (Robert Taft in the early 1950s, the conservative wing of Richard Nixon's coalition in the early 1960s) for not policing their own right flanks more vigorously. The authors of *TRR* may have believed or hoped that the radical right would be *replaced* by a more energetic version of Taft. This new right would reject libertarian as well as populist temptations.

TRR's authors claim that McCarthyism revealed how much of the right was aggressively uncivil. The post-World War II radical right mistrusts authority even when speaking favorably of it (Hofstadter, "The Pseudo-Conservative Revolt," 76–77). When authority figures appear politically unreliable, this right is quick not only to attack individuals but also to attack their institutions and question their legitimacy. From McCarthy on (to Wallace and Buchanan, one might add) this radical right has charged opponents with an elitist domination of American political and cultural life (as in the national media, liberal Protestant denominations, and elite universities).

The Radical Right helps explain why, from the early 1950s on, the most successful elements of the American right have not been committed to temperate and sober modes of conservatism. The civil and responsible conservatives that the authors of *The Radical Right* preferred to the radical right can be found at several points in American politics in later decades. But these forces were not often leaders or victors, as they seem to lack imagination or dynamism. Alone and even as leaders of coalitions they are often easy targets for centrist or center-left modernizers in national politics (Kennedy against Nixon, Carter against Ford, Clinton against Bush). A restrained and temperate conservatism, which mainly emphasizes order, can make little headway on its own without alliances that include other more dynamic forces on the right. In a fluid and unsettled social context, much of the American right will have strong commitments to growth and mobility. This openness to change, in which many conservatives will support calls for thorough transformation and renewal, makes it hard for a conventional party of order to succeed.

The Merit of The Radical Right

The Radical Right is at times marred by overstatement. Its arguments about status politics are imprecise. It pays too little attention to the strategic uses of McCarthyism in national politics. Its use of psychological categories is sometimes partisan. But its virtues are far more important and long-lasting than these defects. *TRR* recognized the novelty and importance of McCarthyism without overstating its reach or potential. It tried to link that political force both to distinctive currents of postwar social and cultural life and to more durable patterns of American politics. Its main arguments about status politics, the limits of traditionalist conservatism, and the ambivalence of the populist tradition in the United States remain productive and interesting. Thus *TRR* provides a valuable point of departure for analyzing the American right and American politics from the early 1960s to the end of the century.

III

The Changing Shape of the Right, 1965–2001

TRR was published soon before a crucial development for the American right—the nomination of Barry Goldwater as Republican candidate for President in 1964. In one sense this event confirmed the analysis of the authors of *TRR*. It demonstrated the growing weakness of moderate conservatives, whose inability to control their own political territory opened the way for more aggressive forces.

The Goldwater Moment

Despite his massive defeat, Goldwater's campaign reduced the marginality of the radical right. His campaign built a new and durable road from the radical right into national politics, and made clear what had to be done to keep this road open. Threats to dismantle all the social welfare policies of the 1930s and 1940s, and to do so soon, had to go. So did loose talk about nuclear confrontation; aggressive claims that major public figures were effectively Communist in their outlook; and claims of conspiracy about everything from the Supreme Court to fluoridated water.[16]

Parts of the radical right of the 1950s and 1960s continued to enter mainstream national politics after the Goldwater campaign. There was mutual influence, as some of the views and elements of the style of the radical right of the first postwar decades were assimilated by leading figures on the broader right in the 1960s and 1970s. The form and extent of this incorporation varied. But radical right elements were dynamic and had a significant role in the successes of notable political actors such as in Wallace's populism, Reagan's antistatism, and later in Buchanan's nativism.

These volatile elements were not simply a burden for the right as a whole. The picture became more complex with the rise of new and vigorous political forces concerned mainly with cultural and social questions. Regarding such issues as abortion, homosexuality, and prayer in school, it became difficult to draw a sharp line between the radical right and more conventional forms of conservatism. After 1964, the distance between the main centers of Republican power and less extreme currents of the radical right (William F. Buckley, Jr., for example) diminished greatly.

Placing the Radical Right

Deep changes have occurred in national politics since *TRR* was published. The political spectrum has moved well to the right, and many whose positions resemble those of the radical right of 1950–62 have gained important national positions. With each overall shift to the right, the space of the radical right has been replenished with new themes and elements. The most militant sections of the radical right have given rise to an ultraright that is fully antagonistic toward public authority and sometimes encourages terrorism. A dynamic of centrism has not prevailed (in which radical tendencies would either moderate or be marginalized in favor of less radical currents), even if some major Republican leaders sincerely employ a centrist political style.

In this context does "radical right" designate a viewpoint or a characteristic political location with respect to other forces? It is not possible to separate these approaches entirely, but the distinction is needed to get a clear image of the radical right in relation to the right as a whole. I start with a relational view and then look at substantive commitments.

In relational terms, the radical right is defined by its place far to the right on the political spectrum. The scale of protest from this area has expanded. In the mid-1950s and early 1960s the predominance and relative coherence of American progressive liberalism in both thematic and institutional terms made it relatively easy to map the forces to its right. To begin, there was the loyal opposition, such as Thomas Dewey. There were constitutional opponents of the regime such as Robert Taft in the early 1950s. They wanted to get rid of Democratic domination but did not routinely attack the loyalties of Democratic leaders and rarely hinted at unconventional forms of politics. Taft disputed the national regime's policies and perspectives, but he did not reject its constitutional right to exist.

Starting with part of Taft's supporters, other forces on the right emphasized the need to make a fundamental break with the Democratic regime. Some claimed that the New Deal order was not only a fertile source of bad policies but also a morally damaged regime whose legitimacy was dubious. *Part of the right defined itself as radical by proposing to end a noxious regime, not only to change particular New Deal policies.*

Thus a radical right rejects the national regime and aims to replace it. In relational terms, a radical right normally includes the most conservative parts of the Republican Party and more conservative positions outside it. *The Radical Right* correctly depicted this force as neither transitory nor an incipient majority. The radical right was a secondary political force in the 1950s and early 1960s, but it did not go away.

The Radical Right's Viewpoint

If we analyze substantive themes rather than relative positions, a different story emerges. Since the early 1960s, political forces that were once marginal have become important.

Views that from the 1930s to the early 1960s were repeatedly defeated became acceptable and sometimes predominant in the 1980s and 1990s. The major shifts to the right of recent decades are signified by these events: Goldwater's nomination in 1964; Nixon's two presidential victories; Reagan's triumphs in 1980 and 1984; and the successes of conservative Republicans in Congress from 1994 on.

After the 1960s a vehement antistatism became respectable and even conventional. By the mid-1980s the New Deal was no longer taken for granted as the framework for American public policy. Political campaigns and initiatives often featured populist attacks on elites, especially those in government and cultural life. Tax revolts surged, and then diminished as special political events while the focus on cutting taxes and reducing government became routine. Political figures often affirmed religious commitments as both a good thing for individuals and a valid part of public life.

Here the main dynamic was not centrist. Instead, the positions initially proposed by the right took up more space and redefined the political center. Further to the right, traditional conservatism grew and its themes spread toward the center. The radical right expanded and then divided between a far right that opposes the regime through legal means and a militant ultraright that sometimes rejects legality.

In this new configuration, views not far to the left of Barry Goldwater in 1964 (absent some of his provocative rhetoric) are now frequently depicted and perceived as centrist, or barely to the right of center (President George Bush). Positions very close to those of Goldwater not only gain respect but sometimes dominate national politics (Reagan, Gingrich).

This process of change is illustrated in Table 1. The overall political spectrum has shifted notably to the right, as from T1 to T4 in the table. Thus a position well to the right of center in the early 1960s (position x) had become centrist as of the 1990s without undergoing deep substantive changes. Within the terms of that shift to the right, a centrist logic operates at any given point. This centrism appears within a broader process of political redefinition. In this context, sec-

DAVID PLOTKE

TABLE 1
MOVING TO THE RIGHT

T_1 _____ X ____

  T_2 _____ X _____

    T_3 _____ X _____

      T_4 _____ X _____

tions of the right can reasonably make the hard choice that is required to shift a political spectrum—they can risk taking positions at or near the center of the political spectrum that they hope to create!

All these changes do not mean that the radical right analyzed in *TRR* has defined a new common sense for the entire American polity. Yet a range of radical right ideas (opposition to virtually all government regulation, rejection of the entire welfare state, etc.) has grown in significance and now appears across a much larger part of the political spectrum. Descendants of those who filled the political zone from Taft to McCarthy can be found not only on the fringes of politics but in powerful and influential positions (such as William Rehnquist and Richard Cheney).

In this process the pro-McCarthy right, the religious far right, the least extreme of the anti-Communist activists of the early 1960s, and their many successors have faced a problem that confronts radicals who find themselves closer to real power than they expected to be. They can join the new regime, or they can oppose it as little better than what it replaced. The first choice has meant supporting Nixon, Reagan, Gingrich, or George W. Bush. Thus major elements among radical right forces have often chosen to ally themselves with leading national Republicans and have thereby been able to gain significant positions and shape policies.

Many of the substantive positions of the postwar radical right now extend much further toward the political center than they did before Goldwater. And the forces that occupy the same location as the radical right of the 1950s and early 1960s have become more radical both in their views and tactics. This space has been refilled with new and striking themes and with more militant conceptions of action. The rightward motion of the overall political spectrum continues, as newer themes of the radical right are readily available to the legitimate right and are influential in the choices of the right-center.

In the last three decades in the United States, the center of American politics has moved notably to the right. The main themes of the legitimate right—defined relationally as that part of the right capable of gaining serious national power and winning office—have also moved further to the right. A wide space has opened for varied forces whose predecessors were well to the right of what was the center of American politics when *TRR* was published.

The Right's Diversity

TRR did not anticipate the overall shift to the right that has occurred, but almost no one did at the time. The authors of *TRR* took the radical right of the early 1950s and early 1960s seriously, and tried to link it to deep tendencies in American social and cultural life.

The shifts noted in the previous section have been driven primarily by the success of substantial parts of the right in defining a distinctive and frequently successful combination of themes. The prevailing formulations have linked strong support for the market in economic and social policy to deeply conservative cultural and social commitments. Reagan articulated this position forcefully. Candidates who take up this stance are not always victorious. But they most often dominate the broad right while they fare at least decently well in two-party competition.

It is properly the subject of another work to try to explain fully the dynamic that drives these large rightward shifts in the national political spectrum. Beyond the right's thematic and organizational efforts, the weaknesses of the American left and center-left after the mid-1960s have been a large part of

the story. Following the achievement of historic reforms in racial politics and the passage of major social welfare legislation, this broad left has lacked the resources required to answer increasingly serious and powerful critiques from various
parts of the right. This has allowed the right to weaken its
mainstream opponents by identifying them with unpopular
forms of leftist radicalism and by insisting loudly on the entire left's exhaustion.

A position committed both to the market and to cultural
conservatism had to be built and developed in order to prevail within the right and to endure as a major national force.
Comparing today's right with Eisenhower or even Taft in the
1950s, or with the Nixon of 1960, it becomes apparent that
large shifts had to occur for leading sections of the right to
consider that affirming traditional cultural values should be a
major political theme.

The combination of antistatist and deeply pro-market economic views and traditionalist cultural and social commitments
is not dictated by any purely conceptual logic. Parts of the left
often tried to weaken this position by pointing out the apparent tension between the aversion to state action in economic
and social welfare policies and the willingness to use government to defend traditional cultural values. This strategy was
more clever than effective. Its proponents often made their critique in place of a substantive response to either half of the
right's perspective. And they most often ignored the vulnerability of the left to the same charge of incoherence, as the
left remained statist in economic policy while becoming nearly
libertarian in cultural matters.

A dynamic combination of antistatism and cultural conservatism took shape in the 1960s and achieved full expression
in the efforts of Reagan in the 1980s and the Congressional
Republicans in the 1990s. (See Table 2.) This position is now
the primary referent of the entire right in the U.S. Its
ascendance is notable in comparative terms. Herbert Kitschelt
has analyzed the contemporary radical right in Western Europe and concluded that its greatest chances of success arise
when it combines pro-market economic policies with social

TABLE 2
POSITIONS ON THE AMERICAN RIGHT

		Economic Issues	
		Regulatory & Welfarist	Market
Cultural Issues	Liberal	Centrist Republicans (Arlen Specter)	Libertarianism (Barry Goldwater 1980s)
	Traditionalist	Conservative Populism (George Wallace 1960s)	Reaganism (R. Reagan, G. W. Bush)

conservatism.[17] The irony is that what Kitschelt meant by success was managing to keep small parties afloat so they can win a few seats in parliament and some local elections. (His book appeared before the Austrian Freedom Party grew large enough to gain power as part of a coalition government in 2000). In the United States a similar combination of views contends for national leadership, and even when it does not win, it still shapes national policy and debate.

From the 1960s to the present the right has been striking for its expansion and differentiation. There remains a traditional conservative right which never accepted the New Deal and vigorously opposes major new government projects. This right is at home in the Republican Party. The lines have been blurred between this part of the right and what is now often called the Republican center. (The latter current is similar to what used to be considered mainstream conservative Republicanism.) Thus, such prominent national figures as President George Bush and Senator Robert Dole are often termed centrist. If we trace these individuals and their allies back to the 1960s and early 1970s, they were clearly on the conservative side of the Republican Party.

Major figures on the contemporary right, such as President George W. Bush and John McCain, are often centrist in their demeanor. As was dramatically the case in McCain's campaign for the Republican presidential nomination in 2000, some of these figures are willing to distance themselves from the most conservative sections of the Republican party and forces to its right. They strive to appeal to what they consider to be the political center, and want to avoid taking steps that would polarize centrist forces against them. Yet in substantive terms these figures are centrist mainly because the overall political spectrum has moved even further to the right. What was once called liberal or centrist Republicanism (Rockefeller) has dwindled and in some regions disappeared altogether.

There has been a substantial populist right, whose recent roots lie partly in George Wallace's presidential campaigns. In the 1970s, the populist right was identified with efforts to limit or halt school desegregation and to cut government spending for social programs. In the 1980s, this force helped to generate a significant group of "Reagan Democrats" among lower middle class and working class whites.

With parts of this populist right, as well as other sections of the right, racial themes have played a major role, even if most of the right now claims to accept core elements of the Civil Rights Act. Racial conservatives who are suspicious of any new reform measures aimed at racial equality dominate the right. They also make communal appeals to whites as a group.

From the 1970s on, an important neoconservative right has been led by intellectuals previously identified with the Democratic center or center-right. Many of these people joined the Republican Party during the 1980s on domestic and foreign policy grounds. Few have returned to the Democratic Party.

There has been a great expansion of political action by conservative religious forces. From a core of evangelical Protestants in the 1970s, this mobilization has broadened to include other Christians who are not evangelical or fundamentalist in their orientation. Forces based on religious conservatism can

TABLE 3
POLITICAL CURRENTS ON THE RIGHT

	Center Right					Far Right
	←					→
Market vs. State Allocation	LR	SC	NC	MR	TC	RR
Choice vs. Values	SC	LR	MR	NC	TC	RR

LR   Liberal Republicanism (Arlen Specter)
SC   Suburban Conservatism (John Rowland)
MR   Mainstream Republicanism (George W. Bush, Jeb Bush)
NC   Neoconservatism (Irving Kristol)
TC   Traditional Conservatism (Robert Dole)
RR   Radical Right (Patrick Buchanan, Helen Chenoweth, Pat
      Robertson)

greatly influence or win many local and state political contests. Yet the religious right is not an unquestioned authority
within the right, even on its core cultural issues. Some of the
disagreement comes from parts of what might be called a suburban right made up of voters in new occupations in newer
cities and suburbs. These people tend to be conservative in
economic matters, but not on social and cultural issues.

This inventory points to both the diversity and scale of the
contemporary right (see Table 3). Along with the successes
come problems. It is not easy to sustain mobilization, bridge
wide thematic differences, and share power and positions
among divergent forces. There is a temptation to reach too far
and imagine that popular support for aspects of Reaganism and
substantial parts of the right's perspective means approval for
the full economic and social programs of the most conservative sections of the right. This temptation plagued Republicans in Congress after their great electoral successes in the
mid-1990s. Newt Gingrich's inability to gauge the bases and
limits of his success was a major reason for his rapid political decline after 1994.

Strong fundamentalist currents flourish on many parts of
the right. They view their principles as wholly coherent and
integrated, and strongly reject compromise. The presence of
fundamentalists gives most strategic problems a sharp edge,

because some of those who must be included in major projects
are likely to reject as betrayal any major compromises of principle or even tacit cooperation with the impure. Fundamentalists also threaten to play a card that is not common in national politics—they may leave the game. If total political victory is out of reach and the world remains corrupt, a retreat
deep into religious and communal networks is an inviting alternative to politics.

Sometimes, as in 1992, fundamentalist currents have been
a large burden for Republican presidential candidates. At other
points these forces have played a mainly positive role in mobilizing and organizing voters. On balance the challenging
presence of fundamentalism has not prevented the broader
right from contending seriously for national power.

IV

From McCarthy to the Militias

To maintain continuity with the analysis of *TRR* and to recognize the expansion and diversity of the contemporary right
requires a new distinction. A deep division has emerged in
what the authors termed the radical right. *Now there exists both
a legitimate far right and a militant and sometimes violent
ultraright.* This ultraright poses problems of explanation similar to those faced by the authors of *TRR*.

The national shift to the right has opened space for many
sections of the radical right to enter party politics. Some have
gained a presence in Congress and in state and local institutions. What can now be called the far right extends from the
right of the legitimate political spectrum and shades off into
marginal and sectarian political thought and activism. The far
right has grown considerably in size, and its location resembles
that of McCarthyism and the less extreme parts of the radical
right of the early 1960s.

Estimating the size of political currents in and around the
two main parties has always been a tricky enterprise. The expansion of the primary system provides an improved basis for
making guesses. In 1992 Patrick Buchanan, whose political

career included service to Republican presidents and activism in the far right, strongly opposed incumbent President George Bush in Republican presidential primaries. He achieved notable successes, such as winning 37 percent of the vote in New Hampshire. Then in 1996 Buchanan ran again, with Robert Dole as his main opponent. In this year Buchanan received 21.6 percent of the total votes cast in Republican primaries. Perhaps Buchanan's national reputation and his skills as a writer and performer inflated his showing. Yet his efforts can also be taken as a good measure of the radical right. To choose Buchanan, voters had to reject a clearly conservative admininstration in 1992 and then vote against a respected Republican conservative in 1996. If one takes Buchanan's support to indicate the size of the radical right, his 21.6 percent of the Republican primary vote in 1996 translates into somewhat more than half of that figure as a proportion of the active national electorate.[18]

The Shape of the Ultraright

Further to the right, more intransigent and militant groups form, mobilize, and splinter. Most of these groups are thoroughly alienated from conventional political life. These ultraright forces call for drastic political change, and at the extreme are willing to countenance violence against an oppressive state.

To cite the radical right of the 1950s and 1960s as a predecessor and source of recent ultraright currents is politically provocative because it highlights the common roots of the contemporary ultraright and the legitimate parts of the far right.

Direct biographical and organizational descent from the radical right of the early 1960s to the contemporary ultraright is hard to demonstrate in a way that has much explanatory force. There are gaps in the organizational forms of the radical right and shifts in the composition of its constituencies.[19]

Yet the new ultraright is in substantial part linked to prior forces on the radical right. The thematic connections between *TRR*'s radical right and the contemporary ultraright are important. The key to making the connection is the intense antistatism of the ultraright of the 1980s and 1990s. This was a founding theme for much of the postwar radical right, and has been expressed more ardently after the end of the Cold War. For many on the radical right, the existence of the Cold War rationalized at least the national security dimension of a vigorous American state. With the end of the Cold War, this justification is no longer plausible.

Today there is more concern with cultural questions on the ultraright, including those raised by feminism, than was typical of McCarthyism or the radical right of the early 1960s. Yet there was little or no feminist movement for the radical right to oppose in the 1950s and early 1960s. The question of abortion was barely on the public agenda. The focus of parts of the ultraright on family and gender matters is consistent with the prevalent cultural orientation of most earlier currents on the radical right (though not all—consistent libertarians would find no home in the contemporary ultraright).

Ultraright Militancy

In the 1990s, notable parts of the ultraright radicalized their demands and tactics. Smaller parts of this current supported political violence and terrorist conspiracies. While extremist militants of the ultraright comprise only a small portion of the radical right's supporters, the numbers involved have been large enough to sustain considerable violence. Moreover, the lines dividing partisan action on behalf of the most radical parts of the Republican Party, sectarian agitation, and antigovernment militancy are not always sharp. This blurring of distinctions is not because any central committee seeks to provide cover for its militants by sowing confusion. It is due instead to the political success achieved by parts of the far right amid the overall rightward shift of American politics.

The most militant and sometimes violent tactics of the ultraright have unfolded along three main dimensions.[20] First, there have been numerous disruptive and violent acts by militia groups and other ultraright currents. They have aimed primarily at challenging and disrupting the activities of the federal government and sometimes of state governments as well.

These tactics have accompanied claims that the federal government is illegitimate. Second, major violence has been directed against medical facilities and medical professionals who provide abortions. Third, episodes of racial violence have been launched from ultraright circles.

The first two of these forms of violence fly under the flag of demands relatively close to those of the broad American right. Calls to cut back the role of the state dramatically and attacks on a wide range of government activities are routine for much of the right. From mainstream Republicans through the far right, these attacks usually propose a deep change of course without claiming that the national state has become illegitimate (much less urging violent resistance). Nonetheless, it is accurate to say that parts of the ultraright propose to take illegal action on behalf of the antistatism that permeates the right as a whole.

With the abortion issue the thematic links are even closer. Proposals to make abortion very difficult if not impossible to obtain are a fixture of Republican national discourse. Many Republican and far right critiques of abortion insist on equating it with murder. If such claims were taken seriously, and abortion really were understood to be murder, then many forms of civil disobedience aimed at blocking the performance of abortions might be reasonable. And at least some militant action against practitioners, if carefully tailored to hinder only their medical activities, would at least merit serious discussion. Thus links between mainstream rightist discourse and ultraright actions are close and substantial.

The third strand of ultraright violence, which targets racial and ethnic minorities, is not directly connected to dominant rightist themes and ultraright actions. Most of the right, including the far right, is now nonracist in principle. Many on the right cite their egalitarian commitments as part of the basis for their opposition to affirmative action and other public efforts at racial reform.

But issues of race and ethnicity are not so simple. The right has consistently rejected reform projects in the area of race, including court-sponsored efforts to desegregate schools, affirmative action in education and employment, and districting plans aimed at increasing the presence of minority representatives in political bodies. In each case they have sought to argue against these projects in terms that are plausibly consistent with a liberal notion of racial equality. Yet a consistent record of opposition to racial reform has made the broad right a magnet for racists old and new. In this context, virulent racism has become part of ultraright politics. Racial violence in recent years has been the work of apparently isolated individuals or very small groups. These people have often been immersed in ultraright political milieus, but they do not appear to be acting on behalf of even the loose networks that exist among the militia or anti-abortion militants.

Ultraright violence from the 1980s on has had the following main features. First, the antigovernment ultraright has sponsored the most dramatic episodes of violence. This current combines radical antistatism with extreme variants of Christian fundamentalism. Second, the most sustained forms of disruption have been carried out by militant sections of the anti-abortion movement. Third, while the discourses of the militias and of Christian identity groups have been aggressive and threatening, the discourses of the most radical sections of the antiabortion movement have been in some ways even more violent. They encourage direct action against abortion providers and facilities beyond what the militia groups usually propose for government officials. Fourth, despite the decline of ultraright violence since Oklahoma City, a tightly organized core of activists remains involved in the militia groups and their peripheries. Fifth, while there has been some thematic convergence between the anti-abortion militants and the anti-government contingents, these currents remain mostly separate.

Bell, Lipset, and other contributors to *TRR* considered the antidemocratic contribution of the radical right mainly in terms of its negative effects on political culture (Lipset, "The Sources of the 'Radical Right,'" 307–08). They regarded it as a source of intolerance and an obstacle to political reflection and deliberation.[21] They did not worry that supporters of McCarthy or members of the John Birch Society would blow up government buildings and shoot federal officials. Now the potential for ultraright violence seems to be durably present both as dramatic large episodes (which entail substantial planning) and as nearly random assaults by individuals.

Explaining the Ultraright

To analyze the radical right today requires accounting for ultraright militancy. The violence of the ultraright, as in militia actions, the bombing in Oklahoma City, and attacks on doctors who provide abortions, has been widely dicussed. But there have been relatively few serious efforts to explain these events. By the time of Timothy McVeigh's execution in 2001, in much of the public discussion he had become an almost pure symbol of remorseless evil. This made his death very interesting as regards the debate about capital punishment in the United States. But his execution was not an occasion for serious reflection on the political origins and meaning of his crimes.

Leading public intellectuals of the right, such as George Will and William Bennett, have criticized the ultraright's violence. But they have not sought to explain or rigorously criticize the political themes and activities of ultraright militants, beyond routine references to frustration and disturbance.[22]

This may be partly due to an aversion to sectarian controversy within the right. Many on the right have spent years blasting away at statism and cultural decay.[23] In this conetxt there is a good chance some will take the assaults too literally and engage in disruption or violence. To reject all those who sympathize with such dire conclusions would mean trying to draw sharp lines between the ultraright and the rest of the right. Yet this effort would cause much turmoil in the far right and beyond.

Political commentators on the left have also given less attention to this violence or to the proximate radical-right discourses than might seem appropriate. Some on the left fear that analyzing conspirators will become conspiracy mongering. This would distort reality by giving too much notice to the most extremist forces, and diverting attention from the main projects of the American right. Others on the left might want to avoid the likely countercharge that the modern American left initiated political violence as a widespread tactic in the 1960s. Analysts with left of center views who focused on the recent violence of the ultraright might be quickly reminded of that decade's urban civil disturbances and of the far left's subsequent terrorism.[24]

Why, given the depth and extent of the shift to the right, have parts of the radical right turned to extrainstitutional and sometimes violent means? Since Lyndon Johnson withdrew from the presidential race in 1968, national politics has been mainly conservative on many fronts. Yet parts of the ultraright are certain that they face an alien and tyrannical state, and act accordingly in opting for sectarian adventures and even terrorism. From Nixon to George W. Bush, Bill Clinton was the president furthest to the left in the last thirty years. This striking fact illustrates a deep rightward shift that should produce a sense of accomplishment if not deep happiness across the right. Instead, a strong and bitter sense of unfinished business often prevails.

To say that the ultraright upsurge is about opposition to welfare statism, abortion rights, affirmative action, and immigration, is accurate in roughly the same limited way that it was correct to claim that McCarthyism was about Communism. The key question is this: *given a broad conservative shift, and so many conservative successes, why did ultraright militancy flourish in the 1990s?*

First, extensive economic and social change occurred from the 1970s on, including major regional and sectoral shifts. There have been phases of strong growth, as from the mid-1990s, along with phases of more limited growth and of recession. Sometimes growth has brought benefits to a majority of the population, while at other points the rewards have been much more narrowly distributed. This unsettled economic and social picture cannot be cited as a direct and sufficient cause of the radical right's expansion or of the choice of parts of that current to launch conspiracies. Yet social and economic change has dislocated many people, some of whom are available for new forms of political mobilization.

Second, the cultural disruption of the last several decades has been at least as great as the economic and social change. Here, the story on one front after another roughly resembles the abortion battles. Major egalitarian changes with libertarian elements occurred in the 1960s and 1970s. Parts of these changes soon gained legal and political legitimacy, so that cultural conservatives found themselves losing a war they had not quite realized was being fought. They have mobilized repeatedly against reforms that they regard as threatening.

The economic changes and cultural conflicts of recent decades provide a framework for the emergence of a new ultraright but do not determine that result. A crucial dynamic derives from the difficulty of coping with political success that is less than total. The sequence Nixon, Ford, Carter, Reagan, Bush signaled a very strong run by the American right. It meant the end of Democratic national domination and provided numerous opportunities for conservatives.

Yet by the standards of the full program of the far right in Reagan's coalition, the world has not really changed. Abortion continues, prayer is still excluded from schools, the national government remains large, and (limited) affirmative action continues. In the 1990s, a centrist Democrat won election twice and upheld liberal policies in many areas regarded as crucial by cultural conservatives. Clinton often bore a certain similarity to Eisenhower, in his moderate administration of someone else's regime, and he often made a virtue of this position by selectively advocating conservative themes.[25] Such ironies were entirely lost on many militants of the right, for whom his electoral successes were simply an infuriating provocation. Especially for cultural and social conservatives, the real changes remain to be made (even after Gore's defeat in 2000).

The resulting sense of anger and political betrayal cannot simply be termed irrational. Republican platforms pledged to ban abortion and smash the welfare state, rather than to restrict access to abortion and curb the growth of state spending. The road to ultraright action starts with the insight that breaking up the old Democratic order and enhancing Republican power did not wholly change the political world. But why not? One answer might be weakness and betrayal by Republican leaders. This answer, while superficial, appeals to the legitimate far right. It recommends a politics aimed at creating a genuine version of the regime that parts of the radical right thought was on its way first with Nixon and then more rigorously with Reagan. Another answer is structural—if changing the government was not enough to change the world, the basic forms of American political life must be deeply corrupt. Because of this corruption, conservative and far right forces failed to deliver what they promised. They could not even stop Clinton from winning two presidential elections. According to this logic, a new political world has to be created—thus militant action begins to seem plausible. Within the ranks of the militant, new divisions arise about how to speed the needed transformation—some conclude that violent action, however unfortunate, will be necessary.

The broader right's prolonged and vigorous attacks on the national state and on liberal culture nourished the durable radicalization that has led part of the far right into sectarian and violent adventures. This is not because Bennett or Buckley counsels disruption. It is because both figures and many others assail the state and the more liberal aspects of American culture in the most severe terms. Most influential figures on the right are careful to distinguish their stringent critiques from a rejection of constitutional methods. But their attacks on policies and institutions have often been so intense as to make constitutionalism seem less important than the need to end great evils and corruption.

Economic and social turmoil and cultural conflict have facilitated the emergence of a militant ultraright. It has taken shape mainly as a political response to the dramatic yet incomplete victories of mainstream conservatives in recent decades. The ultraright proposes to make good on Republican promises and go much further in the same direction. Responsibility for specific acts of violence lies with those who commit them. Nonetheless, the aggressive and destructive elements of radical right themes and arguments have helped to make ultraright militancy appear to some as a reasonable political option.

If recent experience signals future dynamics, ultraright politics is likely to produce more violence and terrorism when the national administration has a centrist or center-left character than when it is center-right or entirely on the right. Ultraright militants may regard these political differences as superficial, and may view the national government as thoroughly corrupt in both cases. However, they will have more trouble acting as though the government is wholly illegitmate when it is under the control of Republicans and conservatives. When there is a centrist or center-left administration, mainstream conservatives and the respectable far right have fewer means of incorporating or disciplining their most radical associates. Is it then fair to conclude that electing a president as conservative as George W. Bush is the simplest way to contain the most extreme forms of ultraright militancy? Perhaps so, but the need of presidents in situations like Bush's to create and sustain governing coalitions may lead to frustration and bitterness relatively soon among the most ardent militants of the ultraright.

V

From Class to Status to Identity

Analytically, much of *The Radical Right* centered on the concept of status politics (Hofstadter, "The Pseudo-Conservative Revolt," 80–85). This approach derived partly from a critique of Marxism and progressive historiography. Several contributors to *The Radical Right* had been socialists or social democrats and were influenced by Marxism. By the time of their encounter with McCarthyism none of them remained Marxists in any orthodox sense. Yet they were still engaged with Marxist views. McCarthyism seemed interesting as well as significant in part because it so clearly illustrated the limits of Marxism as a mode of political analysis.[26]

The status politics argument insists that politics is basically about more than the efforts of groups to seek economic objectives. Hofstadter argues that individuals and groups also compete to establish and secure their positions in a status order. This claim gains theoretical force against a background of Marxian premises about the (class-based) formation and (mainly economic) aims of political groups.

Hofstadter's position had notable referents in social theory and American history. Max Weber's theory was crucial, as he aimed precisely to distinguish class and status as forms of stratification and axes of conflict. The American referent is a political and social history that appears full of conflict about status. McCarthyism and the radical right marked a distinctive moment in a long sequence of battles about such matters as religion, temperance, and evolution.

Hofstadter claims that status politics is prominent in phases of economic prosperity, while class politics dominates in times of economic distress. This formulation reflects the prior three decades' experience: nativism and Prohibition flourished in the prosperous 1920s, an American labor politics dominated the Depression era, and McCarthyism and later the John Birch society surfaced along with prosperity in the 1950s and 1960s.

The concept of status politics greatly increased the possibility of saying something interesting about the radical right. Members of the radical right, in this view, have their own complaints and objectives. They are not simply the hapless tools of reactionary elites. Those who take political steps to pursue status aims are often people whose world and place within it have been severely disrupted. They aim to retrieve lost honor. The status politics view provided a cogent way to describe important elements of the radical right in the first two decades after World War II. In historical terms, Hofstadter argued that similar concerns and dynamics could be found in prior political movements that seemed to share little with the radical right.

Yet analytical problems remain. In *TRR,* the positive content of status politics remains uncertain. Regarding class politics the basic notion seems clear, perhaps because it has been explored so often. The idea is that class-based agents enter politics to seek crucial objectives. Their aims center on improving their own position and thus the position of their class relative to others. These agents want more economic resources, and they want to gain political and social power in order to maintain or increase their resources. When people engage in status politics, what are they trying to do? This key point is elusive, because status is both the name for the agents who fight (status groups) and the name for what these actors want. Class actors do not fight to get class; they fight for power and resources. What is it that status actors are trying to get? Do they want prestige? Recognition by others as worthy? Formal and legal acceptance of a status claim?

One might say that status groups want honor and want their position in society to be esteemed. That seems to be Hofstadter's view in his 1955 essay. But this position is not rich enough to express or account for what the groups are really doing. When status groups seek honor, they usually want particular values and activities to be honored.

Hofstadter and Bell mark status off from class, and doing so always requires a substantial theoretical effort. Yet they do not get much further than making that crucial distinction— Max Weber himself did not get much further in his classic essay on the subject.[27]

TRR had trouble specifying when social groups will tend to engage in status politics. Two main claims were made. One, mentioned earlier, asserts that episodes of status politics occur when economic times are relatively good, while class politics dominates in difficult economic phases (Lipset, "The Sources of the 'Radical Right,'" 308–14). It makes sense to contrast the nativist 1920s and anti-Communist 1950s with the class politics of the 1930s. Yet the turbulence of the Depression called many status positions into question. And some of that decade's movements made status claims as well as raising class issues.

The second claim is mainly about the agents of status politics. Bell and Hofstadter argued that both rising and falling social groups could make their concerns political through presenting them as status conflicts (Bell, "The Dispossessed," 22; "Interpretations of American Politics," 47). This idea is plausible, yet vague. It is plausible because one can see how disorder might lead members of a group to worry about their status relative to others. Yet the United States from the Civil War to the present has been a dynamic society full of change. Many groups rose and fell, while some groups broke apart and new ones emerged.

In *TRR*, the authors who use the concept of status politics do not claim there was a time when status was fixed and stable in the United States. But without means of distinguishing between routine change and more unusual shifts that are likely to yield status politics, the implication is that status politics itself is routine, rather than a function of prosperity. Does the concept then expand to include everything beyond a clearly defined class politics?

If *TRR* provides no clear answer to this question, its main formulations imply that status politics has a long future. Here Bell and Hofstadter take a position distinct from most theories of modernization. In the latter view, when modern social orders take hold they integrate the great majority of the population. Thus, Parsons argues that the radical right is doomed by its refusal to accept modernity (Parsons, "Social Strains in America," 233–34). Yet if status politics is about social change in a modern setting, there are few grounds for expecting it to disappear. As new changes occur, social positions will be disturbed. Then status politics will continue well into the future in any likely version of modernity.

Some formulations in *TRR* expressed a view of modernization as such a strong and determining force that it would render the radical right marginal. This view predominates in the contributions by Talcott Parsons (and appears in Lipset's articles as well). For Parsons, the main line of social cleavage separates groups that are fully integrated in modern social life from partially integrated or displaced groups. This cleavage was expected to give rise to professional politics on the one hand and expressive movements on the other. The protagonists of a modern, professional politics would typically win these conflicts. Most of *TRR*'s authors did not wholly accept this view, though they used its imagery to underline what they took to be the backwardness of the radical right. Hofstadter, Bell, and others affirmed the possibility of new moments of status politics, and by implication, the prospect of new radical movements on the right.

The modernization view predicted much less of a future for the radical right and its successors than did the status politics argument. Yet the authors who relied mainly on the status politics view hesitated to make claims about the likelihood of new forms of radical right politics. Perhaps this was due to a fear of appearing alarmist about the future of McCarthyism or the radical right currents of the early 1960s. Whatever the source of this caution, the result is that the arguments of Hofstadter and Bell in particular are more useful in understanding the subsequent flourishing of far right currents than are their own explicit statements about these matters.

From Status to Identity Politics

Hofstadter's 1963 article revised his earlier view of status politics (Hofstadter, "Pseudo-Conservatism Revisited," 98–99). His revision proposed that status politics is not only about rank but also about the values used to produce the ranking. Status politics concerns defining the honor and value of important attributes and practices.

Here Hofstadter turned toward a concept of cultural politics. If McCarthy was about status politics, the radical right of the early 1960s was also about cultural politics. Radical right groups wanted their cultural commitments to be prevalent, if not entirely dominant. That is different from wanting a group's distinctive features to be recognized. For cultural practices to be properly valued, social life has to be organized in some ways and not others. Those engaged in cultural politics want to reduce the distance between social reality and their own view of an appropriate cultural ordering. Political conflicts readily arise from efforts to gain positive recognition of the value of cultural practices, because such efforts affect everyone and entail government action.

Hofstadter's discussions of status and culture raised questions that remain important. For example, when are the two kinds of issues more or less closely linked? One might sharply distinguish status politics from cultural politics under some conditions. If social positions were relatively fixed, status would refer to the distribution of honor and esteem. Cultural politics would then designate conflicts about values—what ways of life should be regarded as valid and worthy, and why? In a rigid social order, the two sorts of politics might be quite separate. Status conflicts might occur between clearly defined estates or castes, while cultural conflicts might center on religion. But with the notable exception of race, much of the status order in the United States has been fluid and status positions have not been fixed. In this context, status and cultural politics are apt to be intertwined.

TRR's account of status and cultural politics indicates that in the United States today (and in other advanced market countries) we should expect recurrent conflicts about status, honor, and cultural values. Protagonists of new conflicts might include those who have been recently displaced, as well as those who resent their location in a status order. Others will propose to reshape prevailing cultural commitments.

These arguments call into question a deeply influential understanding of politics in which class and distributive conflicts are considered to engage interests, while cultural and status conflicts are understood to focus on desires and norms. To recognize a place for a durable cultural or status politics implies that most major political conflicts involve interests of some sort while they also concern norms, desires, and even fantasies. In this light, class politics is about distributive shares among classes and/or the shape of the class structure itself. Cultural politics is about the evaluation of practices, the distribution of status and esteem, and the shape of a status order or relations among values. In both class and cultural or status politics, there is usually an interplay of interests and norms.

Status Politics and the Status Quo

The Radical Right's account of status and cultural politics was a valuable contribution with the potential for substantial development. But the response to this conception was mixed. This had partly to do with relations between intellectual and political life in the 1960s and 1970s. Soon after *TRR* appeared, neoprogressive and neoMarxist currents in historiography and social science gained prominence. For many proponents of these positions, *TRR*'s focus on status politics and cultural politics wrongly downplayed the extent of class-related political conflict in the United States.

Critics also objected to *TRR*'s account of illiberalism in American political life. In this view, Bell, Lipset, and the other authors depicted normal American political conflict as pitting a radical extreme (such as McCarthyism) against a liberal and modernizing center. They regarded lower middle class and working class groups as a potential source of intolerant and antidemocratic politics. When some analysts rejected *TRR*'s focus on status politics, they also criticized its emphasis on the popular side of McCarthyism because that view meant emphasizing the possible importance of popular threats to democratic liberties. Critics instead stressed the class elements of McCarthyism and its links to traditional Republican politics, and sought to acquit lower status and working class groups of the charge of antiliberalism.

TRR's authors saw McCarthyism and the John Birch Society as threats from the margins of political life. The assaults were launched against a center that had been reshaped and democratized by the New Deal. If this did not amount to the complacency that some critics claimed to find in *TRR*, there was strong skepticism in that work about the liberal commitments and democratic meaning of new movements on the left and right. Moreover, Bell began the 1955 volume by asserting that the entire complex that *The New American Right* had aimed to analyze was framed by the exhaustion of the left of the 1930s and 1940s (Bell, "Interpretations of American Politics, 47).

When a populist and participatory spirit dominated the left in the 1960s and early 1970s, many viewed *TRR*'s skeptical view of populist radicalism as simply a preference for order. This reduction was understandable, if unsubtle. The liberal-labor center that Bell and Hofstadter were willing to defend against McCarthy in the early 1950s looked very different ten or fifteen years later amid conflicts about Vietnam and racial politics.

When neopopulist and neoMarxist critics of *TRR* charged

its authors with fearing the masses, they misunderstood its project. *TRR* drew on Weber while offering a quasi-Marxist account of why a raucous and intense status politics often appears in this country. This conception might have been wrong, but it was neither celebratory nor disinterested in conflict.

While the specific context of these arguments has receded, important issues remain. Is it useful to analyze liberal and democratic themes in American politics in terms of contrasts between a center and peripheries? This question presumes that a recognizable center exists in American political life, which is a point of contention. But if there is a political center in some form, what is its relation to democratic impulses? When and why do major democratic changes occur?[28]

Since World War II, analysts have given three main responses to these questions. For some, democratic change flows primarily from the center. This can be construed positively, as evidence of a systemic capacity for reform guided by thoughtful elites. Or it can be regarded as a sign of the extent of elite manipulation (in contrast to more authentic modes of democratization).

The second view of democratic change emphasizes its popular sources and dynamics. The people—in more or less organized forms—either directly implements democratic changes or forces elites to make them. This analytical point can be taken as locating a problem, because popular forces cause disorder and inefficiency while raising unrealistic expectations. Or it can be seen as finding a virtue, the one means of saving a deeply flawed American regime from sliding into totally decay.

The third way of understanding democratic change focuses on the development of political institutions through processes of legal and political reflection. Here the core image is much less a conflict between center and periphery than a collective effort at constitutional deliberation.

Democratic reform was not the main subject of *The Radical Right*. Yet that book entered the debates of the 1960s and 1970s about the sources of democratic reform primarily because it disrupted what had become a new common sense on the left. For neopopulists, participatory democrats, and (most) American neoMarxists, a strong version of the second position I have sketched was nearly constitutive. Democracy was seen almost entirely as a popular accomplishment, and political problems were seen as requiring more popular involvement and activity.

The arguments of *The Radical Right*, in this context, amounted to claiming that popular impulses and movements were not necessarily democratic in aim or effect. This meant rejecting any notion of a unified people aiming for democratic improvement. It also meant rejecting the idea that nondemocratic and illiberal political practices could be remedied simply by increasing popular engagement in political life.

This was not a message that many on the left wanted to hear in the 1960s or early 1970s. Now it has become a familiar report from many different precincts of American politics, and it is difficult to find serious analysts who claim a simple and unproblematic relation between the popular and the democratic elements in American politics.

It is still reasonable to claim that major democratic changes in the United States require substantial popular engagement and mobilization. Yet one can affirm this point while insisting that there is no exclusive site of democratic virtue. Conventional dichotomies between elites and the people cannot provide much analytical or normative guidance as regards proposals for democratic reform. I have argued elsewhere that democratic changes occur from the joint effects of popular mobilization and elite efforts at reform.[29] That view may or may not be correct. The point here is that *TRR*'s account of the radical right helped to undermine the populist common sense of the new and old lefts in the 1960s, and many were not glad to hear this news.

By now it is not very bold to say that political and economic elites can at times use their power to sustain democratic reforms (as with the judicial defense of abortion rights, or corporate willingness to support some forms of affirmative action). After all, parts of the radical right routinely charge elites with victimizing the people in the name of expanding democracy. Nondemocratic projects also have many sources in the contemporary United States, including the rigorous antiunion efforts of large corporations, anti-immigrant agitation on the right (Buchanan), and obscurantist nationalism on the left (Farrakhan). In this area of dense and passionate arguments, one of *TRR*'s enduring contributions is to provide a stringent antidote to the populist sentimentality that tempts diverse currents in American intellectual and political life, not only on the left.

The Resurgence of Post-Marxism

Sometimes *TRR*'s approach was treated as a premature post-Marxism. Yet from the 1970s on, neoMarxism became less and less orthodox as analysts emphasized that the meaning of political projects cannot be deduced from the economic locations of their members.[30] Arguments about the political force of status, culture, and identity have become increasingly widespread. Whether Weber, Parsons, or Foucault is invoked, claims about the importance of noneconomic elements flourish. In this context, the effort of *TRR* to open analytical space for examining status and cultural politics prefigured the cultural turn that has been so influential in American historiography and parts of the social sciences.

TRR's account of status and cultural politics became even more durably salient than the authors imagined in light of major political and economic developments of the 1970s and 1980s. *TRR*'s account had proposed that class politics would dominate in times of economic distress. Yet this did not occur during the economic troubles of the 1970s. Instead, status and cultural politics flourished along with varied class and nonclass distributive conflicts. While distributive political battles certainly took place, these conflicts were an important element rather than the defining feature of political life.

Since the 1970s numerous cultural conflicts have persisted, such as those concerning the legal status of abortion, the legal and moral position of homosexuality, the cultural meaning of immigration, and the cultural and social dimensions of education. Even fights about evidently distributive matters—

health care, taxes, and social welfare—have been laced with status and cultural elements. Proposals about status and culture have often focused on concepts of identity. This concept provides groups with means both of demanding esteem and of proposing that government action be taken to sustain deeply held values.

Growth and increasing prosperity returned after the 1970s—in partial and uneven forms in the 1980s, and then more broadly in the 1990s. This renewal took place on a scale that exceeded all serious prior predictions. It takes no wisdom to predict an eventual interruption of the powerful growth that occurred in the United States in the 1990s and into the new century. Yet it is hard to imagine how any plausible economic downturn would cause conflicts about status, culture, and identity to become marginal or disappear from political life for an extended period in favor of class politics.

A New Political Sociology?

TRR's analyses raise several theoretical issues, one of which follows directly from the argument about status politics. The field of political sociology has a distinguished history and an uncertain future. Its premise is that social relations can explain a substantial part of politics. The point of departure has often been Marxian.[31] The shift to include status and culture as well as class in accounting for politics might open new lines of inquiry. But the difficulty of the enterprise is evident: if there is no definite relation between class and politics, and there are multiple sources of political mobilization of roughly equal importance, can there still be an explanatory sociology of politics?

TRR made a cogent critique of American progressive historiography and Marxian political sociology. The turn from class toward status and culture does not make explanation simpler, however. It has always been difficult to develop a Weberian political sociology beyond the initial and always useful rejection of economic reductionism. For a new political sociology, what social relations are the basis of politics? What political forces typically arise from the main social groups, and how? In the ensuing political conflicts, who tends to prevail? Are we in fact left without an explanatory political sociology? Should we simply recognize that an open-ended politics has no bases?

Conventional Marxian and progressive accounts of politics—certainly as the authors of *TRR* saw them—are economic or class-based. They posit a one-way causal arrow between class and politics. Both views see parties, unions, and business groups as the main political agents arising from class relations. They expect that the class-based political groups in control of the most resources will normally win political conflicts. *TRR*'s authors rejected that view as a sufficient or adequate guide to explanation, and they remain correct in doing so.

The next option, which is proposed by several authors in *TRR*, augments a class account with a status-based account: politics is about competition over status, as well as about class. This model posits two unidirectional arrows, pointing from both class and status to politics. This approach does not explain when class or status elements are more important for politics. And it gives politics little weight in shaping status or class relations.

A further move is from status toward culture. Status politics often involves claims about how life should be ordered and what should be valued. Groups engaged in status politics are trying to shape the culture. Such efforts, in plural societies, lead to conflicts in which groups claim that a particular cultural form or set of relations is crucial for them to exist in a decent way. Claims about the position of social groups and the value of cultural activities are thus linked. In the last several decades, conflicts about rights and identities have been very important results of linking claims about status and culture.

Each move away from a class determination of politics produces empirical richness. These moves also seem to head toward indeterminacy insofar as an indefinite number of ways of producing political action seem possible and (in principle) of equal importance. Any social difference can be decisive for political organization and action.

The claim that the social bases of politics are diverse is analytically distinct from the idea that politics has no social bases in a causal sense. But the implications of the first view may not be so different from those of the second. If the links between social and political life are indefinitely large and shifting, it is hard to attribute substantial causal significance to any particular link.

The logic of stressing plural connections between the social and the political leads to further questions. Can political practices significantly affect social and cultural relations? Are there political causes of political outcomes? These questions open the way to conceiving political sociology as a source of theories in which class, status, and politics all interact to shape political results. The problems of such an open theory in providing causal accounts do not need restatement. The issue is how to proceed when such a theory seems to be the logical result of a critique of the limits of Marxian and Weberian political sociologies.

Is it possible to develop a causal account of politics that starts from an acknowledgment of systemic complexity and interaction? This means criticizing the project of political sociology as it was understood in much of the Weberian tradition and almost all of the Marxian tradition. In this direction, one starts by recognizing both the range of major social influences on politics and the causal efficacy of politics in producing political outcomes. The danger, of course, is that one will end up with figures so full of causal arrows that nothing can be explained or even much clarified. Yet this direction follows logically from two points that by now seem strongly established: class is not always or necessarily the main social cleavage as regards politics, and political factors matter in causing political results.

VI

TRR and New Themes of American Politics

If politics after the 1960s had returned permanently to an American-style class politics similar to that of the 1930s and

1940s, then *TRR*'s perspective might have had diminishing pertinence. While distributive issues have not disappeared, status politics, cultural politics, and identity politics have all proliferated. *TRR*'s perspective helps to illuminate major ongoing conflicts that have been intertwined with the growth of parts of the right.

Gender Politics After the 1960s

TRR did not say much about the sexual politics of the radical right. It was written before the new wave of feminism appeared in the 1960s. From the 1970s on, the radical right has been resolute and passionate in opposing feminist views of gender, sex, and family, and in fighting legal and political decisions that partly reflect those views.

The status and cultural politics perspectives of *TRR* describe key aspects of gender politics. Dramatic changes weakened and disrupted the status positions defined by the system of gender relations that prevailed after World War II. New identities in gender relations have taken public and explicit forms. The evident relevance of status and identity questions has informed several valuable accounts of battles between feminists and their opponents.[32]

Some of the sharpest conflicts in gender politics, such as those over abortion, have endured well beyond the point at which a general modernization of family and gender relations occurred. The stakes of these conflicts include both status positions and cultural commitments. Proponents of antifeminist views are not doomed to extinction so long as they have some capacity to adapt their perspectives to the pressure of modernizing changes. Parts of the antifeminist right have demonstrated at least this minimal ability, and sometimes considerably more.

Very few accounts of American politics and culture in the late 1950s and early 1960s envisioned anything like the bitter and volatile conflicts over gender issues which have extended over the last three decades. *TRR* was not unusual in failing to discern this major development. It was unusual, however, in providing elements of an approach to analyzing these durable conflicts about gender, family, and sexuality.

Race and Status Politics

Race is mentioned but does not figure prominently in *TRR*. The authors saw it primarily as a legal question and thought that reform leading toward the civic and political inclusion of blacks was under way. They were surprised by the lack of explicitly racist elements in the discourses of the radical right in the 1950s and early 1960s. In that light, it was reasonable for the authors to emphasize that the radical right did not avow racist commitments, though this led them to miss some of the ties between the radical right and segregationists.

The course of racial politics from the mid-1960s on was certainly not predicted, even in broad outline, by the authors of *TRR*. But that book's main arguments can usefully be applied to later events. The distinction between *TRR*'s unremarkable empirical account and its fruitful theoretical approach is clear in Hofstadter's claim: "Because, as a people extremely democratic in our social institutions, we have had no clear, consistent and recognizable system of status, our personal status problems have an unusual intensity" (Hofstadter, "The Pseudo-Conservative Revolt," 83). Empirically, race is the obvious and dramatic exception to this claim. And the analytical point is valuable for understanding racial politics after the Civil Rights Act. If fluid and uncertain status relations encourage an intense status politics, it makes sense that legal and political attacks on caste-like racial relations in the 1960s would unleash torrents of conflict. The new status position of blacks remained to be defined after legal equality was won. The racial status positions of many whites were uncertain and often likely to be devalued by political and legal change. Not surprisingly, parts of the radical right turned toward racial issues during and after the mid-1960s.[33]

The status politics view helps to illuminate aspects of contemporary racial conflict. First, race is a status. Different racial positions receive varying amounts of esteem and honor in an inclusive system in which everyone has a racial definition. Second, racial conflict is not simply determined by economic competition or hardship. While such conflict is sharpened by economic competition among racial groups, it also occurs in periods of growth and relative prosperity. Third, racial conflict can readily become cultural conflict about choosing and sustaining desired forms of order and defining core values and commitments.

Much of modern racial politics appears as contentious forms of status and cultural politics. *TRR*'s authors mainly anticipated a gradual reform of race relations. Yet their perspective implies that deep legal changes like those of 1964 and 1965 would open the way to severe racial conflict, because those changes disrupted a long-standing and highly unequal status order. As that order fell apart, many people (most of them white) experienced a loss of status and tried to recoup their losses through new political and social initiatives.

A New Religious Mobilization

TRR's approach illuminates one of the most important developments of the last thirty years. There has been an extraordinary growth of religious forces in politics, and this growth has occurred mainly on the right. This upsurge marks a departure from the 1950s and early 1960s, when much of the radical right presumed Christian commitments but did not make them a primary thematic focus or a basis for efforts at mobilization.

In this extended political mobilization, status politics is thickly present. This has been clear in conflicts among Protestant denominations, as fundamentalist and evangelical forces have fought with considerable success to reorient American Protestantism. Rather than remaining a contest for status and leadership among Protestants, the religious upsurge of recent decades has become a general cultural conflict. One side includes fundamentalist Protestants, other conservative religious forces within Protestantism, and conservative currents in contemporary Catholicism and Judaism. These forces are suspicious of or hostile toward political liberalism and cultural pluralism, which they see as threatening to religious values and the position of religion per se. They not only demand recognition but also propose to shape the national culture to express their own values and doctrines. In these cultural battles—about abortion, homosexuality, education, and other issues—conservative religious forces often justify their proposals partly by reference to their identities. In a move that is now familiar across the political spectrum, these speakers equate their authenticity and sincerity with the validity of their arguments.

Through assaults on secular liberalism, appeals to tradition, and claims about the legitimacy of religious identities, religious conservatives argue that religious doctrine is a valid basis for making political judgments. Some claim that honest citations of such doctrine should count as legitimate reasoning in public debate. The dangers to liberal politics that *TRR* found in the radical right of the first postwar decades thus reappear, especially when the religious right considers its critics and opponents as corrupt, illegitimate, and malevolent.

TRR had little of interest to say about gender, race, and religion per se, and did not predict their emergence as durable political issues. Yet it is more important to note that *TRR*'s framework provides at least a decent grasp of these major themes of modern American politics. Groups have repeatedly formed and mobilized to achieve status and cultural aims, especially when status relations that were relatively stable have been disrupted. For parts of the American right the focus on culture has gone even further than *TRR*'s framework would suggest. Influential figures such as William Bennett, Robert Bork, and Irving Kristol have come to place primary and sometimes exclusive emphasis on cultural matters.

This cultural emphasis partly reflects the right's great success in conventional matters of political economy. Thus, from the right it would be hard to formulate a strongly critical view of American economic and social policies since Reagan was first elected president without that view being libertarian. But the cultural turn has involved more than a search for new issues. In the 1990s and even after George W. Bush's election, a deep and enduring sense of betrayal emerged in parts of the far right. Many lamented that only the economic parts of their project had succeeded, leaving a morally adrift nation to use the proceeds of successful economic reform for progressively more corrupt and expensive forms of decadence. This cultural and moral critique of American life usually downplays conventional strategies of coalition building based on class or status interests. Instead its proponents launch fierce jeremiads against decay and depravity.

VII

The Right and the Radical Right Today

TRR made a major contribution to understanding the radical right of its time. Today it provides a useful starting point for analyzing the subsequent development of much of the American right. The concept of status politics and the related arguments were a serious effort to outline a post-Marxist political sociology attentive to the shape of American political and social life. That effort offers insights into some of the main themes of American politics in the last three decades, in which battles about status, culture, and identity have played such a large political role. There are notable problems with the book's arguments. For the most part, however, these problems point to difficult analytical and empirical issues that are yet to be resolved. Adequate accounts of the American right of the last half-century, when they are produced, will take *TRR* as a valuable reference point.

Earlier I tried to locate the radical right both in relation to other political currents and in terms of its main themes. I did not directly address a question that often troubles accounts of the political right and left. What do these terms indicate about both the political commitments and the shape of these forces?

TRR did not spend many pages on this issue, with the exception of its discussions of authentic and pseudo-conservatism. Perhaps this was because the massive reordering of American politics produced in the 1930s was still recent, and it could be presumed that left and right retained the clear definitions given by the battles of that decade. Forty years after *TRR* was published, no such clarity exists.

Conventional terms do not capture the forms of the modern right very well. Neither a party nor any specific organization can be taken as a proxy for the right, even given its overlap with the Republican Party. But it would not be accurate to take the right as a name for a coalition among groups who engage in joint action only to achieve their immediate aims. To view the right as a coalition in this sense would make it very hard to explain how such a diverse political force could remain relatively coherent for a long period. Purely instrumental coalitions tend to break up and disappear due to a powerful logic that drives their membership down toward the minimum required to win the next major contest.

The best way to understand the right's forms is via the concept of a political bloc. A political bloc is organizationally and socially diverse, linked by political commitments, and oriented toward gaining political power in a durable way. A political bloc aims to gain power in the service of basic commitments. Thus political blocs are defined by their commitments when the latter frame practical political efforts.

As a political bloc, the American right has included many elements. It has always included large sections of the Republican Party, and sometimes parts of the Democratic Party as well. The right includes interest organizations and lobbies, civic and religious groups, and intellectual currents. These elements have never been wholly unified. But its leading elements have forged positive relations of cooperation and mutual respect. These relations have depended on the understanding of participants that the links among them are valuable and should be sustained.

Given this conception of the right, what commitments are central in defining and unifying it over time?

In the mid-1990s, Norberto Bobbio provided a valuable service by bravely insisting on a definition of left and right organized around a single concept. Many authors throw up their hands at the difficulty of finding a definition—Bobbio's blunt clarity aids discussion. The left, he says, favors equality and the right does not.[34]

While this definition has some merit, it is partisan in form and has only limited value in making sense of American political divisions. Given the democratic revolution in modern politics, to define the left as those who favor equality almost

automatically works to define the left as modern and reasonable. To be defined as against equality means to be against
progress and even against liberty in many modern interpretations of that term. There is clearly something to Bobbio's definition, as many on the right are critical of equality. But it is
too simply a means of defining the left as better than the right.

Bobbio's definition is most plausible in countries where a
right that rejects political and legal equality among citizens is
part of a common political memory, even if such a right is
not easy to find in daily politics. Historically, the United States
has tended to lack a frankly inegalitarian right (such as monarchists, anti-market advocates of an organic society, and fascists), with the exception of racial politics. After 1964, the general acceptance of at least a limited notion of racial equality,
save for extreme sections of the ultraright, makes it even
harder to apply Bobbio's definition of left and right fruitfully.

If we start by asking what the right opposes, we can identify two core elements of the modern American right. "The
right" designates political actors who generally oppose using
the national state to regulate the market, except as an unavoid-
able last resort. These actors almost always oppose using the
state to redistribute resources. "The right" also designates
forces opposed to a further expansion of the number and range
of rights. After the Civil Rights Act of 1964, the American
right remains firmly antistatist. It opposes new rights as well
as new regulation or redistribution.

In positive terms closer to those that its leaders and activists affirm, the right has asserted the value of market orderings—both for efficiency and to foster self-reliance and independent judgment. The right has affirmed efforts to sustain or
reestablish what it regards as valid traditional moral values.
These positive commitments are the basis for opposing state
action aimed at regulation, redistribution, and expanding
rights.

While the right's commitments to the market and traditional
cultural forms are not linked by logical necessity, the links are
thick and meaningful. Intellectuals and politicians on the right

have made serious efforts to link commitments to the market and to traditional values in practical and theoretical terms. The content of "right" can change within and across societies, and the core aims of the American right may eventually change; but that prospect does not make the right's present forms of unity arbitrary or transient.

Given this conception of the American right, it is easier to see what makes the radical right radical. It is not, as Bobbio's definition would suggest, that such forces are deeply devoted to inequality. Some elements may be. But the populist themes of the radical right sometimes make it more egalitarian than other parts of the right. *The radical right is ardently committed to traditional values and deeply in favor of market orderings.* Its leaders and members believe that realizing their commitments will require deep changes in American political institutions and cultural forms. These positions provide grounds for opposing all the political and cultural forces that limit the market or jeopardize traditional values as the radical right understands them. On this basis the radical right has played a large role in national political life over the last three decades, one larger than the authors of *TRR* anticipated.

After 2000

Less than a year after the presidential election of 2000, it is not possible to know the long-term effects of that extraordinary process on the position and prospects of the radical right. Yet both the campaign and its result seem likely to continue the main dynamic discussed above. A general shift to the right gives conservative views a centrist location, while opening space for the less sectarian parts of the radical right to play a large and influential public role.

George W. Bush became President partly because of his adroit management of relations with the radical right, especially the more legitimate sections of the far right. By all indications Bush received the active support of most leaders and activists of the far right. One reason for this success was that many of these actors were very tired of losing presidential elections in the 1990s. They saw strong support for Bush as their best way to prevent another loss. In terms of the vote, exit polls show that Bush received the support of the great majority of conservative Republicans (and of most conservative independents). Bush was a sufficiently attractive candidate to the far right on both strategic and principled grounds that there was little if any room for Patrick Buchanan's independent campaign. At the same time Bush gained the support of about two thirds of liberal Republicans and of those who voted for Perot in 1996.

Bush achieved these results through an even-tempered presentation of traditional conservative positions along with elements of the views and approaches of the far right. This was not a clever trick but a real accomplishment. It resulted from years of debate about how to develop and articulate the right's core themes in broad and open forms, as the Republican platform of 2000 sought to do.

Bush generally avoided provocative formulations of his views, which were almost entirely consistent with prior initiatives from the Republican right. Thus he strongly urged large tax cuts, which he argued for not only on economic grounds but because they would have the benign result of reducing the role of the national government. Reducing the role of the national government was also one dimension of his proposal to restructure and partially privatize social security. Along with these proposals, Bush's campaign expressed conservative communitarian themes about family and social life, while urging that religious organizations become much more active in carrying out and thus in shaping social policies.[35]

In the Bush campaign boundaries were blurred between traditional Republican conservatism and parts of the far right. Numerous advisers and activists bridged and blended these two currents. The tone was centrist; the content was strongly and firmly conservative. Bush's moderate tone won him very little Democratic support, but that was probably not the point. It does seem to have been effective among independents and more liberal Republicans.

Bush's campaign showed that mainstream Republican conservatives regard the support of the radical right (mainly the far right) as very important for electing a Republican president. This support was indeed crucial in defeating Senator John McCain in the Republican primary contest. The far right's support seems to have been significant in defeating Gore in some of the states that voted for Clinton in the 1990s. Bush showed that a highly partisan strategy could produce a Republican victory, even if it was narrow in conception and made few new inroads among mainly Democratic constituencies.

Early in Bush's administration parts of the right drew the conclusion that the unfinished conservative agenda of the mid-1990s could be enacted despite the tenuous Republican majority in Congress. Especially after the loss of Republican control of the Senate, others will regard such an approach as sectarian, given Bush's narrow victory. They may try to develop a broader strategy for drawing significant parts of the center and center-right toward the right in support of Bush's overall program.

Winning yields such difficulties. As the center once again moves to the right, the main elements of the radical right face major choices. For much of the increasingly respectable and influential far right, the opportunity to influence Bush's themes and policies is both appealing and a perceived duty. Other parts of the far right may be more hesitant, doubting that a narrow victory over Gore marks a new political era. The ultraright is apt to be under great pressure to restrain itself—and some will respond by withdrawing from politics. In the near future this will probably mean that ultraright disruption and violence are more limited than they were in the 1990s.

Gore gained little support from his efforts to link Bush with the far right, as his likely voters were already opposed to Bush. If Gore's failure to stigmatize Bush does not really show popular approval of the far right, it registers yet again the blurring of boundaries between traditional Republican conservatism and the legitimate sections of the far right. The presence of the *National Review* in the Bush camp thus surprised no one and scared very few people who were not already opposed to Bush.

Given the shape of the Bush campaign and its success, we

can expect a significant radical right—mainly the legitimate far right—to play an influential role in national politics in the next few years. The radical right has shown the ability to develop and adapt after important defeats. In the 2000 election most of its elements contained their more sectarian impulses at key moments. If the radical right seems unlikely ever to achieve its full program, that reality will sooner or later cause new disappointment and bitterness for its adherents. Yet this surprisingly vigorous political force has survived and at times flourished over the last half century. The radical right has established itself in national politics as a force with enough strength and flexibility to survive the challenges of both incorporation and marginality. It will likely remain on the scene through and beyond the presidency of George W. Bush.

Notes

1. Erik Asard, Daniel Bell, and Michael Kazin made valuable comments on earlier drafts. I benefited from the comments and research assistance of the following students at the Graduate Faculty of New School University: Nancy Wadsworth, Shelley Hurt, Joseph Lowndes, Mark Redhead, and Marcos Soler. Time to work on this essay was one of the many opportunities provided to me as Fulbright Chair at the Swedish Institute for North American Studies at Uppsala University in 1999–2000.

2. *TRR*'s analyses retain a broad comparative significance. In the second half of the 1990s and early in the next decade, parties of what is called the "far right" or the "radical right" in Western Europe made notable advances in several countries, even if their overall success was not impressive. When one such party, the Freedom Party in Austria, helped to form a government in 2000, controversy centered on the inflammatory statements of its leader, Jorg Haider. When he responded by continuing to make similar statements while affirming his commitment to democracy, the key question became clear: How is it possible to distinguish between a party of the right that is happy to employ nativist and racialist discourses but is basically committed to constitutional procedures and democratic liberties, and a party whose core commitments are illiberal and dangerous? This is not precisely the issue that faced the authors of *The Radical Right*, of course, but there are sufficient similarities to make that work of interest to people who are mainly concerned with contemporary comparative politics.

3. On the populist radicalism of the 1930s see Alan Brinkley, *Voices of Protest: Huey Long, Father Coughlin, and the Great Depression* (New York: Alfred A. Knopf, 1982); on American populism, see Michael Kazin, *The Populist Persuasion* (New York: Basic Books, 1995).

4. *The Radical Right* was reviewed widely in 1963 in academic and popu-

lar journals. See *American Political Science Review* (volume 57: 688–89), *The New Yorker* (May 18, 1963), *Saturday Review* (Victor Lasky, "180 Degrees from the Left," June 22, 1963), and *Harpers* (July 1963). For a survey of debates about McCarthyism see Thomas C. Reeves, "McCarthyism: Interpretations Since Hofstadter," *Wisconsin Magazine of History* 60 (autumn 1976): 42–54.

5. On the right's early critical response to *TRR* see George H. Nash, *The Conservative Intellectual Movement in America—Since 1945* second edition (Wilmington, DE: Intercollegiate Studies Institute, 1996): 125–26, 442.

6. Nelson W. Polsby, "Toward an Explanation of McCarthyism," *Political Studies* 8 (1960): 250–71; Michael Paul Rogin, *The Intellectuals and McCarthy: The Radical Specter* (Cambridge: MIT Press, 1967). Polsby and Rogin differ considerably from Nash in their political judgments of McCarthy. However, they share with Nash a view of McCarthy as a conventional, if melodramatic, conservative politician. There is merit in this view as McCarthy sought office and engaged in routine politics. But it understates the aggressive, rageful, and destructive elements of his projects.

7. Polsby emphasizes the diffuseness of the status politics argument in "Toward an Explanation of McCarthyism," 254.

8. In the last decade the opening of ex-Soviet and American intelligence files has produced mounting evidence both of the political and financial dependence of the American Communist Party on the Soviet Union, and of the involvement of a substantial number of Communists in espionage in the 1930s and 1940s. This evidence has helped to spur a retrospective appreciation of McCarthy as basically correct if erratic and excessive. For such efforts, see Arthur Herman, *Joseph McCarthy: Reexamining the Life and Legacy of America's Most Hated Senator* (Free Press: New York, 2000); and William F. Buckley Jr., *The Redhunter—A Novel Based on the Life of Senator Joe McCarthy* (Boston: Little, Brown and Company, 1999). McCarthy is not revalued in this way in the most reliable new work on American Communism and the Soviet Union, which has appeared in a series of volumes by Klehr, Haynes, and co-authors. The most recent of these books is John Earl Haynes and Harvey Klehr, *Venona: Decoding Soviet Espionage in America* (New Haven: Yale University Press, 1999).

9. The actual sequence—in which McCarthy's emergence occurred well into the Cold War—creates difficulties for his defenders. The problem with the pro-McCarthy view is, putting it simply, Truman. By 1950–51 the Marshall Plan was underway and NATO existed. The U.S. was at war against a Soviet ally. The Communist Party was broken as a political organization in the U.S. Why, in this context, was a new and more extensive initiative against domestic Communism required in the United States? How would such an offensive help the U.S. in international politics?

10. *Congressional Record*, 82nd Congress, 1st session, June 14, 1951: 6556–6603. Quoted in Thomas C. Reeves, *The Life and Times of Joe McCarthy: A Biography* (New York: Stein and Day, 1982), p. 372.

11. Interpretations of McCarthy's support based on poll data should be

qualified by noting that the data are thin and their quality is uncertain. Polls in the 1950s mainly asked respondents whether they supported McCarthy or not, without specifying the aspects of McCarthy's views and actions that were in question. Lipset, Polsby, and Rogin were evaluating the same limited polls. These data definitely showed that Republicans more often favored McCarthy than did Democrats. But they also showed significant support for McCarthy among Democrats. Thus, a 1954 Gallup survey cited by Polsby aimed to gauge the extent of support for McCarthy by party. As measured four different ways, from 21 to 30 percent of Democrats supported McCarthy. This was a much lower level of support than among Republicans, but it was nonetheless substantial. Rogin surveyed Gallup Polls in the early 1950s to find that McCarthy gained support from 36 percent of Democrats and 61 percent of Republicans, while 44 percent of Democrats and 25 percent of Republicans opposed him. These data show that McCarthy was more apt to be supported by Republicans than Democrats. But they also show the potential effectiveness of McCarthy in gaining Democratic support without losing too many Republican votes. In two party competition, an initiative that could produce the alignment I have just sketched might be a very attractive one for a party to launch. Imagine an election in which McCarthy was somehow made the only issue and voters were distributed as Rogin indicates. Undecided voters are not counted, and the numbers of Democrats and Republicans are equal. In this imaginary contest, Republicans would get 58 percent of the total vote. (Polsby, "Toward an Explanation of McCarthyism," 262; Rogin, *The Intellectuals and McCarthy: The Radical Specter*, 233–35; Lipset, "Three Decades of the Radical Right," 396, 400).

12. Rogin, *The Intellectuals and McCarthy*, 103, 165–67, 262.

13. There was much debate about the Wallace vote soon after his presidential primary efforts in 1964. For a survey see M. Margaret Conway, "The White Backlash Re-examined: Wallace and the 1964 Primaries," *Social Science Quarterly* 49 (1968): 710–19.

14. An unreasonable political argument in the context of the contemporary United States entails premises or proposals that few if any citizens could accept as compatible with liberal and democratic commitments. But such an argument remains political insofar as it could in principle be adopted as a way of organizing social relations. A purely irrational claim is so evidently unworkable either for the individual or group proposing it or for the polity of which those making the claim are part as to be clearly and directly destructive. These distinctions are necessary, complicated, and partly contextual. See John Rawls, *Political Liberalism* (New York: Columbia University Press, 1993).

15. Karl Mannheim argued that conservatism should be distinguished from traditionalism because the former is a conscious effort to reflect on and reshape tradition in response to the disruptions of modernity. Conservatism is both reactive and creative. Peter Viereck's formulations resemble what Mannheim argued three decades earlier. Mannheim is not cited in *The Radical Right*, but its main authors knew his work. Karl Mannheim, *Conservatism: A Contribution to the Sociology of Knowledge*, edited and introduced

by David Kettler, Volker Meja, and Nico Stehr (London: Routledge & Kegan Paul, 1986): 73, 85, 101–102.

16. On Goldwater's career see Robert Alan Goldberg, *Barry Goldwater* (New Haven, CT: Yale University Press, 1995). Goldberg notes the contributions of Robert Taft and Joseph McCarthy to Goldwater's first campaign for the Senate in 1952 (95–97). Also see Rick Perlstein, *Before the Storm: Barry Goldwater and the Unmaking of the American Consensus* (New York: Hill and Wang, 2001).

17. Herbert Kitschelt in collaboration with Anthony J. McGann, *The Radical Right in Western Europe: A Comparative Analysis* (Ann Arbor, Michigan: University of Michigan Press, 1995): 19, 275.

18. I would place the figure at 12 to 14 percent of the national electorate. This estimate might be deemed high, because the Republican primary electorate is usually regarded as to the right of the Republican national presidential vote. Yet the overall decline in voting rates diminishes the salience of this point. So does the weakening of party identification, which means that someone like Buchanan could expect to obtain support from a number of voters who are registered Democrats, independents, or Republicans who don't vote in primaries.

Poll data on abortion also suggest that estimating the radical right at 12 to 14 percent of the electorate is reasonable. These data find that 15 to 20 percent of those surveyed want to ban abortion. One would expect the anti-abortion figure to be higher than the core strength of the radical right because some people who oppose abortion on Catholic doctrinal grounds are centrist or liberal on other issues. For the figures on Republican primaries, see Gerald M. Pomper, *The Election of 1992* (Chatham House Publishers: Chatham, New Jersey, 1993): 46–50; and Gerald M. Pomper, *The Election of 1996* (Chatham House Publishers: Chatham, New Jersey, 1997): 46–47.

19. On organizations and currents on the radical right (especially the ultraright), see Sara Diamond, *Roads to Dominion: Right-Wing Movements and Political Power in the United States* (New York: The Guilford Press, 1995).

20. Ultraright violence in the 1990s was reported regularly by law enforcement agencies and these reports were collected by several organizations. This information is available in the publications and web sites of the National Abortion and Reproductive Rights Action League and the Southern Poverty Law Center. Both groups have a political interest in stressing the extent of violence, but they have to defend their reports against hostile critics. NARAL claimed on its web site in 1999 that anti-abortion forces committed seven murders since 1993, attempted sixteen murders since 1991, committed over 2,000 reported acts of anti-abortion violence, and engaged in 28,000 acts of disruption at facilities where abortions are performed. The first two figures can readily be checked against other sources. Even if the latter two figures are high estimates, the reality of substantial anti-abortion violence is evident. So is the extent of ultraright anti-government violence, which is the main subject of the reports of the Southern Poverty Law Center. This source focuses

on militia groups and racist groups. It emphasizes and perhaps overstates the convergence between the two. It also seems less reliable than NARAL in its quantitative claims. Thus, a web site in September 1999 cited 435 active "patriot groups" in the U.S. as of 1998–99. When one looks at the list, organized by state, many of the entries refer to bookstores and tiny groups that do not resemble the highly organized and well-armed groups commonly identified as militias. Nonetheless, the Southern Poverty Law Center's reports on episodes of violence are generally accurate and they record a very disturbing experience. These episodes declined after the mid-1990s and their renewal seems unlikely in Bush's first term. Yet the ultraright remains on the scene as both a political current and infrastructure that could lead to new phases of militancy and perhaps new forms of political violence.

21. For a view of the radical right's political effects that expresses elements of *TRR*'s critique, see Edward A. Shils, *The Torment of Secrecy: The Background and Consequences of American Security Policies* (Chicago: Ivan. R. Dee, Publisher, 1996—first published in 1956).

22. Such a broad claim might be disputed by reference to particular columns and articles. I base it on a review of *Commentary, National Review,* and *Weekly Standard* from 1996 through 1999. In these years ultraright activities received very little serious analysis in these important publications.

23. For a collection of such critiques, see Mitchell S. Muncy, editor, *The End of Democracy? The Judicial Usurpation of Politics* (Dallas, Texas: Spence Publishing Company, 1997). The book's core is a symposium published in *First Things* in 1996, in which prominent far right intellectuals questioned and in some cases rejected the legitimacy of the current American regime. In the symposium and responses, William Bennett and the editors of *National Review* countered the provocative assertion of illegitimacy. They agreed with much of the critique of American politics and culture, but counseled respect for constitutional procedures.

24. The left's problem in making a consistent critique of the right's links with illiberal and antidemocratic forces is not only historical. It continued into the 1990s, where it was symbolized by the political figure of Louis Farrakhan. Once it became clear that Farrakhan had some support among constituencies that the left regarded as important, there was great reticence about simply rejecting him altogether, despite the many opportunities that his positions provided for this response.

25. For a valuable study of the domestic policies of the Clinton administrations, see Margaret Weir, editor, *The Social Divide: Political Parties and the Future of Activist Government* (Washington, D.C.: Brookings Institution Press, 1998).

26. Several decades later the emergence and political success of Margaret Thatcher's Conservatives in Britain occasioned a similar process of reflection among left of center analysts in that country. Their rethinking, which was conducted in terms much closer to Marxism, occasioned a vigorous debate about whether Thatcherism had elements of genuine political novelty. See Stuart Hall and Martin Jacques, editors, *The Politics of Thatcherism* (Lon-

don: Lawrence and Wishart, 1983). On the Thatcher experience also see Shirley Robin Letwin, *The Anatomy of Thatcherism* (London: Hutchinson, 1999).

27. Max Weber, "Class, Status, Party," in Hans H. Gerth and C. Wright Mills, editors, *From Max Weber: Essays in Sociology* (New York: Oxford University Press, 1958): 180–195.

28. Diverse efforts have been made in this direction, in such works as Samuel Huntington's *American Politics: The Promise of Disharmony* (Cambridge, Massachusetts: Harvard University Press, 1981) and James Morone's *The Democratic Wish: Popular Participation and the Limits of American Government* (New York: Basic Books, 1990).

29. David Plotke, *Building a Democratic Political Order: Reshaping American Liberalism in the 1930s and 1940s* (New York: Cambridge University Press, 1996).

30. Chantal Mouffe and Ernesto Laclau made an ambitious effort to demonstrate the full analytical separation of class and politics. After their careful effort to retain elements of Marxism within a postmodern framework, the way was open to focus on identity as a plastic and virtually self-created reality for which there are no real social determinants. Ernesto Laclau and Chantal Mouffe, *Hegemony and Socialist Strategy* (London: Verso, 1985).

31. In addition to Marxism, political sociology has non-Marxist roots in the elite theories of the early 20th century produced by Michels, Mosca, and Pareto. These theories made their way into mid-century American social theory via several routes, including Weber's political sociology and Parsons' own work. For an interesting recent effort to reinvigorate political sociology, in which the authors seek to emphasize the causal importance of social cleavages for national politics in the United States, see Jeffrey Manza and Clem Brooks, *Social Cleavages and Political Change: Voter Alignments and U.S. Party Coalitions* (New York: Oxford University Press, 1999).

32. Kristin Luker, *Abortion and the Politics of Motherhood* (Berkeley: University of California Press, 1984) and Jane Mansbridge, *Why We Lost the ERA* (Chicago: University of Chicago Press, 1986).

33. Obviously George Wallace was a key figure. In this area there are a number of important controversies. These concern figures such as Wallace himself, the shape and dynamic of public opinion about race in recent decades, and the relative importance of race as compared with other issues in defining the perspective and activities of various strands of the radical right. Adjudicating the last issue is especially difficult because of deep changes in public discourse on racial matters as a result of which explicitly racist language is rarely used. I do not think it is accurate or useful to claim that the post-Reagan radical right as a whole is racist. Yet what I would call racial conservatism has been a major theme in both the antistatism and social conservatism of the radical right. And the radical right has been a magnet for explicitly racist political forces. On these matters, see: Amy Elizabeth Ansell, *New Right New Racism: Race and Reaction in the United States and Britain* (London: Macmillan Press, 1997); Lawrence D. Bobo and Ryan A. Smith,

"From Jim Crow Racism to Laissez-Faire Racism: The Transformation of Racial Attitudes," in Wendy F. Katkin, Ned Landsman, and Andrea Tyre, *Beyond Pluralism: The Conception of Groups and Group Identities in America* (Chicago: University of Illinois Press, 1998): 182–220; Dan T. Carter, *From George Wallace to Newt Gingrich: Race in the Conservative Counterrevolution, 1963–1994* (Baton Rouge: Louisiana State University Press, 1996); Martin Gilens, *Why Americans Hate Welfare: Race, Media, and the Politics of Antipoverty Policy* (Chicago, University of Chicago Press, 1999); and Paul M. Sniderman and Thomas Piazza, *The Scar of Race* (Cambridge: Belknap Press, 1993).

34. Norberto Bobbio, *Left and Right: The Significance of a Political Distinction* (Chicago: University of Chicago Press, 1996): 58–59. For a valuable effort to characterize the right primarily in relational terms, see Albert O. Hirschman, *The Rhetoric of Reaction: Perversity, Futility, Jeopardy* (Cambridge: Harvard University Press, 1991).

35. See Marvin Olasky, *Renewing American Compassion* (New York: Free Press, 1996); and Marvin Olasky (with an introduction by George W. Bush), *Compassionate Conservatism: What it is, What it Does, and How it Can Transform America* (New York: Free Press, 2000).

PREFACE

The idea for the original edition of this volume, which appeared under the title *The New American Right,* arose in 1954 in a faculty seminar on political behavior, at Columbia University. The subject was McCarthyism, and we sought to bring to bear on this question whatever sophistication the social sciences had achieved. One thing soon became clear: the standard explanations of American political behavior—in terms of economic-interest-group conflict or the role of the electoral structure—were inadequate to the task. (See Chapter 2.) The most fruitful approaches seemed to be those worked out by Richard Hofstadter and Seymour Martin Lipset.

Hofstadter, from a historian's vantage point, argued that a preoccupation with status has been a persistent element in American politics and that McCarthyism as a social phenomenon could best be explained as a form of "status anxiety" in groups that have been "tormented by a nagging doubt as to whether they are really and truly and fully American." He called the individuals in such positions "pseudo-conservatives" because, while claiming to uphold tradition, they were in reality projecting their own fears and frustrations onto society.

Lipset, a sociologist, distinguished between "class politics," which seemed applicable during periods of depression and "status politics," which seemed to predominate during periods of prosperity, when groups were concerned to defend their newly won positions. McCarthyism, he argued, was a species of status politics, and McCarthy's followers were the "radical right"—a term coined by Lipset and used for the first time in the original edition of this book—because they represented a form of extremism, rather than a genuine effort to bespeak the conservative point of view.

A number of essays appearing about this time—by David Riesman and Nathan Glazer, Peter Viereck, and Talcott Parsons—indicated that other writers had independently been engaged in the same kind of analysis, although each with a different emphasis. The congruence was striking enough to suggest a book that would bring together these essays as illustrations of this new conceptual analysis. Hence, *The New American Right*.

When the book appeared in 1955, McCarthy was already sliding toward his downfall. But as the introductory essay noted at that time, "McCarthyism, or McCarthywasm, as one wit put it, may be a passing phenomenon. This book is concerned not with these transiencies, but with the deeper-running social currents of a turbulent mid-century America." The re-emergence of the "radical right" in 1961–62 has justified these fears while confirming our analysis. This is not to say that Birchism, and other aspects of the present radical right, are exactly the same as McCarthyism. As a number of the following essays make clear, there are some distinct dissimilarities as well as some common features. McCarthy was a wrecker—what the Germans call an *Umstürzmensch*, a man who wants to tear up society but has no plan of his own. The radical right of the nineteen-sixties is a movement that fears not only Communism but "modernity," and that, in its equation of liberalism with Communism, represents a different challenge to the American democratic consensus.

In bringing out this new, enlarged edition of *The New American Right*, the authors felt that, rather than rewrite the original essays, they would prefer to let these stand as their judgments at the time, and to add supplementary essays. In American social science, there is a valuable tendency, initiated by Paul Lazarsfeld and Robert K. Merton in their follow-up volume on "The American Soldier," to create "continuities" in research by allowing participants in the original efforts, and others, to comment on that research and to extend the initial analysis. In that sense, this volume represents a "continuity" in which the authors can assess their own work and, at the same time, contribute analyses of the radical right, circa 1962. Thus, the original essays carry the notation "1955" after the title, while the new essays bear the legend "1962."

From the original volume, one essay, "The Polls on Communism and Conformity," by S. M. Lipset and Nathan Glazer, has been eliminated, primarily because it was methodological, while its substantive material, a report on the volume *Communism, Conformity and Civil Liberties,* by Samuel Stouffer, is summarized in the new essay by Herbert H. Hyman.

In addition to the supplementary chapters by the original authors, we have added two new essays to this volume. One, by Alan Westin, is an intensive examination of the ideology and operations of the John Birch Society, which Westin locates in the context of extremist politics, both left and right, in the United States. The second, by Herbert H. Hyman, is a comparison of the climates of political intolerance in England and America. Any general explanation of a social movement has to be rooted in comparative analysis, and Hyman's pioneering work in that direction provides a useful corrective to some of the parochial aspects of the original analyses.

The volume opens with a new chapter by the editor, which seeks to explain the emergence of the radical right of 1961–62 both in its immediate political context and as a reflection of more pervasive social changes in American life; this is followed by the editor's original essay of 1955, which deals with the standard interpretations of political behavior in America. In all other instances, the original essay precedes each author's supplementary chapter.

The stimulus to several of these essays came initially from the Fund for the Republic, and we again acknowledge, gratefully, its courageous and early help. Mr. Lipset's long, supplementary contribution—a monograph in its own right—was aided by a grant from the Anti-Defamation League which is sponsoring, at the University of California at Berkeley, an extended survey of the relationship of political extremism to ethnic prejudice in the United States.

Daniel Bell

Columbia University
June, 1962.

1

THE DISPOSSESSED (1962)*

Daniel Bell

> The American has never yet had to face the trials of Job.
> . . . Hitherto America has been the land of universal
> good will, confidence in life, inexperience of poisons.
> Until yesterday, it believed itself immune from the he-
> reditary plagues of mankind. It could not credit the dan-
> ger of being suffocated or infected by any sinister prin-
> ciple. . . .
>
>
>
> GEORGE SANTAYANA,
> *Character and Opinion
> in the United States*
>
>

In the winter of 1961–62, the "radical right" emerged into
quick prominence on the American political scene. The immediate reasons for its appearance are not hard to understand. The simple fact was that the Republican Party, now
out of power, inevitably began to polarize (much as the
Democrats, if they were out of power, might have split over
the civil rights and integration issue), and the right wing
came to the fore. The right-wing Republicans have an ideology—perhaps the only group in American life that possesses
one today—but during the Eisenhower administration they
had been trapped because "their" party was in power, and
the American political system, with its commitment to deals
and penalties, does not easily invite ideological—or even principled—political splits. An administration in office, possessing
patronage and prestige, can "paper over" the inherent divi-

sions within a party. But out of office, such conflicts are
bound to arise, and so they did within the G.O.P.

Clearly there is more to all this than merely a contest for
power within a party. Something new has been happening
in American life. It is not the rancor of the radical right, for
rancor has been a recurrent aspect of the American political
temper. Nor is it just the casting of suspicions or the conspiracy theory of politics, elements of which have streaked
American life in the past. What is new, and this is why the
problem assumes importance far beyond the question of
the fight for control of a party, is the ideology of this movement—its readiness to jettison constitutional processes and
to suspend liberties, to condone Communist methods in the
fighting of Communism.

Few countries in the world have been able to maintain a
social system that allows political power to pass peacefully
from one social group to another without the threat of hostilities or even civil war. In the mid-twentieth century, we see
such historical centers of civilization as France, let alone
states just beginning to work out viable democratic frame-
works, torn apart by ideological groups that will not accept
a consensual system of politics. The politics of civility, to
use Edward Shils' phrase, has been the achievement of only a
small group of countries—those largely within an Anglo-
Saxon or Scandinavian political tradition. Today, the ideology of the right wing in America threatens the politics of
American civility. Its commitment and its methods threaten
to disrupt the "fragile consensus" that underlies the American political system.

I believe that the radical right is only a small minority,
but it gains force from the confusions within the world of
conservatism regarding the changing character of American
life. What the right as a whole fears is the erosion of its own
social position, the collapse of its power, the increasing in-
comprehensibility of a world—now overwhelmingly technical
and complex—that has changed so drastically within a lifetime.

The right, thus, fights a rear-guard action. But its very

anxieties illustrate the deep fissures that have opened in American society as a whole, as a result of the complex structural changes that have been taking place in the past thirty years or so. And more, they show that the historic American response to social crisis, the characteristic American style, is no longer adequate to the tasks.

I

The Emergence of the Radical Right

Social groups that are dispossessed invariably seek targets on whom they can vent their resentments, targets whose power can serve to explain their dispossession. In this respect, the radical right of the early 1960s is in no way different from the Populists of the 1890s, who for years traded successfully on such simple formulas as "Wall Street," "international bankers," and "the Trusts," in order to have not only targets but "explanations" for politics. What lends especial rancor to the radical right of the 1960s is its sense of betrayal not by its "enemies" but by its "friends."

After twenty years of Democratic power, the right-wing Republicans hoped that the election of Dwight Eisenhower would produce its own utopia: the dismantling of the welfare state, the taming of labor unions, and the "magical" rollback of Communism in Europe. None of this happened. Eisenhower's Labor Secretary courted the unions, social-security benefits increased, and, during the recession, unemployment benefits were extended, while the government, in good Keynesian style, ran a twelve-billion-dollar budgetary deficit. In foreign policy, Secretary of State Dulles first trumpeted a "liberation policy," and then retreated, talked brinkmanship but moved cautiously, announced a policy of "massive retaliation," and, toward the end of his tenure, abandoned even that, so that the subsequent Eisenhower moves toward summitry were no different from, or from a "hard" right line were "softer" than, the Truman-Acheson containment policy. Thus eight years of moderation proved more frustrating than twenty years of opposition.

Once the Democrats were back in office, the charge of
softness in dealing with Communism could again become a
political, as well as an ideological, issue. And the radical
right was quick to act. The abject failure in Cuba—the name
of the landing place for the abortive invasion, the Bay of
Pigs, itself became a cruel historical joke—seemed to reinforce the picture of the United States that emerged out of
the stalemate in Korea a decade ago—of a lurching, lumber-
ing power, lacking will, unsure of its strength, indecisive in
its course, defensive in its posture. The theme of the radical
right was voiced by Rear Admiral Chester Ward (ret.), the
Washington director of the American Security Council, who
declared, "Americans are tired of defeats. They are tired of
surrenders covered up as 'negotiated settlements.' They are,
indeed, tired of so much talk and little action by our leaders.
For the first time in sixteen years of the cold war, a demand
for victory is beginning to roll into Washington."

Thus the stage was set.

The factors that precipitated the radical right into quick
notoriety in early 1961 were the rancor of their attacks and
the flash spread of the movement in so many different places.
McCarthyism in the mid-1950s was never an organized movement; it was primarily an atmosphere of fear, generated by a
one-man swashbuckler cutting a wide swath through the
headlines. In some localities—in Hollywood, on Broadway, in
some universities—individual vigilante groups did begin a
drumbeat drive against Communists or former fellow-travelers, but by and large the main agitation was conducted in
government by Congressional or state legislators, using agencies of legislative investigation to assert their power. In contrast, the radical right of the 1960s has been characterized
by a multitude of organizations that seemingly have been
able to evoke an intense emotional response from a devoted
following.

Three elements conjoined to attract public attention to the
radical right. One was the disclosure of the existence of the
John Birch Society, a secretive, conspiratorial group obedient
to a single leader, Robert Welch, who argued that one could

combat the methods of Communism only with Communist methods. Thus, membership lists were never disclosed, fronts were organized to conduct campaigns (such as the one to impeach Chief Justice Warren, which turned, with heavy-handed jocularity, into calls to "hang" him), and a symbol of patriotism was put forth in the name of an Army captain who had been shot in China by the Communists.

The second was the fashionable spread of week-long seminars of anti-Communist "schools," conducted by evangelist preachers who adapted old revivalist techniques to a modern idiom, which swept sections of the country, particularly the Southwest and California. These schools promised to initiate the student into the "mysteries" of Communism by unfolding its secret aims, or unmasking the philosophy of "dialectical materialism." And, third, there was the disclosure of the existence of extreme fanatic groups, such as the Minutemen, who organized "guerrilla-warfare seminars," complete with rifles and mortars, in preparation for the day when patriots would have to take to the hills to organize resistance against a Communist-run America. Such fringe movements, ludicrous as they were, illustrated the hysteria that had seized some sections of the radical right.

To a surprising extent, much of the radical-right agitation —and the spread of the seminar device—was unleashed by the Eisenhower administration itself. In 1958, the National Security Council issued a directive, as yet still unpublished, which stated that it would be the policy of the United States government, as Senator Fulbright cited it, "to make use of military personnel and facilities to arouse the public to the menace of Communism."[1] Following this directive, the Joint

[1] "Memorandum Submitted to the Department of Defense on Propaganda Activities of Military Personnel," by Senator Fulbright, *Congressional Record,* August 2, 1961, pp. 13436–13442. As the New York *Times* summarized this N.S.C. directive on June 17, 1961, "President Eisenhower and his top policy leaders decreed that the cold war could not be fought as a series of separate and often unrelated actions, as with foreign aid and propaganda. Rather, it must be fought with a concentration of all the resources of the

Chiefs of Staff and the National War College entered into consultation with the Foreign Policy Research Institute of the University of Pennsylvania, and the Institute of American Strategy (a creation of the Richardson Foundation), to plan curriculum and seminars for reserve officers and local businessmen. A basic text was adopted, *American Strategy for the Nuclear Age*, edited by Walter F. Hahn and John C. Neff, of the University of Pennsylvania group. An equally influential text was the book *Protracted Conflict*, by Robert Strausz-Hupe and Colonel William Kintner, which argues that no negotiations with the Russians leading to a stable settlement are really possible. The Strausz-Hupe group is neither part of, nor should it be identified with, the lunatic fringes of the right. Its arguments are serious and subject to the debate and rival assessments of other scholars. But the actions initiated by the Joint Chiefs of Staff did lead to a large number of Projects Alert and indoctrination seminars, carried out by official Navy and Army spokesmen, that went far beyond the original scope of the National Security Council directive, and that brought into these sessions the pitchmen of the radical right.

In August, 1960 (as detailed in the Fulbright memorandum), the United States Naval Air Station, at Glenview, Illinois, sent out invitations to community leaders and businessmen, inviting them to a seminar on "Education for American Security." The announced purpose of the seminar was to stimulate an active force against "moral decay, political apathy and spiritual bankruptcy," and to teach the participants how to create similar schools in other Midwestern communities. The conference was addressed by a number of high-ranking naval officers. But it also included Dr. Fred C. Schwarz, the organizer of the Christian Anti-Communism Crusade; E. Merrill Root, author of *Brainwashing in the High Schools* and *Collectivism on the Campus*, and an en-

---

Government and with the full understanding and support of the civilian population. It was decided, in particular, that the military should be used to reinforce the cold-war effort."

dorser of the John Birch Society; and Richard Arens, former research director of the House Un-American Activities Committee, and a member of Schwarz's Christian Crusade. The speeches during the sessions, according to the *Christian Century*, the liberal Protestant weekly published in Chicago, not only attacked Communism but condemned as well "liberals, modernists, John Dewey, Harvard students, the New York *Times*, the American Friends Service Committee, pacifists, naïve ministers," and so on.

It was this same mixture of official military sponsorship and propagandists of the radical right that characterized dozens of similar seminars around the country. On April 21, 1961, the Chamber of Commerce of Greater Pittsburgh sponsored a Fourth-Dimensional Warfare Seminar, with the coöperation of the commanding general of the 2nd U. S. Army, Lieutenant General Ridgely Gaither, and his staff, at whose sessions the House Un-American Activities Committee film *Operation Abolition* was shown, and the principal speaker, Admiral Chester Ward (ret.), attacked Adlai Stevenson and George Kennan, as advisers to the President whose "philosophies regarding foreign affairs would chill the typical American." A Strategy for Survival conference held on April 14th and 15th in Fort Smith, Fayetteville, and Little Rock, Arkansas, sponsored by the local Chamber of Commerce and promoted by Major General Bullock, the area commander, heard speakers from Harding College, a small institution in Searcy, Arkansas, operated by members of the Church of Christ, which has been the source of much extreme right-wing material. And on the program was the film *Communism on the Map*, prepared by Harding College, which equates Socialism with Communism. A Project Alert was organized at the Pensacola Naval Air Training station, in Florida, based on Harding College materials, and the program was repeated in similar "alerts" in Georgia, South Carolina, and Texas. Dr. Fred C. Schwarz held a seminar at the headquarters of the 8th Naval District, in New Orleans, which was endorsed by the Commandant, Rear Admiral W. G. Schindler. A Houston Freedom Forum was held by Schwarz's

Christian Anti-Communism Crusade at which Admiral F. W. Warder gave the keynote address.

And so it went. In almost every area of the country, seminars, schools, and projects, organized by the military or by business groups in coöperation with the military, spread the propaganda of the radical right and gave a broad aura of authority and legitimacy to such propaganda and to such pitchmen of the radical right as the Reverend Dr. Schwarz and the Reverend Billy Hargis.

II

The Psychological Posture

The psychological stock-in-trade of the radical right rests on a threefold appeal: the breakdown of moral fiber in the United States; a conspiracy theory of a "control apparatus" in the government which is selling out the country; and a detailed forecast regarding the Communist "takeover" of the United States.

Central to the appeal of the radical right is the argument that old-fashioned patriotism has been subverted by the cosmopolitan intellectual. An editorial in the *National Review* on the space flight of astronaut John Glenn sums up this theme in striking fashion. Glenn, said the editorial, is an authentic American hero because he is unashamed to say that he gets a thrill when the American flag goes by and because he will openly acknowledge the guidance of God. "It is 'American' as in older storybooks, as in legends, and myths and dreams—brought up to technological date, of course—as, let's say it plainly, in the pre-1930 Fourth of July celebrations; and the *Saturday Evening Post* covers before they, too, not long ago, went modern; and a touch of soap opera. Yes, a bit corny—for that is the traditional American style. Too corny by far for the Norman Cousinses, Arthur Schlesingers, Adlai Stevensons, Henry Steele Commagers, Max Lerners, John Kenneth Galbraiths, and those others of our enlightened age—so many of them now fluttering around the Kennedy throne—who have long left behind the old provincial corn for a headier global brew."

Here one finds the praise of the "simple virtues"—they are always simple—the evocation of small-town life, the uncluttered Arcadia, against the modern, the sophisticated, the cosmopolitan. But the Glenn flight, according to the editorial, proved more: it proved the victory of "man" against the "mechanical" and, implicitly, against the intellectual. "This and that went wrong, we all learned, with the unbelievably complex mechanism of Glenn's ship, as it whirled through the emptiness of Space," continued the *National Review*.

> The attitude control thingamajigs didn't work right. There were troubles in some of the communication instruments. A signal indicated that the latching of the heat shield was precarious. This and that went wrong with the mechanism, and man took over and brought Friendship 7 to its strange harbor. . . . And that is fine news, though it should hardly be news. It is good technically, because we Americans, with our gadgetry obsession and our wish for too much convenience, safety and comfort, tend to crowd all our machines and vehicles with too immensely many tricky devices. Every additional transistor in these automatic mechanisms means that many more connections to loosen; every valve can fail to open; every fuse can blow. Many sober engineers believe that this over-complication habit accounts for not a few of our missile and space troubles. . . . It is better news still, philosophically, we might say, because it reminds us that there is no such thing, and never will be, as a "thinking" machine. Only man thinks, wills, decides, dares. No machine, on land, in sea, air or space, can do man's job for him: can choose, for good or ill.

The fact that "man" is also the one who designs the machines is, of course, beside the point of the editorial. Its implication is fairly clear: don't let anyone tell us that space (or politics, economics, or life) is complicated; machines can never be perfect ("every valve can fail to open; every fuse can blow"); only "man" (not the scientist, the intellectual, or the unsober engineer) can think. In short, America will be back on an even keel when the simple virtues prevail.

The theme of conspiracy haunts the mind of the radical rightist. It permits him to build up the image of the children of darkness and the children of light. It exempts him from having to specify empirical proofs. General Edwin Walker told a Congressional committee that a "control apparatus" was "selling out the Constitution, national sovereignty and national independence," but when asked to specify the members of the control apparatus, he replied that he could not name the individuals, but that the apparatus could be identified "by its effects—what it did in Cuba—what it did in the Congo—what it did in Korea."

The irony of this reply is that it is cut from the same cloth as vulgar Bolshevik explanation: accident and contingency are ruled out of history, subjective intentions are the prattlings of "bourgeois morality," history is plot and objective consequence. Just as in a concentration camp—or any extreme situation—a victim adopts unconsciously the mode, manner, and even swagger of the aggressor, so men like General Walker seem to have become mesmerized by the enemies they have studied so assiduously and with such horrified fascination.

And to round out their picture of horror, the radical right has given us an exact forecast of things to come. Just as the "enthusiastic" preachers of Baptist fundamentalism would predict with Biblical certainty the date of the end of the world, so the fundamentalists of the radical right make their own predictions of the end of liberty in the United States. Fred Schwarz has named 1973 as the date set by the Communists for the takeover of America. In his lectures, Schwarz builds up the picture of the ultimate fate in store for his audience once the Communists win. "When they come for you, as they have for many others, and on a dark night, in a dank cellar, they take a wide-bore revolver with a soft-nose bullet, and they place it at the nape of your neck. . . ."

A more elaborate fantasy is provided in *The John Franklin*

Letters, a Birchite novel that was circulated in 1959, and then withdrawn.[2] The novel pictures an America Sovietized by the Communists in 1970. The beginning of the end comes in 1963, when the World Health Organization sends in a Yugoslav inspector, under powers granted by the President of the United States, to search any house he chooses. The Yugoslav discovers in the house of a good American a file of anti-Communist magazines, seizes them as deleterious to the mental health of the community, and is shot by the American, who escapes to the woods. But the infiltration continues. By 1970, the United States, thanks to the global do-gooders, has become part of a World Authority dominated by the Soviet-Asian-African bloc, and this Authority suspends the country's right to govern itself because of the "historic psychological genocide" against the Negro race. United Nations administrators, mostly Red Chinese, are sent in to rule. Harlem, triumphant, arises and loots the liquor stores. The city proletariat, its sense of decency destroyed by public housing, begins to raid the suburbs. In short order, twenty million Americans are "done away with," while the people are subjected to torture by blow-torch and rock-'n'-roll—the latter on television.

Meanwhile, the good American begins to fight back. As far back as 1967, John Franklin and his friends had been stockpiling rifles. And now they act. Franklin describes in gory detail a total of fourteen patriotic murders: two by fire, one by hammer, one by strangling, two by bow and arrow, one by defenestration, one by drowning, and the rest by shooting. These brave actions are sufficient to turn the tide—despite the atom bomb, a huge invasion army, and absolute terror. By 1976, the people all over the world go into the streets, and everywhere Communism falls. The assumption is that Communism is so inefficient, it cannot build heavy tanks or heavy weapons. All that is necessary is the courage

[2] I am following here the account of Murray Kempton in the New York *Post*, October 26, 1961.

of a few determined men, practicing the "simple virtues," to overthrow this clumsy Moloch.

"This, of course," as Murray Kempton remarks, "is the Bircher's dream. America slides unresistingly into Communism; a few Mike Hammers find their rifles; and in five years the world is free. The Birch mind is only the Mickey Spillane mind. There is that lingering over and savoring of pure physical violence, the daydream of the disarmed. Reading *The John Franklin Letters* we can recognize Robert Welch's voice. He is Charles Atlas saying to us again that we need only mail the letter and back will come the muscles which we will use to throw the bully off the beach and have the girl turn to us with eyes shining with the sudden knowledge of how special we are."

The distinctive theme of the radical right is that not only is Communism a more threatening force today than at any other time in the past forty years, but that the threat is as great domestically as it is *externally*. If one points out, in astonishment, that the American Communist Party is splintered badly, its membership at the lowest point since the mid-1920s, its influence in the trade-union movement nil, and that not one intellectual figure of any consequence today is a Communist, the rightist replies do not confront these assertions at all. They range from the question that, if this is so, how did it happen that the United States "lost" China, Czechoslovakia, and Cuba to the Communists, to the outright charges, like General Walker's, that the highest officials of the Democratic Party are members of the "Communist conspiracy," or to Robert Welch's claim that former President Eisenhower was a "tool" of the Communists and that his brother Milton is an avowed one. Defeat can be possible only if sinister men were at the helm.[8]

---

[8] Typical of this line is the question constantly reiterated by the Reverend Billy Hargis: "How can you explain the mistakes of our leaders for the last 30 years if there aren't Communists giving them advice?" Hargis is one of the more flamboyant evangelists of the radical right. He publishes *The Weekly Crusader,* which contains a Foreign Intelligence Digest Section, written by Major General

In fact, so great is the preoccupation with the alleged domestic threat that only rarely in the press of the radical right is there any mention of Russia's military prowess, its scientific equipment, or its ability to propel intercontinental ballistic missiles. When such facts are raised, it is often asserted either that such strength is a sham or that whatever knowledge Russia has was "stolen" from the United States (the claim made, for example, by Medford Evans, now an adviser to General Walker, in his book *The Secret War for the A-Bomb*, Chicago, Regnery Press, 1953). For a considerable period of time, in fact, the magazines of the radical right refused to acknowledge that the Russians had sent a sputnik to the moon, or that they had sent a man into space, and, like the *Daily Worker* unmasking a capitalist conspiracy, they gleefully pounced on inconsistencies in news stories to assert that we were all being hoodwinked by a hoax (as were, presumably, the American tracking stations).

The existence of an extreme *internal* threat is crucial to the ideological, if not the psychological, posture of the radical right, for if it admitted that such a threat is dubious, then the debate would have to shift to ground about which it has little comprehension, or rightists would have to admit —as Eisenhower did—that the area of maneuverability in foreign policy is highly limited. If the threat was conceded to be largely external, one would have to support an expanded federal budget, large military expenditures, foreign aid to allies, and also confront the intractable fact that American might alone is insufficient to defeat the Russians—or that victory for anyone would not be possible once war began!— and that the United States has to take into account the forces working for independence in the former colonial world.

The unwillingness of the radical right to recognize Russian military strength as a prime factor in the balance of terror, and the compulsive preoccupation with a presumed internal threat, can perhaps be clarified by a little-under-

Charles A. Willoughby (ret.). Willoughby was General Douglas MacArthur's Intelligence chief in the Pacific.

stood psychological mechanism—the need to create "fear-justifying" threats in order to explain fright that is provoked by other reasons. For example, a child who is afraid of the dark may tell his parents that the creaking noises he hears in the house indicate that there are burglars downstairs. It does not reassure the child if he is told that there is no burglar, or that the noises are harmless, for he needs the story to justify the fear he feels. In fact, it upsets the child to the "reassured." (The simplest answer is to tell the child that *if* there are burglars downstairs, his father is strong enough to handle them or the police are close by.) Similarly, a study by Prasad of rumors in India following an earthquake revealed that people in the areas adjacent to the earthquake, who had heard about the quake but had had no direct experience of it, persisted in believing and spreading rumors that a *new* earthquake was coming. The function of such stories was to justify, psychologically, the *initial* apprehensions, which had little basis in experience.[4] In short, the

[4] For a technical elaboration of this psychological mechanism, see Leon Festinger, *A Theory of Cognitive Dissonance* (Row, Peterson; Chicago, 1957), especially Chapter 10, which reports the study of the rumor. Festinger's theory seeks to explain how individuals try to reconcile—or, technically, "to reduce the dissonance" of—the holding of two inconsistent beliefs at the same time; e.g., the belief that smoking reduces tension and the fear that smoking may produce cancer. When beliefs are specific, denial may be one simple means, conversion to an opposite view follows under certain specifiable conditions, or, if the apprehensions are vague, the creation of "fear-justifying" threats becomes another mechanism.

In the light of Festinger's theory, it would be interesting to confront a sample of the radical right with the problem of explaining the belief in the rising internal threat of Communist infiltration into *government* with the continued presence of J. Edgar Hoover—the one figure who seems to be sacrosanct to the right—as director of the F.B.I. Since Hoover has been in office all through the years when Communism was allegedly growing as an internal threat, how explain the inability of the F.B.I. to cope with it? One could say that the Communists were cleverer than Hoover, but that would tarnish his image. Or one could say that Hoover had been shackled by the successive administrations—even a Republican one. But if that were the case, why would such a stalwart anti-Communist accept such shackles? One could retort that Hoover felt his role in

radical right, having a diffused sense of fear, needs to find some story or explanation to explain, or justify, that fear. One can deny the external reality, and build up the internal threat, through such psychological mechanisms.

One sees among the radical right, particularly among individuals in its upper-middle-class following who have never seen a Communist, the most extraordinary apprehensions about the extent of current Communist infiltration in government. If one asks them to explain these attitudes, one is constantly reminded of Alger Hiss and Harry Dexter White. Yet whatever the actuality of past Communist infiltration in the government—and its extent has been highly distorted as to the actual influence exerted—none of this offers any proof about the current status of Dean Rusk or W. W. Rostow, or any of the present foreign-policy advisers of the Kennedy administration. Yet the *internal* threat is the one that is primarily harped upon, along with suspicions of the "soft" attitudes of the current administration.

It is largely among the extremist fringes of the radical right that such paranoid views are peddled. But most of the radical right, uneasily aware of the difficulty of maintaining the position that the Communist Party alone constitutes the internal threat, has shifted the argument to a different and more nebulous ground—the identification of Communism with liberalism. "I equate the growth of the welfare state," says Dan Smoot, a former F.B.I. agent whose program, *The*

---

office to be more important than a grand gesture of renunciation (such as General Walker's). But if the Communist infiltration has been so enormous as to extend almost to, if not into, the White House, why would he not step out and unmask the plot? But then, since the Communist threat may grow even greater, he would still be needed in office—or, horrors to admit the thought, it may well be that, reversing G. K. Chesterton's *The Man Who Was Thursday*, J. Edgar Hoover is himself the chief agent of the Communist conspiracy in America, and that could explain the protection the conspiracy has received so far. The possibilities of such a thought are clearly quite provoking, and it may well be that Robert Welch, in the privacy of his office, has entertained them. But if that were so, who, then, is immune from the plague?

Dan Smoot Report, is heard on thirty-two television and fifty-two radio stations, "with Socialism and Socialism with Communism." Thus it is argued that the administration is unwilling (for ideological reasons) or incapable (for intellectual reasons) of "getting tough" with Communism. And in this fashion, the foreign-policy issue is tied in with a vast array of right-wing domestic issues, centering around the income tax and the welfare state.

But with this shift in the argument, the nature of the debate becomes clearer. What the right wing is fighting, in the shadow of Communism, is essentially "modernity"—that complex of attitudes that might be defined most simply as the belief in rational assessment, rather than established custom, for the evaluation of social change—and what it seeks to defend is its fading dominance, exercised once through the institutions of small-town America, over the control of social change. But it is precisely these established ways that a modernist America has been forced to call into question.

III

The Crisis in National Style

Every country has a "national style," a distinctive way of meeting the problems of order and adaptation, of conflict and consensus, of individual ends and communal welfare, that confront any society. The "national style," or the characteristic way of response, is a compound of the values and the national character of a country.[5] As anyone who has read travelers' accounts knows, there has long been agreement on the characteristics of the American style.

The American has been marked by his sense of achievement, his activism, his being on the move, his eagerness for

---

[5] The "style" of a country, or of an organization, is in this sense a literary counterpart of the idea of an "operational code"—the do's and don'ts that implicitly prescribe and proscribe permissible modes of action for an organization or a group. For an explicit, technical application of this concept, see Nathan Leites, *The Operational Code of the Politburo* (New York, McGraw-Hill, 1951).

experience. America has always been "future-oriented." Europe represented the past, with its hierarchies, its fixed statuses, its ties to antiquity. The American "makes" himself, and in so doing transforms himself, society, and nature.[6] In Jefferson's deism, God was not a transcendental being but a "Workman" whose intricate design was being unfolded on the American continent. The achievement pattern envisaged an "endless future," a life of constant improvement. Education meant preparation for a career rather than cultivation. When Samuel Gompers, the immigrant labor leader, was asked what labor's goal was, he gauged the American spirit shrewdly in answering, simply, "More."

Hand in hand with achievement went a sense of optimism, the feeling that life was tractable, the environment manipulable, that anything was possible. The American, the once-born man, was the "sky-blue, healthy-minded moralist" to whom sin and evil were, in Emerson's phrase, merely the "soul's mumps and measles and whooping cough." In this sense the American has been Graham Greene's "quiet American" or, to Santayana, "inexperienced of poisons." And for this reason Europeans have always found America lacking in a sense of the esthetic, the tragic, or the decadent.[7]

American achievement and masculine optimism created a buoyant sense of progress, almost of omnipotence. America had never been defeated. America was getting bigger and

[6] One viewpoint argues that national character is rooted in the language system of each society. Thus, as an old joke has it, the Englishman *earns* his living; the Frenchman *gagne* (gains); the German *verdient* (earns—with the connotation of serving); the American *makes* his livelihood; and the Hungarian *keretznenni* (looks for and finds) his living.

[7] The forms of murder and the styles of pornography mirror a society, for they disclose ways in which, actually and vicariously, the society satisfies forbidden desires. Death in the American mode is impersonal, sudden, and violent, rather than a lingering disease, as, say, in *The Magic Mountain*. Pornography in Mickey Spillane (in contrast with the French *L'Histoire d'O*, with its complex account of slavish female submission to sinister erotic wants) is a slashing, compulsive emphasis on brute masculinity—which betrays its own fear of castration or impotence.

better. America was always first. It had the tallest buildings, the biggest dams, the largest cities. "The most striking expression of [the American's] materialism," remarked Santayana, "is his singular preoccupation with quantity."

And all of this was reflected in distinctive aspects of character. The emphasis on achievement was an emphasis on the individual. The idea that society was a system of social arrangements that acts to limit the range of individual behavior was an abstraction essentially alien to American thought; reality was concrete and empirical, and the individual was the moral unit of action. That peculiar American inversion of Protestantism, the moralizing style, found its focus in the idea of reform, but it was the reform of the individual, not of social institutions. To reform meant to remedy the defects of character, and the American reform movement of the nineteenth century concentrated on sin, drink, gambling, prostitution, and other aspects of individual behavior. In politics, the moralistic residue led to black-and-white judgments: if anything was wrong, the individual was to blame. Since there were good men and bad men, the problem was to choose the good and eschew the bad. Any defect in policy flowed from a defect in the individual, and a change in policy could begin only by finding the culprit.

All of this—the pattern of achievement, of optimism and progress, and the emphasis on the individual as the unit of concern—found expression in what W. W. Rostow has called the "classic" American style.[8] It was one of *ad-hoc* compromise derived from an implicit consensus. In the American political debates, there was rarely, except for the Civil War, an appeal to "first principles," as, say, in France, where every political division was rooted in the alignments of the French Revolution, or in the relationship of the Catholic Church to the secular state. In the United States, there were three unspoken assumptions: that the values of the individual were to be maximized, that the rising material wealth would

[8] In *The American Style* (Little, Brown, 1960), ed. by Elting E. Morrison.

dissolve all strains resulting from inequality, and that the continuity of experience would provide solutions for all future problems.

In the last fifteen years, the national self-consciousness has received a profound shock. At the end of World War II, American productivity and American prodigality were going to inspire an archaic Europe and a backward colonial system. But the American century quickly vanished. The fall of China, the stalemate in Korea, the eruption of anti-colonialism (with the United States cast bewilderingly among the archvillains), the higher growth rates in the western European economies at a time when growth in this country has slowed considerably, and the continued claims of Khrushchev that Communism is the wave of the future have by now shattered the earlier simple-minded belief Americans had in their own omnipotence, and have left almost a free-floating anxiety about the future. In a crudely symbolic way, the Russian sputniks trumped this country on its own ground—the boastful claim of always being first. Getting to the moon first may be, as many scientists assert, of little scientific value, and the huge sums required for such a venture might be spent more wisely for medical work, housing, or scientific research, but having set the "rules of the game," the United States cannot now afford to withdraw just because, in its newly acquired sophistication, it has perhaps begun to realize that such competitions are rather childish.

But these immediate crises of nerve only reflect deeper challenges to the adequacy of America's classic national style. That style, with its *ad-hoc* compromise and day-to-day patching, rather than consistent policy formation, no longer gives us guides to action. The classic notion was that rights inhered in individuals. But the chief realization of the past thirty years is that not the *individual* but *collectivities*—corporations, labor unions, farm organizations, pressure groups—have become the units of social action, and that individual rights in many instances derive from group rights, and in others have become fused with them. Other than the thin veil of the "public consensus," we have few guide lines, let alone a principle of distributive justice, to regulate or check the arbitrary power of many of these collectivities.

A second sign that the classic style has broken down appears in the lack of any institutional means for creating and maintaining necessary public services. On the municipal level, the complicated political swapping among hundreds of dispersed polities within a unified economic region, each seeking its own bargains in water supply, sewage disposal, roads, parks, recreation areas, crime regulation, transit, and so on, makes a mockery of the *ad-hoc* process. Without some planning along viable regional lines, local community life is bound to falter under the burdens of mounting taxes and social disarray.

And, third, foreign policy has foundered because every administration has had difficulty in defining a national interest, morally rooted, whose policies can be realistically tailored to the capacities and the constraints imposed by the actualities of world power. The easy temptation—and it is the theme of the radical right—is the tough-talking call for "action." This emphasis on action—on getting things done, on results—is a dominant aspect of the traditional American character. The moralizing style, with its focus on sin and on the culpability of the individual, finds it hard to accept social forces as a convincing explanation of failure, and prefers "action" instead. Americans have rarely known how to sweat it out, to wait, to calculate in historical terms, to learn that "action" cannot easily reverse social drifts whose courses were charted long ago. The "liberation" policy of the first Eisenhower administration was but a hollow moralism, deriving from the lack of any consistent policy other than the need to seem "activist"—again part of the classic style—rather than from a realistic assessment of the possibility of undermining Soviet power in eastern Europe. Until recently, there has been little evidence that American foreign policy is guided by a sense of historical time and an accurate assessment of social forces.

Styles of action reflect the character of a society. The classic style was worked out during a period when America was an agrarian, relatively homogeneous society, isolated from the world at large, so that *ad-hoc* measures were a realistic way of dealing with new strains. As an adaptive mechanism, it served to bring new groups *into* the society. But styles of action, like rhetoric, have a habit of outliving institutions. And the classic style in no way reflects the deep structural changes that have been taking place in American life in the past quarter of a century.

IV

The Sources of Strain

Although the crisis in national style can be detected most forcefully in the realm of foreign policy, there have been, in the past thirty years, deep changes taking place in the social structure that are reworking the social map of the country, upsetting the established life-chances and outlooks of old, privileged groups, and creating uncertainties about the future which are deeply unsettling to those whose values were shaped by the "individualist" morality of nineteenth-century America.

The most pervasive changes are those involving the structural relations between class position and power. Clearly, today, political position rather than wealth, and technical skill rather than property, have become the bases from which power is wielded. In the modes of access to privilege, inheritance is no longer all-determining, nor does "individual initiative" in building one's own business exist as a realistic route; in general, education has become the major way to acquire the technical skills necessary for the administrative and power-wielding jobs in society.

In the older mythos, one's achievement was an individual fact—as a doctor, lawyer, professor, businessman; in the reality of today, one's achievement, status, and prestige are rooted in particular *collectivities* (the corporation, being attached to a "name" hospital, teaching at a prestigious university, membership in a good law firm), and the individual's role is necessarily submerged in the achievement of the collectivity. Within each collectivity and profession, the proliferation of tasks calls for narrower and narrower specializations, and this proliferation requires larger collectivities, and the consequent growth of hierarchies and bureaucracies.

The new nature of decision-making—the larger role of technical decision—also forces a displacement of the older elites. Within a business enterprise, the newer techniques of operations research and linear programming almost amount to the "automation" of middle management, and its displacement by mathematicians and engineers, working either within the firm or as consultants. In the economy, the businessman finds himself subject to price, wage, and investment criteria laid down by the economists in government. In the polity, the old military elites find themselves challenged in the determination of strategy by scientists, who have the technical knowledge on nuclear capability, missile development, and the like, or by the "military intellectuals" whose conceptions of weapon systems and political warfare seek to guide military allocations.

In the broadest sense, the spread of education, of research, of administration, and of government creates a new constituency, the technical and professional intelligentsia, and while these are not bound by some common ethos to constitute a new class, or even a cohesive social group, they are the products of a new system of recruitment for power (just as property and inheritance represented the old system), and those who are the products of the old system understandably feel a vague and apprehensive disquiet—the disquiet of the dispossessed.

V

The Generational Dispossessed

Many of the political changes that have transformed American society originated in measures taken thirty and more years ago. In many instances, the changes have been irrevocably built into the structure of American society. Why then have the consequences of these changes—and the reactions to them—become so manifest, and produced such rancor, at this time?

It was Walter Bagehot who said that the Reform Bill of 1832 was "won" in 1865—that political reforms are secured largely through generational change. New legislation may stipulate a set of reforms, but the administration of the law, its judicial interpretation, and its enforcement are in the hands of an older political generation which may hinder the changes. Only when the new generation comes of age are the judiciary and the bureaucracy taken over, and men educated in the "new spirit of the time" come into the established framework of power.

In this sense, the social enactments of the New Deal came to fruition thirty years later. While the Roosevelt administration created a host of new regulatory agencies, the judiciary, in its values and social outlook, largely reflected the *ancien régime*, and even though there was no entrenched bureaucracy, like those of Germany, France, or Britain, that would impede or distort these reforms, the lack of a broad intelligentsia made it difficult to staff the regulatory agencies without drawing in the business community, the trade associations, and the like. Thus, while the enactments of the Roosevelt administration seemed to many conservatives to be startlingly revolutionary, the business community—the main group whose power was abated—could, through the courts, Congress, and often the administrative agencies, modify substantially the restrictions of the regulations.

The paradoxical fact is that while the New Deal has lost much of its meaning on the ideological or rhetorical level, the fabric of government, particularly the judiciary, has been rewoven with liberal thread so that on many significant issues—civil rights, minority-group protection, the extension of social welfare—the courts have been more liberal than the administrations. Only Congress, reflecting the disproportionate power of the rural areas and the established seniority system, has remained predominantly under conservative control.

In identifying "the dispossessed," it is somewhat misleading to seek their economic location, since it is not economic interest alone that accounts for their anxieties. A small businessman may have made considerable amounts of money in the last decade (in part because he has greater freedom than a large corporation in masking costs for tax purposes), and yet strongly resent regulations in Washington, the high income tax, or, more to the point, his own lack of status. To the extent that any such economic location is possible, one can say that the social group most threatened by the structural changes in society is the "old" middle class—the independent physician, farm owner, small-town lawyer, real-estate promoter, home builder, automobile dealer, gasoline-station owner, small businessman, and the like—and that, regionally, its greatest political concentration is in the South and the Southwest, and in California. But a much more telltale indicator of the group that feels most anxious—since life-styles and values provide the emotional fuel of beliefs and actions— is the strain of Protestant fundamentalism, of nativist nationalism, of good-and-evil moralism which is the organizing basis for the "world view" of such people.[9] For this is the group whose values predominated in the nineteenth century, and which for the past forty years has been fighting a rearguard action.

The present upsurge of American nativism—one aspect of the radical right—is most directly paralleled in the 1920s, in the virulent assaults on teachers' loyalty by the fundamentalist churchmen in the name of God, and by patriotic organizations like the American Legion in the name of country. These conflicts—expressed most directly in the Scopes trial on the teaching of evolution in Tennessee, and the bellicose efforts of Mayor Big Bill Thompson in Chicago to expunge favorable references to Great Britain from the school textbooks—were between "fundamentalists" and "modernists," between "patriots" and "internationalists."

These skirmishes of the 1920s were the first defensive at-

[9] For an earlier discussion of the historical sources of this moralism, see Chapter 2.

tacks of the nativist and the old middle-class elements. They arose in reaction to the entry *into* society of formerly "disenfranchised" elements, particularly the children of immigrants and members of minority ethnic groups—an entry made through the urban political machines, the only major route open to them. In short, it was a reaction to the rise of a mass society.

Until the mid-1920s, America in its top and middle layers had been, politically and culturally, a fairly homogeneous society. As Walter Lippmann pointed out in 1928, in a neglected but prescient account of the times, *American Inquisitors,* "those who differed in religion or nationality from the great mass of the people played no important part in American politics. They did the menial work, they had no influence in society, they were not self-conscious and they produced no leaders of their own. There were some sectarian differences and some sectional differences within the American nation. But by and large, within the states themselves, the dominant group was like-minded and its dominion was unchallenged."[10]

But in time its dominion *was* challenged, and principally from the cities. The year 1920 was the first in American history when a majority of persons lived in "urban territory."[11]

[10] Walter Lippmann, *American Inquisitors* (New York, Macmillan, 1928).

[11] The sociological definition of "urban"—using government statistical data—is a difficult task. Thus, in 1920 about 54,157,000 persons lived in "urban territories" and 51,550,000 in "rural territories." But rural is defined, at the time, as places under 2500 population. Clearly many persons living in small towns partake of "rural" attitudes. Thus, in 1920 sixteen million of those in "urban territories" lived in towns under 25,000 population. If one takes the 25,000 population as the dividing line between "urban" and "small town," then it was only in 1960 that a majority of Americans lived in urban areas. Since 1950, of course, the movement of city dwellers to the suburbs has complicated the definitional problem. If one takes the census definition of a metropolitan area as a guide (i.e., populations living within a county, or group of contiguous counties, possessing at least one city of 50,000 inhabitants), by 1950 slightly more than half of the United States popu-

The children and the grandchildren of the immigrants began to come of political age. The movement to the cities and the gradual cultural ascendancy of metropolitan life over rural areas, accentuated by the rise of the automobile, motion pictures, and radio—creating, for the first time, a national popular culture—began to threaten established customs and beliefs. Thus, there was no longer, as Lippmann pointed out at the time, "a well-entrenched community, settled in its customs, homogeneous in its manners, clear in its ultimate beliefs. There is great diversity, and therefore there are the seeds of conflict."

Faced with the rise of "heretical" beliefs, the religious fundamentalists in Tennessee put forth the argument, self-evident to them, that teaching in the schools ought to conform to the views of the majority. If the people of Tennessee did not believe in evolution, they had a right to demand that it be stopped. And as Lippmann wryly commented, there was warranty for such a populist demand in Jefferson's bill for the establishment of religious freedom in Virginia, in 1786, which declared that "to compel a man to furnish contributions of money for the propagation of opinions which he disbelieves, is sinful and tyrannical."

Intellectually, the fundamentalists were defeated and the modernists won; their views came to predominate in the country. But the fundamentalist temper of the 1920s still holds strong sway in rural-dominated states. As David Danzig has pointed out, "the States that repudiated Darwinianism and Al Smith are today prominent among those nineteen that have passed 'Right to Work' laws since 1950."[12] And, paradoxically, although they have become intellectually and socially dispossessed, the fundamentalist "regions" have risen to new wealth in the last fifteen years or so. The industrialization of the South and Southwest, the boom in real estate,

---

lation lived within metropolitan areas. (For the confirmable data, see *The Historical Statistics of the United States,* Series A, 195–209, and the *Statistical Abstract of the U.S.,* 1960, pp. 14–15.)

[12] "The Radical Right and the Rise of the Fundamentalist Minority," *Commentary,* April, 1962.

the gushing wealth of oil in Texas and Oklahoma have transformed the fundamentalist churches and the Southern Baptist movement into a middle-class and upper-middle-class
group. Small wonder that, possessing this new wealth, the
fundamentalist groups have discovered the iniquity of the
income tax.

The social ideas of fundamentalism are quite traditional
—a return to the "simple" virtues of individual initiative and
self-reliance.[13] In political terms, this means dismantling
much of the social-security program, eliminating the income
tax, reducing the role of the federal government in economic
life, and giving back to the states and local government the
major responsibilities for welfare, labor, and similar legislation.[14]

Until now, much of the political strength of the right has
stemmed from its ability to block the reapportionment of
seats in the state legislatures (and to gerrymander seats for
Congress), resulting in a heavily disproportionate representa-

[13] As for the actual meaning of these ideas, as Richard Hofstadter pointed out in a memorandum for the Fund for the Republic
in 1955, "A casual survey of the contents of some of the right-wing
periodicals will show that the fear of modernity which inspired the
fundamentalist crusades of the 1920s and the dislike of the poly-
glot life of the city, and of Jewish and Catholic immigrants, which
inspired the Ku Klux Klan, is still alive among the extreme right."

[14] The rationalizations for the farm programs of the various administrations—which support farm prices and give the farmer
money *not* to produce—offer a fascinating example of the ideological moralizing of the right. For those reared on fundamentalist
virtues, the idea of being paid not to produce creates considerable
moral queasiness. Yet, given the overproduction in agriculture, the
operation of a free market would serve only to wipe out thousands
of farmers immediately. The function of the acreage restrictions is
to adjust supply to demand, and farm-price supports provide an
"income cushion" in order to ease the lot of the farmer. These programs, costing billions of dollars a year, are defended ideologically
on the ground of protecting private property. But the effort—which
has the same protective function—to help workers through unemployment compensation is attacked as weakening moral fiber, and
the suggestion that technological changes which disrupt the established lives of thousands be retarded is attacked as impeding
progress.

tion of the small-town and rural areas in both assemblies. In Tennessee—whose flagrant failure to act precipitated the Supreme Court decision in April, 1962, ordering the reallocation of seats—although the state constitution specified that a reapportionment be made every ten years, the state legislature, since 1901, had rejected all bills attempting to carry out that mandate. As a result, in the voting for the Tennessee State Senate, one-third of the electorate nominated two-thirds of the legislators. In almost every state of the Union one could point to similarly glaring disproportions—though none so astounding as in California, where the single state senator from Los Angeles represents 6,038,771 persons, while a colleague from a rural area represents 14,294 persons, a ratio of 422.5 to 1. In forty-four states, less than forty per cent of the population can elect a majority of the state legislators; in thirteen states, fewer than a third of the voters can elect a majority. How quickly this will change, now that the federal courts are empowered to act, remains to be seen.

VI

The Managerial Dispossessed

To list the managerial executive class as among the dispossessed may seem strange, especially in the light of the argument that a revolution which is undermining property as the basis of power is enfranchising a new class of technical personnel among whom are the business executives. And yet the managerial class has been under immense strain all through this period, a strain arising in part from the status discrepancy between their power within a particular enterprise and their power and prestige in the nation as a whole.

The old family firm was securely rooted in the legal and moral tradition of private property. The enterprise "belonged" to the owner, and was sanctioned, depending on one's theological tastes, by God or by Natural Law. The modern manager lacks the inherited family justifications, for increasingly he is recruited from the amorphous middle class. He receives a salary, bonus, options, expense accounts, and "perks" (use of company planes, memberships in country clubs), but his power is transitory, and he cannot pass on his position to his son.[15]

In order to justify his position, the manager needs an ideology. In no other capitalist order but the American—not in England, or Germany, or France—has this drive for ideology been so compulsive. This ideology is no longer derived from private property but from enterprise, the argument being that only the American corporate system can provide for economic performance. But if performance is the test, then the American manager more and more finds himself in a sorry position. The growth rate of the American economy in the past decade has been surprisingly small. And the "legitimacy" of the manager—the question of who gives him the right to wield such enormous economic power—has been challenged in a series of powerful arguments by Berle, Galbraith, and others.

Within the enterprise, the new corporation head often finds himself with the vexing problem of trying to "downgrade" the importance of the trade-union leader—in order to raise his own status. In an age when management is deemed to be a great and novel skill, involving the administration of production, research, finance, merchandising, public relations, and personnel, the company president feels that there is little reason now to treat union leaders as equals—especially when labor is, after all, only one of a large number of the "co-ordinates of administration." Labor relations, he feels, should be reduced to their proper dimension, as a concern of the personnel manager.

Yet the corporation head is often unable to obtain even this satisfaction—as has been evident in the steel industry. For years the industry smarted at the union's power, particularly at U. S. Steel, where in 1957 a new management team, headed by Roger Blough, a lawyer with no experience

[15] On the decline of inherited position and nepotism in the large corporation, see Mabel M. Newcomer, *The Big Business Executive* (New York, Columbia University Press, 1955).

in production, took over. Blough's predecessor, Ben Fairless, an old production hand who had come up through the mill, had cleverly sought to assuage the vanity of Dave McDonald, the steel-union president, by joint "walking tours" through the plant. There was talk of "mutual trusteeship" by the managers of capital and the managers of labor. But Blough would have none of this charade, and when it was evident that because of slack demand the industry could take a strike, it did so.

The strike lasted three months and ended only with the intervention of Vice-President Nixon and Labor Secretary Mitchell (after Blough and McDonald met secretly at the Vice-President's home), who feared the political consequences in the 1960 campaign of such a long-drawn-out struggle. The strike proved in this, as in a dozen other areas, that the industry could not escape the checkrein of government—not even in a Republican administration. This was demonstrated even more dramatically by Roger Blough's comeuppance in 1962. In the spring of 1962 the Kennedy administration, in an effort to maintain the wage-price line, brought pressure on the steel union to sign an early contract that provided some small fringe benefits but, for the first time in the union's history, no direct wage increase. Shortly afterward, however, U. S. Steel, followed by most of the industry, announced an immediate price rise. In a burst of fury, the colossal weight of the federal government was mobilized against the big steel firms—through threats of prosecution, cancellation of government purchase orders, and the cajoling of the business community—and in short order the industry gave in.

It is unlikely that the business community will take this crashing demonstration of governmental power without making some countervailing efforts of its own on the political level. Already in 1960 the efforts of a number of corporations, led by General Electric, to go "directly" into politics, in imitation of the unions—by taking a public stand on political issues, by sending out vast amounts of propaganda to their employees and to the public, by encouraging right-to-work referendums in the states—indicated the mood of political dispossession in many corporations. Since then, a significant number of corporations have been contributing financially to the seminars of the radical-right evangelists.[16] Despite the black eye General Electric—the most vocal defender of free enterprise—received when the government disclosed that G.E. as well as a dozen other electrical manufacturing companies had been guilty of illegal price-rigging and cartelization, it is likely that the Kennedy-Blough imbroglio of 1962 will provide an even greater impetus for corporations to finance right-wing political activity in the coming years.

VII

The Military Dispossessed

The irony for the American military establishment is that at a time when, in the new states, the military has emerged as the ruling force of the country (often because it is the one organized group in an amorphous society),[17] and at a

[16] The National Education Program, at Harding College in Arkansas, which prepares films on Communism and materials on free enterprise, has been used extensively by General Electric, U. S. Steel, Olin Mathieson Chemical, Monsanto Chemical, Swift & Co., and others. Boeing Aviation and the Richfield Oil Company have sponsored many of the anti-Communism seminars on the West Coast. The Jones & Laughlin Steel Company has a widespread propaganda program for its employees. One of the most active firms is the Allen Bradley Company, of Milwaukee, which makes machine tools and electrical equipment. The Allen Bradley Company advertises in the John Birch Society magazine and reprinted Dr. Fred Schwarz's testimony before the House Un-American Activities Committee, a reprint which Schwarz claims had "wider distribution than any other government document in the history of the United States, with the possible exception of the Bill of Rights, the Declaration of Independence and the Constitution." The Allen Bradley Company, which constantly extols the virtue of free enterprise, was one of the companies convicted of collusive bidding and illegal price-rigging.

[17] One of the factors that has acted to safeguard democracy in England and the United States is that both countries have never had any permanently large standing armies. The insularity of Eng-

time in American history when the amount of money allocated to military purposes—roughly fifty per cent of the federal budget—is the highest in peacetime history, the military is subject to challenges in its own bailiwick. The problems of national security, like those of the national economy, have become so staggeringly complex that they can no longer be settled simply by common sense or past experience. As a writer in the *Times Literary Supplement* recently put it, "The manner in which weapons systems are likely to develop; the counters which may be found to them; the burdens which they are likely to impose on the national economy; the way in which their possession will affect international relations or their use the nature of war; the technical problems of their control or abolition; all these problems are far beyond the scope of the Joint Planning Staff study or the Civil Service brief."[18]

The fact is that the military establishment, because of its outmoded curriculum, its recruitment and promotion patterns, the vested interests of the different services, and the concentration at the top levels of officers trained in older notions of strategy, is ill equipped to grasp modern conceptions of politics, or to use the tools (computer simulation, linear programming, gaming theory) of strategic planning. As Morris Janowitz has pointed out in his comprehensive study of the military:

land made it place its protection in the Navy, whose forces were always far from shore, and the continental isolation of the United States made it unnecessary to build up any permanent military force. Where large armies have existed, the military, because it has represented an organized bloc whose control over the means of violence could be decisive, has almost invariably been pulled into politics. Thus the German Army in one crucial situation, in 1920, defended the Weimar Republic (against the Putschists of the right), but in a second crucial instance, in 1932 (the machinations of von Schleicher), contributed to its downfall. In Spain in 1936, in France in 1960, and more recently in Argentina, Turkey, Korea, Pakistan, Burma, and so on, the armed forces have been the decisive political element in the society.

[18] "The Military Intellectuals," *Times Literary Supplement* (London), August 25, 1961.

There is little in the curriculum to prepare the officer for the realities of participating in the management of politico-military affairs. While the case-study and war-games approaches give the officer a direct understanding and "feel" for the logistics and organizational apparatus that must be "moved" for military operations, there is no equivalent training for the political dimensions of international relations. . . .

All evidence indicates that both absolutists and pragmatists—in varying degree—overemphasize the potentials of force. The realistic study of international relations involves an appreciation of the limits of violence. Military education does not continually focus on these issues, as it relates both to nuclear and limited conventional warfare. Paradoxically, military education does not emphasize the potentialities of unconventional warfare and political warfare, since these are at the periphery of professionalization.[19]

In the last decade, most of the thinking on strategic problems, political and economic, has been done in the universities or in government-financed but autonomous bodies like the Rand Corporation. A new profession, that of the "military intellectual," has emerged, and men like Kahn, Wohlstetter, Brodie, Hitch, Kissinger, Bowie, and Schelling "move freely through the corridors of the Pentagon and the State Department," as the *T.L.S.* writer observed, "rather as the Jesuits through the courts of Madrid and Vienna three centuries ago."

In structural terms, the military establishment may be one of the tripods of a "power elite," but in sociological fact the military officers feel dispossessed because they often lack the necessary technical skills or knowledge to answer the new problems confronting them. Since the end of World War II, the military has been involved in a number of battles to defend its elite position, beginning in 1945 with the young

[19] Morris Janowitz, *The Professional Soldier* (The Free Press, 1960), p. 429.

physicists and nuclear scientists, down to the present action against the "technipols" (the technicians and political theorists, as the military derisively calls them), whom Secretary McNamara has brought into the Department of Defense.

The first challenge came from the scientists over the issue of continuing military control of atomic energy. In a burst of almost H. G. Wellsian messianism, the scientists moved into the political arena. And, as a result of skillful lobbying by enthusiastic young scientists from Los Alamos, Chicago, and Brookhaven, Congress passed the McMahon Bill, which set up the Atomic Energy Commission under civilian control. J. Robert Oppenheimer, the scientific head of the Manhattan District project, which constructed the atom bomb, became a leading adviser to the State Department and was one of the principal authors of the Baruch plan.

The advent of the Cold War, in 1947–48, raised a number of issues that divided the scientists and the military even further, and for the next four years a "hidden struggle" between the two elites went on in the labyrinthine corridors of Washington. The chief issue was whether or not to build an H-bomb. The scientists in the General Advisory Committee to the A.E.C., in overwhelming majority—including Oppenheimer, Conant, Rabi, duBridge—opposed the construction of the H-bomb, but lost out. A different issue was raised about the need for defense. The Strategic Air Command, the big-bomber striking arm of American power, argued that no defense against atomic attack was possible and claimed that the only effective deterrent against the Russians would be the threat of massive retaliation. In strategy, this would mean reliance solely on heavy atomic bombs. Against the S.A.C., the scientists claimed that continental defense *was* possible— if the United States could be made invulnerable to attack, negotiations with the Russians could be opened from strength —and, furthermore, that western Europe could be defended with limited, tactical atomic weapons, so that the United States was not wholly dependent upon "big-bomb" deterrents.

To test their arguments, the scientists got support—in some cases surreptitiously—from backers in the National Security

Council for a series of "games." Project Lincoln was set up at M.I.T. to study the problems of defense, which resulted later in the radar net of the D.E.W., or early-warning system, in the Arctic. Project Vista, which enlisted some five score scientists from different universities, was set up at the California Institute of Technology to study the use of tactical atomic weapons.

The S.A.C. pooh-poohed both projects, deriding continental defense as a Maginot Line of the air. And it sought to block the distribution of both projects' findings. Eventually, the results from the two laboratories were adopted. An early-warning system was created, and the N.A.T.O. strategy was revised, which meant, in effect, that the S.A.C. monopoly of atomic policy was broken.

Although Robert Oppenheimer had not been the prime instigator of these moves—except in the case of Project Vista —he became the symbol of the scientific opposition to the big-bomber command. In November, 1953, when Lewis Strauss was appointed by President Eisenhower to the chairmanship of the Atomic Energy Commission, Oppenheimer was charged with being a security risk. The basis of the charge—that Oppenheimer had in the later 1930s been sympathetic to a number of Communist fronts—had long been known to the security agencies. But the real inspiration for the A.E.C. action, as is evident from testimony before its special panel, came from men who believed fervently in the theory of strategic air power, who resented Oppenheimer's influence, and could draw only sinister conclusions from his stands on policy.[20]

[20] Major General Roscoe C. Wilson, the former chief of the Air War College, testified that he once "felt compelled to go to the Director of Intelligence to express my concern over what I felt was a pattern of action that was simply not helpful to the national defense." The items cited in this pattern included Oppenheimer's interest in the "internationalizing of atomic energy," his insistence that it was technically premature to build nuclear-powered aircraft, and his conservatism on thermonuclear weapons. (United States Atomic Energy Commission, "In the Matter of J. Robert Oppenheimer," Transcript of Hearings Before the Personnel Security

The Oppenheimer case is now almost a decade behind us, and a shameful instance of national folly; the specific strategic issues regarding the role of manned bombers as the major weight of military power have by now been outmoded by the work on missiles. The originally small scientific community, whose members, drawn from a few university centers, knew each other intimately, has greatly expanded, and with the rise of space exploration, missile technology, and the like, it is no longer dominated by the small group of nuclear physicists who charted the new atomic age. Nor does it any longer, needless to say, have the rough unanimity of outlook that characterized it in the immediate postwar decade. And yet, though the military won the first round of their fight with the nuclear scientists, in the present decade its position as the shaper, as well as the executor, of strategic policy has been consistently eroded. For in present-day decision-making, the nature of strategy involves a kind of analysis for which experience is insufficient. If one takes the complex problem of the choice of "weapons systems," the long lead time that is necessary in the planning and testing, let alone the production, of weapons forces an analyst to construct mathematical models as almost the only means toward rational choices. The recent controversy over the desirability of the RS-70 bomber is a case in point. The systems analysts in the office of the Secretary of Defense, led by Charles Hitch, an economist from Rand who has become

---

Board, Government Printing Office [Washington, 1954], pp. 684–85.)

The decision of the special A.E.C. panel was a curious one. Its chairman, Gordon Gray, president of the University of North Carolina, noted that if the board could use common sense rather than apply the stringent rules of the security regulations, its decision might have been different. But in the light of those regulations, while Oppenheimer's "loyalty" was affirmed, he had to be declared a security risk. The full A.E.C. board, by a four-to-one vote, rendered an even harsher judgment in forbidding Oppenheimer access to all classified material. See also, Robert Gilpin, *American Scientists and Nuclear Policy* (Princeton University Press, 1962), Chap. IV, for a discussion of Project Vista and Project Lincoln.

the comptroller in the Pentagon, decided on the basis of computer analysis that the manned RS-70 bomber would long be outmoded by the time it could come into full production, and that it would be wiser to concentrate on missiles.[21] Dismayed by this decision, the Strategic Air Command and its allies in the aircraft industry invoked Congressional support, and the House Military Affairs Committee voted money for the bomber.

But the "technipols," with McNamara at their head, have gone far beyond the use of linear programming or other planning devices for making more rational choices in the allocation of military resources. The entire Pentagon has been almost completely reorganized so as to reduce the importance of the traditional service arms—Army, Navy, Air Force, and Marines—and to introduce "functional" groupings, whereby missions from each of the services are grouped together for budget and strategic purposes in order to test their effectiveness.

The point of all this is that such reorganization means more than the introduction of modern management practice into a top-heavy bureaucratic structure. For the reorganization on program and mission lines stemmed from a new conception of the strategic distribution of the armed forces—a political conception of the role of limited wars and nuclear capabilities, most of which came from the "technipols," rather than from the military establishment.

The traditional services, and their Chiefs, have reacted to all this with dismay. As an article in *Fortune* put it, "It was at this point that the military professionals began to exhibit real alarm. McNamara did not ignore them; they had their say, as usual, in defense of their service budgets. But his drive, his intense preoccupation with figures and facts, left the Chiefs and their staffs with the feeling that the computers

[21] Much of the newer economic thinking is reflected in the study by Charles Hitch and Roland N. McKean, *The Economics of Defense in the Nuclear Age* (Harvard University Press, 1961), completed at Rand before Hitch was appointed comptroller in the Pentagon.

were taking over." And the *Fortune* article, reflecting the dismay of the service Chiefs, was also a veiled attack on McNamara's penchant for "quantification"; for his failure to respect "the uncomputable that had made Curtis Le May [the head of the big-bomber command] the world's finest operational airman"; for his "inexperience" in military strategy and for his reliance on the technipols, "the inner group of lay experts who were dispersed through State, the White House and Defense." The import of the article was clear: the traditional military professionals were being dispossessed.[22]

On any single set of political or strategic issues, it is an

[22] See "The Education of a Defense Secretary," by Charles J. V. Murphy, *Fortune*, May, 1962. Murphy, the military correspondent of *Fortune*, has consistently reflected the views of the military establishment in its battles with the scientists and other critics of the military. Murphy's comprehensive story of the reorganization of the Pentagon is the first account of the "hidden" conflicts between the traditional services and McNamara that has resulted from the introduction of long-range programming in the Defense Department. As Murphy writes, "So swiftly did he move that the high brass again and again found itself confronted by a McNamara decision while it was still mulling over his initial direction for action. . . .

"In two months McNamara produced blueprints for the Kennedy line of action for both the strategic and the conventional forces. The new requirements in the first area was drawn up by a task force under a former Rand economist, Charles J. Hitch, the Defense Department comptroller. Those for the limited-war forces were developed by another task force under Paul H. Nitze, a former investment banker and State Department planner who was and remains the Assistant Defense Secretary for International Security Affairs.

"The job was pretty much over and done before the military had more than grasped that something unusual was going on. By tradition, the military services had generated their own requirements. It was they who proposed, the civilians who disposed. Under McNamara, however, the system was suddenly turned upside down. Now it was McNamara and his lay strategists who were saying what weapons and what forces in what numbers were needed; the service Chiefs found themselves in the strange position of reviewing weapon systems and force structures they had never formally considered."

exaggeration, of course, to speak of "the military," or "the scientists," or "the military intellectuals," as if these were monolithic entities. On any particular set of issues, or even on fundamental values, members of the scientific community are often sharply at odds (for example, Edward Teller and Hans Bethe), as are the political strategists, from the "pro-tracted-conflict" line of the University of Pennsylvania group (Strausz-Hupe and Kintner) to the various arms-control and bargaining or negotiation schemes advanced by Thomas Schelling and Hans Morgenthau.

But the main point is that the military community is no longer the only, or even the dominant, source from which the strategists are drawn, and the older military leaders par-ticularly, with vested interests in military doctrines and weapons systems derived from their own by now parochial experiences, find themselves in danger of being ignored or shelved. A few—Major General Walker is an example—may feel that all intellectuals are involved in a plot against the nation. No doubt most of the military men will be forced, as is already happening, into the more complex and bureau-cratic game of recruiting particular groups of scientists for their own purposes (in part through the power of the purse), or attempting to make alliances. In the long run, the military profession may itself become transformed through new modes of training, and a new social type may arise.

But one can already see, in the behavior of retired mili-tary officers, the rancor of an old guard that now finds its knowledge outdated and its authority disputed or ignored, and that is beginning to argue, bitterly, that if only "their" advice had been followed, America would not be on the defensive. A surprising number of high-ranking officers on active duty as well as high-ranking retired officers have be-come active in extreme-right organizations. The Institute of American Strategy, which is financed by the Richardson Foundation, has on its board, and among its members, Rear Admiral Rawson Bennett, Chief of Naval Research; Lieutenant General E. C. Itschner, Chief of Engineers; Rear Admiral H. Arnold Karo; Lieutenant General George W. Mundy, Commandant of the Industrial College of the Armed Forces; and General E. W. Rawlings (U.S.A.F., ret.), the executive vice-president of General Mills, Inc. The American Security Council, for example, lists on its national strategy committee such retired officers as Admiral Arthur W. Radford, former chairman of the Joint Chiefs of Staff, who had been one of the leading exponents of "massive retaliation"; General Albert C. Wedemeyer, who served in China; Lieutenant General Edward M. Almond; Admiral Felix B. Stump; Admiral Ben Moreell (now head of the Republic Steel Corporation); and Rear Admiral Chester Ward.

More active as anti-Communist entrepreneurs are some lesser lights who have held Army posts, often in Intelligence work, and who seek political status accordingly. Thus Brigadier General Bonner Fellows (ret.), a wartime aide to General MacArthur, is the national director of a group called For America, and chairman of the Citizens Foreign Aid Committee, which, despite its name, seeks to reduce foreign aid. Lieutenant Colonel Gunther Hartel (ret.), a former Intelligence officer in Europe and the Far East, heads an organization called American Strategy, Inc. These and other retired officers are active in the various "seminars" and public meetings organized by the radical-right groups.

The stock in trade of almost all these individuals is the argument, reinforced by references to their experiences, that negotiation or co-existence with Communists is impossible, that anyone who discusses the possibility of such negotiation is a tool of the Communists, and that a "tough policy"—by which, *sotto voce*, is meant a preventive war or a first strike—is the only means of forestalling an eventual Communist victory.

VIII

The Polarities of American Politics and the Prospects of the Radical Right

A meaningful polarity within the American consensus has always been part of the American search for self-definition and self-identity: Jefferson versus Hamilton, Republicanism versus Federalism, Agrarianism versus Capitalism, the frontier West versus the industrial East. However significant such polarities may have been in the past, there seems to be little meaningful polarity today. There is no coherent conservative force—and someone like Walter Lippmann, whose *The Public Philosophy* represents a genuine conservative voice, rejects the right, as it rejects him—and the radical right is outside the political pale, insofar as it refuses to accept the American consensus. Nor does a viable left exist in the United States today. The pacifist and Socialist elements have been unable to make the peace issue salient. The radicals have been unable to develop a comprehensive critique of the social disparities in American life—the urban mess, the patchwork educational system, the lack of amenities in our culture. Among the liberals, only the exhaustion of the "received ideas," such as they were, of the New Deal remains. It is a token of the emptiness of contemporary intellectual debate that from the viewpoint of the radical right, the Americans for Democratic Action constitutes the "extreme left" of the American political spectrum, and that *Life*, in order to set up a fictitious balance, counterposes the tiny Councils of Correspondence, a loosely organized peace group led by Erich Fromm and David Riesman, as the "extreme left," to the "extreme right" of the John Birch Society.

The politics of conflict in any country inevitably has some emotional dimension, but in the United States, lacking a historically defined doctrinal basis—as against the ideological divisions of Europe—it takes on, when economic-interest-group issues are lacking, a psychological or status dimension. In this psychological polarity, the right has often been splenetic, while the mood of the left has traditionally been one of *ressentiment*. Today the politics of the radical right is the politics of frustration—the sour impotence of those who find themselves unable to understand, let alone command, the complex mass society that is the polity today. In our time, only the Negro community is fired by the politics of resentment—and this resentment, based on a justified demand for equity, represents no psychological polarity to the radical right. Insofar as there is no real left to counterpoise to the right, the liberal has become the psychological target of that frustration.

One of the reasons why psychological politics can flare up so much more easily here than, say, in Great Britain is the essentially "populist" character of American institutions and the volatile role of public opinion. In the ill-defined, loosely articulated structure of American life, public opinion rather than law has been the more operative sanction against nonconformists and dissenters. Though Americans often respond to a problem with the phrase "there ought to be a law," their respect for law has been minimal, and during periods of extreme excitement, whether it be the vigilante action of a mob or the removal of a book from a school library, the punitive sanctions of opinion quickly supersede law. The very openness or egalitarianism of the American political system is predicated on the right of the people to know, and the Congressional committees, whether searching into the pricing policies of corporations or the political beliefs of individuals, have historically based their investigative claims on this populist premise.

It has always been easier to "mobilize" public opinion on legislation here than it is in England, and in the United States the masses of people have a more direct access to politics.[23] The Presidential-election system, (as against a

[23] In the elite structure of British politics, control is not in the constituencies (or, as here, among the hundreds of local political bosses who have to be dealt into the game), but in the small parliamentary caucuses, which have a legal as well as historic independence from mass party control. The British elite, wedded to a

ministerial system), with the candidates appealing to every voter and, if possible, shaking every hand, involves a direct relation to the electorate. And in the Congressional system, individual constituents, through letters, telephone calls, or personal visits, can get through immediately to their representatives to affect his vote. The Congressional system itself, with its elaborate scaffolding of Senatorial prerogative, often allows a maverick like Borah, Norris, or Robert La Follette to dominate the floor, or a rogue elephant like Huey Long or Joseph McCarthy to rampage against the operations of the government.

But while the populist character of the political institutions and the sweeping influence of public opinion allow social movements to flare with brush-fire suddenness across the political timberland, the unwieldy party system, as well as the checks and balances of the Presidential and judicial structures, also act to constrain such movements. In a few instances, notably the temperance crusade, a social movement operating outside the party system was able to enforce a unitary conception of social behavior on the country; and even then prohibition was repealed in two decades. Until recently, the party and Presidential system have exerted a "discipline of compromise" that has put the maverick and the rogue elephant outside the main arena of the political game.

Within this perspective, therefore, what are the prospects of the radical right? To what extent does it constitute a threat to democratic politics in the United States? Some highly competent political observers write off the radical right as a meaningful political movement. As Richard Rovere has written, "The press treats the extreme Right as though it were a major tendency in American politics, and certain politicians are as much obsessed with it as certain others are with the extreme Left. If a day arrives when the extreme Right does become a major movement, the press and the obsessed politi-

---

"politics of civility," tends to dampen any extremism within the top political structure, while the control system keeps the masses outside and makes it difficult for them to be mobilized for direct pressure on the government.

cians may have a lot to answer for. For the time being, there seems no reason to suppose that its future holds anything more than its present. There is no evidence at all that the recent proliferation of radical, and in some cases downright subversive, organizations of a Rightist tendency reflects or has been accompanied by a spread of ultraconservative views. On the contrary, what evidence there is suggests that the organizations are frantic efforts to prevent ultra-conservatism from dying out."[24]

In his immediate assessment, Rovere is undoubtedly right. In the spring of 1962, both former Vice-President Nixon and Senator Goldwater had moved to dissociate themselves from the extremist right. Nixon quite sharply repudiated the Birchites, on the premise that they are already a political liability, and Goldwater did so more cautiously in expressing his concern that, if not the Birchites, then its leader, Robert Welch, may have gone too far. Yet the future is more open than Rovere suggests. It is in the very nature of an extremist movement, given its tensed posture and its need to maintain a fever pitch, to mobilize, to be on the move, to act. It constantly has to agitate. Lacking any sustained dramatic issue, it can quickly wear itself out, as McCarthyism did. But to this extent the prospects of the radical right depend considerably on the international situation. If the international situation becomes stable, it is likely that the radical right may run quickly out of steam. If it were to take a turn for the worse—if Laos and all of Vietnam were to fall to the Communists; if, within the Western Hemisphere, the moderate regimes of Bolivia and Venezuela were to topple and the Communists take over—then the radical right could begin to rally support around a drive for "immediate action," for a declaration of war in these areas, for a pre-emptive strike, or similar axioms of a "hard line." And since such conservatives as Nixon and Goldwater are committed, at least rhetorically, to a tough anti-Communist position, they would either be forced to go along with such an extreme policy or go under.

[24] "Letter from Washington," *The New Yorker*, February 24, 1962.

Yet, given the severe strains in American life, the radical right does present a threat to American liberties, in a very different and less immediate sense. Democracy, as the sorry history of Europe has shown, is a fragile system, and if there is a lesson to be learned from the downfall of democratic government in Italy, Spain, Austria, and Germany, and from the deep divisions in France, it is that the crucial turning point comes, as Juan Linz has pointed out, when political parties or social movements can successfully establish "private armies" whose resort to violence—street fightings, bombings, the break-up of their opponents' meetings, or simply intimidation—cannot be controlled by the elected authorities, and whose use of violence is justified or made legitimate by the respectable elements in society.

In America, the extreme-right groups of the late 1930s—the Coughlinites, the German-American Bund, the native fascist groups—all sought to promote violence, but they never obtained legitimate or respectable support. The McCarthyite movement of the early 1950s, despite the rampaging antics of its eponymous leader, never dared go, at least rhetorically, outside the traditional framework in trying to establish loyalty and security tests. The Birchers, and the small but insidious group of Minutemen, as the epitome of the radical right, are willing to tear apart the fabric of American society in order to instate their goals, and they did receive a temporary aura of legitimacy from the conservative right.

Barbarous acts are rarely committed out of the blue. (As Freud says, first one commits oneself in words, and then in deeds.) Step by step, a society becomes accustomed to accept, with less and less moral outrage and with greater and greater indifference to legitimacy, the successive blows. What is uniquely disturbing about the emergence of the radical right of the 1960s is the support it has been able to find among traditional community leaders who have themselves become conditioned, through an indiscriminate anti-Communism that equates any form of liberalism with Communism, to judge as respectable a movement which, if successful, can only end the liberties they profess to cherish.

2

INTERPRETATIONS OF
AMERICAN POLITICS (1955)

Daniel Bell

This book presents a series of novel essays on some recent political history, notably an examination of the "new American right" which had concentrated for a time around the leadership of Senator McCarthy, and which continues today in large, if inchoate, form. This is not, however, a book about Senator McCarthy, although two of the essays, by Talcott Parsons and S. M. Lipset, offer some fresh insights into the flash-fire spread of McCarthyism. McCarthyism, or McCarthywasm, as one wit put it, may be a passing phenomenon. This book is concerned not with these transiencies, but with the deeper-running social currents of a turbulent mid-century America.

This is a turbulence born not of depression, but of prosperity. Contrary to the somewhat simple notion that prosperity dissolves all social problems, we see that prosperity brings in its wake new social groups, new social strains and new social anxieties. Conventional political analysis, drawn largely from eighteenth- and nineteenth-century American experience, cannot fathom these new social anxieties nor explain their political consequences.

This book, by establishing a new framework, attempts to provide an understanding of these new social problems. This framework is derived from an analysis of the exhaustion of liberal and left-wing political ideology, and by an examination of the new, prosperity-created "status-groups" which, in their drive for recognition and respectability, have sought to impose older conformities on the American body politic. This framework, drawn from some of the more recent thought in sociology and social psychology, represents a new and original contribution which, we feel, extends the range of conventional political analysis. To an extent, this is a "thesis book." It does not present a "total" view of politics nor does it supplant the older categories of political analysis, but it does add a new and necessary dimension to the analysis of American society today. Equally important, and of more immediate relevance perhaps, the application of these concepts may allow us not only to understand some puzzling aspects of the last decade, but also to illuminate the sub-rosa political forces of 1956 and beyond.

Politics in the United States has been looked at, roughly, from three standpoints: the role of the electoral structure, of democratic tradition, and of interest groups, sectional or class.

Perhaps the most decisive fact about politics in the United States is the two-party system. Each party is like some huge bazaar, with hundreds of hucksters clamoring for attention. But while life within the bazaars flows freely and licenses are easy to obtain, all trading has to be conducted within the tents; the ones who hawk their wares outside are doomed to few sales. This fact gains meaning when we consider one of the striking facts about American life: America has thrown up countless social movements, but few political parties; in contradiction to European political life, few of the social movements have been able to transform themselves into political parties. Here is one source of apparent flux that yet makes for stability in American life.

"It is natural for the ordinary American," wrote Gunnar Myrdal, "when he sees something that is wrong to feel not only that there should be a law against it, but also that an organization should be formed to combat it,"—and, we might add, to change it. American reform groups have ranged from Esperantists to vegetarians, from silver-money advocates to conservationists, from trust-busters to Socialists of fifty-seven varieties. These groups, intense and ideologically single-minded, have formed numerous third parties—the Greenback Party, Anti-Monopoly Party, Equal Rights Party, Prohibition Party, Socialist Labor Party, Union Labor Party, Farmer-Labor Party, Socialist Party. Yet none succeeded.

The wheat farmers of the north central plains have a homogeneity of cultural outlook and a common set of economic problems which national boundary lines cannot bisect. Yet in Canada, the wheat farmers formed a Social Credit Party in Alberta and a Cooperative Commonwealth Federation in Saskatchewan, while their brothers in North Dakota could only, at best, form a Non-Partisan League within the Republican Party in order to press their interests.[1]

These factors of rigid electoral structure have set definite limits on the role of protest movements, left and right, in American life. ("Let me make the deals, and I care not who makes the ideals," an American politician has said.) They account in significant measure for the failure of the Lemke-Coughlin movement in 1936, and the Wallace-Progressive Party in 1948. They account for the new basic alliance between the unions and the Democratic Party. Whatever lingering hopes some trade unionists may have held for a labor party in the United States were dispelled by Walter Reuther at the C.I.O. convention in November 1954 when, in answering transport leaders such as Mike Quill, he pointed out that a third party was impossible within the nature of the United States electoral system. This is a lesson that every social movement has learned. And any social movement which hopes to effect or resist social change in the United States is forced now to operate within one or the other of the two parties. This factor alone will place an enormous strain on these parties in the next ten years.

The democratic tradition, the second of the interpretive categories, has played an important role in shaping American political forms. The distinctive aspect of the political tradition in the United States is that politics is the arena of

[1] See also, S. M. Lipset, *Agrarian Socialism* (University of California Press), pp. 224 *passim*.

the *hoi polloi*. Here the "common man" becomes the source
of ultimate appeal if not authority. This was not so at the beginning. The "founding fathers," with the Roman republic,
let alone the state of affairs under the Articles of Confedera-
tion, in mind, feared the "democratic excesses" which the
poor and propertyless classes could wreak against those with
property. Whatever the subsequent inadequacies of the economic interpretation of history in a complex society, it is
clear that in 1787 self-consciousness of property, and a desire to limit the electoral role of the people, were uppermost
in the minds of the "four groups of personality interests
which had been adversely affected under the Articles of Con-
federation: money, public securities, manufactures, and trade
and shipping."[2] This was reflected in the precautions written
into the Constitution: a non-popular Senate, selected by the
States; an appointive judiciary holding office for life, and a
President elected through the indirect and cumbersome means
of an electoral college.

But these barriers soon broke down. The victory of the
Jeffersonians was the first step in the establishment of a "populist" character for the American democracy. The Federalists,
seeing the success of the Jeffersonian methods, realized the
necessity of imitating those "popular, convivial and charitable
techniques." As early as 1802, Hamilton, in a letter to Bay-
ard, outlined a plan for a "Christian Constitutional Society,"
which would appeal to the masses "through a development
of a 'cult' of Washington and benevolent activities."[3] A Washington Benevolent Society was formed in 1808, but it was
too late, the Federalists had already lost. Thirty years later
their spiritual descendants, the Whigs, beat the Democrats
at their own game. Casting aside Henry Clay, whose "Hamil-
tonian" views were too well-established, the Whigs nominated
General William Henry Harrison, the hero of the battle of

[2] Charles A. Beard, *An Economic Interpretation of the Constitution* (New York, 1935 edition), page 324.
[3] See Dixon Ryan Fox, *The Decline of the Aristocracy in the
Politics of New York.*

Tippecanoe, against Andrew Jackson's successor, Martin Van Buren.

"If General Harrison is taken up as a candidate," said Nicholas Biddle, the former head of the National Bank, in some direction to party managers (which might not have echoed so strangely in 1952), "it will be on account of the past. . . . Let him say not one single word about his principles, or his creed—let him say nothing—promise nothing. Let no Committee, no convention—no town meeting ever extract from him a single word about what he thinks or will do hereafter. Let the use of pen and ink be wholly forbidden."[4]

The "cider election" of 1840 was a turning-point in American political life. Harrison traveled from place to place in a large wagon with a log cabin on top, and a barrel of hard cider on tap for the crowds. Daniel Webster, with the fustian of the demagogue, expressed deep regret that he had not been born in a log cabin, although his elder siblings had begun their lives in a humble abode. Whig orators berated Van Buren for living in a lordly manner, accusing him of putting cologne on his whiskers, eating from gold plate, and of being "laced up in corsets such as women in town wear and if possible tighter than the best of them."

The lesson was clear. Politics as a skill in manipulating masses became the established feature of political life, and the politician, sometimes a front-man for the moneyed interests, but sometimes the manipulator in his own right, came to the fore. Increasingly, the upper classes withdrew from direct participation in politics. The lawyer, the journalist, the drifter, finding politics an open ladder of social mobility, came bounding up from the lower middle classes. The tradition of equality had been established. The politician had to speak to "the people" and in democratic terms.

If the politician spoke to the people, he acted for "interests." The awareness of the interest-group basis of politics, the third of the categories, goes far back to the early days of the republic. Madison, in the oft-quoted Number Ten of the

---

[4] Cited in Charles A. Beard, *The Rise of American Civilization* (1940 edition), Vol. 1, page 574.

Federalist Papers, had written, "the most common and durable source of factions has been the various and unequal distribution of property. Those who hold and those who are without property have ever formed distinct interests in society." James Harrington's maxim that "power always follows property," "I believe to be as infallible a maxim in politics, as that action and reaction are equal in mechanics," said John Adams, the outstanding conservative of the time.[5] The threat to property on the part of the small farmer and the landless formed the basis of the first disquiet in American politics. The Shaysites in Massachusetts and other insurgents, General Henry Knox complained to George Washington, "believe that the property of the United States has been protected from the confiscations of Britain by the joint exertions of all." Madison, looking to the future, anticipated that "a great majority of the people will not only be without land, but any other sort of property." When this has occurred, he predicted, the propertyless masses will "either combine under the influence of their common situation; in which case the rights of property and the public liberty will not be secure in their hands; or what is more probable," he continued, with the lessons of the Roman demagogues in mind, "they will become tools of opulence and ambition, in which case, there will be equal danger on the other side."[6]

The early factional struggles in American political life, rustic in form because of the agrarian weight of the population, soon became sectional. This was inevitable since the different regions developed different interests: the rice, tobacco and cotton of the South; the fishing, lumber, commerce of New England. National parties came into being when the Federalists succeeded at first in combining the large planters of the upper and lower South with the commercial interests

---

[5] Cited in "American Individualism: Fact and Fiction," by A. T. Mason. *American Political Science Review*, March, 1952. Professor Mason's paper is the most concise account I know of the struggle between private economic power and popular political control in the United States.

[6] A. T. Mason, *ibid.*, page 5.

of the North Atlantic region, and when Jefferson challenged this combination by uniting the grain growers and other small farmers both North and South into a rival party. Since then, the national parties have been strange alliances of heterogeneous sectional groups: Midwest farmers with the populist, Democratic and Republican parties; the urban immigrant North with the backward, nativist South. Ethnic and functional groups have, often by historic accident, flowed into one of the two parties: the Negroes, because of the Civil War, for sixty years or so voted Republican; the Irish, because of their original relation to Tammany Hall, became Democrats; the Germans, settling in the Midwest, became Republican; the urban Italians, in reaction to their exclusion by the Irish, became Republican.

Within the sectionalism of American political life, arose the narrower, more flexible tactic of the pressure group standing outside the particular party, committed to neither, giving support or winning support on the basis of allegiance to the single issue alone. One of the first skillful innovators of this tactic was George Henry Evans, a confrère of Robert Owen and a leading figure for a time in the reform politics of the 1830s and '40s. Evans had been one of the leaders of the Workingmen's Party in 1829, a New York party that began with moderate success but which faded when ideological differences inflamed a latent factionalism, and when the Democrats "stole their thunder" by adopting some of their immediate demands. Evans who believed that free land would solve the class tensions and plight of the propertyless workers, organized an Agrarian League in the 1840s. His experience had taught him that a minority party could not win by its own votes and that politicians, interested primarily in "deals not ideals," would endorse any measure advocated by a group that could hold the balance of power. Evans "therefore asked all candidates to support his 'sliding measures.' In exchange for such a pledge, the candidate would receive the votes of the workingmen."[7] While the Agrarian League itself

[7] John R. Commons and associates, *History of Labour in the United States*, Vol. 1, page 531.

met with middling success, its tactics paid off in the later passage of the Homestead acts.

In 1933, with the arrival of the New Deal, the feeling arose that a new era was emerging. In a widely-quoted book, Professor Arthur N. Holcombe of Harvard wrote: "The old party politics is visibly passing away. The character of the new party politics will be determined chiefly by the interests and attitudes of the urban population. . . . There will be less sectional politics and more class politics."[8] The emergence of "functional" groups, particularly labor, and the growing assertion of ethnic groups, seemed to underscore the shift. The fact that Franklin Roosevelt was able to weave together these groups, some of whom like the farmers had been allied with the G.O.P., seemed to indicate that some historic realignments were taking place. Some have. The trade union movement, politically articulate for the first time, is outspokenly Democratic; but the working-class vote has usually been Democratic. Ethnic groups which have played a role in politics have, by and large, retained their loyalty to the Democratic Party; but there are many indications that, as a result of rising prosperity and higher social status, significant chunks of these nationality and minority groups are beginning to shift their allegiance.[9] The farmers, despite the enormous supports voted by the New Deal, have returned to the Republican fold.

While sectional politics have somewhat diminished, class politics have not jelled. Elements of both are reflected in the rise of pressure groups and the lobbies. The most spectacular use of the seesaw pressure group tactic was the Anti-Saloon League, which, starting in 1893, was able in two and a half decades to push through a Constitutional amendment prohibiting the manufacture and sale of liquor in the United States. Since then, the pressure group device has been adopted by

[8] A. N. Holcombe, *The New Party Politics* (New York, 1933), page 11.

[9] See Samuel Lubell, *The Future of American Politics* (New York, 1952); Louis Harris, *Is There a Republican Majority?* (New York, 1955).

thousands of organizations, whether it be for tariff reform, opposition to Federal medical programs, or political aid to the state of Israel. In 1949, the Department of Commerce estimated that there were 4000 national trade, professional, civic and other associations. Including local and branch chapters there were probably 16,000 businessmen's organizations, 70,-000 local labor unions, 100,000 women's clubs and 15,000 civic groups carrying on some political education. The enormous multiplication of such groups obviously cancels out many of the threats made to candidates defying one or the other interests.[10] But it makes possible, too, a dextrous art of logrolling, which itself makes it possible for small interest to exert great political leverage. Thus, when peanuts were eliminated from a farm subsidy program in 1955, over one hundred Southern congressmen held up a crop support bill until the subsidy was restored. (Although Georgia peanuts account for less than one half of one per cent of farm income, subsidizing this crop has cost the U.S. 100 million dollars in the past decade.)

The multiplication of interests and the fractioning of groups make it difficult to locate the sources of power in the United States.[11] This political fractioning, occurring simultaneously with the break-up of old property forms and the rise of new managerial groups to power within business enterprises, spells the break-up, too, of older ruling classes in the United States. A ruling class may be defined as a power-holding group that has both an established community of interest and continuity of interest. One can be a member of the "upper class" (i.e. have greater privilege and wealth and be able to transmit that wealth) without being a member of the *ruling group*. The modern ruling group is a coalition whose modes of continuity, other than the political route as such, are still ill-defined.[12]

[10] For an extended discussion of the role of interest groups in American politics, see David Truman, *The Governmental Process* (New York, 1951).

[11] See David Riesman, *The Lonely Crowd* (Anchor edition, pp. 246–59).

[12] The amorphousness of power in contemporary United States and its relationship to the break-up of "family capitalism," in the

More than ever, government in the United States has become in John Chamberlain's early phrase, "the broker state." To say this is a broker state, however, does not mean that all interests have equal power. This is a business society. But within the general acceptance of corporate capitalism, modified by union power and checked by government control, the deals and interest-group trading proceed.

Granting the usefulness of these frames of political analysis —the role of electoral structure in limiting social movements and social clashes; the tradition of popular appeal; and the force of interest-groups in shaping and modifying legislative policy—in understanding "traditional" political problems, they leave us somewhat ill-equipped to understand the issues which have dominated political dispute in the last decade. These categories do not help us understand the Communist issue, the forces behind the new nationalism of say Bricker and Knowland, and the momentary range of support and the intense emotional heat generated by Senator McCarthy.

For Europeans, particularly, the Communist issue must be a puzzle. After all, there are no mass Communist parties in the U.S. such as one finds in France and Italy; the Communist Party in the U.S. never, at any single moment, had more than 100,000 members. In the last five years, when the Communist issue appeared on the national scene, the Communists had already lost considerable political influence and were on the decline—the Communists had been expelled from C.I.O.;[18] the Progressive Party, repudiated by Henry Wallace, had fizzled; the Communists were losing strength in the intellectual community.

United States is developed by the writer in a paper on "The Ambiguities of the Mass Society and the Complexities of American Life," presented at a conference in Milan, Italy, in September, 1955 on "The Future of Freedom." [This paper is included in my essays, The End of Ideology (The Free Press, 1960, paperback edition, Collier Books, 1961).]

[18] By 1952 they controlled unions with fewer than five percent of United States labor membership as against a peak control of unions with 20 percent of union membership in 1944.

It is true that liberals have tended to play down the issue.[14] And some rational basis for its existence was present. There was the surprise of the aggression in Korea and the emotional reaction against the Chinese and Russian Communists which carried over to domestic Communists. The disclosures, particularly by Whittaker Chambers, of the infiltration of Communists into high posts in government and the existence of espionage rings, produced a tremendous shock in a nation which hitherto had been unaware of such machinations. People began realizing, too, that numbers alone were no criteria of Communist strength; in fact, thinking of Communist influence on the basis of statistical calculation itself betrayed an ignorance of Communist methods; in the United States the Communists by operating among intellectual groups and opinion leaders have had an influence far out of proportion to their actual numbers. And, finally, the revelations in the Canadian spy investigations, in the Allan Nunn May trial in Britain and in the Rosenberg case that the Soviets had stolen Unites States atom secrets, themselves added fuel to the emotional heat against the Communists.

When all of this is said, it still fails to account for the extensive damage to the democratic fabric that McCarthy and others were able to cause on the Communist issue—and for the reckless methods disproportionate to the problem: the loyalty oaths on the campus, the compulsive Americanism which saw threats to the country in the wording of a Girl Scout handbook, the violent clubbing of the Voice of America (which under the ideological leadership of such anti-Com-

---

[14] The contradictory stand of the Truman administration compounded these confusions and increased the alarums. On the one hand, leading members of the administration, including Truman himself, sought to minimize the degree of past Communist infiltration, on the other hand, the administration let loose a buckshot security program which itself inflamed the problems. This included the turning of the Attorney-General's list of subversive organizations into a blank check-list to deny individuals passports and even non-government jobs; an unfair loyalty program in which individuals could not even face their accusers; and the prosecution of the Communist Party leaders under the Smith Act.

munists as Foy Kohler and Bertram Wolfe had conducted intelligent propaganda in Europe), the wild headlines and the senseless damaging of the Signal Corps radar research program at Fort Monmouth—in short the suspicion and the miasma of fear that played so large a role in American politics. Nor does it explain the unchallenged position held so long by Senator McCarthy.

McCarthy himself must be a puzzle to conventional political analysis. Calling him a demagogue explains little; the relevant questions are, to whom was he a demagogue, and about what. McCarthy's targets were indeed strange. Huey Long, the last major demagogue, had vaguely attacked the rich and sought to "share the wealth." McCarthy's targets were intellectuals, Harvard, Anglophiles, internationalists, the Army.

His targets and his language do, indeed, provide important clues to the "radical right" that supported him, and the reasons for that support. These groups constituted a strange mélange: a thin stratum of soured patricians like Archibald Roosevelt, the last surviving son of Teddy Roosevelt, whose emotional stake lay in a vanishing image of a muscular America defying a decadent Europe; the "new rich"—the automobile dealers, real estate manipulators, oil wildcatters—who needed the psychological assurance that they, like their forebears, had earned their own wealth, rather than accumulated it through government aid, and who feared that "taxes" would rob them of that wealth; the rising middle-class strata of the ethnic groups, the Irish and the Germans, who sought to prove their Americanism, the Germans particularly because of the implied taint of disloyalty during World War II; and finally, unique in American cultural history, a small group of intellectuals, many of them cankered ex-Communists, who, pivoting on McCarthy, opened up an attack on liberalism in general.

This strange coalition, bearing the "sword of the Lord and Gideon," cannot be explained in conventional political terms. These essays do provide some frame, particularly one to explain the "new rich" and the "rising ethnic" groups. One key concept is the idea of "status politics" advanced by Richard Hofstadter. His central idea is that groups that are upwardly mobile (i.e. that are advancing in wealth and social position), are often as anxious and as politically febrile as groups that have become déclassé. Many observers have noted that groups which have lost their social position seek more violently than ever to impose on all groups the older values of a society which they once bore. Hofstadter demonstrates that groups on the rise may insist on a similar conformity in order to establish themselves. This rise takes place in periods of prosperity, when class or economic interest group conflicts have lost much of their force.[15] The new, patriotic issues proposed by the status groups are amorphous and ideological. This theme is elaborated in the essay by Riesman and Glazer, with par-

---

[15] Before the Civil War and immigration, discrimination in America was almost solely on religious grounds. In the decades that followed, the rising social classes began to create status demarcations. For an excellent account of the turning-point in social discrimination in America, i.e., its emergence in an egalitarian society, see the essay by Oscar Handlin, "The Acquisition of Political and Social Rights by the Jews in the United States," in the *American Jewish Yearbook, 1955.*

In the expansion and prosperity of the 1870s and 1880s, Professor Handlin points out, "many a man having earned a fortune, even a modest one, thereafter found himself laboring under the burden of complex anxieties. He knew that success was by its nature evanescent. Fortunes were made only to be lost; what was earned in one generation would disappear in the next. Such a man, therefore, wished not only to retain that which he had gained; he was also eager for the social recognition that would permit him to enjoy his possessions; and he sought to extend these on in time through his family. . . . The last decades of the nineteenth century therefore witnessed a succession of attempts to set up areas of exclusiveness that would mark off the favored groups and protect them against excessive contact with outsiders. In imitation of the English model, there was an effort to create a 'high society' with its own protocol and conventions, with suitable residences in suitable districts, with distinctive clubs and media of entertainment, all of which would mark off and preserve the wealth of the fortunate families."

For an account of a parallel development in England, see the essay by Miriam Beard in the volume by Graeber and Britt, *Jews in a Gentile World.* For the sources of discrimination in American traditions and populism, see Daniel Bell, "The Grassroots of Jew Hatred in America," *The Jewish Frontier,* June, 1944.

ticular reference to the new rich. But these groups are able to assert themselves, the two sociologists point out, largely because of the exhaustion of liberal ideology—a collapse not from defeat but from "victory." The essay by Peter Viereck traces some of the historical roots of the peculiar rhetoric of the right, showing the sources of the anti-intellectualism and Anglophobia in the egalitarian populism of the last century. Professor Parsons, discussing the nature of social change in the United States, demonstrates how the resultant social strains foster the emergence of the new right. Glazer and Lipset, analyzing the recent study by Professor Stouffer on "Communism, Conformity and Civil Liberties," deal with limitations of "survey methods" in elucidating social attitudes. The long concluding essay by Professor Lipset provides a detailed analysis of the social groups identified with the new right and assesses their strength.

These essays were not written for this volume. All but the reviews of the Stouffer book appeared about the same time, and quite independently. And yet they showed a remarkable convergence in point of view. This convergence itself indicates that some of the recent concepts of sociology and social psychology—the role of status groups as a major entity in American life and status resentments as a real force in politics—were being applied fruitfully to political analysis.

Whether the groups analyzed in this volume form a political force depends upon many factors. Certainly McCarthy himself is, at the moment, at the nadir. By the logic of his own political position, and by the nature of his personality, he had to go to an extreme. And he ended, finally, by challenging Eisenhower. It was McCarthy's great gamble. And he lost, for the challenge to a Republican President by a Republican minority could only have split the party. Faced with this threat, the party rallied behind Eisenhower, and McCarthy himself was isolated. In this respect, the events prove the soundness of the thesis of Walter Lippmann and the Alsops in 1952 that only a Republican President could provide the necessary continuity of foreign and domestic policy initiated and maintained by the Fair Deal. A Democratic President

would only have polarized the parties, and given the extreme
Republican wing the license to lead the attack; the administration of a moderate Republican could act as a damper on the
extreme right.

The lessening of international tensions may confirm Mc-
Carthy's defeat, just as a flare-up of war in Asia, particularly
Chinese Communist action over Formosa, might give him a
platform to come back. Yet McCarthy has to be understood
in relation to the people behind him and the changed political
temper which these groups have brought. He was the catalyst,
not the explosive force. These forces still remain.

The essays in this volume identify and deal with the emergence of the "status groups." Their emergence raises some
further questions regarding the political theory and political
temper of American democracy.

Throughout our history, Americans have had an extraordinary talent for compromise in politics and extremism in morality. The most shameless political deals (and "steals") have
been rationalized as expedient and realistically necessary; yet
in no other country were there such spectacular attempts to
curb human appetites and brand them as illicit—and nowhere
else such glaring failures. From the start America was at one
and the same time the frontier community where "everything
goes," and the fair country of the restrictive Blue Laws (to
the extent, for example, of barring theatrical performances
on Sunday). At the turn of the century the cleavage developed between the big city and the small town conscience:
crime as a growing business was fed by the revenues from
prostitution, liquor and gambling that a cynical urban society
encouraged, and which a middle-class Protestant ethos sought
to suppress with a ferocity unmatched in any other civilized
country. Even in prim and proper Anglican England, prostitution is a commonplace of Piccadilly night life, and gambling one of the largest and most popular industries. But in
America, the enforcement of public morals has been a continuing feature of our history.

The sources of this moralism are varied. This has been a

middle-class culture, and there may be considerable truth to
the generalization of Svend Ranulf that moral indignation is a
peculiar fact of middle-class psychology and represents a dis-
guised form of repressed envy.[16] One does not find moral
indignation a feature of the temper of aristocratic culture.
Moralism and moral indignation are characteristic of religions
that have largely abandoned other-worldly preoccupations and
have concentrated on this-worldly concerns. Religions, like
Catholicism, which are focused on heaven are often quite tolerant of man's foibles, weaknesses, and cruelties on earth;
theft, after all, is only a venial sin, while pride bears the stain
of venality. This is a country, and Protestantism a religion, in
which piety has given way to moralism, and theology to
ethics. Becoming respectable represents "moral" advance-
ment, and regulating conduct, i.e. being "moral" about it, is a
great concern of the Protestant churches in America.

This moralism, itself not unique to America, is linked to
an evangelicalism that was largely unique. There has long been
a legend, fostered for the most part by literary people, and
compounded by sociologists, that America's has been a "puritan" culture. For the sociologists this has arisen out of a mistaken identification of the Protestant ethic with puritan code.
The literary critics have been seduced by the myth of New
England, and the literary revolt initiated by Van Wyck
Brooks which sought to break the hold of puritanism in literature. While puritanism, and the "New England mind,"
have indeed played a large intellectual role in American life,
in the habits and mores of the masses of people, the peculiar
evangelicalism of Methodism and Baptism, with its high emotionalism, its fervor, enthusiasm and excitement, its revivalism,
its excesses of sinning and of high-voltage confessing, has
played a much more important role in coloring the moral
temper of America. Baptism and Methodism have been the
American religious creed because they were the rustic and
frontier religions. In his page on "Why Americans Manifest a
Sort of Fanatical Spiritualism," de Tocqueville observes: "In

16 Svend Ranulf, *Moral Indignation and Middle Class Psychology*, Copenhagen, 1938.

all states of the Union, but especially in the half-peopled country of the Far West, itinerant preachers may be met with who
hawk about the word of God from place to place. Whole families, old men, women and children, cross rough passes and
untrodden wilds, coming from a great distance, to join a camp-
meeting, where, in listening to these discourses, they totally
forget for several days and nights the cares of business and
even the most urgent wants of the body."[17]

The Baptist and Methodist churches grew while the more
"respectable" Protestant bodies remained static, precisely because their preachers went on with the advancing frontier and
reflected its spirit. "In the camp meeting and in the political
gathering logical discourse was of no avail, while the 'language
of excitement' called forth an enthusiastic response," observed
H. Richard Niebuhr.[18]

This revivalist spirit was egalitarian and anti-intellectual. It
shook off the vestments and the formal liturgies and preached
instead the gospel and roaring hymn. This evangelicalism was
reflected in the moralism of a William Jennings Bryan, a religious as well as an economic champion of the West, and in the
urban revivalism of a Dwight Moody and the Y.M.C.A. movement that grew out of his gospel fervor.[19] In their espousal
of social reform, the evangelical churches reflected the peculiar influence of moralism. They were the supreme champions
of prohibition legislation and Sabbath observance. Reform, in
their terms, meant, not as in the New Deal, a belief in welfare
legislation, but the redemption of those who had fallen prey to
sin—and sin meant drink, loose women and gambling.

This moralism, so characteristic of American temper, had
a peculiar schizoid character: it would be imposed with ve-
hemence in areas of culture and conduct—in the censorship
of books, the attacks on "immoral art," etc., and in the realm
of private habits; yet it was heard only sporadically regarding

[17] De Tocqueville, *Democracy in America* (New York, 1945),
Vol. II, page 134.
[18] H. Richard Niebuhr, *Social Sources of Denominationalism*
(New York, 1929), page 141.
[19] See W. W. Sweet, *Revivalism in America* (New York, 1944).

the depredations of business or the corruption of politics. And yet, this has had its positive side. To the extent that moral indignation—apart from its rhetorical use in political campaigns —played so small a role in the actual political arena, the United States has been able to escape the intense ideological fanaticism—the conflicts of clericalism and class—which has been so characteristic of Europe.

The singular fact about the Communist problem is that an ideological issue was raised in American political life, with a compulsive moral fervor only possible because of the equation of Communism with sin. A peculiar change, in fact, seems to be coming over American life. While we are becoming more relaxed in the area of traditional morals (viz., the Supreme Court ruling against censorship in the case of the movie, The Miracle), we are becoming moralistic and extreme in politics. The fact that Senator McCarthy could seek to pin a Communist label on the Democratic Party, and tie it with a tag of "treason"—and be abetted for a time by Attorney General Brownell and the Republican Party is a reflection of a new political temper in America.

The tendency to convert politics into "moral" issues is reinforced by a second fact, the activities of the McCarthyite intellectuals—James Burnham, William Schlamm, Max Eastman, and their minor epigoni. The rise of intellectual apologists for a reactionary right is, too, a new phase in American life. The quixotic fact is that many of these men, ex-Communists, repudiated at first not the utopian vision of Communism, but its methods. In the thirties, the crucial intellectual fight was to emphasize, against the liberal piddlers who sought to excuse the harshness of Stalinism by reference to the historic backwardness of Russia, or the grandeur of the Soviet dream, that in social action there is an inextricable relation between "ends and means," and that consistently amoral means could only warp and hideously distort an end. Yet these men have forgotten this basic point in their defense of McCarthy. Schlamm, the author of a fine book about Stalinism, Die Diktatur der Lüge (The Dictatorship of the Lie), applauds McCarthy as a man who is seriously interested in ideas. John

T. Flynn, the old muckraker, denies McCarthy has ever made use of the lie. Max Eastman, slightly critical at times, worries most not about McCarthy but that the liberals by attacking McCarthy might be playing "the Communist game"; as if all politics were only two-sided, in this case McCarthy or the Communists.

How explain this reversal? Motivations are difficult to plumb. Some of these men, as George Orwell once pointed out in a devastating analysis of James Burnham,[20] slavishly worship power images. *The Freeman,* the old-maidish house organ of the intellectual right, coyly applauded McCarthy as a tough hombre.

Yet one significant fact emerges from this bile: the hatred of the ex-Communist is not so much of the Communist, but of the "liberals," and the root of the problem goes back to the political situation of the thirties. In recent years there has been a growing myth that in the 1930s the Communists dominated the cultural life of America, its publishing houses, Broadway, Hollywood, and the colleges. The myth is a seductive one which grows more plausible with revelation of different "name" personages who the public now discover were once open or covert fellow-travelers. Yet, as Granville Hicks points out, only one anti-Communist book is ever cited as having been suppressed in those years, while anti-Communist authors such as Eugene Lyons, Max Eastman, Freda Utley, Jan Valtin all published anti-Soviet books.[21] The Communists, in fact, felt that the shoe at times was on the other foot. "In the autumn of 1934," says Hicks, "I wrote an article for the *New Masses* in which I argued that the New York *Times* Book Review assigned almost all books on Russia to anti-Communists." The *Nation* book section under Margaret Marshall in those years was anti-Communist. The Communist cells in universities were small; at Harvard in 1938, at the height of the popular front, there were fourteen faculty Communists in all. While the Communists were able to enlist a sizable number of well-known names for their fronts, the Committee for Cul-

[20] *Shooting an Elephant and Other Essays* (New York, 1950).
[21] Granville Hicks, *Where We Came Out* (New York, 1954).

tural Freedom, in issuing a statement in 1939 bracketing the Soviet and Nazi states as equally immoral, displayed a more distinguished roster of intellectuals than any statement issued by a Communist front.

How explain these contrasting images of the Red Decade—the anti-Communists who regarded the Communists as dominating the cultural life and the Communists who complained that they had little influence? The evidence, I would say, lies on Hicks' side.[22] The Communists did not dominate the cultural field, though they wielded an influence far out of proportion to their numbers. What is true, and here I feel Hicks missed the subtle edge of the problem, is that the official institutions of the cultural community—because of the Spanish Civil War, the shock of Fascism, and the aura of New Deal reform—did look at the Communist with some sympathy; they regarded him as ultimately, philosophically wrong, but still as a respectable member of the community. But the vocal anti-Communists (many of them Trotskyites at the time), with their quarrelsome ways, their esoteric knowledge of Bolshevik history (most of the intellectuals were completely ignorant of the names of the Bolsheviks in the dock at the Moscow trials, Zinoviev, Kamenev, Bukharin, Piatakov, Sokolnikov, Rakovsky) seemed extreme and bizarre—and were regarded with suspicion. The anti-Stalinists, by raising "extraneous" issues of a "sectarian" nature, were "sabotaging" the fight against Fascism. Hence, in the thirties, one found the Communist possessing a place in the intellectual world, while the anti-Communists were isolated and thwarted.

Here, in a sense, is the source of the present-day resentment against "the liberals." If one looks for formal or ideological definition "the liberal" is difficult to pin down. To a McCarthyite, "the liberals" dominate the intellectual and publishing community—and define the canons of respectability and acceptance. And once again the knot of ex-Communists, now,

---

[22] I have attempted to assemble some of that evidence in my essay on the history of American Marxist parties in the volume *Socialism and American Life,* edited by Egbert and Persons (Princeton, 1952).

as in the thirties, finds itself outside the pale. At stake is an attitude toward the Communists. *The Freeman* intellectuals want the Communists shriven or driven out of all areas of public or community life. The "liberal" says the effort is not worth the price, since there are few Communists, and the drive against them only encourages reactionaries to exact a conformity of opinion. By refusing to sanction these measures, the liberals find themselves under attack as "soft."

In these strange times, new polar terms have been introduced into political discourse, but surely none so strange as the division into "hard" and "soft." Certainly in attitudes towards the rights of Communists, there are many gradations of opinion among genuine anti-Communists, as the debates in the Committee for Cultural Freedom have demonstrated. But for *The Freeman* intellectuals, there are only two attributes— hard or soft. Even the New York *Post*, whose editor, James A. Wechsler has fought Communists for years, and the Americans for Democratic Action, whose initiating spirit was Reinhold Niebuhr, and whose co-chairman, Arthur Schlesinger, Jr., was one of the early intellectual antagonists of the Communists, before McCarthy ever spoke up on the subject, have been denounced as "soft."

What does the term mean? Presumably one is "soft" if one insists that the danger from domestic Communists is small. But the "hard" anti-Communists insist that no distinction can be made between international and domestic Communism. This may be true regarding intent and methods, but is it equally so regarding their power; is the strength of domestic Communists as great as that of international Communism? It is said, that many liberals refused to recognize that Communists constituted a security problem or that planned infiltration existed. This is rather a blanket charge, but even if largely true, the "hard" anti-Communists refuse to recognize the dimension of time. The question is: *what is the degree of the present-day Communist infiltration?* Pressed at this point some "hard" anti-Communists admit that the number of actual Communists may be small, but that the real problem arises because the liberals, especially in the large Eastern universities, are pre-

dominantly "anti-anti Communists." But what is the content of
this "anti-anti Communism?" That it won't admit that the
Communists constitute a present danger. And so we are back
where we started.

The polarization of images reflects itself in a strange set,
too, of contrasting conceptions about power position. The liberals, particularly in the universities, have felt themselves subject to attack by powerful groups; the pro-McCarthy intellectuals see themselves as a persecuted group, discriminated
against in the major opinion forming centers in the land. A
personal incident is relevant here. A few years ago I encountered Robert Morris, the counsel then for the Jenner Committee on internal subversion. He complained of the "terrible
press" his committee was receiving. What press, he was asked;
after all, the great Hearst and Scripps-Howard and Gannett
chains, as well as an overwhelming number of newspaper
dailies, had enthusiastically supported and reported the work
of the Committee. I wasn't thinking of them, he replied. I was
thinking of the New York *Times,* the Washington *Post,* the St.
Louis *Post-Dispatch.*

The paradoxical fact is that on traditional economic issues,
these "liberal" papers are conservative.[23] All three supported
Eisenhower. Yet, traditional conservative issues no longer
count in dividing "liberals" from "anti-Communists." The only
issue is whether one is "hard" or "soft." And so, an amorphous, ideological issue, rather than an interest-group issue,
has become a major dividing line in the political community.

[23] The sense of being a hunted, isolated minority is reflected
quite vividly in an editorial note in *The Freeman*—June, 1955:
"Since the advent of the New Deal (An Americanized version of
Fabian socialism) the mass circulation media in this country have
virtually closed their columns to opposition articles. For this they
can hardly be blamed; their business is to sell paper at so much a
pound and advertising space at so much a line. They must give the
masses what they believe the masses want, if they are to maintain
their mass circulation business; and there is no doubt that the promises of socialism reiterated by the propaganda machine of the government, have made it popular and dulled the public mind to the
verities of freedom."

The "ideologizing" of politics gains reinforcement from a third, somewhat independent tendency in American life, the emergence of what may be called the "symbolic groups." These are the inchoate, often ill-coordinated entities, known generally, in capital letters, as "Labor," "Business," the "Farmers," *et al.* The assumption is made that these entities have a coherent philosophy and a defined purpose and represent actual forces. But is this true in a society so multi-fractioned and interest-divided?

The utilitarians, the first to give politics a calculus, and thus begin an experimental social science, made a distinction between a social decision (the common purpose) and the sum total of individual self-interest decisions. Adam Smith assumed a natural harmony, if not identity, between the two. But Jeremy Bentham knew that such identity was artificial, although he felt that they could be reconciled by an intelligent legislator through "a well-regulated application of punishments."[24] The distinction between the self-interest and social decisions might be reworded in modern idiom as one between "market" and "ideological" decisions. The first represents a series of choices based on the rational self-interest of the individual or organization, with the aim of maximizing profit or the survival or enhancement of the organization. The second represents decisions, based on some purpose clothed in moral terms, in which the goal is deemed so important as to override when necessary the individual self-interest.[25]

In modern society, the clash between ideological and market decisions is often as intense within groups, as between groups. The "labor movement," for example, has strongly fa-

[24] Jeremy Bentham, *Principles of Morals and Legislation*, Oxford edition, page 3; see also, Elie Halevy, *Growth of Philosophical Radicalism* (New York, 1928); pp. 14–18.

[25] The distinction, thus, is more than one between opinion and behavior. Quite often an ideological decision will have greater weight for a group than immediate self-interest (defined in rational market terms), and the group will act on the basis of ideology. The task of a realistic social psychology is to identify under what circumstances the ideological or market conditions will prevail.

vored lower tariffs and broader international trade; yet the sea-men's union has urged that U.S. government aid be shipped in American, not foreign bottoms, while the textile unions have fought for quotas on foreign imports. Political-minded unionists, like Mike Quill in New York, have had to choose between a wage increase for their members against a rise in transit fares for the public at large. Interest rivalries are often more direct. The teamsters' unions have lobbied against the railroad unions and the coal miners against the oil workers. In every broad group these interest conflicts have taken place, within industry, farm, and every other functional group in the society.

The tendency to convert interest groups into "symbolic groups" derives from varied sources. Much of it comes from "vulgar" Marxist thinking, with its image of a self-conscious, coordinated Business class (as in Jack London's image of "the oligarchs" in his *The Iron Heel,* and the stereotypes of "Wall Street"). Some of this was taken over by the New Dealers with their image of "America's Sixty Families." But the biggest impetus has come from the changing nature of political deci-sion-making and the mode of opinion formation in modern society. The fact that decision-making has been centralized into the narrow cockpit of Washington, rather than the im-personal market, leads groups like the National Association of Manufacturers, the Farm Bureau, the A.F. of L., *et al,* to speak for *"Business,"* for the *"Farmers,"* for *"Labor."* At the same time, with the increased sensitivity to "public opinion," heightened by the introduction of the mass polling technique, the "citizen" (not the specific-interest individual) is asked what "Business" or "Labor" or the "Farmer" should do. In effect, these groups are often forced to assume an identity and greater coherence beyond their normal intramural interest conflicts. A result again is that political debate moves from specific inter-est clashes, in which issues can be identified and possibly com-promised, to ideologically-tinged conflicts which polarize the groups and divide the society.

The essays in this book are primarily analytical. Yet they also point implicitly to a dangerous situation. The tendency to convert issues into ideologies, to invest them with moral color and high emotional charge, invites conflicts which can only damage a society. "A nation, divided irreconcilably on 'principle,' each party believing itself pure white and the other pitch black, cannot govern itself," wrote a younger Walter Lippmann.

The saving glory of the United States is that politics has always been a pragmatic give-and-take rather than a series of wars-to-the-death. One ultimately comes to admire the "practical politics" of a Theodore Roosevelt and his scorn for the intransigents, like Godkin and Villard, who, refusing to yield to expediency, could never put through their reforms. Politics, as Edmund Wilson has described T.R.'s attitude, "is a matter of adapting oneself to all sorts of people and situations, a game in which one may score but only by accepting the rules and recognizing one's opponents, rather than a moral crusade in which one's stainless standard must mow the enemy down."[26]

Democratic politics is bargaining and consensus because the historic contribution of liberalism was to separate law from morality. The thought that the two should be separate often comes as a shock. Yet, in the older Catholic societies, ruled by the doctrine of "two swords," the state was the secular arm of the Church, and enforced in civil life the moral decrees of the Church. This was possible, in political theory, if not in practice, because the society was homogeneous and everyone accepted the same religious values. But the religious wars that followed the Reformation proved that a plural society could only survive if it respected the principles of toleration. No group, be it Catholic or Protestant, could use the state to impose its moral conceptions on all the people. As the party of the *Politiques* put it, the "civil society must not perish for conscience's sake."[27]

These theoretical foundations of modern liberal society were completed by Kant, who, separating legality and morality, de-

[26] Edmund Wilson, in *Eight Essays* [New York, 1954 (Anchor Books, page 213).]

[27] See Harold J. Laski, *The Rise of Liberalism* (New York, 1938), pp. 43–51. Also, Franz Neumann, *Behemoth* (New York), pp. 442–47.

fined the former as the "rules of the game" so to speak; law dealt with procedural, not substantive issues. The latter were private matters of conscience with which the state could not interfere.

This distinction has been at the root of the American democracy. For Madison, factions (or interests) were inevitable and the function of the republic was to protect the causes of faction, i.e., liberty and "the diversity in the faculties of men." As an interpreter of Madison writes, "free men, 'diverse' man, fallible, heterogeneous, heterodox, opinionated, quarrelsome man was the raw material of faction."[28] Since faction was inevitable, one could only deal with its effects, and not smother its causes. One curbed these effects by a federal form of government, by separation of powers, *et al*. But for Madison two answers were central: first, an *extensive republic*, since a larger geographical area, and therefore a larger number of interests, would "lessen the insecurity of private rights," and second, the guarantee of representative government.

Representative government, as John Stuart Mill has so cogently pointed out, means representation of all interests, "since the interest of the excluded is always in danger of being overlooked." And being overlooked, as Calhoun pointed out, constitutes a threat to civil order. But representative government is important for the deeper reason that by including all representative interests one can keep up "the antagonism of influences which is the only real security for continued progress."[29] It is the only way of providing the "concurrent majorities" which, as Calhoun knew so well, were the solid basis for providing a check on the tyrannical "popular" majority. Only through representative government can one achieve consensus and conciliation.

This is not to say that the Communist "interest" is a legiti-

---

[28] See Neal Riemer, "James Madison's Theory of the Self-Destructive Features of Republican Government," *Ethics*, Vol. 65, Oct. 1954, pp. 34–43.

[29] See John Stuart Mill, *Representative Government* (Everyman's Library, 1936), pp. 201, 209.

mate one, or that the Communist issue is irrelevant. As a conspiracy, rather than as a legitimate dissenting group, the Communist movement is a threat to any democratic society. And, within the definition of "clear and present danger," a democratic society may have to act against that conspiracy. But these are questions to be handled by law. The tendency to use the Communist issue as a political club against other parties or groups (i.e. to provide an ideological guilt by association), or the tendency to convert questions of law into issues of morality (and thus shift the source of sanctions from courts and legitimate authority to private individuals), imposes a great strain on democratic society.

In almost 170 years since its founding American democracy has been rent only once by civil war. We have learned since then, not without strain, to include the "excluded interests," the populist farmers and the organized workers. These economic interest groups take a legitimate place in the society and the ideological conflicts that once threatened to disrupt the society, particularly in the New Deal period, have been mitigated. The new divisions created by the status anxieties of new middle-class groups pose a new threat. The rancor of McCarthyism was one of its ugly excesses. Yet, the United States, so huge and complex that no single political boss or any single political grouping has ever been able to dominate it, may in time diminish these divisions. This is an open society, and these status anxieties are part of the price we pay for that openness.

3

THE PSEUDO-CONSERVATIVE REVOLT (1955)

Richard Hofstadter

Twenty years ago the dynamic force in American political life came from the side of liberal dissent, from the impulse to reform the inequities of our economic and social system and to change our ways of doing things, to the end that the sufferings of the Great Depression would never be repeated. Today the dynamic force in our political life no longer comes from the liberals who made the New Deal possible. By 1952 the liberals had had at least the trappings of power for twenty years. They could look back to a brief, exciting period in the mid-thirties when they had held power itself and had been able to transform the economic and administrative life of the nation. After twenty years the New Deal liberals have quite unconsciously taken on the psychology of those who have entered into possession. Moreover, a large part of the New Deal public, the jobless, distracted and bewildered men of 1933, have in the course of the years found substantial places in society for themselves, have become home-owners, suburbanites and solid citizens. Many of them still keep the emotional commitments to the liberal dissent with which they grew up politically, but their social position is one of solid comfort. Among them the dominant tone has become one of satisfaction, even of a kind of conservatism. Insofar as Adlai Stevenson won their enthusiasm in 1952, it was not in spite of, but in part because of the air of poised and reliable conservatism that he brought to the Democratic convention. By comparison, Harry Truman's impassioned rhetoric, with its occasional thrusts at "Wall Street," seemed passé and rather embarrassing. The change did not escape Stevenson himself. "The strange alchemy of time," he said in a speech at Columbus, "has somehow converted the Democrats into the truly conservative party of this country—the party dedicated to conserving all that is best, and building solidly and safely on these foundations." The most that the old liberals can now envisage is not to carry on with some ambitious new program, but simply to defend as much as possible of the old achievements and to try to keep traditional liberties of expression that are threatened.

There is, however, a dynamic of dissent in America today. Representing no more than a modest fraction of the electorate, it is not so powerful as the liberal dissent of the New Deal era, but it is powerful enough to set the tone of our political life and to establish throughout the country a kind of punitive reaction. The new dissent is certainly not radical—there are hardly any radicals of any sort left—nor is it precisely conservative. Unlike most of the liberal dissent of the past, the new dissent not only has no respect for non-conformism, but is based upon a relentless demand for conformity. It can most accurately be called pseudo-conservative—I borrow the term from the study of *The Authoritarian Personality* published five years ago by Theodore W. Adorno and his associates—because its exponents, although they believe themselves to be conservatives and usually employ the rhetoric of conservatism, show signs of a serious and restless dissatisfaction with American life, traditions and institutions. They have little in common with the temperate and compromising spirit of true conservatism in the classical sense of the word, and they are far from pleased with the dominant practical conservatism of the moment as it is represented by the Eisenhower administration. Their political reactions express rather a profound if largely unconscious hatred of our society and its ways—a hatred which one would hesitate to impute to them if one did not have suggestive clinical evidence.

From clinical interviews and thematic apperception tests, Adorno and his co-workers found that their pseudo-conservative subjects, although given to a form of political expression that combines a curious mixture of largely conservative with occasional radical notions, succeed in concealing from themselves impulsive tendencies that, if released in action, would be very far from conservative. The pseudo-conservative, Adorno writes, shows "conventionality and authoritarian submissiveness" in his conscious thinking and "violence, anarchic impulses, and chaotic destructiveness in the unconscious sphere. . . . The pseudo-conservative is a man who, in the name of upholding traditional American values and institutions and defending them against more or less fictitious dangers, consciously or unconsciously aims at their abolition."[1]

Who is the pseudo-conservative, and what does he want? It is impossible to identify him by class, for the pseudo-conservative impulse can be found in practically all classes in society, although its power probably rests largely upon its appeal to the less educated members of the middle classes. The ideology of pseudo-conservatism can be characterized but not defined, because the pseudo-conservative tends to be more than ordinarily incoherent about politics. The lady who, when General Eisenhower's victory over Senator Taft had finally become official, stalked out of the Hilton Hotel declaiming, "This means eight more years of socialism" was probably a fairly good representative of the pseudo-conservative mentality. So also were the gentlemen who, at the Freedom Congress held at Omaha over a year ago by some "patriotic" organizations, objected to Earl Warren's appointment to the Supreme Court with the assertion: "Middle-of-the-road thinking can and will destroy us"; the general who spoke to the same group, demanding "an Air Force capable of wiping out the Russian Air Force and industry in one sweep," but also "a material reduction in military expenditures";[2] the people who a few years

[1] Theodore W. Adorno *et al., The Authoritarian Personality* (New York, 1950), pp. 675–76. While I have drawn heavily upon this enlightening study, I have some reservations about its methods and conclusions. For a critical review, see Richard Christie and Marie Jahoda, eds., *Studies in the Scope and Method of "The Authoritarian Personality"* (Glencoe, Illinois, 1954), particularly the penetrating comments by Edward Shils.

[2] On the Omaha Freedom Congress see Leonard Boasberg, "Radical Reactionaries," *The Progressive*, December, 1953.

ago believed simultaneously that we had no business to be fighting communism in Korea, but that the war should immediately be extended to an Asia-wide crusade against communism; and the most ardent supporters of the Bricker Amendment. Many of the most zealous followers of Senator McCarthy are also pseudo-conservatives, although there are presumably a great many others who are not.

The restlessness, suspicion and fear manifested in various phases of the pseudo-conservative revolt give evidence of the real suffering which the pseudo-conservative experiences in his capacity as a citizen. He believes himself to be living in a world in which he is spied upon, plotted against, betrayed, and very likely destined for total ruin. He feels that his liberties have been arbitrarily and outrageously invaded. He is opposed to almost everything that has happened in American politics for the past twenty years. He hates the very thought of Franklin D. Roosevelt. He is disturbed deeply by American participation in the United Nations, which he can see only as a sinister organization. He sees his own country as being so weak that it is constantly about to fall victim to subversion; and yet he feels that it is so all-powerful that any failure it may experience in getting its way in the world—for instance, in the Orient—cannot possibly be due to its limitations but must be attributed to its having been betrayed.[8] He is the most bitter of all our citizens about our involvement in the wars of the past, but seems the least concerned about avoiding the next one. While he naturally does not like Soviet communism, what distinguishes him from the rest of us who also dislike it is that he shows little interest in, is often indeed bitterly hostile to such realistic measures as might actually strengthen the United States vis-à-vis Russia. He would much rather concern himself with the domestic scene, where communism is weak, than with those areas of the world where it is really strong and threatening. He wants to have nothing to do with the democratic nations of Western Europe, which seem to draw more of his ire than the Soviet Communists, and he is opposed to all "give-away

[8] See the comments of D. W. Brogan in "The Illusion of American Omnipotence," *Harper's*, December, 1952.

programs" designed to aid and strengthen these nations. Indeed, he is likely to be antagonistic to most of the operations of our federal government except Congressional investigations, and to almost all of its expenditures. Not always, however, does he go so far as the speaker at the Freedom Congress who attributed the greater part of our national difficulties to "this nasty, stinking 16th [income tax] Amendment."

A great deal of pseudo-conservative thinking takes the form of trying to devise means of absolute protection against that betrayal by our own officialdom which the pseudo-conservative feels is always imminent. The Bricker Amendment, indeed, might be taken as one of the primary symptoms of pseudo-conservatism. Every dissenting movement brings its demand for Constitutional changes; and the pseudo-conservative revolt, far from being an exception to this principle, seems to specialize in Constitutional revision, at least as a speculative enterprise. The widespread latent hostility toward American institutions takes the form, among other things, of a flood of proposals to write drastic changes into the body of our fundamental law. Last summer, in a characteristically astute piece, Richard Rovere pointed out that Constitution-amending had become almost a major diversion in the Eighty-third Congress.[4] About a hundred amendments were introduced and referred to committee. Several of these called for the repeal of the income tax. Several embodied formulas of various kinds to limit non-military expenditures to some fixed portion of the national income. One proposed to bar all federal expenditures on "the general welfare"; another, to prohibit American troops from serving in any foreign country except on the soil of the potential enemy; another, to redefine treason to embrace not only persons trying to overthrow the government but also those trying to "weaken" it, even by peaceful means. The last proposal might bring the pseudo-conservative rebels themselves under the ban of treason: for the sum total of these amendments might easily serve to bring the whole structure of American society crashing to the ground.

[4] Richard Rovere, "Letter from Washington," *The New Yorker,* June 19, 1954, pp. 67–72.

As Mr. Rovere points out, it is not unusual for a large number of Constitutional amendments to be lying about somewhere in the Congressional hoppers. What is unusual is the readiness the Senate has shown to give them respectful consideration, and the peculiar populistic arguments some of its leading members have used to justify referring them to the state legislatures. While the ordinary Congress hardly ever has occasion to consider more than one amendment, the Eighty-third Congress saw six Constitutional amendments brought to the floor of the Senate, all summoning simple majorities, and four winning the two-thirds majority necessary before they can be sent to the House and ultimately to the state legislatures. It must be added that, with the possible exception of the Bricker Amendment itself, none of the six amendments so honored can be classed with the most extreme proposals. But the pliability of the senators, the eagerness of some of them to pass the buck and defer to "the people of the country," suggests how strong they feel the pressure to be for some kind of change that will give expression to that vague desire to repudiate the past that underlies the pseudo-conservative revolt.

One of the most urgent questions we can ask about the United States in our time is the question of where all this sentiment arose. The readiest answer is that the new pseudo-conservatism is simply the old ultra-conservatism and the old isolationism heightened by the extraordinary pressures of the contemporary world. This answer, true though it may be, gives a deceptive sense of familiarity without much deepening our understanding, for the particular patterns of American isolationism and extreme right-wing thinking have themselves not been very satisfactorily explored. It will not do, to take but one example, to say that some people want the income tax amendment repealed because taxes have become very heavy in the past twenty years: for this will not explain why, of three people in the same tax bracket, one will grin and bear it and continue to support social welfare legislation as well as an adequate defense, while another responds by supporting in a matter-of-fact way the practical conservative leadership of the moment, and the third finds his feelings satisfied only by the angry conspiratorial accusations and extreme demands of the pseudo-conservative.

No doubt the circumstances determining the political style of any individual are complex. Although I am concerned here to discuss some of the neglected socio-psychological elements in pseudo-conservatism, I do not wish to appear to deny the presence of important economic and political causes. I am aware, for instance, that wealthy reactionaries try to use pseudo-conservative organizers, spokesmen and groups to propagate their notions of public policy, and that some organizers of pseudo-conservative and "patriotic" groups often find in this work a means of making a living—thus turning a tendency toward paranoia into a vocational asset, probably one of the most perverse forms of occupational therapy known to man. A number of other circumstances—the drastic inflation and heavy taxes of our time, the dissolution of American urban life, considerations of partisan political expediency—also play a part. But none of these things seem to explain the broad appeal of pseudo-conservatism, its emotional intensity, its dense and massive irrationality, or some of the peculiar ideas it generates. Nor will they explain why those who profit by the organized movements find such a ready following among a large number of people, and why the rank-and-file janizaries of pseudo-conservatism are so eager to hurl accusations, write letters to congressmen and editors, and expend so much emotional energy and crusading idealism upon causes that plainly bring them no material reward.

Elmer Davis, seeking to account for such sentiment in his recent book, *But We Were Born Free*, ventures a psychological hypothesis. He concludes, if I understand him correctly, that the genuine difficulties of our situation in the face of the power of international communism have inspired a widespread feeling of fear and frustration, and that those who cannot face these problems in a more rational way "take it out on their less influential neighbors, in the mood of a man who, being afraid to stand up to his wife in a domestic argument, relieves his feelings by kicking the cat."[5] This suggestion has the merit of both simplicity and plausibility, and it may begin to account for a portion of the pseudo-conservative public. But while we may dismiss our curiosity about the man who kicks the cat by remarking that some idiosyncrasy in his personal development has brought him to this pass, we can hardly help but wonder whether there are not, in the backgrounds of the hundreds of thousands of persons who are moved by the pseudo-conservative impulse, some commonly shared circumstances that will help to account for their all kicking the cat in unison.

All of us have reason to fear the power of international communism, and all our lives are profoundly affected by it. Why do some Americans try to face this threat for what it is, a problem that exists in a world-wide theater of action, while others try to reduce it largely to a matter of domestic conformity? Why do some of us prefer to look for allies in the democratic world, while others seem to prefer authoritarian allies or none at all? Why do the pseudo-conservatives express such a persistent fear and suspicion of *their own government,* whether its leadership rests in the hands of Roosevelt, Truman or Eisenhower? Why is the pseudo-conservative impelled to go beyond the more or less routine partisan argument that we have been the victims of considerable misgovernment during the past twenty years to the disquieting accusation that we have actually been the victims of persistent conspiracy and betrayal—"twenty years of treason?" Is it not true, moreover, that political types very similar to the pseudo-conservative have had a long history in the United States, and that this history goes back to a time when the Soviet power did not loom nearly so large on our mental horizons? Was the Ku Klux Klan, for instance, which was responsibly estimated to have had a membership of from 4,000,000 to 4,500,000 persons at its peak in the 1920s, a phenomenon totally dissimilar to the pseudo-conservative revolt?

What I wish to suggest—and I do so in the spirit of one setting forth nothing more than a speculative hypothesis—is that

[5] Elmer Davis, *But We Were Born Free* (New York, 1954), pp. 35–36; cf. pp. 21–22 and *passim.*

pseudo-conservatism is in good part a product of the rootless-
ness and heterogeneity of American life, and above all, of its
peculiar scramble for status and its peculiar search for secure
identity. Normally there is a world of difference between one's
sense of national identity or cultural belonging and one's social
status. However, in American historical development, these
two things, so easily distinguishable in analysis, have been
jumbled together in reality, and it is precisely this that has
given such a special poignancy and urgency to our status-
strivings. In this country a person's status—that is, his relative
place in the prestige hierarchy of his community—and his ru-
dimentary sense of belonging to the community—that is, what
we call his "Americanism"—have been intimately joined. Because, as a people extremely democratic in our social institutions, we have had no clear, consistent and recognizable system of status, our personal status problems have an unusual
intensity. Because we no longer have the relative ethnic homogeneity we had up to about eighty years ago, our sense of
belonging has long had about it a high degree of uncertainty.
We boast of "the melting pot," but we are not quite sure what
it is that will remain when we have been melted down.

We have always been proud of the high degree of occupational mobility in our country—of the greater readiness, as
compared with other countries, with which a person starting
in a very humble place in our social structure could rise to a
position of moderate wealth and status, and with which a person starting with a middling position could rise to great emi-
nence. We have looked upon this as laudable in principle, for
it is democratic, and as pragmatically desirable, for it has
served many a man as a stimulus to effort and has, no doubt,
a great deal to do with the energetic and effectual tone of our
economic life. The American pattern of occupational mobility, while often much exaggerated, as in the Horatio Alger
stories and a great deal of the rest of our mythology, may
properly be credited with many of the virtues and beneficial
effects that are usually attributed to it. But this occupational
and social mobility, compounded by our extraordinary mobility from place to place, has also had its less frequently recog-

nized drawbacks. Not the least of them is that this has become a country in which so many people do not know who they are or what they are or what they belong to or what belongs to them. It is a country of people whose status expectations are random and uncertain, and yet whose status aspirations have been whipped up to a high pitch by our democratic ethos and our rags-to-riches mythology.[6]

In a country where physical needs have been, by the scale of the world's living standards, on the whole well met, the luxury of questing after status has assumed an unusually prominent place in our civic consciousness. Political life is not simply an arena in which the conflicting interests of various social groups in concrete material gains are fought out; it is also an arena into which status aspirations and frustrations are, as the psychologists would say, projected. It is at this point that the issues of politics, or the pretended issues of politics, become interwoven with and dependent upon the personal problems of individuals. We have, at all times, two kinds of processes going on in inextricable connection with each other: *interest politics*, the clash of material aims and needs among various groups and blocs; and *status politics*, the clash of various projective rationalizations arising from status aspirations and other personal motives. In times of depression and economic discontent—and by and large in times of acute national emergency—politics is more clearly a matter of interests, although of course status considerations are still present. In times of prosperity and general well-being on the material plane, status considerations among the masses can become much more influential in our politics. The two periods in our recent history in which status politics has been particularly prominent, the

[6] Cf. in this respect the observation of Tocqueville: "It cannot be denied that democratic institutions strongly tend to promote the feeling of envy in the human heart; not so much because they afford to everyone the means of rising to the same level with others as because these means perpetually disappoint the persons who employ them. Democratic institutions awaken and foster a passion for equality which they can never entirely satisfy." Alexis de Tocqueville, *Democracy in America*, ed. by Phillips Bradley (New York, 1945), Vol. I, p. 201.

present era and the 1920s, have both been periods of prosperity.

During depressions, the dominant motif in dissent takes expression in proposals for reform or in panaceas. Dissent then tends to be highly programmatic—that is, it gets itself embodied in many kinds of concrete legislative proposals. It is also future-oriented and forward-looking, in the sense that it looks to a time when the adoption of this or that program will materially alleviate or eliminate certain discontents. In prosperity, however, when status politics becomes relatively more important, there is a tendency to embody discontent not so much in legislative proposals as in grousing. For the basic aspirations that underlie status discontent are only partially conscious; and, even so far as they are conscious, it is difficult to give them a programmatic expression. It is more difficult for the old lady who belongs to the D.A.R. and who sees her ancestral home swamped by new working-class dwellings to express her animus in concrete proposals of any degree of reality than it is, say, for the jobless worker during a slump to rally to a relief program. Therefore, it is the tendency of status politics to be expressed more in vindictiveness, in sour memories, in the search for scapegoats, than in realistic proposals for positive action.[7]

[7] Cf. Samuel Lubell's characterization of isolationism as a vengeful memory. *The Future of American Politics* (New York, 1952), Chapter VII. See also the comments of Leo Lowenthal and Norbert Guterman on the right-wing agitator: "The agitator seems to steer clear of the area of material needs on which liberal and democratic movements concentrate; his main concern is a sphere of frustration that is usually ignored in traditional politics. The programs that concentrate on material needs seem to overlook that area of moral uncertainties and emotional frustrations that are the immediate manifestations of malaise. It may therefore be conjectured that his followers find the agitator's statements attractive not because he occasionally promises to 'maintain the American standards of living' or to provide a job for everyone, but because he intimates that he will give them the emotional satisfactions that are denied them in the contemporary social and economic set-up. He offers attitudes, not bread." *Prophets of Deceit* (New York, 1949), pp. 91–92.

Paradoxically the intense status concerns of present-day politics are shared by two types of persons who arrive at them, in a sense, from opposite directions. The first are found among some types of old-family, Anglo-Saxon Protestants, and the second are found among many types of immigrant families, most notably among the Germans and Irish, who are very frequently Catholic.

The Anglo-Saxons are most disposed toward pseudo-conservatism when they are losing caste, the immigrants when they are gaining.[8]

Consider first the old-family Americans. These people, whose stocks were once far more unequivocally dominant in America than they are today, feel that their ancestors made and settled and fought for this country. They have a certain inherited sense of proprietorship in it. Since America has always accorded a certain special deference to old families—so many of our families are *new*—these people have considerable

[8] Every ethnic group has its own peculiar status history, and I am well aware that my remarks in the text slur over many important differences. The status history of the older immigrant groups like the Germans and the Irish is quite different from that of ethnic elements like the Italians, Poles and Czechs, who have more recently arrived at the point at which they are bidding for wide acceptance in the professional and white-collar classes, or at least for the middle-class standards of housing and consumption enjoyed by these classes. The case of the Irish is of special interest, because the Irish, with their long-standing prominence in municipal politics, qualified as it has been by their relative non-acceptance in many other spheres, have an unusually ambiguous status. In many ways they have gained, while in others, particularly insofar as their municipal power has recently been challenged by other groups, especially the Italians, they have lost some status and power. The election of 1928, with its religious bigotry and social snobbery, inflicted upon them a status trauma from which they have never fully recovered, for it was a symbol of the Protestant majority's rejection of their ablest leadership on grounds quite irrelevant to merit. This feeling was kept alive by the breach between Al Smith and F.D.R., followed by the rejection of Jim Farley from the New Deal succession. A study of the Germans would perhaps emphasize the effects of uneasiness over national loyalties arising from the Hitler era and World War II, but extending back even to World War I.

claims to status by descent, which they celebrate by membership in such organizations as the D.A.R. and the S.A.R. But
large numbers of them are actually losing their other claims
to status. For there are among them a considerable number
of the shabby genteel, of those who for one reason or another
have lost their old objective positions in the life of business
and politics and the professions, and who therefore cling with
exceptional desperation to such remnants of their prestige as
they can muster from their ancestors. These people, although
very often quite well-to-do, feel that they have been pushed
out of their rightful place in American life, even out of their
neighborhoods. Most of them have been traditional Republicans by family inheritance, and they have felt themselves
edged aside by the immigrants, the trade unions, and the urban machines in the past thirty years. When the immigrants
were weak, these native elements used to indulge themselves
in ethnic and religious snobberies at their expense.[9] Now the
immigrant groups have developed ample means, political and
economic, of self-defense, and the second and third generations
have become considerably more capable of looking out for
themselves. Some of the old-family Americans have turned to
find new objects for their resentment among liberals, left-
wingers, intellectuals and the like—for in true pseudo-conservative fashion they relish weak victims and shrink from asserting
themselves against the strong.

New-family Americans have had their own peculiar status
problem. From 1881 to 1900 over 8,800,000 immigrants came
here, during the next twenty years another 14,500,000. These
immigrants, together with their descendants, constitute such a
large portion of the population that Margaret Mead, in a
stimulating analysis of our national character, has persuasively
urged that the characteristic American outlook is now a third-

[9] One of the noteworthy features of the current situation is that
fundamentalist Protestants and fundamentalist Catholics have so
commonly subordinated their old feuds (and for the first time in
our history) to unite in opposition to what they usually describe
as "godless" elements.

generation point of view.[10] In their search for new lives and new nationality, these immigrants have suffered much, and they have been rebuffed and made to feel inferior by the "native stock," commonly being excluded from the better occupations and even from what has bitterly been called "first-class citizenship." Insecurity over social status has thus been mixed with insecurity over one's very identity and sense of belonging. Achieving a better type of job or a better social status and becoming "more American" have become practically synonymous, and the passions that ordinarily attach to social position have been vastly heightened by being associated with the need to belong.

The problems raised by the tasks of keeping the family together, disciplining children for the American race for success, trying to conform to unfamiliar standards, protecting economic and social status won at the cost of much sacrifice, holding the respect of children who grow American more rapidly than their parents, have thrown heavy burdens on the internal relationships of many new American families. Both new and old American families have been troubled by the changes of the past thirty years—the new because of their striving for middle-class respectability and American identity, the old because of their efforts to maintain an inherited social position and to realize under increasingly unfavorable social conditions imperatives of character and personal conduct deriving from nineteenth-century, Yankee-Protestant-rural backgrounds. The relations between generations, being cast in no stable mold, have been disordered, and the status anxieties of parents have been inflicted upon children.[11] Often parents en-

[10] Margaret Mead, *And Keep Your Powder Dry* (New York, 1942), Chapter III.

[11] See Else Frenkel-Brunswik's "Parents and Childhood as seen through the Interviews," *The Authoritarian Personality*, Chapter X. The author remarks (pp. 387–88) concerning subjects who were relatively *free* from ethnic prejudice that in their families "less obedience is expected of the children. Parents are less status-ridden and thus show less anxiety with respect to conformity and are less intolerant toward manifestations of socially unaccepted behavior. . . . Comparatively less pronounced status-concern often goes hand

tertain status aspirations that they are unable to gratify, or that they can gratify only at exceptional psychic cost. Their children are expected to relieve their frustrations and redeem their lives. They become objects to be manipulated to that end. An extraordinarily high level of achievement is expected of them, and along with it a tremendous effort to conform and be respectable. From the standpoint of the children these expectations often appear in the form of an exorbitantly demanding authority that one dare not question or defy. Resistance and hostility, finding no moderate outlet in give-and-take, have to be suppressed, and reappear in the form of an internal destructive rage. An enormous hostility to authority, which cannot be admitted to consciousness, calls forth a massive overcompensation which is manifest in the form of extravagant submissiveness to strong power. Among those found by Adorno and his colleagues to have strong ethnic prejudices and pseudo-conservative tendencies, there is a high proportion of persons who have been unable to develop the capacity to criticize justly and in moderation the failings of parents and who are profoundly intolerant of the ambiguities of thought and feeling that one is so likely to find in real-life situations. For pseudo-conservatism is among other things a disorder in relation to authority, characterized by an inability to find other modes for human relationship than those of more or less complete domination or submission. The pseudo-conservative always imagines himself to be dominated and imposed upon because he feels that he is not dominant, and knows of no other way of interpreting his position. He imagines that his own government and his own leadership are engaged in a more or less continuous conspiracy against him because he has come to think of authority only as something that aims to manipulate and deprive him. It is for this reason, among others, that he enjoys seeing outstanding generals, distinguished

---

in hand with greater richness and liberation of emotional life. There is, on the whole, more affection, or more unconditional affection, in the families of unprejudiced subjects. There is less surrender to conventional rules. . . ."

secretaries of state, and prominent scholars browbeaten and humiliated.

Status problems take on a special importance in American life because a very large part of the population suffers from one of the most troublesome of all status questions: unable to enjoy the simple luxury of assuming their own nationality as a natural event, they are tormented by a nagging doubt as to whether they are really and truly and fully American. Since their forebears voluntarily left one country and embraced another, they cannot, as people do elsewhere, think of nationality as something that comes with birth; for them it is a matter of *choice*, and an object of striving. This is one reason why problems of "loyalty" arouse such an emotional response in many Americans and why it is so hard in the American climate of opinion to make any clear distinction between the problem of national security and the question of personal loyalty. Of course there is no real reason to doubt the loyalty to America of the immigrants and their descendants, or their willingness to serve the country as fully as if their ancestors had lived here for three centuries. None the less, they have been thrown on the defensive by those who have in the past cast doubts upon the fullness of their Americanism. Possibly they are also, consciously or unconsciously, troubled by the thought that since their forebears have already abandoned one country, one allegiance, their own national allegiance might be considered fickle. For this I believe there is some evidence in our national practices. What other country finds it so necessary to create institutional rituals for the sole purpose of guaranteeing to its people the genuineness of their nationality? Does the Frenchman or the Englishman or the Italian find it necessary to speak of himself as "one hundred per cent" English, French or Italian? Do they find it necessary to have their equivalents of "I Am an American Day?" When they disagree with one another over national policies, do they find it necessary to call one another un-English, un-French or un-Italian? No doubt they too are troubled by subversive activities and espionage, but are their countermeasures taken under the name of committees on un-English, un-French or un-Italian activities?

The primary value of patriotic societies and anti-subversive ideologies to their exponents can be found here. They provide additional and continued reassurance both to those who are of old American ancestry and have other status grievances and to those who are of recent American ancestry and therefore feel in need of reassurance about their nationality. Veterans' organizations offer the same satisfaction—what better evidence can there be of the genuineness of nationality and of *earned* citizenship than military service under the flag of one's country? Of course such organizations, once they exist, are liable to exploitation by vested interests that can use them as pressure groups on behalf of particular measures and interests. (Veterans' groups, since they lobby for the concrete interests of veterans, have a double role in this respect.) But the cement that holds them together is the status motivation and the desire for an identity.

Sociological studies have shown that there is a close relation between social mobility and ethnic prejudice. Persons moving downward, and even upward under many circumstances, in the social scale tend to show greater prejudice against such ethnic minorities as the Jews and Negroes than commonly prevails in the social strata they have left or are entering.[12] While the existing studies in this field have been focused upon prejudice rather than the kind of hyper-patriotism and hyper-conformism that I am most concerned with, I believe that the typical prejudiced person and the typical pseudo-conservative dissenter are usually the same person, that the mechanisms at work in both complexes are quite the same,[13] and that it is merely the expediencies and the strategy of the situation today that cause groups that once stressed racial discrimination to find other scapegoats. Both the displaced old-American type

[12] Cf. Joseph Greenblum and Leonard I. Pearlin, "Vertical Mobility and Prejudice" in Reinhard Bendix and Seymour M. Lipset, eds., *Class, Status and Power* (Glencoe, Illinois, 1953), pp. 480–91; Bruno Bettelheim and Morris Janowitz, "Ethnic Tolerance: A Function of Personal and Social Control," *American Journal of Sociology*, Vol. IV (1949), pp. 137–45.

[13] The similarity is also posited by Adorno, *op. cit.*, pp. 152ff., and by others (see the studies cited by him, p. 152).

and the new ethnic elements that are so desperately eager for reassurance of their fundamental Americanism can conveniently converge upon liberals, critics, and nonconformists of various sorts, as well as Communists and suspected Communists. To proclaim themselves vigilant in the pursuit of those who are even so much as accused of "disloyalty" to the United States is a way not only of reasserting but of advertising their own loyalty—and one of the chief characteristics of American super-patriotism is its constant inner urge toward self-advertisement. One notable quality in this new wave of conformism is that its advocates are much happier to have as their objects of hatred the Anglo-Saxon, Eastern, Ivy League intellectual gentlemen than they are with such bedraggled souls as, say, the Rosenbergs. The reason, I believe, is that in the minds of the status-driven it is no special virtue to be more American than the Rosenbergs, but it is really something to be more American than Dean Acheson or John Foster Dulles —or Franklin Delano Roosevelt.[14] The status aspirations of some of the ethnic groups are actually higher than they were twenty years ago—which suggests one reason (there are others) why, in the ideology of the authoritarian right-wing, anti-Semitism and such blatant forms of prejudice have recently been soft-pedaled. Anti-Semitism, it has been said, is the poor man's snobbery. We Americans are always trying to raise the standard of living, and the same principle now seems to apply to standards of hating. So during the past fifteen years or so, the authoritarians have moved on from anti-Negroism and anti-Semitism to anti-Achesonianism, anti-intellectualism, anti-nonconformism, and other variants of the same idea, much in the same way as the average American, if he can manage it, will move on from a Ford to a Buick.

Such status-strivings may help us to understand some of the

[14] I refer to such men to make the point that this animosity extends to those who are guilty of no wrongdoing. Of course a person like Alger Hiss, who has been guilty, suits much better. Hiss is the hostage the pseudo-conservatives hold from the New Deal generation. He is a heaven-sent gift. If he did not exist, the pseudo-conservatives would not have been able to invent him.

otherwise unintelligible figments of the pseudo-conservative ideology—the incredibly bitter feeling against the United Nations, for instance. Is it not understandable that such a feeling might be, paradoxically, shared at one and the same time by an old Yankee-Protestant American, who feels that his social position is not what it ought to be and that these foreigners are crowding in on his country and diluting its sovereignty just as "foreigners" have crowded into his neighborhood, and by a second- or third-generation immigrant who has been trying so hard to de-Europeanize himself, to get Europe out of his personal heritage, and who finds his own government mocking him by its complicity in these Old-World schemes?

Similarly, is it not status aspiration that in good part spurs the pseudo-conservative on toward his demand for conformity in a wide variety of spheres of life? Conformity is a way of guaranteeing and manifesting respectability among those who are not sure that they are respectable enough. The nonconformity of others appears to such persons as a frivolous challenge to the whole order of things they are trying so hard to become part of. Naturally it is resented, and the demand for conformity in public becomes at once an expression of such resentment and a means of displaying one's own soundness. This habit has a tendency to spread from politics into intellectual and social spheres, where it can be made to challenge almost anyone whose pattern of life is different and who is imagined to enjoy a superior social position—notably, as one agitator put it, the "parlors of the sophisticated, the intellectuals, the so-called academic minds."

Why has this tide of pseudo-conservative dissent risen to such heights in our time? To a considerable degree, we must remember, it is a response, however unrealistic, to realities. We do live in a disordered world, threatened by a great power and a powerful ideology. It is a world of enormous potential violence, that has already shown us the ugliest capacities of the human spirit. In our own country there has indeed been espionage, and laxity over security has in fact allowed some spies to reach high places. There is just enough reality at most points along the line to give a touch of credibility to the melo-dramatics of the pseudo-conservative imagination.

However, a number of developments in our recent history make this pseudo-conservative uprising more intelligible. For two hundred years and more, various conditions of American development—the process of continental settlement, the continuous establishment in new areas of new status patterns, the arrival of continuous waves of new immigrants, each pushing the preceding waves upward in the ethnic hierarchy—made it possible to satisfy a remarkably large part of the extravagant status aspirations that were aroused. There was a sort of automatic built-in status-elevator in the American social edifice. Today that elevator no longer operates automatically, or at least no longer operates in the same way.

Secondly, the growth of the mass media of communication and their use in politics have brought politics closer to the people than ever before and have made politics a form of entertainment in which the spectators feel themselves involved. Thus it has become, more than ever before, an arena into which private emotions and personal problems can be readily projected. Mass communications have aroused the mass man.

Thirdly, the long tenure in power of the liberal elements to which the pseudo-conservatives are most opposed and the wide variety of changes that have been introduced into our social, economic and administrative life have intensified the sense of powerlessness and victimization among the opponents of these changes and have widened the area of social issues over which they feel discontent. There has been, among other things, the emergence of a wholly new struggle: the conflict between businessmen of certain types and the New Deal bureaucracy, which has spilled over into a resentment of intellectuals and experts.

Finally, unlike our previous postwar periods, ours has been a period of continued crisis, from which the future promises no relief. In no foreign war of our history did we fight so long or make such sacrifices as in World War II. When it was over, instead of being able to resume our peacetime preoccupations, we were very promptly confronted with another war. It is hard for a certain type of American, who does not think much about the world outside and does not want to have to do so, to understand why we must become involved in such an unremitting struggle. It will be the fate of those in power for a long time to come to have to conduct the delicate diplomacy of the cold peace without the sympathy or understanding of a large part of their own people. From bitter experience, Eisenhower and Dulles are learning today what Truman and Acheson learned yesterday.

These considerations suggest that the pseudo-conservative political style, while it may already have passed the peak of its influence, is one of the long waves of twentieth-century American history and not a momentary mood. I do not share the widespread foreboding among liberals that this form of dissent will grow until it overwhelms our liberties altogether and plunges us into a totalitarian nightmare. Indeed, the idea that it is purely and simply fascist or totalitarian, as we have known these things in recent European history, is to my mind a false conception, based upon the failure to read American developments in terms of our peculiar American constellation of political realities. (It reminds me of the people who, because they found several close parallels between the NRA and Mussolini's corporate state, were once deeply troubled at the thought that the NRA was the beginning of American fascism.) However, in a populistic culture like ours, which seems to lack a responsible elite with political and moral autonomy, and in which it is possible to exploit the wildest currents of public sentiment for private purposes, it is at least conceivable that a highly organized, vocal, active and well-financed minority could create a political climate in which the rational pursuit of our well-being and safety would become impossible.

4

PSEUDO-CONSERVATISM REVISITED:
A POSTSCRIPT (1962)

Richard Hofstadter

At the time these essays appeared, many critics objected to an assumption that I believe underlies all of them—the assumption that the radical right is a response to certain underlying and continuing tensions in American society. It was held that the authors of these essays were being intellectually fancy and oversubtle. There was no need to go so far around the bend to find new explanations for these phenomena, critics complained, when the important explanations were obvious: the anxiety arising from the Korean stalemate, coming as it did right on the heels of the sacrifices of a major war; a series of startling revelations about Communist espionage; the long wartime and postwar inflation, the continuing high level of taxation, the frustration of the Republican Party shut out of the White House for twenty years. With all these things on tap to account for right-wing discontent, why invoke sociological forces whose relation to the issues seemed less direct?

Such criticism, I believe, was based upon a fundamental misconception of what these essays were trying to do. I can speak only for myself, but I doubt that any of the authors would deny that the Korean War was in the foreground of radical-right thinking, or that taxation had a good deal to do with its economic discontents. But the authors of these essays were curious about something in which their critics do not seem to have been interested—and that is the whole complex of forces that underlay the responses of the public to the frustrations of the 1950s. After all, not every wealthy American demanded the repeal of the income-tax amendment; not every Republican responded to the twenty-year period of Democratic ascendancy by branding the Democratic Party as treasonous; not every American who was wearied by the Korean stalemate called for all-out war at the risk of starting World War III— and, indeed, some Americans who expressed violent impatience over the conduct of the Korean War were those who were in fact benefiting from it economically. What puzzled us was how to account for the complex of forces in the structure of American society, in American traditions, that made it possible for men and women who were sharing the same experiences and the same disorders to call for drastically different types of remedies. After six or seven years of additional observation of the extreme right, it now seems more probable that our original approach was correct.

One aspect of my own essay that may be of enduring use and yet that now seems to require some modification is the concept of status politics. That there is a need for some such concept I have little doubt. My generation was raised in the conviction that the basic motive power in political behavior is the economic interest of groups. This is not the place to discuss at length the inadequacies of that view of the world, but it may be enough to say that we have learned to find it wanting as an account of much of the vital political behavior of our own time. However much importance we continue to attach to economic interests or imagined economic interests in political action, we are still confronted from time to time with a wide range of behavior for which the economic interpretation of politics seems to be inadequate or misleading or altogether irrelevant. It is to account for this range of behavior that we need a different conceptual framework, and I believe that the extreme right wing provides a pre-eminent example of such behavior.

However, it now seems doubtful that the term "status politics," which apparently was used for the first time in this essay, is an adequate term for what I had in mind. No doubt, social status is one of the things that is at stake in most political behavior, and here the right wing is no exception. But there are other matters involved, which I rather loosely assimilated to this term, that can easily be distinguished from status, strictly defined. The term "status" requires supplementation. If we were to speak of "cultural politics" we might supply part of what is missing. In our political life there have always been certain types of cultural issues, questions of faith and morals, tone and style, freedom and coercion, which become fighting issues. To choose but one example, prohibition was an issue of this kind during the twenties and early thirties. In the struggle over prohibition, economic interests played only the most marginal role; the issue mobilized religious and moral convictions, ethnic habits and hostilities, attitudes toward health and sexuality, and other personal preoccupations. There are always such issues at work in any body politic, but perhaps they are particularly acute and important in the United States because of our ethnic and religious heterogeneity. As I indicated in my essay, they loom larger during periods of prosperity, when economic conflicts are somewhat muted, than they do during periods of depression and economic discontent. Hard times mobilize economic group antagonisms; prosperity liberates the public for the expression of its more luxurious hostilities.

But this brings us to another aspect of the matter: at times politics becomes an arena into which the wildest fancies are projected, the most paranoid suspicions, the most absurd superstitions, the most bizarre apocalyptic fantasies. From time to time, movements arise that are founded upon the political exploitation of such fancies and fears, and while these movements can hardly aspire to animate more than a small minority of the population, they do exercise, especially in a democratic and populistically oriented political culture like our own, a certain leverage upon practical politics. Thus, today, despite the presence of issues of the utmost gravity and urgency, the American press and public have been impelled to discuss in all seriousness a right-wing movement whose leaders believe that President Eisenhower was a member of the "Communist conspiracy." It seems hardly extravagant to say that the true believers in a movement of this sort project into the arena of politics utterly irrelevant fantasies and disorders of a purely personal kind. Followers of a movement like the John Birch Society are in our world but not exactly of it. They intersect with it, they even have effects on it that could become grave, but the language they speak is a private language; they can compel the rest of us to listen to this language because they are just numerous enough, and because the structure of political influence is loose enough for them to apply a political leverage out of proportion to their numbers. They represent a kind of politics that is not exactly status politics or cultural politics, as I have defined them, but that might be called "projective politics." It involves the projection of interests and concerns, not only largely private but essentially pathological, into the public scene.

In action, of course, considerations of status and cultural role become intertwined with the content of projective politics, and what may be well worth making as an analytical distinction is not necessarily so clear in the actual world of political controversy. One of the reasons why the term "status" now seems to me to be inadequate to suggest the full complex of realities that I had in mind is that several considerations are woven together in an unusually complex social fabric. One thing that has been at stake is the problem of an American identity, which has an especial poignance because of the heavy immigrant composition of our population and its great mobility. Many Americans still have problems about their Americanness and are still trying, psychologically speaking, to naturalize themselves. Ethnicity is in itself partly a status problem because American life does contain a status hierarchy in which ethnic background is important. Finally, because of the great mixture of religious and moral strains in our population, there is a constant argument over the social legitimacy of certain roles and values.

One of the facets of my own essay which I am disposed to regret is its excessive emphasis on what might be called the clinical side of the problem. Whether or not the psychological imputations it makes prove to be correct or not, I think a good deal more might have been said on purely behavioral and historical grounds to establish the destructive and "radical" character of pseudo-conservatism. The political character of this movement can be helpfully delineated by comparing it with true conservatism. The United States has not provided a receptive home for formal conservative thought or classically conservative modes of behavior. Lacking a formidable aristocratic tradition, this country has produced at best patricians rather than aristocrats, and the literature of American political experience shows how unhappy the patricians (for example, Henry Adams) have been in their American environment. Restless, mobile both geographically and socially, overwhelmingly middle-class in their aspirations, the American people have not given their loyalty to a national church or developed a traditionally oriented bar or clergy, or other institutions that have the character of national establishments. But it is revealing to observe the attitude of the extreme right wing toward those institutions that come closest here to reproducing the institutional apparatus of the aristocratic classes in other countries. Such conservative institutions as the better preparatory schools, the Ivy League colleges and universities, the Supreme Court, and the State Department—exactly those institutions that have been largely in the custodianship of the patrician or established elements in American society—have been the favorite objects of right-wing animosity.

And while the ring-winger dislikes the social type that might be called conservative—a type represented by men like Dean Acheson, John Foster Dulles, Adlai Stevenson, and Harry L. Stimson—it also dislikes what might be called the practical conservatism of our time, as represented by the Eisenhower administration and by the eastern Dewey-Willkie-Eisenhower wing of the Republican Party. The Chicago *Tribune* expressed the dominant right-wing view some years ago when it lumped together "the nationalist, the Demi-Reps, the Truman Republicans, and the New Dealers, who . . . played footie-footie with the Communist for years." When the Democrats were finally ousted in the election of 1952, nothing less than a complete *bouleversement* in government would have satisfied the extreme right. Most of them were already highly suspicious of Eisenhower, and they felt they were justified when his administration neither uprooted the welfare reforms of the previous twenty years nor reversed the general strategy of American foreign policy. As the Chicago *Tribune* said of Eisenhower's 1955 State of the Union message, "Welfare statism and a tender if meddlesome solicitude for every fancied want of a once self-reliant citizenry were pyramided and compounded in this message."

Perhaps what is more to the point—though it is conjecture and not history—is that if Robert A. Taft had been nominated and elected in 1952, his administration might have been almost as disappointing to the hard core of the extreme right as Eisenhower's. The extreme right really suffers not from the policies of this or that administration, but from what America has become in the twentieth century. It suffers, moreover, from an implacable dislike and suspicion of all constituted authority. In part this is because, entertaining expectations that cannot be realized, it is bound to be dissatisfied with any regime. But still more decisive, in my opinion, is that the extreme right wing is constituted out of a public that simply cannot arrive at a psychological modus vivendi with authority, cannot reconcile itself to that combination of acceptance and criticism which the democratic process requires of the relationship between the leaders and the led. Being uncomfortable with the thought of any leadership that falls short of perfection, the extreme right is also incapable of analyzing the world with enough common sense to establish any adequate and realistic criterion for leadership. The right wing tolerates no compromises, accepts no half measures, understands no defeats. In this respect, it stands psychologically outside the frame of normal democratic politics, which is largely an affair of compromise. One of the most fundamental qualities, then, in the right-wing mentality of our time is its implicit utopianism. I can think of no more economical way of expressing its fundamental difference from the spirit of genuine conservatism.

If this essay were to be rewritten today, there is one force in American life, hardly more than hinted at in my original formulation, that would now loom very large indeed, and that is fundamentalism. The little that we know from the press about the John Birch Society, the Christian Crusade of Dr. Fred Schwarz, and the activities of the Reverend Billy Hargis has served to remind us how much alive fundamentalism still is in the United States, and how firmly it has now fixed its attention on the fight against Communism, as it once concentrated on the fight against evolution. To understand the Manichaean style of thought, the apocalyptic tendencies, the love of mystification, the intolerance of compromise that are observable in the right-wing mind, we need to understand the history of fundamentalism as well as the contributions of depth psychology; and those who would understand it will do well to supplement their acquaintance with Rohrschach techniques or the construction of the F-scale with a rereading of the Book of Revelations. To the three sources of right-wing sentiment that are commonly enumerated—isolationism (or anti-Europeanism), ethnic prejudice, and old-fashioned "liberal" economics—one must add the fundamentalist revolt against modernity, and not by any means as a minor partner.

5

THE INTELLECTUALS AND THE DISCONTENTED CLASSES (1955)

David Riesman and Nathan Glazer

In the nineteen-thirties, Maury Maverick, who died in 1954, was a quite exceptional but far from untypical representative of the Texas political outlook: free-swinging, red-tape cutting, "a man's a man for a' that." Born to a famous Texas name which had entered the common speech, he enjoyed living up to it by defending the downtrodden: the Spanish-Americans of San Antonio; the small businessmen; and, most courageously, the Communists and their right to be heard in the municipal auditorium. In the Maverick era, Texas was reputed to be the most interventionist state in the Union, providing some of the firmest support to Roosevelt's foreign policy. Its influential Congressional delegation, which included Sam Rayburn as well as Senator Tom Connally and a less cautious Lyndon Johnson, were Roosevelt's stalwarts as often in domestic as in foreign policy. But not many years later Maverick had turned into a political untouchable, and Texas competed with the North Central isolationist belt in violent opposition to the old Roosevelt policies no less than to the policies of Truman, his successor and legitimate heir.

Texas demonstrates in extreme form the great shift in the character of American politics and political thinking since the Second World War. We can date the change more precisely than that. In the election of 1948, Harry Truman, more unequivocally and guilelessly committed to many New Deal policies and attitudes than F.D.R., won an election against a candidate far more liberal and capable, if less appealingly homespun, than Eisenhower. Even as late as the beginning of 1950, the special political tone of the Roosevelt era continued to influence public life. We need only recall the mood of the Democratic Senators investigating McCarthy's charges of Communist infiltration into the State Department early that year. The transcript shows them at ease, laughing away McCarthy's charges, taking it for granted that the country was with them, and that McCarthy was another Martin Dies. Four years later, another group of Democratic Senators sat in judgment on McCarthy. They were tense and anxious, seeking the protective cover of J. Edgar Hoover, trying to seem just as good Communist-hunters—indeed, better Republicans—than any of their colleagues. In the last years of Truman's term, while many demagogic anti-Communist steps were taken by a reluctant administration—as well as many effective ones under Acheson's bedeviled auspices—the general climate of Washington still remained comparatively easygoing. Congress was a partially manageable menace and General Vaughan still could get along without knowing the difference between Harry Dexter White and Adolf Berle.

Many explanations have been offered for what appears to be a decisive shift in the American mentality. Fear of the Soviet Union is alleged by some to be the cause; others blame McCarthy, his allies, and his victims; others look for cynical explanations, while still others think that Americans have abandoned liberal traditions for good and all. In this essay we attempt to estimate the real extent of the shift, to delineate some factors, previously neglected, which may be relevant, and to offer some very tentative interpretations pointing toward the revival of a liberal political imagination.

I

Detectable and decisive shifts of political mood can occur, of course, without affecting the majority. And this seems to be what has happened in this country. The less educated part of the population takes a long time learning to form an opinion about any international matter and even more time to change it. It is not easily accessible to new information and is not trained to alter its opinions under exposure to the public interpretation of events.[1] Thus, the World War II alliance with the Soviet Union did little to change the suspicion and distrust with which (apart from sheer apathy) the poor and less educated in this country have always regarded Russia—indeed, all foreign countries; these people were "protected" by their fatalism, generalized suspiciousness, and apathy from the wartime messages of the movies, the OWI, and like agencies. Consequently, the worsening of relations with the Soviet Union found the "backward" strata already holding the appropriate attitudes toward Russia—no change was demanded of them, and little change occurred.

The less educated of whom we speak are of course literate; they have radios and TV and buy newspapers; and to an Asiatic they must appear to move with fabulous speed. Certainly, in non-political matters (where the "voter" has at hand the ready mechanism of a retail store) fashions spread with ever faster waves, and the "backward" buy "modern" in furniture long before they will buy it in elections. Yet it is the educated, the readers of editorial pages, who have customarily been responsible for the major changes in American political position. For example, the shift of this group from neutrality to intervention in 1940 and 1941 allowed the Lend Lease Act to slip through. It also supplied the cadre under Averell Harriman which then energetically did the actual "lending."

The odd situation today, however, is that such a change does not suffice to explain what happened between 1950 and 1952. Many of the intelligent (i.e., college-educated) and articulate minority still in the main are not unsympathetic to Roosevelt's and Truman's foreign policies. They believe that the alliances with Britain and France must be maintained; they do not regard Communist infiltration as a serious problem; they do regard the threat to civil liberties by Communist

---

[1] For data on the negligible influence of political campaigns, see Paul Lazarsfeld, Bernard Berelson, and Hazel Gaudet, *The People's Choice* (Harper's, New York, 1948).

hunters as a serious problem. If they do not always say so, this is partly for protective coloration, partly because, as we shall see, they have been put on the defensive not only strategically but also within themselves. (There are of course others of the college-educated who have always hated Truman and Roosevelt, largely for domestic "that man" reasons; they are not averse to using foreign policy as a heaven-sent means of vindication.)

As we have seen, the shift has not been among the inarticulate—they have always held their present attitudes. The decisive factors, we suggest, have been twofold, and interconnected. On the one hand, the opinion leaders among the educated strata—the intellectuals and those who take cues from them—have been silenced, rather more by their own feelings of inadequacy and failure than by direct intimidation. On the other hand, many who were once among the inarticulate masses are no longer silent: an unacknowledged social revolution has transformed their situation. Rejecting the liberal intellectuals as guides, they have echoed and reinforced the stridency of right-wing demi-intellectuals—themselves often arising from those we shall, until we can find a less clumsy name, call the ex-masses.

II

During the New Deal days a group of intellectuals led and played lawyer for classes of discontented people who had tasted prosperity and lost it, and for a mass of underprivileged people who had been promised prosperity and seen enough mobility around them to believe in it. Today, both sources of discontent have virtually disappeared as a result of fifteen years of prosperity.[2] This same prosperity, and its attendant inflation, has hit many elderly and retired people who cannot

[2] To be sure, there are enclaves where the underprivileged can still be found, as in the Southern Alleghenies or the rural Deep South. And, as we shall see, the fact that "everyone" has moved up means that mobility may not have kept pace with aspiration, one reason why the slogan "you never had it so good" is a poor campaign weapon.

adjust financially, politically, or psychologically to the altered value of a dollar—people, who, though they have the money, cannot bring themselves to repair their homes because they have not been brought up to "do it yourself" nor to pay three dollars an hour to someone else for doing it. Among the youth, too, are many people who are at once the beneficiaries and the victims of prosperity, people made ill-at-ease by an affluence not preceded by imagining its reality, nor preceded by a change to a character-structure more attuned to amenity than to hardship. The raw-rich Texas millionaire appears often to be obsessed by fears that "they" will take his money away— almost as if he were fascinated by a fatality which would bring him, as it were, back to earth.

These people, whether suddenly affluent or simply better off, form a new middle class, called out of the city tenements and the marginal small towns by the uneven hand of national prosperity; many have moved to the fringes of urban centers, large and small. This has been described in *Fortune* as a new middle-class market, which will play a great role in keeping the economy prosperous. But in politics, these former masses do not have so benign an influence—we shall call them the *discontented classes*.

Their discontent is only partially rooted in relative economic deprivation. Many of them, it is true, forgetting their condition of fifteen years ago, see only that the salaries and income they would once have thought princely do not add up to much. Politically, such people, thinking in terms of a relatively fixed income (in this case, of course, not from capital, save occasional rentals, but from salaries and wages) against a standard of variable expenses, are generally conservative. And their conservatism is of a pinched and narrow sort, less interested in the preservation of ancient principles than in the current reduction of government expenditures and taxes. It is the conservatism we usually associate with provincial France rather than with the small-town venture capitalist of the older Yankee sort. This conservatism helps create the particular posture of the discontented classes vis-à-vis America's foreign role; they are mad at the rest of the world for bothering them, hate to waste money in spankings and cannot stand wasting money in rewards.

But more significant, and more difficult to understand and grapple with, is a discontent which arises from the mental discomforts that come with belonging to a class rather than a mass—discomforts founded less on economic than on intellectual uncertainty. If one belongs to the middle class one is supposed to have an opinion, to cope with the world as well as with one's job and immediate surroundings. But these new members have entered a realm where the interpretations of the world put forth by intellectuals in recent decades, and widely held among the educated, are unsatisfying, even threatening. Having precariously won respectability in paycheck and consumption style, they find this achievement menaced by a political and more broadly cultural outlook tending to lower barriers of any sort—between this nation and other nations, between groups in this nation (as in the constant appeals to inter-ethnic amity), between housing projects reserved for Negroes and suburbs reserved for whites; many families also cannot stand the pressure to lower barriers between men and women, or between parents and children.

When this barrier-destroying outlook of the intellectuals promised economic advance as well as racial equality, many of the impoverished could accept the former and ignore the latter. Now, having achieved a modicum of prosperity, the political philosophy of the intellectuals, which always requires government spending, taxes, and inflation, is a threat—and the racial equality, which could be viewed with indifference in the city tenement or homogeneous small town, is a formidable reality in the new suburbs. When the intellectuals were developing the ideology justifying cutting in the masses on the bounties of American productivity, they were less apt to be called do-gooders and bleeding hearts—the grown-up version of that unendurable taunt of being a sissy—than now when the greater part of the masses needing help are outside the nation's boundaries.[8]

[3] The concept of "intolerance of ambiguity," developed by Else Frenkel-Brunswik and co-workers, is relevant here: these newly

Very often, moreover, the individuals making up the discontented classes have come, not to the large civilizing cities, but to the new or expanding industrial frontiers—to Wichita and Rock Island, to Jacksonville or the Gulf Coast, to Houston or San Diego, to Tacoma or Tonawanda. Even those who become very rich no longer head automatically for New York and Newport. Whereas the Baptist Rockefeller, coming from Cleveland where he was educated, allowed Easterners to help civilize him by giving away his money, as Carnegie and Frick also did, these new rich lack such centralized opportunities for gratuitous benevolence, being constrained by the income tax and the institutionalization of philanthropy. And their wives (whatever their secret and suppressed yearnings) no longer seem to want the approval of Eastern women of culture and fashion; they choose to remain within their provincial orbits, rather than to become immigrants to an alien cosmopolitan center. Indeed, the airplane has made it possible for the men —and *Vogue* and Neiman-Marcus for the women—to share in the advantages of New York without the miseries, expenses, and contaminations of living there. Howard Hughes, for example, can do business operating from a plane, yacht, or hotel room.

All this, however, puts some complex processes too simply. New big money in America has always tended to unsettle its possessors and the society at large. For one thing, the absence of an aristocracy means that there is no single, time-approved course of buying land, being deferential to the values of those already on the land, and earning a title by good behavior. Though Rockefeller tried philanthropy, he was still hated, still needed the services of Ivy Lee. Yet he lived at a time when the aristocratic model, in Europe if not here, provided certain guide-posts. Today, the enormously wealthy new men of Texas have not even the promise of an assured well-traveled road, at the end of which stand duchesses, Newport, and gatekeepers

---

prosperous ones want to see the world clearly bounded, in blacks and whites; they have been brought up conventionally, to make use of conventional categories, and fluidity of boundaries threatens their self-assurance and their very hold on reality.

like Ward McAllister. Instead, such men may prefer to buy a
television program for McCarthy, or to acquire the publishing
firm of Henry Holt, or, on behalf of an anti-Wall Street business demagogue, the very railroad which once helped cement
New York "Society."

Moreover, the partial and uneven spread of cosmopolitan
values to the lower strata and to the hinterland has as one
consequence the fact that rich men can no longer simply spend
their way to salvation. Conspicuous underconsumption has replaced conspicuous consumption as the visible sign of status,
with the result that men who have made enough money to
indulge the gaudy dreams of their underprivileged youth learn
all too fast that they must not be flamboyant. This is a trick
that the older centers of culture have played on the newer
centers of wealth. The latter can try to catch up; Baylor and
Houston Universities, and the Dallas Symphony, have not done
too badly. Or they can enter the still gaudy forum of politics
to get back at those they suspect of ridiculing their efforts. Perhaps there was something of this in Hearst, as there is in some
of the newer magnates of the media. Senator McCarthy, with
his gruff charm and his Populist roots, seems made to order
for such men; and he has attracted some of the political
plungers among the new underprivileged rich,[4] a task made
easier by the fact that they have too few intellectuals and idea
men to divide and distract them.

Furthermore, a great many Americans, newly risen from
poverty or the catastrophe of the Depression, are much more
fearful of losing their wealth than are scions of more estab-

[4] It is at this point that the lack of connection between the small
cadre of truly conservative intellectuals and any sizable anti-liberal
audience becomes a major factor in the present political scene. For
patronage politics and for the untutored businessman, writers like
Allen Tate or Russell Kirk have nothing but contempt; their "conservatism" (as some critics have pointed out) is based on an irrelevant landed-gentry and professional-class model. With a few
exceptions, the pseudo-conservatives who have a radical and nihil-
istic message for the untutored have to face little intellectual competition, save from occasional socially conscious clergymen and
priests.

lished families already accustomed to paying taxes, to giving to charity, and to the practice of *noblesse oblige*. We know many men who made their money in war orders, or through buying government-financed plants, or through price supports, who hate the federal government with the ferocity of beneficiaries —and doubtless want to cut off aid from the ungrateful French or British! Such men cannot admit that they did not make "their" money by their own efforts; they would like to abolish the income tax, and with it the whole nexus of defense and international relations, if only to assert their own anachronistic individualism the more firmly. They are likely to be clients, not only of lawyers who specialize in the capital gains tax, but also of prophets and politicians specializing in the bogeys of adults.

The rapid and unanticipated acquisition of power seems to produce a sense of unreality—people are "up in the air." We face the paradox that many Americans are more fearful today though more prosperous than ever before and though America is in some ways more powerful.

III

It is the professional business of politicians, as of other promoters and organizers, to find in the electorate or other constituency organizable blocs who will shift their allegiance to them, who will respond with passion in the midst of indifference, and with identification in the midst of diffuse and plural ties. In the pre-World War I days of the great outcry against the Trusts, it was possible to find a few old and dislocated middle-class elements which resented the new dominance by big and baronial business—in some respects, these were precursors of the present discontented classes, though with more to hope for and less to fear. In the thirties, the way had already in large measure been prepared for an appeal to unemployed factory workers and Southern and Western farmers on the basis of Wilsonian and Populist rhetoric, made into a heady brew by more recent infusions of radicalism, native and imported. These discontented masses showed in their voting be-

havior (in NLRB and Agricultural Adjustment Act elections
as well as at the polls) that the appeal, whatever it meant
to those who made it, hit home in terms of the listeners' wants
and situation.

How can the discontented classes of today be welded into
a political bloc? This is the question that haunts and tempts
politicians. The uncertainty of the Democrats faced with Stevenson and of the Republicans faced with McCarthy signifies
not only disagreements of principle but also doubts as to
whether a proper appeal has as yet been found on which a
ruling or controlling coalition can be built. As geologists cover
the earth prospecting for oil, so politicians cover the electorate
prospecting for hidden hatreds and identities.

In local elections campaigns can be waged on the promise
to hold down taxes and build no more schools. And many
people in national affairs will respond to a promise to hold
down inflation or to create more jobs. But when voters feel
insecure in the midst of prosperity, it is not an economic appeal that will really arouse them. For it is not the jobs or goods
they do not have that worry them; indeed, what worries them
is often that they do not know what worries them, or why,
having reached the promised land, they still suffer. Sharply felt
needs have been replaced by vague discontents; and at such a
time programs or clear-cut ideas of any kind are worse than
useless, politically speaking. This is one reason why the appeal
to the discontented classes is so often more a matter of tone
than of substance—why a gesture of retroactive vindictiveness
like the Bricker Amendment can arouse angry Minute Women
and small-town lawyers, why on the whole the pseudo-conservative right has so small a program and so belligerent a
stance. In this situation, ideology tends to become more important than economics.[5]

[5] Strictly speaking, there is no such thing as an "economic" appeal, nor is a well-paying job a "natural" need of mankind. Rather,
the present insistence of the American workingman that he is entitled to such a job is the outgrowth of recent experience, clarified
and interpreted for him by his leaders. These combine into a
demonstration that depressions are not necessary (though perhaps

And when one must resort to ideology in a prosperous America, one must fall back on the vaguely recalled, half-dreamlike allegiances and prejudices serving most people for ideology. Americanism, of course, will play a major role; but, paradoxically enough, so do those underground half-conscious ethnic allegiances and prejudices which, as Samuel Lubell has shown, still play a large part in American politics. In much that passes for anti-Communism these strands are combined, as for instance for many Irish or Polish Catholics whose avid anti-Communism enables them to feel more solidly American than some less fanatical Protestants who, as earlier arrivals, once looked down on them; similarly, a good deal of Mc-Carthy's support represents the comeback of the German-Americans after two world wars. A haunting doubt about Americanism and disloyalty, however, affects not only those of recent enemy or socially devalued stocks but also those many businessmen forced to operate under government regulations of price and materials control, or under defense contracts. As Talcott Parsons has observed (see Chapter 9), these men are constantly being asked, on grounds of patriotism, to obey government norms which they are as constantly opposing and evading; for them it is convenient to discover that it is not they who are ambivalent toward defense, but those others, the Reds or the State Department or the Democrats. Many of these men, especially perhaps in small business, are victims of a prosperity which has made them rich but neither as enlightened as many big business managers nor as independent as their ideology expects them to be.

Not all members of the discontented classes come from similar backgrounds or arrive at similar destinations; nevertheless, mobility—a fast rise from humble origins, or a transplantation to the city, or a move from the factory class to the white-collar class—is a general characteristic. They or their parents are likely to have voted Democratic sometime between 1930 and 1948, and such a memory makes them more sus-

wars are), and that therefore jobs and all that goes with them are necessary.

ceptible to ideological appeals, for in rising above their impoverished or ethnically "un-American" beginnings, they have found it "time for a change" in identification: they would like to rise "above" economic appeals ("don't let them take it away") to ideological ones—or, in more amiable terms, "above" self-interest to patriotism. Such people could not be brought in one move into the Republican Party, which would seem too much like a betrayal of origins, but they could be brought to take a stand "above party"—and to vote for a nonpartisan general whom the Democrats had also sought. According to a recent study reported by Professor Malcolm Moos, in two counties outside Boston the self-declared "independent" voters now outnumber the Republicans and Democrats combined—a reflection of this roving background of discontented classes which has become the most dynamic force in American political life.[6] Recently, a woman who had campaigned for Eisenhower (while her husband voted for Stevenson) told one of us how much she admired Ike's sincerity, adding, "Actually I don't know enough about politics to identify myself with either one [major party], and I am a—what do you call it—an independent." Of course, not all independents stand in this sort of proud ignorance above parties and above the politicians who may have helped their parents with jobs or visas or the warmth of recognition.

Just as many among the newly prosperous tend at present to reject the traditional party labels (while others seek, perhaps after a split ticket or two, the protective coloration of the GOP), so they also reject the traditional cultural and educational leadership of the enlightened upper and upper-middle

[6] According to a study of the 1952 election by the Survey Research Center of the University of Michigan, only two groupings in the population were resistant to these appeals and went more strongly Democratic than in 1948: these were the Negroes on the one extreme of the social spectrum and the college-educated, upper income, and professional and managerial strata at the other extreme—the latter also produced more Republican votes, as the result of a decline in the non-voters. See Angus Campbell, Gerald Gurin, and Warren E. Miller, *The Voter Decides* (Row, Peterson and Co., Evanston, 1954), Table 5.1.

classes. They have sent their children to college as one way of maintaining the family's social and occupational mobility. Some of these children have become eager strivers for cosmopolitanism and culture, rejecting the values now held by the discontented classes. But many of those who have swamped the colleges have acquired there, and helped their families learn, a half-educated resentment for the traditional intellectual values some of their teachers and schoolmates represented. While their humbler parents may have maintained in many cases a certain reverence for education, their children have gained enough familiarity to feel contempt. (Tragically, the high schools and colleges have often felt compelled at the same time to lower their standards to meet the still lower level of aspiration of these youngsters, no eager beavers for learning, but too well off to enter the labor force.) In many local school board fights, the old conservative and hence intellectually libertarian elites have been routed by lower-middle-class pressure groups who, often to their surprise, discovered the weakness of the schools and their defenders—in many of these fights, much as on the national scene, ethnic elements helped identify the combatants. Once having seen the political weakness, combined with social prestige, of the traditional cultural values, the discontented classes, trained to despise weakness, became still less impressed by the intellectual cadres furnishing much of the leadership in the Thirties.

The high school and college training has had a further effect of strengthening the desire of the graduates to take some part in political life, at least by voting: we know that non-voting and non-participation generally is far more common among the uneducated. Even more, it has strengthened their need for an intellectual position to give a name, an identity, to their malaise. Whatever they think of intellectuals as such, they cannot do without them, and sustenance rejected in the form of the adult education work of the Ford Foundation is sought or accepted from mentors like Hunt's Facts Forum whose tone reflects their own uneasiness and yet gives it a factual, "scientific" cast. Thus they repay their "education for citizenship."

We have spoken earlier of the xenophobia and slowness in altering opinions characteristic of the lower classes. If in a survey people are asked, "Do you think it wise to trust others?" the less educated are always the more suspicious; they have in the course of life gained a peasant-like guile, the sort of sloganized cynicism so beautifully described by Richard Wright in *Black Boy.* In a hierarchical society, this distrust does not become a dynamic social and political factor; except insofar as it prevents the organization of the masses it remains a problem only for individuals in their relations with other individuals. But when the mistrustful, with prosperity, are suddenly pushed into positions of leverage, attitudes previously channeled within the family and neighborhood are projected upon the national and international scene.

Recent psychoanalytically-oriented work on ethnic prejudice provides possible clues as to why overt anti-Semitism has declined at the same time that attacks on Harvard and other symbols of Eastern seaboard culture seem to have increased. In their valuable book, *The Dynamics of Prejudice,* Bruno Bettelheim and Morris Janowitz make the point that in America Jews and Negroes divide between them the hostilities which spring from internal conflict: The super-ego is involved in anti-Semitism, since the Jew is felt to represent the valued but unachieved goals of ambition, money, and group loyalty ("clannishness"), whereas fear and hatred of the Negro spring from id tendencies which the individual cannot manage, his repressed desires for promiscuity, destruction of property, and general looseness of living. (In Europe, the Jews must do double duty, as the outlet for both id and super-ego dynamisms.) Today, on the one hand, the increasing sexual emancipation of Americans has made the Negro a less fearsome image in terms of sexuality (though he remains a realistic threat to neighborhood real estate and communal values) and, on the other hand, prosperity has meant that the Jew is no longer a salient emblem of enviable financial success. Thus, while the KKK declines the former "racial" bigot finds a new threat: the older educated classes of the East, with

their culture and refinement, with "softness" and other amenities he does not yet feel able to afford.[7]

Furthermore, the sexual emancipation which has made the
Negro less of a feared and admired symbol of potency has
presented men with a much more difficult problem: the fear
of homosexuality. Indeed, homosexuality becomes a much
more feared enemy than the Negro. (It may also be that
homosexuality is itself spreading or news of it is spreading, so
that people are presented with an issue which formerly was
kept under cover—another consequence of enlightenment.)
How powerful, then, is the political consequence of combining
the image of the homosexual with the image of the intellectual
—the State Department cooky-pusher Harvard-trained sissy
thus becomes the focus of social hatred and the Jew becomes
merely one variant of the intellectual sissy—actually less important than the Eastern-educated snob! Many people say of
McCarthy that they approve of his ends but not of his methods. We think this statement should be reversed to read that
they approve of his methods, which are so obviously not sissi-
fied, but care little about his ends, which are irrelevant provided that the targets are drawn with the foregoing constellation in mind.

As a result of all this, the left-wing and liberal intellectuals,
who came forward during the New Deal and who played so
effective a role in the fight against Nazism and in "prema-
turely" delineating the nature of the Communist as an enemy,
today find themselves without an audience, their tone depre-
cated, their slogans ineffectual.

IV

Apart from this central social change, much has happened
to reduce the intellectuals to a silence only temporarily broken by such a clamor as that over McCarthy.

[7] Professor Richard Hofstadter, to whose work we are indebted,
reminds us of the status gain involved in being able to bait old-
family Anglo-Saxons on the ground they are un-American—a
greater gain than is to be won by demonstrating superiority simply
to the Jews. (See Chapter 3.)

For one thing, the success of the New Deal has silenced
them. The New Deal as a triumphant movement at once of
the "folk," liberal government officials, and the intellectuals,
came to an end in 1937. By this time the major reforms, such
as the NLRB and Social Security, had already been institutionalized, and many of the remaining unspent energies of the
movement were dissipated in the Court-packing fight—nominally waged to preserve the reforms. After this, the crusading
spirit could only work on modifications and defenses of an
extant structure (for instance, the last major New Deal bill,
the Wages and Hours Act of 1938). This vacuum of goals
was concealed by affairs in Europe; Fascism in Spain and
Germany, and its repercussions in this country, absorbed many
New Dealers, the intellectuals, and their allies among the cultivated, and provided them with an agenda. But it was assumed that, once the war was over, the New Dealers and their
allies could return to the unending problem of controlling the
business cycle and reforming the economy. The business cycle,
however, refused to turn down, or did not turn down very far.
The one postwar victory based on something like the old New
Deal approach and coalition—that of 1948—owed more to the
anger of well-to-do farmers at the sag in agricultural prices
than it did to the self-interested voting of the city workers.
Had the depression come, the alliance forged by Roosevelt
might have emerged unimpaired from the wartime National
Unity front. But it turned out to be "too easy" to control the
business cycle: Keynesianism was no longer esoteric knowledge but the normal working doctrine of administrators, liberal or conservative, and even the Republicans, as was demonstrated in 1953–54, could keep a down-turn in the business
cycle under control.

What was left on the home front? One could raise the floor
under wages, but in a time of prosperity and inflation that
could not excite many beyond those, like the Textile Workers
Union, who spoke for the worst-paid workers. One could press
for socialized medicine, but this had little of the force of the
old New Deal campaigns. One could denounce Wall Street
and the interests, but it looked old-fashioned, and more, it

divided the liberal intellectuals from those who, on the issues that still counted, were natural allies. For Wall Street was closer to the liberal intellectuals on the two domestic issues that were still alive—civil rights and civil liberties—and on the whole range of issues related to foreign policy than were the former allies of the liberal intellectuals, the farmers and the lower classes of the city, both in their old form as factory workers and in their new form as white-collar workers.

Indeed, what has happened is that the old issues died, and on the new issues former friends or allies have become enemies, and former enemies have become friends. Thus: the liberal intellectuals have had to switch their attitudes toward Wall Street—as symbolizing both the great financiers and the giant corporations they organize—and toward "small business." By 1940, one could no longer speak of Wall Street as "the enemy." Demographic shifts and the Depression, along with the increasing ability of industry to finance expansion from reserves, had already weakened the hegemony of Eastern capital. The New Deal, by rhetoric and by such legislation as the SEC and the Holding Company Act, weakened it further, in comparison with the growing power of mid-continent businessmen (not to speak of tax-privileged oil and gas men). And the war had the same effect, for the small businessmen and tougher big businessmen of the Midwest paid less taxes and less attention to OPA and WPB. Wall Street lawyers Stimson and McCloy (perhaps Wendell Willkie might be added), Wall Street bankers Forrestal, Lovett, and Harriman, all have had a far greater cosmopolitanism and tolerance for intellectuals than do, for example, the big and little car dealers and other "small businessmen" of the Eisenhower administration.[8] In general, Wall Streeters, like the British Tories, are a chastened lot—and an easy symbol of abuse for pastoral and Populist simplifications. But, while Harry Hopkins and Tommy Corcoran recruited such men for Roosevelt, many New Dealers

[8] In the perspective employed here, "Engine Charlie" Wilson's Detroit provides a smaller and less cosmopolitan environment than Secretary Humphrey's Cleveland.

and their journalist and intellectual supporters resented their entrance.

They also resented the military, who were frequently similarly chastened men, sensitive to the limits of "free enterprise." The liberal political imagination in America, with its tendency to consider generals and admirals hopeless conservatives, and its tendency to consider war an outmoded barbarity that serious thinkers should not concern themselves with, was incapable of seeing that military men, like Wall Streeters, might be natural allies in the new epoch, and that military issues would become at least as important as the domestic economic issues of the New Deal era. What could be more crucial today than the outcome of the struggle between the Strategic Air Command and the Army Ground Forces? Yet who concerns himself with it? (The self-styled conservatives, being so often isolationists with overtones of manifest-destiny jingoism, have been on the whole even less well prepared to consider such issues.)

When the comments on policy of intellectuals and academic people are dated by ignorance, the military man who might be guided by thoughtful civilians—and there are many such—feels the hopelessness of communication; he must, in spite of himself, resort to pressure and public relations to defend his service and with it his country. Aside from a few journalists like the Alsops, several able magazine editors, and a handful of academic people like Bernard Brodie and the late Edward Mead Earle, only atomic scientists (and their occasional sociological counselors such as Edward A. Shils) have made serious efforts to grapple with such factors.

Today, the Federal defense budget is so large as to leave little room for major socio-cultural argument; in Washington, at least, anything outside of it can be no more than a fringe benefit. As Eliot Janeway has pointed out, we are now in a defense cycle rather than a business cycle; and Daniel Bell, tracing this out in terms of the capital expansion consequences of military commitments, has emphasized how many of the conventional areas of business and social decision are foreclosed. If a depression permitting reshaping of political thinking is unlikely, so also is a huge surplus the spending of which could lead to a healthy controversy outside the warring military services and their highly placed civilian partisans. Everywhere we look, then, there is room for change only within a narrow margin, if we interpret change in terms traditional among intellectuals.

At home, indeed, only the cause of racial emancipation remains to arouse enthusiasm. And this cause differs politically from the old New Deal causes in that it represents for many liberals and intellectuals a withdrawal from the larger statist concerns—it is a cause which is carried into personal life and into the field of culture where it attracts many reflective young people who appear apathetic to civic and electoral politics. By its nature, the field of race is one in which everyone can have a hand: institutionalization has not proceeded nearly so far as it has with economic underprivilege. Thus, every state has some form of social security, but only a few have an FEPC; and, as many Americans become more sensitive to interpersonal considerations, they feel it imperative to work for the amelioration of racial slights that would not have troubled an earlier generation. But as we have indicated, the demand for tolerance of Negroes cannot replace, politically, the demand for "economic equality": it is a very great and aggravating demand to make on children of white immigrants who are paying off the mortgage on their first suburban house.

V

Thus, for liberal intellectuals in the postwar era the home front could not be the arena for major policies, mobilizing a majority coalition, that it was in the 1930s; the focus had shifted to foreign policy. But for this the New Dealers and the intellectuals were generally unprepared. In particular, they were not prepared to view the Communists and the Soviet Union as the enemy in the way they had earlier recognized Fascism as the enemy, and for this failure they were to suffer seriously. Not many New Dealers had actually been pro-Soviet: the liberal politicians, lawyers, and civil servants had little in common with Popular Front writers, who were contemptuous of reform and addicted to slogans about Marx, the proletariat, and the Revolution. Indeed, the New Dealers were almost too ready to dismiss both the Stalinists and their left-wing sectarian critics; preoccupied with domestic reforms and anti-fascism, they formed no clear-cut image of Communism. They did not sympathize with it, let alone accept it, but they did not see it as a major enemy.

Understandably, they could not be as ebullient in carrying on a policy in which Communism was the major enemy as they could be in attacking depression and the interests. True, they did what was necessary: Truman's Point IV program and the Marshall Plan were the major postwar achievements of the American political imagination. However, these brilliant anti-Communist measures have not succeeded in saving the New Dealers from the taint of fellow-traveling. Moreover, these measures were not able to arouse among intellectuals, and sensitive young people, very much enthusiasm, even in the hearts of those active in administration of the aid program. For one thing, with the whole planet sending in distress signals, Point IV seems a drop of milk in a rusty Malthusian bucket— to be defended more for what it symbolizes at home than for its often ambiguous blessings (lowered death rates and uncontrollable population growth) abroad. For another thing, all these measures of international hope and help have been launched and caught up in the spirit of cold-war public relations. Thus, no one knows any longer whether he supports a program because it is worthwhile and an expression of humaneness, or because it is necessary to harry Soviet satellites or win over neutralists in Europe and Asia, or because it is necessary to appear tough-minded vis-à-vis congressmen and Philistines generally. A military "angle" has been discovered in, for instance, the work of anthropologists seeking to mediate the coming of industry to Indonesia. While such practical compromises and dual motives are always involved in reform, in this case they have often served to confuse the reformers, who deny, even to themselves, that they are motivated by anything visionary; hence the intellectual climate becomes less and less open to political imagination.[9]

As the hope of solving our foreign problems by indiscriminately and rapidly raising the standard of living of the rest of the world has waned, the more informed critics of contemporary politics have had to fall back on an austerity program —a program promising less and requiring more: more money, more soldiers, more arms, more aid, hence more taxes. All this is required, of course, not for redistribution within America, though a good deal of this does ensue, but to provide a new carrier (it costs as much as a Valley Authority) or a radar early-warning defense (as costly as socialized medicine). This program divides the intellectuals among themselves—many still agitate for socialized medicine—but divides them still more grievously from the poor and uneducated—for the latter, whatever the bellicose consequences of their xenophobia and love of verbal violence, always oppose war and sacrifice.

It is perhaps in reaction to these dilemmas that one new issue—that of the protection of traditional civil liberties—has risen in recent years to monopolize almost completely the intellectuals' attention. But this, too, is an issue which demands sacrifice from the uneducated masses—not financial sacrifice but the practice of deference and restraint which is understood and appreciated only among the well-to-do and highly educated strata.[10] Thus, a focus on civil liberties and on for-

[9] Commenting on an earlier draft of this paper—and we are indebted to such comments for many important revisions—Arthur Schlesinger, Jr., reminds us of utopian thinkers still alive and kicking, such as Stringfellow Barr, Clarence Streit, and the United World Federalists. We feel that the spectrum here is not wide or the proposals terribly imaginative; moreover, many of the proposals are counsels of despair, to avoid world catastrophe, rather than of hope, to improve American or planetary life.

[10] It was evident in the first opinion polls of the thirties that the conventional notion of the rich as conservative and the poor as radical was correct in the realm of government, labor, and distributive policy—thus, the poor have no objection to government ownership—but false in the realm of civil liberties and foreign policy where the greater impact of mistrust and fear of the strange and the stranger among the poor came to light.

eign policy tends, as we have seen, to make intellectuals seek allies among the rich and well-born, rather than among the workingmen and farmers they had earlier courted and cared about; indeed, it tends to make them conservative, once it becomes clear that civil liberties are protected, not by majority vote (which is overwhelmingly unsympathetic), but by traditional institutions, class prerogatives, and judicial life-tenure.

At the same time, the protection of civil liberties has had to cope with the Communist issue, much as other liberal causes have. The Sacco-Vanzetti case united the liberals; the Rosenberg case divided them. The great civil liberties cases of the post-Enlightenment era were not fought to save the Czar's spies and police from detection and punishment; they were fought for anarchists, for socialists and liberals, for professors teaching evolution or economics; and it takes either a case-hardened and sometimes disingenuous naïveté about Communists or a subtle strategic decision about where to draw the line to muster much enthusiasm for the defense of intellectuals who plead the Fifth Amendment. In this situation, the defense becomes at best a rear-guard action, but cannot hope to be a "positive" program—a demand on the basis of which political identities can be reshaped.

Where do the college-bred young stand in all this? In the late Thirties they were offered blood, sweat, and tears in the fight against Nazism. Some sought and accepted the agenda. But the fight against Nazism was made real by its domestic opponents: one saw almost all that was despicable—anti-Semites, fascists, Europe-haters, the bigoted and the crackpot —lined up on the pro-Nazi side. Today, the pathetic passel of domestic Communists cannot be compared with these fascists who organized street gangs or shook down businessmen; and many of the Communists' allies are decent, if misguided, "liberals who haven't learned." In international politics, we must accept alliances with despots no more savory than our erstwhile domestic fascists. Thus, the young are asked to fight international Communism not on the basis of street experience but of what they are taught. Cool in spirit generally, they can hardly be expected to show enthusiasm. Indeed, a holding game against the Communists is a reality and a prospect to sober the most enthusiastic. The question of appeasement that most thoughtful people could reject offhand in the pre-atom-bomb era now becomes more insistent intellectually even while it becomes outlawed politically.

If we leave substance aside, and consider the tone of politics, we realize that the loss of initiative by intellectuals is coupled with a change of emotional accent. The conservative and ascetic program just sketched is not avant-garde; it is dull; there is no hope in it of saving the world; it assumes the world is well enough and only wishes the Communists thought so too.

Demands are the basis of politics: the demands of a group or class, formulated by its intellectual leaders—or, more accurately, the demands create and identify the group or class which then is led. When a group is either satisfied or exhausted, when for whatever reason it no longer makes demands, then it has lost the *élan* which can attract new forces. It can only hope that the institutions and battalions that have been built up by the vanished *élan* of the past are large enough to withstand the onslaught of those who do make new demands.

VI

It is not only the dilemmas of policy that have been responsible for the decline of enthusiasm and vitality among the liberal intellectuals in the last decade or so. Another factor is hard to discuss without sounding like E. A. Ross, Henry Pratt Fairchild, and other pre-World War I opponents of immigration from Eastern and Southern Europe; yet it seems evident to us that the American crusading spirit has been sustained in considerable measure by the non-conformist conscience of New England and its offshoots in the Western Reserve and the Far West.[11] As long as the new immigrants looked up to this

[11] In addition, the Southern Scotch-Irish Presbyterians, such as Woodrow Wilson, have played a great role, especially in the Democratic and in splinter parties.

model, they tended to imitate the benign as well as the sharp-shooting doctrines and practices of the Yankees, but in a cumulative process which is only now reaching its end, the New Englanders themselves have run out of confidence and prestige: their land is now Vacationland, rather than the source of Abolitionist and other gospel; in the home territory, surrounded by Irish, Italians, Poles, French Canadians, Portuguese whom they have influenced more than either party will admit, they feel defeated and out of control in the charter institutions.[12]

This is not the place to trace the complex relations between the New England conscience and pragmatic reform. The remaining possessors of that conscience are still a national asset, but there are fewer of them proportionately; their wealth is smaller proportionately; and, scattered throughout the country, they are more remote from the centers of ideas. New ideas have their headquarters in New York. They often originate with, or are mediated by, Jews who have more reasons for hesitation and are perhaps psychologically as well as sociologically more vulnerable to pressure than the New Englanders—just as the newer media (movies and broadcasting) in which they are influential are weaker in the face of censorship than the older media (book publishing and the press) in which they play less part than the Yankees do. To be sure, there are many affinities between Jews and Puritans—both are

---

[12] On the whole, the English settlements over the globe indicate that the non-conformist conscience needs to be surrounded by other such consciences if it is to remain effective. The English Methodist who goes to Kenya or Australia to make his fortune is likely to retain the values he went out with, and not be prodded towards wider social sympathies, so that eventually his descendants will be estranged from Colonial Office officials representing his cousins who have stayed, and moved intellectually and morally forward in the Old Country. Similarly, the New Englanders who have left New England, the Quakers who have left Pennsylvania, may not—despite relative ease of intranational movement—keep up with developments in the original centers of cultivated morality. Indeed, New Englanders marooned in the Midwest (the late Robert Taft came of such stock) have been the source of much soured high-principled reaction—the "colonial" conscience at its worst.

people of the Book—and a political and intellectual alliance of the sort that Holmes and Brandeis once typified is still to be found, especially in smaller communities.

On the whole, as Americanization spreads, the old Puritan families have been slowly losing status. Some have responded by eccentricity, leadership, intellectuality, and liberalism; others have joined angry "pro-America" movements—where, ironically enough (save in the DAR), they meet the very Irish or Italian or other newer elements who have displaced or jostled them.[13] Since they can no longer safely snub these ex-Wops, ex-Shanty Irish, and ex-Hunkies, they displace their animus onto the weak targets provided by intellectuals, "left-wingers," "one-worlders," and so on.[14] And they can blame these latter people for the very social changes that have brought the descendants of lowly immigrants into the top councils of what was once, in some areas, the ethnically rather exclusive club of the Republican Party. Their blame, moreover, is not entirely misplaced, for the New Deal, along with the war, did help bring prosperity and mobility and reputability to Catholics and Jews.

After the war, the recognition of the Communist menace still further boosted the status of Catholics by making them almost automatically charter members of the anti-Communist crusade. By the same token, the intellectuals, their limited links with Communism continuously and extravagantly exposed, became more vulnerable. We believe that Granville Hicks in *Where We Came Out* presents a reasonably just picture of the actual extent of Communist influence in the Thirties —an influence much less than is now often supposed even among intellectuals; indeed, his picture does not take sufficient account of the infinitesimal extent of Party effectiveness outside the major seaboard cities. The New Dealers, as we

[13] The Jews, so largely beneficiaries of inflation and gainers of middle-class and professional status, have overwhelmingly remained Roosevelt Democrats, though a kind of "leakage" has provided some of the leadership and newspaper support for the new right.

[14] See Richard Hofstadter's excellent essay, "The Pseudo-Conservative Revolt" (Chapter 3).

have already said, were even less affected than the intellectuals, but they shared with the latter some personal and journalistic ties; this, plus some dramatic cases like those of Harry Dexter White and Alger Hiss and the belated fellow-traveling of Henry Wallace, made it politically possible—though fantastic—to damn the New Deal as a Communist-front organization. This has created a situation obviously quite different from that of earlier decades, when though liberal intellectuals and New Dealers were also called Communists, they only became as a result firmer and angrier. Today such libel is not only a disaster for public relations but cause for an anxious inner scrutiny. For as it becomes clear that few of the causes liberals have espoused have been immune to exploitation by the Communists, the liberal intellectuals lose their former sure conviction about their causes and are put, inside as well as out, on the defensive. One evidence of this is the strategy of continuous balancing so many of us engage in: if one day we defend Negroes (one of the few causes which, though taken up by Communists, still gets relatively unambiguous attention from intellectuals), then the next day we set the record straight by calling for more aid to Indo-China—not, let us repeat, merely for protective coloration but to make clear to ourselves that we are not fools or dupes of fellow-traveler rhetoric.

The intellectuals themselves are further weakened—in their own minds, at least—by the fact that their ideas, even where relevant to contemporary discontent, are quickly taken over by the mass media and transmuted into the common stock of middlebrow conceptions. They can no longer control, even by intentional opacity, the pace of distribution. Thus, what they produce soon becomes dissociated from them and their immediate coteries; in the division of labor, the middlebrows take over the function of dissemination and translation, and this alienation from their "product" leaves the intellectuals, even when they may reach a wider audience with more dispatch than ever before in history, with a feeling of impotence and isolation.

And, finally, the self-confidence of the liberal intellectuals is weakened by their own egalitarian ideology, which has led them not only to attack ethnic and class barriers but to defer to the manners and mores of the lower classes generally. Whereas in the days of Eastern seaboard hegemony the masses sought to imitate the classes, if they sought to rise at all, today imitation is a two-way process, and intellectuals are no longer protected by class and elite arrogance (and the strategic ignorances arrogance protects) against the attitudes of their enemies.[15] We find, for example, the cynicism of the lower strata reflected in the desire of the intellectuals to appear tough-minded and in their fear to be thought naïve. Such tough-mindedness in turn may then require acceptance of belligerent and vindictive attitudes in domestic and foreign affairs, and a further weakening of any visionary hopes and motives.

What the left has lost in tone and initiative, the right has gained. The right has believed, ever since "that man" entered the White House, in the utter deviltry of the New Deal. But what was once a domestic misanthropy has now been writ large upon the globe: the right has hit on what it regards as an unquestioned truth, which needs only to be spread (the utter sinfulness, the total evil, of the idea of Communism and the total perfection of the idea of Americanism); it maintains the zeal of missionaries in propagating this truth; it feels today it possesses a newer, better, altogether more avant-garde knowledge, even though about so limited a subject as the influence of Communists on American culture and politics (look

[15] We ourselves had an experience of this when we undertook to write a criticism of Norman Dodd's report as Staff Director of the Reece Committee investigating foundations. We criticized not only the crackpot notions that socialists and the great foundations had plotted to take America over on behalf of education and the Federal government—a plot somehow connected with "empiricism" and the prestige-laden "name" universities—but we also ridiculed the illiteracy, the demi-educated vein in which the report was written. Then we had misgivings about pulling the rank of our own education and relative fluency, and withdrew our comments on the style of the report. It is no longer comfortable (or expedient) to bait the hillbilly, the hick, the Negro preacher, or the night-school lawyer—so, too, with the political *arriviste*. The ridicule that greeted Bryan in Tennessee did not greet Congressman Reece.

at *The Freeman* and *The American Mercury,* or at *McCarthy and His Enemies* for illustration). Moreover, this new right possesses that convenient and perhaps essential feeling of martyrdom which its very presence gives to many liberal intellectuals: it sees itself as a minority suffering for its desire to enlighten the people (Peter Viereck has referred to the "bleeding hearts of the right").[16]

But the parallel is far from complete. For the left and the liberals in their days of influence really wanted something: they had specific reforms in mind, and specific legislation. The new right, with its few intellectuals trying to create a program for it, wants at best an atmosphere: it really has no desire to change the face of the nation; it is much more interested in changing the past, in rewriting the history of the New Deal, of the Second World War and its aftermath, or in more ambitious efforts, of the whole modern movement. Here again the comparison of the new right with the Communists is instructive, for the latter, too, in this country have been preoccupied with a state of mind: they have aimed, if not to make Americans sympathetic to the Soviet Union, at least unsympathetic toward its enemies here and overseas. To this end, their greatest efforts have been in rewriting recent and current history, in presenting a certain picture of the world in which big business, on the one side, supported fascism and anti-Semitism, while the Soviet Union, on the other side, fostered Negroes, Jews, and other minorities, and defended the work-

---

[16] When not long ago we heard Frank Chodorov, a leading organizer and publicist of the right, speak to a businessmen's luncheon, we felt that he bore much the same relation to his audience that, for instance, a speaker sent out by the American League for Peace and Democracy might have borne to a meeting of a Unitarian Sunday evening forum: he was more extreme, and therefore seemed more daring, but he shared enough of the values and verbal tags of the group to disguise somewhat the extent to which he was pushing their logics and rhetorics to fanatical limits. Indeed, Communist organizing tactics have often given lessons to rightists, and the little library in a New Hampshire town that might have received, from an anonymous donor, a copy of a novel by Howard Fast or a subscription to *The National Guardian* will now get the Buckley and Bozell book or *The Freeman.*

ing class. American domestic politics have been useful to the Communists in providing object-lessons for this general theory and in recruiting stalwarts for its further propagation. In the same way, one can read or listen to the organs of the new right and find nothing that amounts to a legislative program: the bills they want passed are those which give expression to their feelings about the past, such as the Bricker Amendment,[17] or withdrawing Hiss's pension and otherwise harassing Communists (often in ways that such veteran Communist-hunters as Governor Dewey think unjust and unwise)—the fight for these measures is an educative fight in re-interpreting the past. When it comes to coping with world Communism, this group has nothing to propose in the way of strengthening anti-Communists abroad—nothing but withdrawal or muted quasi-suicidal hints of preventive war. In fact, the hatred this group feels for the modern world, as manifested at home, in America, is so huge that there is little energy left over for the rest of the globe—rather, there is an aimless destructiveness in which legislative and local battles simply focus and dramatize resentment.

Nevertheless, this group now possesses the enthusiasm and momentum previously held by liberals. Its leaders cannot channel discontent; they can interpret it: they can explain why everything has gone wrong—for the while, that is enough. Thus, the picture today in American politics is of intelligence without force or enthusiasm facing force and enthusiasm without intelligence.

How much longer can this pattern last? International de-

[17] The Minute Women of America who buttonholed Senators on behalf of the Bricker Amendment are of course quite different in social position from the lower-class women who, in a few interviews a student supervised by one of us conducted by telephone, praised Senator McCarthy as the only one in Washington who was cleaning out the crooks and the Commies: they saw him as a kind of Lone Ranger, bravely fighting an all-powerful "they." Throughout this paper, we have had to collapse such distinctions to form general categories; we hope to stimulate further discussion of the coalitions—and the contradictions—that we lump as the discontented classes.

velopments will probably be determinative—the belligerence coupled with isolationism of this rightist group may tempt or frighten the Soviet Union into further adventures and incidents, finally touching off a war of annihilation (we think this most unlikely, and assuredly not inevitable). But the present leadership of the discontented classes has to do more than symbolize their disorientation and lack of satisfying political loyalties if it is to solidify new allegiances. For this, no intellectual reserve of demands appears in the offing. Instead, the leadership is continually subject to the temptation to fall back on the more developed intellectual positions of laissez-faire or of various brands of fascism—but these, it knows, will lose them much of their potential following, which is neither conservative in the older free enterprise sense nor on the lookout for, though tempted by, civil commotion and foreign adventure. It is not surprising that Congress represents the peak of strength of this group, since Congress is a sounding-board for mood—and an extraordinarily democratic one—as much as it is a machine for pork-processing and bill-passing. A tone, however, soon becomes monotonous and, if not institutionalized when at its shrillest, fades away.

In sum, the earlier leadership by the intellectuals of the underprivileged came about through a program of economic changes; and this program demonstrated an ability in the leaders to interpret the situation of the unorganized workers, of minority groups, and of marginal farmers. Today, a different group of classes (including many of these former underprivileged groups, now risen to middle-income status) wants something, but their wants (partly for the very reason that these people are now above subsistence or disfranchisement) are much less easily formulated. These new groups want an interpretation of the world; they want, or rather might be prepared to want, a more satisfying life.

It is the unsatisfying quality of life as they find it in America that mostly feeds the discontent of the discontented classes. Their wealth, their partial access to education and fuller exposure to the mass media—indeed, their possession of many of the insignia they have been taught to associate with the good life—these leave them restless, ill at ease in Zion. They must continually seek for reasons explaining their unrest—and the reasons developed by intellectuals for the benefit of previous proletariats are of course quite irrelevant.

Is it conceivable that the intellectuals, rather than their enemies, can have a share in providing new interpretations and in dissipating, through creative leadership, some of the resentment of the discontented classes? What kind of life, indeed, is appropriate to a society whose lower classes are being devoured faster by prosperity than Puerto Rican immigration can replenish? We have almost no idea about the forms the answers might take, if there are answers. But we do recognize that one obstacle to any *rapprochement* between the discontented classes and the intellectuals is the fact that many of the latter are themselves of lower-middle-class origin, and detest the values they have left behind—the dislike is not just one way. They espouse a snobbery of topic which makes the interests of the semi-educated wholly alien to them—more alien than the interests of the lower classes. Only in the great new melting pot of the Army would there appear to be instances where intellectuals discover that individuals in the discontented classes are "not so bad," despite their poisonous tastes in politics and culture—instances where the great camaraderie of the male sex and the even greater one of the brass-haters bridge the gap created by the uneven development of social mobility and cultural status. Of course, to suppose that the intellectuals can do very much to guide the discontented classes by winning friends and influencing people among them is as ridiculous as supposing that Jews can do much to combat political anti-Semitism by amiability to non-Jews. Nevertheless, there is only one side from which understanding is likely to come, and that is their own.

6

THE INTELLECTUALS AND THE
DISCONTENTED CLASSES:
SOME FURTHER REFLECTIONS (1962)*

David Riesman

As time marches on, our own understanding of the past shifts, not only with new evidence and new interpretations, but also with the impact of our own experience of life. So it is with the foregoing essay: Nathan Glazer and I sought to explain McCarthyism, especially its attack on the intellectuals, not so much in terms of the Korean War and the problems of foreign policy as in terms of endemic strains in American life and the discovery that charges of domestic Communism gave political leaders a way to seem active, strong, and rough without actually having a program. What follows is a re-examination of the essay, to correct what now seems mistaken in it and to add a few comments concerning more recent developments.

The original essay was criticized by a number of readers for seeking the sources of American discontent primarily in America, and especially in socio-psychological and cultural developments, rather than viewing this discontent as a rational response to Communist aggressions. Similarly, Margaret Mead, in her essay "The New Isolationism,"[1] criticizing Richard Hofstadter's essay as well as ours, wrote:

> There might be no atom bomb, no hydrogen bomb, no explicit insistence on a polarized world, no Communist China to alter the attitudes of the American people, to

[1] *The American Scholar*, Summer, 1955, pp. 378–82.

pinch and prune their luxuriant sense of national assurance, to plunge the mobile young into an orgy of grabbing at opportunities which they are sure will be snatched from them by conscription, to tear people loose from the certainties of their old invincibilities.

Far from denying the relevance of our contentions in general, what troubled Margaret Mead was the emphasis of our essay, and our tendency to criticize the Americans for reacting anxiously and aggressively to a world situation only partly of our own making. Undoubtedly, without the cold war and the revolutionary ferment in the world that both feeds on it and inflames it, the radical right would have far less of a colorable focus for its resentments: one cannot build a national movement out of an attack on the income tax, on allegedly Keynesian professors, or even on desegregation. Nevertheless, I still think that Hofstadter, Glazer, and I were right to emphasize strains endemic to American life. For the more we read American history, the more we are struck by the persistence of a secularized crusading spirit, seldom managing to seize power but frequently distorting the political spectrum and creating a climate in which the range of discussion and the possibilities for peaceful change have been foreshortened.[2] Even since we wrote the article, there have been internal developments, only marginally influenced by events abroad, that have shifted the locale of politically relevant discontent. I think especially of the increasing pace of change in the South, including the fight over desegregation, the decline of export-oriented farming, and the rise of tariff-oriented industry; I think also of the increasing gap between the generations produced by differential education and experience, and of the consequences of electing an activist Irish Catholic to the Presidency.

To take the last of these first, the election has seemed to open the possibility of an alliance, attempted but never consummated prior to the Korean War: that between Protestant

[2] Cf. Roger Hagan, "American Response to Change," *Contact* No. 9, Vol. III, No. 1 (September, 1961), pp. 7–17.

and Catholic fundamentalism. A relatively small minority of Catholics found Kennedy too much of a Harvard man, too liberal, to be a true ethnic anti-Communist patriot. (A few of them have turned up in the ranks of the John Birch Society, named after a vehemently fundamentalist Protestant missionary.) As long as Eisenhower was President, Catholics who had turned Republican and Protestants who had always been Republican could feel that they were not totally powerless and devoid of influence. Furthermore, as a conservative and an at least nominal Republican, a General and a man of old-fashioned budget-balancing morality, Eisenhower could for a time reassure various old guards in American life that they need not bother their heads about politics. Such people might crusade locally to prevent the fluoridation of water (which some regarded as a Communist-capitalist plot and an invasion of the "states' rights" inherent in every human body). And such people might make sure that there were various subjects, such as the recognition of Red China, that it was impolitic for schoolteachers, librarians, or Congressmen to raise. However, public-opinion pollers in the 1956 Presidential election campaign reported a widespread torpor, even an incipient "era of good feeling," and in the early Eisenhower era the call for national purpose trumpeted by a few intellectuals and publicists seemed as out of place as an evangelist at a country club.

As Samuel Lubell has pointed out on the basis of his surveys, this complacency was jarred first by sputnik, then by the dramatic rise of Khrushchev, and most recently by Castro. President Kennedy fought his campaign on the basis of an ascetic insistence on sacrifice, reminiscent of Theodore Roosevelt's belief in strenuousness, in American destiny, and in the responsibility owed the nation by patricians and intellectuals. As has already been suggested, Kennedy's victory released the Republican radical right (never quite happy with Nixon in any case) and the fundamentalist Democrats North and South from many of the mild restraints that Eisenhower's presence had imposed. At the same time, the new administration brought into office a number of the most influential spokesmen for liberalism within the Democratic Party; and these

men, though not exactly "muzzled," have not only been removed from the ranks of the liberal and radical opposition
but have taken part in the President's effort to reach a bi-
partisan consensus, especially in foreign policy, to secure passage of necessary measures in Congress, and to create the
strong working majority not provided by the election itself.
The presence of intellectuals and academicians in the new administration, and its cosmopolitan style and dash, have helped
persuade many liberals that they have access to power, that
the country is once again in purposeful, intelligent hands, and
that the fight against the radical right doesn't need their
energies.

I think there is some truth in this optimism, but also a considerable element of illusion. I define intellectuals as a group
of men who, whatever their field, take part in and contribute
to general ideas and speculative thought. This group must be
distinguished analytically, if not in concrete cases, from the
many intelligent professional and academic men who serve
the government or devote themselves to questions of public
policy. In the limited definition I have used, there are not
many intellectuals in America (or in any country), and of
these, not many have the political acumen, personal assertive-
ness, or relative insensitivity to criticism that would open
political or administrative careers to them. There has, however, developed in this country a group of lucid, well-educated, widely traveled men, recruited from the universities or
the mass media or occasionally from the law, who are committed to shaping a global mission for America, sometimes a
stabilizing and sometimes an expanding or policing one. Their
belief, reminiscent in some ways of the early Puritans, that
the country, like an individual, needs a purpose; their insistent
charges that America is too affluent and indolent; and that
we are in a race with world Communism that can be won only
by tireless and resourceful activity—all this is in many respects
a new morality, quite out of keeping with Abilene or even
the traditional service academies (even though, as I have indicated, one can find precursors of it in the first Roosevelt and
also, if we put aside his more insistent moralism, in Woodrow

Wilson). President Kennedy presents himself in this context as the principal hope of American liberals in fending off attacks from the troublesome minority of American Poujadists, and also as the hope of those who want this country to be more active on the world scene, employing its military, economic, and propaganda powers more effectively.

Thanks to the continuing prosperity that rests so dangerously on the Keynesian multiplier of a war economy, it would seem that the center of gravity of discontent has shifted upward in the status system. True, hidden beneath the growing middle of our middle-class society are millions of disinherited citizens, the aged and infirm and unskilled, the Negroes and Puerto Ricans and Southern poor whites—large numbers of all of whom are unemployed or underemployed. But save for the increasingly vigorous Negro protest movements (including the Negro version of the radical right, the Black Muslim movement), most of these millions are isolated and unorganized, as yet unavailable as constituencies for radical political leadership. In Senator McCarthy's movement, there were elements of a soured obscurantist populism; in many parts of the country McCarthy—the fighter, the good Joe, the exposer of Establishment shams—had a working-class and lower-middle-class following that responded not to his program, for he had none, but to his methods, his tone and targets. Today's radical right wing, in contrast, appears to draw much of its membership as well as its financial and polemical backing from far more well-to-do strata. It would seem that the small businessmen who belong to the John Birch Society are on the whole, like the Texas oil-rich who backed McCarthy, *small* businessmen in the sense of having limited educations and little experience as corporate managers in a complex world—but they are not poor. One can own a small trucking or real-estate firm or candy company and still amass millions—and be encouraged to believe that one did it all by oneself. Even more menacing are the indications that a few large corporations have found that anti-Communism is no longer "controversial" but can bring in sales and good will, so that hitherto cautious corporate officials who undoubtedly supported Eisenhower and, after him, Nixon now may listen to the peddlers of propaganda films and educational materials like those General Walker thought his division in Germany required. Furthermore, while many of the scientists and other staff men who work for the big missile and electronics companies are apolitical and at times quite cynical about their work (and a very few actively favor arms limitation), others may be grateful for the ideological justification provided by that right-wing brain trust, swelled by former Communists who have seen the light, without which Senator McCarthy himself would not have known the First Amendment from the Fifth Amendment or a Trotskyite from a Social Fascist.

To be sure, it remains true that the growing minority of old people who feel rejected, disoriented, impoverished and resentful are ready to applaud an anti-political movement that promises to reorganize the world so that the old folks can understand it again. Many of them, less well educated than their children or even the entertainers who nightly abuse them on television, are grateful for the simplistic, evangelistic messages of anti-Communism, which affirm to their hearers that the latter are the really good Americans, whatever their ethnicity, whatever their failure to live up to the American dream of youthfulness, competence, love, and success. These devalued elders, moreover, may be willing to applaud a speaker who denounces the income tax, though the vigor of denunciation matters even more to them than the topic. But it remains a question whether the rich reactionaries and the poor oldsters can form a united front around the anti-Communist issue when what they actually want from society is something so different.

In many communities, notably in the South and Southwest, extremely rapid urbanization and industrialization (often based on or growing out of defense activities) have disrupted the already fragile social structure so that there is no old elite sufficiently in charge of affairs to say "nobody's going to beat up Freedom Riders in this town and nobody, in the name of anti-Communism, is going to push librarians and schoolteachers around either." It is notable that perhaps the first public opposition to the John Birch Society came in Santa Barbara, from a very old man, a newspaper publisher who had grown up with the community and who assumed responsibility for civic decency when no one else would. (Papers that are owned by the staff or by a chain are often too faceless for this sort of free enterprise.) The fluid social structure in many expanding communities creates anxiety and bewilderment as well as opening opportunities for aggressive political activism among the newly awakened and the newly rich, who suddenly have discovered the uses of literacy. The situation allows new converts to the dangers of domestic Communism to practice their skills of intimidation locally: heckling at SANE meetings, expunging a textbook that mentions the United Nations, or setting students to spy on their professors at the teachers' college. Meanwhile, they watch the political horizon in search of a national leader comparable to McCarthy, appraising Senators Goldwater and Thurmond, hopeful about General Walker, but not yet solidified behind a single leader.[3]

But they have found a national—and nationalistic—cause in an anti-Communism, the belligerent frenzy and fanaticism of which is often vaguely reminiscent of the extravagances of Frenchmen in Algeria or of Japanese militarists before Pearl Harbor. Since this country has never been seriously hurt by war, except for the one it fought with itself (the memory of which we are now turning into a nostalgic celebration), and since most Americans have been in my opinion grossly miseducated about the world during the cold-war years, the radical right can always insist that the administration is following a policy that is insufficiently belligerent, insufficiently tough and dynamic. In fact, Kennedy during his campaign shared the right-wing picture of an America pushed around by Khrushchev and Castro, and suffering defeat after defeat in

[3] This is a perennial problem of the right wing and perhaps of all extremist groups. The authoritarianism, suspiciousness, and even mild paranoia that drive people into the right wing also drive them into suspicion of each other. Hitler's accomplishment lay in part in bringing to his banner the gifted Goebbels and Goering and, later, Speer, whereas the American right wing has not yet been able to unite behind a team with such diversified abilities.

the cold war, a tendentious picture that ignores the troubles of the Communists in the Congo and elsewhere and that proceeds from tacit premises either of omnipotence or of total rather than limited containment. The real chance of the right wing will come, it would seem, as this picture is highlighted through further changes in world alignments that can be interpreted as defeats for us and victories for a monolithic Communism. While it may generally be true that the ordinary citizen is averse to policies requiring war and sacrifice, it is possible that if the fear of Communism and nuclear war becomes sufficiently intense, many Americans will leap eagerly to short-cuts that promise to get things over with.

This jumpiness is enhanced by the fact that many Americans find it hard to realize, with full emotional awareness, that nuclear war is not simply a quantitative extrapolation of previously terrible near-total wars. The very term "war" puts it in a familar category, as do the common terms "all-out war" or "shooting war" or "hot war." In the face of right-wing attacks, the administration denies that it is pursuing a "no win" policy; it argues instead that it is just as combative, only more clever or roundabout. It is true, as public opinion polls have shown, that perhaps the majority of Americans intellectually recognize the catastrophic nature of what strategists sometimes refer to as a nuclear "exchange," and will tell an interviewer that they do not expect to survive. But these same Americans see no legitimate way to deal with what they regard as the encircling, crescent dangers of world Communism, other than by applying misread lessons of Munich and Pearl Harbor. And even now, against their better judgment, they find it hard to believe that this broad country, shielded by right and might, could be damaged beyond recognition: things have gone well with them as individuals (as the polls also show) and, outwardly, with the country.

A psychologically and politically expedient "solution" for these dilemmas is to find a scapegoat who can be ostracized and bullied because he stands for the bigger Soviet bully who is at once less available and more threatening. As already argued, the extreme right wing occupies itself very largely with domestic scapegoats of this sort, finding an inexhaustible supply among vulnerable liberals even when the supply of actual (non-FBI-agent) Communists and even fellow travelers does not meet the demand. Castro has become such a scapegoat. No German Jew, he may have welcomed this role. It binds more firmly to him the Communist powers, on whom he has become dependent. And the role may also be welcome to a Latin-American revolutionary who wants to break with the soberer reformism of men like Muñoz Marin, Betancourt, or Haya de la Torre, and whose provocativeness may have a touch of the cult of *machismo,* or maleness, that appeals to many students in Latin America, and to a few in this country. The chances seem all too good that we will continue to make Castro a scapegoat, and that the latter will be able, by frightening and aggravating us, to do precisely what we most resent and fear, namely, to allow our adversaries to limit our freedom of action by pushing us into violent counter-aggression. Indeed, Kennedy in his campaign was driven toward this very trap, not only by his specific denunciation of Communism "ninety miles from home," but also by his general assault on the do-nothing character of the administration.[4]

[4] Another consequence of the election campaign was apparently to make more difficult the re-election of a number of liberal Congressmen, and a number of those who had belonged in Congress to the small, brave, but not willful band of "peace Congressmen" —such as Byron Johnson, Charles Porter, and William Meyer—were defeated. The jingoism of the campaign might have been a factor in their defeat; also reflected was the way in which Protestant fundamentalist bigotry against a Catholic in the White House was aroused against Democratic candidates generally, even in areas where it was all right for a Catholic to occupy the statehouse. Cf., however, Tris Coffin, "The Political Effects of the Liberal Project" (*Newsletter of the Committee of Correspondence,* May, 1962), pointing out that these defeated Congressmen ran ahead of President Kennedy and calling attention to local factors both in their earlier victories and their later defeats.

Since this postscript was written, the attack by Senator Barry Goldwater and by the Chairman of the Republican National Committee and other right-wing Congressmen on *The Liberal Papers,* a collection of essays on foreign policy, edited by Congressman James Roosevelt and prepared for the Liberal Project, has served

In the last years of the Eisenhower presidency, Eisenhower's supporters themselves had tended to grow somewhat restless and disaffected. Though their Republican ideology favored decentralization and federal inaction, even men who would have enjoyed Eisenhower's company at golf or hunting or bridge in South Georgia had become uneasy at the growing signs that the United States could no longer play world policeman with impunity, and that we might someday be unable to roll back the tide of Communist advance while going about our business as before. Hence the propaganda about national purpose began to hit home among those who once would have thought a national purpose a violation of laissez-faire and perhaps a form of spurious religiosity as well—as if the new nationalism of the rising nations (including the Communist ones) were being echoed here at home just as other militant nationalistic tactics were becoming attractive in the name of freedom. Thus Eisenhower left to the country, and to his successor, a legacy of feeling that there ought to be someone in charge—and this feeling perhaps was heightened by the new awareness that there was obviously no one in charge of our sprawling me-

---

to underline the ability of the right wing in marginal Congressional districts to intimidate its opposition and to narrow the discussion of alternatives. *The Liberal Papers,* to which I was one of the contributors, includes a number of reasonably scholarly essays exploring various foreign-policy issues, but the attack on the book has been so ferocious, accusing it of being a blueprint for an American Munich or the left-wing equivalent of the John Birch Society's *Blue Book,* that a number of the Democratic Congressmen who had originally taken part in the Project have understandably disidentified themselves with it. The defeats of 1960 have not helped the morale of these men, all of whom come from close districts, and it is hard to criticize their lack of solidarity when it is realized that each Congressman seeking re-election is on his own, facing an irreducible minimum of right-wing opinion in his home district (often well financed and in control of the local media) and unable to explain to his constituents why he has taken it on himself to sharpen foreign-policy issues that are not his main concern—and that aren't their main concern either. Political analysts have observed that few Congressmen are in fact defeated because of stands they have taken on issues, but they can be defeated if they seem far out, or inattentive to local preoccupations.

tropolises, our wasting natural resources, and our increasingly complicated and ambiguous ties with the rest of the globe. There are still powerful currents of evangelical fervor in America. These currents may in fact be exacerbated by a prosperity that is associated with cities, complexity, "softness," irreligion, and skepticism toward traditional virtues. And while President Eisenhower's election owed something to that fervor, which is not confined to rural areas and small towns, many who had voted for him could not rest comfortably with what they felt was a somewhat shaky and uneven prosperity. Such people might still not be prepared to make real sacrifices, let alone the unimaginable sacrifices even of "tactical" nuclear war, but they might be prepared to listen to calls for sacrifice to reassert national control and supremacy against the apparently unequivocal Communist successes. Furthermore, as suggested in the earlier essay, an evangelical counterattack by proponents of American Puritan virtues could allow Catholics and other newer Americans thus to establish their superiority to older, better-educated, but "decadent" families. The counterattack itself, calling for "action" but securing it at present only in symbolic doses, provides a sense of momentum.

Activist lay leaders in fundamentalist churches sometimes have an opportunity to conduct their church work with a single-minded, businesslike efficiency and pep from which they are restrained in the conduct of business itself by having to cope with labor unions, customers, tax collectors and other government officials. So, too, when such men and their wives as well get into political work, their local community may offer a wide range of relatively easy victories, exciting rallies, and dramatic, seemingly dangerous vicissitudes reminiscent on a higher income and educational level of Ku Klux Klan attractions. Quite generally, it would seem, when such right-wingers attend a Unitarian or other liberal-church meeting to picket or heckle, and are asked who they are, they reply with some right-wing version of the Fifth Amendment; e.g., "I am a loyal American." They may hand out a mimeographed statement, but they will refuse to give their names, sometimes indicating that they fear Communist reprisal. The rich and the

poor fundamentalists have this much in common: they fear
the way the world is going, at home or abroad; they resent
those more cosmopolitan people who appear to understand the
world less badly and who seem less ill at ease with all the different kinds of people who mingle in our big cities or at the
United Nations. Moreover, whatever sectarian or doctrinal
differences divide the discontented from each other in theological terms, all can agree on the gospel of Americanism.[5]
(Of course, it should be clear that I speak of right-wing fundamentalism, but I am not suggesting that all fundamentalists
in religion are right-wingers in politics. Many reject politics
as one of the things of this world that is alien to the devout
and otherworldly; many others find in the Gospels the basis
for often courageous Christian social action for peace or racial
integration.)

Seven years ago, it appeared to Mr. Glazer and me that a
holding game against the Communists would be frustrating
but endurable. Since then, Soviet Communism has broken
away from Stalin's paranoia, caution, and brutality and seems
at once more flexible and more difficult to understand; it is
also much better armed, militarily if not ideologically. At the
same time, as I have sought to emphasize, President Kennedy
has broken out of the limits imposed on American policy by
the provincial, benign—but restrictive—morality of his predecessor. President Kennedy brings to this task exceptional gifts
of virtuosity, drive, charm, and impatience, and he and his
advisers have a grasp of the world far more differentiated
and supple than the narrow moralism of John Foster Dulles.
In addition, the new administration is deeply and energetically
committed to civil rights as both a domestic- and a foreign-
policy imperative, and it is naturally drawn toward support
for civil liberties by its ties to academic and intellectual values

---

[5] I recall in this connection an extremely revealing and disturbing study done at a junior college on the West Coast, which indicated that education served to moderate the anti-minority ethno-
centrism of students (many of whom were planning to become
teachers) but, if anything, to increase their nationalism. In other
words, a certain tolerance for minorities within this country has,
as it were, been gained at the cost of a greater chauvinism.

and by its view of what is fitting for a civilized and sophisticated society. President Kennedy himself is anything but a demagogue, as his debates with Nixon showed, nor is he an indignant and fanatical ideologue. Nevertheless, his rhetoric of activism speaks to the mood of many in the discontented classes, and since he has in some measure freed himself from his predecessor's budgetary and other controls,[6] the anti-Communism of the radical right can always appear to be an extension of the administration's doctrine to its logical conclusion—a conclusion from which, as the right would say, the administration itself draws back only from softness, inconsistency, treason, or incompetence. The effect of this pressure from the radical right, in the absence of anything like comparable pressures from the left, is to shift the whole climate of political contest and discussion toward the right (a process of which the men of intellect and intelligence in the administration may not be fully aware, protected as they are by their metropolitan locale and contacts).

At the present writing (winter, 1962), President Kennedy appears to have satisfied all but the wildly irrational right wing (plus the Republicans and the racketeers who hope to get money or office by playing on the fears and hopes of this group) that he is pursuing a vigorous yet cautious anti-Communism and that he can not only "stand up to Khrushchev," as at Berlin, but outpoint him in the ring. Grateful in spite of themselves for forcefulness and direction, many conservatives have come to realize that President Kennedy, outside of the field of civil rights and discounting rhetoric and personal sym-

---

[6] While President Kennedy's rhetoric is less budget-minded than that of President Eisenhower, his administration would appear to be almost as orthodox in fiscal matters, limited not only by fear of offending the financial community but also by the balance-of-payments problem. Even so, the radical right is frightened by the liberal speeches of the Democrats, and I believe the latter are in fact less able than the Republicans to use the budget as a tacit form of arms control. There has been left very little budget surplus to use as a political weapon in domestic controversy—after armaments, and associated foreign-aid programs, nearly everything else becomes a fringe benefit.

pathies, is himself quite conservative, and not a reborn New Dealer.[7] Thus the President would seem to have absorbed some of the right-wing's drive and to have rendered it relatively harmless on the national scene, whatever its power to punish dissenters locally. But in a fluid national and international setting, the problem cannot be left at this point. In moods of crisis, militancy, where it is not too ideological or complicated, is an attractive quality to Americans. Older, more tolerant, or more acquiescent men who are not themselves militant may be influenced more than they realize by militant subordinates or critics, especially if the latter combine an apparently hardheaded realism (e.g., a skepticism about the possibilities of peaceful coexistence) with the quiet sincerity and fervor of their dedication. This constellation may help press the administration toward policies (that are also attractive on other grounds) of responding to the nuclear stalemate by energetic non-nuclear military actions, whether in Cuba or in South Vietnam, or in the domestic para-military step of an expanded civil-defense program.[8]

Such measures, whatever justification each standing in isolation may have, antagonize much of the rest of the world, especially the non-white formerly colonial world. And this

[7] There is some evidence that the Kennedy-Nixon TV debates, by compelling Nixon supporters to see the latter's opponent (rather than shut him out, as partisans so often do with the opposition), prepared them to realize that the enemy candidate was no monster and thereby to be won over after the inauguration.

[8] I recognize that there are reasons, perhaps in one or another case sufficient ones, for each of these actions, quite apart from domestic politics. Thus we are pressured to act in South Vietnam by Communist-guerrilla tactics (and the hope of finding a way of repulsing these everywhere else) and by fear for all our Asian allies with whom we are linked in military pacts. And we are pressed to act in Cuba by shaky Central and South American states. Moreover, the administration would deny that civil defense, though shifted to the Pentagon, is a para-military measure (though it is clearly this in the minds of some counterforce strategists), being simply a rational effort at insurance. What I am emphasizing in this essay as in the preceding one are the domestic pressures that are one factor in the American response to the cold war and to the momentum and forms in which that war is carried on.

antagonism seems to Americans both utterly bewildering and grossly ungrateful, detaching us still further from the rest of the world and thus feeding discontent simultaneously at home and abroad. Indeed, it may well be that this administration, far more cosmopolitan and world-minded than the country at large, may serve to isolate us from the world more than did an administration dominated by the fiscal conservatism and small-mindedness of men like George Humphrey and "Engine Charley" Wilson. This is all the more likely since Communism is no longer confined within the limited bounds of Stalin's mistrustful isolationism. And can anyone foretell the reaction here at home, or the situation abroad, when the Chinese Communists gain nuclear weapons? While we and the Soviet Union are running an accelerated arms race, nationalistic and discontented groups within each adversary of the two superpowers or their allies help provoke their opposite numbers in each country, and thus lend justification to a program of increased militancy at home and abroad.

In this perspective, it appears that in the earlier essay Mr. Glazer and I may have underestimated somewhat the effect of foreign policy and of such issues as "who lost China" in the support of McCarthyism. But what I still would stress is that we deal here not with foreign affairs in the abstract but with specifically American reactions to solutions that must be imperfect, or indeed to any ambiguous and tragic situations.

As C. Vann Woodward pointed out a few years ago, only the South is "un-American" in having suffered defeat, in having lacked the dynamic of industrialism, and in having gained in these ways some skepticism about the doctrine of progress. Yet despite much talk of states' rights and individual freedom, the South does not today seem aware of the consolations of being a defeated power.[9] It has certainly made no effort to control its own booming industralization or its combination of sectional Irredentism and nationalist belligerence. And while

[9] As W. J. Cash angrily reminds his readers in *The Mind of the South*, not even before the Civil War was the South the stable social order, governed by Tidewater gentry, that magnolia mythology describes.

before the Second World War the South was perhaps the most pro-British, pro-free-trade, interventionist part of the country, today it may be the most tariff-minded and the most anti-British (whenever Britain tries to moderate the cold war).[10]

The Southern white college students, as a number of surveys have shown, seldom share either the prejudices or the passions of their vocal elders. And the Negro college students increasingly fail to adopt the passivities and covert compromises of their elders. Our earlier essay was written before the desegregation decision had made itself felt in the South, and shortly thereafter, in connection with the Fund for the Republic study of academic freedom,[11] I visited, though only for a day, the Greensboro Agricultural and Technical College, where a few years later the first sit-ins began. From my visit and from what I was told by other observers, I would not have expected the sit-ins to start in an institution where most of the students appeared to be satisfied to enter the lower ranks of the "black bourgeoisie" and where their apparently docile patriotism comforted and confirmed the established leadership, Negro and white alike. That same year, I analyzed several hundred interviews of college seniors at twenty colleges and universities throughout America in which the students had described what they looked forward to in life fifteen years hence; I noted complacency, amiability, tolerance, and a lack of ideological and political concerns on the part of most of these respondents.[12] From such material I certainly did not expect the sudden growth on many campuses of student pro-

[10] The South (not counting Texas) was also anti-McCarthy, while today it offers support to various right-wing crusaders who, whatever their nominal political color, are opposed to the Democratic Party of President Kennedy. I recognize that the voting South is a minority, and that those who claim to speak for the South speak for a minority; the entire South has perhaps changed less rapidly than its articulate and organized cadres.

[11] Cf. Paul F. Lazarsfeld and Wagner Thielens, Jr., *The Academic Mind: Social Scientists in a Time of Crisis* (Glencoe, Illinois: The Free Press, 1958).

[12] See "The Found Generation," *The American Scholar*, Vol. 25, 1956, pp. 421–36.

test movements, today still small in number but not small in vigor and impact. When I came to Harvard in 1958, an effort to found a Committee to Study Disarmament was temporarily abandoned thanks to disruption by a group of Young Republicans (who intervened much as Communists used to take over liberal organizations); in February, 1962, as I write these lines, Harvard students are taking active leadership in planning a demonstration in Washington, and three hundred students at this notably skeptical, cool, and sophisticated college have volunteered to go.

Students in America are not a class, nor do they speak for a class (though in the Negro community they are able, perhaps, to speak for a race). At times their tendency to act outside of conventional parliamentary channels may represent a feeling that they are living in an occupied country—and indeed those students who have been abroad, whether in the Peace Corps or in such predecessors of it as the Experiment in International Living, are often well aware that the climate of debate in this country on cold-war issues has become extremely constricted.

It is generally thought that the debate is more open and uncensored now than it was at the height of McCarthyism. In some respects, this is so: there is, for instance, more give and take with the Communist countries, and more awareness of the fact that these countries are not all alike or unalterable, either ideologically or in terms of social organization. Yet in other respects, the bi-partisan consensus with respect to foreign policy has served to impose more complex and subtle restraints on free discussion of alternatives than McCarthyism did. For the very virulence, unpleasantness, and demagoguery of McCarthy led, if not to counterattack or even to solidarity, at least to a common feeling of disgust and distrust among liberal intellectuals and many conservatives.

McCarthy, however, was not interested in the cold war but only in dissatisfactions within America, including the exploitable grievances of rising ethnic minorities. Today, in contrast, the Kennedy administration focuses much, if not most, of its attention on the cold war, and the very attractiveness and *élan* of this administration tend to mute liberal and radical dissent. World Communism is a real and not a factitious adversary, and perhaps it is easier to unify the country against Communism abroad than against people who are extravagantly alleged to be Communists at home. In any case, many leading intellectuals have been hesitant to plumb the depths of their misgivings about the Kennedy administration. In the nuclear age their anxiety about the future has a nightmarish quality, and as the cold-war consensus develops, they understandably fear the prospect of becoming alienated and powerless. When the President expresses their more utopian hopes, as he sometimes does, they are cheered; when he moves in the opposite direction, they blame his advisers or—not unreasonably—Congress or the mass media or an electorate responsive to slogans.

The young radical students, in contrast, have in many cases been more quickly alienated from the administration. Because so many of them believed that the Democrats in the North are the party of virtue, their expectations were perhaps too high, and the Cuban invasion began for a number of them a drastic disenchantment, ending with the view that Kennedy's administration is more clever but also more dangerous and militaristic than Eisenhower's.[13] In the eyes of the young, the older generation of intellectuals has succeeded almost too well in dissecting and demolishing Communism and its fronts—and liberal hopefulness and trust also. I have sometimes found that young activists do not want to be warned about the duplicities of domestic Communists and fellow-travelers. They are impatient with our prudence and historical awareness, which they regard as pussyfooting at best and witch-hunting at worst. The enormous changes that have overtaken America in the last generation, particularly in the last few years, have separated many young people from their elders rather more than generations are usually divided, and each generation in the presence of the other feels insecure and perplexed.

[13] Since they fear being again disillusioned, there is sometimes a tendency wholly to disregard the efforts toward disarmament and the reduction of tensions that President Kennedy has in fact made, in alternation with his efforts to secure "positions of strength."

At the same time the dominant academic liberalism of the major metropolitan centers, combined with the vitality and activity of the new protest groups, has helped bring into being new organizations of right-wing students for whom in an earlier day college would have been simply the dormitory and locale for fun and games. In the past, students who identified themselves as conservative did not feel threatened in the campus social climate that supported their prankish and ordinarily unreflective activities. Many such students can still be found; perhaps they are the majority in the country as a whole. In the past, the fraternities and sororities could protect such students from having to come to terms with the academic culture, while remaining on relatively good terms with the values of their parents and of the alumni, whose ranks they would soon join. Increasingly today, however, these protections against the larger intellectual world do not suffice, any more than the Atlantic and Pacific suffice to protect America itself from the fear of destruction. On the larger campuses, at least a few students can usually be found who possess the forensic ability, the desire for individualism, and the eagerness to fight fire with fire that can propel them into organizing right-wing groups; articulate journals such as the *National Review* provide ammunition.

These right-wing students (and some of the more sober and ideologically committed conservatives as well) are armored with facts and are often able to cite Communist abuses and treacheries around the globe with a debater's skill. Such students, on graduation if not before, are capable of taking part in the many seminars, schools, and more or less intellectual apparatuses of today's anti-Communist movements. (To be sure, there are still plenty of less articulate right-wingers who are satisfied to shout "Better dead than Red" or "We want more bombs," but these are seldom found among the educated —just as Southern segregationist mobs include few from the educated strata.)

I speak here on the basis of rough impressions and cannot adequately document the changes that I sense. Father Coughlin had his followers gather in small groups or cells to listen to his broadcasts and receive instructions, but his sermons made little attempt at intellectual analysis. Senator McCarthy's speeches and hearings made more of an effort to give the appearance of analysis, with the constant waving of documents and citing of supposed facts. Members of the John Birch Society and enrollees at various anti-Communist seminars sometimes appear to be people of the book, and a portion of the literature aimed at them blends exigent secularized fundamentalism with the witch-doctor academese ("each and every Harvard graduate"; "known Comsymp") that helps make such pamphleteering attractive for some of the uneasy new rich whose achievements have outrun their anticipations. It is not clear to me where to draw the line between the radical right and extreme conservatives. Senator Goldwater's sometimes humorous and genial tone is very different from that of the more obviously sectarian and suspiciously secretive groups. But he is capable of simplifications, such as the demand for total victory in the battle with world Communism, which speak to the malaise of the more angrily discontented.[14]

Nor is it clear to me what weight ideology possesses in these various fragmentary movements. The sit-in and disarmament groups often reject ideology[15] and complexity in preference for a single issue simply seen—though some of the groups are scholarly and searching, particularly in the field of disarma-

[14] Goldwater was picketed at a recent meeting by members of a radical-right organization who carried signs saying, "We want war. . . . Red Russia must not survive." Such exhortations are alien to much of the literate prose of the *National Review*. At some Catholic colleges, Goldwater may be a drawing card for students who find the priests and other religious who teach at their college departing from the doctrine or liturgical practice of their diocesan priest and threatening the students with complexity, much as they are threatened on secular campuses.

[15] Rejecting ideology, like rejecting abstraction or being sincere and natural, is more easily said than done. There is always a tacit ideology. Furthermore, there has been a flourishing of student liberal and radical journalism (the active leaders are often graduate students) which both reviews what is happening in the world and seeks to interpret it in a neo-Marxist, existentialist, or other contemporary perspective.

ment and foreign policy. On the radical right, as just suggested, there is a stronger attempt than before to support attitudes with ideology or at least with slogans and superficial information; there is more fanaticism and less fooling around. As people become aware of their national defenselessness in the nuclear age, the militant may feel they need ideas even while they fear them. The educational and intellectual upgrading of our population as a whole forces right-wing groups to pay more attention to ideas or to their semblance.

Efforts to explain even in social psychological terms a political or cultural movement risks making it appear too rational, too much a direct response to external events. I now think that in our earlier effort to understand the radical-right mentality we placed too much emphasis on the ties between New Dealers and a few Communists or alleged Communists such as Alger Hiss and Harry Dexter White. For the discovery of a few actual spies and compromised bureaucrats had slight importance, perhaps, among the fanatical true believers of the radical right, convinced of their own powerlessness and cynical about politicians and big shots; among such an audience even so inveterate an anti-Communist as Dean Acheson could be made to appear traitorous. Beyond these circles, with their crusading wildness, however, such events as the Hiss case did have an important effect, giving McCarthy and his allies a gloss of rationalism and demoralizing many liberals, whether or not they had had any contact with front organizations. Looking inward at their own mistakes, moreover, as lack of power often leads the vulnerable and reflective to do, some articulate and self-conscious intellectuals who left the Communist Party or various splinter groups have remained perhaps unduly preoccupied with liberal guilt, innocence, or disingenuousness vis-à-vis Communism in the 1930s and 1940s. In my judgment, both Communists and anti-Communists have a stake in exaggerating the importance of the Communists in this period, and the ready gullibility of liberals to Communist-front organizations. But (as Hannah Arendt pointed out in *The Origins of Totalitarianism*) fronts look both ways, and it is arguable that labor unions and other movements for social betterment exploited the Communists' fanaticism while the Communists believed that they were the exploiters. It seems to me that many liberal intellectuals have become fixated on the past, yet without seeing it in perspective, and are distracted from imagining a better future by the gnawing desire to cope with vestiges of domestic Communist contamination and with the still potent dangers of McCarthyism. In practical politics—for instance, in the peace movement—the two issues create difficult questions for strategy, ethics, and clarity, but they offer diminishing returns to our understanding of the dangers and the opportunities of the future.

If we must wait until we understand ourselves, we are unlikely to get out of the nuclear age, indeed may not get out of it whatever we do. But clearly one requirement for getting out is a less oppressive domestic climate, and achieving this would seem to entail drastic re-education, and measures on many fronts abroad and at home, to give Americans a feeling of creativity in the discovery of a political equivalent that would also be a moral equivalent for war.

In the light of all these crescent dangers, the earlier article seems to me today too detached and somewhat complacent an essay. Since it was written, intelligence and discontent have both gained much more importance in American life. Emerging from the sordid and frightening distraction provided by Senator McCarthy—though not by any means from all the legacies of his procedures and his view of the world—the intellectuals regained some confidence. And in the last years of the Eisenhower presidency, despite Stevenson's two defeats, men began to run for Congress and the Senate and to take part in political life who were as much at home in the world of ideas as their colleagues and predecessors were in the courthouse crowd or the Masonic Lodge of small-town Republicanism. Indeed, the discussion of disarmament and foreign policy in the United States has become more open, more sophisticated, and more widespread in the last few years; preoccupations once confined to the *Bulletin of the Atomic Scientists* and a few other specialized or sectarian groups can now be shared with a far wider audience, inside as well as outside the administration. The difficulty, as so often in history, is that events seem to be outpacing the rapid growth of understanding and the rather slower development of political concepts and forms that might bring about a more creative domestic and foreign policy. The spirit of McCarthyism reflects long-standing discontents and bellicosities in America, for our society is one where men and groups are accustomed to mobility, to expansion, to progress and secular growth, and the cold war now provides a wider stage for the drama of winning and losing, of growth and senescence.[16]

The antibodies against McCarthyism are not hardy. But what makes the radical right so ominous now is less its impact on civil liberties and domestic affairs, which can be held in check with the resiliency of politics, than its potential power, in co-operation with mindless militancy in other countries, to jeopardize, at least in the northern latitudes, the human enterprise itself. Political plagues become devastating when a single plane or Polaris submarine can carry more death than all the bombs of World War II.

[16] Cf., for fuller discussion, Riesman and Michael Maccoby, "The American Crisis," in James Roosevelt, ed., *The Liberal Papers* (New York: Doubleday Anchor Books, 1962), pp. 13–47.

7

THE REVOLT AGAINST THE ELITE (1955)

Peter Viereck

Defeat of western silver.
Defeat of the wheat.
Victory of letterfiles
And plutocrats in miles
With dollar signs upon their coats
And spats on their feet.
Victory of custodians,
Plymouth Rock,
And all that inbred landlord stock.
Victory of the neat. . . .
Defeat of the Pacific and the long Mississippi. . . .
And all these in their helpless days
By the dour East oppressed, . . .
Crucifying half the West,
Till the whole Atlantic coast
Seemed a giant spiders' nest. . . .
And all the way to frightened Maine the old East
    heard them call, . . .
Prairie avenger, mountain lion,
Bryan, Bryan, Bryan, Bryan,
Smashing Plymouth Rock with his boulders from the
    West.

—from Vachel Lindsay's "higher vaudeville" imitation of how a sixteen-year-old Bryanite Populist radical in 1896 would have viewed the revolt of western mass egalitarianism against Atlantic Coast traditionalism and aristocracy. Note the stress on revenge ("avenger, mountain lion") for having been humiliated and patronized intellectually or socially by "that inbred landlord stock" of Plymouth Rock; this emotion of revenge for humiliation is often shared by recent immigrants in Boston and the east as well as by the Populist older stock in Wisconsin and the west.

During the Jacobin Revolution of 1793, in those quaint days when the lower classes still thought of themselves as the lower classes, it was for upper-class sympathies and for *not* reading "subversive leftist literature" that aristocrats got in trouble.

Note the reversal in America. Here the lower classes seem to be the upper classes—they have automobiles, lace curtains and votes. Here, in consequence, it is for alleged lower-class sympathies—for "leftist" sympathies—that the aristocrats are purged by the lower class.

In reality those lower-class sympathies are microscopic in most of that social register (Lodge, Bohlen, Acheson, Stevenson, and Harvard presidents) which McCarthy is trying to purge; even so, leftist sympathies are the pretext given for the purge. Why is it necessary to allege those lower-class sympathies as pretext? Why the pretext in the first place? Because in America the suddenly enthroned lower classes cannot prove to themselves psychologically that they are now upper-class unless they can indict for pro-proletariat subversion those whom they know in their hearts to be America's real intellectual and social aristocracy.

Ostensibly our aristocrats are being metaphorically guillotined for having signed, twenty years ago, some pinko-front petition by that egghead Voltaire (a typical reversal of the 1793 pretext) and for having said, not "Let them eat cake," but "Let them read books" (violation of loyalty oath to TV). Behind these ostensible pretexts, the aristocratic pro-proletarian conspirators are actually being guillotined for having been too exclusive socially—and, even worse, intellectually—at those fancy parties at Versailles-sur-Hudson. McCarthyism is the revenge of the noses that for twenty years of fancy parties were pressed against the outside window pane.

In Populist-Progressive days and in New Deal days, those

same noses were pressed with openly radical, openly lower-class resentment. During 1953 and 1954, the same noses snorted triumphantly with right-wing Republicanism. This demagogue's spree of symbolically decapitating America's intellectual and social upper class, but doing so while shouting a two hundred per cent upper-class ideology, suggests that McCarthyism is actually a leftist instinct behind a *self-deceptive* rightist veneer. This combination bolsters the self-esteem of sons of Democratic urban day laborers whose status rose into stuffy Republican suburbia. Their status rose thanks to the Communism-preventing social reforms of Roosevelt. Here for once is a radicalism expressing not poverty but sudden prosperity, biting the New Deal hand that fed it.

What figure represents the transition, the missing link, between the often noble, idealistic Populist-Progressives (like that truly noble idealist, La Follette) and the degeneration of that movement into something so different, so bigoted as McCarthyism? According to my hypothesis, that transition, that missing link is Father Charles Coughlin. All liberals know that Coughlin ended by defending Hitler in World War II and preaching the vilest anti-Semitism. They sometimes forget that Coughlin began his career by preaching social reforms to the left of the New Deal; his link with Populism and western Progressivism emerges from the fact that Coughlin's chief panacea was the old Populist panacea of "free silver," as a weapon against Wall Street bankers, eastern seaboard intellectuals, and internationalists, three groups hated alike by democratic Populists and by semi-fascist Coughlinites. And Coughlin's right-wing fascist anti-Semitism sounds word for word the same as the vile tirades against "Jewish international bankers" by the left-wing egalitarian Populist, Ignatius Donnelly.

On the surface, Senators like Wheeler and Nye (originally Progressives and campaigners for La Follette) seemed to reverse themselves completely when they shifted—in a shift partly similar to Coughlin's—from "liberal" Progressives to "reactionary" America Firsters. But basically they never changed at all; throughout, they remained passionately Anglophobe, Germanophile, isolationist, and anti-eastern-seaboard, first under leftist and then under rightist pretexts. Another example is Senator McCarran, who died in 1954. McCarran ended as a McCarthyite Democrat, hating the New Deal more than did any Republican. This same McCarran had been an eager New Dealer in 1933, voting for the Wagner Act and even for the NRA. Yet throughout these changes, he remained consistently anti-internationalist, anti-British, anti-eastern-intellectual.

Broadening the generalization, we may tentatively conclude: the entire midwest Old Guard Republican wing of today, journalistically or vulgarly referred to as "conservative," does not merit that word at all. Theirs is not the traditional conservatism of a Winston Churchill or of a Burke or of our own *Federalist* papers. Theirs is not true American conservatism in the sense in which Irving Babbitt defines indirect democracy (in his great book *Democracy and Leadership*), as opposed to plebiscitarian, Tom Painean direct democracy. "Conservative" is no proper label for western Old Guard Republicans, nor for their incongruous allies among the status-craving, increasingly prosperous, but socially insecure immigrants in South Boston and the non-elite part of the east. What all these groups are at heart is the same old isolationist, Anglophobe, Germanophile revolt of radical Populist lunatic-fringers against the eastern, educated, Anglicized elite. Only this time it is a Populism gone sour; this time it lacks the generous, idealistic, social reformist instincts which partly justified the original Populists.

Many of our intellectual aristocrats have helped to make the McCarthyite attack on themselves a success by denouncing McCarthyism as a rightist movement, a conservative movement. At first they even denounced it as a Red-baiting, anti-Communist movement, which is exactly what it wanted to be denounced as. By now they have at least caught on to the fact that it is not anti-Communist, has not trapped a single Red spy —whether at Fort Monmouth, the Voice of America, or the State Department—and is a major cause of the increased neutralism in Europe, McCarthy being the "Typhoid Mary" of anti-Americanism.

But although American liberals have now realized that McCarthyism is not anti-Communist (which is more than many American businessmen and Republicans have realized), they have still not caught on to the full and deep-rooted extent of its radical anti-conservatism. That is because they are steeped in misleading analogies with the very different context of Europe and of the European kind of fascism. Partly they still overlook the special situation in America, where the masses are more bourgeois than the bourgeoisie. I am speaking in terms of psychology, not only of economics. A lot more is involved psychologically in the American ideal of the mass man than the old economic boast (a smug and shallow boast) that simply "everybody" is "so prosperous" in America. "Every man a king" is not true of America today. Rather, every man is a king except the kings.

The real kings (the cultural elite that would rank first in any traditional hierarchy of the Hellenic-Roman West) are now becoming declassed scapegoats: the eggheads. The fact that they partly brought that fate on themselves by fumbling the Communist issue does not justify their fate, especially as the sacred civil liberties of everybody, the innocent as much as the guilty, must suffer for that retribution.

America is the country where the masses won't admit they are masses. Consequently America is the country where the thought-controllers can self-deceptively "make like" patriotic pillars of respectability instead of admitting what they are: revolutionaries of savage direct democracy (Napoleon plus Rousseau plus Tom Paine plus the Wild West frontier) against the traditional, aristocratic courts and Constitution and against the protection of minority intellectual elites by the anti-majoritarian Bill of Rights. The McCarthyites threaten liberty precisely because they are so egalitarian, ruling foreign policy by mass telegrams to the Executive Branch and by radio speeches and Gallup Poll. The spread of democratic equal rights facilitates, as Nietzsche prophesied, the equal violation of rights.

Is *liberté* incompatible with sudden *égalité?* It was, as people used to say in the Thirties, "no accident that" an American Legion meeting in New York in July, 1954, passed two resolutions side by side—the first condemning another Legion branch for racial discrimination (the "Forty and Eight" society) and the second endorsing McCarthyism. This juxtaposition is noted not in order to disparage the long overdue anti-bigotry of the first resolution. Rather, the juxtaposition is noted in order to caution the oversimplifying optimism of many liberal reformers who have been assuming that the fight for free speech and the fight for racial tolerance were synonymous.

Admittedly not all nationalist bigots have yet "caught on" to the more lucrative new trend of their own racket. Many will continue to persecute racial minorities as viciously as in the past, though surely decreasingly and with less profit. Because of the Southern atmosphere of Washington, the anti-segregation resolution could not be repeated when the Legion met there a month later.

Often untypical or tardy about new trends, the South is more opposed to the good cause of Negro rights and to the bad cause of McCarthyism than the rest of the nation. One Southerner (I am not implying that he represents the majority of the South) told me he regards as Communistic the defenders of the civil liberties of any of our several racial minorities; then he went on to reproach the North for "not fighting for its civil liberties against that fascist McCarthy."

The same day I heard that statement, I read an account of a McCarthy mass meeting in the North at which racial discrimination was denounced as un-American and in which anyone defending civil liberties against McCarthy was called Communistic. At the same meeting, a rabbi accused the opposition to Roy Cohn of anti-Semitic intolerance. Next, Cohn's was called "the American Dreyfus Case" by a representative of a student McCarthyite organization, Students for America. This young representative of both McCarthyism and racial brotherhood concluded amid loud applause: "Roy Cohn and Joe McCarthy will be redeemed when the people have taken back their government from the criminal alliance of Communists, Socialists, New Dealers, and the Eisenhower-Dewey Republicans."

This outburst of direct democracy[1] comes straight from the leftist rhetoric of the old Populists and Progressives, a rhetoric forever urging the People to take back "their" government from the conspiring Powers That Be. What else remained but for Rabbi Schultz, at a second Cohn-McCarthy dinner, to appeal to "the plain people of America" to "march on Washington" in order to save, with direct democracy, their tribune McCarthy from the big bosses of the Senate censure committee?

Bigotry's New Look is perhaps best evidenced by McCarthy's abstention, so far, from anti-Semitic and anti-Negro propaganda and, more important, by countless similar items totally unconnected with the ephemeral McCarthy. A similar juxtaposition occurs in a typical New York *Times* headline of September 4, 1954, page one: PRESIDENT SIGNS BILL TO EXECUTE PEACETIME SPIES; ALSO BOLSTERS BAN ON BIAS. Moving beyond that relatively middle-of-the-road area to the extremist fringe, note the significant change in "For America." This nationalist group is a xenophobic and isolationist revival of the old America First Committee. But instead of appeasing the open Nazis who then still ruled Germany, as in the old-

[1] What do we mean by "direct democracy" as contrasted with "indirect democracy?" Let us re-apply to today the conservative thesis of Madison's tenth *Federalist* paper and of Irving Babbitt's *Democracy and Leadership.*

Direct democracy (our mob tradition of Tom Paine, Jacobinism, and the Midwestern Populist parties) is government by referendum and mass petition, such as the McCarthyite Committee of Ten Million.

Indirect democracy (our semi-aristocratic and Constitutionalist tradition of Madison and the *Federalist*) likewise fulfills the will of the people but by *filtering* it through parliamentary Constitutional channels and traditional ethical restraints.

Both are ultimately majority rule, and ought to be. But direct democracy, being immediate and hotheaded, facilitates revolution, demagogy, and Robespierrian thought control, while indirect democracy, being calmed and canalized, facilitates evolution, a statesmanship of *noblesse oblige,* and civil liberties.

fashioned and blunter days of Father Coughlin, "For America" began greatly expanding its mass base in 1954 by "quietly canvassing Jewish and Negro prospects."

And so it goes. From these multiplying examples we may tentatively generalize: Manifestations of ethnic intolerance today tend to decrease in proportion as ideological intolerance increases. In sharp contrast, both bigotries previously used to increase together.

If sociologists require a new term for this change (as if there were not enough jargon already), then at least let it be a brief, unponderous term. I would suggest the word "transtolerance" for this curious interplay between the new tolerance and the new intolerance. Transtolerance is ready to give all minorities their glorious democratic freedom—provided they accept McCarthyism or some other mob conformism of Right or Left. I add "or Left" because liberals sometimes assume conformism is inevitably of the Right. Yet "Right" and "Left" are mere fluctuating pretexts, mere fluid surfaces for the deeper anti-individualism (anti-aristocracy) of the mass man, who ten years ago was trying to thought-control our premature anti-Communists as "warmongers" and who today damns them as "Reds" and who ten years from now, in a new appeasement of Russia, may again be damning them as "Wall Street warmongers" and "disloyal internationalist bankers."

Transtolerance is the form that xenophobia takes when practiced by a "xeno." Transtolerant McCarthyism is partly a movement of recent immigrants who present themselves (not so much to the world as to themselves) as a two hundred per cent hate-the-foreigner movement. And by extension: Hate "alien" ideas. Transtolerance is also a sublimated Jim Crow: against "wrong" thinkers, not "wrong" races. As such, it is a Jim Crow that can be participated in with a clear conscience by the new, non-segregated flag-waving Negro, who will be increasingly emerging from the increased egalitarian laws in housing and education. In the same way it is the Irishman's version of Mick-baiting and a strictly kosher anti-Semitism. It very sincerely champions against anti-Semites "that American Dreyfus, Roy Cohn"; simultaneously it glows with the same mob emotions that in all previous or comparable movements have been anti-Semitic.

The final surrealist culmination of this new development would be for the Ku Klux Klan to hold non-segregated lynching bees.

At the same moment when America fortunately is nearer racial equality than ever before (an exciting gain, insufficiently noted by American-baiters in Europe and India), America is moving further from liberty of opinion. "Now remember, boys, tolerance and equality," my very progressive schoolma'am in high school used to preach, "come from cooperation in some common task." If Orwell's 1984 should ever come to America, you can guess what "some common task" will turn out to be. Won't it be a "team" (as they will obviously call it) of "buddies" from "all three religions" plus the significantly increasing number of Negro McCarthyites, all "cooperating" in the "common task" of burning books on civil liberties or segregating all individualists of "all three" religions?

It required Robespierre to teach French intellectuals that *égalité* is not synonymous with *liberté*. Similarly, Joseph McCarthy is the educator of the educators; by his threat to our lawful liberties, he is educating American intellectuals out of a kind of liberalism and back to a kind of conservatism. The intellectual liberals who twenty years ago wanted to pack the Supreme Court as frustrating the will of the masses (which is exactly what it ought to frustrate) and who were quoting Charles Beard to show that the Constitution is a mere rationalization of economic loot—those same liberals today are hugging for dear life that same court and that same Constitution, including its Fifth Amendment. They are hugging those two most conservative of "outdated" institutions as their last life preservers against the McCarthyite version of what their Henry Wallaces used to call "the century of the common man."

Our right to civil liberties, our right to an unlimited non-violent dissent, is as ruggedly conservative and traditional as Senator Flanders and the mountains of Vermont. It is a right so aristocratic that it enables one lonely individual, sustained by nine non-elected nobles in black robes, to think differently from 99.9 per cent of the nation, even if a majority of "all races, creeds, and colors," in an honest democratic election, votes to suppress the thinking of that one individual.

But what will happen to that individual and his liberties if ever the 99.9 per cent unite in direct democracy to substitute, as final arbiter of law, the white sheets for the black robes?

II

Asians and Europeans ought never to confuse genuine American anti-Communism, a necessary shield for peace and freedom against aggression, with the pseudo-anti-Communism of the demagogues, which is not anti-Communism at all but a racket. American anti-Communism, in the proper sense of the term, usually turns out to be a surprisingly sober and reasonable movement, fair-minded and sincerely dedicated to civil liberties. Indeed, when you consider the disappointed hopes and the murderous provocations suffered by an unprepared public opinion in the five years between Yalta illusions and Korean causalty lists, there emerges a reality more typical and impressive than the not-to-be-minimized existence of racketeers and thought-controllers; and that impressive reality is the sobriety, the reasonableness of America's genuine anti-Communists, whether Eisenhower, Stevenson or Norman Thomas.

Pro-Communist periodicals in Europe have been linking American anti-Communists and McCarthy, as if there were some necessary connection. The zany rumor that McCarthyism is anti-Communism may be spread by honest ignorance, but it may also be spread maliciously: to give anti-Communism a bad name abroad, to make anti-Communism as intellectually disreputable as it seemed during the Popular Front era. But the fact that pro-Communists find it strategic to link the McCarthy methods with American anti-Communism is no reason for our American anti-Communists to do so, or to allow even the hint of such a linkage to continue.

To move to a different but overlapping problem: There is likewise no reason for philosophical conservatives (disciples of Burke, Coleridge, Tocqueville, Irving Babbitt and the Federalists, rather than of President McKinley or Neville Chamberlain) to condone even the hint of any linkage between our philosophical conservatism and that *rigor mortis* of Manchester liberalism known as the Old Guard of the Republican Party.

I now propose to develop the above two generalizations. First, if McCarthyism does not represent anti-Communism, what does it represent? Second, if the present Republican Party does not merit the support of philosophical (Burkean or Federalist) conservatives, then who does merit that support in 1956?

To a certain extent, the new nationalist toughness ("McCarthyism") is the revenge of those who felt snubbed in 1928, when the man with the brown derby lost the election, and who felt snubbed a second time in 1932, when the nomination went to his victorious rival from Groton and Harvard.

But even more important than that old wound (the Irish Catholic role in McCarthyism being intolerantly overstressed by its liberal foes) is the McCarthy-Dirksen-Bricker coalition of nationalism, Asia Firstism and Europe-Last isolationism; and what is this coalition but a Midwest hick-Protestant revenge against that same "fancy" and condescending east? That revenge is sufficiently emotional to unite a radical wing with a reactionary wing. The revenge-emotion of McCarthyism has united the old Midwest Populist instincts on the down-with-everybody Left (barn-burners from way back and distrusters of Anglicized highbrow city-slickers) with the rich Chicago *Tribune* nationalists on the authoritarian Right. Both these Midwest groups are Protestant, not Catholic. Both are against an east viewed as Europe First and Asia Last—shorthand for an east viewed as aristocratic, internationalist, overeducated, and metaphorically (if rarely literally) Grotonian.

By itself and without allies, the resentment of lower-middle-class Celtic South Boston against Harvard (simultaneous symbol of Reds and Wall Street plutocrats) was relatively powerless. (Note that no serious mass movement like McCarthy's was achieved by the earlier outburst of that resentment in Coughlinism.) It was only when the South Boston resentment coalesced with the resentment of flag-waving Chicago isolationists and newly-rich Protestant Texans (still denied *entrée* into the *chicté* of Wall Street) that the American seaboard aristocracy was seriously threatened in its domination of both governmental and intellectual public opinion and in its domination of its special old-school-tie preserve, the Foreign Service. Against the latter, the old Populist and La Follette weapon against diplomats of "you internationalist Anglophile snob" was replaced by the deadlier weapon of "you egghead security-risk"—meaning, as the case might be, alleged unbeliever and subverter or alleged homosexual or alleged tippler and babbler. All of these allegations have been made for centuries by pseudo-wholesome, "pious" peasants against "effete" noblemen.

What is at stake in this revolt? Liberty or mere economic profit? Probably neither. Nobody in any mass movement on any side in any country is really willing to bear the burden of liberty (which is why liberty is preserved not by mass-will nor by counting noses but by tiny, heroic natural-aristocracies and by the majesty—beyond mob majorities—of moral law). As for economic profit, there is enough of *that* lying around in lavish America to keep both sides happily glutted, in defiance of both Marx and Adam Smith. Instead, the true goal of both sides—the McCarthyite rebels and the seaboard aristocracy —is the psychological satisfaction of determining the future value-pattern of American society.

As a pretext for its drive toward this true goal, the first side uses "anti-Communism." (Falsely so, because nothing would please the Communists more than a victory of the Bricker, McCarthy and Chicago *Tribune* side, thereby isolating America from Western Europe.) As a counter-pretext, the second side uses "civil liberties."

The latter is not solely a pretext but valid enough at the moment, now that this side is seeing its own ox being gored. But ultimately much of its oratory about civil liberties rings as false as that of self-appointed anti-Communism, if only you consider the silence of the second side about "civil liberties" when the gored ox was not their own pet Foreign Service aristocrats and professors but the violated civil liberties of thousands of interned Japanese-Americans during World War II or the Minneapolis Trotskyites jailed under the Smith Act (in both cases under Roosevelt), not to mention the hair-raising precedent of currently denying a passport to the anti-Stalinist Marxist, Max Schachtman. With some honorable exceptions, the internment of friendless Japanese-Americans, of un-"forward-looking" conscientious objectors and of presumably un-chic Trotskyites has evoked fewer decibels of "witch-hunt, witch-hunt!" from fashionable liberals, fewer sonorous quotations of what Jefferson wrote to Madison about free minds, than does the current harassing of a more respectably bourgeois and *salonfähig* ex-Stalinoid from the Institute of Pacific Relations. Thus does snobbism take precedence over ideology in the conformism known as "anti-conformism."

In every American community, picture some eagle scout of "anti-Communism" battling some village Hampden of "civil liberties." What a spectacle! Insincerity or self-deception on both sides.

Which of the two unattractive alternatives can be sufficiently improved and matured to become not merely a lesser evil but a positive good? Since the noble pretexts of both sides ring so hollow, why do I favor (while retaining an independent third position) a victory by the second of these two sides? Not for its *beaux yeux*—not, that is, for its comic snobbism, its mutually contradictory brands of "progressive" political chic, *avant-garde* cultural chic, and Eastern-college, country-club social chic. Even its trump card, namely, the ethical superiority to McCarthyism of its upper-class educated liberals, remains badly compromised by the 1930s—the silence, because of expediency, during the Moscow Trials and the business-baiting McCarthyism-of-the-Left of too many New Deal agitations and investigations. Still, despite everything, the heritage known as "New England" (a moral rather than sectional term and diffused through all sections) does inspiringly combine the two things that mean most to me in determining my choice: respect for the free mind and respect for the moral law.

This combination of moral duty and liberty may by 1956 have a new birth of nationwide appeal, owing to the providential emergence of the leadership of Adlai Stevenson, a blender of New England and Middle West, an intellectual uncompromised by Popular Frontist illusions or by the era of Yalta appeasement.

No "great man" theories, no determinism: Let us take Stevenson merely as symbolizing imperfectly a still potential goal, a new era that may or may not be attained by his very diverse followers. For intellectuals, he symbolizes the mature outgrowing and discarding of what in part was their bad and silly era. A bad era insofar as they sacrificed ethical means to a progress achieved by Machiavellian social engineering. (Defined metaphysically, the ethical double standard of many toward Russia was a logical consequence of the initial false step of seeking a short-cut to material progress outside the moral framework.) A silly era insofar as they alternated this expediency with the opposite extreme, that of idealistic *a priori* blueprints and abstractions; these lack the concrete context of any mature, organically evolved idealism. An oscillation between these extremes was likewise characteristic of the eighteenth-century liberal intellectuals, oscillating between impractical utopian yearnings and an all-too-practical softness (double standard) toward Jacobin social engineering.

Here is one extremely small but revealing example of the new, maturer kind of intellectual leadership: Stevenson did not have his name listed to endorse the *Nation* magazine (that Last Mohican from the liberal illusions of the 1930s), even though such routine endorsements in past years came automatically from the highest liberal intellectuals and New Dealers. Today, most liberal intellectuals have learned to distinguish between the "liberalism" of certain double-standard *Nation* experts (even while rightly defending their free speech against McCarthyism or thought control) and the valid liberalism of, say, the *New Republic, The Progressive,* or the *Reporter*. Five years ago, when I began writing the chapter about the *Nation* in *Shame and Glory of the Intellectuals*, that ethical distinction was still unclear to most liberal intellectuals. How much saner America would be today if those businessmen who would like to be "conservatives" had some Republican version of Mr. Stevenson to teach them the comparable quality of distinguishing between endorsing genuine anti-Communism and endorsing the "anti-Communism" of the McCarthys, Jenners and Dirksens!

What businessman today—whether in the New York-Detroit axis or even in Chicago *Tribune*land—sees anything radical or even liberal about the SEC or insurance of bank deposits? These and other New Deal cushionings of capitalism have become so traditional, so built-in a part of our eastern business communities that their old feud with the New Deal becomes a fading anachronism, a feud dangerous only if it still hampers their support of Eisenhower's "New Deal Republicans" against the isolationist nationalist Republicans.

Though the partly unintentional effect of such New Deal reforms has been conservative, this does not mean we can go to the opposite extreme and call the New Deal as a whole conservative. In contrast with its Communism-preventing social reforms, its *procedures* of agitational direct democracy were occasionally as radical as the business world alleged them to be, by-passing the Supreme Court, the Constitution, and the rest of our indirect democracy. Further, the Popular Front attitude of expediency toward the sheer evil of Communism, though it mesmerized New Deal talkers in New York more than actual New Deal doers in Washington, was as radical an anti-ethics on the Left as is—on the Right—the similar anti-ethics of a Popular Front with McCarthyism.

It is the bad and silly aspects of the New Deal, the procedural and unethical aspects, which have been rightly outgrown in new leaders like Stevenson, who rightly retain the valuable humane and conservative aspects. This refreshing development, by which—unlike its nationalist Republican foes—a fallible movement outgrows its own errors, is the decisive argument for supporting Stevenson and the Democrats in the

Presidential election of 1956. The same support was actually earned by them already in 1952, but less obviously then, owing to the then legitimate hope that Eisenhower could help the Republicans to similarly outgrow their errors.

Despite the magnificent personal intentions of our decent and kindly President, the present Republican Administration —when considered as a whole, Knowland, Nixon and all—has obviously failed to evoke a world-minded, responsible American conservatism. Instead, the Republican leadership has left to others (like the bipartisan Watkins Committee) its own plain duty of restraining its wild men of the Right, whose activity was defined by the ever perceptive Will Herberg (*New Leader*, January 18, 1954) as "government by rabble-rousing, the very opposite of a new conservatism." Such revolutionary agitators would never be tolerated in the more truly conservative party of Eden, Butler and Churchill.

A conservative kind of government would bring the following qualities: a return to established ways, relaxation of tension and calm confidence, reverence for the Constitution and every single one of its time-hallowed amendments and liberties, orderly gradualism, protection of the Executive Branch from outside mob pressure. The conservative kind of government would bring an increased respect—even to the point of pompous stuffiness—for time-honored authority and for venerable dignitaries. Specifically, that would mean an increased respect for such dignitaries as Justices of the Supreme Court, famous generals decorated for heroism or with a Nobel Prize for statesmanship, past Presidents (because of the impersonal dignity of that office and because of the traditionalist's need of historical continuity), and any present President and his top appointments, especially in such a snobbishly aristocratic preserve as the Foreign Service. The above qualities are the stodgier virtues. They are not invariably a good thing, nor is conservatism in every context a good thing. All I am saying is that these happen to be the qualities of conservative rule, and the Republican Administration has not brought us a single one of them.

The Democrats were voted out of office partly because the

country was fed up (and rightly so) with certain of the more radical notions and agitations of the New Deal 1930s. Yet, it now appears, by contrast, that those now-nostalgic "twenty years of treason" gave America a bit more of old-fashioned conservative virtues than the present self-styled anti-soapboxing of Republican soapboxers.

Unless one of two unexpected events occurs, the Republican Party has forfeited its claim to retain in 1956 those decisive votes of non-partisan independents which gave it victory in 1952. The unexpected events are either a far firmer assertion of presidential leadership over the anti-Eisenhower barn-burners and wild men in the Senate, or else their secession into a radical third party. If either of these blessings occurs, there will again be good reason for independents to vote for Eisenhower: on moral grounds if he asserts his leadership, on strategic grounds if there is a McCarthy third party. The latter would save the Republicans in the same unexpected way that the secession of pro-Communists into the Progressive Party saved Truman in 1948.

If neither of these unlikely blessings occurs for the Republicans, then the last remaining obstacle has been cleared away for all thoughtful conservatives and independents, as well as liberals and Democrats, to support Adlai Stevenson for President in 1956. Though neither giddy optimism nor personal hero-worship is in order, at least there is a good chance —in proportion to our own efforts to make it a good chance— that a Stevenson party, outgrowing the bad and the silly aspects of the 1930s will lead America beyond the two false alternatives of Babbitt Senior Republicans and Babbitt Junior liberals. Ahead potentially lies an American synthesis of Mill with Burke, of liberal free dissent with conservative roots in historical continuity.

Of two American alternatives with bad records, the slanderous wild nationalists and the sometimes double-standard civil-libertarians, only the second alternative is capable of outgrowing a bad and silly past. The 1956 elections can bring it a better and wiser future under the better and wiser intellectualism of Stevenson. Here ends a cycle once partly symbol-

ized by Alger Hiss ("a generation on trial"). Here, symbolized by Adlai Stevenson, begins potentially a new cycle of
the glory, not the shame, of the eggheads.

III

In view of America's present mood of prosperous moderation, the McCarthy revolution and all other extremes of right
and left will almost certainly lose. All that might rescue them
is the emotionalism that would accompany a lost or costly war
in China. But, luckily, the stakes are neither that high nor
that desperate. America is no Weimar Republic, and Mc-
Carthyism tends to be more a racket than a conspiracy, more
a cruel publicity hoax (played on Fort Monmouth, the Voice
of America, the State Department) than a serious "fascist"
or war party. Despite demagogic speeches ("speak loudly and
carry a small stick"), the nationalist wing of the Republicans
cares no more about really blockading and fighting the Red
Chinese despotism than Hamlet's vehement player cared about
Hecuba. Our indispensable European allies need not fear that
Americans, even our nationalist wild men, will become pre-
ventive-warriors or trigger-happy. The struggle to be the new
American ruling (taste-determining) class is a domestic struggle, in which foreign policy and Our Boys in China merely
furnish heartless slogans to embarrass the older ruling class.

In this struggle, two points emerge about diction: First,
"nationalism" is less often a synonym of "national interest"
than an antonym; second, no alchemy has yet been invented by
which a loud repetition of the word "anti-Communism" transforms a Yahoo into a Houyhnhnm.

That the McCarthy movement normally accuses only non-
Communists of "Communism" is one of the main rules of
the game. Why? Not because the Communist menace to
America has decreased (it has increased since Malenkov),
but because McCarthy is not after the scalps of Communists
in the first place but after the scalps of all those traditionalists who, like Senators Watkins and Flanders, favor government by law. And the reason why emotional McCarthyism,

more by instinct than design, simply *must* be against traditionalists, conservatives and government-by-law is explained by its
unadmitted but basic revolutionary nature. It is a radical
movement trying to overthrow an old ruling class and replace
it from below by a new ruling class.

I use "ruling class" not in the rigid Marxist sense but to
mean the determiners of culture patterns, taste patterns, value
patterns. For in America classes are fluid, unhereditary,
and more psychological than economic. As suggested earlier,
our old ruling class includes eastern, educated, mellowed
wealth—internationalist and at least superficially liberalized,
like the Achesons of Wall Street or the Paul Hoffmans of the
easternized fraction of Detroit industrialists. The new would-
be rulers include unmellowed plebeian western wealth (Chicago, Texas, much of Detroit) and their enormous, gullible
mass-base: the nationalist alliance between the sticks and the
slums, between the hick-Protestant mentalities in the west
(Populist-Progressive on the Left, Know-Nothing on the
Right) and the South Boston mentalities in the east. The latter
are, metaphorically, an unexplored underground catacomb,
long smoldering against the airy, oblivious palaces of both
portions (liberal and Wall Street) of the eastern upper world.

Nobody except McCarthy personally can bridge this incongruous alliance of sticks and slums, and likewise span both
sides of their respective religions. Too many commentators
assume that the censured McCarthy, being increasingly discredited, will now be replaced by a smoother operator, by a
more reliably Republican type like Nixon. To be sure, an Arrow collar ad like Nixon, eager-eyed, clean-shaven and grin-
ning boyishly while he assesses the precise spot for the stiletto,
is socially more acceptable in the station-wagons of all kinds
of junior executives on the make. However, even though the
Vice President's tamer version of the McCarthy drama would
flutter more lorgnettes in respectable suburbia, that gain
would be counterbalanced by the loss of the still more numerous South Boston mentalities. The latter would thereupon
revert to the Democratic party, from which only a "prole-

tarian," non-Protestant McCarthy, never a bourgeois Rotarian Nixon, can lure them.

A fact insufficiently stressed is that McCarthy himself was originally a member of the Wisconsin "Democrat Party." The otherwise similar Senator Pat McCarran preferred to remain, at least nominally, a Democrat to the end. Here, clearly, is a function of voter-wooing—namely, wooing to Republicanism the slummier part of the thought-control bloc—which only a McCarthy and not even the most "glamorous" Nixon or Dirksen can perform for the wealthy, suburban, Republican anti-civil-libertarians. I would, therefore, disagree with Adlai Stevenson when he equates Nixon's appeal with McCarthy's.

No one but McCarthy can combine these incompatibles of Catholic slums and Protestant sticks into one movement, not to mention scooping up *en passant* the scattered lunatic fringes that emerged from anti-anti-Fascist isolationism during World War II. Therefore, it is premature to write McCarthy off as finished. What will indeed destroy him in the long run is the fact that his organizing ability does not keep pace with his publicizing ability, and that the left (New Deal) and right (Wall Street) wings of the old aristocracy can today partly team up whenever they need to protect their common interests. The wealthy Wall Street lawyer Acheson symbolized this team-up under Truman and was hated for it; his aristocratic, old-school-tie, Anglicized mannerisms were a Red flag to the McCarthyite plebeian revolution.

The New Deal and Wall Street battled in the 1930s when their imagined interests seemed irreconcilable. (I say "imagined" and "seemed" because it was hardly a threat to Wall Street when the New Deal reforms immunized workers against that lure of Communism to which French workers succumbed.) But the common Anglophilism of the internationalist, educated eastern seaboard united them (fortunately for the cause of liberty) on the interventionist, anti-Nazi side during World War II. And, by today, the New Deal reforms have become so deeply rooted and traditional a part of the *status quo*, so conservative in a relative (though not absolute) sense, that the new plebeian money from the Midwest can no longer count on a split between social chic (eastern money in New Canaan and Long Island) and progressive chic (clichés of "forward"-looking uplift). Whether under Eisenhower Republicans or Stevenson Democrats, there will be no such split. And, unless there is a lost war, this partial unity between the financial and the liberal wings of aristocracy will fortunately smash the McCarthyite plebeian insurrection of "direct democracy" (government by mass meetings and telegrams).

The partial *rapprochement* between Wall Street and a now middle-aged New Deal is evidenced by the many recent books by veteran New Dealers on the advantages of enlightened "bigness" in business—books, for example, by David Lilienthal, J. K. Galbraith and Adolf Berle. These three valuable writers I profoundly admire on most points, but I disagree on the following rhetorical question: While fully recognizing the harmful snob-motives of the medieval feudal mind, was there not, nevertheless, some sound moral core within its "reactionary" distrust of the cash-nexus bourgeois?

Are liberal intellectuals, in a mirror-image of their former Left Bank stance, now suddenly to become joiners, good sports, success-worshipers, members of The Team? Will it next be a triumph of their adaptability to suffer in silence, without the old "holy indignation," the spectacle of a Republican auto dealer patronizing a great scientist as if he were his clerk instead of approaching him cap in hand? In that case, who on earth, if *not* the intellectuals, will resist the periodic stampedes to entrust American culture to the manipulators of gadgets? This resistance to stampedes ought to express not the conformism of "non-conformism," flaunted to pose as a devil of a fellow, but the sensitivity of a deeper and finer grain, an ear conforming not to bandwagon-tunes but to the finer, older, deeper rhythms of American culture.

A few years ago, liberal intellectuals were reproaching me for refusing to bait Big Business—and today (in several cases) for refusing to equate it with Santa Claus. Why do either? Business-baiting was and is a cheap bohemian flourish, a wearing of one's soulfulness on one's sleeve, and no substitute for seriously analyzing the real problem: namely, the compulsion of modern technics (whether under capitalist bigness or a socialist bigness) to put know-how before know-why.

When the alternative is the neo-Populist barn-burners from Wisconsin and Texas, naturally I ardently prefer Big Business, especially a *noblesse*-obligated and New Dealized Big Business. For its vanity (desire to seem sophisticated) makes a point of allowing a lot more elbowroom to the free mind. But what a choice! All America's great creative spirits of the past, like Melville (who spoke of "the impieties of Progress") and conservative Henry Adams, would turn in their graves, as indignantly as would liberal Abraham Lincoln, at even the hint that no noble third alternative remained for a nation boasting of itself as the freest on earth.

Insofar as they refute the old Stalinist lie about America's imaginary mass poverty and the imaginary prosperity of the Soviet slave kennels, let us welcome the belated liberal conversions to anti-business-baiting. But what when they go to the other extreme of white-washing almost everything, from the old robber barons to the new "bigness?" What when the paeans to economic prosperity ignore the psychological starvation, the cultural starvation, the mechanized mediocrity of too-efficient bigness? At that point, the value-conserver must protest: Judge our American elephantiasis of know-how not solely in contrast with the unspeakably low values of Soviet Communism but also in contrast with our own high anti-commercial traditions of Hawthorne, Melville and Thoreau, all of whom knew well enough that the railroad rides upon us, not we on the railroad.

Where the Communist police state is the alternative, let us continue to emphasize that American Big Business is an incomparably lesser evil. But beyond that special situation no further concessions, least of all unnecessary ones. Let us frankly embrace as enjoyable conveniences the leisure and services resulting from IBM efficiency. But must the embrace be corybantic? Shall intellectuals positively wallow in abdicating before a bigness which admittedly gives Americans economic prosperity and, at present, a relative political freedom but which robotizes them into a tractable, pap-fed, Reader's-Digested and manipulated mass-culture?

Too utilitarian for a sense of tragic reverence or a sense of humor, and prone (behind "daring" progressive clichés) to an almost infinite smugness, one kind of bourgeois liberal is forever making quite unnecessary sacrifices of principle to expediency—first to the fellow-traveling Popular Front line in the 1930s, now to the opposite line in the 1950s. But there comes a time when lasting values are conserved not by matey back-slapping but by wayward walks in the drizzle, not by seemingly practical adjustments but by the ornery Unadjusted Man.

8

THE PHILOSOPHICAL
"NEW CONSERVATISM" (1962)

Peter Viereck

The author's preceding chapter of 1955, in the symposium book *The New American Right*, treats this new right as mainly the right-wing radicals of McCarthyism and of Midwest neo-populist Republicanism. Hence, the 1955 chapter fails to deal with something far more serious intellectually—the non-Mc-Carthyite, non-thought-controlling movement known as "the new conservatism." The latter movement, being non-popular and being burdened with partly merited philosophical pretensions, is restricted mainly to the campuses and the magazine world, even though it sometimes lends ghost-writers and an egghead façade to the popular political arena outside.

The extreme McCarthy emphasis of the 1955 chapter was justified in the exceptional context of the early 1950s. It is perhaps no longer justified in the context of this 1962 edition. As for over-publicized groups like the John Birch Society, fortunately they have no chance of attaining anything like the mass base attained by McCarthy, Coughlin, or Huey Long. This is because they lack the demagogic populist or pseudo-socialist economic platform without which chauvinist thought-control movements have no chance of success. Note that Hitler called himself not merely a nationalist but a National Socialist. Note that Huey Long ("every man a king"), Coughlin ("free silver"), and McCarthy ("socialistic" farm subsidies) had a similar rightist-leftist amalgam rather than a purely rightist or nationalist platform.

Though the pseudo-conservatism of Long-Coughlin-Mc-

Carthy seems dead for the time being, and though that of the John Birchers seems stillborn, the philosophical "new conservatism" is still—on its admittedly smaller scale—alive. Alive whether for better or worse, its merits and defects being approximately equal. Since the present author furnished the first postwar book of the new conservatism—*Conservatism Revisited: The Revolt Against Revolt* (1949, reprinted by Collier Books, 1962)—he bears a certain responsibility: again, "whether for better or worse." Hence, since the new conservatism is still alive and since it was not included in the preceding chapter of 1955, the following supplementary chapter seems in order.

I

In the 1930s, when the present author, still a student, was writing an article for the *Atlantic Monthly* urging "a Burkean new conservatism in America," and to some extent even as late as his *Conservatism Revisited* of 1949, "conservatism" was an unpopular epithet. In retrospect it becomes almost attractively amusing (like contemplating a dated period piece) to recall how violently one was denounced in those days for suggesting that Burke, Calhoun, and Irving Babbitt were not "Fascist beasts" and that our relatively conservative Constitution was not really a plot-in-advance, by rich bogeymen like George Washington and the Federalist Party. For example, the author's *Atlantic* article, written in prewar student days, was denounced more because the word used ("conservative") was so heretical than because of any effort by the Popular Frontist denouncers to read what was actually said. It was the first-written and worst-written appeal ever published in America for what it called a "new" conservatism ("new" meaning non-Republican, non-commercialist, non-conformist). This new conservatism it viewed as synthesizing in some future day the ethical New Deal social reforms with the more pessimistic, anti-mass insights of America's Burkean founders. Such a synthesis, argued the article, would help make the valuable anti-Fascist movement among literary intellectuals simultaneously anti-Communist also, leaving behind the Popular Frontist illusions of the 1930s.

As the liberal Robert Bendiner then put it, "Out of some 140,000,000 people in the United States, at least 139,500,000 are liberals, to hear them tell it. . . . Rare is the citizen who can bring himself to say, 'Sure I'm a conservative.' . . . Any American would sooner drop dead than proclaim himself a reactionary." In July, 1950, a newspaper was listing the charges against a prisoner accused of creating a public disturbance. One witness charged, "He was using abusive and obscene language, calling people conservatives and all that."

When conservatism was still a dirty word, it seemed gallantly non-conformist to defend it against the big, smug liberal majority among one's fellow writers and professors. In those days, therefore, the author deemed it more helpful to stress the virtues of conservative thought than its faults, and this is what he did in the 1949 edition of *Conservatism Revisited*. But in the mood emerging from the 1950s, blunt speaking about conservatism's important defects no longer runs the danger of obscuring its still more important virtues.

The main defect of the new conservatism, threatening to make it a transient fad irrelevant to real needs, is its rootless nostalgia for roots. Conservatives of living roots were Washington and Coleridge in their particular America and England, Metternich in his special Austria, Donoso Cortés in his Spain, Calhoun in his antebellum South, Adenauer and Churchill in the 1950s. American conservative writings of living roots were the *Federalist* of Hamilton, Madison, Jay, 1787–88; the *Defense of the Constitutions* of John Adams, 1787–88; the *Letters of Publicola* of John Quincy Adams, 1791; Calhoun's *Disquisition* and *Discourse*, posthumously published in 1850; Irving Babbitt's *Democracy and Leadership*, 1924. In contrast, today's conservatism of yearning is based on roots either never existent or no longer existent. Such a conservatism of nostalgia can still be of high literary value. It is also valuable as an unusually detached perspective about current social foibles. But it does real harm when it leaves literature and enters short-run politics, conjuring up mirages to conceal sordid realities or to distract from them.

In America, southern agrarianism has long been the most gifted literary form of the conservatism of yearning. Its most important intellectual manifesto was the Southern symposium *I'll Take My Stand* (1930), contrasting the cultivated human values of a lost aristocratic agrarianism with Northern commercialism and liberal materialism. At their best, these and more recent examples of the conservatism of yearning are needed warnings against shallow practicality. The fact that such warnings often come from the losing side of our Civil War is in itself a merit; thereby they caution a nation of success-worshippers against the price of success. But at their worst such books of the 1930s, and again of today, lack the living roots of genuine conservatism and have only lifeless ones. The lifeless ones are really a synthetic substitute for roots, contrived by romantic nostalgia. They are a test-tube conservatism, a lab job of powdered Burke or cake-mix Calhoun.

Such romanticizing conservatives refuse to face up to the old and solid historical roots of most or much American liberalism. What is really rootless and abstract is not the increasingly conservatized New Deal liberalism but their own utopian dream of an aristocratic agrarian restoration. Their unhistorical appeal to history, their traditionless worship of tradition, characterize the conservatism of writers like Russell Kirk.

In contrast, a genuinely rooted, history minded conservative conserves the roots that are *really there*, exactly as Burke did when he conserved not only the monarchist-conservative aspects of William III's bloodless revolution of 1688 but also its constitutional-liberal aspects. The latter aspects, formulated by the British philosopher John Locke, have been summarized in England and America ever since by the word "Lockean."

Via the Constitutional Convention of 1787, this liberal-conservative heritage of 1688 became rooted in America as a blend of Locke's very moderate liberalism and Burke's very moderate conservatism. From the rival Federalists and Jeffersonians through today, all our major rival parties have continued this blend, though with varied proportion and stress. American history is based on the resemblance between moderate liberalism and moderate conservatism; the history of Continental Europe is based on the difference between extreme liberalism and extreme conservatism.

But some American new conservatives import from Continental Europe a conservatism that totally rejects even our moderate native liberalism. In the name of free speech and intellectual gadflyism, they are justified in expounding the indiscriminate anti-liberalism of hothouse Bourbons and czarist serf-floggers. But they are not justified in calling themselves American traditionalists or in claiming any except exotic roots for their position in America. Let them present their case frankly as anti-traditional, rootless revolutionaries of Europe's authoritarian right wing, attacking the deep-rooted American tradition of liberal-conservative synthesis. Conservative authority, yes; right-wing authoritarianism, no. Authority means a necessary reverence for tradition, law, legitimism; authoritarianism means statist coercion based only on force, not moral roots, and suppressing individual liberties in the Continental fashion of czardom, Junkerdom, Maistrean ultra-royalism.

Our argument is not against importing European insights when applicable; that would be Know-Nothing chauvinism. The more foreign imports the better, when capable of being assimilated: for example, the techniques of French symbolism in studying American poetry or the status-resentment theory of Nietzsche in studying the new American right. But when the European view or institution is neither applicable to the American reality nor capable of being assimilated therein, as is the case with the sweeping Maistre-style anti-liberalism and tyrannic authoritarianism of many of the new conservatives, then objections do become valid, not on grounds of bigoted American chauvinism but on grounds of distinguishing between what can, what cannot, be transplanted viably and freedom-enhancingly.

The Burkean builds on the concrete existing historical base, not on a vacuum of abstract wishful thinking. When, as in America, that concrete base includes British liberalism of the 1680s and New Deal reforms of the 1930s, then the real American conserver assimilates into conservatism whatever he finds lasting and good in liberalism and in the New Deal. Thereby he is closer to the Tory Cardinal Newman than many of Newman's American reactionary admirers. The latter overlook Newman's realization of the need to "inherit and make the best of" liberalism in certain contexts:

> If I might presume to contrast Lacordaire and myself, I should say that we had been both of us inconsistent;— he, a Catholic, in calling himself a Liberal; I, a Protestant, in being an Anti-liberal; and moreover, that the cause of this inconsistency had been in both cases one and the same. That is, we were both of us such good conservatives as to take up with what we happened to find established in our respective countries, at the time when we came into active life. Toryism was the creed of Oxford; he inherited, and made the best of, the French Revolution.[1]

How can thoughtful new conservatives, avoiding the political pitfalls that so many have failed to avoid, apply fruitfully to American life today what we have called non-political "cultural conservatism"—the tradition of Melville, Hawthorne, Thoreau, Henry Adams, Irving Babbitt, William Faulkner? In order to conserve our classical humanistic values against what he called "the impieties of progress," Melville had issued the following four-line warning to both kinds of American materialists: (1) the deracinating, technology-brandishing industrialists; their so-called freedom and progress is merely the economic "individualism" of Manchester-liberal pseudo-conservatism; and (2) the leftist collectivists; their unity is not a rooted organic growth of shared values[2]

---

[1] From the appendix of the second edition (London, 1865) of Newman's *Apologia Pro Vita Sua*.
[2] Here to be defined as "archetypes."

but a mechanical artifact of apriorist blueprint abstractions,[8] imposed gashingly upon concrete society by a procrustean statist bureaucracy. The last-named distinction—between a unity that is grown and a unity that is made—differentiates the anti-cash-nexus and anti-rugged-individualism of "Tory Socialists" (in the aristocratic Shaftesbury-Disraeli-F.D.R.-Stevenson tradition) from the anti-capitalism of Marxist Socialists or left-liberal materialists. Here, then, is Melville's little-known warning to both bourgeois and Marxist materalists:

> Not magnitude, not lavishness,
> But Form—the site;
> Not innovating wilfulness,
> But reverence for the Archetype.

A scrutiny of the plain facts of the situation has forced our report on the new conservatives to be mainly negative. But a positive contribution is indeed being made by all those thinkers, novelists, and poets in the spirit of this Melville quotation today (whether or not they realize their own conservatism) who are making Americans aware of the tragic antithesis between archetypes and stereotypes in life and between art and technique in literature. Let us clarify this closely related pair of antitheses and then briefly apply them to that technological brilliance which is corrupting our life and literature today. Only by this unpopular and needed task, closer in spirit to the creative imagination of a Faulkner or an Emily Dickinson than to the popular bandwagons of politics, can the new conservatism still overcome its current degeneration into either (at best) Manchester-liberal economic materialism or (at worst) right-wing nationalist thought control. And only via this task can America itself humanize and canalize its technological prowess creatively, instead of being dehumanized and mechanized by it in the sense of Thoreau's "We do not ride on the railroad; it rides upon us."

Every outlook has its own characteristic issue of moral

---

[8] Here to be defined as "stereotypes."

choice. For thoughtful conservatives today, the meaningful moral choice is not between conforming and nonconforming but between conforming to the ephemeral, stereotyped values of the moment and conforming to the ancient, lasting archetypal values shared by all creative cultures.

Archetypes have grown out of the soil of history—slowly, painfully, organically. Stereotypes have been manufactured out of the mechanical processes of mass production—quickly, painlessly, artifically. They have been synthesized in the labs of the entertainment industries and in the blueprints of the social engineers. The philistine conformist and the ostentatious professional nonconformist are alike in being rooted in nothing deeper than the thin topsoil of stereotypes, the stereotypes of Babbitt Senior and Babbitt Junior respectively.

The sudden uprooting of archetypes was the most important consequence of the worldwide industrial revolution. This moral wound, this cultural shock was even more important than the economic consequences of the industrial revolution. Liberty depends on a substratum of fixed archetypes, as opposed to the arbitrary shuffling about of laws and institutions. The distinction holds true whether the shuffling about be done by the apriorist abstract rationalism of the eighteenth century or by the even more inhuman and metallic mass production of the nineteenth century, producing new traumas and new uprootings every time some new mechanized stereotype replaces the preceding one. The contrast between institutions grown organically and those shuffled out of arbitrary rationalist liberalism was summed up by a British librarian on being asked for the French constitution: "Sorry, sir, but we don't keep periodicals."

Every stereotyped society swallows up the diversities of private bailiwicks, private eccentricities, private inner life, and the creativity inherent in concrete personal loyalties and in loving attachments to unique local roots and their rich historical accretions. Apropos the creative potential of local roots, let us recall not only Burke's words on the need for loyalty to one's own "little platoon" but also Synge's words, in the Ireland of 1907, on "the springtime of the local life," where the imagination of man is still "fiery and magnificent and tender." The creative imagination of the free artist and free scientist requires private elbowroom, free from the pressure of centralization and the pressure of adjustment to a mass average. This requirement holds true even when the centralization is benevolent and even when the mass average replaces sub-average diversities. Intolerable is the very concept of some busybody benevolence, whether economic, moral, or psychiatric, "curing" all diversity by making it average.

Admittedly certain kinds of diversity are perfectly dreadful; they threaten everything superior and desirable. But at some point the cure to these threats will endanger the superior and the desirable even more than do the threats themselves. The most vicious maladjustments, economic, moral, or psychiatric, will at some point become less dangerous to the free mind than the overadjustment—the stereotyping—needed to cure them.

In the novel and in the poem, the most corrupting stereotype of all is the substitution of good technique for art. What once resulted from the inspired audacity of a heartbreakingly lonely craftsman is now mass-produced in painless, safe, and uninspired capsules. This process is taking over every category of education and literature. The stream of consciousness for which James Joyce wrestled in loneliness with language; the ironic perspective toward society that Proust attained not as entertainment but as tragedy; the quick, slashing insights for which a Virginia Woolf bled out her heart, all these intimate personal achievements of the unstandardized private life are today the standard props of a hundred hack imitators, mechanically vending what is called "the *New Yorker*-type story." Don't underestimate that type of story; though an imitation job, it is imitation with all the magnificent technical skill of America's best-edited weekly. And think of the advantages: no pain any more, no risk any more, no more nonsense of inspiration. Most modern readers are not even bothered by the difference between such an efficient but bloodless machine job and the living product of individual heart's anguish.

What, then, is the test for telling the coffee from the Nes-café—the true artistic inspiration from the jar of Instant Muse?

The test is pain. Not mere physical pain but the exultant, transcending pain of selfless sacrifice. The test is that holy pain, that brotherhood of sacrifice, that aristocracy of crea-tive suffering of which Baudelaire wrote, *"Je sais que la douleur est l'unique noblesse."* In other words, in a free democracy the only justified aristocracy is that of the lonely creative bitterness, the artistically creative scars of the fight for the inner imagination against outer mechanization—the fight for the private life.

II

Nationalist demagogy, whether McCarthy style or John Birch style, would never have become such a nuisance if lib-eral intellectuals and New Dealers had earlier made them-selves the controlling spearhead of American anti-Commu-nism with the same fervor they showed when spearheading anti-fascism. Only because they defaulted that duty of equal leadership against both kinds of tyranny, only because of the vacuum of leadership created by that default, were the bullies and charlatans enabled partly to fill the vacuum and partly to exploit the cause of anti-Communism. Such had been the thesis of my book *Shame and Glory of the Intellectuals*—a thesis entirely valid for the postwar Yalta era of illusions about Communism among the Henry Wallace kind of liberal and New Dealer.

Today that era is long over. It is ironic that Johnny-come-lately anti-Communists like McCarthy and the Birchers did not attack New Dealers until after the latter had got over the pro-Communist illusions that some of them undoubtedly and disastrously had. Today it is no longer in the interest of our two political camps to go on forever with such recriminations of the past. What is to the co-operative interest of both parties is to make sure that both are not replaced (after an intervening Kennedy era) by the "rejoicing third"—some new movement of nationalist demogogy. Conservatives have no more excuse to refuse to co-operate with liberals and New Dealers against right-wing nationalist threats to our shared liberties than to refuse to co-operate against comparable left-wing threats.

Fortunately, many Burkean new conservatives—Raymond English, Chad Walsh, Thomas Cook, Clinton Rossiter, J. A. Lukacs, August Heckscher, Will Herberg, Reinhold Niebuhr, and other distinguished names—have always been active and effective foes of the thought-control nationalists. Every one of these names achieved a record of all-out, explicit anti-McCarthyism in the days when that demagogue still seemed a danger and when it still took courage, not opportunism, to attack him. The same cannot be said of other, often better-known "new conservatives." They failed the acid test of the McCarthy temptation of the 1950s in the same way that the fellow-traveler kind of liberal failed the acid test of the Communist temptation of the 1930s. Both temptations were not only ethical tests of integrity but also psychological tests of balance and aesthetic tests of good taste.

Apropos such tests, Clinton Rossiter concludes, in his book *Conservatism in America*, "Unfortunately for the cause of conservatism, Kirk has now begun to sound like a man born one hundred and fifty years too late and in the wrong country." But it is pleasanter to see the positive, not only the negative, in a fellow-writer one esteems. Let us partly overlook Kirk's silence about the McCarthy thought-control menace in Chicago. Let us partly overlook his lack of silence in supporting as so-called "conservatives" the Goldwater Manchester liberals of old-guard Republicanism (as if historic Anglo-American conservatism, with its Disraeli-Churchill-Hughes-Roosevelt tradition of humane social reform, could ever be equated with the robber-baron kind of *laisser-faire* capitalism). Fortunately, Kirk's positive contribution sometimes almost balances such embarrassing ventures into practical national politics. His positive contribution consists of his sensitive, perceptive rediscovery of literary and philosophical figures like Irving Babbitt and George Santayana for a true humanistic conservatism today.

Even at its best, even when avoiding the traps of right-wing radicalism, the new conservatism is partly guilty of causing the emotional deep-freeze that today makes young people ashamed of generous social impulses. New conservatives point out correctly that in the 1930s many intellectuals wasted generous emotions on unworthy causes, on Communist totalitarianism masked as liberalism. True enough—indeed, a point many of us, as "premature" anti-Communists, were making already in those days. But it does not follow, from recognizing the wrong generosities of the past, that we should today have no generous emotions at all, not even for many obviously worthy causes all around us, such as desegregation. Not only liberals but conservatives like Burke (reread his speeches against the slave trade) and John Adams and John Quincy Adams (among America's first fighters for Negro rights) have fought racism as contradicting our traditional Christian view of man.

The cost of being a genuine Burke-Adams conservative today is that you will be misrepresented in two opposite ways— as being really liberals at heart, hypocritically pretending to be conservatives; as being authoritarian reactionaries at heart, hypocritically pretending to be devoted to civil liberties. So far as the first misrepresentation goes: devotion to civil liberties is not a monopoly of liberals. It is found in liberals and Burkean conservatives alike, as shown in the exchange of letters in their old age between the liberal Thomas Jefferson and his good friend, the conservative John Adams. So far as the second misrepresentation goes: the test of whether a new conservative is sincere about civil liberties or merely a rightest authoritarian is the same as the test of whether any given liberal of the 1930s was sincere about civil liberties or merely a leftist authoritarian. That test (which Senator Goldwater fails) is twofold, involving one question about practice, one question about theory. In practice, does the given conservative or liberal show his devotion to civil liberties in deeds as well as words? In theory, does he show awareness of a law we may here define as the law of compensatory balance? The law of compensatory balance makes the exposure of Communist fellow-traveling the particular duty of liberals, the exposure of right-wing thought-controllers the particular duty of conservatives.

Here are some further implications of the law of compensatory balance. A traditional monarchy is freest, as in Scandinavia, when anticipating social democracy in humane reforms; an untraditional, centralized mass democracy is freest when encouraging, even to the point of tolerating eccentricity and arrogance, the remnants it possesses of aristocracy, family and regional pride, and decentralized provincial divergencies, traditions, privileges. A conservative is most valuable when serving in the more liberal party, a liberal when serving in the more conservative party. Thus the conservative Burke belonged not to the Tory but the Whig Party. Similarly Madison, whose tenth *Federalist* paper helped found and formulate our conservative Constitutionalist tradition of distrusting direct democracy and majority dictatorship, joined the liberal Jeffersonian party, not the Federalist Party. Reinhold Niebuhr, conservative in his view of history and anti-modernist, anti-liberal in theology, is not a Republican but a New Dealer in political-party activities.

III

Our distinction between rooted conservatives and rootless, counterrevolutionary doctrinaires is the measure of the difference between two different groups in contemporary America: the humanistic value-conservers and the materialistic old-guard Republicans. The latter are what a wrong and temporary journalistic usage often calls "conservative." It is more accurate to call them nineteenth-century Manchester liberals with roots no deeper than the relatively recent post-Civil War "gilded age." Already on May 28, 1903, Winston Churchill denied them and their British counterparts the name of conservatives when he declared in Parliament:

The new fiscal policy [of high tariffs] means a change,
not only in the historic English parties but in the conditions of our public life. The old Conservative Party with
its religious convictions and constitutional principles will
disappear and a new party will arise . . . like perhaps
the Republican Party in the United States of America
. . . rigid, materialist and secular, whose opinions will
turn on tariffs and who will cause the lobbies to be
crowded with the touts of protected industries.

The Churchill quotation applies well to Senator Goldwater
today. This charming and personable orator is a *laisser-faire*
Manchester liberal when humane social reforms are at stake.
But, as is Churchill in the above quotation, he is ready to
make an exception against *laisser-faire* when protection of
privileged industry is involved. The Burkean conservative today cherishes New Deal reforms in economics and Lockean
parliamentary liberalism in politics, as traditions that are here
to stay. Indeed, it is not the least of the functions of the new
conservatism to force a now middle-aged New Deal to realize
that it has become conservative and rooted, and that therefore
it had better stop parroting the anti-Constitutional, anti-traditional slogans of its youth. These slogans are now being practiced instead, and to a wilder extent than even the most extreme New Deal liberal ever envisaged, by the Republican
radicals of the right, with their wild-eyed schemes for im-
peaching Justice Warren or abolishing taxes.

The best-rooted philosophical conservatives in America derive from the anti-material-progress tradition of Melville and
Irving Babbitt; they are found mainly in the literary and educational world, the creative world at its best, the non-political
world. Politics will not be ready for their ideas for another
generation; they should shed their illusions on that score. The
normal time lag of a generation likewise separated the literary
and university origin of Coleridge's conservatism from its
osmosis into the politics of Disraeli Toryism.

Sir Henry Maine (1822–1888), one of the world's leading
authorities on constitutions, called America's Constitution

the most successful conservative bulwark in history against majority tyranny and mass radicalism and on behalf of traditional liberties and continuity of framework. Later scholars like Louis Hartz prefer to derive our free heritage not from the Burkean and Federalist ideas of Adams and the Constitution but from eighteenth-century Lockean liberalism. Both sides are partly right and need not exclude each other. For Locke's liberalism is a relatively moderate and tradition-respecting brand when compared with the Continental, anti-traditional liberalism of Rousseau, not to mention the Jacobins. So we come full circle in America's political paradox; our conservatism, in the absence of medieval feudal relics, must grudgingly admit it has little real tradition to conserve except that of liberalism—which then turns out to be a relatively conservative liberalism.

The need for new conservatives to maintain continuity *also* with well-rooted liberal traditions does not mean conservatism and liberalism are the same. Their contrast may be partly and briefly defined[4] as the tragic cyclical view of man, based on a political secularization of original sin, versus the optimistic faith in the natural goodness of man and mass and the inevitability of linear progress. In Coleridgian terms, conservatism is the concrete organic growth of institutions, as if they were trees, while rationalist liberalism is an abstract, mechanical moving around of institutions as if they were separate pieces of furniture. Conservatism serves "growingness" and moves inarticulately and traditionally, like the seasons; liberalism serves "progress" and moves consciously and systematically, like geometry. The former is a circle, the latter an ever-advancing straight line. Both are equally needed half truths; both are equally inherent in the human condition, liberalism on a more rational level and conservatism on a perhaps deeper level. It may be generalized that the conserva-

[4] Longer, more complete definition, with all the needed specific examples in political and intellectual life, is attempted in the first three chapters of the present writer's Anvil paperback, *Conservatism from John Adams to Churchill* (Van Nostrand Company, Princeton, 1956).

tive mind does not like to generalize. Conservative theory is anti-theoretical. The liberal and rationalist mind consciously articulates abstract blueprints; the conservative mind unconsciously incarnates concrete traditions. Liberal formulas define freedom; conservative traditions embody it.

Even while philosophical conservatives support liberals in day-to-day measures of social humaneness or of Constitutional liberties against rightist or leftist radicals, the above basic contrast between the two temperaments will always remain. For these contrasts are symbolized by contrasting spokesmen in our history. George Washington, John Adams, and the Federalists are not the same as apriorist egalitarians like Paine, or believers in natural goodness like Jefferson. John Calhoun is not the same as Andrew Jackson. Barrett Wendell, Irving Babbitt, Paul Elmer More are not the same as the spokesmen of our liberal weeklies or of the New York *Post*. Charles Evans Hughes is not the same as La Follette or even Woodrow Wilson. No, the need for conservative continuity with America's institutionalized liberal past does not mean identity with liberalism, least of all with optimism about human nature, or utilitarian overemphasis on material progress, or trust in the direct democracy of the masses. Instead, conservative continuity with our liberal past simply means that you cannot escape from history; history has provided America with a shared liberal-conservative base more liberal than European Continental conservatives, more conservative than European Continental liberals.

This shared liberal-conservative base is a rooted reality, not a rightist nostalgia for roots, and from it grows the core of the New Deal and of the Kennedy program, as opposed to the inorganic, mechanical abstractions of either a Karl Marx or an Adam Smith. So let new conservatives stop becoming what they accuse liberals of being—rootless doctrinaires.

IV

When asked by President Teddy Roosevelt what the justification was of Austria's supposedly outdated monarchy, the old Hapsburg emperor Francis Joseph replied, "To protect my peoples from their governments." Similarly Disraeli—like Lord Bolingbroke of the early eighteenth century—defended the Crown and the Established Church as bulwarks of the people's rights against ephemeral politicians. The throne, whether Hapsburg or British, serves to moderate excesses of nationalistic or economic pressure groups against individual rights. In non-monarchic America, this same indispensable protection of liberty against the mob tyranny of transient majorities is performed by the Supreme Court, that similarly hallowed and aloof inheritor of the monarchic aura.

So conservatism fights on two fronts. It fights the atomistic disunity of unregulated capitalism. It fights the merely bureaucratic, merely mechanical unity of modern Socialism. It fights both for the sake of organic unity—but thereby runs the risk of creating a third threat of its own. For within its organic unity lies the totalitarian threat whenever the free individual is sacrificed totally and without guarantees (instead of partly and with constitutional guarantees) to that unity. Such a total sacrifice of individual to society took place in German romanticism; organic unity there became an anti-individual cult of the folk-state (*Volk*). This cult took place already in the nineteenth century. It not only unbalanced German conservatism toward extreme statism (via Hegel) but unwittingly prepared the German people psychologically for Hitler's gangster unity.

The proper conservative balance between individual diversity and organic social unity has been best formulated by Coleridge, in 1831:

> The difference between an inorganic and an organic body lies in this: in the first—a sheaf of corn—the whole is nothing more than a collection of the individual parts or phenomena. In the second—a man—the whole is everything and the parts are nothing. A State is an idea intermediate between the two, the whole being a result from, and not a mere total of, the parts,—and yet not so

merging the constituent parts in the result, but that the individual exists integrally within it.

Coleridgian conservatism, the height of the conservative philosophy, lies in the above intermediate "and yet," which saves the "individual integrally" while linking him organically. The folk romanticism of Germany and the "Third Rome" heritage of czarist Russia upset that balance in favor of "the whole is everything, the parts nothing," thereby paving the way for Nazism and Communism respectively. On the opposite extreme, America upset that Coleridgian balance in favor of "the whole is nothing" ("a sheaf of corn")—after the chaotic robber-baron individualists emerged as the real victors of the Civil War. So the proper rebalancing ("intermediate between the two") would promote an almost exaggerated individualism in Germany and Russia and an almost exaggerated "socialistic" or New Deal unity in America, not for its own sake but to even the scales.

Therefore in America it is often the free trade unions who unconsciously are our ablest representatives of the word they hate and misunderstand—conservatism. The organic unity they restore to the atomized "proletariat" is the providential Coleridgian "intermediate" between doctrinaire capitalism and doctrinaire Socialism. In the words of Frank Tannenbaum in *A Philosophy of Labor,* 1952:

> Trade unionism is the conservative movement of our time. It is the counter-revolution. Unwittingly, it has turned its back upon most of the political and economic ideas that have nourished western Europe and the United States during the last two centuries. In practice, though not in words, it denies the heritage that stems from the French Revolution and from English liberalism. It is also a complete repudiation of Marxism. . . .
>
> In contrast with [Communism, Fascism, and *laisser-faire* capitalism] the trade union has involved a clustering of men about their work. This fusion [the new, medieval-style organic society] has been going on for a long time. It has been largely unplanned. . . . There is a

great tradition of humanism and compassion in European and American politics, philosophy, and law, which
counters, at first ineffectively, the driving forces operating
for the atomization of society and the isolation of man.
That tradition in England includes such names as Cobbett, Shaftesbury, Romilly, Dickens, Byron, Coleridge,
Carlyle, Ruskin, Charles Kingsley. . . . The trade union
is the real alternative to the authoritarian state. The trade
union is our modern "society," the only true society that
industrialism has fostered. As a true society it is concerned with the whole man, and embodies the possibilities of both the freedom and the security essential to human dignity.

This Tannenbaum passage is both conservative and new.
Yet it would fill with horror the Kirk-Goldwater kind of mind
that today claims to speak for "the new conservatism." Such
horror is not an argument against Tannenbaum nor against a
new conservatism. It is an argument against the misuse of
language. And it is an argument against that old-guard wing
of the Republican Party which has yet to learn the anti-right-
ist warning spoken in 1790 by the conservative Burke: "A
state without the means of some change is without the means
of its conservation."

What about the argument (very sincerely believed by the
National Review and old-guard Republicans) that denies the
label "conservative" to those of us who support trade union-
ism and who selectively support many New Deal reforms?
According to this argument, our support of such humane and
revolution-preventing reforms in *politics*—by New Dealers and
democratic Socialists—makes us indistinguishable in *philosophy* from New Dealers and democratic Socialists. Similarly
our support of the liberal position on civil liberties in politics
supposedly makes us indistinguishable from liberals in philosophy. Shall we then cease to call ourselves philosophical
conservatives, despite our conservative view of history and
human nature?

The answer is: Children, don't oversimplify, don't pigeonhole; allow for pluralistic overlappings that defy abstract blueprints and labels. Trade unionists (and some of the new humanistic, non-statist Socialists that are evolving in England and West Germany) may be what Frank Tannenbaum calls "the conservative counter-revolution" despite themselves (a neo-medieval organic society) and against their own conscious intentions. Meanwhile, self-styled conservatives are often unconscious anarchic wreckers and uprooters (from the French O.A.S. to America's second generation of campus neo-McCarthyites). Moreover, the same social reform in politics may be supported for very different philosophical reasons. To cite an old example newly relevant today, the support of the workingman's right to vote and right to strike by both the Chartists and the Tory Disraeli merely means that some support a reform as a first step to mass revolution while others support the same reform to woo the masses away from revolution and to give them a sense of belongingness by changing them from masses to individuals.

Finally, there is the distinction between what is done and how it is done. This distinction differentiates the conservative from the democratic Socialist and from the New Deal bureaucrat even when they all vote the same ticket (as so many of us could not help but do, given the Republican alternative, in the case of Roosevelt, Stevenson, and Kennedy). This distinction, this clarification of the proper use of "conservative," is found in an important and much-discussed essay by August Heckscher, at that time the chief editorial writer of the New York *Herald Tribune* and in 1962 appointed President Kennedy's Consultant for Cultural Affairs. Writing in the Harvard magazine *Confluence* in September, 1953, Mr. Heckscher said:

> The failure to understand the true nature of conservatism has made political campaigns in the United States signally barren of intellectual content. In debate it is difficult at best to admit that you would do the same thing as the opposition, but in a different way. Yet the spirit in which things are done really does make a dif-

ference, and can distinguish a sound policy from an unsound one. Social reforms can be undertaken with the effect of draining away local energies, reducing the citizenry to an undifferentiated mass, and binding it to the shackles of the all-powerful state. Or they can be undertaken with the effect of strengthening the free citizen's stake in society. The ends are different. The means will be also, if men have the wit to distinguish between legislation which encourages voluntary participation and legislation which involves reckless spending and enlargement of the federal bureaucracy.

It is easy to say that such distinctions are not important. A conservative intellectual like Peter Viereck is constantly challenged, for example, because in a book like *Shame and Glory of the Intellectuals* he supports a political program not dissimilar in its outlines from that which was achieved during twenty years of social renovation under the Democrats. But the way reforms are undertaken is actually crucial. Concern for the individual, reluctance to have the central government perform what can be done as well by the state or to have the public perform what can be done as well by private enterprise—these priorities involve values. And such values (upheld by writers like Mr. Viereck) are at the heart of modern conservatism. . . . So conservatism at best remains deeper and more pervasive than any party; and a party that does claim it exclusively is likely to deform and exploit it for its own purposes.

In conclusion, let us broaden the discussion from America into certain worldwide considerations about the nature of despotism. They are considerations about which all men of good will can agree as a strategy of freedom, whether New Deal social democrats or Manchester-liberal Republicans or Burkean conservatives. If there is no such agreement, then the epitaph on the tombstone of freedom may appropriately be these lines of Yeats:

Things fall apart; the center cannot hold. . . .
The best lack all conviction, while the worst
Are full of passionate intensity.

According to the neo-Stalinist wing in Russia today, almost all intellectuals and reformers are secret agents of western capitalism. According to the right wing today in America, almost all intellectuals and reformers are secret agents of eastern Communism. Mirror images, of course. And wrong twice.

Each mirror image needs the other and reflects on the other. They need each other as bogeymen. They reflect on each other because each leftist extreme frightens waverers into the rightist camp; each rightist extreme frightens waverers into the leftist camp. McCarthyism used to frighten European liberals into being fellow-travelers with Communism. Communism frightens American conservatives into being fellow-travelers with the pseudo-conservative nationalist thought controllers.

Neither mirror image is strong enough to destroy freedom by itself. Freedom is destroyed when both attack at the same time. Lenin was able to seize power in November, 1917, only because the new Duma government had been weakened by right-wing authoritarians, the John Birchers of Russia, who slandered it as "Red" and who had undermined it by the Kornilov Putsch in September. Hitler was able to seize power in 1933 only because the Weimar Republic had been weakened by Communist authoritarians, who slandered it as "Social Fascist" and who had undermined it by postwar Putsches. In 1962 in France, the anti-de Gaulle Communists and the O.A.S. rightists are examples of the same process in our own time. So are the Gizenga leftists and Tshombe rightists in the Congo.

In both Congo and California, in France today as in Kerensky's Russia yesterday, the fellow-traveler left and the thought-control right are still needing each other and feeding each other, as against the center. Meanwhile in every country the Burke-style conservatives, who revere a rooted constitution, and the Mill-style liberals, who revere civil liberties, likewise need each other: to unite against what Metternich called "the white radicals" of the right as well as the red radicals. Hence this slogan to end all slogans: "LIBERTARIANS OF THE WORLD, UNITE! YOU HAVE NOTHING TO LOSE BUT ABSTRACTIONS. YOU HAVE A WORLD TO CHAIN."

Liberties versus "liberty." Concrete liberties, preserved by the chains of ethics, versus abstract liberty-in-quotes, betrayed by messianic sloganizing, betrayed into the far grimmer chains of totalitarianism. "Man was born free" (said Rousseau, with his faith in the natural goodness of man) "but is everywhere in chains." "In chains, and so he ought to be," replies the thoughtful conservative, defending the good and wise and necessary chains of rooted tradition and historic continuity, upon which depend the civil liberties, the shared civil liberties of modern liberals and conservatives, and parliamentary monarchists, and democratic Socialists. Without the chaos-chaining, the id-chaining heritage of rooted values, what is to keep man from becoming Eichmann or Nechayev—what is to save freedom from "freedom"?

9

SOCIAL STRAINS IN AMERICA (1955)

Talcott Parsons

To the relatively objective observer, whether American or foreign, it seems clear that the complex of phenomena that have come to be known as "McCarthyism" must be symptoms of a process in American society of some deep and general significance. Some interpret it simply as political reaction, even as a kind of neo-fascism. Some think of it as simply a manifestation of nationalism. The present paper proposes to bring to bear some theoretical perspectives of sociology in an attempt to work out an interpretation which goes beyond catchwords of this order.

McCarthyism can be understood as a relatively acute symptom of the strains which accompany a major change in the situation and structure of American society, a change which in this instance consists in the development of the attitudes and institutional machinery required to implement a greatly enhanced level of national political responsibility. The necessity for this development arises both from our own growth to an enormous potential of power, and from the changed relation to the rest of the world which this growth in itself, and other changes extraneous to American development, have entailed. The strains to which I refer derive primarily from conflicts between the demands imposed by the new situation and the inertia of those elements of our social structure which are most resistant to the necessary changes.

The situation I have in mind centers on the American position in international affairs. The main facts are familiar to all. It is not something that has come about suddenly, but the impact of its pressures has been cumulative.

The starting point is the relative geographical isolation of the United States in the "formative" period of its national history, down to, let us say, about the opening of the present century. The Spanish-American War extended our involvements into the Spanish-speaking areas of the Caribbean and to the Philippines, and the Boxer episode in China and our mediation of the Russo-Japanese War indicated rapidly growing interests in the Orient. Then the First World War brought us in as one of the major belligerents, with a brief possibility of taking a role of world leadership. From this advanced degree of international involvement, however, we recoiled with a violent reaction, repudiating the Treaty of Versailles and the League of Nations.

In the ensuing period of "normalcy," until the shock of Pearl Harbor settled the question, it could still be held that the "quarrels" of foreign powers beyond the Americas were none of our concern, unless some "arbitrary" disturbance impinged too closely on our national interests. By the end of the Second World War, however, this attitude could not again be revived by any body of opinion which pretended to depend upon a realistic appraisal of our situation. Our own strength, in spite of our massive disarmament and demobilization, had grown too great; the defeat of France and the disorganization of Germany destroyed such continental European balance of power as had existed; Britain, though victorious, was greatly weakened in the face of world-wide commitments; and Soviet Russia emerged as a victorious and expanding power, leading with a revolutionary ideology a movement which could readily destroy such elements of stability favorable to our own national values and interests as still remained in the world. Along with all this have come developments in military technology that have drastically neutralized the protections formerly conferred by geographical distance, so that even the elementary military security of the United States cannot now be taken for granted apart from world-wide political order.

The vicissitudes of American foreign policy and its relations to domestic politics over this period show the disturbing effect of this developing situation on our society. We have twice intervened militarily on a grand scale. With a notable difference of degree, we have both times recoiled from the implications of our intervention. In the second case the recoil did not last long, since the beginnings of the Cold War about 1947 made it clear that only American action was able to prevent Soviet domination of the whole continent of Europe. It can, however, be argued that this early and grand-scale resumption of responsibility imposed serious internal strains because it did not allow time for "digesting" the implications of our role in the war.

The outstanding characteristic of the society on which this greatly changed situation has impinged is that it had come to be the industrial society par excellence—partly because the settlement of the continental area coincided with the later industrial revolution, partly because of the immense area and natural resources of the country, but partly too because of certain important differences between American and European society. Since the United States did not have a class structure tightly integrated with a political organization that had developed its main forms before the industrial revolution, the economy has had a freedom to develop and to set the tone for the whole society in a way markedly different from any European country or Japan.

All highly industrialized societies exhibit many features in common which are independent of the particular historical paths by which their developments have taken place. These include the bureaucratic organization of the productive process itself, in the sense that the roles of individuals are of the occupational type and the organizations in which they are grouped are mainly "specific function" organizations. Under this arrangement the peasant type of agricultural holding, where farming is very closely bound up with a kinship unit, is minimized; so too of small family businesses; people tend to look to their productive function and to profit as a measure of success and hence of emancipation from conflicting ties and claims; the rights of property ownership are centered primarily in the organization which carries functional responsibility, and hence permits a high degree of segregation between private life and occupational roles for production purposes; contract plays a central part in the system of exchange, and para-economic elements tend to be reduced in importance.

Outside the sphere which touches the organization of the economy itself, industrialism means above all that the structures which would interfere with the free functioning of the economy, and of their adaptation to it, are minimized. The first of these is family and kinship. The American family system, chiefly characterized by the isolation of the nuclear or conjugal family, has gone farther than in any European society toward removing all interferences with the occupational roles of the breadwinning members, and with occupational mobility. A second field is religion. The American combination of federalism and the separation of church and state has resulted in a system of "denominational pluralism" which prevents organized religion from constituting a monolithic structure standing in the way of secular social developments. The third field concerns the matter of social stratification. The United States of course has a class structure; but it is one which has its primary roots in the system of occupational roles, and in contrast to the typical European situation it acts as no more than a brake on the processes of social mobility which are most important to an industrial type of occupational system. Under an effective family system there must be some continuity of class status from generation to generation, and there cannot be complete "equality of opportunity." In America, however, it is clearly the occupational system rather than kinship continuity that prevails.

Linked to this situation is our system of formal education. The United States was among the pioneers in developing publicly supported education; but this has taken place in a notably decentralized way. Not only is there no Department of Education in the Federal government, but even the various state departments are to a large extent service organizations for the locally controlled school systems. Higher education further has been considerably more independent of class standards which equate the "scholar" with the "gentleman" (in a class sense) than has been the case in Europe. Also a far larger proportion of each age-group attends institutions of higher education than in European countries.

Politically the most important fact about American industrialism is that it has developed overwhelmingly under the aegis of free enterprise. Historically the center of gravity of the integration of American society has not rested in the political field. There came to be established a kind of "burden of proof" expectation that responsibilities should not be undertaken by government unless, first, the necessity for their being undertaken at all was clearly established, and second, there was no other obviously adequate way to get the job done. It is therefore not surprising that the opening up of vast new fields of governmental responsibility should meet with considerable resistance and conflict.

The impact of this problem on our orientation to foreign relations has been complicated by an important set of internal circumstances. It is a commonplace that industrialism creates on a large scale two sets of problems which uniformly in all industrialized countries have required modifications of any doctrinaire "laissez-faire" policy: the problems of controlling the processes of the economy itself, and of dealing with certain social repercussions of industrialization.

As the process of industrialization has developed in America there has been a steady increase in the amount of public control imposed on the economy, with the initiative mainly in the hands of the Federal government. This trend was accelerated in the latter years of the nineteenth century, and has continued, with interruptions, through the New Deal. The New Deal, however, was more concerned with the social repercussions of industrialization, rather than with more narrowly economic problems. The introduction of a national system of social security and legislation more favorable to labor are perhaps the most typical developments. This internal process of government intervention has not gone far enough to satisfy European socialists, but it certainly constitutes a great modification of the earlier situation. Moreover, in broad lines it can be regarded as firmly established. It is significant that the major political parties now tend to vie with each other in promoting the extension of social security benefits, that there is no likelihood of repeal of the Federal Reserve Act, and that there is no strong movement to place the unions under really severe legal restraints.

On the whole, business groups have accepted the new situation and cooperated to make it work with considerably more good faith than in Continental Europe. Nevertheless, these internal changes have been sufficiently recent and far-reaching to keep the strains attendant on them from being fully resolved. Moreover they have created an important part of the problems with which this examination is chiefly concerned, problems touching the composition of the higher strata of the society, where the primary burden of responsibility must fall.

By contrast with European countries, perhaps in some ways particularly Britain, the United States has been conspicuous for the absence or relative weakness of two types of elite elements. The first of these is a hereditary upper class with a status continuous from pre-industrial times, closely integrated with politics and public service. The second is an occupational elite whose roots are essentially independent of the business world—in the independent professions, the universities, the church, or government, including civil and military services.

In America the businessmen have tended to be the natural leaders of the general community. But, both for the reasons just reviewed and for certain others, this leadership has not remained undisputed. On the whole the business community has, step by step, resisted the processes of internal change necessitated by industrialization rather than taken the leadership in introducing them. The leadership that has emerged has been miscellaneous in social origin, including professional politicians, especially those in touch with the urban political machines, leaders in the labor union movement and elements in close touch with them. An important part has been played by men and women who may be said to exhibit a more or less "aristocratic" tinge, particularly in the Eastern cities, President Roosevelt of course having been among them. An important part has been played by lawyers who have made themselves more independent of the business connection than the typical corporation lawyer of a generation ago. Under the pressure of emergency, there has been a tendency for high military officers to play important roles in public life.

Another important group has been composed of "intellectuals"—again a rather miscellaneous assembly including writers, newspapermen, and members of university faculties. In general the importance of the universities has been steadily enhanced by the increasingly technical character of the operations of the economy; businessmen themselves have had to be more highly educated than their predecessors, and have become increasingly dependent on still more highly trained technicians of various kinds.

The important point is that the "natural" tendency for a relatively unequivocal business leadership of the general community has been frustrated, and the business group has had to give way at many points. Nevertheless, a clearly defined non-business component of the elite has not yet crystallized. In my opinion, the striking feature of the American elite is not what Soviet propaganda contends that it is—the clear-cut dominance by "capitalists"—but rather its fluid and relatively unstructured character. In particular, there is no clear determination of where political leadership, in the sense including both "politics" and "administration," is to center.

A further feature of the structure of American society is intimately related to the residual strains left by recent social changes. There is a continuing tendency for earlier economic developments to leave a "precipitate" of upper groups, the position of whose members is founded in the achievements of their ancestors, in this case relatively recent ones. By historical necessity these groups are strongest in the older parts of the country. Hence the cities of the Eastern seaboard have tended to develop groups that are the closest approach we have—though still very different from their European equivalent—to an aristocracy. They have generally originated in business interests, but have taken on a form somewhat similar to the mercantile aristocracies of some earlier European societies, such as the Hanseatic cities. In the perspective of popular democratic sentiments, these groups have tended to symbolize at the same time capitalistic interests and social snobbery. In certain circumstances they may be identified with "bohemianism" and related phenomena which are sources of uneasiness to traditional morality.

As the American social and economic center has shifted westward, such groups in the great Middle Western area and beyond have been progressively less prominent. There the elites have consisted of new men. In the nature of the case the proportional contribution to the economy and the society in general from the older and the newer parts of the country has shifted, with the newer progressively increasing their share. But at the same time there is the sense among them of having had to fight for this share against the "dominance" of the East. A similar feeling permeates the lower levels of the class structure. A major theme of the populist type of agrarian and other radicalism had combined class and sectional elements, locating the source of people's troubles in the bankers and railway magnates of the East and in Wall Street. It must not be forgotten that the isolationism of the between-the-wars period was intimately connected with this sectional and class sentiment. The elder La Follette, who was one of the principal destroyers of the League of Nations, was not a "conservative" or in any usual sense a reactionary, but a principal leader of the popular revolt against "the interests."

It must also not be forgotten that a large proportion of the American population are descendants of relatively recent immigrants whose cultural origins are different from the dominant Protestant Anglo-Saxon elements. A generation and more ago the bulk of the new immigration constituted an urban proletariat largely dominated by the political machines of the great cities. By now a great change has taken place. The children of these immigrants have been very much Americanized, but to a considerable degree they are still sensitive about their full acceptance. This sensitivity is if anything heightened by the fact that on the whole most of these elements have risen rapidly in the economic and social scale. They are no longer the inhabitants of the scandalous slums; many have climbed to lower-middle-class status and higher. They have a certain susceptibility to "democratic" appeals which are directed against the alleged snobbery of the older dominant elements.

Finally, the effect of the great depression of the 1930s on the leading business groups must not be forgotten. Such a collapse of the economy could not fail to be felt as a major failure of the expectation that business leaders should bear the major responsibility for the welfare of the economy as a whole and thus of the community. In general it was not the businessmen but the government, under leadership which was broadly antagonistic to business, which came to the rescue. Similarly, the other great class of American proprietors, the farmers, had to accept governmental help of a sort that entailed controls, which in turn inevitably entailed severe conflicts with the individualistic traditions of their history. The fact that the strains of the war and postwar periods have been piled so immediately on those of depression has much to do with the severity of the tensions with which this analysis is concerned.

My thesis, then, is that the strains of the international situation have impinged on a society undergoing important internal changes which have themselves been sources of strain, with the effect of superimposing one kind of strain on another. What responses to this compound strain are to be expected?

It is a generalization well established in social science that neither individuals nor societies can undergo major structural changes without the likelihood of producing a considerable element of "irrational" behavior. There will tend to be conspicuous distortions of the patterns of value and of the normal beliefs about the facts of situations. These distorted beliefs and promptings to irrational action will also tend to be heavily weighted with emotion, to be "overdetermined" as the psychologists say.

The psychology of such reactions is complex, but for present purposes it will suffice to distinguish two main components. On the negative side, there will tend to be high levels of anxiety and aggression, focused on what rightly or wrongly are felt to be the sources of strain and difficulty. On the positive side there will tend to be wishful patterns of belief with a strong "regressive" flavor, whose chief function is to wish away the disturbing situation and establish a situation in phantasy where "everything will be all right," preferably as it was before the disturbing situation came about. Very generally then the psychological formula tends to prescribe a set of beliefs that certain specific, symbolic agencies are responsible for the present state of distress; they have "arbitrarily" upset a satisfactory state of affairs. If only they could be eliminated the trouble would disappear and a satisfactory state restored. The role of this type of mechanism in primitive magic is quite well known.

In a normal process of learning in the individual, or of developmental change in the social system, such irrational phenomena are temporary, and tend to subside as capacity to deal with the new situation grows. This may be more or less easily achieved of course, and resolution of the conflicts and strains may fail to be achieved for a long period or may even be permanently unsuccessful. But under favorable circumstances these reactions are superseded by an increasingly realistic facing of the situation by institutionalized means.

Our present problem therefore centers on the need to mobilize American society to cope with a dangerous and threatening situation which is also intrinsically difficult. It can clearly only be coped with at the governmental level; and hence the problem is in essence a matter of political action, involving both questions of leadership—of who, promoting what policies, shall take the primary responsibility—and of the commitment of the many heterogeneous elements of our population to the national interest.

Consequently there has come to be an enormous increase in pressure to subordinate private interests to the public interest, and this in a society where the presumptions have been more strongly in favor of the private interest than in most. Readiness to make commitments to a collective interest is the focus of what we ordinarily mean by "loyalty." It seems to me that the problem of loyalty at its core is a genuine and realistic one; but attitudes toward it shade all the way from a reasonable concern with getting the necessary degree of loyal cooperation by legitimate appeals, to a grossly irrational set of anxieties about the prevalence of disloyalty, and a readiness to vent the accompanying aggression on innocent scapegoats.

Underlying the concern for loyalty in general, and explaining a good deal of the reaction to it, is the ambivalence of our approach to the situation: The people in the most "exposed" positions are on the one hand pulled by patriotic motives toward fulfillment of the expectations inherent in the new situation; they want to "do their bit." But at the same time their established attitudes and orientations resist fulfillment of the obligation. In the conflict of motives which ensues it is a natural consequence for the resistance to be displaced or projected on to other objects which function as scapegoats. In the present situation it is precisely those parts of our population where individualistic traditions are strongest that are placed under the greatest strain, and that produce the severest resistances to accepting the obligations of our situation. Such resistances, however, conflict with equally strong patriotic motives. In such a situation, when one's own resistance to loyal acceptance of unpalatable obligations, such as paying high taxes, are particularly strong, it is easy to impute disloyal intentions to others.

Our present emotional preoccupation with the problem of loyalty indicates above all that the crisis is not, as some tend to think, primarily concerned with fundamental values, but rather with their implementation. It is true that certain features of the pattern of reaction, such as tendencies to aggressive nationalism and to abdication of responsibilities, would, if carried through, lead to severe conflict with our values. But the main problem is not concerned with doubts about whether the stable political order of a free world is a goal worth sacrificing for, but rather with the question of how our population is rising or failing to rise to the challenge.

The primary symbol that connects the objective external problem and its dangers with the internal strain and its structure is "Communism." "World Communism" and its spread constitute the features of the world situation on which the difficulty of our international problem clearly centers. Internally it is felt that Communists and their "sympathizers" constitute the primary focus of actual or potential disloyalty.

With respect to the external situation, the focus of the difficulty in the current role of Soviet Russia is of course reasonable enough. Problems then arise mainly in connection with certain elements of "obsessiveness" in the way in which the situation is approached, manifested for instance in a tendency to subordinate all other approaches to the situation exclusively to the military, and in the extreme violence of reaction in some circles to the Chinese situation, in contrast to the relative tolerance with which Yugoslavia is regarded.

Internally, the realistic difficulty resides mainly in the fact that there has indeed been a considerable amount of Communist infiltration in the United States, particularly in the 1930s. It is true that the Communist Party itself has never achieved great electoral success, but for a time Communist influence was paramount in a number of important labor unions, and a considerable number of the associations Americans so like to join were revealed to be Communist-front organizations, with effective Communist control behind the public participation of many non-Communists. Perhaps most important was the fact that considerable numbers of the intellectuals became fellow-travelers. In the days of the rise of Nazism and of the popular front, many of them felt that only Soviet Russia was sincere in its commitment to collective security; that there was a Franco-British "plot" to get Germany and Russia embroiled with each other, etc. The shock of the Nazi-Soviet pact woke up many fellow-travelers, but by no means all; and the cause was considerably retrieved by Hitler's attack on Russia.

Two other features of the Communist movement which make it an ideal negative symbol in the context of the present loyalty problem are the combination of conspiratorial methods and foreign control with the progressive component of its ideological system. On the one hand the party has drastically repudiated the procedures of constitutional democracy, and on this issue has broken with all the democratic socialist parties of Europe; it claims the protection of democratic procedures and civil liberties, but does not hesitate to abuse them when this seems to be advantageous. There has further never been any question of the American party determining its own policies by democratic procedures. Perhaps in fact the knowledge of the extent to which the "front" organizations have been manipulated from behind the scenes has been the most disillusioning aspect for liberal Americans of their experience with Communism at home.

At the same time the movement had a large content of professed idealism, which may be taken to account for the appeal of Communism before the Cold War era for such large elements of liberal opinion in the United States, as in other Western countries. Marx was, after all, himself a child of the Enlightenment, and the Communist movement has incorporated in its ideology many of the doctrines of human rights that have formed a part of our general inheritance. However grossly the symbols of democracy, of the rights of men, of peace and brotherhood, have been abused by the Communists, they are powerful symbols in our own tradition, and their appeal is understandable.

Hence the symbol "Communism" is one to which a special order of ambivalence readily attaches. It has powerful sources of appeal to the liberal tradition, but those who are out of sympathy with the main tradition of American liberalism can find a powerful target for their objections in the totalitarian tactics of Communism and can readily stigmatize it as "un-American." Then, by extending their objections to the liberal component of Communist ideology, they can attack liberalism in general, on the grounds that association with Communist totalitarianism makes anything liberal suspect.

These considerations account for the anti-Communist's readiness to carry over a stereotype from those who have really been party members or advanced fellow-travelers to large elements of the intellectuals, the labor movement, etc., who have been essentially democratic liberals of various shades of opinion. Since by and large the Democratic Party has

more of this liberalism than has the Republican, it is not surprising that a tendency to label it as "sympathizing" with or
"soft toward" Communism has appeared. Such a label has
also been extended, though not very seriously, to the Protestant
clergy.

But there is one further extension of the association that is
not accounted for in these terms, nor is the failure to include
certain plausible targets so accountable. The extension I have
in mind is that which leads to the inclusion as "pro-Communist" of certain men or institutions that have been associated
with political responsibility in the international field. Two
symbols stand out here. The first is Dean Acheson. Mr.
Acheson has for years served the Democratic Party. But he
has belonged to the conservative, not the New Deal wing of
the party. Furthermore, the coupling of General Marshall
with him, though only in connection with China, and only by
extremists, clearly precludes political radicalism as the primary objection, since Marshall has never in any way been
identified with New Deal views. The other case is that of
Harvard University as an alleged "hot-bed" of Communism
and fellow-traveling. The relevant point is that Mr. Acheson
typifies the "aristocrat" in public service; he came of a wealthy
family, he went to a select private school (Groton) and to
Yale and Harvard Law School. He represents symbolically
those Eastern vested interests, against whom antagonism has
existed among the new men of the Middle West and the
populist movement, including the descendants of recent immigrants. Similarly, among American universities Harvard
has been particularly identified as educating a social elite, the
members of which are thought of as "just the type," in their
striped trousers and morning coats, to sell out the country to
the social snobs of European capitals. It is the combination
of aristocratic associations—through the Boston Brahmins—
and a kind of urban-bohemian sophistication along with its
devotion to intellectual and cultural values, including precisely its high intellectual standards, which makes Harvard a
vulnerable symbol in this context.

The symbol "Communism," then, from its area of legitimate application, tends to be generalized to include groups in the population who have been associated with political liberalism of many shades and with intellectual values in general and to include the Eastern upper-class groups who have tended to be relatively internationalist in their outlook.

A second underlying ambivalent attitude-structure is discernible in addition to that concerning the relation between the totalitarian and the progressive aspects of Communism. On the one hand, Communism very obviously symbolizes what is anathema to the individualistic tradition of a business economy—the feared attempt to destroy private enterprise and with it the great tradition of individual freedom. But on the other hand, in order to rise to the challenge of the current political situation, it is necessary for the older balance between a free economy and the power of government to be considerably shifted in favor of the latter. We must have a stronger government than we have traditionally been accustomed to, and we must come to trust it more fully. It has had in recent times to assume very substantial regulatory functions in relation to the economy, and now vastly enhanced responsibilities in relation to international affairs.

But, on the basis of a philosophy which, in a very different way from our individualistic tradition, gives primacy to "economic interests," namely the Marxist philosophy, the Communist movement asserts the unqualified, the totalitarian supremacy of government over the economy. It is precisely an actual change in our own system in what in one sense is clearly this direction that emerges as the primary focus of the frustrations to which the older American system has been subjected. The leaders of the economy, the businessmen, have been forced to accept far more "interference" from government with what they have considered "their affairs" than they have liked. And now they must, like everyone else, pay unprecedentedly high taxes to support an enormous military establishment, and give the government in other respects unprecedentedly great powers over the population. The result of this situation is an ambivalence of attitude that on the one hand demands a stringent display of loyalty going to lengths far beyond our tradition of individual liberty, and on the other hand is ready to blame elements which by ordinary logic have little or nothing to do with Communism, for working in league with the Communist movement to create this horrible situation.

Generally speaking, the indefensible aspect of this tendency in a realistic assessment appears in a readiness to question the loyalty of all those who have assumed responsibility for leadership in meeting the exigencies of the new situation. These include many who have helped to solve the internal problems of the control of the economy, those who in the uneasy later 'thirties and the first phase of the war tried to get American policy and public opinion to face the dangers of the international situation, and those who since the war have tried to take responsibility in relation to the difficult postwar situation. Roughly, these are the presumptively disloyal elements who are also presumptively tainted with Communism. Here again, admittedly, certain features of our historical record and attitudes provide some realistic basis for this tendency. In fact many elements in both parties have failed lamentably to assess correctly the dangers of the situation, both internally and externally. New Dealers have stigmatized even the most responsible elements of the business world as economic royalists and the like, while many elements in business have clung long past a reasonable time to an outmoded belief in the possibility of a society with only a "night watchman" government. In foreign affairs, some members of the Democratic Party have been slow to learn how formidable a danger was presented by totalitarian Communism, but this is matched by the utopianism of many Republicans about the consequences of American withdrawal from international responsibilities, through high tariffs as well as political isolationism. The necessity to learn the hard realities of a complex world and the difficulty of the process is not a task to be imposed on only part of the body politic. No party or group can claim a monopoly either of patriotic motive or of competent understanding of affairs.

In a double sense, then, Communism symbolizes "the intruder." Externally the world Communist movement is the obvious source of the most serious difficulties we have to face. On the other hand, although Communism has constituted to some degree a realistic internal danger, it has above all come to symbolize those factors that have disturbed the beneficent natural state of an American society which allegedly and in phantasy existed before the urgent problems of control of the economy and greatly enhanced responsibility in international affairs had to be tackled.

Against this background it can perhaps be made clear why the description of McCarthyism as simply a political reactionary movement is inadequate. In the first place, it is clearly not simply a cloak for the "vested interests" but rather a movement that profoundly splits the previously dominant groups. This is evident in the split, particularly conspicuous since about 1952, within the Republican Party. An important part of the business elite, especially in the Middle West and in Texas, the "newest" area of all, have tended in varying degrees to be attracted by the McCarthy appeal. But other important groups, notably in the East, have shied away from it and apparently have come to be more and more consolidated against it. Very broadly, these can be identified with the business element among the Eisenhower Republicans.

But at the same time the McCarthy following is by no means confined to the vested-interest groups. There has been an important popular following of very miscellaneous composition. It has comprised an important part of those who aspire to full status in the American system but have, realistically or not, felt discriminated against in various ways, especially the Mid-Western lower and lower middle classes and much of the population of recent immigrant origin. The elements of continuity between Western agrarian populism and McCarthyism are not by any means purely fortuitous. At the levels of both leadership and popular following, the division of American political opinion over this issue *cuts clean across the traditional lines of distinction between "conservatives" and "progressives,"* especially where that tends to be defined, as it so often is, in terms of the capitalistic or moneyed interests as against those who seek to bring them under more stringent control. McCarthyism is *both* a movement supported by certain vested-interest elements *and* a popular revolt against the upper classes.

Another striking characteristic of McCarthyism is that it is highly selective in the liberal causes it attacks. Apart from the issue of Communism in the labor unions, now largely solved, there has been no concerted attack on the general position of the labor movement. Further, the social program aimed toward the reduction of racial discrimination has continued to be pressed, to which fact the decision of the Supreme Court outlawing segregation in public education and its calm reception provide dramatic evidence. Nevertheless, so far as I am aware there has been no outcry from McCarthyite quarters to the effect that this decision is further evidence of Communist influence in high circles—in spite of the fact that eight out of nine members of the present court were appointed by Roosevelt and Truman.

Perhaps even more notable is the fact that, unlike the 1930s, when Father Coughlin and others were preaching a vicious anti-Semitism, anti-Semitism as a public issue has since the war been very nearly absent from the American scene. This is of course associated with full employment. But particularly in view of the rather large and conspicuous participation of Jewish intellectuals in the fellow-traveling of the 1930s, it is notable that Jewishness has not been singled out as a symbolic focus for the questioning of loyalty. A critical difference from German Nazism is evident here. To the Nazis the Jew was the *primary* negative symbol, the Communist the most prominent secondary one. But it must also be remembered that capitalism was symbolically involved. One of the functions of the Jew was to *link* Communism and capitalism together. This trio were the "intruders" to the Nazis. They symbolized different aspects of the disturbance created by the rapid development of industrialism to the older preindustrial *Gemeinschaft* of German political romanticism. It was the obverse of the American case—a new economy destroying an old political system, not new political responsibilities interfering with the accustomed ways of economic life.

Negatively, then, the use of the symbol "Communism" as the focus of anxiety and aggression is associated with a high order of selectivity among possibly vulnerable targets. This selectivity is, I submit, consistent with the hypothesis that the focus of the strain expressed by McCarthyism lies in the area of political responsibility—not, as Marxists would hold, in the structure of the economy as such, nor in the class structure in any simple, Marxian-tinged sense.

The same interpretation is confirmed by the evidence on the positive side. The broadest formula for what the McCarthyites positively "want"—besides the elimination of all Communist influence, real or alleged—is perhaps "isolationism." The dominant note is, I think, the regressive one. It is the wishful preservation of an old order, which allegedly need never have been disturbed but for the wilful interference of malevolent elements, Communists and their sympathizers. The nationalistic overtones center on a phantasy of a happy "American way" where everything used to be all right. Naturally it is tinged with the ideology of traditional laissez-faire, but not perhaps unduly so. Also it tends to spill over into a kind of irritated activism. On the one hand we want to keep out of trouble; but on the other hand, having identified an enemy, we want to smash him forthwith. The connection between the two can be seen, for example, in relation to China, where the phantasy seems to be that by drastic action it would be possible to "clean up" the Chinese situation quickly and then our troubles would be over.

The main contention of these pages has been that McCarthyism is best understood as a symptom of the strains attendant on a deep-seated process of change in our society, rather than as a "movement" presenting a policy or set of values for the American people to act on. Its content is overwhelmingly negative, not positive. It advocates "getting rid" of undesirable influences, and has amazingly little to say about what should be done.

This negativism is primarily the expression of fear, second-arily of anger, the aggression which is a product of frustration. The solution, which is both realistically feasible and within the great American tradition, is to regain our national self-confidence and to take active steps to cope with the situation with which we are faced.

On the popular level the crisis is primarily a crisis of con-fidence. We are baffled and anxious, and tend to seek relief in hunting scapegoats. We must improve our understanding and come to realize our strength and trust in it. But this cannot be done simply by wishing it to be done. I have consistently ar-gued that the changed situation in which we are placed de-mands a far-reaching change in the structure of our society. It demands policies, and confidence, but it demands more than these. It demands above all three things. The first is a revision of our conception of citizenship to encourage the ordinary man to accept greater responsibility. The second is the de-velopment of the necessary implementing machinery. Third is national political leadership, not only in the sense of indi-vidual candidates for office or appointment, but in the sense of social strata where a traditional political responsibility is ingrained.

The most important of these requirements is the third. Un-der American conditions, a politically leading stratum must be made up of a combination of business and nonbusiness elements. The role of the economy in American society and of the business element in it is such that political leadership without prominent business participation is doomed to ineffec-tiveness and to the perpetuation of dangerous internal conflict. It is not possible to lead the American people *against* the leaders of the business world. But at the same time, so varied now are the national elements which make a legitimate claim to be represented, the business element cannot monopolize or dominate political leadership and responsibility. Broadly, I think, a political elite in the two main aspects of "politicians" whose specialties consist in the management of public opin-ion, and of "administrators" in both civil and military serv-ices, must be greatly strengthened. It is here that the practical consequences of McCarthyism run most directly counter to the realistic needs of the time. But along with such a specifically political elite there must also be close alliance with other, predominantly "cultural" elements, notably perhaps in the universities, but also in the churches.

In the final sense, then, the solution of the problem of McCarthyism lies in the successful accomplishment of the social changes to which we are called by our position in the world and by our own domestic requirements. We have already made notable progress toward this objective; the current flare-up of stress in the form of McCarthyism can be taken simply as evidence that the process is not complete.

10

SOCIAL STRAINS IN AMERICA:
A POSTSCRIPT (1962)

Talcott Parsons

I think that the diagnosis I put forward originally can stand. McCarthyism was essentially a crisis of national solidarity in the face of what, for us as a nation, were accumulating and unprecedented political demands and responsibilities. The precipitating factor was the Korean War, which, acting as a "last straw," frustrated the expectations of relaxation that many Americans held after the end of the big war, a war that itself was entered into only after serious internal division and conflict. The focus of the strain was the problem of national loyalty. But the very insistence on national loyalty created a paradox that Edward Shils, in his *The Torment of Secrecy*, has highlighted more clearly than anyone else, in that the very demand for nearly absolute national loyalty undermined our national capacities for effective action.

One of the most striking features of the McCarthy movement was its intensity while it lasted, and the rapidity with which it subsided when the "bubble" finally burst. Though more deep-rooted and underlying strains may have been involved—and may still be—McCarthyism as a social threat was more clearly analogous to a financial panic, say, than to a long-drawn-out depression. Putting the situation in terms of that analogy may help to clarify the ways in which the strain operated. When there is a run on the bank by depositors the tendency is, in a cumulative regression, to more and more "elementary" monetary transactions. In the ordinary course of business "cash" is only a minor convenience, for most transactions are carried out essentially by exchange of deposits within a credit system. But if too many depositors want payment all at once, these demands cannot be honored and the credit system maintained. "Logically" the end of the line of monetary deflation, of course, is a return to species payments, or the use of metal, the toting of which would make any commercial transaction quite weighty. Such a downward spin can only be checked by a restoration of "confidence," which means willingness to accept payment other than "hard" cash—the return to credit. In short, there has to be a foundation of trust for the credit system to operate.

McCarthyism was such a "deflationary spiral." The "credit" repudiated was the ordinary level of commitment of the citizen to the national interest, which in a pluralistic society is virtually never total. What the McCarthyites demanded of those who claimed to be "trustworthy" was not fulfillment of ordinary obligations, but an absolute guarantee that no other commitment could conceivably compete with what *they* called "loyalty" to the government.

Obviously this pressure generated a special kind of conflict in American society. We have a tradition that the claims of government on the individual are relatively minimal, and the presumptive morality is one of defense of individual rights against government. In the 1950s we were made acutely aware of the serious threats to national security and of the necessity of strengthening the government in ways that, in some sense, involved a sacrifice of private rights.

In such a situation there will necessarily be widespread ambivalence, and it was to be expected that the phenomenon of scapegoating would be prominent. It was my view, as stated in the original paper, that the most prominent scourgers would be those who had a strong—moral as well as "material"—vested interest in limiting the powers of government, and that the victims would be those who had on the whole taken the initiative in realistic attempts to meet the situation. From this point of view it was not unintelligible that the men who had entered government service were the ones most victimized. (This is perhaps analogous to the banker who, having taken the responsibility for lending "other people's money" is then, by populistic demand, subjected to the most rigorous checking, so that even any minor loss through error of judgment comes to be attributed to his bad faith.)

The question may now be raised whether the most recent phase of development of the radical right is a repetition of McCarthyism or something different. There is, it seems to me, a common substratum, but in many respects the current flare-up has markedly different features.

The common substratum seems to lie in the tendency to polarization that derives from the main pattern of developmental change in American society. In the broadest sense—which can be made to correspond only approximately to political-party divisions—the "right" is the protest against the fact that American society is changing, and against the direction of change. The United States is a society that has been evolving toward increasing complexities and scale of its organization and functions; a greater concentration of population and activities in complex communities; increasing responsibility in the world political system; and a higher order of technology, knowledge, sophistication, and the like. The conservatives are the rear-guard resistance to this trend.

Common to all the multifarious aspects of the right wing is a certain type of "individualism." It has such facets as the individualism of the small unit as against the large—the independent entrepreneur versus the large corporation, and similarly the rural and small town versus the city and the metropolis. As regards international relations, this individualism romanticizes our earlier lack of involvement in the complex world of power relations, when America could be left to work out its own destiny. Most generally perhaps this individualism is the idealization of pristine simplicity as against organizational and other complexity.

In the general picture, the current right seems to be the more regressive of the two, and for that very reason possibly less threatening, since the radical wing of conservatism is likely to be excluded from power. In understanding its salience it should also be remembered that while McCarthyism started during the latter part of the Truman administration, it came to a head under a Republican administration. The so-called "resurgence" of the right in the past year is, in part, undoubtedly a simple function of the Republican Party's again going into opposition.

In spite of this common substratum, in an important sense the current rightist preoccupations, typified perhaps by the John Birch Society, are the obverse of the McCarthyites. The right of the 1960s shares, of course, the symbol of Communism as the source of all evil, but its meaning has been shifted in a way that brings to the fore the other side of an ambivalent motivational complex.

An important symptom of the difference between McCarthyism and Birchism is the shift in the geographical center of gravity.[1] This is a move from the Middle West to the Southwest. (Texas, to be sure, is the common sector in both movements, and to some extent the same is true of that perennial hothouse of the exotic, Southern California.) This is no accident; the Southwest is the nearest thing left to a frontier, or, more specifically, Texas and Southern California are the sections that, despite a rapidly burgeoning urban civilization, still cherish the illusion that the old frontier is alive.

The essential point about the frontier is that it was the situation—in legend at least—of the predominance of self-help. Here a man—who was allegedly *really* a man—was most obviously "on his own." If "bad" men were about, he had to defend himself—and of course the good women—with his bare fists or his six-shooter. He made his living "honestly"—by wrestling with nature in the form of recalcitrant soils, drought, storm, and "ornery" beasts—so that no one could say when he won that it was because he was dependent on anyone.[2]

[1] For emphasizing this point, as well as considerable contribution to the general pattern of analysis outlined here, I am indebted to Dr. Winston White.

[2] A paradigmatic case of this frontier mentality is described in E. Z. Vogt, Jr., *Modern Homesteaders* (Harvard University Press), a study of "Texan" migrants into a semi-arid section of New Mexico.

It seems to me that it is this fierce and hence "defensive" independence which is the hallmark of the most recent right.[8] The good life is to be completely untamed by the disciplines of complex society. From the point of view of this individualism, the income tax is a "tribute" exacted by a "foreign" usurper; namely, the urban, and more or less European, America. The income tax—attacks on which were by no means absent from the ideology of the McCarthy era (cf. the views of the late Representative Carroll Reece)—has been upgraded to become almost the central symbol of evil; i.e., the first entering wedge of "Communism." The reason why it is unexceptionably "Communist" is simply that it presumes to assert the authority of government. By taking away what "belongs to" the taxpayer, it symbolizes the arbitrariness in almost any regulation of the complete freedom of the individual to "do what he will with his own," and defend himself against comers who challenge his rights.

This is the essential structure of the ambivalence. The McCarthyites demanded absolute subordination of all private rights to the government. McCarthy was in effect the most drastically radical "Socialist" imaginable. The Bircher demands nearly absolute immunity from any type of public control over his independence.

In this regard, the image of Communism is somewhat different in the two cases. In the original paper I argued that for the McCarthyites the aggression against the source that called for the development of government was the key to its pattern. To meet the threat of real Communism, there was a strengthening of responsible government and more centralized authority. To fight "Communism," which stands for the total state, McCarthy demanded even more centralized government. This is a motivational mechanism operating analogously to the normal oedipal situation—the resentment against the "father" as the symbolic source of the pressure to grow up, but also an identification with him. The McCarthyites, by demanding absolute loyalty, were in fact promoting a kind of

[8] Another interesting manifestation of this complex is the part it plays in the opposition to the fluoridation of water supplies.

distorted identification with government. The identification was carried out in a destructive way so as to threaten the many altogether legitimate pluralistic loyalties and associations, to subordinate them altogether too drastically to the one national loyalty, and in the process to attack large numbers of completely innocent persons and in general spread an atmosphere of unwarranted distrust.

Except for the readiness in quick anger to deal summarily with sources of frustration, and hence to demand total victory over international Communism, the new right movements seem to lack this element of identification. Hence they are more regressive than McCarthy, in that they apparently seek, without qualification, to preserve the socially "infantile" state of everything "little." Their influence is even more drastically "deflationary" than the McCarthyite, in the constriction of commitments to the more highly organized sectors of society. This includes the extensive functions of government, but it also goes beyond them. Even the large corporation is in some sense felt to be vaguely "Socialistic," in that it interferes with the complete independence of the small man.

In this sense, the Birchers are the extreme wing of a much more ramified complex. The central focus of it seems to be the political rear-guard action (and its roots in the social structure) of the rural and small-town elements in the society, which have been able to "dig in," above all through legislative refusal to redistrict, first for the House of Representatives, but even more for the state legislature. In this connection, the question of "equal protection of the laws" through fair representation is slowly building up to becoming the most important internal political question of the society, a question that crosscuts many of the older bases of political differentiation and segmentation, most conspicuously, of course, underlying the coalition of Republicans and Southern Democrats.[4]

But one must see, too, that "individualism" is by no means confined to a complex of what I have here called "regres-

[4] The decision of the Supreme Court to restrict the legislatures' freedom to avoid redistricting may prove to be a highly important factor in this situation.

sive" attitudes. There is an opposite group whose orientation, though "ideological," presents a very different case from that of the reactionary individualists. These are the intellectuals whom Winston White has called the Moralizers.[5] Regarding themselves as liberals, or left of center, they deplore many of the features of contemporary society, in particular what they hold to be the increasing pressures to "conformity," but they also stress the importance of the responsibility of the individual, not for "self-help," but for the welfare of the society, and hence for the collective interest of the nation as a whole. They stand in an obverse relation to the Birchers, but in a quite different direction from that of the McCarthyites. The element of acceptance of the developing social order, of "identification" with it, as described above, is stronger for them than for the McCarthyites. It does not, however, involve a coerced loyalty, but the opposite—a free acceptance of individual responsibility to the point of often being utopian about the necessity for formal organization and for authority that can implement important collective goals. Whereas the Birchers are drastically "deflationary" with respect to any sort of social responsibility, the Moralizers are "inflationary," in that they seem to hold that full commitment of the individual is enough—the practical organization and know-how are secondary.

But there is a third, and indeed a very different type of individualism that is focal to the whole American pattern of values and attitudes—the strong emphasis on freedom and responsibility of the individual *within* a framework of both normative order and collective organization. This is what on occasion I have called "institutionalized individualism," using Durkheim's famous analysis of the relation between contractual agreements and the "non-contractual" institutional elements of contract as a prototype.[6] In this point of view, we can see society as providing for more complex, more technical, and more "professional" jobs; allowing for more

[5] *Beyond Conformity* (Free Press, 1961).
[6] Cf. Emile Durkheim, *The Division of Labor in Society*, Bk. I, Ch. 7.

variety of choices, in occupation and in culture, and providing greater diversity within the framework of organization. It is my strong conviction that the main trend of development in the society is individualistic in *this* sense.[7]

The regressive individualism of which the Birchers are the extreme examples is very different from this. Regressive individualism resists the processes of institutional change by virtue of which a more complex and hence more effective division of labor or differentiation has been developing, by which there has developed an increasingly ramified system of pluralistic collective solidarities and enterprises (including, of course, the enterprises of government but by no means confined to them[8]), and, finally, by which there has been developing a more generalized and elaborated system of norms, especially at the level of law, through which the inevitably complex relations of such a society come to be regulated. Seen in this perspective, the Birchers are the generic type of the true "reactionary." The phrase that has already been rather widely applied to them and to groups like them—that they want to "repeal the twentieth century"—seems to sum them up very well indeed.

[7] Perhaps the fullest statement of the sense in which this is the case yet published is Parsons and White, "The Link Between Character and Society," in Lipset and Lowenthal, editors, *Culture and Social Character* (Free Press, 1961).

[8] Durkheim was one of the few to see clearly that the "division of labor" in the private sector must proceed concomitantly with increasing elaboration of the functions of government. Cf. Durkheim, *op. cit.*

11

THE JOHN BIRCH SOCIETY: "RADICAL RIGHT" AND "EXTREME LEFT" IN THE POLITICAL CONTEXT OF POST WORLD WAR II (1962)*

Alan F. Westin

In April of 1961, the Gallup Poll asked a nationwide sample of Americans whether they had heard of the John Birch Society. The poll indicated that thirty-nine million persons—an extraordinary number, according to Gallup—had read or heard of the Birchers. Of these, 44 per cent had an unfavorable estimate of the Society, 9 per cent were favorable, and 47 per cent had not yet reached a judgment. In one sense, these figures suggest a five-to-one rejection of the Birchers. But the figures also indicate that at the moment when the Society was receiving highly damaging publicity—when the mass media were featuring the charge by Birch founder Robert Welch that President Eisenhower was "a dedicated, conscious agent of the Communist conspiracy"—a projected three and a half million persons still perceived the Society as a commendable, patriotic anti-Communist organization. If the undecided 47 per cent were to be divided in the same proportion as those who had reached a judgment (and this might underweight pro-Birch sentiment), another three and a half million persons would be added to the ranks of the approving. By this estimate, as many as seven million Americans from among the most public-affairs-conscious forty million of our adult population seemed to be favorably impressed with the John Birch Society.

Between this poll and the beginning of 1962, virtually the entire religious, civic, and political Establishment of the nation rose to denounce the John Birch Society by name. Exposés filled the general and special media, while Robert Welch continued to contribute outlandish accusations to feed the exposés and dismay his conservative well-wishers. Yet when the Gallup Poll again asked a nationwide sample about the Birchers, in February, 1962, 8 per cent of the now fifty-six million who had heard of the Society were still favorably impressed. (43 per cent were unfavorable and 49 per cent had no opinion.) This represents a projected four and a half million approving citizens, with a potential among the undecided of another five million, making a "hard core" of nine and a half million Americans who are assumed to see the Birch Society as a useful organization in the anti-Communist cause.†

The explanation of this high degree of interest is that the Birch Society had become, for the while, the most appealing, activist, and efficient movement to appear on the extreme right since the fertile decade of the 1930s. Birch membership in 1962 was estimated by most observers at sixty thousand and was distributed widely throughout the nation, with particular strength in traditional centers of fundamentalism like Houston, Los Angeles, Nashville, Wichita, and Boston. This membership provided an annual-dues income of $1,300,000. Life membership at $1000, special donations by wealthy supporters, and sales of Society literature added perhaps $300,-000 more, giving the group a working fund of $1,600,000 a year. As of early 1962, the Society, by its own count, had 41 staff workers in its home offices in Belmont, Massachusetts; 35 fully salaried and expenses-paid traveling "co-ordinators"; and 70 partially paid "volunteer" co-ordinators. The staff payroll alone was $12,000 a week, or $625,000 a year. During 1961 and 1962, the effect of this well-financed, well-staffed, and well-led apparatus had been felt in the civic and

† For a more detailed breakdown of this survey, see pp. 415–23.

political life of dozens of local communities, and "Bircher" had become an instantly recognized term of political description. Such a phenomenon is worth close attention and analysis.

I

However much factors like urbanization, the cold war, and status insecurities may have provided a new setting for native fundamentalists, a large and irreducible corps of such people has always existed in the United States. Unlike American liberals and conservatives—who accept the political system, acknowledge the loyalty of their opponents, and employ the ordinary political techniques—the fundamentalists can be distinguished by five identifying characteristics:

(1) They assume that there are always solutions capable of producing international victories and of resolving our social problems; when such solutions are not found, they attribute the failure to conspiracies led by evil men and their dupes.

(2) They refuse to believe in the integrity and patriotism of those who lead the dominant social groups—the churches, the unions, the business community, and the like—and declare that the American Establishment has become part of the conspiracy.

(3) They reject the political system; they lash out at "politicians," the major parties, and the give and take of political compromise as a betrayal of the fundamental Truth and as a circus to divert the people.

(4) They reject those programs for dealing with social, economic, and international problems that liberals and conservatives agree upon as minimal foundations. In their place, the fundamentalists propose drastic panaceas requiring major social change.

(5) To break the net of conspiracy, they advocate "direct action," sometimes in the form of a new political party, but more often through secret organizations, push-button pres-

sure campaigns, and front groups. Occasionally "direct action" will develop into hate-propaganda and calculated violence.

Today, right-fundamentalism spans a broad spectrum. At one pole is the "hate" right, led by the Conde McGinleys, Gerald L. K. Smiths, Admiral Crommelins, Father Terminellos, John Kaspers, and George Rockwells, who offer various combinations of anti-Semitic, anti-Catholic, and anti-Negro sentiment. These groups are thoroughly discredited in contemporary America, and the major problem they present is a matter of defining the line that our law should draw between deviant expression and hate-mongering or advocacy of violence. At the other pole is the semi-respectable right. Here we encounter a variety of different political and educational organizations including the Foundation for Economic Education, the Daughters of the American Revolution, the Committee for Constitutional Government, and the White Citizens Councils of the South. Socially prominent figures belong to such groups, which are well financed, often have connections with local and national major-party factions, and exercise substantial lobbying influence. Their supporters and leaders may long to break with the two-party system and start a rightist party, but they are restrained by the knowledge that this would isolate them and thus diminish their present effectiveness.

The John Birch Society stands between the "hate" right and the semi-respectable right. In order to get a precise picture of its ideology and tactics, I examined the published works issued by the Society since its formation in 1958: the 1961 annotated edition of the *Blue Book of the John Birch Society*, its operating manual and theological fount; the monthly *Bulletin*, which is sent to members and contains the agenda of activities (the 1960 issues of the *Bulletin* are available in a bound edition entitled *The White Book of the John Birch Society*); those writings of Robert Welch that have been officially incorporated into and reprinted by the Society (e.g., *The Life of John Birch, May God Forgive Us, A Letter to the South on Segregation*); and every issue of

American Opinion, the monthly publication edited by Robert Welch for the Society, published before 1958 under the title *One Man's Opinion.*

Measured by its official materials, the authenticated accounts of Welch's speeches, and public comments by members of the Society's Council, the Society emerges as a pure-bred specimen of American right-fundamentalism.

(1) *Its image of world events and American politics is wholly conspiratorial.* In the July, 1960, *Bulletin,* Welch explains that the "key" to the advance of world Communism "is treason right within our government and the place to find it is right in Washington." The danger, Welch says in the *Blue Book,* "is almost entirely internal." And it is "a certainty," he writes in *May God Forgive Us,* that there are "more Communists and Communist sympathizers in our government today than ever before." As recently as January, 1961, Welch was informing his supporters that "Communist influences are now in almost complete control of our Federal Government."

Each year since 1958, Welch and his "board of experts" have published a "score board" rating all the nations of the world according to the "present degree of Communist influence and control over the economic and political affairs" of the country. In 1958, the United States was rated as 20–40 per cent under Communist control; in 1959, the United States went up to 30–50 per cent; and in 1960, the figure climbed to 40–60 per cent. (At that pace, we will reach the 80–100-per-cent mark in 1964.) England's rating went from 20–40 per cent in 1958 to 50–70 per cent in 1960. Israel is presently rated as 40–60 per cent controlled; Egypt 80–100 per cent.

Everywhere, the Birchers advise, Communists are at the heart of events, even among some events that might seem to less skilled observers remote from Kremlin direction. In an open letter to Khrushchev in 1958, Welch said, "Your hands played the decisive unseen part" in the run on American banks and their closing in 1933. It was the Communist-contrived recognition of the Soviets in 1933 that "saved them from financial collapse." The "very idea of American foreign

aid was dreamed up by Stalin, or by his agents for him." The
"trouble in the South over integration is Communist-contrived"; the Communists have invented a "phoney 'civil rights'
slogan to stir up bitterness and civil disorder, leading gradually to police-state rule by federal troops and armed resistance
to that rule." The United States Supreme Court "is one of
the most important agencies of Communism." The Federal
Reserve system is a "realization" of "Point 5" of the *Communist Manifesto*, calling for centralization of credit in the
hands of the state. The purpose of proposed legislation requiring registration of privately owned firearms is to aid the
Communists in making "ultimate seizure of such by the government easier and more complete." Everywhere, Welch concludes, the Communists are winning—in "the press, the pulpit,
the radio and television media, the labor unions, the schools,
the courts, and the legislative halls of America."

All the above descriptions of conspiratorial trends have
been cited from official Birch Society literature, what Welch
calls the Society's "steps to the Truth." But the picture grows
darker when one turns to the *Black Book*, or, as it is more
commonly known, *The Politician*—the book-length "letter"
that Welch circulated "privately" to hundreds of persons but
that the Society has carefully rejected as an official document. *The Politician* is to the Society what Leninist dogma is
to the Communist-front groups in Western or neutralist nations—it is the ultimate truth held by the founder and his hard
core, but it is too advanced and too powerful to present,
as yet, to the "masses" being led. In *The Politician*, Welch
names names. Presidents Roosevelt, Truman, and Eisenhower;
Secretary of State John Foster Dulles; C.I.A. Director Allen
Dulles; Chief Justice Warren—all of these men are called
knowing instruments of the Communist conspiracy.

It is worth noting that Eisenhower and his administration
draw the strongest venom in *The Politician*. For Welch, the
Eisenhower administration was a betrayal that could only
have had Communists at its source. "For many reasons and
after a lot of study," Welch writes, "I personally believe
[John Foster] Dulles to be a Communist agent." "Allen

Dulles is the most protected and untouchable supporter of Communism, next to Eisenhower himself, in Washington." Arthur F. Burns's job as head of the Council of Economic Advisers "has been merely a cover-up for Burns's liaison work between Eisenhower and some of his Communist bosses." "The chances are very strong that Milton Eisenhower is actually Dwight Eisenhower's superior and boss within the Communist Party." As for Dwight Eisenhower himself, Welch states unequivocally: "There is only one possible word to describe [Eisenhower's] purpose and actions. That word is treason." "My firm belief that Dwight Eisenhower is a dedicated, conscious agent of the Communist conspiracy," he continues, "is based on an accumulation of detailed evidence so extensive and so palpable that it seems to put this conviction beyond any reasonable doubt." Discussing what he terms Eisenhower's "mentality of fanaticism," Welch even refuses to accept the thought that Ike may just be an "opportunistic politician" aiding the Communists. "I personally think he has been sympathetic to ultimate Communist aims, realistically willing to use Communist means to help them achieve their goals, knowingly accepting and abiding by Communist orders, and consciously serving the Communist conspiracy for all of his adult life."

(2) *The Birchers impugn the integrity and patriotism of those at the head of the major social and economic groups of the nation.* In a supplement to the February, 1961, *Bulletin,* Welch announced that "Communist influences" are "very powerful in the top echelons of our educational system, our labor-union organizations, and of almost every important segment of our national life. Insidiously but rapidly the Communists are now reaching the tentacles of their conspiracy downward throughout the whole social, economic, and political pyramid." Thus, the National Council of Churches of Christ is Communist-minded, and from three to five per cent of the Protestant clergy have been called actual Communists. "Treason," Welch further declares, "is widespread and rampant in our high army circles." The American Medical Association has been "took" and can no longer be depended

upon for support in the fight against Socialism. So too with the United States Chamber of Commerce, which has been preaching dangerously liberal and internationalist doctrines in its courses on practical politics. (When Chamber leaders protested this slur, Welch replied that their outraged reaction was exactly like that of the State Department in the 1940s, when charges of Communist infiltration were first raised.) The leadership of our universities, corporations, foundations, communications media—all are riddled with Communists, or "Comsymps" (a word Welch coined to avoid having to say whether a given person was a real party member or only a sympathizer).

Naturally, Welch and his colleagues are certain that these "Comsymp" elites are out to destroy him and his movement. References to persecution and images of martyrdom abound in Birch literature, ranging from incessant mention of how the patron saint (Senator McCarthy) was driven to his death, to suggestions that Welch may be murdered one day by the Communists.

(3) *The Birchers are convinced that the Communists have gone so far in penetrating American politics that there is little hope in the existing political system.* In his letter to Khrushchev, Welch wrote that the Communists obviously intended to "maintain and increase [their] working control over both our major political parties." We cannot count on "politicians, political leadership or even political action." Though he advocates the nomination, on an American Party ticket, of Senator Barry Goldwater for President and J. Strom Thurmond for Vice-President in 1964, Welch has warned his followers that even Goldwater—the most "Americanist" figure around in politics at the moment—is "still a politician" and therefore not to be relied upon. Welch has also had some things to say about "Jumping Jack" Kennedy. According to Welch, the nation received "the exact Communist line . . . from Jack Kennedy's speeches, as quickly and faithfully as from the *Worker* or the *National Guardian*. . . ."

(4) *Most of the Birch Society's positive program consists of advocating the repeal of things or the removal of the*

nation from something or somewhere. A partial list of the things that the Society describes as wicked, Communist, and dangerous includes: U.S. membership in the United Nations, the International Labor Organization, the World Health Organization, the International Trade Organization, UNICEF (the United Nations International Children's Emergency Fund); membership in GATT (the General Agreement on Trades and Tariffs); reciprocal trade agreements; the "useless and costly" NATO; "so-called defense spending"; all foreign aid; diplomatic relations with the Soviet Union and all other Communist nations; the National Labor Relations Act; social security; the graduated income tax; the Rural Electrification Administration, the Reconstruction Finance Corporation, and the T.V.A.; government wage and price controls; "forced integration"; "deliberately fraudulent" U.S. government bonds; the Federal Reserve System; urban renewal; fluoridation; metro government; the corporate-dividend tax; the "mental-health racket"; federal aid to housing; and all programs "regimenting" farmers.

(5) *Finally, the Birch Society advocates both "direct action" and "dirty tactics" to "break the grip of the Communist conspiracy."* Unlike those right-fundamentalist groups that have energetic leaders but passive memberships, the Birchers are decidedly activist. "Get to work or learn to talk Russian" is a slogan Welch recommends to his followers, and they are certainly hard at work. From national headquarters in Belmont, Massachusetts, Welch formulates a set of complementary national and local action programs, then issues them to members through directives in the *Bulletin* and contacts with chapter leaders. A mixture of traditional and fundamentalist techniques is prescribed. The local programs include infiltration of community organizations such as the P.-T.A. ("to take them away from the Communists"); harassment of "pro-Communist" speakers at church meetings, political gatherings, and public forums; creation of local front groups (e.g., the Committee Against Summit Entanglements, College Graduates Against Educating Traitors at Government Expense, the Committee to Impeach Earl Warren, and the

Committee to Investigate Communist Influences at Vassar College); campaigns to secure endorsement of Birch positions and signatures for Birch petitions in all groups that Birch members belong to (e.g., veterans and business organizations); letters and telephone calls to local public officials, leading citizens, and newspapers who support what the Society opposes or oppose the Society directly; monthly telephone calls to the local public library to make sure it has copies of the five right-wing books recommended by Welch every month.

The national campaigns are carefully pinpointed efforts. They range from letter—and postcard—writing to national advertising campaigns. In the past two years, Birchers have been told to write the National Boy Scouts director and demand to know why the president of the National Council of Churches addressed their National Jamboree; insist personally and in writing each time a member flies American, United, or Eastern Airlines that they stock *Human Events* and the *National Review* on their planes; protest to the N.B.C. network and the Purex Corporation for sponsoring a TV drama favorable to Sacco and Vanzetti; circulate petitions and write letters to Congress to impeach Chief Justice Warren and thereby "give the Communists a setback."

Welch also sends out the copy for punchy postcards to be addressed to national political leaders. To cite instances in 1960 alone: to Ambassador Henry Cabot Lodge, Jr., at the U.N., "Two questions, Mr. Lodge—Who Murdered Bang-Jensen? And Which Side Are You On?"; to Secretary of State Christian Herter, "Castro is a Communist. Trujillo is an anti-Communist. Whose Side Are You On?"; and to President Eisenhower, on the eve of the scheduled summit conference, "Dear President Eisenhower—If you go, don't come back."

The last postcard stirred some protests from Society members, who felt that Welch's savage little message to the President was a bit too strong. Welch set them straight in the *Bulletin:* "It is one of our many sorrows that, in fighting the evil forces which now threaten our civilization, for us to be *too*

civilized is unquestionably to be defeated." The Communists, he continued, want us to be "too gentle, too respectable . . . [but] this is not a cream-puff war . . . and we do
mean business every step of the way." Welch admitted that
the technique of planted and loaded questions and the disruption of meetings was a "dirty trick," but he still defended it as
another vital tactic.

To stimulate compliance by members with the local and
national efforts prescribed each month in the *Bulletin*, Welch
has devised the MMM system, or "Member's Monthly
Memos." These forms are filled out by the member detailing
what he or she has done and including sundry observations
on the "Americanist fight." They are then collected by the
chapter leader and transmitted to Belmont. Welch and his
staff, according to the *Bulletin*, spend much time going over
the MMMs.

In its first years, the Birch Society was successful in attracting to it some highly substantial figures in local communities
—physicians, stockbrokers, retired military officers, lawyers,
businessmen (particularly small and middle-sized manufacturers in the Midwest and the South),[1] and professionals,

---

[1] Despite alarmist cries of a corporate-Birch alliance, there is no
evidence that the Birch Society has attracted support from the large
publicly owned, executive-managed companies of the Standard Oil,
General Motors, American Telephone & Telegraph type. While sixteen of the twenty-five members of the Birch Society's National
Council are top executives or former heads of corporations—including Frank Masland, President of H. Masland & Sons, the car-
pet firm; William Grede, President of Grede Foundries; F. G.
Chance, President of A. B. Chance & Sons; A. G. Heinsohn,
President of Cherokee Textile Mills; Fred Koch, President of the
Rock Island Oil & Refining Co.; and Cola G. Parker, former
President of Kimberley-Clark—a close look at these names, and
those of other corporate supporters, shows that these are either
family firms or companies headed by a single "I did it myself"
entrepreneur. Executives from major publicly held companies are
almost always retired figures, like Welch himself, and the two
former presidents of the N.A.M. on the Birch Council are obviously no longer presidents of that organization. The attitude of the
major "blue-chip" companies was indicated by a leading corporate
public-affairs newsletter in 1962 that lashed out at radical-right

many of whom have become local chapter leaders and state co-ordinators. The Council of the Society is a veritable board of directors of right-fundamentalism: men like Colonel Lawrence Bunker, Cola G. Parker, T. Coleman Andrews, Clarence Manion, and Spruille Braden. Among the contributing editors and editorial advisory committee for *American Opinion* have been J. B. Matthews, William S. Schlamm, Kenneth Colegrove, J. Bracken Lee, Ludwig von Mises, Adolphe Menjou, J. Howard Pew, and Albert C. Wedemeyer. In several communities, observers of the Society have noted a significant number of thirty-to-forty-year-olds joining the organization. Welch has stated that half of the Society's membership is Catholic,[2] that there are some Jewish members, and that there are Negroes also—two segregated locals in the South and integrated chapters in the North.

Press reports suggest that most of the Society's members already had strong affiliations with other right-wing groups before the Birch Society was formed. What Welch hoped to do was to build a one-million-member organization by welding together the masses of right-fundamentalist joiners into the fighting educational and pressure arm of the John Birch Society. In the *Bulletin* and *American Opinion*, Welch continually offers flattering salutes to various right-wing groups, publications, and personalities, stressing that "Americanists" can work in several forums at once for the cause. In May, 1961, for example, Welch listed two pages of "other anti-Communist groups" that he endorsed and urged Birchers to support. These included the American Coalition of Patriotic Societies, the American Council of Christian Laymen,

---

groups such as the Birch Society for taking money away from the Republican Party, trying to capture its local machinery, supporting primary candidates who endanger the position of conservatives, and giving President Kennedy the chance to associate the Republican Party and conservatism with "extremism."

[2] Catholic writers in *America* (the Jesuit organ) and in several diocesan newspapers have challenged Welch's figures about Catholic membership, but 30,000 Catholic Birch members do not seem an unlikely quantity.

the Cardinal Mindszenty Foundation, the Catholic Freedom
Foundation, the Christian Crusade, the Freedom Club (of
Los Angeles), Freedom in Action (Houston), the Intercollegiate Society of Individualists, the Network of Patriotic Letter Writers (Pasadena), and We, The People! (Chicago). In
turn, Welch's appearances are often sponsored by such
groups: the Freedom Club of Reverend James Fifield ar-
ranged his Los Angeles rally, and the Sons of the American
Revolution sponsored his Houston appearance.

To a large extent, Welch's personal selflessness and his
salesmanship made him a rallying point for the fundamentalist right, and no recent right-wing group comes to mind
that has achieved so large and solid a dues-paying and working membership. In a world of Communist advances in Asia
and Africa, pressures on Berlin, vast changes in the relation
of white to colored populations throughout the world, the
Birch Society has developed a thoroughly satisfying way for
the thin-lipped little lady from Wichita or the self-made
manufacturer of plumbing fixtures in North Carolina to work
in manageable little daily doses against "the Communists."
The cancer of the unquestioned international Communist
menace and the surgery of local pressure on the P.-T.A. and
the public library—here is a perfect appeal for right fundamentalism. This highlights the fact that the Society's most
successful efforts to date have not been on the national scene
but on the "soft underbelly" of American democracy—those
places where a minimum of pressure can often produce
maximum terror and restrictive responses. Welch has stressed
that school boards, city colleges, local businesses, local clergy,
and similar targets are the ones to concentrate on. Above all,
Welch has brought *co-ordination* to the fundamentalist right
—co-ordinated targets, co-ordinated meetings and rallies, and
co-ordinated pressure tactics. "All of a sudden," the director
of a Jewish Community Council in one city reflected, "the
right-wingers began to function like a disciplined platoon.
We have had to contend with precision and saturation ever
since."

II

If this is what the Society advocates and how it functions, what are its prospects? The Society has already lost one of its most potent weapons—the element of secrecy. Those in local communities who felt the sting of Birch campaigns during 1959–61 report that it was the factor of surprise at these sudden fundamentalist pressures and the unawareness of their organizational source that threw them off balance. Now, however, the Society has been brought into public view. Its authoritarian character and extremist statements have been attacked in both liberal and conservative newspapers; by important Catholic, Protestant, and Jewish leaders; and by political figures as diverse as Richard Nixon, President Kennedy, Attorney General Robert Kennedy, Representative Sam Rayburn, Senator Thomas E. Dodd, and even Senator Barry Goldwater himself. The fact that a prominent leader of the Society who had been chosen as Washington lobbyist for the American Retail Federation was hastily discarded by the Federation because of his Birch affiliation indicates that publicity has damaged the Society's claim to respectability. One Midwestern Congressman known for his open advocacy of right-wing movements felt it wise recently to seek out liberal leaders from his community and explain privately that he did *not* support the Birch movement. Increasingly, those "solid" figures who joined the group when it was operating privately have had to face public disapproval of the Society, and this probably has caused some falling away among borderline conservatives.

In the longer perspective, there are three specific factors that deserve mention in assessing the Society's future. The first is the authoritarian character of the group and the centralized control exercised by Robert Welch (a situation that has led Senator Goldwater to criticize Welch directly). According to the charter of the Society, Welch is the absolute leader; there is no accounting of dues or contributions; there is no representative process or democratic system for selecting programs or defining positions; and Welch has the power (which he has used) to expel any member or chapter for reasons sufficient to him, without right of hearing or appeal on the expulsion. This has produced widespread criticism of Welch as a "little Hitler" and the Society as a group run on Fascist lines. However, Welch has stressed again and again that members can disagree with him; that he doesn't expect any member to carry out a project which violates his conscience; and that the Society definitely opposes an "enforced conformity" within its ranks. The controls, Welch explains, are needed to prevent Communist infiltration of the Society (which he believes has already begun or will certainly begin as the Society becomes more effective) and infiltration by hate-mongers. This blend of leader-principle and group self-protection has great appeal to right-fundamentalists and even to some right-wing conservatives. The authoritarian setup makes fine ammunition for liberal and mainstream-conservative fire, but this is not likely to harm Welch a bit in his recruiting among fundamentalists.

A second factor is Welch himself. The fantastic allegations he has made in *The Politician*—even though the book has not been endorsed by the Council and is, indeed, repudiated by some members—have branded him as an unbalanced figure and convinced many staunch conservatives that Welch is a truly dangerous leader. The conservative Los Angeles *Times* did a thorough exposé of the Society and ran a stinging editorial that read Welch out of the conservative camp. Out of self-defense, Republicans in California joined in with the *Times* (especially in condemning Welch's attacks on Eisenhower), for the Birchers were proving so effective in pulling the Republican Party to the far right that some counterattack was felt to be essential. Welch himself has been highly equivocal about *The Politician*. He insists that it was a "private" letter and never published, though he does not deny its authenticity. In the May, 1961, issue of the *Bulletin,* he alludes to "questions or criticism from some of our most loyal members" relating to *The Politician*. To these, he replies that "the considerations involved in connection with many such matters are varied, over-lapping, involved, and with too many ramifications to be explained in short compass. There are even times when, for reasons of strategy, we take an oblique approach to a specific objective, and fully to explain every step of our course would seriously handicap our effectiveness." Having decided not to say anything at all, Welch assured members that if he "could give . . . the whole background of events," then objections might turn into approval, and with this he dropped the subject of his magnum opus.

As Welch led his cadres on during 1962, he forced even those who applauded the Birch Society to speak out against Welch personally. The arch-conservative Manchester (N.H.) *Union-Leader*, published by William Loeb, called on Welch to resign in February of 1962, citing Welch's praise for Batista and Trujillo as examples of his "nonsense." Russell Kirk, Congressman Walter Judd, Senator Thomas Dodd, and even Fulton Lewis, Jr., joined in suggestions that Welch's statements were wild, his presence a burden for "the cause," and his retirement highly desirable. The fullest attack came from the *National Review* on February 13, 1962, in a documented complaint that Welch "persists in distorting reality and in refusing to make the crucial moral and political distinction . . . between 1) *an active pro-Communist,* and 2) *an ineffectually anti-Communist Liberal."* After discussing *The Politician,* the *National Review* editorial added such examples of recent Welchery as these: "The Cuban invasion was a plot by Fidel Castro and his friends in the U. S. Government. The invasion was planned by Castro and his friends in our government to make Castro stronger throughout Latin America [and to] reduce U.S. prestige"; the United States is now "50–70+%" under "Communist-control"; "the government of the United States is under operational control of the Communist Party." The *National Review* also cited Welch's claims that the Tito break with Stalin was "completely stage-managed and phoney"; that Nasser was as much a Kremlin agent "as . . . Mao Tse Tung"; that the Soviets "deliberately precipitated" the Polish and Hungarian revolts of 1956; that the C.I.A. "is on the [Communist] side"; NATO is a Communist "hoax"; Willy Brandt is a "hypocritical Comsymp"; and on, and on. The editorial concluded by noting that the John Birch Society could be a superb organization, and "might have had many millions" of members, but for Welch's misleadership. Now, he should resign.

Not every Birch Society supporter joined this bandwagon of criticism, however. Congressman John Rousselot (Rep., Calif.), a Birch Society member and frank advocate, issued a statement on February 15, 1962, urging Welch's retention. "Robert Welch is an intense foe of Communism and the fact that he is the anti-Communist most often attacked in *Pravda* as well as other Communist publications throughout the United States and the rest of the world, attests to the validity of his thesis." Representative Rousselot added, "It seems unrealistic to me to ask any segment of our conservative, anti-Communist movement to be removed from the battle line at the time when we are beginning to win and just because we do not agree with every item."

As of the spring of 1962, Welch had not resigned. He is subject to no election or governing board, and it is arguable whether he or his critics best express the ideas of the Society's membership. In any event, his talents as organizer, salesman, and unifier of fundamentalist ranks made the Birch Society, and he has shown no intention of surrendering his apparatus.

A third factor relating to the Birch Society's immediate prospects is the question of anti-Semitism. Repeated charges have been made that the Society is a genteel endorser of such anti-Semitic publications as Russell Maguire's *American Mercury* and Merwin K. Hart's *Economic Council Newsletter*. Hart—who often talks about a conspiracy of "Zionists and their confederates" controlling America and whose organization was described by a Congressional committee investigating lobbying as one that relies on "an ill-concealed anti-Semitism"—is presently leader of the Birch Society's Manhattan Chapter No. 26. In addition, such openly anti-Semitic spokesmen as Conde McGinley have rushed to endorse the Birch Society. In the March 15, 1961, issue of *Common Sense*, McGinley wrote, "Inasmuch as we have received many inquiries from all over the United States regarding the John Birch Society, we want to go on record. We believe this to be an effective, patriotic group, in good hands."

On the other hand, Welch has always appealed to all religions, has urged Jews to join the Society, and has warned that it is a "Communist tactic to stir up distrust and hatred between Jews and Gentiles, Catholics and Protestants, Negroes and Whites." Much of the April, 1961, issue of his *Bulletin* is devoted to a discussion of the allegation that the Society is anti-Semitic, and what Welch has to say there is well worth close examination.

He opens by noting that "the most vicious" charges leveled against him have come from "such notorious anti-Semites as Lyrl Clark Van Hyning (*Women's Voice*) and Elizabeth Dilling (the *Dilling Bulletin*) on the grounds that my various committees and supporters are nothing but a 'bunch of Jews and Jew-kissers.' . . ." He then cites the names of Jewish members of the Society such as Willi Schlamm, Julius Epstein, Morrie Ryskind, the late Alfred Kohlberg, and Rabbi Max Merritt, and indicates that it has been endorsed by the American Jewish League Against Communism (a Jewish right-fundamentalist group). Next, Welch explains that he probably has "more good friends of the Jewish faith than any other Gentile in America." When he was in the candy-manufacturing business in Massachusetts, he recalls, he had many Jewish customers; he drank coffee in their kitchens at midnight, borrowed money from them and lent them money in return, and engaged in every kind of business and social activity with Jews.

Turning to some specific accusations, Welch admits that he used a pamphlet by Joseph Kamp as a source for his book *May God Forgive Us*, and also paid Kamp a hundred dollars to go through *The Life of John Birch* to find errors. This was in 1954. But later, he says, he became "aware of both the fact and the weapon of anti-Semitism in America, and I wanted no part of the whole argument." He had nothing further to do with Kamp after the 1954 contact, but he adds that he still simply doesn't know enough to say whether Kamp is really anti-Semitic.

Welch goes on to relate that a person who had been trying to convert one local chapter into "a hotbed of anti-Semitism" was dropped from the Society, and he pledges that the Society will never become a haven for anti-Semitic feeling "so long as I am directing its policies." After several additional paragraphs explaining why no member of the Jewish faith can also be a Communist (and pointing out that Karl Marx was "probably the most vicious anti-Semite of all times"), Welch concludes with the following warning:

> There is only one real danger in the charge of anti-Semitism today, to the man who actually is not anti-Semitic. It is that the utter (and in some cases malicious) unfairness of the charge may cause him to react with anger against Jews in general, and then begin to let some of his feeling creep into his writings or his speeches. That brings on even more vitriolic attacks, with a few more straws to support them. And so the development continues until the man in question winds up actually becoming violently anti-Semitic. And he seldom realizes that this was the Communist game and purpose all along, of which the majority of Jews who innocently helped the Reds to implement it were as unaware and innocent as the ordinary Methodist who supports the National Council of Churches. And many an anti-Communist fighter of great promise in America has had his career ruined and his effectiveness destroyed by letting himself fall into that carefully prepared trap.

This will never happen to him, Welch declares; to his "thousands of Jewish friends" he pledges, "I shall remain your friend, no matter what happens. . . ."[3] Furthermore, despite clear atmospheres of anti-Semitism at some of his public meetings and anti-Semitic questions from the floor,

[3] One other bit of information bearing on Welch's attitude is that he has been consistently anti-Nasser, viewing the Arab nationalists as aiding the Communists in gaining control of the Middle East.

Welch has refused to give his estimate of how many American rabbis are Comsymps, though he has given definite figures for the Protestant and Catholic clergy.

All the evidence available at the moment suggests the presence of a certain ambivalence in the Birch Society on the matter of anti-Semitism. Welch himself seems to be personally without bias toward Jews, and he wants the Society to reflect this position. Yet there is no doubt that some local leaders and members are well-known anti-Semites. With one after another of the rabbinical associations and major Jewish civic groups speaking out in complete condemnation of Welch and his movement, there will be rising pressures to respond to the "Jewish attacks." Probably, Welch will continue to allow some light flirtation with the more sophisticated anti-Semitic spokesmen. But it is a testimony to American maturity and the activities of Jewish defense agencies that open anti-Semitism is seen as a dead end today for any "middle-of-the-road right-wing organization."

One final aspect of the Society should be noted. Welch's writings have a remarkable combination of fantastic allegation and sweet reasonableness. Along with his proposals advocating drastic action against the Communist agents all over America will go reminders to be polite while making menacing telephone calls to local officials, to exercise self-restraint when attacked unfairly, and to take no action that violates "moral Principles." "It is a major purpose of the John Birch Society," he often explains, one "never to be overlooked by its members, to help in every way we can—by example as well as precept—to restore an abiding sense of moral values to greater use as a guide of conduct for individuals, for groups, and ultimately for nations." If there are some right-fundamentalists to whom this sort of passage sounds a bit like the National Council of Churches, the total blend of warmhearted, main-street vigilantism is still appealing to the majority of Welch's followers.

III

Whatever the specific prospects for the Birch Society, the 1960s will surely be years of expansion for the fundamentalist right in this country. Several things point toward this conclusion.

First, this will be a decade of immense frustration for American foreign policy. We will witness increased neutralism among the new nations; increased militancy among the non-white peoples over questions of color; constant military and scientific pressures from the Russians and, soon, the Chinese Communists; diminished American influence in the United Nations; greater conflict in Latin America; and continued outlays of foreign assistance that do not "buy loyalties" or "deliver votes" on critical issues. If the United States can simply prevent these situations from exploding, most informed students of diplomacy would think we had done well. But cutting losses inflicted by the stagnant 1950s and preparing hopeful future positions is not going to appeal to the right-fundamentalist masses (or to the frantic pacifist variety on the left, either). The right is unshakable in its faith in unilateral solutions and its belief that each loss for America can be traced to a Communist agent or "Comsymp" in the C.I.A., on the New York *Times,* in the Cathedral of St. John the Divine, or at the Yale Law School. And the inescapable strategic retreats of the early 1960s (Laos is a good example) will lend fuel to the fires on the right.

Second, the domestic racial issue also poses a serious threat of a rise in right-fundamentalism. In the 1960s, the struggle for Negro equality will move increasingly into areas outside the South. Lower-middle-class and middle-class resentments against Negro neighbors and Negro competitors are bound to increase. The crescendo of Negro militancy and the spreading use of government power to enforce civil rights will peel away the already thinned layers of toleration in many sectors of the Northern and Western population. In this area of public policy, groups like the Birch Society—which are not explicitly anti-Negro but oppose compulsory integration—have a promising position, and the reservoirs of white hostility, unless carefully and wisely channeled by both white and Negro liberal leaders, could fill the well of the fundamentalist right to overflowing.

Third, there exists the distinct possibility of an unprecedented coalition of Catholic and Protestant right-fundamentalists in the 1960s. Only those who know little about the history of American Catholicism think this is a monolithic community. Yet many factors suggest that the 1960s may see an even deeper division of American Catholics into warring ideological factions than has obtained at any time in the past. Already some influential Catholics are complaining bitterly that President Kennedy has joined the "Liberalist Establishment," that he has been "selling out" Catholic Church interests, and that the administration of the first Catholic President may go down in history as the "softest on Communism." This is far from the dominant view among American Catholics. Indeed, it may represent the last thrashing of the old, super-loyalist element in the American Catholic community—a group that will be goaded to extremism by the sight of an a-clerical, literate, sophisticated Catholic liberal in the White House. Under these conditions, and with the magic memory of Joseph McCarthy to help bridge the chasm of the Reformation, the fundamentalist Protestants and the fundamentalist Catholics may enter into alliance (possibly inside the Birch Society).

The Catholic Bishops at their annual meeting in 1961 denounced reckless radical-right charges, and a host of powerful clergy and writers within the Church have attacked Birch membership as inconsistent with Catholic ideals and responsibilities. Nevertheless, such Catholic journals as the *Tidings* (Los Angeles) and the *Tablet* (Brooklyn) remain pro-Birch, and Father Ginder remains on the Society's National Council.

Probably the most important long-range factor that will determine the future of the Birch Society and its potential imitators or replacement in the 1960s will be the position taken by conservatives—especially businessmen, conservative civic groups, and the Republican Party. On that question, and on the larger historical significance of the Birchers, it is useful to compare the radical right of the 1960s with the extreme left of 1945–48, since the ideologies, programs, strategies, and tactics of the two movements are remarkably similar.

In 1946, the pro-Communist left saw its wartime hopes for a perfect world—for total disarmament, an economy of abundance, a harmonious United Nations, and fraternal United States-Soviet relations—shattered by the rise of severe tensions between the United States and Russia. The cause of these tensions, this grouping of the left concluded, was not Soviet imperialism or the "natural" conflicts of nation-states but a "Fascist conspiracy" within the United States. The danger was basically *internal*. "Nazis are running the American government," Henry Wallace declared at one passionate moment in 1948. Our two major parties had "rotted," and Wall Street, the military clique, labor "misleaders," "red-baiting" intellectuals, and even the churches had become part of a program to "betray" peace and progress. Unless "the people" rose and shook off this conspiracy, this left warned, the country faced an imminent Fascist takeover, and American foreign policy would serve only dictator regimes and the former Fascist nations.

Compare this ideological image with that of the new radical right. Its dream of perfection was that a Republican administration in 1952 (preferably led by MacArthur or Taft rather than Eisenhower) and a green light for Senators McCarthy and McCarran that would bring an end to the "appeasement" and "defeats" of the "Yalta-Acheson" decades. American prestige would soar upward, the Soviet empire would be pushed back to the borders of Russia, and the Soviet regime itself would probably collapse. All this would be accomplished while we were "restoring free enterprise" at home, erasing the "Socialist" measures of the New and Fair Deals, and balancing the budget.

However, when Soviet power rose rather than fell in the middle 1950s, when the forces of nationalism and neutralism increased, and when "Socialist" measures like the T.V.A. and social security remained and were even extended, the radical right exploded. Beginning about 1958, when the Birch Society was organized and other radical-right groups began to expand, the cause of our troubles was perceived: a vast "Communist conspiracy" at home, even under the Eisenhower administration. Our major parties, with their "left-wing tendencies" and reliance on "minority groups," the "Socialist" unions, Communist-infiltrated churches, even leaders of American business—all had been saturated with Communist ideas and were in the hands of Communist conspirators.

Sharing these perspectives, the two movements attacked the foreign and domestic policies of "treason." The pro-Communist left attacked the basic international programs of the United States in the late 1940s as *too* "anti-Communist." It opposed American policy toward the U.N. as based upon cold-war power politics, and demanded that we abandon the regional "war pacts" in which we were supposedly engaging as contrary to the U.N. charter. The pro-Communist left opposed what it called the Martial Plan for Europe (as well as military aid to Greece, Turkey, and Iran), warning that we were shoring up decadent regimes and that "the people" in these countries would not be bought for our "cold-war mercenaries." Defense spending and rearmament were violently denounced as warlike, costly, and the death knell for domestic reform. To meet the might of Soviet power, the pro-Communist left urged us to rely on our overpowering moral example as a peace-loving nation and to trust the prospects of Soviet reasonableness at the conference table. A book describing these views was entitled *High Treason*.

In its own terms, the radical right is mounting an identical attack on the nation's international position today. Now our policies are not "anti-Communist" enough. Our participation in the U.N. is rejected because we cannot use the world body as a cold-war agency. The radical right rejects American alliances and friendly relations with all governments that are not "firmly anti-Communist," a list that includes Mexico, India, Ghana, Burma, and other countries that are "playing along with the Communists." Foreign aid is bitterly assailed as "pouring money down Communist ratholes," wasting hard-earned and heavily taxed American dollars that should be given back to private enterprise at home. Balanced defense programs and overseas military establishments are regarded as "useless" measures that could be replaced by far smaller expenditures for "massive retaliation"; if the Soviets were only taught that we mean business, that would solve the problems of the arms race. This, after all, is the radical right's basic key to American foreign policy: "Mean business! Really mean business!" After that, the U.N., foreign aid, NATO—all would be unnecessary, and a resolute America would turn back the Sino-Soviet tides by the stern announcement of our will to be Dead Rather Than Red.

In terms of basic strategy, the pro-Communists in 1946–48 aimed at winning influence within two key sectors of American civic life which were considered ripe for penetration—the labor movement and organized liberalism. Communists and Progressives had secured important positions in the union movement between 1935 and 1945; they hoped to operate outward from unions controlled by them, such as the United Electrical Workers, the International Longshoremen's Union, and the Mine, Mill, and Smelter Workers, to bring the unions like the United Auto Workers and the C.I.O. itself into the "Progressive camp."

Pro-Communists and their Progressive allies reasoned that control of the C.I.O. and organized liberalism would give them access to power in the Democratic Party. At the least, the Progressives would exercise a veto power in the formulation of foreign and domestic policy by the Democrats; with luck, they could replace the "Truman cold-war" leadership of the Democrats with old New Deal figures who shared some of their perspectives.

Such a figure was soon found in a first-term New Deal Cabinet member, a former Vice-President under Roosevelt, and a man who left the Truman Cabinet because of disagreement over the national anti-Communist consensus—Henry A. Wallace. It was Wallace who gave the pro-Communist left its respectability in 1946–47, and it was Wallace who led that "left" to found the Progressive Party in 1948, and break openly with the "two old parties."

While the radical right is still in its "1946" rather than its "1948" phase strategically, its basic objectives are clear enough. It is aiming at the "soft" areas of the business community and organized conservatism. The newer groups of the radical right, such as the Birch Society and We, The People and older organizations such as the National Economic Council and the Constitutional Educational League, already had influential business figures in their ranks and as their financial patrons. And as we shall see, the support of the business community has been increasing in recent months.

As for the established conservative groups, the themes of the radical right have been echoing in such conservative strongholds as the National Association of Manufacturers, the National Association of Real Estate Boards, the American Legion, and the Daughters of the American Revolution. Other conservative groups, such as the American Medical Association, the American Bar Association, and the American Farm Bureau Federation, are now facing ideological penetration.

If it can rally enough business and conservative group support, the radical right can look forward to influence in the Republican Party. At the least, it could push Republicans in a far right direction, and it might lead the Republicans to nominate a rightist in 1964 or 1968. If this is not possible, there is the distinct possibility of a third-party campaign by the radical right, as some of its leaders have already demanded. Obviously Senator J. Strom Thurmond, a nominal Democrat, would be delighted to lead this movement, just as he led the Dixiecrats in 1948.

Unlike Senator McCarthy and the loose apparatus of McCarthyism, the radical right is fervently organizational today. Once people attending radical-right rallies have been alarmed by tales of Communist betrayal in Washington and imminent collapse of the nation—as those of the pro-Communist "Left" were alarmed by tales of impending fascism—the organizers carefully follow up by leading the new recruits into a total "life-way" apparatus. Followers are put to work in "Americanist" cadres. In the Birch Society, there are home-study groups where tape recordings are played and films are shown; radical-right books and pamphlets are assigned and discussed under the careful direction of a chapter leader; members report on their activities and are given regular assignments to conduct pressure campaigns against their community's "Communists"—e.g., local ministers, school-board members, library committees, and newspaper editors.

In a lovely parallel with the American Communist Party, there are now bookstores throughout the nation that serve as nerve centers for local radical-right activity: the Betsy Ross Bookshop in Los Angeles; the Pro-Blue Patriotic Book Store in Torrance, California; and the Anti-Communist Bookstore in Fort Lauderdale, Florida, are only a few of the dozens now in existence. The functions of such places were recently described by a New York *Times* report on radical-right bookstores in California: radical-right books and pamphlets are sold, speakers' names listed, rallies advertised, petitions left for signing, and membership and mailing lists traded among various local groups.

Like the old Communist Left, the radical right knows how to manipulate the appeals of martyrdom. The radical right begins with Senator McCarthy, the patron saint driven to his death by the Communists, and moves on to "Americanists" such as General Edwin A. Walker who are "hounded" from positions in the military, the colleges, the communications media, and the government because they dare to tell "the Truth." Thus a leading article in *American Opinion*, the Birch organ, could have cribbed a paragraph from a radical-left organ of 1946 in its lament that today America sees "Witch-hunting of patriots . . . character assassination, and wild accusations against anybody who dares ask questions and insist upon answers." It is also an article of faith for both movements that all of these powerful persecuting forces can be wiped out in a flash by revealing "the Truth" to an "angry people." The Birchers will triumph, and soon, *American*

Opinion states, because it is the movement of "the revolted, misinformed, deceived, abused, angry American. . . ."

These are some of the deadly parallels of ideology, program, strategy, and tactics between the extreme left in 1946 to 1948 and the present radical right. But in using this comparison, two things should be said immediately. First, I am not suggesting that the two movements are identical. History provides complex and suggestive analogies at times, but no photographic reproductions, and obviously there are great differences. The most important of these is the fact that no hostile nation and its puppet party within the United States are guiding the radical right, as the Soviet Union and the American Communist Party came to infiltrate the pro-Communist left. There is no secret espionage and infiltration apparatus linked to the radical right, despite Robert Welch's airy pledges to set up Birch "front groups" such as the Committee Against Summit Entanglements or College Graduates Against Educating Traitors at Government Expense. And there is less unity and single-mindedness on the radical right than there was on the radical left, for all the efforts of Billy Hargis and Kent Courtney to establish a national Anti-Communist Federation. Yet in its own way the radical right does present a unified and pointed danger to the national consensus.

Second, I hope it is clear that I do not regard departures from the "national anti-Communist consensus" as automatically putting all critics in the radical left or radical right. Nor is this an argument that national progress comes only from "moderate" and "unvisionary" ideas. Obviously there can be legitimate, far-reaching criticisms of our internal-security measures, welfare programs, alliance policies, military strategy, disarmament position, U.N. policies, and the like. Thus Norman Thomas and the Committee for a Sane Nuclear Policy are legitimate participants in our national debates, as are Russell Kirk and the American Enterprise Association. The all-important distinction is that their criticisms are made within the framework of rational discourse and civic responsibility. They do not rest on cries of grand hidden conspiracies, allegations of traitorous leadership, and dangerously millennial proposals. Nor do they include bullying tactics in the civic marketplace, whether Communist or Birchite. With this as a guide, it should be clear that talk of Americans for Democratic Action or the N.A.A.C.P. as the radical left of today is absurd.

One of the uses of this analogy is to recall what happened when this leftist movement arose after 1945. Between 1946 and 1948, after a pitched battle marked by a few misadventures for liberalism (such as the Alger Hiss case), American labor and the American liberal community thoroughly repulsed the pro-Communist left. The C.I.O. expelled the partyline unions, eliminated pro-Communist staff members such as the C.I.O.'s General Counsel, Lee Pressman, and pressed "left-leaning" union chiefs like Mike Quill and Joseph Curran to break loose from the party line. Liberal organizational leaders such as Mrs. Eleanor Roosevelt, Reinhold Niebuhr, Walter Reuther, and Arthur Schlesinger, Jr., formed Americans for Democratic Action to focus the opposition of American liberals to the Communists. And, by a painful process, the American Veterans Committee showed that liberals could save their organizations from Communist infiltration. On the left itself, there were a number of vocal, if small, anti-Stalinist groups that fought the Communists and the Progressives— *The New Leader* magazine, for example, and Norman Thomas's Socialist Party, and many of the writers and intellectuals who previously had been supporters of Trotsky in the thirties.

The result of these various actions was that the pro-Communist left was isolated from either political or civic respectability in the nation. The Truman administration was able to execute the Marshall Plan, create NATO, and meet the explosion of the Korean War. And American liberalism emerged from the 1945-to-1948 period purged of the misunderstandings of Soviet Communism that had marked the thirties.

The future of the Birch Society and the radical right will very largely be shaped by the way business, conservatives, and the Republican Party police the boundaries of conservatism. There is every indication that the traditions of the

democratic center are at work and that the containment of
the radical right is at hand. But it will always be containment,
rather than extinction, as the Gallup figures cited earlier
suggest. The radical right and the extreme left are annoying
endemic features of American political life. But it is wise to
remember that they represent the price we pay for freedom of
thought, speech, and association in America; that resistance
to their destructive proposals through public debate and defense of policies serves to toughen the muscles of an often
flabby Establishment; and that the drawing together of liberal and conservative groups against the spear thrusts of the
radicals is a highly useful process for a nation waging a
global battle for peace, freedom, and security.

12

ENGLAND AND AMERICA: CLIMATES OF TOLERANCE AND INTOLERANCE (1962)*

Herbert H. Hyman

During the 1950s, a climate of political intolerance existed in the United States. While working on various surveys of this climate, I began to feel that our understanding of this phenomenon would be greatly enlarged by an examination of the English scene. Both countries are in that same broad temperate zone of the world where the balance of nature, forces of history, political geography, and law should have affected us equally. Yet England appeared to be a region that continued to be favored by a climate of political tolerance in sharp contrast to the unfavorable changes America had become exposed to. A comparative study to determine whether there was, in fact, a difference, and what the factors accounting for it might be, was planned, and the exploratory phases of it were conducted by field studies undertaken in 1961.

I

Some clarification of the concept involved in "a climate of political intolerance" is a necessary prelude. Our ultimate concern is with the widespread intolerance manifested in actions against political nonconformists. The *overt intolerance* may be regarded as a reflection of a *climate of opinion*—a

* The support of the Guggenheim Foundation and the Social Science Research Council is gratefully acknowledged. The research assistance of Miss Harriet Zuckerman in the United States and the co-operation of Dr. Mark Abrams in England are also acknowledged with thanks.

pervasive pattern of beliefs and attitudes in a society—about political nonconformity. This, in turn, may be seen as embedded in a more fundamental system of belief and attitude involving *generalized intolerance* toward political groups, ethnic groups, and other groups within the country or outside its boundaries. To assume that these three phenomena are the same, or naturally flow and blend into one another, is to obscure the important questions of the processes by which they become linked. Thus, it is equally possible that generalized intolerance can become focused on or diverted from a particular object, and, once focused, can be translated or not into various forms of action against that object. Some of the differences in England might derive from fundamental differences in climates of opinion or might instead derive from factors that altered the focus of such opinions, or their translation into action.

A climate of political intolerance is a problem of deep concern, for it may generate in society an atmosphere of fear and distrust. Dissenters of all varieties—not only Communists —may become afraid to engage in innocent forms of behavior, expressions of attitude, or perhaps even to hold "dangerous" opinions. Such feelings may also be subsumed under the concept of a climate of opinion, but here again a correspondence between a climate of political intolerance and an atmosphere of fear should not be assumed. Whether such fears become pervasive or remain restricted to particular groups and the way they manifest themselves may depend on many factors, some that sustain possible victims of intolerance, and others that contain the intolerance itself. The measurement of the English atmosphere and the exploration of such factors formed the second purpose of the comparative study.

II

A brief review of some studies of America in the 1950s is necessary for comparison. The American conclusions can pose questions to be checked against the English experience. And by seeing what questions the American studies left unanswered, the crucial role of comparative studies in regions of tolerance and intolerance can be conveyed.

The many scholarly analyses of the American security programs have pointed out inadequacies in the criteria and legal procedures employed, and have documented the cases of injury and injustice to individuals in government and teaching.[1] To demonstrate the climate of opinion in the general public and the extent of fear, one must turn, however, to various surveys.

In a national survey in 1954, Samuel Stouffer demonstrated that the level of public intolerance, not only toward Communists but toward milder kinds of political nonconformists, was strikingly high.[2] But the widespread intolerance was not matched by any widespread fear among the people about expressing views in their everyday life. One must recall that the public merely reported their intolerant *opinions* and did not always act them out, and this implies that a climate of intolerance requires stimulation and mobilization in order to work its social effects.

On this score, Stouffer's parallel inquiry among *local* community leaders, mainly those in *legitimate* positions of authority, had revealed that these persons, when asked to venture opinions in their roles as private individuals, were more tolerant than the public, although not as tolerant as one might hope. Thus, legitimate local leadership, which might mobilize popular sentiments, was not as rampant as the public, and

[1] See, for example, various works cited below. One finds no equivalent to this extensive literature for the British security programs. While this may represent the bent of English scholarship or the complacency of English scholars, it also suggests that there was very little provocative enough to call for the attention of analysts. Two of the very few treatments of the British program are, interestingly enough, by American scholars. See E. Bontecou, "The English Policy as to Communists and Fascists in the Civil Service," *Columbia Law Review,* 51, 1951, pp. 564–86; H. H. Wilson, and H. Glickman, *The Problem of Internal Security in Great Britain, 1948–1953,* Doubleday Short Studies in Political Science, 1954.

[2] S. A. Stouffer, *Communism, Conformity, and Civil Liberties* (New York: Doubleday, 1955).

acted as a partial check on possibly unbridled actions. Other psychological findings of Stouffer's study help resolve the paradox. The normal apathy of the public provided some restraint on violent action against possible victims and also made the public less responsive to appeals to intolerance from national figures. The Army-McCarthy hearings, via one mass medium or another, had reached an estimated audience of some eighty-five million adults. Yet Stouffer found that thirty per cent of the national sample could not name any of the senators who had been investigating Communism, not even McCarthy. Such is one of the blessed social functions of ignorance!

Stouffer's prime finding, the widespread intolerance in the public, leads one to develop certain models of the way intolerance must be distributed within a population for it to generate maximum fear. The many who are intolerant do not fear the climate of opinion they themselves create; they are the agents of intolerance, not the victims. The more their numbers increase, the fewer are left over who hold the kind of opinions that would be a cause for fear—although as the minority weighs the odds, the fears might become more intense. Various models to represent such social processes might be elaborated along ecological lines, since the assumption that the national population is the meaningful social entity may be unwarranted. However one refines these models, it tends to become clear that preponderant intolerance in a society does not create the widest repercussions of fear.

But while the *general* public did not exhibit what Stouffer termed a "national anxiety neurosis," studies of *specialized* population groups did document an atmosphere of fear in response to the felt climate of intolerance. Marjorie Fiske's study of librarians in California showed that the librarians engaged in many self-imposed restrictive practices so as to avoid sanctions.[3] Lazarsfeld and Thielens in 1955 surveyed a large sample of social scientists in colleges throughout the country and documented the incidents of social pressure

[3] M. Fiske, *Book Selection and Censorship* (Berkeley and Los Angeles: University of California Press, 1959).

against political nonconformity that in turn had led to considerable apprehension and cautionary activity on the part of teachers.[4] In 1954 Marie Jahoda studied a small sample of personnel then currently employed in the broadcasting industry and showed that the climate of intolerance, as channeled through the institution of the blacklist, had created a preponderant pattern of fear among such individuals, so that they had restricted their opinions, activities, and associations.[5] A similar pattern of findings was evident in an earlier study by Jahoda and Cook, conducted in 1951, among a small sample of Washington civil servants; they demonstrated that the loyalty-and-security issue had become of such pervasive concern to these individuals that in response to the total climate of formal government procedures and informal pressures, these individuals showed much fear and cautionary activity.[6] These and other specialized studies provide substantial evidence that, while the masses were not made afraid by the climate of intolerance, particular strategic groups who had been objects of attack were definitely prone to fear.[7]

[4] P. F. Lazarsfeld and W. Thielens, *The Academic Mind* (Glencoe: Free Press, 1958).

[5] M. Jahoda, "Anti-Communism and Employment Policies in Radio and Television," in J. Cogley, *Report on Blacklisting*, II, *Radio-Television* (The Fund for the Republic, 1956), pp. 221–81.

[6] M. Jahoda and S. Cook, "Security Measures and Freedom of Thought," *Yale Law Journal*, 61, 1952, pp. 295–333.

[7] In the Stouffer study, respondents who had reported that people did not feel as free to express opinions as formerly were asked which kinds of people felt less free. The leadership sample included individuals in local government and on the school and library boards, thus giving them an obvious vantage point for making observations of these sectors of personnel. The major differences in the responses to this sub-question for the leadership as against the general population was in the tendency of leadership to mention people in public life, educators, and intellectuals. (*Op. cit.*, p. 79.) An illustration of the climate of fear among civil servants during that period was reported by Chief Justice Warren: "A few days ago I read in the newspaper that a group of state employees . . . charged with responsibility for determining what announcements could be posted on the employees' bulletin board refused to permit the Bill of Rights to be posted on the ground that it was a controversial document. It was reported that the altercation became

All of these studies exploited their resources to the full, but were limited empirically to certain forms of analysis. By comparing groups within the sample, the analysts indicated the factors accounting for differences in intolerance and sensitivity to fear that were of an individual or psychological nature. They were also able to establish the differences in the situations—the milieu or community setting, and still larger factors of a sub-societal or sub-cultural nature—which shaped the responses. But these many diverse analyses, based as they were on an inquiry at a particular time or place within the one society, did not provide any empirical test of *macroscopic* factors, such as the cultural and historical, economic, political, and administrative, which might account for the *over-all* findings about the American climate of opinion.

A comparative national study can provide some test of such factors. And the comparison with England commends itself as an almost model experiment. The external threat of the Soviet Union and the cold war had affected both countries. The dangers of internal subversion existed in both countries and led to official programs of security promulgated at about the same time in 1948–49. If anything, England labored under handicaps that should have aggravated the security problem. England was weaker militarily and economically, and in terms of proximity was in even greater danger from the Soviet Union. Various English trade unions were threatened by Communist domination, including some strategic unions of civil servants.[8] England had had its own notorious cases of

intense, and that only after the Governor, in writing, vouched for its non-controversial character was the Bill of Rights permitted to occupy a place along with routine items of interest to state employees. And this happened in the United States of America on the 15th day of December, 1954, the 163rd anniversary of our Bill of Rights, declared by proclamation of President Eisenhower to be Bill of Rights Day." Quoted by John Lord O'Brian, *National Security and Individual Freedom* (Cambridge: Harvard University Press, 1955), p. 68.

[8] It is obviously very difficult to find a simple and appropriate index of the strength of the Communist Party and the dangers it presented for the internal security of England or the United States,

espionage to stimulate official and public concern with problems of security and loyalty. Yet this very same complex of objective events led in the United States to McCarthyism, but in England, despite even more compelling conditions, it did not. Obviously, there is much more to it than these objective circumstances.

III

It may hardly appear to be a discovery that there are more subtle factors involved. Obviously, an objective threat to a society can be perceived in many different ways and need not always lead to the same demands that political dissent within the society be restricted. The findings from comparable surveys conducted in 1953 among samples of teachers in seven western European countries showed that the relation between "threat orientation" and tolerance of internal dissent varied among the countries, and that *each* of these variables was itself complex and could have a different psychological structure from country to country.[9] Yet the value of a simple con-

---

and to obtain the statistical evidence to compute the index. Some sense of the comparative situation is afforded by various facts. Within the United States, estimates of membership at various times have not run higher than 100,000, and a reasonable estimate for the period in question, the early fifties, would place it at under 50,000. The vote, which might provide a better index of popular support, at least in the pre-war years when the Communist Party was on the ballot, generally ran under 50,000 and in the peak year was about 103,000, a fractional value of one per cent of the total vote. In the postwar years, the total third-party vote ran less than .1%, not counting the 1948 vote for Henry Wallace. In the postwar period in England, the Communist Party vote was also a fractional value of one per cent of the total vote cast, but was higher in magnitude than the corresponding American vote. The voting statistics for the United States are taken from conventional sources. For England, see *Whittaker's Almanac, 1962* (London: Whittaker's, 1962), p. 316.

[9] V. Aubert, B. Fisher, S. Rokkan, "A Comparative Study of Teachers' Attitudes to International Problems and Policies: Preliminary Review of Relationships in Interview Data from Seven Western European Countries," *Journal of Social Issues,* 10, No. 4, 1954,

clusion about objective threat should not be discounted. It has
the practical virtue of showing that a tradition of civil liberties
can survive such obstacles. From the point of view of social
research, there would be no way of establishing the exact
contribution of threatening events without recourse to some
type of comparative design, and their importance has been
strongly argued in past analyses of the American climate. For
example, it has been suggested that Alger Hiss was "a heaven-
sent gift. If he did not exist, the pseudo-conservatives would
have not been able to invent him."[10] How plausible it sounds
to claim that such a case aggravated public irrationality and
intolerance. But if America had an Alger Hiss, the English
had their Fuchs, their Pontecorvo, their Burgess and MacLean,
and still others, and still the consequences in intolerance did
not ensue. These cases are not sufficient causes, although they
may be necessary ones.

If we must turn to other factors besides the objective threat
to account for the difference in the extent of intolerance, the
comparative study of the two countries narrows down our
search considerably, for many other factors are also equated
in what seems a fortunate natural experimental design. A

---

pp. 25–39. Comparable national surveys in England, the United
States, and other countries yield estimates of perception of external
threat from such indicators as expectation of war, belief that Russia
is gaining over the United States, belief that the U.N. can maintain peace, or the belief that Russia is trying for world domination.
Such beliefs fluctuate over time; in some instances the Americans
are more prone to perceive external threat, but at other times the
total English population has been more threat-oriented, and their
upper classes have been much more threat-oriented than their
American counterparts. See *Where Stands Freedom: A Report on
the Findings of an International Survey of Public Opinion* (New
York: *Time* Magazine, April, 1948); for a summary of other results, see Otto Klineberg, *Tensions Affecting International Understanding* (New York: Social Science Research Council, 1950),
Bull. 62, pp. 131–32, 174–75.

[10] In a recent discussion of "The Rampageous Right," Alan
Barth, a long-time student of the problem, quotes and attributes
the statement to Richard Hofstadter. See the *New York Times
Magazine*, Nov. 26, 1961.

history of legal guarantees of civil liberties is common to both countries; if anything, some of the protections that are most relevant are *stronger* in America. The American Civil Service, a focus for McCarthyism, has greater *legal* rights to employment. The English civil servant has no statutory protection and his employment is not within the jurisdiction of the courts. He serves by the prerogative of the Crown or the government. In the parliamentary discussions of the English security program in 1948, many issues were reviewed and debated, but on the point of the government's right to terminate the employment of a civil servant there was no argument.[11] Law aside, the traditional norms and values that are taught as guides to conduct are much the same in both countries—justice, liberty, fair play, freedom of expression and belief—and if norms, not law, governed the phenomenon, the outcomes should have been the same.

It may be argued that what is written on the books counts less than what gets written on the mind. Perhaps the Americans do not really hold to the values. The values that are *internalized* are certainly relevant to the problem, and afford one illustration of a host of socio-psychological formulations that have been advanced to account for the American climate of intolerance. Whether they are, in fact, valid descriptions of American character is one issue, and this can be established from the comprehensive surveys that have been conducted in America. But the more important issue is the explanatory power of such formulations. Equivalent comparative data on the values of Englishmen would tell us whether such national value systems are crucial to the climates that emerged, for it might be the case that the values are widely honored, in the breach or the observance, in *both* places, and are not enough to account for the different outcomes.

[11] R. H. Pear, an English political scientist, makes the point eloquently in a discussion of security problems when he remarks that it is "brutally obvious in England that government employees have no rights to their governmental employment." See "People, Government and Security," *Northwestern University Law Review*, 51, 1956, p. 107.

Whatever direction these socio-psychological formulations take, they should be tested twice, once for their validity as descriptions of American character, and again for their validity as explanations of the climate of political intolerance. The comparative study serves the second test.

Many American surveys have shown that the public espoused general democratic values in the abstract, but did not apply them to particular concrete cases where they might be expected to apply. Values have to be *engaged,* have to be seen as relevant to particular situations, before a public uses them as guides to conduct.[12] Perhaps the English and American publics differ in the degree to which their common value system has been seen as relevant to the treatment of political nonconformity. Comparative description of values must be accompanied by research into the cognitive processes of value-engagement.

England provides an ideal testing ground for other socio-psychological constructs that have figured in discussions of the American climate of intolerance. For example, consider Alan Barth's recent characterization of the 1960-style McCarthyites as the "rampageous right": they see things simplistically; they do not make distinctions; the tensions and frustrations under which we live make them angry and less prone to reason.[18] There is nothing wrong with the description. But how adequate is it to explain the prominence of these groups in America? The English live in a similar world of tensions. They too are likely to draw oversimple cognitive maps to guide them toward a better world. Yet the English conservative does not go on a rampage against political nonconformists.

[12] For one of many illustrations of the lack of engagement of a value, see the Cornell studies, which establish that students who endorse democratic values do not apply them consistently to a series of concrete instances where they might logically be regarded as applicable. R. K. Goldsen, M. Rosenberg, R. Williams, and E. Suchman, *What College Students Think* (Princeton: Van Nostrand, 1960).

[18] Barth, *op. cit.*

What remains problematical is why the oversimplifications of thought have taken on a particular content in America. Why do the political nonconformist and the Communist in our midst figure so prominently in the American cognitive map? Why is the boundary line between the two so fuzzy on the American map? Doctrinal distinctions are not simple, but the wild assortment of criteria for identifying a Communist that Stouffer compiled from the responses of his sample seem hardly to represent the limits of ordinary American intelligence.[14] Comparative study might reveal some of the factors that have encouraged oversimplification in thought and have shaped its content.

Or consider the influential body of theory organized around the concepts of "status politics" and "status anxiety" —which were central to the original edition of this volume— in which McCarthyism was seen as the accompaniment of social mobility, of the displacement of some groups by others rising in the social order.[15] The upward mobile in their status-anxiety become conservative and conforming, and become intolerant because they must display their conformity by demanding it from others. By other psychodynamic routes, the downward mobile, the status-deprived, also arrive at intolerance. Certainly, the social location of McCarthy's support in America, and similar kinds of structural analyses of survey data, might give inferential support to such theories. But there are some stubborn facts about England that are hard to reconcile with the theory. The English postwar social order was mangled as much if not more than ours. They have their *nouveaux riches,* their "Texas millionaires," who should have felt a need to validate themselves by excessive loyalty and zeal about others' loyalty. Contrary to usual belief, social mobility in Britain, both upward and downward, has been

[14] Stouffer, *op. cit.,* pp. 156–78.
[15] For many elaborations of this theory, see the original essays in this volume. The statement of the theory above does not do full justice to all the subsidiary propositions in the theory, but seems a not unreasonable statement of the heart of the argument.

substantial and not very different in magnitude from mobility in the United States.[16]

IV

The contemplation of the comparative study provides a corrective for theories that employ some form of psychologi-

[16] Such comparisons involve many technical complexities, but the evidence is substantial and the conclusions in general agreement. See, for example, D. V. Glass, ed., *Social Mobility in Britain* (London: Routledge and Kegan Paul, 1954), pp. 260–66; S. M. Lipset and H. Zetterberg, "A Theory of Social Mobility," *Trans. Third World Cong. Sociol.*, 1956, III, pp. 155–77; B. Barber, *Social Stratification* (New York: Harcourt, Brace, 1957), 469–77; S. M. Lipset and R. Bendix, *Social Mobility in Industrial Society* (Berkeley: University of California Press, 1959), pp. 17–28. Admittedly, these theories demand more subtle types of measurement. For the upward mobile, the conservatism, conformity, and intolerance might be construed as a kind of anticipatory socialization, and so would call for some evidence on subjective class affiliation. But even here the English data show that forty per cent of manual workers identify themselves as middle class, and over half of these vote conservative. Mark Abrams, "Social Class and British Politics," *Public Opinion Quarterly*, 25, 1961, pp. 342–50. For comparative data for an earlier postwar period, in which the size of the subjectively defined middle class is fairly close for the two countries and the amount of false consciousness not markedly different, see W. Buchanan and H. Cantril, *How Nations See Each Other* (Urbana: University of Illinois Press, 1953), pp. 13–17. Ironically, these findings indicate a *smaller* "subjective" middle class in England and the United States than was found in eight other countries surveyed in the same inquiry. Other relevant data are based on a comparative study of former Communist Party members in the two countries. Downward social mobility, when subjectively appraised as deprivational, has figured in theories on the psychodynamics of Communist affiliations as well as in theories of intolerance. Comparing his small samples of former Communists on a variety of subtle indicators of status deprivation, Almond shows that his English subjects have deteriorated more from the status of their parents than his American subjects, exhibit somewhat less career dissatisfaction than the Americans, and exactly equal "personal damage" due to events and misfortunes. See G. Almond, *The Appeals of Communism* (Princeton: Princeton University Press, 1954), pp. 194–98.

cal analysis of the American past. The investigator finds the forerunners of the new intolerance of political nonconformists in such passages in our history as the Alien and Sedition Acts, the Know-Nothing Movement, the raids on Reds after World War I, the Ku Klux Klan, the rough and tough of the frontier, or some other gory item out of the American past from which one postulates a persistent streak of intolerance in American character. Comparison with England reveals the incompleteness of the argument. The scene there is one of lawfulness and restraint punctuated, only on occasion, by some brutal racial intolerance.[17] But the English past was full of excess, punitive laws, lawlessness, and the victimization of types of nonconformists. We had our past oaths for teachers, but they had their acts of uniformity against teachers. At Oxford, religious tests were not completely abolished until 1871. We had our anti-Semitism, but the legal disabilities placed on Jews in England persisted well into the latter half of the nineteenth century, and were not completely removed until about 1890. Paralleling our Alien and Sedition Acts—at about the same time and in similar response to the French Revolution, they had their Sedition trials.[18] They had their violence. A widely traveled anthropologist and student of the English character, Geoffrey Gorer, puts the matter vividly. "No society in the world I know of had such persistently cruel and violent amusements and diversions as the people of Elizabethan Eng-

[17] See, for example, "A Short Talk with a Fascist Beast," a young English laborer who took part in the beating of Negroes in the race riots in 1958. Quoted in S. M. Lipset, *Political Man* (New York: Doubleday, 1960), p. 98.

[18] How up-to-date, perhaps even American, the English prosecutor of 1793 sounds in his address to the jury. ". . . he used constantly to be reading seditious publications in the back shop;—it was there, in that cathedral of sedition, he sat like a spider, weaving his filthy web to ensnare the unwary. . . . Even the poor organist could not pass the house of this demon of mischief but he must be stopped and desired to play *ça ira*—a tune which is made use of in that unhappy country, France, as a signal for blood and carnage." A. E. Sutherland, "British Trials for Disloyal Association During the French Revolution," *Cornell Law Quarterly*, 34, 1948–49, pp. 313–14.

land; the bull-baiting, the bear-baiting, the cock-fighting, the public executions and floggings, the teasing of the insane in Bedlam." By 1800, the scene is still lurid: "six women were publicly flogged for hedge-pulling till the blood ran down their backs, and the public flogging of women was only made illegal in 1817."[19] The English parallel suggests that there is something questionable in the logic of explanations that appeal to a historical streak of general intolerance to account for the recent climate of political intolerance. History is obviously a record of discontinuities and changes in social character as well as a record of continuities. Somebody or something can break or extend the historical thread.

The blemishes on the English record, which we normally forget, suggest too that there may be something arbitrary in the sampling procedure used to support such theories about American intolerance. American History may be read as a record of periodic intolerance, violence, encroachment on civil liberties, but it is equally appropriate to draw opposite conclusions by judicious selection. In between the bad episodes, there were plenty of other things happening—native radicalism that was tolerated, utopian communities that survived unharmed, communistic communities founded by foreigners, reformers who were read and listened to, tracts on Socialism and even anarchism that were not burned or censored.[20] There are many strands to the American past. Perhaps one must look in England and America at the forces that bring out any particular inchoate aspect of national character.

Another psychological construct that often figured in the discussion of McCarthyism was the theme of conformity in the American character. Political intolerance certainly exacts as its price a conformity from its victims, but the argument appeals to a notion that there is a more fundamental and

[19] G. Gorer, *Exploring English Character* (New York: Criterion Books, 1955), pp. 13–15.

[20] See, for example, V. L. Parrington, Jr., *American Dreams: A Study of American Utopias* (Providence: Brown University Press, 1947); L. Filler, *Crusaders for American Liberalism* (New York: Harcourt, Brace, 1939).

generalized conformity that shapes the political demands for conformity and makes the victims compliant. Certainly, there is plenty of evidence of *individual* differences in compliance with social pressures, and recently there has appeared some evidence of national differences in compliance under *experimentally* created social pressures.[21] That Americans as a people demand more conformity from others than English people do, and that these demands must of necessity focus on the *political* sphere still remains unexamined and unproven. The seven-country study of teachers showed that the English subjects were among the highest in their *disapproval* of dissent on military matters, which was hardly suggestive of mildness when it came to conformity demands on matters of high importance,[22] while some American data from the Detroit area studies had suggested that the politically intolerant were inclined to *gentle* forms of persuasion of nonconformists, rather than to harsh measures.[23]

What we take as typifying the lack of English pressures for conformity, as some of my informants have suggested, is their tolerance of eccentricity, of the amateur engaged in odd hobbies; perhaps playing with politics is regarded as an innocent kind of nonconformity. The question whether a particular realm of behavior is defined as innocent or dangerous nonconformity is central to an understanding of the climate of intolerance in a society, and perhaps directs us to the definition of "dangerous" that is urged upon the ordinary man.[24]

[21] A recent study obtained differences between Norwegian and French subjects. See S. Milgran, "Nationality and Conformity," *Scientific American*, 205, Dec. 1961, pp. 45–51. For an earlier study in which the English findings were inconclusive, see S. Schachter *et al.*, "Cross Cultural Experiments on Threat and Rejection: A Study of the Organization for Comparative Research," *Human Relations*, 7, 1954, pp. 403–39.

[22] Aubert, *et al.*, p. 33.

[23] *A Social Profile of Detroit, 1956* (Ann Arbor: Survey Research Center, 1957), pp. 57–62.

[24] Analyses of the American climate of intolerance in terms of susceptibility to compliance with social pressures also distract attention from two important features of the recent period. Most American adults did not have to comply in their attitudes—they

In these many ways, the planning of a comparative study led me to reappraise the large body of speculations about McCarthyism. The hypotheses that withstood this reappraisal became the guide to my travels and observations. The research design ideally would have followed a particular sequence of stages. The general climate of opinion—the pervasive pattern of values, beliefs and attitudes that characterized the British public—should be described first on the basis of adequate survey data. If the British public differed in their dispositions toward intolerance, the psychological hypotheses that had been advanced to account for the American climate of political intolerance would have greater plausibility. If, however, the British public were equally disposed toward intolerance, then one should explore the political and structural factors that had held the intolerance in check. Was the British elite even more tolerant than Stouffer had found the stratum of American leadership to be? Had particular political institutions prevented the mobilization of intolerant sentiments? What influence did events and situations have in shaping the forms of intolerance? And if the British public were disposed toward intolerance, had an atmosphere of fear been generated, particularly among the kinds of groups that had been found to be vulnerable in the American studies?

Some of these hypotheses about climates of political intolerance could have been tested by another type of research design. Long-term trend surveys conducted within one society, the United States, would also have provided a comparison of political intolerance under conditions of changing events and national situations.[25]

---

weren't nonconformists to begin with—and the sustained pressures on the few who were nonconformists to start with were so severe that strength of character would have been little help. One may argue that in the formation of their original attitudes, a conformity process had already worked on the majority, but it seems valuable to distinguish such developmental phases of early socialization from later conformity processes, in which a change in opinion or action is coerced.

[25] Ideally, comparative-trend surveys in both countries could be conducted, thus demonstrating changes in national climates of

From trend questions on public intolerance asked by the National Opinion Research Center periodically over a decade, plus other survey data, Paul Sheatsley and I reported in 1953 considerable public intolerance long before the rise of McCarthy, but we also showed that this was correlative with events. With the cold war, public intolerance had grown and the relative tolerance of the more educated strata had been undermined.[26] McCarthyism declined, but the cold war did not abate. Some questions, therefore, were in order. How long does it take for the fears of the nonconformists to be dissipated? Have the social scientists, the civil servants, broadcasters, and librarians remained as apprehensive as they were? Has the public remained as intolerant in the years between McCarthy and Robert Welch, and, if so, what forms has such intolerance taken?

With these thoughts in mind, Sheatsley and I extended the trend line on two of the N.O.R.C. tolerance questions in surveys conducted in December, 1956, and April, 1957. At the

opinion as the respective contexts changed, and the differential response of national groups to situational factors. Earlier comparative national surveys provide one base-line point. In February, 1948, prior to the announcement of the British security program, surveys were conducted by Elmo Roper in nine European countries and the United States. One question asked was whether people did not have "today to a satisfactory degree" five specific freedoms. The British sample, in contrast to the Americans, very frequently mentioned the lack of the right to work at a job of one's choice or to private ownership of business, suggesting that the responses were discriminating. However, on the two freedoms relevant to our discussion—"the right to say or write what one believes without fear of punishment" and "protection from unreasonable interference by police"—the aggregate results are almost identical in the two countries, with only a small minority asserting that such freedoms were infringed. Comparisons between the American and the British educated strata, containing those individuals who would be more likely to be sensitive to and knowledgeable about such problems, reveal almost identical distributions, with only a small minority questioning the existence of such freedoms. *Where Stands Freedom, op. cit.*

[26] H. Hyman and P. B. Sheatsley, "Trends in Public Opinion on Civil Liberties," *Journal of Social Issues*, 9, No. 3, 1953, pp. 6–16.

height of McCarthyism, the earlier trend point had established in January, 1954, when 81 per cent of the national sample declared they would not allow Communist Party members to speak on the radio, a steady rise from a figure of 40 per cent in 1943. Three years later, in December, 1956, the figure was 73 per cent, and in April, 1957, it was 75 per cent. Similarly, we had reported in 1954 that 45 per cent would not allow Socialists to publish newspapers in peacetime, a rise from a figure of 25 per cent in 1943. In December, 1956, 38 per cent still endorsed this policy and in April, 1957, the figure was 39 per cent.[27] Such fragmentary data suggested that the sentiments of the American public continued to be intolerant, but simply had become *latent* in the absence of forces to activate, focus, or mobilize opinions.

If fragmentary findings over a short span can be suggestive, it would be much more illuminating to have longer trends to juxtapose against radical changes in events and political institutions. Under different leadership conditions, would the same pattern of sentiments have become mobilized into action? The fifties seem to have been a period when the actions of elected officials such as Senator McCarthy and some administrative officers in government, and the lack of action of other officials against intolerance, gave a new legitimacy to such behavior. In the sixties, by contrast, the legitimacy of such social movements and climates of opinion has been questioned by the strong actions of the President.[28] One wonders what difference this has made in the incidence, virulence,

[27] The earlier trend data are reported in Hyman and Sheatsley, *op. cit.* The 1954 trend point was reported in Stouffer, *op. cit.,* p. 56. The 1956–57 data are as yet unpublished.

[28] I have in mind not only President Kennedy's California speech of November, 1961, but also other episodes such as the recent rebuke accorded a reporter who questioned the loyalty of two State Department employees. A chain of events was thus set in motion in which the broadcast networks made an official inquiry to determine whether a lawsuit would follow if the story were carried, and the Under-Secretary of State left the parties in suspense. N.B.C. deleted the item from its transcription of the President's news conference, and the reporter declined to make any further public comment. The New York *Times,* Jan. 25, 1962, p. 12.

and forms of public intolerance and in the fears of nonconformists.[29] Alas, the interest of sponsors and of researchers
has diminished, as the problem of intolerance appeared less
problematical, and no one thus far has seen fit to repeat the
studies of Stouffer or Lazarsfeld or Fiske. Applied social research seems oriented to the immediate issue rather than
being problem-oriented. The latent aspects of an issue are
neglected and trend designs for surveys have lost prestige.

V

The first stage of my research strategy, as already indicated,
was to find systematic survey data on the British climate of
opinion. Occasional bits of such data that I had seen over the
years had led me to doubt the image of a tolerant English
public. If this were really so, I could then eliminate that variable as an explanation of the different climates of political
tolerance, and concentrate on the other hypotheses. In England, huge volumes of data had been collected on all sorts of
matters, but only a few questions had been asked on civil
liberties and political nonconformity. To the question why,
the survey people replied that they had no problem of Mc-
Carthyism, so why bother to study it?[30]

There was, however, enough survey data from a number of
countries, varying in the effective climates of political tolerance, to show that the sentiments of the common man every-

[29] Some evidence is provided by a comparison of Gallup Poll
findings on public opinion toward the John Birch Society with findings the Poll obtained on public approval of McCarthy in the early
fifties.

[30] This is a rather interesting example of a self-fulfilling proph-
ecy among research workers. You can't find out that you do have
a problem you think you don't have, if you don't study it. More
generally, as I have suggested elsewhere, we will never be able to
work toward a "theory of public opinion" until we have data
showing how a new opinion emerges from an earlier state in which
there were no opinions of that particular type held. Survey research
here again shows how it has identified what is problematic for study
almost exclusively with what is an issue, a *hot* problem, and this
has been to its disadvantage.

where are often intolerant, thus suggesting that other factors explain the different outcome. For example, in Norway, a relatively tolerant country, a probability sample of the City of Oslo was studied in 1951–52. Thirty-two per cent felt Communists should not have the right to publish their own newspaper, even if it were carefully controlled by the authorities, and proportions ranging between 40–50 per cent felt Communists should be denied such positions as teachers, non-leading positions in states and municipalities, and trade-union offices.[31] Surveys done by the Canadian Institute of Public Opinion in 1950 showed that the magnitude of public intolerance of Communists was about the same as Stouffer demonstrated for the American public in 1954.[32] The Australian Institute of Public Opinion had found in 1951 that about two-thirds of the public approved a ban on the Communist Party. Yet the ironical fact was that a national referendum had been held in September, 1951, on the issue of a ban and the ban had lost. One might have cast doubt on the validity of the surveys or argued for a last-minute shift in opinion. But in a survey conducted after the referendum, in December, 1951, the same finding was demonstrated. The finding was so startling that the survey was replicated once more and the exact same result obtained.[33] While one can explore other technical reasons for the difference between the vote and the popular opinion, what is suggested is that the relation between opinion and action is complicated by other variables, and an effective climate of opinion does not necessarily mirror popular sentiment.

[31] C. Bay, I. Gullvag, H. Ofstad, and H. Tonnessen, *Nationalism* (Oslo, Institute of Social Research, 1953), III, pages not numbered. While this was a period of military build-up, following Norway's joining NATO and the Korean War, and a period in which legislation for "preparedness" was being debated, it should also be noted that there was much criticism of such legislation, and a good deal of it was abandoned. Also, the effective climate of opinion allowed for much dissent and the expression of nonconformist opinion.

[32] See the releases of the Canadian Institute of Public Opinion.

[33] See various releases of the Australian Institute of Public Opinion.

Lacking exact survey data on the English public, I had to turn in other directions: to inquiry of informants, analysis of documents, and to an examination of concrete events. I attempted to find out what had actually happened to freedom of opinion, to political nonconformists, to Communists and so-called Communists in the schools, universities, civil service, and community. And it became abundantly clear to me as these bits of evidence accumulated that there had been many fewer overt actions against nonconformists. While this might be seen as a reflection of a climate of tolerant political opinion, the reverse may be argued. The lack of such actions may well alter the climate, and it might still be asserted that the general English public initially held as intolerant sentiments as are found in other countries. And the lack of actions may easily account for the reduction in an atmosphere of fear.

Consider the scope of *official* investigative activities in the United States in the mid-fifties. At that time, approximately six million American adults were covered by the *civilian* personnel-security programs of the federal government. These included about 2,300,000 employees of the federal government, some three million employees in private industries engaged in defense work, plus other personnel who came under special federal legislation concerned with security problems in the Atomic Energy Commission, the United Nations, and in maritime trades. The *military* personnel-security program covered an additional three million, for a total of nine million *adults* subject to investigation in 1955.[34] But even these figures seriously understate the extent to which official governmental scrutiny of security and loyalty touched the American people, for given the normal turnover of employment, subsequent occupants of the same positions would also be subject to investigation. Thus, depending on the span of years involved, the number of American adults might total considerably higher than nine million.

[34] These summary figures are taken from the *Report of the Special Committee on the Federal Loyalty-Security Program of the Association of the Bar of the City of New York* (New York: Dodd Mead, 1956), *passim*.

Investigations by committees of the Senate and the House of Representatives sometimes covered government agencies and the military, but other inquiries into the teaching professions and the communications industries brought under official scrutiny some considerable number of additional persons in non-federal employment. In addition, the loyalty of other individuals employed in the private sector came under official scrutiny through the requirement of a loyalty oath attached to various research grants made by the federal government, although such individuals were not actually subject to investigative procedures. To these millions, add the additional number whose political views came under scrutiny as a result of the security and loyalty programs of the various state governments. The two most populous states, New York and California, focused extensive investigative programs on teachers, and no less than a dozen other states had legislation covering various classes of employees.[35] Municipalities added their weight to the numbers by their own investigative activities.

The total number of individuals whose loyalty or security had been subject to *official* scrutiny by some organ of American *government* clearly extended into the many millions. The number of American *families* who had been affected by inquiry about one of their family members, and the additional number of families who had encountered such an inquiry through a field investigation of one of their acquaintances,

[35] For detailed accounts of activities in two of the states, see L. H. Chamberlain, *Loyalty and Legislative Action: A Survey of Activity by the New York State Legislature, 1919–1949* (Ithaca: Cornell University Press, 1951); E. L. Barrett, Jr., *The Tenney Committee: Legislative Investigation of Subversive Activities,* (Ithaca: Cornell University Press, 1951). For a brief summary of activities of states, see Ralph S. Brown, Jr., "Loyalty-Security Measures and Employment Opportunities," *Bulletin of Atomic Scientists,* XI, No. 4, 1955, pp. 113–17. Brown reports that "about half the states required test oaths of their employees, including teachers," and he estimates the number of state and local government employees subject to tests at about two million.

friends, or relatives must have been so large as to make quite
a dent in the consciousness of the American people.

In contrast, investigations in England were focused on a
much smaller group, those employed in sensitive posts in government or industry, and the aim was not to bar the individual
from all employment, but merely to decide whether he should
be transferred to a less sensitive position. The recent case of
Henry Houghton, found guilty in 1960 of selling secret information to agents of the Soviet Union, dramatically illustrates the difference in the British security program. Houghton
had been a clerk in the office of the naval attaché in Warsaw
in 1951, and was returned from this post to London on account of his drinking habits. Despite the potential security
risk, he was appointed a year later to a post in the Underwater
Detection Establishment of the British Navy, from which
agency he stole the secret papers leading to his ultimate conviction. While the report of the Romer Committee, which was
appointed to review security procedures following the revelation of these spy cases, strongly criticized the security practices employed by the Admiralty, it notes that "given the
security criteria of the time, no legitimate criticism can be
made of Houghton's subsequent appointment in 1952 to a
post in the Underwater Detection Establishment at Portland
which *did not in itself involve access to secret material.*"[36]

Comprehensive evidence on the exact scope of the official
British security program is not easy to obtain. Official documents and statistical summaries of cases suggest that the program has been limited to a narrow sphere of employment and
to a limited number of individuals. One can say that a much
larger sphere and population could in fact be affected since
investigations may be conducted secretly; witnesses similarly
protected by secrecy; the real grounds for dismissal, transfer,
or lack of promotion of employees not revealed; and decisions
on job applicants not disclosed. To estimate the magnitude
of this covert sphere is, in the nature of the case, impossible.
If one turns to sources other than the official ones, evidence is

[36] Manchester *Guardian,* June 14, 1961, p. 1:1. (Italics ours.)

impressionistic, much of it qualitative material involving selected cases, and all of it difficult to evaluate. Organizations
representing various classes of employees, teachers' and professors' associations, and unions of civil servants were vigilant
about their interests and well informed on grievances. This
increased the estimates but might still understate the extent
of the problem, since some victims of improper security
practices might be unsuspecting and occasional others might
prefer, on grounds of self-interest, to hush up the matter.
Interest groups concerned with problems of civil liberties, and
varying in their ideology and militancy, contributed additional
evidence on the extent of the security program.

From these sources, plus interviews with informants, I arrived at an approximate picture of the total scope, probably
missing only those ramifications of official-security programs
so secret that no member of the public was aware of them.
Secrecy, so secret, cannot alter the climate or create an atmosphere of fear, although it certainly frees investigators from
constraint and violates canons of law.[37]

The English security program, when first instituted in 1948,
was expressly limited to only a part of the civil service—to
those "employed in connection with work the nature of which
is vital to the security of the state." Additional security procedures introduced in 1952 for government employees involved in "exceptionally secret work, especially work involving access to secret information about atomic energy," applied
only to some 14,000 employees.[38] After the Burgess and Mac-
Lean case, a conference of Privy Councillors on Security

---

[37] Of greater concern as a possible source of bias in my findings
was the extent of investigation known or believed to be practiced
but whose detailed nature remained unknown to my informants.
This latter type of investigation, because of its "semi-secret" character, could have profound psychological effects and would be the
perfect device to create an atmosphere of anxiety. While anxiety
stemming from such a psychological source is readily reported and
is relevant to the study, its basis in objective reality cannot be determined because the facts are not known.

[38] Quoted in R. H. Pear, "People, Government and Security,"
Northwestern University Law Review, 51, No. 1, 1956, pp. 105–11.

suggested a strengthening of the security program and urged especially stringent precautions in the Foreign Service, and the defense and atomic-energy fields; these recommendations were accepted by the government. One informed estimate put the number of employees brought within the scope of these recommendations at about 120,000. Between 1948–61, a total of 163 professional civil servants were involved in official cases arising out of all these procedures. Of these the largest group, 83, were transferred to non-secret positions, and 32 were reinstated.[89]

The changes in the procedures introduced in 1956, however, may be more sweeping than they appear. The reports of the Campaign for the Limitation of Secret Police Powers, representing a committee of distinguished individuals, including a considerable number of M.P.s, have criticized the newer procedures, especially the secrecy involved and the fact that the normal safeguards against arbitrary action by Ministers provided by the principle of parliamentary responsibility cannot apply under a veil of secrecy. This committee refers to cases in their files involving personnel in the Merchant Navy, the Central Office of Information, the Post Office, private industry involved in defense contracts, and military personnel seeking commissions. The number of these cases is difficult to estimate from their report.[40] The annual reports of the National Council for Civil Liberties make reference to only a very small number of such incidents, and all such reports taken together hardly convey the impression of magnitude that one obtains from equivalent accounts of American cases summarized by scholars or by American organizations concerned with civil liberties.[41] By way of illustration,

[89] *State Service, Journal of the Institution of Professional Servants,* XLI, No. 4, 1961, p. 102.

[40] Campaign for the Limitation of Secret Police Powers, *A Year with the Secret Police.*

[41] See the National Council for Civil Liberties, Annual Reports for the years, 1955–1961. For equivalent American accounts of cases, see, for example, E. Bontecou, *The Federal Loyalty-Security Program* (Ithaca: Cornell University Press, 1953), pp. 101–56; A. Yarmolinsky, Comp., *Case Studies in Personnel Security* (Wash-

one summary by the American Civil Liberties Union abstracts and lists some seventy-five cases arising merely out of investigations by the House Un-American Activities Committee. In contrast, the annual report of the British National Council for 1956–57 remarks on "one or two disquieting reports of political discrimination creeping into employment where no security issue could by any stretch of the imagination be said to exist." The difference conveyed seems hardly accountable in terms merely of stylistic or expressive differences in annual report writing. On balance, it would appear that official English investigations of personnel in government and war-related industry have been limited in extent.[42]

Turning from the civil service and war-related industry to other occupational spheres, the contrast persists. In comparison with the extent of American investigation of the loyalty of teachers, the personnel of English elementary and secondary schools appears to be almost free from official governmental scrutiny. One major case clearly constitutes an exception, but in its very character is most informative for our purposes.[43] Beginning in 1950, the Middlesex County Education

---

ington: Bureau of National Affairs, 1955); Jahoda and Cook, *op. cit.;* American Civil Liberties Union, Mimeo Report, n.d.

[42] Discussions in print and conversations with informants often mention the very same case, that of Mr. J. H. A. Lang, the Assistant Solicitor of Imperial Chemical Industries, who was forced to resign as a result of threats to refuse the company government contracts, the official reason being that his wife had once been a Communist. By contrast, the same research procedure applied in the United States would no doubt have turned up a much more varied list of cases. Perhaps this reflects the notoriety of the Lang case, but it also suggests that informants and critics have a much more limited population of cases to draw upon for evidence of miscarriages of the British security program.

[43] It is exceedingly difficult to determine the full extent of discrimination on political grounds exercised by local authorities in the appointment, continuation, or promotion of teachers. Officials of the National Union of Teachers, whose membership includes about seventy-five per cent of all teachers, report that the number of such grievances brought to their attention are very few, and probably reflect the true number of occurrences. Only one such case is cited in the reports of the National Council for Civil Lib-

Authority imposed a political test on all *applicants* for the position of head Teacher or for a staff position in teacher-training colleges, with the intent to debar past or present Communists or Fascists. It should be noted that this imposition occurred in only one of a hundred and forty-six Local Education Authorities in England and Wales, was restricted to a limited number of posts, and applied only to applicants, rather than incumbents. Moreover, it represented an action of a county authority that was expressly criticized by both the former and the then current National Ministers of Education, the current Minister even attempting by conference to persuade the local authority to reconsider its policy. In the years from 1950 to 1955, this test remained in force, but was finally withdrawn when a new local government was voted into power. This one major exception in the record of English schools was a passing thing, and the circumstances surrounding the reversal of policy are also informative for our inquiry.

It has been argued that the relative freedom of English teachers and scholars from investigations into security and loyalty reflects the militancy of their opposition to political tests. Yet, in this particular case, the national executive of the Teachers Union expressed itself strongly, attempted to exert persuasion through higher political authorities, and made attempts to persuade candidates running for office in the course of two local elections during the period 1950–55, and all to no avail. From one other episode it is clear that the sentiments of the rank-and-file members of the union, the teachers themselves, were neither militant nor important in the final outcome. After other procedures had failed, the union leadership contemplated the extreme action of a teachers' strike, which before being called required a referendum from the membership. The vote on the referendum was three to one against a strike.

---

erties in the period studied. See Annual Report, 1956–57, p. 6. The publication "A Year with the Secret Police," issued by the Campaign for the Limitation of Secret Police Powers, alludes to cases in the teaching profession, but cites no instances in detail.

With respect to British universities, comprehensive and detailed facts on the degree to which political considerations have affected the actual appointment or promotion of teachers are, in the nature of the case, difficult to determine. Such criteria could operate through informal and subtle means. But clearly it is the case that *government* has not attempted to intervene and apply official pressures to those remaining in university positions, despite the fact that all British universities in the recent period have been dependent on the state for the largest part of their support.

There does appear to have been a certain amount of interference exercised indirectly by the English authorities over the international travel of *liberal* students and scholars, and their appointments to posts in other countries. These individuals, including one world-famous scholar, have found that the host country denies them entry or employment on grounds of information that presumably must have been transmitted by English police authorities. Thus, there is evidence that such dossiers are compiled for teachers, in some unknown number. How frequent the practice has been and whether it represents conventional police co-operation with requests initiated by other national governments or was initiated by the English authorities is not easy to evaluate.[44]

One rather exceptional case occurred in the fifties, in which the government intervened and indirectly terminated the employment of a lecturer at Birmingham University. The peculiar circumstances are especially revealing for a comparison of British and American practices. In the case of Dr. J. H. Cort, an American citizen having a permit to reside in Great Britain, the Home Secretary terminated the permit upon pressures from the United States government.[45] While the issues of the case are complex, it is interesting to note that the original

[44] See the cases cited by the Campaign for the Limitation of Secret Police Powers.

[45] For a brief account of the complex legal and political aspects of the case, see Lord Chorley, "Dr. Cort and the Association of University Teachers," *University Review*, 27, 1954, pp. 3–7.

source of the action was not British but stemmed from our side of the Atlantic.

The British university teacher, like his American counterpart, has been subject to interrogation by government investigators who seek to assess the reliability of students who might enter government employment. The British Association of University Teachers took an official stand against questions concerning the political beliefs and associations of students; their spokesman, Lord Chorley, made a protest in Parliament, and the association provided their members with a special printed label to be attached as a reply to such inquiry whereby the teacher can register his disapproval of the investigation. The action of the organization hardly suggests a response of fear or compliance.

There does appear to be one area of official investigation and activity that violates traditional civil liberties and creates pressures against the free expression of opinion. The police, by invoking various regulations, have created difficulties for various public demonstrations and meetings. There are periodic reports of police surveillance of those in attendance at political meetings and police investigation of the organization of such meetings, plus reports of rough treatment by police of public demonstrators.[46] Such police activity, in contrast with security procedures applied to specialized sectors such as the civil service or defense industries, would impinge on members of the general public and might diffuse an atmosphere of fear. Without denying the significance of such occurrences, it is likely that their impact is limited to a small circle within the public that is activist and that has nonconformist opinions. Evidence on this is provided by a national survey conducted in connection with the inquiry of the Royal Commission on the Police in late 1960. The sample includes but underrepresents young people aged 18–21, a group that may be more prominent among those involved in recent political demonstrations. The time of interviewing coincided

[46] See, for example, *National Council for Civil Liberties, Annual Reports for 1957–58, 1958–59.* See also this organization's *Submission to the Royal Commission on Police,* November, 1960.

with some demonstrations of the Committee for Nuclear Disarmament, an organization that had figured earlier in the cases reported above of police intervention. Only five per cent of the total sample thought that the police often exercised too much force in handling people. Only four per cent knew personally of such instances, but about half of them had occurred in the distant past, and most of the instances did not involve demonstrators or participants in public meetings.[47]

In summary, it appeared that official-security procedures in England had been applied to a much smaller number of individuals within a relatively narrow sector of the society. The law of parsimony would suggest that the differences in the climate of political intolerance and the corollary atmosphere of fear in the fifties in the United States and England were a simple function of the magnitude of official investigation rather than a product of complex social, historical, and psychological variables. Those who know they are free of the danger of investigation have no reason to be afraid. When millions of individuals, located everywhere, are brought under official scrutiny as possible security risks, it validates the belief that everyone ought to be regarded with suspicion, and it legitimates the idea of investigation itself, whether performed by professional officials or by amateurs. It thus encourages in the public at large a climate of intolerance toward those who may exhibit nonconformist opinions.

The suggestion seems congruent with the fact that pressures originating from outside of government, whether by the general public or specialized groups, and directed at nonconformists seem to have been minimal in England. There seem to have been few if any public pressures against teachers. The Middlesex County issue provided an obvious focus for public sentiment, was brought to public awareness by the press, and yet produced no resonance on the part of the public. One case occurred in 1950 in which a lecturer was dismissed from the University of London, and it was alleged

[47] The Social Survey, COI, *The Relations between the Police and the Public*, SS 321, December, 1960, p. 66.

that political grounds were involved.[48] Apart from this instance, informants report little or no pressure on the part of the general or special publics against university teachers and students for their politics.[49] In 1949, the John Lewis department stores announced a policy of excluding Communists from employment, one instance of privately organized action against individuals in non-sensitive employment on the ground of their politics. The reaction in Parliament was to introduce motions condemning the policy, which served to undermine the legitimacy of such private pressures.[50] Apart from many instances within the British trade-union movement of pressures exerted on Communist Party members, there seems to be little evidence that private individuals or groups have harassed others for nonconformist opinions. Indirect evidence in support of this evaluation is provided by data from a survey conducted in June, 1959. While two-thirds of the sample reported that there were some people with whom they would not discuss politics, of these fewer than four per cent (some two per cent of the total sample) gave the reason that it might jeopardize their job, and only about .2 per cent gave the reason that it could lead to trouble with authorities.[51]

[48] The Association of University Teachers in its review of the case claimed that no evidence of political discrimination was demonstrable. *University Review*, 23, 1950, No. 1, p. 5.

[49] Consider a recent item in the British press in which the chairman of the Ruskin College Communist Club at Oxford remarks of future club plans, "We expect to draw considerable support. We've been making tentative inquiries with the University Authorities and anticipate no opposition from them." In the same article, it is reported that the Oxford University Communist Club will resume its activities, lapsed since 1956, having found a new senior faculty sponsor in the person of a Roman Catholic, not himself a Communist, who was Professor of Religion. The Manchester *Guardian*, June 10, 1961.

[50] Quoted in Bontecou, *op. cit.*, pp. 256–57.

[51] These data were made available to me by Gabriel Almond from his Comparative Survey of Citizenship, and are gratefully acknowledged.

VI

The parsimonious explanation for the rarity of intolerant actions on the part of the British public, and the absence of an atmosphere of fear, is based on the character of the official-security programs. But I was unable to establish empirically whether the British public really held intolerant sentiments that remained latent because of political restraints. Systematic survey data, as noted, were not available to me, and a rigorous judgment would be that a diagnosis of British popular sentiment in this area is not possible. But certainly suggestive evidence is on the side of the second hypothesis. Even if such sentiments exist, very little has been done to agitate them, and a great deal has been done to keep them latent.

Political exploitation of the Communist issue, which could contribute to a climate of intolerance, has been negligible. Within the Parliament, debate, if anything, has focused on questions or excesses in the security program. In the election campaigns over the last decade, political exploitation of the issue to smear one's opposition seems also to have been almost nonexistent. The General Election of 1959 provides a dramatic illustration of such restraint in that the manifestoes of the Labour Party and Communist Party coincided on a number of policy issues, a similarity the Conservatives could readily have exploited but did not.[52]

[52] A series of definitive volumes on the general elections of the last decade are available, and reading of these bears out the general conclusion above. There are occasional instances where the issue of domestic Communists arose, but the nature of the assertions, ironically enough, would serve usually not to smear the opposition at all, but perhaps to lose whatever advantage was implicit in the issue. See H. G. Nicholas, *The British General Election of 1950* (London: Macmillan, 1951); D. E. Butler, *The British General Election of 1951* (London: Macmillan, 1952); D. E. Butler and Richard Rose, *The British General Election of 1959* (London: Macmillan, 1960). An episode reported in a study of the Greenwich constituency during the 1950 General Election will illustrate the restraints. The Conservative candidate and his agent drafted a leaflet exploiting the fact that the Labour candidate, a Mr. Reeves,

Contrast the American handling of the issue in recent campaigns. In 1948, the cases of Alger Hiss and others had just come to light and became a hot campaign issue, leading the Chairman of the Republican National Committee to announce, "Once the Dewey-Warren Administration takes over, we will see the greatest housecleaning in Washington since St. Patrick cleaned the snakes out of Ireland." The Lieutenant Governor of New York predicted with pride that if Dewey were elected, "no one will be exempted from scrutiny as to their loyalty to the country. No one will be so high that they cannot be brought down and no one so hidden that they cannot be uncovered. We will have Americanism in the highest meaning of the word when Mr. Dewey becomes President."[53] The 1950 elections saw Senator McCarthy exploiting the Communist issue, and the 1952 elections may well have been a high point in the extravagant use of this issue for campaign purposes.

Now, it may be argued that the difference between Britain and the United States in the extent of political exploitation of the Communist issue is only part of the solution to our problem, and that the other part of the answer involves the psychology of the public. Perhaps the English public would not have been susceptible to such appeals if they had been made, and the American public has the latent intolerance that makes them especially responsive to such political oratory. The formulation would again require empirical evidence on British sentiments of intolerance, which, as previously

---

had made certain speeches in the Commons that were sympathetic to the Soviet Union. The leaflet carried the slogan "Reeves and Crypto-Communism." The Conservative Party chairman had been against the publication and, following its appearance, he closed the committee room, removed the posters from the windows, and did not reopen until "some very strong words had passed between candidate and chairman." See, M. Benney, A. P. Gray, and R. H. Pear, *How People Vote* (London: Routledge, 1956), pp. 95–96.

[53] Quoted in Bontecou, *op. cit.,* pp. 102–3. A content analysis of forty speeches by Dewey and Truman revealed that about ten per cent of their remarks dealt with the Communist issue, domestic and foreign. See B. Berelson, P. F. Lazarsfeld, and W. N. McPhee, *Voting* (Chicago: University of Chicago Press, 1954), p. 236.

noted, is not available, and thus seems imponderable. But its plausibility can be questioned, for it is clear from extensive American survey data that the bulk of Americans showed no special responsiveness in the 1952 election to the issue of domestic Communism, despite the lavishness of the campaign appeals.

Following their study of that election, the Survey Research Center demonstrated that the issue was not *salient* to the voters, "only 3 per cent of the population mentioned the argument that the Democratic Administration has been 'soft to Communism.' "[54] The 1956 survey data indicate that the "issue had virtually disappeared."[55] Thus, any great significance that might be imputed to an American character structure as an explanatory principle seems unwarranted. For all one knows, the English might have been more susceptible to such appeals if they had been exploited![56] This is not to

[54] A. Campbell, G. Gurin, and W. E. Miller, *The Voter Decides* (Evanston: Row, Peterson, 1954), p. 52. Louis Harris gives more weight to the issue of domestic Communism in the 1952 election, but he also indicates that it was far from salient, in that it was not volunteered by more than eleven per cent as a major national issue. See L. Harris, *Is There a Republican Majority?* (New York: Harper, 1954), p. 32. Cf. also the findings cited earlier from Gallup Polls on the far from universal appeal of Senator McCarthy.

[55] A. Campbell, P. Converse, W. Miller, and D. Stokes, *The American Voter* (New York: John Wiley, 1960), p. 51.

[56] Mark Abrams, a distinguished English survey-research expert and political analyst, conducted a special survey in 1960 "to establish those attitudes and social values which have led the electorate to turn away steadily from the Labour Party over the past ten years." In the course of this survey, a list of sixteen political goals was presented to the sample, and they were asked to choose the four that were most important in a good political party. Obviously, the sixteen were designed to cover the spectrum of political values that might possibly be important to Englishmen and that might have been inadequately supported by the Labour Party's past actions. As Abrams remarks, "The sixteen formed a reasonably comprehensive coverage of current political values." The issue of domestic Communism was not included, suggesting that it is of no special significance to the British working-class universe. But here again it is unfortunate, from our theoretical point of view, that no empirical evidence was obtained. See Abrams, *op. cit.*

deny the significance of such campaign tactics for the emergence of a climate of intolerance and the corresponding atmosphere of fear, for while the issue never became highly salient to the general American public, it may have cut deep into the minds of a smaller attentive public, and it may well have struck fear into the hearts of those who were sensitive and vulnerable to possible attack.

Three of the celebrated British loyalty cases within the last decade represented potential focuses of political debate and, in turn, for public repercussions that might have altered the climate of tolerance. Here again one notes particular political structures and institutions which served as mechanisms to cool the atmosphere and reduce the consequences on the climate of tolerance. The Burgess and MacLean case certainly shook Parliament and aroused much discussion. In answer to the many questions asked, the government showed a good deal of reticence, and with respect to criticisms of laxity, the government countered that Burgess and MacLean had legal rights. It reacted by establishing in November, 1955, the Conference of Privy Councillors on Security, which did not present its findings until March, 1956. As noted, the report urged more stringent security procedures, but it reaffirmed the principle that no extra powers to detain suspects or withdraw passports should be sought.[57] It may be urged that such reticence and delay mask incompetence and endanger internal security—or, alternatively, that such secrecy masks an insidious and extensive security program. Nevertheless these procedures also served to maintain the tolerant climate.

Again in 1961, two spy cases followed the same course. The Houghton-Gee-Lonsdale case, in March, 1961, led to the appointment of the Romer Committee, which rendered a report in June, 1961. Only a summary of this report was made public; the Prime Minister remarked that it would not serve the public interest to disclose the full report. The Blake case, resulting in a conviction in May, 1961, led to the ap-

[57] *Statement on the Findings of the Conference of Privy Councillors on Security* (London: Her Majesty's Stationery Office, March, 1956), CMD No. 9715.

pointment of the Radcliffe Committee. A report of their findings was not made public until April, 1962, and the full findings were again withheld on the ground that it would not serve the public interest.[58]

A feature of the British security program provides another mechanism to reduce public sentiments below a fever point, and to minimize the fears of those who might be injured or stigmatized by the program. The decisions are not publicized. Individuals may be transferred quietly, or removed from a sensitive job. This is certainly a cause for suffering, but it is at least partially mitigated by the likelihood that the persons involved can remain in the community or obtain other work, since the reasons are not made public. Contrast this with the pattern of American legislative investigations of suspects, where publicity is a common accompaniment of any accusation.[59] Correspondingly, the publicity can aggravate the intolerance of the American public.[60]

It appears to me, then, that such political procedures and

[58] *Security Procedures in the Public Service* (London: Her Majesty's Stationery Office, April, 1962), CMD No. 1681. It is very difficult to summarize the findings of this rather lengthy report of about forty pages. The American newspaper accounts stressed those aspects of the report that refer to the dangers from Communists in the Civil Service and among the officials in the Civil Service trade unions. Yet the recommendations did not suggest the extension of security procedures to all government departments, "many of which by the nature of their work have little or no need for special security measures" and the committee urged that "security arrangements . . . will be the more effective the more limited is the field to be protected."

[59] See, for example, accounts by the American Civil Liberties Union of the activities of the House Un-American Activities Committee. There is even the suggestion that findings of security investigations by federal administrative agencies have on occasion been communicated to potential private employers. See Bontecou, *op. cit.*, pp. 64–66.

[60] It might be suggested that the English people hold strongly the value of privacy, and thus accept and do not invade the domain of secret investigations of security. For an interesting discussion of the concepts publicity and secrecy, and the third concept, privacy, as they affect the problems of climates of opinion, see Edward Shils, *The Torment of Secrecy* (Glencoe: Free Press, 1956).

institutions as I have described explain the differences in the English climate of political tolerance. In the absence of systematic evidence on the underlying opinions of the British public, one must still acknowledge the possibility that there are prior restraints internalized within the English character. However, it is also clear that the political mechanisms would act as *external* restraints on any latent public intolerance.

One may well ask: Why *these* particular political mechanisms? Those in power could have behaved so as to encourage latent intolerance. And there were and are in England other individuals clamoring for political power, some of them fanatical on the problem of Communism and security, and some who press their argument from a privileged position within the British elite.[61] One must analyze the political structures that guide and discipline the behavior of their members and into which the more fanatical individuals cannot insinuate themselves.[62] One must also examine the prevailing beliefs and values, the inner directives, that guide the conduct of the political elite—but on these unfortunately, systematic survey data were not available.

If, as I have conjectured, there is widespread intolerance in the British public, what insulates the elites and political structures from popular pressures? What frees them to follow their own inner directives? In contrast with the American public, the English public may well accord more privacy and more

[61] For a case study of one such attack by a member of the elite, see the account of Lord Vansittart's 1950 speech in the House of Lords against Communism in the B.B.C. (Wilson and Glickman, *op. cit., passim.*) In part, the behavior of the legitimate political elite and of fringe leaders is restrained to some extent by the severe English libel laws. Thus, for example, Atlee brought a libel suit against the National Workers Party in 1936, which was settled in his favor. Similarly, Lord Camrose brought suit against Mosley's British Union of Fascists in 1937 and received heavy damages. See David Riesman, "Democracy and Defamation: Fair Game and Fair Comment I," *Columbia Law Review*, 42, 1942, pp. 1085–1123.

[62] I have in mind not only the formal analysis of political structures but the obvious consequences of the fact that one of the major parties is the Labour Party.

deference to the elite.[68] Here is the focus for a most useful inquiry into the values of the English public. At the popular level, it may be in the area of deference, not tolerance, that we will find one key to the puzzle of the climate of political tolerance that emerged in England in the fifties.

[63] I am indebted to Gabriel Almond for various suggestions about features of English political culture that could be relevant to the problem. His forthcoming comparative study, based on surveys of the publics of England and four other nations, will contribute much-needed evidence.

13

THE SOURCES OF THE "RADICAL RIGHT" (1955)[1]

Seymour Martin Lipset

In the last five years we have seen the emergence of an important American political phenomenon, the radical right. This group is characterized as radical because it desires to make far-reaching changes in American institutions, and because it seeks to eliminate from American political life those persons and institutions which threaten either its values, or its economic interests. Needless to say, this movement is opposed to the social and economic reforms of the last twenty years, and to the internationalist foreign policy pursued by the successive Administrations in that period.

The activities of the radical right would be of less interest if it sought its ends through the traditional democratic procedures of pressure-group tactics, lobbying, and the ballot box. But, while most individuals and organizations which we shall consider as part of the radical right do use these means, many use undemocratic methods as well. The singular fact is that radical right agitation has facilitated the growth of practices which threaten to undermine the social fabric of democratic politics. The threats to democratic procedure which are, in

[1] The intellectual sources of this paper are far more numerous than the footnote references acknowledge. In particular, I am indebted to Richard Hofstadter, whose "The Pseudo-Conservative Revolt" forms Chapter 3 of this volume, and Immanuel Wallerstein's "McCarthyism and the Conservative" (M.A. thesis in the Department of Sociology, Columbia University, 1954). This paper is Publication No. A169 of the Bureau of Applied Social Research, Columbia University, one of a series prepared for the Fund for the Republic.

part, an outgrowth of radical right agitation involve attempts
to destroy the right of assembly, the right of petition, the freedom of association, the freedom to travel, and the freedom to
teach or conduct scholarly research without conforming to
political tests.[2] This movement, therefore, must be seriously
considered by all those who would preserve democratic constitutional precedures in this country.

In evaluating the activities of the radical right, this chapter
is divided into three sections: Part 1 deals with continuing
sources of extremist politics in America as they have their
sources in American history; Part 2 analyzes the social groups
which are more prone than others to support the radical right
today; and Part 3 deals with the specific character of Mc-
Carthyism as the principal expression of radical right ideology
on the current scene.

I

Status and Class Politics

Any analysis of the role of political extremism in the United
States must recognize two fundamental political forces operating under the varying historical conditions of American society. These forces may be distinguished by the terms *status
politics* and *class politics*. Class politics refers to political division based on the discord between the traditional left and the
right, i.e., between those who favor redistribution of income,
and those favoring the preservation of the *status quo*. Status
politics, as used here, refers to political movements whose

[2] I do not assert that every or even most individuals or groups I
classify in the radical right are involved in, or sympathetic to
efforts to reduce personal freedom. In fact, as is made clear later
in this paper, the ideology of the radical right is a belief in as much
laissez-faire as possible. Most supporters of radical right politics
believe that they are helping to increase democratic rights for everyone. The point is, however, that the nature of their attacks on
political opponents, the definition they make of liberal or left politics as illegitimate, un-American, creeping socialism, fellow-traveling or worse, does have the consequence of encouraging the denial
of civil liberties to their political opponents.

appeal is to the not uncommon resentments of individuals or groups who desire to maintain or improve their social status.[3]

In the United States, political movements or parties which stress the need for economic reform have usually gained strength during times of unemployment and depression. On the other hand, status politics becomes ascendant in periods of prosperity, especially when full employment is accompanied by inflation, and when many individuals are able to improve their economic position. The groups which are receptive to status-oriented appeals are not only those which have risen in the economic structure and who may be frustrated in their desire to be accepted socially by those who already hold status, but also those groups already possessing status who feel that the rapid social change threatens their own claims to high social position, or enables previously lower status groups to claim equal status with their own.

The political consequences of status frustrations are very different from those resulting from economic deprivation, for while in economic conflict the goals are clear—a redistribution of income—in status conflict there are no clear-cut solutions. Where there are status anxieties, there is little or nothing which a government can do. It is not surprising, therefore, that the political movements which have successfully appealed to status resentments have been irrational in character, and have sought scapegoats which conveniently serve to symbolize the status threat. Historically, the most common scapegoats in the United States have been the minority ethnic or religious groups. Such groups have repeatedly been the victims of political aggression in periods of prosperity, for it is precisely in these times that status anxieties are most pressing.[4]

---

[3] For a discussion of class and status politics in another context see, S. M. Lipset and R. Bendix, "Social Status and Social Structure," *British Journal of Sociology*, II (1951), especially pp. 230–33. Similar concepts are used by Richard Hofstadter in Chapter 3.

[4] It is important to note that scapegoat and ethnic prejudice politics have not been exclusively the tactic of prosperity-based movements. Anti-Semitic movements, in particular, have also emerged during depressions. The Populist movement and Father Coughlin's National Union for Social Justice are perhaps two of

American political history from this perspective emerges in a fairly consistent pattern. Before the Civil War, there was considerable anti-Catholic and anti-immigrant activity. Such agitation often took the form of organized political parties, the most important of which was the Know-Nothing or American Party. And it was during a prosperous decade that these parties and movements were at their height. The Know-Nothings who polled one fourth of the total popular vote for President in 1856 reached their greatest power in a period of widespread prosperity and inflation and practically vanished in the depression year 1857.[5] The American Protective Association (A.P.A.), which emerged in the late 1880s, was the next major organized anti-Catholic movement and it too arose in a period of renewed prosperity. A contemporary analyst of this movement has pointed to the status concerns which motivated many of the members of the A.P.A.

Latter day Know-Nothingism (A.P.A.ism) in the west,

---

the most significant ones. It should be noted, however, that both of these movements focused primarily on proposed solutions to economic problems rather than racism. Initially, these groups were concerned with solving economic problems by taking away control of the credit system from the private bankers. Anti-Semitism emerged in both as a means of symbolizing their attack on eastern or international financiers. It is interesting to note that many movements which center their explanation of the cause for depressions on the credit system often wind up attacking the Jews. The Social Credit movement is the most recent example of this pattern. Apparently the underlying cultural identification of the international financier with the international Jew is too strong for these groups to resist. In each case, however, Populism, Coughlinism, and Social Credit, the economic program preceded anti-Semitism.

[5] Historians have traditionally explained the decline of the Know-Nothings as a result of their inability to take a firm position on the slavery issue. Recent research, however, suggests that the depression may have been even more important than the slavery agitation. Detailed study of pre-Civil War electoral behavior indicates that the slavery issue played a minor role in determining shifts from one party to another. Evidence for these statements will be found in a forthcoming monograph by Lee Benson of the Bureau of Applied Social Research, Columbia University.

was perhaps due as well to envy of the growing social
and industrial strength of Catholic Americans.

In the second generation American Catholics began to
attain higher industrial positions and better occupations.
All through the west, they were taking their place in the
professional and business world. They were among the
doctors and the lawyers, the editors and the teachers of
the community. Sometimes they were the leading merchants as well as the leading politicians of their locality.[6]

Interestingly enough, the publisher of many anti-Catholic
A.P.A. works was also the publisher of the Social Register,
which was first copyrighted in 1887, the year in which the
A.P.A. was organized,[7] a fact which suggests a possible link
between this mass organization and the desire of high-status,
old family Americans to resist the upward mobility of the
second generation Catholics. A large number of individuals
listed in the Social Register were among the important financial supporters of the A.P.A., as well as of other anti-immi-
gration organizations.

The Progressive movement, which flourished from 1900 to
1912, is yet another protest movement which attracted the
interest and participation of large numbers of Americans during a period of high prosperity. This movement, while differing considerably from the others, since it was concerned with

[6] Humphrey J. Desmond, *The A.P.A. Movement* (Washington:
The New Century Press, 1912), pp. 9–10.

[7] While the A.P.A. arose and won strength in a prosperous era,
it continued to grow during the depression of 1893. Gustavus
Myers, however, suggests that one of the major reasons for its
rapid decline in the following two or three years was the fact that
many of its leaders and members became actively involved in the
class politics which grew out of this depression. That is, many
A.P.A.ers either joined the Bryan movement or actively supported
McKinley, depending on their socio-economc position. Thus, the
decline of the A.P.A., also, may be laid in large part to the fact
that a depression accentuates economic issues and makes status
concerns less important.

See Gustavus Myers, *History of Bigotry in the United States*
(New York: Random House, 1943), pp. 244–45.

liberal social reforms, may, nevertheless, be a reflection of status politics. Richard Hofstadter has suggested that it was based in large measure on the reaction of the Protestant middle class against threats to its values and status.[8] The Progressive movement had two scapegoats—the "plutocrat" millionaires, and the immigrants.[9] The rise of the "robber barons," the great millionaires and plutocrats of the late nineteenth and early twentieth centuries, served to challenge the status of many old, upper-middle-class American families which had previously considered themselves the most impor-

[8] R. Hofstadter, *The Age of Reform* (New York: Alfred A. Knopf, 1955).

[9] Quantitative evidence which fits in with this interpretation of the Progressive movement may be found in an unpublished paper, "The Genteel Revolt Against Politics—A study of the New York State Progressive Party in 1912," by Richard Ravitch. He summed up his statistical analysis as follows:

"It would be wrong to assume that the Progressives were anti-Catholic, but it was unusual for a political party in New York to have only one Catholic in its midst. Several Bull Mooses [Progressives] had belonged to the Guardians of Liberty, an organization which attacked the Church; but they withdrew to avoid the political repercussions. Certainly it can be said that the overwhelming religious affiliation was that of the Conservative [high status] Protestant sects.

"They were men conspicuous for their lack of association with the two groups which were slowly becoming the dominant forces in American life—the industrialist and the union leader. They were part of an older group which was losing the high status and prestige once held in American society. The Progressives represented the middle-class of the nineteenth century with all its emphasis on individualism and a set of values that was basically provincial. Resenting the encroachment on 'his' America by the corporations and urban masses, the formation of the Progressive Party may be considered his way of protesting what was now his defensive position in the bewildering 'drift' which characterized 20th-century society."

Evidence that anti-Catholic sentiment was strong during the pre-World War I prosperity may also be adduced from the fact that a leading anti-Catholic paper, *The Menace,* had a circulation of 1,400,000 in 1914.

Emerson H. Loucks, *The Ku Klux Klan in Pennsylvania* (Harrisburg, Pennsylvania: The Telegraph Press, 1936), p. 16.

tant group in society; these new millionaires were able to outdo them in philanthropy and in setting new styles of life. The Progressive movement, like previous expressions of status politics, was also opposed to immigration. It viewed the immigrant and the urban city machines based on immigrant support as a basic threat to American middle-class Protestant values.

And finally the Ku Klux Klan, which vigorously attacked the rights of minority groups, also emerged in prosperous times, the 1920s. It is important to note, however, that while the Klan was against Jews, Catholics and Negroes, it also represented the antagonism of the small town and provincial city Protestant lower-middle class and working class against the "cosmopolitanism" of the upper classes. The upper-class, largely metropolitan-centered, Protestant churches were a frequent target of Klan attack. The English minister of a high Protestant church, divorced women who were accused of "playing around," physicians who had allegedly engaged in sexual irregularities with patients, were among those subjected to Klan violence.[10]

At its height, the Klan had the support of millions of individuals, and dominated political life in Indiana, Maine, Colorado, Oklahoma, Texas, Oregon, Arkansas, Ohio, and California. It would be rash to give any simplified interpretation of the factors underlying such an important social movement. If, however, one asks what had occurred on the American scene to encourage such a mass expression of provincial resentment, one important factor is the growing predominance of the large metropolitan centers, which were centers of Catholics, Jews, and high-status Protestants. In the changing

[10] This discussion is based largely on an unpublished paper by Nathan Glazer. For documentation of the various points made here see John Moffat Mecklin, *The Ku Klux Klan: A Study of the American Mind* (New York: Harcourt Brace and Co., 1924); E. H. Loucks, *op. cit.;* Henry Fry Peck, *The Modern Ku Klux Klan* (Boston: Small, Maynard and Co., 1922); Frank Bohn, "The Ku Klux Klan Interpreted," *American Journal of Sociology*, January 1925, pp. 385–407.

world of post-World War I America, the fundamentalist provincial was faced with the fact that he and his communities had lost much of their independence and status. The war boom, and later, the prosperity of the twenties, made it possible for many individuals to rise economically, including members of previously lower-class minority groups such as the Jews and Catholics. The Catholics were also beginning to get national political power. These changes were paralleled by a seeming decline in basic morality, and a growth in religious cynicism. The Klan, with its attack on metropolitan "cosmopolitanism" and the more traditional minority ethnic scapegoats, seems to have provided an outlet to the frustrated residents of provincial America, who felt their values, power, and status slipping away.

The hypothesis that the Klan represented the reaction of a large section of provincial America to the frustrations of boom-time social change may, of course, be questioned in view of the fact that it declined considerably as an organization after 1926, before prosperity ended. This decline, however, seems in large measure to be related to the fact that the overwhelming majority of Klan leaders were publicly exposed as obvious charlatans, who were using the organization to feather their own nest, and to the social pressure directed against the Klan by the upper class and every section of the press. The loss of respectability led to a rapid withdrawal from the organization by its middle-class adherents, and the jailing for fraud of some of its leaders soon disillusioned the large section of working-class supporters.

The 1928 Presidential election campaign, however, witnessed a new outburst of bigotry directed against the Catholic Democratic candidate, Al Smith (which showed that the sentiments which gave rise to the Klan had not vanished). In this election, the Democratic Party increased its vote in the large metropolitan centers, while reaching its lowest point in decades in the smaller communities.

These four movements, Know-Nothings, A.P.A., Progressives, and Ku Klux Klan, all illustrate the way in which American society has thrown up major protest movements in periods of prosperity, thus confounding the general assumption that protest politics are primarily products of depressions. The prosperity movements differ from those groups who are products of economic crises in that they find "scapegoats" who threaten their value system, while other protest groups have direct economic targets. The Progressives, a group one does not normally see this way, were concerned with the manner in which the *nouveaux riches* and the immigrants were corrupting American institutions, while the Klan, a status-resentment group par-excellence, attacked the "cosmopolitanism" of Catholics, Jews, and the metropolitan elite, which undermined the middle-class Protestant virtues. Perhaps the most significant single fact concerning the strength of the Klan and the role of organized bigotry in America is that every effort to build a mass social movement based on bigotry during the great depression of the 1930s had little success. It is the common concern with the protection of "traditional" American values that characterizes "status politics" as contrasted with the regard for jobs, cheap credit, or high farm prices, which have been the main emphases of depression-born "class politics."

If we assume that this is a pattern in American politics, it is not surprising that the continuing prosperity of the late nineteen forties and early fifties should also have developed a political movement resembling the four discussed above. McCarthyism, like its predecessors, is characterized by an attack on a convenient scapegoat, which is defined as a threat to American institutions, and also involves an attempt to link "cosmopolitan" changes in the society to a foreign plot.[11]

[11] It is interesting to note in this connection that much of the earlier extremist agitation also dealt with supposed plots of foreign agents. For example, the agitation leading to the Alien and Sedition Acts before 1800, the anti-Catholic movements, all involved claims that agents of a foreign power or of the Pope sought to subvert American life and institutions. The leaders of these movements all argued that men with loyalties to foreign institutions had no claim to civil liberties in America. "Can a Romanist be a good citizen of America . . . ? Romanism is a political system—as a political power it must be met. . . . *No ballot for the man who takes his*

The State of Tolerance in America

A second important factor to consider in evaluating present trends in American politics is the traditional attitude toward tolerance in American society. The historical evidence, some of which has been cited above, indicates that, as compared to the citizens of a number of other countries, especially Great Britain and Scandinavia, Americans are not a tolerant people. In addition to discrimination against ethnic and religious minorities, each war and most prewar situations have been characterized by the denial of civil liberties to minorities, often even of minorities which were not opposed to the war. Abolitionists, for example, faced great difficulties in many areas, North as well as South, before the Civil War. Many were fired from schools and universities. During World War I, German-Americans and Socialists often experienced personal physical attacks, as well as economic discrimination. In the last war, the entire Japanese-American population on the West Coast was denied the most elementary form of personal freedom.[12]

Political intolerance has not been monopolized by political extremists or wartime vigilantes. The Populists, for example, discharged many university professors in state universities in states where they came into power in the 1890s. Their Republican opponents were not loath to dismiss teachers who believed in Populist economics. Public opinion polls, ever since they first began measuring mass attitudes in the early thirties, have repeatedly shown that sizable numbers, often a majority, of Americans oppose the rights of unpopular political minorities.[18] In both 1938 and 1942, a majority of the

---

politics from the Vatican." Reverend James B. Dunn, leader of the A.P.A. quoted in Myers, op. cit., p. 227. (Emphasis in Myers.)

The present situation, of course, differs from these past ones in that there is a foreign directed conspiracy, the Communist Party. But today, as in the past, the new right seeks to link native, non-Communist expression of dissent to foreign powers as well.

[12] Morton Grodzins, Americans Betrayed, Politics and the Japanese Evacuation (Chicago: University of Chicago Press, 1949).

[18] See Herbert Hyman and Paul Sheatsley, "Trends in Public

American public opposed the right of "radicals" to hold meetings.

The state of current attitudes toward civil liberties has been reported on in detail in a study by Samuel Stouffer, based on interviews with a random sample of Americans in the spring of 1954. Large sections of the American population opposed the rights of atheists,[14] Socialists,[15] and Communists[16] to free speech and free publication.

One important factor affecting this lack of tolerance in American life is the basic strain of Protestant puritanical morality which has always existed in this country. Americans believe that there is a fundamental difference between right and wrong, that right must be supported, and that wrong must be suppressed, that error and evil have no rights against the truth. This propensity to see life in terms of all black and all white is most evident, perhaps most disastrous, in the area of foreign policy, where allies and enemies cannot be gray, but must be black or white.[17]

Opinion on Civil Liberties," *Journal of Social Issues,* IX (1953), No. 3, pp. 6–17.

[14] Samuel A. Stouffer, *Communism, Conformity, and Civil Liberties* (New York: Doubleday & Co., 1955), p. 32–33; see the summary and discussion of his findings in Chapter 6.

[15] *Ibid.,* pp. 28–31.

[16] *Ibid.,* pp. 39–46.

[17] David Riesman has suggested that the factors sustaining extreme moralism in American life are declining as more and more Americans are becoming "other-oriented," more concerned with being liked than being right. While Riesman's distinction between inner-oriented and other-oriented people is useful for analytical purposes, I still believe that viewed cross-culturally, Americans are more likely to view politics in moralistic terms than most Europeans. No American politician would say of an ally, as did Churchill of Russia, that I will ally with the "devil, himself," for the sake of victory. The American alliance with Russia had to be an alliance with a "democrat" even if the ally did not know he was democratic. Both the liberal reaction to the possibility of alliance with Chiang Kai-shek and Franco, and the conservative reaction to recognition of Communist China are but the latest examples of the difficulty which morality creates for our international diplomacy. See David Riesman, *The Lonely Crowd* (New Haven: Yale University Press,

The differences in fundamental economic philosophy and way of life between the Democrats and Republicans in this country are far less than those which exist between Conservatives and Socialists in Great Britain. Yet political rhetoric in this country is comparable in Europe only for those campaigns between totalitarians and their opponents. While McCarthy has indeed sunk American political rhetoric to new depths, one should not forget that his type of invective has been used quite frequently in American politics. For example, Roosevelt called some of his isolationist opponents, "Copperheads," a term equivalent to traitor.[18] If various impressionistic accounts are to be believed, many Republicans, especially Republican businessmen, have a far deeper sense of hatred against Roosevelt and the New Deal, than their British or Scandinavian counterparts have against their socialist opponents.

Although Puritanism is probably one of the main sources of American intolerance, there are certainly many other elements which have contributed to its continuance in American life. The lack of an aristocratic tradition in American politics helped to prevent the emergence of a moderate rhetoric in political life. Almost from the start of democratic politics in America with the early adoption of universal male suffrage, the political machines were led by professional politicians, many of whom were of lower-middle-class or even poorer origins, who had to appeal to a relatively uneducated electorate. This led to the development of a campaign style in which any tactic that would win votes was viewed as legitimate. Thus, Jefferson was charged with "treason," and with being a

---

1950), for a discussion of the decline of such morality; and George Kennan, *American Diplomacy, 1900–1950* (New York: New American Library, 1952). Gabriel A. Almond, *The American People and Foreign Policy* (New York: Harcourt, Brace & Company, 1950), Ch. III, "American Character and Foreign Policy"; Raymond Aron, *The Century of Total War* (London: Derek Verschoyle, 1954), pp. 103–4, for analysis of the way in which morality in politics hampers our foreign policy.

[18] See Will Herberg, "Government by Rabble-Rousing," *The New Leader*, January 18, 1954.

French agent before 1800, while Republicans waved the "bloody shirt" against the Democrats for decades following the Civil War. In order to involve the masses in politics, politicians have sought to make every election appear as if it involved life or death for the country or for their party.

Another factor which has operated to diminish tolerance in this country has been mass immigration. The prevalence of different cultural and religious ways of life has always constituted a threat to American stability and cultural unity. In order to build a nation, it was perhaps necessary that men should be intolerant of the practices of newcomers, and should force them to assimilate. All through world history, the intermingling of people from different cultural backgrounds has resulted in strife. Such conflict is obviously not conducive to the emergence of a tradition of civic discipline, in which everyone has the right to live out his life as he sees fit, and in which minorities are protected.

The minority immigrant groups themselves have contributed to the support for conformity. One of the principal reactions of members of such groups to discrimination—to being defined as socially inferior by the majority culture—is to attempt to assimilate completely American values, to reject their past, and to overidentify with Americanism. They tend to interpret indiscrimination against their ethnic group as a consequence of the fact that they are foreign and they behave differently, that in short they are insufficiently American. Many of those who adopt the assimilationist solution attempt to enforce conformity within their own group, and are intolerant of those who would perpetuate foreign ways and thus earn the enmity of those of Anglo-Saxon origin.[19]

[19] It is true, of course, that there has been an alternative nationalist reaction, such as Zionism among the Jews, the Garvey movement among the Negroes, and identification with national societies among other groups. In large measure, however, these patterns have been the reaction of lower-status, usually foreign-born members of immigrant groups. Once assimilated, and accepted, immigrant groups often adopt the so-called "third generation" pattern in which they attempt to re-identify with their past national traditions. While this pattern would seem to conflict with assump-

At least one other element may be suggested as having operated against the development of tolerance: those situations which have encouraged or required men to take the law into their own hands in order to enforce the moral values of the dominant groups in society. Such events occurred in the South after the Civil War, and in the West continuously with the expansion of the frontier. In the South, as Myrdal has pointed out, the conservative groups have resisted legal procedures in order to maintain white supremacy. On the western frontier, many men considered it necessary to engage in vigilante activities to eliminate lawlessness. Both of these traditions, especially the continuing Southern one, have helped to destroy civic discipline.

Americanism as an Ideology: Un-Americanism

A third element in American life related to present political events is the extent to which the concept of Americanism has become a compulsive ideology rather than simply a nationalist term. Americanism is a creed in a way that "Britishism" is not.

The notion of Americanism as a creed to which men are converted rather than born stems from two factors: first, our revolutionary tradition which has led us to continually reiterate the superiority of the American creed of equalitarianism, of democracy, against the old reactionary, monarchical and more rigidly status-bound systems of European society; and second, the immigrant character of American society, the fact that people may become Americans—that they are not simply born to the status.

But if foreigners may become Americans, Americans may become "un-American." This concept of "un-American activities," as far as I know, does not have its counterpart in other countries. American patriotism is allegiance to values, to a creed, not solely to a nation. An American political leader could not say, as Winston Churchill did in 1940, that the Eng-

tion that conformity is the norm, I would suggest that it fits into the needs of individuals in a mass urban culture to find symbols of belongingness which are smaller than the total society.

lish Communist Party was composed of Englishmen, and he did not fear an Englishman.[20]

Unless one recognizes that Americanism is a political creed, much like Socialism, Communism or Fascism, much of what is currently happening in this country must remain unintelligible.[21] Our national rituals are largely identified with reiterating the accepted values of a political value system, not solely or even primarily of national patriotism. For example, Washington's Birthday, Lincoln's Birthday, and the Fourth of July are ideological celebrations comparable to May Day or Lenin's Birthday in the Communist world. Only Memorial Day and Veteran's Day may be placed in the category of purely patriotic, as distinct from ideological, celebrations. Consequently, more than any other democratic country, the United States makes ideological conformity one of the conditions for good citizenship. And it is this emphasis on ideological conformity to presumably common political values that legitimatizes the hunt for "un-Americans" in our midst.

The Multiple Elites

While factors persistent in the culture have exerted great pressure towards conformity to the creed of Americanism, yet the rapid growth, and size, of the United States has prevented American society from developing an integrated cultural or power structure similar to those in smaller and older tradition-oriented European nations. One cannot, for example, speak of *an* American elite, be it economic, political or cultural. The elites that exist are fractioned regionally, ethnically, and culturally, so that friction and competition constantly arise among these segmented groups: West against East, North against South, new rich versus old rich, Anglo-Saxons against minority ethnics, the graduates of Ivy League schools against others, etc.

[20] Churchill made this statement in the House, in defending his refusal to declare the Communist Party, then opposed to the war, illegal.

[21] See Leon Samson. *Toward a United Front* (New York: Farrar and Rinehart, 1933).

This segmentation has facilitated the emergence of new social movements, religions, and cultural fads. But it also has prevented any one of them from engulfing the country. Each new movement is opposed by some segment of a rival elite, as well as that part of the general population which follows it. Thus Populism, the Ku Klux Klan, the abortive labor and socialist parties, the Progressive movement, and the Know-Nothings, have all had important successes within specific regions, communities, or ethnic groups; but each died away without coming to national power. In the United States, seemingly, with the exception of prohibition, it has been impossible to build a durable national movement on a single issue, or on an appeal to a single interest group.

While the heterogeneity and sheer size of the United States apparently bar any extremist ideological group from coming to national power, it also promotes the emergence of such groups on a more parochial base since any can almost always find enough supporters, leaders, and financial backers to make an impression on the body politic. Any appeal, be it anti-Catholicism, anti-Semitism, Huey Long's "Share the Wealth movement," Townsend's Old Age pension crusade, monetary reform, Technocracy, or others such as those mentioned earlier, will have some appeal. It is almost an axiom of American politics that any movement can find some millionaire backing, and it does not take many millionaires to set up an impressive looking propaganda apparatus. Each of the various radical groups, the Socialist Labor Party, the Socialist Party, and the Communist Party, has had its millionaires. In recent decades, the Communists were more successful than others on the left in this regard.

The fact that it is relatively easy to build a new political or economic reform movement in America has often been overlooked by many observers because of the failure of every effort to construct a third major political party—a difference, obviously, between the ease of a *movement* and the difficulty of a *party*. The failure of third-party efforts has been a consequence, however, of the American electoral system with its requirement that only one party can control the executive branch of the government at one time. Actually, the two major American parties are coalitions, and the underlying base of American politics is much closer to the French multi-party system than it is to the British two-party political structure. American parties are coalitions of distinct and often conflicting factions, and no one interest group is able to dominate the government. As in France, however, it is relatively simple for a new ideological or interest group to gain representation, but it is almost impossible for it to secure majority control of the government.[22] For example, in the 1920s many Klan-backed individuals were elected to Congress, state legislatures, and some governor's office. At about the same time, the quasi-socialist Non-Partisan League won control of the Republican Party and the state government in North Dakota, and had considerable influence in a number of other midwest states, while an offshoot of it captured the Democratic Party and the governor's chair in Oklahoma. In the 1930s the Democratic Party of California, Oregon and Washington, was captured temporarily by Socialist factions—i.e., Upton Sinclair's EPIC movement in California, and the Cooperative Commonwealth Federation in the other two coast states. At the same time, three Northern midwestern states were actually governed by left-wing offshoots of the Republican Party—the Non-Partisan League in North Dakota, the Progressive Party in Wisconsin, and the Farmer-Labor Party in Minnesota. Townsend, Huey Long, Father Coughlin, and the Communists were also able to send some men to Congress through the mechanism of winning primary contests in one of the major parties. Today, as in the past, various ideological or interest factions strive to increase their representation in government through rather than against the traditional parties.

The fact that the leaders of American political parties have much less influence over the men whom they elect than do the heads of parties in the British Commonwealth also facilitates the emergence of dissident political tendencies. A Labor or

[22] For further comments on this theme see S. M. Lipset, "Democracy in Alberta," *The Canadian Forum*, November and December 1954, pp. 175–77, 196–98.

Tory member of the British parliament could never engage in a one-man crusade with a power comparable to control of a Senate committee such as Senators Langer, La Follette, and McCarthy have done at different times.

The tendency of American society to throw up new movements or organizations is, of course, not limited to the political field. De Tocqueville, more than a century ago, called attention to the American propensity, as compared with the greater lassitude of Europeans, to form organizations for various purposes. The reason for this distinctive pattern lay in the fact that America did not have a distinct aristocratic elite which could fulfill the functions of organization and leadership performed by the elite in Europe. And, de Tocqueville argued, the very multitude of existing voluntary associations facilitated the emergence of new ones, since the older associations, because they train men in the skills of organization, provide a resource when some new need or new social objective is perceived.[23] What little comparative data exist, suggest that this empirical generalization is still valid.[24]

It is hardly surprising, therefore, that Americans who regard Communism as a great evil should form associations to combat it. These groups are but one more manifestation of American political and moral activity, much like the popular attempts to ban liquor, gambling, or immorality in comic strips. One may point to similar developments in the sphere of religion. Perhaps no other country, including Israel, has thrown up so many new religious sects. Spiritualism, the Mormon Church, Jehovah's Witnesses, Seventh Day Adventists, Christian Science, and the Churches of God, are but some of the sects with over 100,000 church members which were born in the United States.

The various dissident social and religious movements have

[23] Alexis de Tocqueville, *Democracy in America* (London: Oxford University Press, 1946), pp. 376–81.
[24] Arnold Rose, "Voluntary Associations in France," in *Theory and Method in the Social Sciences* (Minneapolis: University of Minnesota Press, 1954), pp. 72–115. Mass Observation, *Puzzled People* (London: Victor Gollancz, 1947), pp. 119–22.

reflected the openness of the American social order. Conventional morality is not supported by a cohesive system of social control since there are, in effect, a variety of moralities. This generalization does not contradict the previous discussion of intolerance in American life, for intolerance to be effective on a national scale must represent the will of a majority or all-powerful group. Fortunately, with the exception of groups which are defined as agents of a foreign actual or potential military enemy, it has been impossible for any group to convince the country to actively support restrictions against others who do not conform to the beliefs of one or another segment of American society. A Canadian sociologist, S. D. Clark, has commented on this aspect of American society. He suggests that the much tighter political and social control structure of Canada frustrates efforts at dissident movements before they can develop, while the United States permits them to emerge, but frustrates their dreams of power:

> Critics outside the country [the United States] might well pause to consider not the intolerance which finds expression in McCarthyism but the tolerance which makes it possible for McCarthyism to develop. In Canada it would be hard to conceive of a state of political freedom great enough to permit the kind of attacks upon responsible political leaders of the government which have been carried out in the United States. More careful examination of the American community in general, and perhaps of the academic community in particular, would probably reveal that, in spite of the witch hunts in that country, the people of the United States enjoy in fact a much greater degree of freedom than do the people of Canada.[25]

The Shift to the Right

Four aspects of American society have been suggested as contributing to an understanding of extremist political devel-

[25] S. D. Clark, "The Frontier and Democratic Theory," *Transactions of the Royal Society of Canada*, XLVII, III, June 1954, p. 72.

opments in the United States: the role of the status-driven during periods of prosperity, their fear of other groups which threaten their status; the absence of a firm tradition of civic discipline or tolerance; the definition of Americanism in ideological terms; and the lack of an integrated cultural and political social control structure.

In order to understand the recent manifestations of political intolerance, however, it is necessary to discuss a fifth factor, the consequences of a liberal or conservative climate of opinion on the power of extremist groups. The period from 1930 to 1945 saw the predominance of liberal sentiment in American politics. This was largely the result of two factors, the depression and the threat of Fascism. The depression emphasized the need for socio-economic reforms and helped to undermine the legitimacy of conservative and business institutions. It was followed immediately by a war which was defined as a struggle against Fascism. Since Fascism was a rightist movement, this fact tended to reinforce the political predominance of leftist liberal sentiments.

During this period the political dynamic in most democratic countries was in the hands of the left, and it used this strength to undermine the prestige of conservatism. In the United States, for example, several Congressional Committees conducted exposés of "undemocratic" activities of big business. In the thirties, the Nye Committee "exposed" the way in which Wall Street bankers had helped plunge the United States into World War I in order to maintain their investments, while the La Follette Committee revealed that large corporations employed labor spies and gangsters to prevent their employees from forming trade unions. The famous Truman Committee often exposed big business profiteering during World War II. All three committees helped to foster an anti-business and anti-conservative climate of opinion. It is quite true that the House Un-American Activities Committee operated at the same time as the liberal committees, but though it secured considerable publicity, it was relatively unimportant compared with the role of anti-subversive committees in the post-war years.

The period of liberal supremacy was also marked by a great growth in the influence of the Communist Party. In the United States, the Communists were concerned with penetrating and manipulating liberal and moderate left groups, rather than with building an electoral party. The Communists, by concealing their real objectives, by acting positively for liberal causes, by being the best organizers of the left, were able to penetrate deeply into various liberal organizations and into the labor movement. An index of their success may be seen in the fact that close to a dozen Congressmen, one state governor, many members of the staffs of liberal Congressmen and Congressional Committees, and a number of high-ranking civil servants, showed by their subsequent political behavior that they were close followers of the Communist Party.

The post-war period, on the other hand, has seen a resurgence of conservative and rightist forces. This has resulted from two factors, a prolonged period of prosperity and full employment, and second, the change in foreign policy. Where once we warred against Fascism, which is identified with the "right," we now war against Communism, which identifies with the "left." And while Fascism and Communism are much closer to each other in moral consequences and actual practice than either is to the democratic right or left, by the general populace, the one is considered right and the other left.[26] And just as the Communists were able to secure considerable influence during the period of liberal ascendancy, right-wing

[26] That this is somewhat legitimate may be seen by analyzing the social bases of support of these totalitarian movements. In general, Communists, where strong, receive support from the same social strata which vote for democratic socialist or liberal groups in countries with weak Communist movements. Conversely, Fascist and right authoritarians, such as De Gaulle, have received their backing from previous supporters of conservative parties. There is little evidence of an authoritarian appeal *per se*. Rather, it would seem that under certain conditions part of the conservative group will become Fascists, while under others, part of the support of the democratic left will support the Communists. See S. M. Lipset, et al., "Psychology of Voting," in Gardner Lindzey, ed., *Handbook of Social Psychology* (Cambridge: Addison Wesley, 1954), pp. 1135–36.

extremists have been able to make considerable headway during the conservative revival. Thus, the period from 1947–48 to 1954 presents a very different picture from the previous decade and a half. The conservatives and the extreme right are now on the offensive. The "free enterprise" system which provides full employment is once more legitimate. Liberal groups feel in a weak position politically, and now wage a defensive battle, seeking to preserve their conquests of the thirties, rather than to extend them.

It is striking to observe the similarities in the rhetoric of the liberals and conservatives when on the offensive. In the thirties, conservatives, isolationists, business leaders, Republican Senators and Congressmen were criticized by some liberals as being semi-Fascist, or with being outright Fascists. Similarly in the last half-decade, many conservatives have waged an attack on liberals, Democrats and opponents of a vigorous anti-Russian foreign policy for being pro-Communist, or "creeping Socialists." The sources of the violent attack on conservatism in the earlier period came in large measure from the Communists and their fellow-travelers, although it was voiced by many liberals who had no connection with the Communist Party and were unaware of the extent to which they had absorbed a Communist ideological position. More recently, the extreme right wing, the radical right of the American political spectrum, has been successful in setting the ideological tone of conservatism.

It is important to note the parallelism in the rhetoric employed by liberals when criticizing the State Department's policy toward the Loyalists in the Spanish Civil War of 1936–39, and that used by many extreme rightists toward the policy of the same department a few years later in the Chinese Civil War. The liberal left magazines portrayed an American foreign office staffed by men who were sympathetic to extreme conservatism if not outright Fascism, and who tricked Roosevelt and Hull into pursuing policies which helped Franco. Various individuals, some of whom are still in the State Department, such as Robert Murphy, were labeled as pro-Franco. The recent right-wing accusations that our Chinese policies were a result of Communist influence in government sound like a rewritten version of the Fascist conspiracy of the thirties. The same allegations about the social background of State Department members, that many of them come from Groton, Harvard, and the Brahmin upper class, were used by the Communists in the thirties to prove that the State Department was ultra-rightist in its sympathies, and are used today by McCarthy and other radical rightists to account for presumed sympathies with Communism.[27] The State Department's re-

[27] For a discussion of the way in which the radical right systematically attacks the Brahmin upper class in the State Department, see pp. 210–11 of this essay. Even as late as 1952, the left-wing journalist I. F. Stone attempted to bolster his attack on American policy in Korea by calling attention to the fact "that Acheson on making his Washington debut at the Treasury before the war, had been denounced by New Dealers as a 'Morgan man,' a Wall Street Trojan Horse, a borer-from-within on behalf of the big bankers." I. F. Stone, *The Hidden History of the Korean War* (New York: Monthly Review Press, 1952), p. 204.

It should be noted that, insofar as education at Harvard, Yale or Princeton is an indicator of upper-class background, the extremist critics of the State Department are correct in their claim that persons with a high-status background are disproportionately represented in the State Department. A study of 820 Foreign Office Officers indicated that 27 per cent of them graduated from these institutions, while only 14 per cent of high-ranking civil servants in other departments had similar collegiate background. (R. Bendix, *Higher Civil Servants in American Society* [Boulder: University of Colorado Press, 1949] pp. 92–93.)

Some evidence that elite background is even of greater significance in the higher echelons of the State Department may be found in a recent article published in the *Harvard Alumni Bulletin:*

"The new United States Ambassador to the Federal Republic of Germany (James B. Conant, Harvard '14, and former president of the University) will find, if he looks about him, fellow alumni in comparable positions. Across the border to the south and west, the Belgian ambassador is Frederick M. Alger, Jr. '30, and the French ambassador is C. Douglas Dillon, '31. Down the Iberian Peninsula the ambassadors to Spain and Portugal are John D. Lodge '25, and James C. H. Bonbright '25. A bit to the north, Ambassador Conant will find Ambassador Robert D. Coe '23 in Denmark and John M. Cabot '23 in Sweden. In the forbidden land to the east of him is Charles E. Bohlen '27, Ambassador to the U.S.S.R. Near at hand, across the Channel, is the senior member of Harvard's ambassado-

fusal to aid Loyalist Spain was presented as convincing proof of the presence of Fascist sympathizers within it. In the same way, the radical right now refuses to acknowledge that men may have made honest errors of judgment in their dealing with the Russians or the Chinese Communists.

So similar are the political approaches of the radical right and the Communists that one may fittingly describe the radical right doctrine as embodying a theory of "Social Communism" in the same sense as the Communists used the term "Social Fascism" in the early thirties. The Communists, before 1934, argued that all non-Communist parties including the Socialists were "Social Fascists," that is, they objectively were paving the way for Fascism. The principal organ of the radical right today, *The Freeman,* contends that all welfare state and planning measures are "objectively" steps toward the development of a totalitarian Communist state. The New Deal, Americans for Democratic Action, the C.I.O. Political Action Committee, all are charged with "objective" totalitarianism. Both the Communists and writers for *The Freeman* have argued that the "social" variety of Fascism or Communism is more dangerous than the real thing, for the public is more easily deceived by a sugar-coated totalitarian program. The Communists in pre-Hitler Germany concentrated their fire not on the Nazis, but on the "Social Fascists," the socialists and liberals, and *The Freeman* and other sections of the radical right let loose their worst venom on the American liberals.

An example of the violent character of this ideology may be seen in a 1950 *Freeman* article which contended that, "This new political machine, which . . . rules the old Democratic Party is an outgrowth of the C.I.O.'s Political Action Committee (PAC)." It further claimed that "every single element in the Browder [Communist Party] program was incorporated in the PAC program. It has been the policy of the Administration ever since." The labor movement organized around Tru-

---

rial galaxy, Winthrop W. Aldrich '07, LL.D. '53, Ambassador to Great Britain. . . . There seem to be enough Harvard ambassadors for a baseball team in Europe. . . ." ("Ambassadors" in *Harvard Alumni Bulletin,* Vol. 57, May 21, 1955, p. 617.)

man because of the Taft-Hartley Act. Why, asked this *Free-man* writer, did labor unite against this act, which though it "injured the Communists . . . certainly did not injure the workers." . . . Because the Communists executed another strategic retreat. They let go of their prominent offices in the C.I.O. but they still had control of the press, and the policy-making and opinion-forming organs. Then they got their ideas into the opinion-forming agencies of the AFL, especially its League for Political Education.

"How could the AFL be captured by the Communist policy-makers? It had a great tradition, but in face of C.I.O. 'gains,' its leaders thought they had to 'do something.' And the Communists were ready and waiting to tell them what to do—policies nicely hidden behind the cloak of higher wages, more benefits, but still fitting perfectly the symbols laid down to guide policy-makers by Earl Browder in 1944."

The article went on to ask, "What proof have we that the Politburo in Moscow wanted the election of Wallace? Wallace certainly did not poll the total Communist vote. For eight years they had worked on getting control of a major party. Why give up the Truman party? . . .

"Practically every word of Truman's campaign came, again, from Browder's pattern of 1944, which is the policy of the PAC. Practically every word of his attack on the 80th Congress can be found earlier in the pages of the *Daily Worker* and the *People's Daily World*.

"What then was the role of Wallace and the third party? It was the old Communist dialectic. By setting up Wallace as the 'left,' the Communists could make Truman's platforms and speeches look like the 'center.' "[28]

Here is a picture of the real world that should be placed side by side with that of the Communists. As they see a country controlled by a self-conscious plot of Wall Street magnates, of two "capitalist" parties competing just to fool the people, this radical rightist sees a nightmarish world in which the Communists also have two political parties in order to fool

[28] Edna Lonergan, "Anatomy of the PAC," *The Freeman*, November 27, 1950, pp. 137–39.

the people, in which Wallace's million votes only represented a presumably small part of total Communist strength.

In both periods, the thirties and the fifties, the extremists have been able to capitalize on sympathetic predispositions. These ideological predispositions have not reflected sympathy with extremism by the average liberal or conservative, but rather led men to view with sympathy any attack directed against their principal political opponents. The lack of any normative restrictions against violent political rhetoric in American politics, to which attention was called earlier, facilitated the adoption by basically unideological politicians of terminology which in large part resembles that used by rival totalitarians in Europe. In effect, the extreme left and right have been able to influence the ideological setting of American politics since the early thirties. The radical right today, like the Communists before them, have been able to win influence far outweighing their numerical support in the general population, because they have seemingly been the most effective fighters against those policies and groups which are repugnant to all conservatives.

II

The Two Conservatives

The conservative elements in American society can be divided into two groups, the moderate conservatives and the radical right. These two may be differentiated by their attitude toward the New Deal era. The moderates are generally willing to accept the past within limits, that is, they do not want "to turn the clock back." They accept various Roosevelt reforms; they tolerate the labor movement; they tend to be internationalist in ideology and to accept the policies of Roosevelt in the last war. Moderate conservatives also believe in constitutional processes, civil liberties, and due process.

The radical right, on the other hand, refuses to accept the recent past, or is radical in the quixotic sense that it rejects the status quo. Most, though not all of the radical right are opposed to: (1) the welfare state; (2) the labor movement; (3) the income tax; (4) World War II—the radical right sees the war as an avoidable mistake, and prefers in retrospect a policy of Russia and Germany fighting it out alone.[29]

In a larger sense, the radical right views our entire foreign policy from the recognition of Russia to Potsdam as appeasement, treason and treachery. It is opposed to membership in the United Nations, and to entangling foreign commitments. It is Asia-oriented, rather than Europe-oriented. It is suspicious of Great Britain as a Machiavellian power which has manipulated us into two wars, and now refuses to back us in our time of need.

Since the radical right believes that both our domestic and foreign policies over the last twenty years have represented tremendous setbacks for the country, it seeks an explanation of these calamitous errors, and finds it in the penetration of the government and the agencies of opinion formation by the

[29] A good example of extreme right ideology is contained in the newspaper report of a speech delivered at a meeting of Alliance, Inc., a right-wing group sponsored by Archibald Roosevelt:

"Gov. J. Bracken Lee of Utah declared last night that 'We have in Washington what to my mind amounts to a dictatorship.'

"Asserting that high spending was heading the country toward poverty, he . . . [said] that the end result of all dictatorships was the same. 'They end up with a ruling class and all the rest of us are peons.' . . .

"There was no difference, he continued, between the Government in Russia and an all powerful central government in Washington. . . .

". . . all the trouble in Washington began when a constitutional amendment authorized the income tax. He assailed the United Nations, foreign aid and Federal grants to the states.

"He appealed to those who felt the way he did 'to speak up now.' When a voice in the audience asked, 'How,' he replied: 'If you feel that McCarthy's on our side say so.' This reference to Senator Joseph R. McCarthy of Wisconsin evoked applause, cheers and whistles."

See "Governor of Utah Sees Dictatorship," New York *Times,* February 18, 1955, p. 19.

For a description of the ideology of the radical right, or as he calls them, the ultra-conservatives, see Clinton Rossiter, *Conservatism in America* (New York: Alfred A. Knopf, 1955), pp. 183–86.

Communist movement. The radical right is far from having a unified ideology. Some groups are more concerned with our past and present foreign policy, others with domestic affairs. But the common denominator which unites the radical right is the identification of the policies which it opposes, either in the economic or foreign sphere, with the "softness" of Franklin Roosevelt and the Democratic Party to the Soviet Union and the American Communist Party.

To some extent the two principal sources of bitter opposition to Roosevelt and the Democrats, the extreme economic conservatives and the isolationists, have tended to come together and adopt each other's ideologies. For example, rightwing Texans were ardent advocates of American entry into World War II. The Texas legislature by an almost unanimous vote passed a resolution telling Charles Lindbergh that he was not welcome in Texas during his leadership of America First. Today, however, many of the same Texans regard our participation in World War II as a blunder. On the other hand, a number of isolationists, such as Burton K. Wheeler, William Henry Chamberlain, and others, who were liberal or radical in economic matters, have become domestic conservatives. John T. Flynn is perhaps the outstanding example. He wrote regularly for the *New Republic* during the thirties and criticized Roosevelt's domestic and international policies from a left-wing point of view. With the onset of World War II, Flynn joined the America First movement. This action subjected him to vicious smears from liberal interventionists, who charged that he cooperated with Fascists.[30] He found increasingly that

[30] One hypothesis which may explain the subsequent bitterness of some of the former liberals and leftists who broke with Roosevelt over his foreign policies is contained in a defense of the Moscow trials of the 1930s written by John T. Flynn in his more leftist days.

"Americans found it difficult to believe that the old Bolsheviks recently executed in Russia, after all their years of warfare against capitalism, could have been really guilty of intriguing with Italy and Germany to destroy Stalin. That seemed unbelievable. *This incredulity struck me as possible only by ignoring the strange distance which the human mind and heart can lead a man of strong*

his audiences and the magazines that would accept his articles were right-wing conservatives, and gradually in joining with the right in foreign policy, he accepted their position on economic issues as well.

It is difficult to demonstrate that similar changes in political ideology have occurred among sections of the general population. A cursory inspection of election results in Wisconsin and other midwest states, however, indicates that many voters who once supported liberal isolationists are now backing right-wing nationalists. It would be interesting to know, for example, what proportion of those who supported the isolationist but progressive Bob La Follette in Wisconsin now backs Mc-Carthy. Conversely, some of the economic radical rightists such as the new millionaires of Texas, or men who were involved in the Liberty League in the thirties, have accepted the isolationist interpretation of the past, even though they were not isolationists before World War II.

Increasingly, a coherent radical right ideology has emerged which attacks past Democratic foreign policy as pro-Soviet, and criticizes New Deal economic policy as Socialist or Communist inspired. What are the sources of the support of the radical right in this country? It is difficult to answer this question since the groups who back the efforts to suppress the civil rights of men with whom they disagree, do not themselves agree on all or even most issues. The common denominator on which all the supporters of extremist action in the political arena agree is vigorous anti-Communism. This issue, today, has replaced anti-Catholicism or anti-immigrant senti-

---

feeling when they begin to generate hatreds. Now we have a weird case of it in our own far more composed country. Would anyone have believed, four years ago for instance, that in 1937 we would behold John Frey, of the A.F.L.—as fine a person as one would care to meet—actually consorting with a company union in steel to defeat and destroy a singularly successful industrial union movement led by John L. Lewis? Yet this fantastic thing has occurred. It is no stranger than a Russian editor full of hatred of Stalin seeking to circumvent that gentleman's plans by teaming up for the moment with Hitler." *New Republic*, March 24, 1937, pp. 209–10 (my emphasis).

ment as the unifying core for mass right-wing extremist action. One can identify some of the groups which play important roles in the anti-Communist crusade. These include groups reacting to the need for status policies, both the upward mobile ethnic population, and some of the downward mobile old American groups; groups responding to economic as well as status appeals; the *nouveaux riches,* and the insecure small businessmen; the traditionalist and authoritarian elements within the working-class groups whose values or ties to groups in other countries make them especially vulnerable to anti-Communist appeals (such as the Catholics or people coming from countries occupied by the Communists); and the traditional isolationists, especially those of German ancestry.

Status Politics and the Radical Right

One traditional source of extreme conservatism in the United States is the derivation of status from a claim to the American past—the people who belong to such filio-pietistic organizations as the Daughters of the American Revolution, the Colonial Dames, veterans' organizations, historical commemoration societies, patriotic groups, etc. The point one must always recognize in considering such organizations is that few of them are actually what their name implies. That is, most of these organizations which supposedly contain all those who have a right to membership in the groups by virtue of their own actions or those of their ancestors only are supported by a minority of those who are eligible. The Daughters of the American Revolution, for example, do not contain all the female descendants of Revolutionary soldiers, but only a small segment, those who choose to identify themselves in that fashion.[31] The same point may be made about the membership

[31] It is worth noting that existing evidence suggests that there is a substantial difference in the reactions of men and women to the radical right. Women are much more likely to support repressive measures against Communists and other deviant groups than are men as measured by poll responses, and many of the organizations which are active in local struggles to intimidate school and library boards are women's groups. In part this difference may be related to the fact that women are more explicitly concerned with family

of groups commemorating the War of 1812, the Civil War, the Confederacy, and other comparable groups. Further, in practice, the members who are active in these groups, who set policy, constitute an infinitesimal minority of the total membership.

---

status in the community than are men in the American culture, and hence, may react more than the men do to status anxieties or frustrations. The organizations of old family Americans which are concerned with claiming status from the past are predominantly female. Hence, if the thesis that status concerns are related to rightist extremism and bigotry is valid, one would expect to find more women than men affected by it.

Secondly, however, evidence from election and opinion studies in a number of countries indicates that women are more prone to be concerned with morality in politics. They are much more likely to support prohibition of liquor or gambling, or to vote against corrupt politicians than men. This concern with morality seems to be related to the greater participation in religious activities by the female sex. Since Communism has come to be identified as a moral crusade against evil by every section of American public opinion, one should expect that women will be more likely to favor suppression of evil, much as they favor suppression of liquor and gambling. The propensity to support efforts to repress "corrupt ideas" is probably intensified by the fact that much of the concern with the activities of Communists is related to their potential effect on the young. See H. Tingsten, *Political Behavior: Studies in Election Statistics* (London: P. S. King, 1937), pp. 36–75 for a report of comparative data on women's attitudes and political behavior. In the 1952 Presidential election in the United States, more women voted Republican than Democratic for the first time in many years. It has been suggested that this was a product of the raising of strong moral issues by the Republicans. See L. Harris, *Is There a Republican Majority?* (New York: Harper & Brothers, 1954), Chapter VI.

The recent Stouffer study of attitudes toward civil liberties further tends to validate these inferences. The data indicate clearly that in 1954 women were much more intolerant of Communists, critics of religion, and advocates of nationalized industry than men. Similarly, presidents of women's clubs were less tolerant than any other group of community leaders interviewed with the exception of officers of the D.A.R. and the American Legion. (See S. A. Stouffer, *op. cit.*, pp. 131–55, 52.) Part of the difference in attitudes between men and women reported in this study is accounted for by the fact that women are more religious than men, and religious

What is the minority deriving status and other gratifications from such membership? Various sociological insights may be of some help here although unfortunately there is little or no research on their membership. It has been suggested that individuals who participate in such societies tend disproportionately to be people who have little other claim to status. They may be members of families which once were important, but whose present position is such that on the basis of personal achievement alone they would have little right to social prestige. Many such individuals tend to magnify this one claim to status, a claim to history, a claim to lineage, an identification with a heroic American past, which other people cannot have. It is their defense against the newcomers, against the rising minority ethnic groups. And consequently, such individuals and their organizations make a fetish out of tradition and past styles of life, and tend to be arch-conservative. Thus the groups which have the greatest sense of status insecurity will oppose both economic reform and internationalism, both of which are viewed as challenges to tradition.

While on one hand, the status-threatened old-family American tends to over-emphasize his identification with American conservative traditions, and thus be potentially or actually a supporter of the radical right, the new American, the minority ethnic, also is in strong need of asserting his status claims. For while the old American desires to maintain his status, the

---

people are more likely to be intolerant than the non-religious. However, even when religious participation is held constant, women are more likely to be intolerant than are men. I would suggest that part of this difference is related to the fact that women are more likely than men to reflect the political concerns derived from status. Unfortunately, the Stouffer study does not attempt to measure the effect of status concerns on political beliefs. For an excellent study which does attempt to do this in the context of analyzing the electoral support of British political parties see Mark Benney and Phyllis Geiss, "Social Class and Politics in Greenwich," *British Journal of Sociology,* 1950, Vol. I, pp. 310–24. The authors of this study found that women were more likely to report themselves in a higher social class than men at the same occupational level, and those who reported themselves to be higher status were more conservative.

new American wishes to obtain it, to become accepted. This is particularly true for those members of the minority groups who have risen to middle or upper class position in the economic structure. These groups, having entered at the bottom, tend to view the status hierarchy as paralleling the economic ladder; they believe that one need only move up the economic scale to obtain the good things of the society. But, as they move up economically, they encounter social resistance. There is discrimination by the old-family Americans, by the Anglo-Saxon against the minority ethnics. The Boston Brahmins, for example, do not accept the wealthy Irish.[32] As Joseph Kennedy, father of the present Senator and former Ambassador to Great Britain, once put it in reaction to the fact that the Boston press continually made reference to him as Irish: "I was born here, my children were born here. What the hell do I have to do to be an American?" All through the country, one can find ethnic groups, often composed of third and fourth generation Americans, who have developed their own middle and upper classes, but who are still refused admittance into the social circles of Anglo-Saxon Protestants. One of the major reactions to such discrimination, as indicated earlier, is to become overconformist to an assumed American tradition. Since many members of these ethnic groups do not want to be defined as European, they also tend to become isolationist, ultra-patriotic, and even anti-European. For them, as for the old American traditionalist, the positive orientation towards Europe of liberals, of moderate conservative internationalists, creates a challenge to their basic values and to their rejection of Europe. Thus the status-insecure old-family American middle class, and the status-striving minority ethnics, both arrive at similar political positions.

But to return at this point to the theme developed in the earlier discussion of status politics, status insecurities and status aspirations are most likely to appear as sources of frustration, independent of economic problems, in periods of prolonged

[32] For an excellent description of the reactions of the Boston Brahmins to the Irish, see Cleveland Amory, *The Proper Bostonians* (New York: E. P. Dutton and Company, 1947), p. 346.

prosperity. For such times make it possible for individuals and groups who have moved up to constitute a visible threat to the established status groups; while at the same time the successfully mobile begin to search for means of improving their status. It is obvious that there are always many who do not prosper in periods of prosperity. And it is precisely members of the older prestigeful groups who are disproportionately to be found among the rentier class economically, with many living on fixed incomes, old businesses and the like—sources of income which are prone to decline in their relative position.[33]

Thus, clearly, prosperity magnifies the status problem by challenging the economic base of the older groups, and accentuating the claim to status of the emerging ones. As a general hypothesis I would suggest that the supporters of the radical right in the 1950s come disproportionately from both the rising ethnic groups, and those old-family Americans who are oriented toward a strong identification with the past.[34]

[33] In an article written shortly before his death, Franz Neumann suggested that one of the social sources of political anxiety which led to individuals and groups accepting a conspiracy theory of politics is social mobility:

"In every society that is composed of antagonistic groups there is an ascent and descent of groups. It is my contention that persecutory anxiety—but one that has a real basis—is produced when a group is threatened in its prestige, income, or its existence. . . .

"The fear of social degradation thus creates for itself 'a target for the discharge of the resentments arising from damaged self-esteem.' . . .

"Hatred, resentment, dread, created by great upheavals, are concentrated on certain persons, who are denounced as devilish conspirators. Nothing would be more incorrect than to characterize the enemies as scapegoats, for they appear as genuine enemies whom one must extirpate and not as substitutes whom one only needs to send into the wilderness. The danger consists in the fact that this view of history is never completely false, but always contains a kernel of truth and, indeed, must contain it, if it is to have a convincing effect."

Franz L. Neumann, "Anxiety in Politics," *Dissent*, Spring 1955, pp. 141, 139, 135.

[34] One study of McCarthy's appeal indicates that, among Protestants, he gets much more support from persons of non-Anglo-

The Economic Extremists

A second source of support for extreme right-wing activities, here as in other countries, is the important group of newly wealthy individuals thrown up by great prosperity. New wealth most often tends to have extremist ideologies, to believe in extreme conservative doctrines in economic matters.[35] The man who makes money himself feels more insecure about keeping it than do people who possess inherited wealth. He feels more aggrieved about social reform measures which involve redistribution of the wealth, as compared with individuals, still wealthy, who have grown up in an old traditionalist background, which inculcates the values of tolerance traditionally associated with upper-class aristocratic conservatism. It is not without reason that the new millionaires, such as those in Texas, have given extensive financial support to radical right movements, politicians, and to such propaganda organizations as Facts Forum.

While the most important significance of the newly wealthy lies in the power which their money can bring, rather than in their numbers, there is a mass counterpart for them in the general population, the small independent businessmen. Sta-

---

Saxon ancestry than from those whose forefathers came from Britain. The polls are not refined enough to locate old Americans who support patriotic organizations, but the activities of groups which belong to the Coalition of Patriotic Societies are what would be expected in terms of the logic of this analysis. See Wallerstein, *op. cit.*

[35] These observations about the *nouveaux riches* are, of course, not new or limited to current American politics. William Cobbett commented in 1827:

". . . this hatred to the cause of public liberty is, I am sorry to say it, but too common amongst merchants, great manufacturers, and great farmers; especially those who have risen suddenly from the dunghill to chariot."

G. D. H. Cole and Margaret Cole, eds., *The Opinions of William Cobbett* (London: The Cobbett Publishing Co., 1944), pp. 86–87; see also Walter Weyl, *The New Democracy*, (New York: The Macmillan Co., 1912), pp. 242–43 for similar comments on the American *nouveaux riches*, in the late nineteenth and early twentieth centuries.

tistical data on social mobility in the United States indicates a great turnover in the ranks of these groups.[36] A large proportion, if not a majority of them, come from other social strata: the small storekeepers and businessmen often are of working-class origin; the small manufacturer often comes out of the ranks of executives, white collar or government workers.

These small businessmen, perhaps more than any other group, have felt constrained by progressive social legislation and the rise of labor unions. They are squeezed harder than large business, since their competitive position does not allow them to pay increases in wages as readily as can big firms. Governmental measures such as social security, business taxes, or various regulations which require filling out forms, all tend to complicate the operation of small business. In general, these people are oriented upwards, wish to become larger businessmen, and take on the values of those who are more successful, or perhaps more accurately, they tend to take over their *image* of the values of more powerful groups, values which are often those of the radical right. Thus, as an hypothesis, it may be suggested that in terms of economic interest motivation, the principal financial support of the radical right comes from those who have newly acquired wealth, and from small business.[37]

[36] See S. M. Lipset and Reinhard Bendix, "Social Mobility and Occupational Career Patterns II. Social Mobility," *American Journal of Sociology*, Vol. LVII (March 1952), pp. 494–504.

[37] Again, poll data fit this hypothesis. Material from a 1952 Roper poll shows that the most pro-McCarthy occupational group in the country is small businessmen. See Wallerstein, *op. cit.* For an excellent discussion of the reactionary politics of upward mobile small business, see R. Michels, "Psychologie der anti-Kapitalistischen Massenbewegungen," *Grundriss der Sozialekonomik*, Vol. IX, No. 1, p. 249. A recent study of post-war elections in Great Britain also suggests that small businessmen react more negatively to welfare state politics than any other occupational group. John Bonham reports that a larger proportion of small businessmen shifted away from the Labor Party between 1945 and 1950 than any other stratum. See the *Middle Class Vote* (London: Faber and Faber, 1954), p. 129.

Extreme conservatism on economic matters is, of course, not new. During the thirties it was represented by the Liberty League, and by various measures of organized business groups to block the development of trade unions. In general, one could probably safely say that most big business was willing to use undemocratic restrictive measures, such as labor spies and thugs, to prevent the emergence of trade unions in the twenties and thirties. The basic difference between the radical right and the moderate right, at present, however, is that the moderate right, which seemingly includes the majority of big business, has come to accept the changes which have occurred in the last twenty years, including trade unions and various social reforms, whereas the radical right still looks upon these as basic threats to its position. In practice economic rightists' efforts to turn the clock back have been successful in many states which are characterized by the lack of metropolitan areas, by rural and small-town predominance in the legislatures. In such states, laws have been passed outlawing the closed union shop, the amendment to repeal the income tax amendment to the Constitution has been endorsed by the legislature, and other legislation designed to destroy the reforms of the thirties and forties has been enacted. The fact remains, however, that the bulk of the reforms and institutions the liberal left created in the thirties and forties remain intact, and the business conservatives and the radical right cannot feel secure or victorious.

The "Tory" Worker

The previous sections have dealt with factors differentiating middle- and upper-class supporters of right-wing extremism from those who back more moderate policies. The stress on the radical right backers in these strata does not mean that the principal support of this type of politics lies here. In fact, survey as well as impressionistic data suggest that the large majority of these classes adhere to moderate politics, principally those of the moderate conservative, and that the overwhelming majority of the middle and upper groups have been consistently opposed to McCarthy and the whole radical right movement. The various studies of attitudes toward civil liberties and McCarthy suggest that the lower a person is in socioeconomic status or educational attainment, the more likely he is to support McCarthy, favor restrictions on civil liberties, and back a "get tough" policy with the Communist states.[38]

The lack of tolerance exhibited by large sections of the lower classes as compared with the middle classes is, of course, quite understandable. Support of civil liberties or tolerance for persons with whom one strongly disagrees requires, one would guess, both a high degree of material and psychic security, and considerable sophistication. As compared with the bulk of the middle and upper classes, the working class

[38] There is a considerable body of evidence which indicates that economic liberalism (support of the labor movement, government planning, and so forth) is correlated inversely with socio-economic status, while non-economic "liberalism" (support of civil liberties, and internationalism), is associated positively with socio-economic status. That is, the poor are for redistribution of wealth, while the more well-to-do are liberal in non-economic matters. See G. H. Smith, "Liberalism and Level of Information," *Journal of Educational Psychology*, February 1948, pp. 65–81; Hyman and Sheatsley, *op. cit.*, pp. 6–17; reports of the American Institute of Public Opinion, *passim*.

These findings are paralleled by various reports which suggest that lower status and education are associated with high scores on scales designed to measure degree of authoritarianism. See H. H. Hyman and P. B. Sheatsley, "The Authoritarian Personality—A Methodological Critique," in M. Jahoda and R. Christie, *Studies in the Scope and Method of "The Authoritarian Personality"* (Glencoe, Ill.: The Free Press, 1954), p. 94; R. Christie, "Authoritarianism Re-examined," in *ibid.*, pp. 169–75.

Janowitz and Marvick have reported the interesting finding based on a national sample that the two most "authoritarian" groups are the poorly educated lower class, and the poorly educated lower middle class. See M. Janowitz and D. Marvick, "Authoritarianism and Political Behavior," *Public Opinion Quarterly*, Summer 1953, pp. 185–201.

The Stouffer study reports results similar to these earlier ones. In addition it indicates that leaders of community organizations, most of whom are drawn from the upper part of the class structure and are college educated, are much more favorable to civil liberties than the general population. See S. A. Stouffer, *op. cit.*, pp. 28–57, and *passim*.

lacks these attributes. The consequences of these differences are manifest not only in the political arena, but in religion as well, for chiliastic evangelical religions have tended to draw their support from the lower classes, while liberal "tolerant" denominations have almost invariably been middle- and upper-class groups.

When one attempts, however, to go beyond the variables of economic status and education, in distinguishing between support or opposition to McCarthy or greater or less tolerance in civil liberties among the lower classes, the principal differentiating factors seem to be party allegiance, and religious beliefs. In the United States and Great Britain, the conservative workers, those who back the Tory or Republican parties, tend to have the most intolerant attitudes. Comparative impressionistic data suggests that these differences are not inherent in varying social strata, but rather are a consequence of partisan identifications and values. That is, the Democratic and Labour parties are more concerned with propagating a civil libertarian value system than are the conservative parties. Within the Democratic and Labour parties, however, the working class is more intolerant than the middle class.[39]

[39] Zetterberg in an unpublished study of attitudes toward civil liberties in a New Jersey community found that working-class respondents were much more intolerant on civil-liberties questions than middle-class respondents, and that working-class Republicans were somewhat more anti-civil libertarian than working-class Democrats. Similar conclusions may be deduced from various reports of the American Institute of Public Opinion (Gallup Poll) and the Stouffer study. The first indicates that lower-class respondents are more favorably disposed to McCarthy than middle and upper class, but that Democrats are more likely to be anti-McCarthy than are Republicans. Stouffer reports similar findings with regard to attitudes toward civil liberties. Unfortunately, neither the Gallup Poll nor Stouffer have presented their results by strata for the supporters of each party separately. See S. A. Stouffer, *op. cit.*, pp. 210–15. A survey study of the 1952 elections indicates that at every educational level, persons who scored high on an "authoritarian personality" scale were more likely to be Eisenhower voters than were those who gave "equalitarian" responses. Robert E.

The support which a large section of the American working class gives to right-wing extremism today may also be related to the greater sense of status deprivation felt by "failures" in periods of prosperity discussed earlier. Workers who fail to get ahead while some friends, classmates, and fellow war

---

Lane, "Political Personality and Electoral Choice," *American Political Science Review,* March 1955, p. 180.

In Britain, Eysenck reports that "middle-class Conservatives are more tender-minded [less authoritarian] than working-class Conservatives; middle-class Liberals are more tender-minded than working-class Liberals; middle-class Socialists more tender-minded than working-class Socialists, and even middle-class Communists are more tender-minded than working-class Communists." H. J. Eysenck, *The Psychology of Politics* (London: Routledge and Kegan Paul, 1954), p. 137. Similar findings are indicated also in a Japanese study which reports that the lower classes and the less educated are more authoritarian than the middle and upper strata and the better educated, but the supporters of the socialist parties are less authoritarian than those who vote for the two "bourgeois" parties. See Kotaro Kido and M. Sugi, "A Report on Research on Social Stratification and Social Mobility in Tokyo (III). The Structure of Social Consciousness," *Japanese Sociological Review,* January 1954, pp. 74–100. See also National Public Opinion Research Institute (of Japan) Report No. 26, *A Survey of Public Attitudes Toward Civil Liberty.*

An as yet unpublished secondary analysis of German data collected by the UNESCO Institute at Cologne yields similar results for Germany. The working classes are less favorable to a democratic party system than are the middle and upper classes. However, within every occupational stratum men who support the Social-Democrats are more likely to favor democratic practices than those who back the more conservative parties. The most antidemocratic group of all are workers who vote for non-Socialist groups. (This analysis was done by the author.)

It is also true that the working class forms the mass base of authoritarian parties in Argentina, Italy, and France. Ignazio Silone is one of the few important Socialists who have recognized that recent historical events challenge the belief that the working class is inherently a progressive and democratic force.

". . . the myth of the liberating power of the proletariat has dissolved along with that other myth of the inevitability of progress. The recent examples of the Nazi labor unions, those of Salazar and Peron . . . have at last convinced of this even those who were reluctant to admit it on the sole grounds of the totalitarian degen-

veterans do, are also likely to feel embittered. This prosperity-born bitterness should result in more varied forms of protest in America than in Europe, since American workers, unlike European ones, do not have a Socialist ideology which places the blame for individual failure on the operation of the social system.[40] While the lower strata constitute the largest section of the mass base of the radical right, especially of McCarthy, who, as we shall see later, makes a particular appeal to them, in power terms they are the least significant. Up to now, there are no organized working-class groups, other than some of the fundamentalist churches, which support radical right activities.[41] And unlike the middle- and upper-class supporters of rightist opinions in the area of civil liberties, and foreign policy, who are also economic conservatives, many of the lower-class followers of radical-right leaders are in favor of liberal economic policies. Those workers who tend to back extreme right policies in economic as well as civil liberties and foreign policy areas tend to be the most traditionalistic and apolitical in their outlook. The principal significance of lower-class attitudes, therefore, lies in the votes and responses to public polls which they contribute to the radical right rather

---

eration of Communism. . . . The worker, as we have seen and as we continue to see, can work for the most conflicting causes; he can be Blackshirt or partisan." Ignazio Silone, "The Choice of Comrades," *Dissent,* Winter 1955, p. 14.

It may in fact be argued that the lower classes are most attracted to chiliastic political movements, which are necessarily intolerant and authoritarian. Far from workers in poorer countries being Communists because they do not realize that the Communists are authoritarian, as many democratic Socialists have argued and hoped, they may be Communists because the evangelical "only truth" aspect of Communism is more attractive to them than the moderate and democratic gradualism of the social democracy.

[40] See R. K. Merton, "Social Structure and Anomie," in his *Social Theory and Social Structure* (Glencoe, Ill.: Free Press, 1949), Chapter IV.

[41] The large Catholic working class, although predominantly Democratic, also contributes heavily to the support of extremist tendencies on the right in questions dealing with civil liberties or foreign policy. This pattern stems in large measure from their situation as Catholics, and is discussed in a later section.

than in their potential utilization as part of a mass base for an organized movement.[42]

The Isolationists

A fourth basis of strength of the radical right has developed out of the old isolationist-interventionist controversy. The traditional isolationists have become, in large measure, a base of the radical right. If one looks over the background of isolationism in this country, it seems largely rooted in ethnic prejudices or reactions, ties to the homeland, and populist xenophobia. Samuel Lubell, for example, suggests, "The hard core of isolationism in the United States has been ethnic and emotional, not geographic. By far the strongest common characteristic of the isolationist-voting counties is the residence there

[42] It is interesting to note in this connection that the large group of persons who are inactive politically in American society tend to be the most conservative and authoritarian in their attitudes. These groups, largely concentrated in the lower classes, do, however, contribute to the results of public opinion polls since they are interviewed. Consequently such polls may exaggerate greatly the effective strength of right-wing extremism. Stouffer reports that those less interested in politics are less tolerant of the civil liberties of Communists and other deviants than are those who are interested. See S. A. Stouffer, *op. cit.*, pp. 83–86. Sanford, who found a negative relationship between socio-economic status and authoritarian attitudes, states: "We have data showing that authoritarians are not highly participant in political affairs, do not join many community groups, do not become officers in the groups they become members of." F. H. Sanford, *Authoritarianism and Leadership* (Philadelphia: Stephenson Brothers, 1950), p. 168; see also G. M. Connelly and H. H. Field, "The non-voter—Who he is, what he thinks," *Public Opinion Quarterly*, Vol. 8, 1944, pp. 175–87. Data derived from a national survey in 1952 indicate that when holding education constant, individuals who score high on an "authoritarianism" scale are more likely to belong to voluntary associations than those who score low. The high "authoritarians," however, are less likely to engage in political activity or have a sense that they personally can affect the political process. Robert E. Lane, *op. cit.*, pp. 178–79. On the other hand Bendix suggests that the apathetic traditionalist group was mobilized by the Nazis in the final Weimar elections; see R. Bendix, "Social Stratification and Political Power," *American Political Science Review*, Vol. 46, 1952, pp. 357–75.

of ethnic groups with a pro-German or anti-British bias. Far
from being indifferent to Europe's wars, the evidence argues
that the *isolationists* are oversensitive to them."[43]

During two wars, the pro-German ethnic groups have been
isolationists. In addition to the Germans, and some midwestern
Scandinavian groups tied to them by religious and ecological
ties, many Irish also have opposed support of Britain in two
wars. Because German influence was concentrated in the Midwest, and in part because isolationist ideologies were part of
the value system of agrarian radicalism, isolationism has been
centered in the Midwest, especially among once-radical agrarians. The agrarian radicals of the Midwest tended to be xenophobic, suspicious of eastern and international finance capitalism. The various agrarian movements regarded efforts to
involve the United States in European conflicts as motivated
by the desire of eastern bankers to make money. The radical
agrarian character of isolationism, however, gradually began
to change for at least two reasons: (1) numerically its mass
Midwest base became less and less rural as the farm population declined, and more and more small-town middle class in
character; and (2) interventionism was identified with the New
Deal and social reform.[44] Thus the small-town midwestern
middle class was anti-New Deal, conservative and isolationist;

[43] Samuel Lubell, *The Future of American Politics* (New York:
Harper and Bros., 1952), p. 132. Lubell's thesis has been challenged by R. H. Schmuckler, "The Region of Isolationism," *American Political Science Review*, June 1953, pp. 388–401. Schmuckler
denies that the statistical evidence proves that any one factor is
basically correlated with voting behavior of isolationist members
of Congress. Lubell, however, uses other indicators of the effect of
ethnic attitudes on voting on foreign policy issues, the changes in
the election of 1940. Regardless of who is correct, the basic
hypothesis that feelings about past American policy which are
linked to the position of different ethnic groups, affect the current political behavior of these groups may still be valid.

[44] Among once liberal Midwest isolationist politicians who were
first liberals and became extreme rightists were Senators Nye,
Wheeler and Shipstead.

this all added up to a fervent opposition to Roosevelt and his domestic and foreign policy.

This former isolationist group, especially its German base, was under a need to justify its past, and to a certain extent, to gain revenge.[45] The Germans, in particular, were considered disloyal by the Yankees and other native American stock in two wars. Consequently, campaigns which seem to demonstrate that they were right and not disloyal would obviously win their support. The way in which one can understand the resentment against the UN and other international agencies is that these organizations are symbolic of American foreign policy and especially of the foreign policy of World War II, of collective security, of internationalism, of interventionism; and thus the attack on UNESCO, the attack on the UN is an attack on the past, an attack on Roosevelt, an attack on our whole foreign policy from '33 on.

The common tie which binds the former isolationist with the economic radical conservative is on the one hand the common enemy, Roosevelt and the New Deal, and secondly, the common scapegoat with which they can justify their past position. Both can now suggest that they were right, right in opposing the foreign policy or correct in opposing certain economic policies because these past policies were motivated or sustained by Communism or the Communist Party. Thus, both have an interest in magnifying the Communist plot, in identifying liberal and internationalist forces in American society with Communism.

The Catholics

A fifth source of mass support for the radical right in the recent period are many Catholics. As a rapidly rising group

[45] "The memory of opposition to the last war seems the real mainspring behind present-day isolationism. What really binds the former isolationists is not a common view on foreign policy for the future, but a shared remembrance of American intervention in the last war. The strength of the Republican appeal for former isolationist voters is essentially one of political revenge." Lubell, *op. cit.,* p. 152.

which was largely low status until recently, Catholics might
be expected to be vulnerable to status-linked political appeals.
In addition and probably more significant, however, Catholics
as a religious group are more prone to support anti-Communist
movements than any other sect with the possible exception of
the fundamentalist Protestant churches.[46] This predisposition
derives from the long history of Catholic opposition to Socialism and Communism, an organized opposition which has been
perhaps more formalized in theological church terms than in
almost any other group. This opposition has, in recent years,
been magnified by the fact that a number of countries taken
over by the Communists in eastern Europe are Catholic, and
it is notable that in Europe those countries which are most in
danger of Communist penetration are, in fact, Catholic.

In the past, however, Catholics in the United States and
other English-speaking countries, have been traditionally allied
with more left-wing parties. For example, in Great Britain,
Australia and New Zealand, the Catholics tend to support the
Labor Party. In the United States, they have backed the Democratic Party, while in Canada they support the Liberal Party.[47]

The identification of Catholicism with the left in the English-
speaking countries, as compared with its identification with the
right in Western Europe, is related to the fact that the Catholic
Church is a minority church in the English-speaking countries, and has been the church of the minority ethnic immigrants who have been largely lower class. As a lower-status
group, Catholics have been successfully appealed to by the
out-party, by the party of the lower class.

The rise of the Communist threat, however, and the identification of Communism with the left has created a conflict for

[46] Various national surveys have indicated that Catholics are
more likely to be favorable to Senator McCarthy than adherents
of other denominations. (See the reports of the American Institute
of Public Opinion.) The recent survey of attitudes toward civil
liberties reports that outside of the South, church-going Catholics
are more intolerant than church-going Protestants. See S. A. Stouffer, *op. cit.*, pp. 144–45.

[47] See S. M. Lipset, et al., *op. cit.*, p. 1140; Eysenck, *op. cit.*,
p. 21.

many Catholics. Historically, this ideological conflict has developed just as the Catholic population in most of these countries has produced a sizable upper and middle class of its own, which in economic terms is under pressure to abandon its traditional identification with the lower-class party. The Republican Party in the United States and the (conservative) Liberal Party in Australia as well, it is interesting to note, are now given an opportunity to break the Catholics from their traditional political mores. The conservatives face the problem in the era of the welfare state, that welfare politics obviously appeal to lower-class people. Consequently, for the conservatives to gain a majority (and here I speak not only of the radical right but of the moderate conservatives as well), they must have some issues which cut across class lines, and which can appeal to the lower classes against the party of that class. Traditionally, nationalism and foreign policy issues have been among the most successful means for the conservatives to break through class lines. In this specific case, if the conservatives can identify the left with Communism they may gain the support of many Catholics, both lower and middle class. This combination of the party desire to win elections plus the general desire of conservatives to dominate the society has led them to adopt tactics which normally they would abhor.

It may be appropriate to recall that the use of bigotry as a tactic by the conservatives to gain a political majority is not unknown in American history. The Whig Party before the Civil War, faced with the fact that increased immigration, largely Catholic, was constantly adding to the votes of the Democratic Party, realized that they might never obtain a majority. (They were in much the same position as the Republican Party from 1932 to 1952.) The Whigs, led largely by the so-called aristocratic elements in American society, upper-class Protestants both north and south, supported mass movements which were anti-Catholic and anti-immigrant, because of the belief that this would be the only way to win elections against the party of the "Demagogues," as they described the Democratic Party.

The upper-class Whigs hoped to break lower-class white

Protestants from their support of the Democratic Party by identifying that party with the immigrants and with the Catholics. Today, of course, the position is reversed. The attempt is not so much to break Protestants from the Democrats, but to win the Catholics from the Democrats. The Republicans wish to break the Democratic allegiance of the Catholics, rather than use them as a scapegoat to secure lower-class Protestant voters.[48]

It is also interesting to note that, since liberal groups draw so much support from the Catholics, it is an exceedingly delicate matter for them to defend themselves against the charge that they once made common cause with the Communists. American liberals are under pressure to deny their past, rather than defend it. To admit that liberals ever had sympathy for the Soviet Union, or that they ever in any way collaborated with Communists would be akin to confession, at least so far as their Catholic supporters are concerned, of collaboration with the Devil. In order to defend itself and to retain its Catholic base, the liberal left must either outdo the right in Communist charges, or at least tacitly agree with it. It fears that a large part of its mass base agrees with the radical right on the Communist question.[49]

The introduction of a bill to outlaw the Communist Party

[48] A similar effort is being made at the current time by the Australian conservatives who are attacking the Labor Party for alleged softness towards Communism, and for allowing itself to be penetrated by the Communists. The presence of a large Catholic population in these countries, traditionally linked to the more liberal party, is probably one of the most important factors affecting the reluctance of the moderate conservative politicians to oppose the tactics of the extremists on their own side.

[49] In Canada, also, the Catholics have provided the main dynamic for threats to civil liberties, which are presented as necessary parts of the struggle against Communism. The government of the Catholic province of Quebec passed legislation in the thirties which gave the government the right to invade private homes in search of Communist activities and to padlock any premises which have been used by the Communists. Civil liberties groups in Canada have charged that these laws have been used against non-Communist opponents of the government especially in the labor movement.

by the most liberal members of the United States Senate is an example of this phenomenon. Many of them are vulnerable to the charge of Communist collaboration. Paul Douglas, as a Socialist, visited the Soviet Union, and was addressed as Comrade by Stalin. This interview was published by the Communist Party. Wayne Morse was strongly backed by Harry Bridges in his election to the United States Senate. Hubert Humphrey was elected to the Senate by the Democratic-Farmer-Labor Party, shortly after the Communists captured the old Minnesota Farmer-Labor Party, and merged it with the Democratic Party of the state. None of these men ever supported the Communist Party, or even has any record of fellow-traveling for a brief period. Nevertheless, facts such as these would be difficult to explain without these men giving repeated evidence of their being strongly anti-Communist.

The situation in the Catholic community, today, is similar to conditions in the Jewish community during the thirties. The Jews, concerned with the growth of Nazism, felt the need to do something about it. Nazism became an important political issue for them. This situation played into the hands of the Communists who used the fight against Nazism as their principal appeal. And it is a fact that the Communists had considerable success among the Jews in this period.[50] Perhaps even more important was the fact that this influence often affected the political ideology and tactics of Jewish organizations which were in no way Communist.

Today the Catholics face the Communist issue as the Jews did Nazism. Even unscrupulous anti-Communism, the sort which is linked to motives and policies unrelated to the problem of fighting Communists, can win support within the Catho-

[50] There is, of course, no reliable quantitative way of measuring this influence, although all students of the Communist movement agree that its success was greatest among Jews. In Canada, where under a parliamentary system, the Communist Party was able to conduct election campaigns in districts where they had hopes of large support, they elected members to the Federal House and provincial legislatures from Jewish districts only. Similarly, in Great Britain, one of the two Communists elected in 1945 came from a London Jewish district.

lic community. And just as the Communists were able to press forward various other aspects of their ideology among the Jews in the 1930s, so the radical right, stressing the anti-Communist issue, is able to advance other parts of its program. The radical right uses the anti-Communist issue to create or sustain hostility among the Catholics against the New Deal, against social reform, at the same time identifying liberalism with Communism.

It is, therefore, impossible to analyze the impact of the radical right on American life without considering the vulnerability of the Catholics to the Communist issue, and the effect of this Catholic sensitivity on the political strategy of both Republican and Democratic politicians in their reactions to the radical right. For politic reasons many existing analyses of the radical right have found it convenient to ignore the Catholics, and attempts have been made to interpret the problem in terms of other variables or concepts, some of which, like the minority ethnic's reaction to status deprivation, have been suggested in this chapter as well. While such processes are important, it should not be forgotten that the majority of Catholics is still proletarian, and not yet in a position to make claim to high status. The role of the Catholic vulnerability to the radical right today, like the similar reaction of the Jews to the Communists a decade ago, must be considered independently of the fact that both groups have also reacted to the situation of being an ethnic minority.[51]

[51] It is possible to suggest another hypothesis for Catholic support of political intolerance in this country which ties back to the earlier discussion of the working class. All existing survey data indicate that the two religious groups which are most anti-civil libertarian are the Catholics and the fundamentalist Protestant sects. Both groups are predominantly low status in membership. In addition, both fall under the general heading of extreme moralizing or Puritanical religions. In the past, and to a considerable extent in the present also, the fundamentalists played a major role in stimulating religious bigotry, especially against Catholics. It is important, however, to note also that a large part of the American Catholic church is dominated by priests of Irish birth or ancestry. French Catholic intellectuals have frequently referred to the American Catholic church as the Hibernian American church. Irish

The Catalytic Elements

No analysis of the social strata and political tendencies which make up the radical right can be complete without a discussion of the catalytic elements, members of near Fascist and so-called borderline organizations, or individuals who though never members of such groups have maintained right-wing authoritarian sentiments. These groups and individuals have advocated extremist right-wing ideologies for a long time. Although their number may vary and their strength may fluctuate, they remain as a chronic source of potential extremist sentiments and organization. During the thirties, there were many avowedly authoritarian Fascist and racist organizations. Racism, at least in the form of anti-Semitism, lost much of its appeal during and following World War II. But while racism became even less useful politically than it ever had been, exposés of Communist plots, a traditional activity of most right-wing authoritarians, fitted in with the popular mood. It is probable that the neo-Fascist groups and individual authoritarians today use the Communist issue instead of anti-Semi-

---

Catholics, like French Canadians, are quite different from those in the European Latin countries. They have been affected by Protestant values, or perhaps more accurately by the need to preserve the church in a hostile Protestant environment. One consequence of this need has been an extreme emphasis on morality, especially in sexual matters. Studies of the Irish have indicated that they must rank high among the sexually repressed people of the earth. The church in Ireland has tended to be extremely intolerant of deviant views and behavior. The pattern of intolerance among the American Irish Catholics is in large measure a continuation in somewhat modified form of the social system of Ireland. Thus the current anti-Communist crusade has united the two most morally and sexually inhibited groups in America, the fundamentalist Protestants and the Irish Catholics. I am sure that much could be done on a psychoanalytical level to analyze the implications of the moral and political tone of these two groups. For a good report on morality and sex repression among the Irish in Ireland and America, see John A. O'Brien, ed., *The Vanishing Irish* (New York: McGraw-Hill, 1953); see also C. Arensberg and S. Kimball, *Family and Community in Ireland* (Cambridge: Harvard University Press, 1948).

tism.[52] For many of them hunting Communists with the seeming approval of society is much more palatable than attacking Jews. Engaging in attacks on alleged Communists or subversives may now serve to enhance their status, while attacks on minority groups meant accepting the role of a political and social deviant.

Here again, the analogy may be made with the role of the Communists in the late thirties and early forties. Being pro-New Deal and anti-Fascist, political values which were held by a large part of the population, made it psychologically much easier for Communists to operate than when they were primarily engaged in an avowed struggle for Communism. A number of former Communists have reported that many of the party members and leaders seemed much happier in this role in the late thirties and early forties than in their earlier phase as avowed revolutionaries. In this latter period, the

[52] Many, however, still make Aesopian references to the Jews. For a good current report on the anti-Semitic fringe within the radical right see James Rorty, "The Native Anti-Semite's 'New Look,'" *Commentary*, November 1954, pp. 413–21.

In reporting on the Madison Square Garden rally called by the Ten Million Americans Mobilizing for Justice, a group formed to fight the move to censure McCarthy, James Rorty suggests that many of the participants were individuals who had taken part in Fascist rallies in the thirties.

"Edward S. Fleckenstein, an American agitator and associate of neo-Nazis whom Chancellor Adenauer had the State Department oust from Germany, had worked overtime to mobilize his Voters Alliance of German Ancestry. So successful were his efforts that Weehawken, Secaucus, and other northern New Jersey communities had sent delegations so large that, according to organizer George Racey Jordan, it had been necessary to limit their allotment of seats, to avoid giving an 'unrepresentative' character to the meeting." James Rorty, "What Price McCarthy Now?", *Commentary*, January 1955, p. 31.

I was present at this rally, and from my limited vantage point, would agree with Rorty. Men who sat near me spoke of having attended "similar" rallies ten and fifteen years ago. Perhaps the best indicator of the temper of this audience was the fact that Roy Cohn, McCarthy's counsel, felt called upon to make a speech for brotherhood, and reiterated the fact that he was a Jew. One had the feeling that Cohn felt that many in his audience were anti-Semitic.

Communist movement was much more effective in initiating campaigns which appealed to large sections of the population.

While there is no right-wing conspiracy equivalent to that of the Communist Party (the various organizations and groups are disunited and often conflict with each other), nevertheless, there is an amorphous radical right extremist movement which receives the support of many who are not open members of extremist organizations. These may be termed the fellow-travelers of the radical right. In sociological terms, these groups should come disproportionately from the categories discussed earlier, that is, from the status-threatened or the status-aspiring, from the *nouveaux riches*, from the small businessmen, from the ardent Catholics. However, it may be suggested that some of the research findings of studies such as the *Authoritarian Personality*[53] are relevant in this context. The *Authoritarian Personality* and similar studies suggest that for a certain undefined minority of the population various personality frustrations and repressions result in the adoption of scapegoat sentiments. Such individuals are probably to be found disproportionately among the members of various patriotic and anti-Communist societies, in the crackpot extremist groups, and significantly in the committees of various Communist-hunt groups, for example, in the un-American activities committees of local Legion posts, and other groups. No one can object to people fighting Communists. If a minority in an organization denounces individual X or Y as a Communist, one may expect a general tendency for other members of the group to accept the charge in terms of their identification with the organization. Thus, with the climate of opinion shifted to the right, and with the Communist issue important to many people, that minority of individuals who for one reason or another feel the need to hunt out local subversive conspirators will be supported by many individuals and groups, who left alone would rarely engage in such activities.[54]

[53] See T. W. Adorno, et al., *The Authoritarian Personality* (New York: Harpers, 1950). See also Richard Christie, *op. cit.,* pp. 123–96, for a summary of more recent work in this field.

[54] Stouffer reports that individuals who support "authoritarian

One other group is important in the development of the radical right since World War II: the ex-Communists. Some of them, along with some other former non-Communist radicals, have given a coherent tone and ideology to the radical right. Basically, the radical right is unintellectual. Its leaders know very little about Communism or international affairs, and as a matter of fact, have little interest in international affairs. The former radicals and Communists can pinpoint for the ideologists and spokesmen of the radical right those areas in American life where Communists have been important, those aspects of American foreign policy which are most vulnerable to attack. Perhaps the best example of this phenomenon is to be found in *The Freeman*. Many of the writers for this magazine have been former leftists, such as James Burnham, William Schlamm, John Chamberlain, Ralph De Toledano, J. B. Matthews, Freda Utley, Eugene Lyons, John T. Flynn, George Schuyler, and Charlotte Haldane.

Before concluding this review of general tendencies, one interesting and important contradiction between radical right ideology in the United States and the consequences of its promulgation should be stressed. Most of the intellectual and political spokesmen of the radical right proclaim a belief in complete liberty for all. *The Freeman* reads like a philosophical anarchist magazine. Its present editor, Frank Chodorov, has proclaimed the libertarian gospel in two recent books, *One Is a Crowd*, and *The Income Tax: Root of All Evil*. The New Deal is often denounced for having endangered civil liberties and individual freedom by increasing the power of the state and trade unions. Many of the speakers at the November 29, 1954 Madison Square Garden rally to protest the Senate censure of Senator McCarthy demanded the preserva-

---

. . . child-rearing practices" and respond positively to the statement: "People can be divided into two classes—the weak and the strong," are prone to also advocate strong measures against Communists, supporters of nationalized industry, and critics of religion. These questions are similar to the ones used on various psychological scales to locate "authoritarian personalities." S. A. Stouffer, *op. cit.*, pp. 94–99.

tion of a "government of limited powers." Writers for *The Freeman* often criticized the tariff. Basically, the ideology of extreme conservatism in this country is *laissez-faire*. McCarthy's young intellectual spokesman, William Buckley, strongly supported the doctrines of Adam Smith in the same book in which he demanded a purge of American university faculties of left-wingers.[55] In a real sense, the radical right is led by the Frondists of American society, those who want to turn the clock back to a golden age of little government.

III

McCarthyism: The Unifying Ideology[56]

Extreme conservatism cannot ever hope to create a successful mass movement on the basis of its socio-economic program alone. Except during significant economic crisis, the majority of the traditional middle- and upper-class conservative elements are not likely to support extremist movements and ideologies, even when presented in the guise of conservatism, and the lower classes do not support movements in defense of privilege. The problem of the radical right is to develop a political philosophy which will have appeal to its traditional rightist support, but will also enable it to win a mass base. Nazism was able to do this in Germany by combining a strong nationalist appeal to the status-threatened German middle and upper class, together with an "attack on Jewish international capitalism" designed to win over those most concerned with economic reform. As a number of European political commentators have suggested, anti-Semitism has often been the extreme rightist equivalent for the Socialist attack on capitalism. The Jewish banker replaces the exploiting capitalist as the scapegoat.

In the United States, the radical right had to find some comparable method of appealing to the groups which have a

[55] William Buckley, *God and Man at Yale* (Chicago: Henry Regnery and Co., 1951).

[56] Much of the data in this section are drawn from Wallerstein, *op. cit.*

sense of being underprivileged, and McCarthy's principal contribution to the crystallization of the radical right in the 1950s has been to locate the key symbols with which to unite all its potential supporters.[57] McCarthy's crusade is not just against the liberal elements of the country, cast in the guise of "Creeping Socialist"; he is also campaigning against the same groups midwest Populism always opposed, the Eastern conservative financial aristocracy. In his famous Wheeling, West Virginia speech of February 9, 1950, McCarthy began his crusade against internal Communism by presenting for the first time an image of the internal enemy:

> The reason why we find ourselves in a position of impotency is not because our only potential enemy has sent men to invade our shores, but rather because of the traitorous actions of those who have been treated so well by this nation. It is not the less fortunate, or members of minority groups who have been selling this nation out, but rather those who have had all the benefits the wealthiest nation on earth has had to offer—the *finest homes,* the *finest college educations,* and the *finest jobs* in the government that we can give. This is glaringly true in the State Department. There the *bright young men who are born with silver spoons in their mouth are the ones who have been worse.*[58]

This defense of the minority groups and the underprivileged, and the attack on the upper class has characterized the speeches and writings of McCarthy and his followers. McCarthy differs considerably from earlier extreme right-wing anti-Communists. He is rarely interested in investigating or

[57] I am not suggesting that McCarthy or the radical right are Fascists or even precursors of Fascism. For reasons wh:ch are discussed below, I do not believe they could build a successful social movement even if they wanted to. Rather, however, I do suggest that the extreme right in all countries, whether Fascist or not, must find a program or issue which can appeal to a section of the lower middle class, if not the working class, if it is to succeed.

[58] *Congressional Record,* February 20, 1950, p. 1954. (My emphasis.)

publicizing the activities of men who belong to minority ethnic groups. The image of the Communist which recurs time and again in his speeches is one of an easterner, usually of Anglo-Saxon Episcopalian origins, who has been educated in schools such as Groton and Harvard.

The attack on the elite recurs frequently in the current writings of the radical right. *The Freeman* magazine writes that "Asian coolies and Harvard professors are the people . . . most susceptible to Red propaganda."[59] Facts Forum describes intellectuals as the group most vulnerable to Communism, and defines intellectuals as, "lawyers, doctors, bankers, teachers, professors, preachers, writers, publishers."[60] In discussing the Hiss case, Facts Forum argued that the forces defending Hiss which were most significant were not the Communists, themselves, but "the American respectables, *the socially pedigreed*, the culturally acceptable, the certified gentlemen and scholars of the day, dripping with college degrees. . . . In general, it was the 'best people' who were for Alger Hiss."[61] In discussing McCarthy's enemies, *The Freeman* stated: "He possesses, it seems, a sort of animal, negative-pole magnetism which repels alumni of Harvard, Princeton, and Yale. And we think we know what it is: *This young man is constitutionally incapable of deference to social status.*"[62]

Over and over again runs the theme, the common men in America have been victimized by members of the upper classes, by the prosperous, by the wealthy, by the well educated. When specific names are given, these are almost invariably individuals whose names and backgrounds permit them to be identified with symbols of high status. As McCarthy could attack other individuals and groups, this concentration on the Anglo-Saxon elite is no accident. What are the purposes it serves?

Since McCarthy comes from Wisconsin, where for forty years isolationism and attacks on eastern business and Wall

[59] *The Freeman*, Vol. I, No. 1, p. 13.
[60] *Facts Forum Radio Program*, No. 57.
[61] *Ibid.* (My emphasis.)
[62] *The Freeman*, November 5, 1951, p. 72. (My emphasis.)

Street were staple political fare, he may have been searching for an equivalent to the La Follette appeal. Much of the electorate of Wisconsin, and other sections of the Midwest, the German-Americans and those who were sympathetic to their isolationist viewpoint, have been smarting under the charge of disloyalty. McCarthy has argued that it was not the isolationists, but rather those who favored our entry into war with Germany who were the real traitors, since by backing Great Britain they had played into the hands of the Soviet Union. The linkage between the attacks on Anglo-Saxon Americans and Great Britain may be seen in McCarthy's infrequent speeches on foreign policy; these invariably wind up with an attack on Great Britain, sometimes with a demand for action (such as economic sanctions, or pressure to prevent her from trading with Red China).[63] Thus McCarthy is in fact attacking the same groups in the United States and on the world scene, as his liberal predecessors.

On the national scene, McCarthy's attacks are probably much more important in terms of their appeal to status frustrations than to resentful isolationism. In the identification of traditional symbols of status with pro-Communism the McCarthy followers, of non-Anglo-Saxon extraction, can gain a feeling of superiority over the traditionally privileged groups.

[63] "Where have we loyal allies? In Britain? I would not stake a shilling on the reliability of a government which, while enjoying billions in American munificence, rushed to the recognition of the Chinese Red regime, traded exorbitantly with the enemy through Hong Kong and has sought to frustrate American interests in the Far East at every turn." Joseph R. McCarthy, *The Story of General George Marshall, America's Retreat from Victory* (No. publ., 1952), p. 166.

"As of today some money was taken out of your paycheck and sent to Britain. As of today Britain used that money from your paycheck to pay for the shipment of the sinews of war to Red China. . . .

"Now what can we do about it. We can handle this by saying this to our allies: If you continue to ship to Red China, while they are imprisoning and torturing American men, you will not get one cent of American money." Joseph R. McCarthy, quoted in the New York *Times*, November 25, 1953, p. 5: 1–8.

Here is a prosperity-born equivalent for the economic radicalism of depressions. For the resentment created by prosperity is basically not against the economic power of Wall Street bankers, or Yankees, but against their status power. An attack on their loyalty, on their Americanism, is clearly also an attack on their status. And this group not only rejects the status claims of the minority ethnics, but also snubs the *nouveaux riches* millionaires.

The celebrated Army-McCarthy hearings vividly presented to a national television audience the differences between the McCarthyites and their moderate Republican opponents. Every member of McCarthy's staff who appeared on television, with but one exception, was either Catholic, Jewish or Greek Orthodox in religion, and Italian, Greek, Irish, or Jewish in national origin. The non-military spokesmen of the Eisenhower administration on the other hand were largely wealthy Anglo-Saxon Protestants. In a real sense, this televised battle was between successfully mobile minority ethnics and, in the main, upper-class Anglo-Saxon Protestants.

It is also interesting to note that McCarthy is probably the first extreme rightist politician in America to rely heavily on a number of Jewish advisors. These include George Sokolsky, the Hearst columnist, Alfred Kohlberg, a Far-Eastern exporter, and of course, his former counsel, Roy Cohn. (These Jewish McCarthyites are, however, unrepresentative of the Jewish population generally, even of its upper strata, since all survey data as well as impressionistic evidence indicate that the large majority of American Jews are liberal on both economic and civil liberties issues.)

An attack on the status system could conceivably antagonize groups within the radical right: such as the patriotic societies, the Daughters of the American Revolution, and members of old upper-status families like Archibald Roosevelt, who chaired a testimonial dinner for Roy Cohn. Yet, attacks on the Anglo-Saxon Yankee scapegoat do not have this effect because they are directed against majority elements in the society. Criticism of Jews or the Irish, or Italians or Negroes, would have resulted in an immediate response from members of the attacked group. Anglo-Saxon white Protestants, as a majority group, however, are not sensitive to criticism, they are not vulnerable to being attacked, nor do they expect attack. McCarthy, on the one hand, can throw out symbols and images which appeal to the minority ethnics, to the Germans, to the Irish, and the Italians, without at the same time securing the hostility of radical rightists who also are members of the D.A.R., the Sons of the American Revolution, the Patriotic Dames or any other comparable group.[64] And in spite of his populist-type symbols, he can retain the support of these groups and the cooperation of some big businessmen. This is his peculiar power. To the status-deprived he is a critic of the upper class; to the privileged, he is a foe of social change and Communism.

Anti-Communism: The Weakness of a Single Issue

In spite of its early successes in intimidating opponents, and gaining widespread support behind some of its leaders, the radical right has not succeeded in building even one organization of any political significance. And without organizing its backing, it cannot hope to secure any lasting power. This failure is not accidental, or a result of inept leadership, but stems from the fact rather that the only *political* issue which unites the various supporters of radical right politicians is anti-Communism.[65] It is only at the leadership level that

[64] It is, of course, possible that Anglo-Saxon Protestant supporters of McCarthy react similarly to the members of minority ethnic groups to the mention of Groton, Harvard, striped-pants diplomats, and certified gentlemen, that is, that they too, take gratification in charges which reduce the prestige of those above them, even if they are also members of the same ethnic group. In large measure, I would guess that it is the middle-class, rather than the upper-class members of nationalistic and historical societies who are to be found disproportionately among the supporters of the radical right. Consequently, they too, may be in the position of wanting the high and mighty demoted.

[65] In addition much if not most of the support for radical right policies reported by the polls comes from groups which normally show the lowest levels of voting or other forms of political partici-

agreement exists on a program for domestic and foreign policy. The mass base, however, is far from united on various issues. For example, as McCarthy well knows, the dairy farmers of Wisconsin want the government to guarantee 100 per cent parity prices. But this policy is an example of government regimentation to some of the extremist elements on his side.

The Catholic working class remains committed to the economic objectives of the New Deal, and still belongs to trade unions. While McCarthy and other radical rightists may gain Catholic support for measures which are presented under the guise of fighting Communism, they will lose it on economic issues. And should economic issues become important again as during a recession, much of the popular support for McCarthyism will fall away. As a result any attempt to build a radical right movement which has a complete political program is risky, and probably will not occur.

The radical right also faces the problem that it unites bigots of different varieties. In the South and other parts of the country, fundamentalist Protestant groups which are anti-Semitic and anti-Catholic back the radical right in spite of the fact that McCarthy is a Catholic.

One illustration of the way in which these contradictions among his supporters can cause difficulty is a statement which appeared in the New York *Journal-American:* "I think Joe owes the Army an apology but I doubt if our soldiers will get it. The Senator has sure lost his touch since he took up with those oil-rich, anti-Catholic Texas millionaires. They are the

---

pation, women, members of fundamentalist sects, and conservative workers. These groups are the most difficult to organize politically.

It is unfortunate that most American politicians as well as the general intellectual public do not recognize that the public opinion poll reports on civil liberties, foreign policy, and other issues are usually based on samples of the total adult population, not of the electorate. Consequently, they probably greatly exaggerate the electoral strength of McCarthyism. For a related discussion see David Riesman and Nathan Glazer, "The Meaning of Opinion," in D. Riesman, *Individualism Reconsidered* (Glencoe, Ill.: The Free Press, 1954), pp. 492–507.

very same gang which threw the shiv at Al Smith back in 1928."[66]

Perhaps the greatest threat to the political fortunes of the radical right has been the victory of Eisenhower in 1952. As long as the Republican Party was in opposition the radical right could depend upon covert support, or at worst, neutrality from most of the moderate conservative sections of the Republican Party. Even when they viewed the methods of the radical right with distaste, the party leadership saw the group as potential vote gainers. The frustration of twenty years in opposition reduced the scruples of many Republicans, especially those who were involved in party politics.

The differences between the radical right and the moderate right are evident indeed and open factionalism existed in the party long before the election of Eisenhower. Nevertheless, the evidence is quite clear that a large proportion, if not the majority of the moderate Republicans, did not view McCarthy or the radical right as a menace to the party, until he began his attack upon them. Walter Lippmann once persuasively argued that when the Republicans were in office they would be able to control the radical right, or that the radical right would conform for the sake of party welfare. Most Republicans probably at the time agreed. However, the program of Eisenhower Republicanism has not been one of turning the clock back, nor has it fed the psychic needs of the radical right in domestic or foreign policy. Eisenhower's policies in the White House have certainly not reduced the needs of radical right groups for political action, for scapegoatism. They have not reduced McCarthy's desires to capitalize upon popular issues to maintain power and prestige in the general body politic. As a result, the radical right is now forced to struggle openly with the moderate conservatives, essentially the Eisenhower Republicans, who in large measure represent established big business.[67] This is a fight it cannot hope to win, but

[66] Frank Conniff in the *Journal-American,* quoted in *The Progressive,* April 1954, p. 58.

[67] The cleavage in the Republican Party revealed by the vote in the United States Senate to censure McCarthy largely paralleled

the danger exists that the moderates in their efforts to resist charges of softness to Communism, or simply to defeat the Democrats, will take over some of the issues of the radical right, in order to hold its followers, while destroying the political influence of its leaders.

The development of open warfare between the moderate Republican, high status, and big business groups on one hand, and McCarthy and the radical rightists on the other, has probably represented the turning point in the power of the latter. Thirty years earlier, the Ku Klux Klan was severely crippled by the emerging antagonism of the traditional power groups. As was pointed out earlier, many of its middle-class members dropped out of the organization when they discovered that such membership would adversely affect their status and economic interest. Today as in 1923–24, the moderate conservative upper-class community has finally been aroused to the threat to its position and values represented by the radical right.[68]

---

the lines suggested in this paper. The party divided almost evenly in the vote, with almost all the Republican Senators from eastern states plus Michigan voting against McCarthy, while most of the Republicans from the Midwest and far western states voted for him. The cleavage, in part, reflects the isolationist and China-oriented section of the party on one side, and the internationalist eastern wing on the other. From another perspective, it locates the Senators with the closest ties to big business against McCarthy, and those coming from areas dominated by less powerful business groups on the other. There are, of course, a number of deviations from the pattern.

An indication of the temper of the right wing of the Republican Party may be seen from the speeches and reaction at a right-wing rally held in Chicago on Lincoln's Birthday. Governor J. Bracken Lee of Utah stated, "We have gone farther to the left in the last two years [under Eisenhower] than in any other period in our history. I have the feeling that the leadership in Washington is not loyal to the Republican Party." Brigadier General William Hale Wilbur, U. S. Army, retired, charged that the "great political victory of 1952 is being subverted. . . . American foreign policy is no longer American." McCarthy drew loud cheers while denouncing the evacuation of the Tachens. Senator George W. Malone of Nevada stated that Washington is "the most dangerous town in the United States." New York *Times,* February 13, 1955, p. 54.

[68] Perhaps the most interesting event in the extremist versus

It is extremely doubtful that the radical right will grow beyond the peak of 1953–54. It has reached its optimum strength in a period of prosperity, and a recession will probably cripple its political power. It cannot build an organized movement. Its principal current significance, and perhaps permanent impact on the American scene, lies in its success in overstimulating popular reaction to the problem of internal subversion, in supplying the impetus for changes which may have lasting effects on American life, e.g., the heightened security program, political controls on passports, political tests for schoolteachers, and increasing lack of respect for an understanding of the Constitutional guarantees of civil and juridical rights for unpopular minorities and scoundrels.

It is important, however, not to exaggerate the causal influence of the radical right on the development of restrictions on civil liberties in American life. More significant than the activities of any group of active extremists are the factors in the total political situation which made Americans fearful of Communism. Perhaps most important of all these is the fact that for the first time since the War of 1812, the United States has been faced with a major foreign enemy before whom it has had to retreat. The loss of eastern Europe, of China, the impasse in Korea, Indo-China and Formosa, the seeming fiasco of our post-war foreign policy, have required an explanation. The theory that these events occurred because we were

---

moderate conservative battle occurred in the 1954 senatorial elections in New Jersey. There, a liberal anti-McCarthyite, Clifford Case, former head of the Fund for the Republic, ran on the Republican ticket on a platform of anti-McCarthyism. A small group of right-wingers urged "real Republicans" to repudiate Case and write in the name of Fred Hartley, coauthor of the Taft-Hartley Act on the ballot. This campaign began with considerable publicity, but soon weakened. One reason for its rapid decline was that a number of the largest corporations in America put direct economic pressure on small businessmen, lawyers, and other middle-class people active in Hartley's behalf. These people were told that unless they dropped out of the campaign, they would lose contracts or business privileges with these corporations. It is significant to note that one of the few remaining groups vulnerable to direct old-fashioned pressure from big business is the middle-class backers of right-wing extremism.

"stabbed in the back" by a "hidden force" is much more palatable than admitting the possibility that the Communists have stronger political assets than we do. The fear and impotence forced on us by the impossibility of a nuclear war requires some outlet. And a hunt for the internal conspirators may appear as one positive action. Political extremists are capitalizing on our doubts and fears, but it is the situation which creates these doubts and fears, rather than the extremists, that is mainly responsible for the lack of resistance by the political moderate.

Every major war in American history has brought with it important restrictions on civil liberties. Recognition of this fact has often led Americans who were primarily concerned with the preservation of civil liberties to oppose our entry into war. Before World War II, such ardent anti-Fascists as Robert Hutchins and Norman Thomas opposed an interventionist policy, on the grounds that entry into a prolonged major war might result in the destruction of American democracy. History fortunately records the fact that they were mistaken. The current situation, however, is obviously more threatening than any previous one, for one can see no immediate way for the United States to win the fight against Communism. And we now face the serious danger that a prolonged cold war may result in the institutionalization of many of the current restrictions on personal freedom which have either been written into law, or have become normal government administration procedure. Those who regard extremist anti-civil libertarian phases of American history as temporary and unimportant in long-range terms should be cautioned that one of the consequences of the Ku Klux Klan and the post-World War I wave of anti-radical and anti-foreigner hysteria was the restrictive immigration laws based on racist assumptions. The Klan died and the anti-radical hysteria subsided, but the quota restrictions based on the assumption of Nordic supremacy remained. Clearly the recent defeat of Senator McCarthy and the seeming decline of radical right support have not resulted in an end or even modification of many of the measures and administrative procedures which were initiated in response to radical right activity. Consequently if the cold war continues, the radical right, although organizationally weak, may play an important role in changing the character of American democracy.[69]

[69] The stress in this paper on the radical right should not lead to ignoring the contribution of the Communist Party to current coercive measures. The presence of a foreign controlled conspiracy which has always operated partially underground, and which engages in espionage has helped undermine the basis of civil liberties. Democratic procedure assumes that all groups will play the game, and any actor who consistently breaks the rules endangers the continuation of the system. In a real sense, extremists of the right and left aid each other, for each helps to destroy the underlying base of a democratic social order.

14

THREE DECADES OF THE RADICAL RIGHT: COUGHLINITES, McCARTHYITES, AND BIRCHERS[1] (1962)*

Seymour Martin Lipset

The three most prominent "radical-right" movements of the past three decades have been Coughlinism, which figured prominently in the political life of the 1930s; McCarthyism, which flared up in the early 1950s; and the John Birch Society, which has occasioned much controversy in the beginning of the 1960s. The following is a report of research into the social bases of these three movements. The three have been extremely nationalistic in different ways, opposing the philosophy of liberal internationalism as applied to the politics of

* Copyright © 1962, 1963 by Seymour Martin Lipset.
[1] This paper is a first report of an effort to investigate the sources of political extremism in American life, and its possible relationship to forms of religious and ethnic prejudice, which is now under way at the Survey Research Center of the University of California under a grant of funds from the Anti-Defamation League. I am especially grateful for assistance in the analysis of the quantitative data to Charles Gehrke, Natalie Gumas, Louise Johnson, Gary Marx, and Nancy Mendelsohn. The analysis of the materials dealing with the support of Father Coughlin is reported in greater detail in Gary Marx, *The Social Basis of the Support of a Depression Era Extremist: Father Charles E. Coughlin* (M.A. thesis, Department of Sociology, University of California at Berkeley, 1962). I am particularly indebted to a number of research agencies for providing the data from various surveys for use in this analysis. These include the Roper Public Opinion Research Center at Williams College, the American Institute of Public Opinion Research (Gallup Poll), and the California Poll.

their time. The political focus of their attack has been primarily though not exclusively the Democratic Party.[2]

The political ideologies shared by these three movements are not, however, what makes them a matter of special concern. Right-wing conservatism and nationalism are political doctrines that have a legitimate place within any democratic polity. What distinguishes these groups in particular is that they are *extremist* tendencies, and as such have rejected the basic rules of democratic society. Edward Shils has described these attributes well:

> An extremist group is an alienated group. . . . It cannot share that sense of affinity to persons or attachment to the institutions which confine political conflicts to peaceful solutions. . . . The romantic reactionaries, aristocratic and populistic . . . allege that they wish to conserve tradition. In practice they regard tradition as dead or corrupt or pernicious and they think that they must wipe out all that exists in order to re-create the right kind of tradition. Neither . . . the Christian Front [of Father Coughlin] nor the most zealous populist followers of Senator McCarthy at his height found the living traditions of the society in which they lived worthy of conservation. They were convinced that they had fallen into the hands of corrupt politicians and had themselves become corrupt. . . .
>
> The ideological extremists [of the left and right]—all extremists are inevitably ideological—because of their isolation from the world, feel menaced by unknown dangers. The paranoiac tendencies which are closely associated with their apocalyptic and aggressive outlook make them think that the ordinary world, from which their devotion to the ideal cuts them off, is not normal at all; they think it is a realm of secret machinations. What goes on in the world of pluralistic politics, in civil society, is a secret to

[2] Coughlin, of course, was antagonistic to conservative Republicans of the Hoover variety, while the Birch Society sees treason present among liberal Republicans.

them. It is a secret which they must unmask by vigorous publicity. Their image of the "world" as the realm of evil, against which they must defend themselves and which they must utimately conquer, forces them to think of their enemy's knowledge as secret knowledge.[8]

But if these three rightist groups have many similarities, they differ greatly too. A large part of the differences may be attributed to the varying circumstances under which they arose. Coughlinism clearly was a response to the unsettled economic conditions of the 1930s, and to the international tensions of the period—the rise of Fascism, the Spanish Civil War, and, eventually, World War II. McCarthyism, as the original essays in this book make abundantly clear, developed in a period characterized domestically by prosperity and twenty years of Democratic Party rule, and internationally by the growing world power of Communism.[4] The John Birch Society was formed in the late 1950s, and came to general public attention as a political force in the 1960s. This period resembles the heyday of McCarthyism. There has been a relatively high level of economic prosperity combined with frustration in the international struggle with Communism.

To a considerable degree, the ideological differences among the three rightist movements reflect these variations in time of origin. Father Charles Coughlin began his political career as a radical monetary reformer, and came to national attention with his attacks on the bankers and the financial system for creating the Great Depression of the 1930s.[5] He supported

---

[3] Edward A. Shils, *The Torment of Secrecy* (Glencoe: The Free Press, 1956), pp. 231–34.

[4] See also W. Millis, "The Rise and Fall of the Radical Right," *Virginia Law Review*, 44 (1958), pp. 1291–1300; Oscar Handlin, "Do the Voters Want Moderation?", *Commentary*, 22 (1956), pp. 193–98; and Frank Thistlethwaite, "What Is Un-American?", *Cambridge Journal*, 5 (1952), pp. 211–24. Two books on the subject, one pro and the other con, are William Buckley and L. B. Bozell, *McCarthy and His Enemies* (Chicago: Regnery, 1954), and Richard H. Rovere, *Senator Joe McCarthy* (New York: Harcourt, Brace, 1959).

[5] Discussions of Coughlin may be found in Victor C. Ferkiss,

Franklin Roosevelt during his first years in office, but then
turned on him in 1935 and launched a third party, the Union
Party, in the Presidential elections of 1936. This party secured
only 900,000 votes nationally, and Coughlin withdrew temporarily from politics. He returned to the air in 1937. Franco
and the Spanish Civil War had become major issues, and
Coughlin backed Franco against the "Communist" Loyalists.[6]
Accompanying the latter issue was a general commitment to
isolationism and opposition to an anti-Nazi foreign policy. All
these attacks were linked to extreme denunciations of President Roosevelt, the C.I.O., and liberal Democrats as having
done little to reduce the economic misfortunes caused by the
depression. And in the middle of 1938, he began to war openly
and continuously against Jewish influence in politics and business.[7] In a real sense, he attempted to build an anti-elitist,

---

"Populist Influences on American Fascism," *Western Political
Quarterly*, 10 (1957), pp. 359–67; James P. Shenton, "The Coughlin Movement and the New Deal," *Political Science Quarterly*, 73
(1958), pp. 352–73; Arthur M. Schlesinger, Jr., *The Politics of
Upheaval* (Boston: Houghton Mifflin, 1960), pp. 16–23, 244–49,
553–61, 626–30.

[6] At one point he threatened to fight "in Franco's way if neces-
sary." (Shenton, *op. cit.*, p. 372.) An analysis of Coughlin's
speeches may be found in Alfred McClung Lee and Briant Lee,
The Fine Art of Propaganda (New York: Harcourt, Brace, 1939).
Coughlin is also discussed in John Roy Carlson, *Under Cover: My
Four Years in the Nazi Underworld of America* (New York: E. P.
Dutton, 1943).

[7] Coughlin actually gave voice to various anti-Semitic statements
while he was still backing Roosevelt in the early years of his administration. "[His] hatred of the moneylenders spilled over to an
identification of bankers with Rothschilds, Warburgs, and Kuhn-
Loebs. . . . Mentioning Alexander Hamilton, he would casually
add, 'whose original name was Alexander Levine.' He freely attacked those 'who, without either the blood of patriotism or of
Christianity flowing in their veins, have shackled the lives of men
and of nations with the ponderous links of their golden chain.'"
(Schlesinger, *op. cit.*, pp. 26–27.) Another historian cites a speech
in which Coughlin criticized Roosevelt as early as 1934 and attacked "godless capitalists, the Jews, Communists, international
bankers, and plutocrats." (Walter Johnson, *1600 Pennsylvania
Avenue* [Boston: Little, Brown, 1960], p. 85.) During the 1936

anti-liberal, nationalist movement, similar in many ways to the movements of Perón and Vargas in Argentina and Brazil.

If Coughlin sought to win the support of those whose social and economic position had been worsened by a prolonged depression, McCarthy, as the essays in this book indicate, appealed to the resentments of prosperity. Although he was a Republican Senator, he devoted little of his public discourse to domestic social and economic problems. Rarely after 1950 did he discuss welfare legislation, trade unions, pensions, or other major domestic issues. His attacks were concentrated on domestic Communism. Unlike Coughlin he never criticized Jews or other minority ethnic groups. Rather, McCarthy's ideal-typical Communist enemy was an upper-class Eastern Episcopalian graduate of Harvard employed by the State Department. The threat to our way of life was embodied in upper-class, well-educated Easterners and New Deal liberals, the dominant forces controlling American political life in both parties.

Although McCarthy was in no sense a Fascist, his appeal was nevertheless similar to those of European Fascist movements, which attacked the upper class, big business, and the Socialists.[8] Fascist movements, however, explicitly ap-

---

Presidential campaign, in a speech discussing Christian Brotherhood, he said, "I challenge every Jew in this nation to tell me that he does or doesn't believe in it." And his paper, *Social Justice*, editorialized in October, 1936, "If certain groups of politically-swayed Jews . . . care to organize against Father Coughlin or the National Union they will be entirely responsible for stirring up any repercussions which they will invite." (Cited in Schlesinger, *op. cit.*, p. 628.) He insisted, however, that he was not anti-Semitic at this time. In a private interview he said, "Jew-baiting won't work here. Fascism is different in every country." (*Loc. cit.*) A detailed description of Coughlin's anti-Semitic activities from the summer of 1938 to his withdrawal from politics after Pearl Harbor may be found in Gustavus Myers, *History of Bigotry in the United States* (New York: Capricorn Books, 1960), pp. 375–415.

[8] For a discussion of these ideological components of European fascism, see S. M. Lipset, *Political Man* (New York: Doubleday, 1960), pp. 131–76. In this book, I have also elaborated on the similarities between the ideologies of McCarthyism, Poujadism,

pealed to the economic and status interests of the lower middle class; McCarthy never attempted an economic-interest appeal. Rather, wittingly or not, he directed his appeal to the status resentments occasioned by prosperity. However, his policies were a reflection of the post-war international crises. He dealt largely with the internal Communist conspiracy that had caused the loss of China, had involved us in the then ongoing Korean War, was preventing us from winning it, and had earlier been responsible for the seemingly pro-Russian foreign policy of World War II. Essentially, McCarthy functioned as a critic of New Deal Democratic Party policies and personnel. His fulminations against members of the Eisenhower administration of 1953 and 1954 were directed against their naïveté in not recognizing the need to clean out New Deal-appointed Communists from government, and their insistence on retaining the rules of due process when dealing with alleged subversion.

Some four years after McCarthy was censured by the Senate, the John Birch Society arose, seemingly in response to the failure of the Republican administration to eliminate the "Socialist" policies of its New Deal predecessors, and to its failure to cope adequately with the continued strength of international Communism. For the Birch Society, the liberal Republicans have been as much a danger to American institutions as the New Deal Democrats. Avowed Communists are not the main problem. Rather, the liberals in both parties have been sapping the moral strength of America by continuing the welfare state at home and refusing to fight Communism and Socialism abroad.

In a real sense, therefore, the three "radical-rightist" movements have differed in their domestic ideological approach. Coughlin appealed to the economically outcast against a major symbol of big economic power, the banks. Although opposed to Roosevelt, he did call for greater government aid to the underprivileged, particularly through manipulation of

---

and variants of Fascist movements without suggesting that either McCarthy or Poujade were Fascists.

the credit system, restrictions on foreclosures, and the like. McCarthy, though a Republican, concentrated his attack on symbols of upper-class status as well as on the Democratic Party as such. He rarely criticized trade unions, and ignored or praised minority ethnic groups. Of the three leaders, Robert Welch of the Birch Society has been the most explicit in rejecting certain aspects of the democratic process, including universal suffrage, and in openly acknowledging his desire to imitate Communist political tactics, while at the same time proposing an uninhibited and pure version of economic conservatism. Hence, one might be justified in suggesting that the appeal of the first movement was to the underprivileged strata normally associated with leftism; that the second attracted the middle classes, who have preferred center politics in the European sense (that is, against both the organized left and the upper classes and big business); and that the third, the Birch Society, which espouses economic conservatism, should have its greatest success with the more privileged strata.[9] On other issues, of course, the three have shared similar orientations: isolationism, extreme nationalism, strong emphasis on the internal as well as the external Communist threat, and a lack of respect for due process in dealing with problems of domestic Communism.

Generalizations such as these concerning presumed support can be made from an examination of the speeches and programs of the diverse radical-right groups. To what extent they conform to reality has been a moot question. Although public-opinion-survey organizations have been gathering information concerning the attitudes of the general population since 1935, few scholars have attempted to find out who has supported groups such as these. This lack of knowledge is particularly true with regard to Coughlinism and other movements of the 1930s. Some limited use has been made of the rather large number of surveys conducted by polling organiza-

[9] I have elaborated the thesis of three different types of "rightist" movements—those oriented to the lower strata, to the centrist middle classes, or to the privileged conservative strata—in *Political Man*, pp. 131–76.

tions regarding attitudes toward McCarthy. Until the essays in this volume, nothing much has been published with regard to public support of the John Birch Society. An effort is now under way at the Survey Research Center of the University of California to analyze the nature of political extremism in the United States, through a study that will be based in part on an analysis of public-opinion-survey data dealing with such politics. The study is as yet in a very early stage, but I feel that some preliminary findings that bear on the hypotheses discussed in the first edition of this book ought to be submitted to readers of the second.

I

The Coughlinites

The analysis of the supporters of Father Coughlin is based on two surveys conducted by the Gallup organization in April and December, 1938. Although conducted seven months apart, they show no significant differences with respect to the social characteristics of those indicating approval of Coughlin. Approximately 25 per cent of each sample stated that they supported Father Coughlin.[10]

TABLE 1
OPINION OF FATHER COUGHLIN
(GALLUP)

	Approve	Disapprove	No Opinion	Total in Sample
April 1938	27%	32%	41%	(2864)
December 1938	23	30	47	(2068)

The fact that so many stated that they were in favor of Father Coughlin does not mean that such large proportions of

[10] A latter survey conducted by the Gallup Poll in July of 1939 indicated that Coughlin's support declined in that year. Only 15 per cent stated that they agreed with his ideas, or with what he said, while 38 per cent stated they disagreed with his ideas, and 31 per cent indicated disagreement with what he said. See Hadley Cantril, *Public Opinion 1935–1946* (Princeton: Princeton University Press, 1951), p. 148.

the population had Coughlinite attitudes on any specific issues. For example, only 8 per cent of those who approved of him reported having voted for the Union Party's presidential candidate, William Lemke, in 1936. Many who favored Coughlin were also pro-Roosevelt and, in some cases, were sympathetic to Loyalist Spain. Although Coughlin turned openly anti-Semitic in July of 1938, and was sharply attacked by his liberal critics as early as 1935 for being pro-Fascist and sympathetic to racism, some of the Jews in the sample and one-half of the Negroes approved of him in the December survey. It would seem that Coughlin was never perceived by the bulk of the American people as a Fascist and anti-Semite, and that much of his support came from people who disapproved of much of what he advocated.[11]

The single most important correlate of support for Father Coughlin in 1938 was religion. Although many Catholic priests and bishops openly opposed him and attacked many of his views as being in conflict with Catholic doctrine, there can be little question that Catholics were much more in favor of him than were Protestants.[12] As the data in Table 2 suggest, over two-fifths of the Catholics supported him and one-quarter opposed him in December, 1938.[13] Among Protestants, less than one-fifth favored Coughlin, while almost one-third expressed disapproval. Coughlin was better known among Catholics than among Protestants; 33 per cent of the former had no opinion of him, as contrasted with over 50 per cent of the

[11] Such contradictions between the opinions of leaders and followers may, of course, be reported for almost every major figure and political party. In some European countries, survey data indicate that 10–15 per cent of those who vote conservative believe in nationalization of most industries, while a much larger proportion of Socialist voters in these nations opposes such measures.

[12] Most of the American hierarchy and the Vatican were in fact deeply troubled by Coughlin's political activities. (See Schlesinger, op. cit., pp. 628–29, and Shenton, op. cit., pp. 364–66, 371.) One Catholic estimate of the politics of the hierarchy reported that at least 103 of the 106 American bishops voted for Roosevelt in 1936. (Ibid., p. 367.)

[13] The April, 1938, study did not inquire as to respondents' religion.

latter. Clearly, as we shall see later in the analysis of
McCarthy, it is difficult to separate out any judgment concerning a prominent Catholic figure from attitudes toward him
as a prominent member of that group.

TABLE 2

RELATION OF RELIGIOUS AFFILIATION TO ATTITUDES
TOWARD COUGHLIN—DECEMBER, 1938

(GALLUP)

Attitudes To Coughlin	Catholics	Religious Affiliation Protestants	Jews	No Religious Choice
Approve	42%	19%	10%	19%
Disapprove	25	31	63	28
No opinion	33	50	27	53
	(380)	(1047)	(67)	(560)

As might be expected, Protestants varied according to denomination in their opinions on Coughlin (see Table 3).
Episcopalians, Congregationalists, and Baptists showed the
highest excess of disapproval over approval; Methodists and
Presbyterians occupied a middle position, somewhat more opposed than favorable; Lutherans were the one Protestant
group in which supporters outnumbered opponents.[14] The opposition to Coughlin of Episcopalians and Congregationalists
may reflect their position as the churches of high-status, old-
stock Americans. The Coughlin support among Lutherans may
be due to the fact that Lutherans were often of recent German
origin, and hence likely to be isolationists in the years preceding World War II. As will be noted subsequently, the Protestant groups differed similarly among themselves with respect to
McCarthy.

The second major factor that differentiated supporters of
Coughlin from opponents was economic status. Among both
Catholics and Protestants, the lower the economic level, the

[14] In reading these tables, it should be noted that the important
measure of support or opposition is the difference in per cent between those opposing and supporting. The presence of a large and
varying group with "no opinion" makes reliance on the proportion
supporting alone misleading.

TABLE 3

ATTITUDES TOWARD COUGHLIN AMONG DIFFERENT
PROTESTANT GROUPS—DECEMBER, 1938

(GALLUP)

Attitudes to Coughlin	Religious Affiliation						
	Bap.	Meth.	Luth.	Pres.	Episc.	Cong.	Other Prot.
Approve	16%	20%	29%	20%	21%	21%	12%
Disapprove	30	29	21	27	45	43	33
No Opinion	54	51	50	53	33	36	55
	(147)	(293)	(125)	(164)	(84)	(47)	(190)
Excess of approval over dis- approval in per cent	—14	—9	+8	—7	—24	—22	—21

greater the proportion of supporters to opponents (see Table 4).

Among Catholics of above average means, the proportion approving was only slightly more (4 per cent) than those disapproving, while among poor Catholics, many more (19 per cent) favored Coughlin than opposed him. The same relation-

TABLE 4

RELATIONSHIP OF RELIGION AND SOCIO-ECONOMIC
STATUS TO ATTITUDES TOWARD COUGHLIN—
DECEMBER, 1938

(GALLUP)

	Attitudes toward Coughlin							
	Catholics				Protestants and No Religious Choice*			
Socio- Economic Status	App.	Disapp.	No. Op.	Difference[a]	App.	Disapp.	No. Op.	Difference[a]
Above av.	38%	34	28	+ 4 (40)	13%	48	39	—35 (264)
Average	41%	28	31	+13 (121)	17%	33	51	—16 (609)
Poor+	46%	25	29	+21 (48)	21%	29	50	— 8 (209)
Poor	42%	23	35	+19 (77)	19%	18	63	+ 1 (277)
On Relief	41%	20	39	+21 (98)	24%	24	52	0 (245)

* As a group those of no choice were like the total Protestant group.
[a] Per cent difference between approval and disapproval.

ship with economic status held among Protestants. Protestants of above average economic level indicated great disapproval, while the proportion approving and disapproving was about the same among poorer Protestants. Occupational variations (not presented here) showed about the same pattern. Manual workers, those on government public works (W.P.A.), and the unemployed were most likely to be Coughlin supporters among both Catholics and Protestants, while in both religious groups, professionals and those in business revealed the least approval and the most opposition.

For some reason, the relative position of white-collar workers differed according to religion. Catholic white-collar workers were among the high-support groups, as high or higher than the manual workers. Among Protestants, white-collar occupations resembled the professionals and businessmen, giving little support to Coughlin. Farmers, both Catholic and Protestant, tended to be high on the Coughlin side. Although the number of cases in each analytic cell becomes small, the pattern holds when three variables—religion, occupation, and income—are held constant: within a given religious and occupational group, approval of Coughlin increased as economic status decreased.

The combination of socio-economic position and religion explain much of the difference between supporters and opponents, but other factors, of course, played a role. Age was important as a source of differentiation; older people were more likely to back Coughlin than others, holding both religion and income constant. Also, men seem to have been slightly more favorable to Coughlin than women.

Rural areas and small towns have traditionally been identified as centers of conservatism, populism, and anti-Semitism in the United States and other countries. This pattern held true regarding attitudes toward Coughlin. The ratio between support and opposition was most favorable for Coughlin in rural areas and small towns. Only 6 per cent of Catholics living on farms disapproved of Coughlin, as compared with 28 per cent opposed among those living in urban areas. Regionally, Coughlin's support followed the pattern one might expect from a spokesman in the populist and social-credit tradition, and his greatest support came from the West Central region of the country (Wisconsin, Minnesota, Iowa, Missouri, South Dakota, Nebraska, and Kansas). New England, with its high concentration of Irish Catholics, was second highest. The areas of least Coughlin support were the West Coast and the South.

Although public-opinion surveys did not secure information on ethnic background during the 1930s, and hence it is impossible to relate these findings to ethnicity, other sources suggest that the regional support for Coughlin may have reflected his specific ethnic appeal to German and Irish Catholics. An ecological analysis of the 1936 vote for Coughlin's presidential candidate, Lemke, indicates that it was concentrated in areas that were disproportionately Irish and German Catholic.

> Outside of North Dakota [his home state], Lemke got more than 10 per cent of the vote in thirty-nine counties. Twenty-one of these counties are more than 50 per cent Catholic. In twenty-eight of these thirty-nine counties the predominant nationality element is German.
>
> The only four cities where Lemke got more than 5 per cent of the vote are also heavily German and Irish Catholic.[15]

The analysis of the demographic background factors suggests clearly that Coughlin was strongest among Catholics and Lutherans in contrast to other Protestants and to Jews, among the less well-to-do, among farmers and those living in small communities, among older people as compared with young ones, and among those living in the Midwest and New England, as contrasted with the Far West and the South.

The surveys permit some limited specification of the attitudes of Coughlin's supporters. The best available measure of opinion on foreign policy at the time is the attitude toward the protagonists in the Spanish Civil War. Religious affiliation played a major role in affecting the opinions of both supporters and opponents of Coughlin. Catholics as a group favored the

[15] Samuel Lubell, *The Future of American Politics* (New York: Doubleday Anchor Books, 1956), p. 152.

Rebels (40 per cent for Franco, 20 per cent for the Loyalists); Protestants backed the Loyalists (40 per cent to 10 per cent). Among both Catholics and Protestants at each economic level, Coughlin supporters were more disposed to favor Franco than were those who disapproved of the radio priest. However, in spite of Coughlin's repeated concentration on the Spanish Civil War issue, only 43 per cent of his Catholic supporters and a mere 18 per cent of his Protestant followers espoused his position regarding Franco. Seemingly, concern with the Communist issue in the Spanish Civil War was not a major source of Father Coughlin's popular appeal.

Analysis of attitudes toward domestic issues suggests that, religious identification apart, Coughlin's support was due in large part to economic dissatisfaction. Coughlin backers at every economic level were much more discontented with their lot, with the economic state of the country, and with prospects for the future than were his opponents. For example, two-thirds of his supporters felt their personal economic situation had been declining, while among those opposed to Coughlin slightly less than one-half felt that their situation had worsened.

The antagonism expressed by Coughlin to the existing business system, to exorbitant profits, to bankers (Jewish and others), and the fact that his support came largely from the lower class would lead one to expect that Coughlinites would express greater antipathy to Republicans and conservatism than to Democrats and liberalism. The data do not bear out this assumption. Those who approved of Coughlin in 1938 were more likely to support the G.O.P. than the Democratic Party, and conservatism rather than liberalism. Supporters of Coughlin were only slightly more favorable to a third party than his opponents (11 per cent as compared to 8 per cent). The party preferences of Coughlin supporters may be inferred from responses to a question posed in the April, 1938, survey: "If you were voting for a Congressman today, would you be most likely to vote for the Republican, the Democrat, or a third party Candidate?" Among Coughlin supporters who expressed a partisan choice, 40 per cent preferred the Democrats, while 55 per cent of Coughlin's opponents backed the Democrats. These differences are evident within each economic category as well (see Table 5).

TABLE 5
RELATIONSHIP BETWEEN ATTITUDE TOWARD COUGHLIN
AND VOTE INTENTION—APRIL, 1938
(GALLUP)

Attitudes toward Coughlin

	APPROVE OF COUGHLIN				DISAPPROVE OF COUGHLIN			
					1938 Vote Intention			
			Third				*Third*	
Income Level	*Repub.*	*Dem.*	*Party*	*N*	*Repub.*	*Dem.*	*Party*	*N*
Above average	66%	25	9	(69)	57%	37	6	(128)
Average	58%	34	8	(203)	39%	52	9	(285)
Poor+	46%	45	9	(111)	36%	57	7	(132)
Poor	47%	40	13	(124)	24%	67	9	(115)
On relief	24%	61	15	(85)	15%	72	13	(69)
Total	49%	40	11	(592)	37%	55	8	(729)

Approval of Coughlin may have meant sharply different things to those of differing economic position. Though at every level Coughlin backers were more often for the Republicans than were those who opposed him, the percentage of those who preferred the Democratic Party and also endorsed Coughlin increased with lower income. The same pattern occurred with respect to attitude toward President Roosevelt; that is, most of the poor and those on relief who approved of Coughlin supported Roosevelt.

The data on party support and opinion of Roosevelt presented in Table 6 suggest that many poor people who backed Coughlin did so in spite of, or without knowledge of, his attitude toward Roosevelt. It is likely that among the less educated and the underprivileged both Coughlin and Roosevelt were viewed in similar lights. Those who felt friendly to Father Coughlin were clearly not of one political persuasion, and he failed to get more than a small minority of them to back his third-party candidate. It seems evident that his well-to-do supporters were a different group ideologically than his lower-strata backers. The former may have found him to their liking because of his antagonism to Roosevelt and the New

TABLE 6
RELATIONSHIP BETWEEN ATTITUDES TOWARD COUGHLIN
AND ROOSEVELT—APRIL, 1938
(GALLUP)

Income Level	Proportion Opposed to Roosevelt Attitudes toward Coughlin	
	Approve	Disapprove
Above average	74% (79)	58% (157)
Average	62 (246)	37 (341)
Poor+	52 (142)	30 (155)
Poor	42 (157)	20 (135)
On relief	25 (99)	18 (82)

Deal, his opposition to the rise of the C.I.O. unions, and his advocacy of militant action to block the rise of Communist forces at home and abroad. For his lower-class supporters, Coughlin's attacks on capitalism, the banks, Jewish financiers, and inept government handling of the depression may have been crucial. Though he failed to build his own party or movement, he did reach a large audience every Sunday on the radio and was regarded favorably by a considerable section of the populace, many of whom were traditional Catholic and working-class Democrats. One might speculate, therefore, as to whether the issues raised by Coughlin may have contributed to the drop-off in Democratic support, particularly among Catholics, in 1938 and 1940. Coughlin may have been instrumental in transferring support from the Democratic to the Republican Party.

Evidence tending to confirm this hypothesis may be found in comparisons between the 1936 Presidential vote and 1938 opinion on parties and candidates. In the latter year, Coughlin supporters who had voted for Roosevelt in 1936 were more likely to have changed their opinion concerning the President than were Roosevelt voters who disapproved of the radio priest.

The same relationship holds in a comparison of the 1936 vote with the party choice of voters in the 1938 Congressional elections. Among those who voted for Roosevelt in 1936 and approved of Coughlin in 1938, only 50 per cent said they would vote Democratic, while among Roosevelt voters who disapproved of Coughlin, 64 per cent remained faithful to the Democrats.

TABLE 7

RELATIONSHIP BETWEEN 1936 PRESIDENTIAL VOTE
AND 1938 CONGRESSIONAL VOTE—APRIL, 1938

(GALLUP)

	1936 Presidential Vote							
	ROOSEVELT				LANDON			
Attitudes to	1938 Party Choice							
Coughlin	Rep.	Dem.	3rd	N.O.	Rep.	Dem.	3rd	N.O.
Approve	21%	50%	9%	20% (342)	78%	5%	4%	14% (256)
Disapprove	9	64	9	19 (509)	73	11	2	11 (323)
No Opinion	13	64	4	19 (477)	84	2	3	14 (231)

Coughlin has often been considered a prototype of American fascism.[16] Nevertheless, it is clear that the 15 or 25 per cent of the population who in 1938 and 1939 supported him did not actually believe in Fascism. There may be some question as to whether most of Coughlin's supporters agreed with his anti-Semitism. Unfortunately none of the surveys inquiring about attitudes toward Coughlin solicited opinions about the Jews. Other surveys made during this period did, however, contain questions on anti-Semitism, and these permit some estimate of the relationship of Coughlin support to expressed prejudice, since it is possible to examine the beliefs of Union Party voters. As expected, most of those who reported in 1938 that they had voted for Lemke in the previous Presidential election indicated approval of Coughlin. Lemke voters were

[16] In an interview with a journalist in 1936, Coughlin stated that this was the last free election that the United States would have, that the country would have to choose between Communism and Fascism, and he said, "I take the road of Fascism." (Schlesinger, *op. cit.*, p. 629.) He also "praised Mussolini and Hitler over the radio. . . ." (Johnson, *op. cit.*, p. 114.) As has already been noted, he ardently backed Franco during the Spanish Civil War, and after war broke out in Europe, he supported Japan in Asia and the Axis powers in Europe. (See Shenton, *op. cit.*, p. 372.)

more likely to indicate anti-Semitic beliefs than the rest of the population, but the difference was not large. The data from two 1939 Gallup surveys that asked whether respondents would support "a campaign against Jews" indicate that 21 per cent of 1936 Lemke voters, 12 per cent of Roosevelt supporters, and 8 per cent of Landon voters were overtly anti-Semitic. Further, in national surveys both before and after Coughlin began his anti-Semitic attacks, the same proportion (12 per cent) reported they would support a campaign against Jews. While these findings suggest that Coughlin's backers were probably more anti-Semitic than the population in general, it is well to keep in mind that the large majority of his Union Party supporters did not give anti-Semitic responses to the survey questions.[17]

The data concerning the social characteristics of Coughlin's followers challenge the generalizations expressed by some that Coughlinism as a form of proto-Fascism appealed primarily to the middle class.[18] As contrasted with European Fascist

[17] It seems clear also that many anti-Semites were also anti-Catholic and thus may have been anti-Coughlin. A Gallup Survey conducted in November, 1938, asked a national sample whether they approved of the Nazis' treatment of Jews in Germany, and similarly whether they approved of the treatment of Catholics. Among non-Catholics who approved of the persecution of the Jews, almost half, 43 per cent, also favored the Nazis' attacks on Catholics, 45 per cent opposed them, and 12 per cent had no opinion. This finding suggests that about half the extreme anti-Semites were also anti-Catholic.

[18] Schlesinger, for example, wrote that the "followers of the demagogues [Coughlin, Townsend, and Long] mostly came from the old lower-middle classes, now in an unprecedented stage of frustration and fear, menaced by humiliation, dispossession, and poverty. . . . They came, in the main, from the ranks of the self-employed, who, as farmers or shopkeepers or artisans, felt threatened by organized economic power, whether from above, as in banks and large corporations, or from below, as in trade unions." (*Op. cit.*, p. 68.)

Victor Ferkiss also described the movements led by Huey Long, Father Coughlin, and Gerald L. K. Smith as "designed to appeal to a middle class composed largely of farmers and small merchants which feels itself crushed between big business—and especially big finance—on the one hand, and an industrial working class . . . on

movements, which recruited disproportionately from the middle strata (small business and white-collar elements), Coughlin, religious appeal apart, drew his support from manual workers and the unemployed. The one common link between the class base of the Coughlin movement and that of the European Fascists was the farmers. Populist antagonism toward the bankers together with general anti-elitist and anti-cosmopolitan attitudes may have accounted for this support. If Coughlin's movement was a Fascist movement, then it represented a version of "proletarian" fascism more comparable to that of Perón and Vargas than to those of Hitler and Mussolini.

II

The Social Base of McCarthyism

It is extremely difficult to ascertain from survey data the proportion of "McCarthyites" in the population during the Senator's heyday. Part of the difficulty arises from the varying meanings that might be attached to the questions posed. Some queries centered on general issue of the prevalence and threat of domestic Communism, while others focused more specifi-

---

the other. . . ." It appealed also "to those members of the urban lower-middle class (especially the white-collar workers) who were unwilling to identify themselves with organized labor and feared its power almost as much as they feared that of big business." (*Op. cit.*, pp. 350, 360.)

A contemporary account of Coughlin described him as having a program which "appeals simultaneously to agriculture, the middle class, and the big employer." Raymond Gram Swing, *Forerunners of American Fascism* (New York: Julian Messner, 1935), p. 51.

These observers all clearly have been unaware that Coughlin's mass base came largely from the urban working class and the very poor, particularly the unemployed and those on relief. Although it may have seemed logical to assume that the urban self-employed were among his supporters, the evidence does not justify this assumption. However, Gustavus Myers did point out that public-opinion data indicated that "Coughlin's followers were mostly in the stratum of low incomes." (*Op. cit.*, p. 388.) This work was first published in 1943.

cally on Senator McCarthy and approval and disapproval of his tactics. Questions phrased in general terms of whether McCarthy's allegations about Communists in government were largely true or not usually produced a rather large proportion of "pro-McCarthy" replies. But questions implying a more direct evaluation of the Senator himself—e.g., how McCarthy's endorsement of a candidate would affect one's vote—produced a very different pattern of response. When attitude toward the existence of Communists in government was not mentioned, somewhere between 10 and 20 per cent were favorable, while about 30 to 40 per cent were opposed to the Wisconsin Senator. Once in existence, McCarthyism became a much more salient issue to the liberal enemies of the Senator than to his conservative or militantly anti-Communist friends. The Communist issue apart, many more people reacted negatively to the mention of his name than positively. His seeming popularity was a result of his riding the existing powerful anti-Communist bandwagon, whose popular influence he may have ultimately reduced rather than enhanced by alienating the militant anti-Communists who believed in due process.[19] This conclusion

[19] A related point was made in the original edition of *The New American Right* in urging the need for a distinction between "the *intolerant*—those who will say 'Kill the Communists' as easily as they will say 'Jail the sex deviants' and 'Fire a teacher who is a free thinker'—and the *concerned*—those who are sincerely worried about Communism, and think strong measures are necessary to deal with it." See Nathan Glazer and S. M. Lipset, "The Polls on Communism and Conformity," in the original edition of *The New American Right,* p. 152. A somewhat similar differentiation among McCarthy supporters has been drawn by John Fenton, an editor of the Gallup Poll. He reports that the Poll's data from two 1954 surveys suggest "two separate wings" of McCarthy supporters. The first "was based primarily on the fact he was anti-Communist," and often disliked his "high-handed and ruthless tactics," while the "second wing liked McCarthy as much for his methods as they did for his anti-Communism. These . . . admired McCarthy because he was 'a fighter' and 'had the guts to stand up to them.'" According to Fenton, as McCarthy lost support in 1954 as a result of his fight with the Army, he "lost ground generally with voters across the country. His sharpest losses, however, tended to come from persons who would fall in the first, or anti-Communist wing. He lost

does not mean that McCarthyism did not exist as a political force. There was a significant minority of Americans who strongly identified with the Senator from Wisconsin, and who approved of any and all methods he used to fight the Communist enemy. Some of them presumably were attracted to, or at least accepted, his attack on the Eastern upper-class elite and on internationalism. But this group of "McCarthyites" was probably always a minority, much smaller than the "anti-McCarthyites," who saw in him and his followers a basic threat to the democratic process once the symbol of McCarthyism had been created as a political issue.

Many of the political policies discussed in the original edition of this book as aspects of McCarthyism clearly have to be differentiated from the symbolic role the Wisconsin Senator played in American political life. The original essays were generally concerned with the sentiment for anti-Communist controls in government, university, and private life. However, sources of support for such policies have always existed independently of the activities of Senator McCarthy. Many, if not most, of those who have favored strong internal security measures have not differentiated as to which agencies should have primary jurisdiction. Many have felt that any public, legitimate anti-Communist activity is worthwhile; every time a crisis brings the issue of Communist subversion to the fore, they indicate their approval of anti-Communist activities if interviewed or called upon to vote in a referendum.

---

fewer friends among the second wing—when the hearings were over, Joe was still the fighter who had 'stood up to them' to many in this wing." (*In Your Opinion* [Boston: Little, Brown, 1960], pp. 135–37.)

Similar results are indicated by a study of mail to Senator Flanders, a prominent critic of McCarthy's. As McCarthy came under severe attack and lost public support in 1954, there "is a significant decline in the literacy quality of the pro-McCarthy mail. . . . The decline in literacy quality of the pro-McCarthy mail is accompanied by an increase in the number of emotionally toned and unsigned letters. . . ." Stanley C. Plog, "McCarthy and Democracy," unpublished paper (dittoed, Neuropsychiatric Institute, U.C.L.A. Medical Center, 1962), pp. P2–P3.

Even in the New Deal period, survey data indicated that the bulk of the population supported the outlawing of the Communist Party and approved of the original House Un-American Activities Committee, led by Martin Dies. In November, 1937, 54 per cent of a national Gallup sample favored a law permitting the police to "padlock places printing Communist literature"; only 35 per cent opposed such a measure. In June, 1938, 53 per cent of a national sample indicated they were against allowing Communists to hold meetings in their community, while only 35 per cent were willing to give Communists this right. In November, 1939, 68 per cent were opposed to allowing "leaders of the Communist Party [to] make speeches to student groups" and only 24 per cent approved. In June of 1942, at a time when the Soviet Union was a military ally of the United States, 50 per cent favored a law preventing membership in the Communist Party, while 36 per cent were against the proposed act. A number of surveys that inquired in 1938 and 1939 whether respondents approved of continuing the Dies Committee reported that approximately three-quarters favored the committee.[20]

Popular awareness of the international Communist threat undoubtedly increased in the late 1940s and early 1950s, with the advent of the Berlin blockade in 1948, the fall of China in 1949, and the outbreak of the Korean War in 1950, but public acceptance of civil liberties for Communists never approached majority sentiment.

McCarthy differed from other anti-Communist investigators in a number of ways. He was more successful in gaining personal attention through his claims to specific knowledge of numerous Communists in government agencies. His attack on the Eastern elite groups as the major source of Communist infiltration was unique. And he was probably more identified than other anti-Communist politicians with efforts to link Democratic international policies with the growth of international Communism. Consequently, he appealed to the isolationists and other antagonists of American foreign policy. Like Father

[20] See Cantril, *op. cit.,* pp. 130, 164, 244.

Coughlin, he was an Irish Catholic and may have also had symbolic significance to the Catholic Irish, and other ethnic groups, which felt resentment in a society dominated by an old American Anglo-Saxon elite. These groups have tended to be isolationist as a result of ethnic identifications with "old-country" issues, and, as Catholics, have been especially sensitive to the Communist issue.

A number of quantitative analyses of the sources of McCarthy's support have been published since the original edition of this book appeared. A summary of the findings of many of these studies is contained in an article by Nelson Polsby.[21] His report indicates that McCarthy received disproportionate support from Catholics, New Englanders, Republicans, the less educated, the lower class, manual workers, farmers, older people, and the Irish.

These findings coincide, on the whole, with the original assumptions of the authors of these essays, but Polsby suggests that the evidence from these surveys and from an examination of the results of different election campaigns in which McCarthy or McCarthyism were issues indicate that most of McCarthy's support can be attributed to his identification as a Republican fighting Democrats. In other words, the vast bulk of his backing came from regular Republicans, while the large majority of Democrats opposed him. And Polsby notes that while survey results do sustain the original hypotheses, "this

[21] Nelson W. Polsby, "Towards an Explanation of McCarthyism," *Political Studies*, 8 (1960). Polsby lists as his sources various published Gallup surveys and the results of his own re-analysis of one 1954 Gallup Poll. See also Louis Bean, *Influences in the Mid-Term Election* (Washington, D.C.: Public Affairs Institute, 1954); and Louis Harris, *Is There a Republican Majority?* (New York: Harper & Brothers, 1954). In reporting Harris's findings, Polsby states that Harris found that the Irish were not disproportionately pro-McCarthy. In my judgment, he misinterpreted Harris's finding. Harris reports that the Irish in his 1952 sample divided evenly between support and opposition to McCarthy. Since, however, McCarthy was only supported by a minority of the entire sample, a group that was evenly split on him was more *favorable* than most other ethnic groups, and hence Harris should be recorded as finding the Irish disproportionately in favor of McCarthy.

relatively meagre empirical confirmation is unimpressive when set against comparable figures describing the two populations [pro- and anti-McCarthy] by their political affiliations."

Undoubtedly Polsby is correct in stressing the linkage between party identification and attitude toward McCarthy. Some confirming evidence was reported in a study of the 1954 election by the University of Michigan's Survey Research Center, which showed the positive relationship between degrees of party commitment and attitude toward McCarthy.

TABLE 8
RELATIONSHIP OF PARTY IDENTIFICATION TO ATTITUDE
TOWARD McCARTHY—OCTOBER, 1954

Attitudes to McCarthy			Party Commitment				
	Strong Dem.	Weak Dem.	Ind. Dem.	Ind.	Ind. Rep.	Weak Rep.	Strong Rep.
Pro-McCarthy	10%	9%	8%	12%	12%	12%	25%
Neutral	37	44	42	54	50	47	43
Anti-McCarthy	50	40	41	21	32	33	27
Other Responses	3	7	9	13	6	8	5
	100%	100%	100%	100%	100%	100%	100%
Excess of Antis Over Pros	40	31	33	9	20	21	2
N	(248)	(288)	(97)	(82)	(68)	(159)	(146)

Based on replies to question: "If you knew that Senator McCarthy was supporting a candidate for Congress, would you be more likely to vote for that candidate, or less likely to vote for that candidate, or wouldn't it make any difference to you?"

Angus Campbell and Homer C. Cooper, *Group Differences in Attitudes and Votes* (Ann Arbor: Survey Research Center, University of Michigan, 1956), p. 92.

The association between McCarthy support and Republicanism does not, of course, tell us how many former Democrats and Independents may have joined Republican ranks *prior* to 1954, because their social situation of personal values made them sympathetic to McCarthy's version of radical right ideology. As has been noted, a considerable section of Coughlin's 1938 backing came from individuals who had supported Roosevelt in 1936, but had later rejected him. There is no reliable means of demonstrating the extent to which Coughlin or McCarthy contributed to a move away from the Democrats, but the available evidence is at least compatible with the hypothesis that they were to some extent influential. A 1954 study by the International Research Associates (I.N.R.A.) inquired as to the respondent's votes in 1948 and 1952. A comparison of the relationship between 1948 voting, attitude toward McCarthy, and 1952 Presidential vote indicates that over half of those who voted for Truman in 1948 and subsequently favored McCarthy voted for Eisenhower in 1952, while two-thirds of the anti-McCarthy Truman voters favored Stevenson (Table 9). A similar relationship between supporting McCarthy and shifting away from the Democrats is suggested in a study by the Roper public-opinion organization.[22]

TABLE 9

RELATIONSHIP BETWEEN 1948 AND 1952 PRESIDENTIAL VOTE
AND ATTITUDES TOWARD McCARTHY
(INRA)

| 1952 Vote | 1948 Vote | | | |
| | Truman | | Dewey | |
	Pro-McCarthy	Anti-McCarthy	Pro-McCarthy	Anti-McCarthy
Eisenhower	53%	31%	99%	95%
Stevenson	47	69	1	5
	(506)	(1381)	(563)	(732)

A more detailed analysis of the sources of McCarthy's support, conducted along the lines of the analysis of Coughlin's

[22] A 1952 Roper survey that was taken in May, before either party had nominated their Presidential candidates, indicates this clearly:

1952 VOTE INTENTION ACCORDING TO TRADITIONAL
PARTY ALLEGIANCE AND ATTITUDE TOWARD McCARTHY

| | Traditional Party Preference | | | |
| | Democrat | | Republican | |
1952 Vote Intention	Pro-McC.	Anti-McC.	Pro-McC.	Anti-McC.
Republican	28%	20%	90%	85%
Democrat	39	45	2	2
Undecided	33	35	8	13
N	(389)	(524)	(40)	(344)

backing, however, belies the suggestion that party affiliation had more bearing on approval or disapproval of McCarthy than other explanatory variables. The 1952 Roper study and the 1954 I.N.R.A. survey both suggest that the most important single attribute associated with opinion of McCarthy was education, while a 1954 national study conducted by the University of Michigan's Survey Research Center indicated that religious affililiation was of greater significance than party. Table 10 below shows the relationship between education, party identification, and attitude toward McCarthy.[23]

TABLE 10

SUPPORT FOR McCARTHY BY EDUCATION
AND PARTY PREFERENCE[a]—1954

(INRA)

Education		Party Identification	
	Democrat	Independent	Republican
Graduate School	—59	—44	—28
College	—44	—24	—19
Vocational	—41	—20	—19
High School	—27	—8	—5
Grammar	—18	—8	+6

a Cell entries refer to percentage differences between approval and disapproval of McCarthy. For example, among grammar-school Republicans, 24% were pro-McCarthy and 18% were anti-McCarthy; among Democrats with graduate education, 8% were pro-McCarthy, 67% anti-McCarthy.

[23] The analysis of McCarthy's support in the remaining part of this section is largely based on the data from four surveys: a Roper study of 3000 respondents made in May, 1952; an eleven-state survey taken by International Research Associates (I.N.R.A.) in August–September, 1954, three months before the Senate censured Senator McCarthy; the 1954 election survey of the University of Michigan's Survey Research Center, cited earlier; and a study conducted by the Gallup organization in December, 1954, after McCarthy had been censured by the Senate, asking a national sample its opinion of the censure. The I.N.R.A. survey presented the analytic advantage of furnishing the largest sample, since it had been designed to report on opinion in 11 states—California, Michigan, Minnesota, Massachusetts, Iowa, New Mexico, Illinois, Ohio, Oregon, Pennsylvania, and New Jersey. The total sample was 9852. While this survey cannot be considered as representative of the national population, there seems no good reason to assume that sub-

The relationship between less education and support of McCarthy is consistent with what is known about the effect of education on political attitudes in general; higher education often makes for greater tolerance, greater regard for due process, and increased tolerance of ambiguity. The less educated were probably attracted, too, by the anti-elitist, anti-intellectual character of McCarthy's oratory, replete with attacks on the "socially pedigreed."[24]

The findings from the surveys with respect to occupation are what might be anticipated, given the preceding results. Those non-manual occupations that require the highest education—i.e., professional and executive or managerial positions—were the most anti-McCarthy (Table 11). And as was suggested in my original essay, independent businessmen were the most favorable to McCarthy among middle-class or non-manual occupations. Workers (including those engaged in personal service) were more favorable to McCarthy than were those in the middle-class occupations, with the exception of independent businessmen.

Farmers were also a pro-McCarthy group, according to three out of the four surveys and the many studies summarized by Polsby. When viewed in occupational categories, McCarthy's main opponents were to be found among professional, managerial, and clerical personnel, while his support was dis-

group variations (e.g., religion, education, party, etc.) within these 11 states were not characteristic of reactions to McCarthy generally. One of its questions concerning reactions to McCarthy was identical with that of the University of Michigan's national study, and the distribution of replies was almost the same.

[24] John Fenton's analysis of Gallup data indicates that those among McCarthy's supporters who approved of his anti-Communism, but were "sometimes repelled by the Senator's high-handed and ruthless tactics," were "often professional or business people with college educations." Those who approved of his methods, who admired him for being tough in his fight against an unspecified "them," who felt that "you can't use kid gloves for that kind of stuff," were disproportionately "from the working classes and with grade-school education." (See Fenton, *op. cit.*, pp. 135–36.)

TABLE 11
RELATIONSHIP BETWEEN OCCUPATION AND ATTITUDES
TOWARD McCARTHY

Per Cent Difference between Approvers and Disapprovers[a]

I.N.R.A.—1954[b]			Roper—1952[c]		
Professional	—35	(731)	Prof. & Exec.	—17	(219)
Exec. & Manager	—24	(511)	Small Bus.	0	(123)
White Collar	—19	(1144)	Cler./Sales	—11	(387)
Ind. Bus.	—14	(583)	Factory Labor	—3	(317)
Supervisor &			Non-Fac. Labor	—6	(235)
Foreman	—16	(405)	Services	—4	(178)
Skilled	—14	(2323)	Farm Own./Mgr.	—6	(184)
Unskilled	—14	(1019)	Gallup—Dec. 1954[d]		
Personal Serv.	—10	(677)	Professional	—44	(163)
Farmers	—21	(824)	Executive	—24	(154)
Retired	—3	(709)	Cler./Sales	—23	(188)
Students	—34	(59)	Skilled	—10	(237)
Michigan—1954[d]			Unskilled	8	(286)
Prof. & Bus.	—40	(246)	Labor	7	(68)
Cler. & Sales	—44	(102)	Service	—10	(103)
Skilled	—30	(337)	Farm Owner	—9	(165)
Unskilled	—16	(144)			
Farmers	—17	(104)			

a Cell entries represent per-cent difference between approval and disapproval of McCarthy. The more negative the entry, the greater the predominance of anti-McCarthy sentiment.

b Occupation of respondent recorded, or of chief wage earner if respondent is a housewife.

c Occupation of respondent recorded; housewives omitted from table.

d Occupation of head of household recorded.

proportionately located among self-employed businessmen, farmers, and manual workers.[25]

In the I.N.R.A. survey, it was possible to examine the attitudes of two groups not in the labor force—students and retired persons. Students were overwhelmingly opposed to McCarthy, while retired persons were among the groups least opposed to the Senator. These findings presumably reflect the combined

[25] These differences among occupational categories continue to hold when Democrats and Republicans are examined separately. Thus, Democratic businessmen in the I.N.R.A. survey were less anti-McCarthy than Democratic professionals, executives, or even manual workers. On the other hand, they were much more anti-

influences of age and education. The attitudes of the retired may have been influenced by several factors associated with age—e.g., particular sensitivity to the rise of Communism and the decline of American prestige; greater political conservatism; and greater rigidity. Moreover, retired persons probably feel most acutely the effects of status deprivation because of both their decline in social importance and their disadvantageous economic position in a period of moderate inflation.

Thus far, the analysis suggests that McCarthy's support was in many ways similar to Father Coughlin's. Both men derived strength from the lower classes and the rural population. They differed only in the relatively greater appeal of the Senator to self-employed businessmen. These results would suggest that the differences in the ideologies of the two men are not paralleled by differences in the character of their support. However, when socio-economic status rather than occupation is taken as an indicator of class, differing patterns of support emerge for the Senator and for Coughlin. The Coughlin analysis indicated a high correlation between socio-economic status (a measure of the style of life of the respondent, largely reflecting income) and approval of the priest. Those of low status were much more likely to approve of him than those of high status. When the corresponding comparison is made for McCarthy, we find a much smaller, almost insignificant, association. Lower-status persons were slightly less likely to support McCarthy than the more privileged ones. This result is initially quite surprising, since both education and occupation, themselves highly correlated with socio-economic status, were, as we have seen, related to attitudes toward McCarthy. The solution to this apparent puzzle lies in the finding that when either education or occupation is held constant—that is, when we compare those high or low on socio-economic status *within* the same educational or occupational categories—the data show that *the higher*

McCarthy than businessmen who consider themselves Republicans or Independents. Republican workers, the "Tory workers" in my original essay, were the group most favorable to McCarthy within their party.

the socio-economic-status level, the greater the proportion of McCarthy supporters. This finding holds true particularly among Republicans; in general, the socio-economic-status level had little effect on attitude toward McCarthy among Democrats of a given occupational or educational level. Thus, while lower educational and occupational status were associated with support for the Wisconsin Senator, within either category *higher* socio-economic status made for greater receptivity to his message among Republicans.[26] Perhaps the higher-income people within lower occupational or educational strata were precisely those who were most drawn to an ideology that attacked as pro-Communist both liberal lower-class-based politics and moderate, conservative old upper-class-elitist groups.

Some of the original essays suggested that McCarthy's strength reflected the frustrations inherent in status discrepancies. In periods of full employment and widespread economic opportunity, some who rise economically do not secure the social status commensurate with their new economic position. Conversely, others, whose financial position has not improved at a corresponding rate (or has worsened), find their social status relatively higher than their economic position. Such status incongruities were presumed to have created sharp resentments about general social developments, which predisposed individuals to welcome McCarthy's attack on the elite and on the New Deal. Efforts to test these hypotheses with the data now available proved unfruitful. For the most part, these analytic efforts took the form of contrasting persons whose status attributes were discordant—e.g., high education and low occupational status—with those whose status determinants were consistent, both high or both low. Seemingly, either the original hypotheses were inadequate or these

[26] The evidence underlying this analysis is not presented in this preliminary report, since it would involve presenting a larger number of complicated analytic tables. The Coughlin studies did not include a question on education, but they did have information on both occupation and socio-economic status. And as was noted in the discussion of his support, within occupational categories, higher socio-economic status was associated with *antagonism* to Coughlin, the opposite of its effect on McCarthy sentiment.

indicators are not refined enough to reflect serious status tensions.

One as yet unpublished study, however, did find some empirical support for these assumptions. Robert Sokol attempted to see whether the subjective perception of status discrepancy ("felt status inconsistency") was related to Mc-Carthyism.[27] The analysis indicated that conscious concern with status inconsistency and McCarthyism were related: "The more strain, the greater will be the tendency to be a Mc-Carthy supporter; with 62 per cent of the high-strain men being pro-McCarthy, in contrast with 47 per cent of those feeling a little strain and 39 per cent of those without any concern about the relative ranks of their statuses." These findings held within different analytic sub-groups. While much more work remains to be done to analyze the relationship between status strain and political protest, and between objective discrepancy and subjective strains, Sokol's research suggests that the general assumptions about the relationship of the status strains of an open society and the type of political protest represented by McCarthy may have some validity.

The findings concerning the relation of education and occupational status to support of McCarthy seem to confirm the hypothesis presented in the original essays concerning stratification factors and McCarthyism. Another hypothesis was that McCarthyism also reflected strains inherent in the varying statuses of different ethnic and religious groups in American society. It was assumed that Catholics and other recent immigrant groups with relatively low status, or with ethnic ties to neutral or Axis nations, were disposed to favor McCarthy, while those of high status or with ethnic links to Allied nations

[27] See Robert Sokol, *Rank Inconsistency and McCarthyism: An Empirical Test* (unpublished paper, Dartmouth College). This was done by asking respondents, "Does the money you receive for your job seem higher, the same or lower than what you'd expect a person with your education to receive?" Those who answered higher or lower were then asked, "How much have you thought about this difference between your income and your education—a great deal, sometimes, or never?" Based on answers to these questions, men were ranked on a scale with seven positions.

opposed the Senator. These generalizations also tend to be supported by survey data. It is clear, as has already been noted, that Catholics as a group were more pro-McCarthy than Protestants, who in turn were somewhat more favorable to him than were Jews. The strong relationship between religious affiliation and attitude toward McCarthy among supporters of the two parties may be seen in Table 12, taken from the University of Michigan study.[28]

TABLE 12
ATTITUDES TOWARD McCARTHY ACCORDING TO RELIGION AND PARTY IDENTIFICATION—1954
(MICHIGAN SURVEY)

Attitudes on McCarthy	Protestants				
	Strong Dem.	Weak Dem.	Ind.	Weak Rep.	Strong Rep.
Pro	7%	6%	7%	11%	23%
Anti	55	45	35	33	28
Excess of Anti over Pro	—48	—39	—28	—22	—5
N	(184)	(213)	(173)	(128)	(123)

Attitudes on McCarthy	Catholics				
	Strong Dem.	Weak Dem.	Ind.	Weak Rep.	Strong Rep.
Pro	18%	23%	19%	20%	39%
Anti	33	20	21	28	23
Excess of Anti over Pro	—15	+3	—2	—8	+16
N	(51)	(58)	(55)	(25)	(18)

SOURCE: Campbell and Cooper, *op. cit.*, p. 149.

Within the Protestant group, the ranking of the different denominations with respect to sentiment toward McCarthy corresponded on the whole to their socio-economic status. As Table 13 shows, the higher the status of the members of a

[28] With but one exception, all the surveys reported by Polsby, *op. cit.*, and those examined here agree on variations in religious backing for McCarthy. The survey that indicates little difference is the 1952 Roper study.

denomination, the more antagonistic the group was toward the Wisconsin Senator.

TABLE 13
PROTESTANT DENOMINATIONAL SUPPORT
FOR McCARTHY—1952
(ROPER)

Attitudes toward McCarthy

	Per Cent of Group High in SES	Agree	Disagree	Don't Know	Difference between Agrees and Disagrees	N
Episcopalians	40%	29%	44%	27%	—15%	(157)
Congregationalists	32	33	44	23	—11	(89)
Methodists	19	29	33	38	—4	(509)
Presbyterians	27	37	36	27	+1	(208)
Lutherans	23	33	31	36	+2	(207)
Baptists	12	28	24	49	+4	(471)

Methodists constitute an exception to this generalization: although a relatively low-status group, they were more anti-McCarthy than the Lutherans or Presbyterians. The rank order of denominations in terms of McCarthy support is, with the exception of the Baptists, identical with that reported earlier for Coughlin (see Table 14). Baptists ranked relatively high

TABLE 14
RANK ORDER OF DIFFERENT PROTESTANT DENOMINATIONS
IN SUPPORT OF COUGHLIN AND McCARTHY

	Coughlin—1938	*McCarthy—1952*
High Support	Lutherans	Baptists
	Presbyterians	Lutherans
	Methodists	Presbyterians
	Baptists	Methodists
	Congregationalists	Congregationalists
Low Support	Episcopalians	Episcopalians

in opposition to Coughlin and in support for McCarthy. It is difficult to suggest any plausible explanation for this change in the position of the Baptists other than that they may have been particularly antagonistic to the Catholic Church, and hence unwilling to approve the political activities of a priest, yet not deterred from supporting a Catholic Senator.

Both the I.N.R.A. and Roper surveys contain information concerning the ethnic origins of respondents which permits an elaboration of the relationship between ethnic and religious identification and McCarthy support (see Table 15). Unfor-

TABLE 15
RELATIONSHIP BETWEEN RELIGION AND ETHNIC BACK-GROUND AND ATTITUDES TO McCARTHY

Per Cent Difference between Approvers and Disapprovers

Roper—1952			I.N.R.A.—1954		
Catholics	(N)		Catholics	(N)	
4th Generation Amer.	(198)	—11	No Answer	(252)	—2
Ireland	(81)	+18	Ireland	(545)	+5
Italy	(61)	+16	Italy	(393)	+8
Germany	(54)	+13	Germany & Austria	(424)	—6
Great Britain	(13)	*	Great Britain	(272)	+4
Poland	(36)	—6	Poland	(246)	—2
Protestants			Protestants		
4th Generation Amer.	(1190)	—2	No Answer	(1037)	—22
Ireland	(29)	+7	Ireland	(487)	—21
Germany	(172)	+2	Germany & Austria	(1266)	—19
Great Britain	(102)	—8	Great Britain	(1814)	—25
Scandinavia	(68)	—3	Scand. & Holl.	(851)	—25
Jews	(96)	—6	Jews	(245)	—54
Negroes	(252)	—7	Negroes	(438)	—13

* Too few cases for stable estimates

tunately, the two studies differed greatly in the wording of questions on ethnicity. Because I.N.R.A. asked for the country of ancestors, while Roper asked for the country of the respondents' grandparents, the Roper survey reported many more Protestants as simply "American" in background. Among Catholics, too, the Roper survey reported a smaller proportion with German or British ancestry than did the I.N.R.A. survey. On the other hand, I.N.R.A.'s request for country of ancestors produced a large "don't know" or "no answer" group. About 20 per cent of the whites did not reply to the question.

Differences in attitude among the ethnic groups were more pronounced among Catholics than Protestants in both the Roper and the I.N.R.A. studies. In the Roper survey, Irish Catholics were 18 per cent more favorable to the Senator than unfavorable, while "old American" Catholics were 11 per cent more negative than positive. Among Protestants, on the other hand, those of German origin were the most pro-McCarthy (2 per cent), while those of British ancestry were most opposed (−8 per cent).

Results from both surveys show that Irish and Italian Catholics were among the most pro-McCarthy groups. The Roper data indicate that Germans, both Catholic and Protestant, were disproportionately in favor of McCarthy, but the I.N.R.A. materials do not confirm this finding. The explanation for this seeming inconsistency may lie in the differing formulation of the questions on ethnicity. It may be that McCarthy appealed successfully to the "Roper" Germans whose family had emigrated to the United States within the past three generations, and consequently retained emotional ties to Germany that made them receptive to McCarthy's isolationist appeal. "I.N.R.A." Germans are more likely to have been old-stock Americans and, like other "old American" groups, predisposed to disapprove of the Wisconsin Senator.

In summary, it appears that the findings concerning ethnic and religious factors agree with the hypotheses suggested in the original essays—that is, McCarthy was generally opposed by descendants of old American Protestant families, and he drew disproportionately from Catholics of recent immigrant background. The two minority groups whose circumstances have led them to identify with liberal Democratic groups and leaders, the Jews and the Negroes, were among those most strongly opposed to McCarthy.

Thus far, the discussion has centered on the relationship between attitudes toward McCarthy and various background characteristics. Many of the original interpretations of the

Senator also posited certain attitudinal and personality characteristics as being linked to support for or opposition to McCarthy. It has been argued that he appealed to isolationists, to those who were most hostile to international Communism, to ardent economic conservatives, to "authoritarian personalities," and to the bigoted. To specify the exact relationship between such attitudes and McCarthy support would require a more detailed analysis than is possible in this preliminary report. At this stage, I would like to summarize the relationships found between certain attitude items and opinions concerning McCarthy.

There seems little doubt that isolationists—i.e., those who opposed aid to foreign countries, disliked support of the United Nations, and favored strong unilateral measures in dealing with the Russians—were more disposed to back the Wisconsin Senator than those who took a more internationalist position on such issues.

McCarthy also drew disproportionately from economic conservatives. Measures of such attitudes as position on liberalism in general, laws to prevent strikes, a federal health program, and support of private development of national resources all indicate that the conservative position on these issues was associated with greater support for McCarthy.

Perhaps more significant than the fact that support of McCarthy correlated with conservative and isolationist political attitudes is that these relationships are on the whole so weak. Clearly, many persons who opposed the Senator's views on important issues reported that they approved of him, his committee, or his charges. Referring to the December, 1954, Gallup survey, completed after McCarthy was censured by the Senate, we find that many still supported him while holding opinions contrary to his. For example, one-third of those who preferred a peaceful-coexistence policy or who favored the United Nations were opposed to the Senate censure. With respect to domestic matters, thirty per cent of those who described their political views as liberal rather than conservative were favorable toward McCarthy at the end of 1954. Thus a significant minority of liberals and internationalists were for

TABLE 16
RELATIONSHIP BETWEEN OPINIONS ON VARIOUS FOREIGN POLICY ISSUES AND ATTITUDES TOWARD McCARTHY

Issues	*Attitudes toward McCarthy*			Source
	Pro	Con	N	
Break Off Diplomatic Relations with Russia				I.N.R.A.—1954
Yes	21%	32%	(3641)	
No	14	43	(2550)	
Withdraw from the United Nations				I.N.R.A.—1954
Yes	28	26	(870)	
No	14	38	(6291)	
Peaceful Coexistence Policy				Gallup—Dec. 1954
Favor	32	55	(694)	
Oppose	46	46	(399)	
U.S. Should Support U.N.				Gallup—Dec. 1954
Favor	33	55	(1042)	
Oppose	47	34	(231)	
How to Handle the Russians				Roper—1952
Offensive War	37	28	(274)	
Keep Strong	32	34	(1923)	
Peaceful Settlement	26	42	(343)	
Korean War Policy for U.S.				Roper—1952
Do as we did	23	40	(577)	
Keep trying for peace	21	43	(665)	
Go further militarily	37	34	(1284)	
Be tough	35	32	(1585)	
Pull out of Korea	31	26	(378)	
Give Economic Aid to Under-Developed Nations				I.N.R.A.—1954
Yes	16	37	(5343)	
No	20	32	(1620)	
Blockading the Coast of Communist China				Gallup—Dec. 1954
Approve	43	43	(495)	
Disapprove	31	60	(550)	
Withdraw Foreign Aid From Nations Which Refuse to Co-operate with U.S.				Gallup—Dec. 1954
Approve	37	46	(1059)	
Disapprove	29	58	(258)	

the Senator throughout his brief career as a leader of the radical right. Conversely, most of those who took conservative and isolationist positions on these issues were opposed to or had no opinion concerning his political activities, though on any given issue they supported him more than did liberals or internationalists.

A more complex relationship between opinion on domestic issues and McCarthyism than is indicated by this preliminary analysis of national survey data has been suggested by a study of attitudes toward McCarthy in a Vermont city. Martin Trow has suggested that the support of McCarthy by small business-men reflected their perception of him as an opponent of the power elite as well as of unions and the liberal welfare state. He argued that those who fear the "growing concentration of economic power in government, unions, and business enter-prises" saw these as "McCarthy's often thinly concealed tar-gets."[29] To test this assumption, Trow divided his respondents into four political categories on the basis of their attitudes toward big business and trade unions. These were: (1) labor-liberals—those who were favorable to trade unions and hostile to large corporations; (2) nineteenth-century liberals—those who were opposed to trade unions *and* to large corporations; (3) moderate conservatives—those who supported trade unions but were also favorable to large business; and (4) right-wing conservatives—those who were hostile to unions and favorable to big business. In terms of this typology, the "nineteenth-century liberals"—anti-big business and anti-trade unions—should be most pro-McCarthy. Trow's data indicate that this combination of attitudes was in fact held more widely by small businessmen than by any other occupational stratum, and that those who held it, whether businessmen or not, were most likely to favor McCarthy. Three-fifths, or 60 per cent, of the "nineteenth-century liberals" approved of McCarthy's meth-ods, while among those in the other three categories, be-tween 35 and 38 per cent indicated approval for McCarthy's

[29] Martin Trow, *Right-Wing Radicalism and Political Intolerance* (unpublished Ph.D. thesis, Department of Sociology, Columbia University, 1957), pp. 30–31.

methods.[30] Efforts at partial replication of Trow's analysis with the I.N.R.A. data did not yield comparable results since the labor-liberals were the most anti-McCarthy group, while the other three groups, though somewhat more pro-McCarthy, were almost identical in their degree of support.

At the moment, all that can be said is that two surveys made at different times in different places, and using different indicators of McCarthy sentiment and political attitudes, yielded differing results. The hypothesis must be placed in the category of the not proven.

Efforts to account for adherence to extremist political ideologies, and to McCarthyism in particular, have suggested that such groups cannot be explained solely or even primarily by an analysis of the values and interests of their supporters. Rather, it has been argued that the support for extremist ideologies and conspiracy theories of politics is also related to personality structure—i.e., that certain types of people find such politics congruent with their psychological needs. These hypotheses have often been linked to the findings in *The Authoritarian Personality*,[31] which suggested there is a definite personality type that is oriented toward strong leadership, is intolerant, dislikes ambiguity, and so forth.

Some of the essays reprinted here speculated along these lines with regard to the sources of McCarthy's support, suggesting, as I did, that he drew disproportionately from those with "personality frustration and repressions [that] result in the adoption of scapegoat sentiments." One of the earliest analyses of McCarthy support, Harold Hodges' study of a Wisconsin town, reported that "the statistically typical Mc-

[30] These materials are also reported in Martin Trow, "Small Businessmen, Political Tolerance, and Support for McCarthy," *American Journal of Sociology*, 64 (1958), pp. 277–78. I have previously discussed Trow's findings in the context of a general analysis of right-wing movements in *Political Man, op. cit.*, pp. 167–70.

[31] T. W. Adorno, Else Frenkel-Brunswik, Daniel Levinson and R. Nevitt Sanford, *The Authoritarian Personality* (New York: Harper & Brothers, 1950).

Carthy supporter . . . is more conformistic, agreeing that there are too many 'oddballs' around, that the 'good' American doesn't stand out among his fellow Americans, and that children should not develop hobbies which are rare or unusual. . . . He expresses a more misanthropic social outlook, concurring with the statement that 'people are out to cheat you' and that there is 'wickedness, cheating and corruption all about us.' "[32] The Sokol community survey, discussed earlier, also reported a strong relationship between personality traits and support of McCarthy. Those who were more intolerant of ambiguity were also more pro-McCarthy. This relationship held even when examined within the categories of education and religious affiliation, two variables that have been shown to affect such attitudes.[33] To test these hypotheses on a broader scale, data taken from a national survey made by the National Opinion Research Center (N.O.R.C.) in 1953, which contained items taken from the original Authoritarian Personality scale, have been reanalyzed here.[34]

Propensity to agree with items designed to measure authoritarian predispositions correlated highly with attitudes toward McCarthy within educational, occupational, or religious groupings. For example, within the three educational categories of

[32] Harold M. Hodges, "A Sociological Analysis of McCarthy Supporters" (unpublished paper, San José State College), pp. 2–3.

[33] See H. H. Hyman and Paul Sheatsley, " 'The Authoritarian Personality'—A Methodological Critique," in R. Christie and M. Jahoda, editors, *Studies in the Scope and Method of "The Authoritarian Personality"* (Glencoe: The Free Press, 1954), pp. 94–96.

[34] The 1953 N.O.R.C. study used the following items as a measure of "authoritarian" predisposition:

1. The *most important* thing to teach children is *absolute obedience* to their parents.

2. Any good leader should be *strict* with people under him in order to gain their respect.

3. Prison is *too good* for sex criminals. They should be publicly whipped or worse.

4. There are two kinds of people in the world: the weak and the strong.

5. No decent man can respect a woman who has had sex relations before marriage.

college, high school, and grammar school, those high on the Authoritarian Personality scale were much more likely to have approved of the McCarthy committee in June, 1953, than those with low scores (Table 17). Seemingly, reactions to the Senator were not only a function of social position, perception of self-interest, or party identification, but were also affected by that component of "character" that the Authoritarian Personality scale measures.

It is significant to note that the largest differences in response to McCarthy occurred within the category of the college-educated. Those among them who were low on the Authoritarian Personality scale were least likely to approve of the Senator, but the college-educated who were high on the measure of authoritariansim gave more support to the McCarthy committee than any segment of those who had not gone beyond grade school. Since various studies have indicated that propensity to give an authoritarian response is inversely related to education, this finding suggests that the Authoritarian Personality scale serves best as a predictor of attitude predispositions among the well educated. Among the less educated, a high authoritarianism score reflects in some part attitudes common to the group, which are also subject to modification by more education. If someone is well educated and still gives authoritarian responses, then the chances are that he really has a basic tendency to react in an authoritarian fashion. However, as Table 17 indicates, there is a relationship between propensity to give "authoritarian" responses and support of McCarthy within the three education groups.

Although McCarthy never attacked minority ethnic groups and seemed to have consciously tried to avoid linking Jews to Communism, many of his critics have felt certain that McCarthyism appealed to religious and racial bigots. Liberals have generally believed that anti-Semitism and rightist politics are associated, and have therefore assumed that, while any given form of right-wing extremism may not be overtly anti-Semitic, such movements attract anti-Semites. With respect to McCarthyism, there has been the further assumption that those who believed in Jews as a hidden source of social ills would also be disposed to believe in a hidden domestic Communist conspiracy that had infiltrated the government. The evidence available from the various studies bearing on this issue, however, does not bear out these assumptions.

TABLE 17
RELATIONSHIP BETWEEN ATTITUDES TOWARD THE
McCARTHY COMMITTEE AND SCORE ON AN
"AUTHORITARIAN PERSONALITY" SCALE WITHIN
EDUCATIONAL GROUPINGS—1953
(N.O.R.C.)

Education and Authoritarianism	*Attitudes toward McCarthy Committee*				
	Difference between Approvers and Disapprovers	*Approve*	*Disapprove*	*Don't Know*	*N*
Grammar School					
High Authoritarian	42	56%	14%	30%	(183)
Middle	43	57	14	29	(229)
Low	28	44	16	39	(57)
High School					
High	68	78	10	12	(139)
Middle	49	65	16	19	(252)
Low	37	61	24	15	(188)
College					
High	75	85	10	5	(20)
Middle	46	66	20	14	(84)
Low	10	49	39	11	(132)

High equals an authoritarian response on at least four items; medium means an authoritarian score on two or three items; low indicates no or one authoritarian response out of the five items.

The I.N.R.A. pre-election study in 1954 asked respondents whether they would be more or less likely to vote for a Congressional candidate if they knew he was Jewish. About 3 per cent said they would be more likely to vote for a Jewish candidate; 17 per cent gave an anti-Semitic response, saying that they would be more likely to oppose a Jewish candidate; while the remaining four-fifths of the sample said knowledge of Jewish background would not affect their vote decision. Comparing the relationship between sentiments toward Jewish Congressional candidates and attitudes to candidates who were pro- or anti-McCarthy produced the startling result that the small group of philo-Semites—those who were favorable to Jewish candidates—were much more likely to be pro-McCarthy than those who were against Jewish Congressional candidates. The latter were also much more likely to be anti-McCarthy than those who said their vote would not be influenced by the candidate's being Jewish.

TABLE 18
RELATIONSHIP BETWEEN ATTITUDES TOWARD A JEWISH
CONGRESSIONAL CANDIDATE AND TOWARD McCARTHY—
1954
(I.N.R.A.)
(Jews Omitted)

Attitudes to McCarthy	Attitudes toward a Jewish Candidate		
	More Likely to Vote for	Immaterial Whether Jew or Not	More Likely to Vote Against a Jew
Pro	26%	16%	12%
Anti	29	30	38
Difference between pro and anti responses	—3	—14	—26
N	(234)	(7557)	(1640)

This result is so surprising as to suggest the existence of an intervening factor associated with one or the other attitude so as to produce a spurious result. To check on such a possibility, the relationship between McCarthyism and anti-Semitism was analyzed within education groups, religious groups, and party-identification groups. The finding, however, still occurred in all. Among the college-educated, as among the high-school- or grammar-school-educated, the same pattern held up—the small per cent of those who were philo-Jewish were more pro-Mc-Carthy. Catholics were less anti-Semitic than Protestants, but within both religious groups McCarthy support and anti-Semitism were inversely related. The relationship was also sustained within the three political categories of Democrats, Republicans, and Independents.[35]

[35] The possibility that the relationship is a function of a response set is challenged by the fact that one of the three questions that measured sentiment toward McCarthy was worded so that a pro-

If we assume that there is some reliability in this result, that it truly measured popular attitudes at the time, it is conceivable that the result is a product of McCarthy's association with various minority ethnics including Jews. The I.N.R.A. study was made after McCarthy's association with Roy Cohn and David Schein, two men publicly identified as Jews, had become a matter of public discussion and controversy. This identification may have led many rank-and-file supporters of the Senator to perceive Jews as being on their side. All this is highly speculative, but the fact remains that the I.N.R.A. results do produce a result that reverses any assumptions about a positive relationship between McCarthyism and anti-Semitism.

The finding that McCarthy supporters were not prone to accept anti-Semitic beliefs is reinforced by a report of a November, 1954, N.O.R.C. study based on a national sample of 1200 Christian respondents. This survey found no relationship between attitudes toward McCarthy and willingness to accept Jews as next-door neighbors. When educational differences were controlled, no consistent linkage between the two attitudes could be observed.[86] (However, since writing this article, my own further analysis of the data of this study has indicated that there is a slight relationship between rejecting Jews as neighbors and being pro-McCarthy in the total sample.)

The lack of a positive relationship between McCarthyism and anti-Semitism may reflect a more general absence of any relationship between ethnic prejudice and McCarthy support. A 1954 Gallup survey inquired, "Would you object to having

---

McCarthy sentiment required a "no" answer. On the whole, those who said "No," they would not support a candidate who opposed McCarthy, replied "Yes," they would back one who favored the Senator.

[86] Charles H. Stember, *Education and Attitude Change* (New York Institute of Human Relations Press, 1961), pp. 109, 118. Since this paper went to press, I have secured a set of the I.B.M. cards of this survey for further analysis. This indicates that in the sample as a whole, those favorable to McCarthy are somewhat less willing to accept Jewish neighbors than were his opponents.

your children attend a school where the majority of pupils are Negro?" Over half of the sample (about 55 per cent) indicated they would object. When the sample was divided between followers and opponents of McCarthy within educational categories, there was no consistent relationship between the willingness to send one's children to a predominantly Negro school and attitudes toward McCarthy. The followers of the Senator were no more and no less liberal on this issue than his opponents.[37]

But if these surveys challenge the liberal intellectuals' belief that McCarthyites were generally intolerant people, there is some evidence to suggest that at least one type of anti-Semitism may have contributed to a small part of McCarthy's support. Data from the 1953 N.O.R.C. survey suggest that those individuals who believed that Jews were disproportionately apt to be Communists were somewhat more likely to approve of the McCarthy committee than those who did not mention Jews. This survey, taken early in the Senator's career as chairman of the Senate investigating committee on government operations, found that a majority (60 per cent) approved of his committee. Of the 8 per cent in the sample who mentioned Jews as being disproportionately Communist, 69 per cent approved of the committee, while among respondents who did not list Jews, 59 per cent reacted favorably to McCarthy. While these results differ from those found in the other surveys, further specification of the relationship within social categories reduces their significance as indicators of greater anti-Semitic sentiments among McCarthyites. When elementary-school-, high-school-, and college-educated respondents are examined separately, the relationship holds among those who did not go beyond elementary school. Of this low-educated group, those who were pro-McCarthy more often mentioned Jews as being Communist than did those who were anti-McCarthy. Within the category of the high-school-educated, there was no relationship between propensity to identify Jews with Communists and attitudes toward the McCarthy committee, while among the

[37] *Ibid.*, pp. 136, 143.

college-educated the relationship was *reversed*. In this stratum, presumably the best informed of the three, the anti-McCarthy group more often saw Jews as disproportionately Communist.

The four surveys are not, of course, directly comparable, for many reasons. Cohn and Schein were not an issue when the 1953 N.O.R.C. interviews were taken, but had become a major source of controversy by the time of the 1954 studies, at which period McCarthy had lost considerable support. More important perhaps is the fact that the studies were asking very different questions. The 1954 surveys were touching on general attitudes toward Jews, while the 1953 poll was tapping the reactions of the very small group who see Jews as more Communistically inclined than non-Jews. Most of the respondents felt that "only a few" Jews are Communists.[38] In fact, studies of the social base of American Communism indicate that while the overwhelming majority of Jews have opposed Communism, Jews have contributed disproportionately to the support of the American Communist Party.[39] Those, therefore, who mention Jews as Communists may be reflecting greater knowledge and concern about Communism rather than anti-Semitism as such.

Analysis of other data in the 1953 N.O.R.C. survey tends to sustain the interpretation that the fact that McCarthy supporters were more likely to mention Jews as disproportionately Communist reflects concern with the Communist issue rather than anti-Semitism. Respondents were asked whether they had heard any criticism of Jews in the last six months. About one-fifth, 21 per cent, reported that they had heard such criticism. Those whose acquaintances included critics of Jews were proportionately *less* favorable to McCarthy than those who did not report hearing anti-Semitic remarks.[40] The respondents

[38] *Ibid.*, pp. 18–19.

[39] Nathan Glazer, *The Social Basis of American Communism* (New York: Harcourt, Brace, 1961), pp. 130–68.

[40] Such evidence cannot be taken as supporting the thesis that anti-McCarthy people were more anti-Semitic than pro-McCarthy people since positive replies to this question do not necessarily indicate greater anti-Semitism. Rather, it has been argued that those individuals who know more people, who have more contacts with

mentioned the specific types of attacks they heard. These break down into a variety of criticisms of Jews as having too much political or economic power, being unscrupulous in business, being socially clannish, *and* those involving charges that Jews are more likely than others to be Communists, or spies and traitors. Most of the anti-Jewish criticisms reported, however, did not concern Communism or spying. Individuals who mentioned hearing anti-Semitic comments not involving Communism were most likely of all to be anti-McCarthy, while the small group that mentioned having heard that Jews were Communists tended to show a larger than average support for the Wisconsin Senator. These results suggest that "normal anti-Semitic" stereotypes—that is, those concerning presumed negative Jewish economic or social traits—were more common in the social environment of people who were against the Senator than of those who were for him.

Given the limitations of the measures of anti-Semitism and the varying results in the three surveys, it is impossible to draw any conclusions about a relationship between anti-Semitism and propensity to support or oppose McCarthy.[41] The available evidence clearly does not sustain the thesis that McCarthy received disproportionate support from anti-Semites.

The findings from the various surveys reported on in this section tend to sustain many of the generalizations made in

---

others, are more likely to hear more of every kind of attitude. And since increased social relations outside of one's intimate family circle are associated with higher education and status, the fact that opponents of McCarthy are higher on these social attributes may account for the finding. To investigate this possibility, these replies were compared among people with varying amounts of education, and the relationship still held. Among the grammar-school-, high-school-, and college-educated, those opposed to McCarthy were more likely to report having heard anti-Semitic comments than those who were pro-McCarthy.

[41] Hodges, in his study, based on a sample of 248 in a small Wisconsin town, reports that those who were pro-McCarthy were more likely to subscribe "more frequently to anti-Semitic statements," but also tended "to reject statements which are anti-Negro in content." (*Op. cit.*, p. 3.)

the original essays. McCarthy's support was differentially based on the lower strata of manual workers, the less educated, and, within the middle class, farmers and self-employed business-men. From a political standpoint, he recruited more heavily from the conservative groups, from Republicans, backers of right-wing policies on domestic issues, isolationists, and those most concerned with the need for a "tough" anti-Russian policy. In terms of religious and ethnic characteristics, he was disproportionately backed by his Catholic co-religionists, by members of lower-status Protestant denominations, and by those of recent immigrant stock, particularly Irish and German Catholics.

The evidence does not bear out any assumptions about a link between ethnic prejudice, particularly anti-Semitism, and McCarthyism. It does, however, argue for the thesis that Mc-Carthy drew disproportionate support from those whose per-sonality traits or social background led them to give "authori-tarian" responses to items from the Authoritarian Personality scale—that is, persons who were generally intolerant of ambiguity, approved of strong leadership, and favored harsh punishment for violations of social norms.

It is difficult to state whether these and other results reported earlier sustain the generalization that the appeal of McCarthy-ism reflected the status strains endemic in an open, prosperous society in which many individuals change their relative economic status. Sokol's study, specifically designed to test these hypotheses, does bear them out on a subjective level. In the Massachusetts community studied, those most concerned with the problem of status discrepancy were more favorable to McCarthy. However, his data and the studies analyzed here do not validate the assumption with respect to "objective" sources of status strain (high education and low economic position, for example). The evidence bearing on the belief that McCarthy appealed to traditional "populist" ideology, directed against organized labor and big business, also produces con-tradictory or ambiguous results.

In concluding the discussion about McCarthy, it may be worth noting again that the evidence indicates that McCarthy did not have widespread support either in 1952 or in 1954. Only 10 per cent of those questioned by Roper in 1952 felt that most of those accused by McCarthy were actually Communists. More significant, when asked in the same survey who among a list of names had done the best job of handling the Communist problem "here in America," only 7 per cent mentioned McCarthy, while from the same list 19 per cent singled him out for unsatisfactory handling of the problem. Thus, long before Eisenhower's election, intense negative feelings about McCarthy were seemingly much more common than strong favorable sentiments. And in the 1954 pre-election I.N.R.A. survey, 32 per cent gave anti-McCarthy reponses on an index based on three questions about McCarthy, while only 15 per cent gave favorable answers. It seems clear from these and other surveys that the form of radical rightism represented by McCarthy, while more politically palatable than that of Coughlin or the John Birch Society, nevertheless, like them, aroused much more hostility than support.

III

The Supporters of the John Birch Society

The analysis of the supporters of the John Birch Society presents some special problems, requiring that it be handled differently from the way in which the two earlier "radical-rightist" tendencies were treated. Because it lacks a nationally known leader, espouses a virulent and extremist ideology which gives rise to attacks on the moderate leaders of both major parties as Communists, and upholds an economic program promoting the interests and values of the small stratum of moderately well-to-do businessmen and professionals, it has appealed to a much smaller segment of the general public than did Coughlin or McCarthy. Further, the Society is only dimly known to many people. For example, a Gallup Survey that inquired into attitudes toward the John Birch Society in the beginning of 1962 found that over two-thirds of those interviewed had not heard of it, or else had no opinion of it (Table

19). Among those who did express opinions, negative judgments outnumbered positive ones by five to one: 5 per cent favored the Society and 26 per cent opposed it.

TABLE 19
OPINION OF A NATIONAL SAMPLE
ON THE BIRCH SOCIETY—
FEBRUARY, 1962
(GALLUP)

Favorable to the Society	5%
Unfavorable	26
No Opinion	27
Have Not Heard of the Society	42
	100%
	(1616)

These results were obtained four years after the Society was first organized, and over a year after it began to receive widespread attention in the general press, as well as sharp criticism from liberal political leaders and journals.

Because the bulk of the national sample had no opinion on the Birchers, certain limitations are imposed in drawing conclusions from the data. Comparisons between population subgroups, as presented for the Coughlin and McCarthy data, must be interpreted with extreme caution, since they may at times be quite misleading. In analyzing support for the Birchers in terms of such categories, it is necessary to compare such small percentages as three per cent pro-Birch among Democrats and seven per cent among Republicans. Such comparisons are made all the more difficult because the proportion of respondents without opinions varies widely from sub-group to sub-group, following the pattern typically associated with political knowledge, opinion, and participation.

As Table 20 shows, the proportion without an opinion is 44 per cent among those who went to college, but 85 per cent among the grammar-school-educated. Further examination of the table discloses that the college-trained have a higher proportion of Birch supporters—and also Birch opponents—than do the grade-school-educated. To take another example, pro-

TABLE 20
ATTITUDES TOWARD BIRCH SOCIETY BY SELECTED
CHARACTERISTICS IN PER CENT—FEBRUARY, 1962
(GALLUP)

Characteristics	Pro	Con	Attitudes on Birch Society Don't Know, Haven't Heard	N
PARTY				
Democrat	3%	21	76	(787)
Independent	5%	34	61	(368)
Republican	7%	28	65	(444)
RELIGION				
Protestant	4%	24	72	(1108)
Catholic	5%	27	68	(390)
Jewish	6%	48	46	(54)
REGION				
Northeast	4%	34	62	(460)
Midwest	4%	20	76	(538)
South	4%	19	77	(359)
West	7%	35	58	(259)
EDUCATION				
Grade	2%	13	85	(428)
High	5%	25	70	(889)
College	8%	48	44	(294)
INCOME				
Low	4%	16	80	(509)
Medium	5%	24	71	(605)
High	6%	39	55	(483)
SEX				
Men	5%	30	65	(784)
Women	4%	22	74	(820)
OCCUPATION				
Professional	9%	51	40	(166)
Business, executive	6%	33	61	(176)
Clerical, sales	7%	34	57	(193)
Skilled labor	5%	19	76	(258)
Unskilled, serv.	3%	18	79	(381)
Farmer	1%	14	85	(173)
Non-labor force	5%	22	73	(235)
Non-manual	7%	39	54	(535)
Manual	4%	19	77	(639)
AGE				
21–29	5%	23	72	(232)
30–49	3%	29	68	(700)
50 and over	6%	23	71	(623)
TOTAL SAMPLE	5%	26	69	(1616)

fessionals appear much more pro-Birch than farmers, if one looks only at the percentage of the two occupations that is favorable to the Society; however, 60 per cent of the professionals expressed an opinion, as contrasted with 15 per cent of the farmers. (To emphasize the differing contributions of various population sub-groups to opinion, both pro and con, on the Birch Society, Table 21 is included, based on the same data as Table 20, but showing the relative contribution of sub-groups to the pro-Birch and anti-Birch groups, rather than the opinion distribution of the sub-groups on the Birch issue.)

The low level of opinion on the Society has additional implications for an analysis of Birch support. These concern the extent of possible latent support. One cannot assume that, because the low-income element (family income under $4000) of the population divided 4 to 1 against the Birchers in 1962, the same division of opinion would obtain at a time when, perhaps, a majority of these persons will know of, and have views regarding, the Birchers. At the time of the Gallup Survey, only 20 per cent of low-income respondents had an opinion on the organization. One cannot guess whether the balance of judgment would remain the same if 50 per cent—or 80 per cent—of this group had opinions to offer. In short, under different conditions arising either within the country or outside it, and with different policies and techniques pursued by the Society itself, the Birchers may come to the attention of segments of the population they are not presently reaching, and the relative distribution of supporters and opponents within different analytic categories may become quite different.

Given these difficulties in interpreting the results of the national survey, I shall not discuss them in great detail. It is possible, however, to specify some of the factors that are associated with opinion toward the Society by concentrating on an analysis of attitudes within the one state in the Union in which the Society has become an important election issue and source of controversy—California. The California Poll, a state-wide survey organization, reports that in January, 1962, 82 per cent of a sample of 1100 Californians had heard of

TABLE 21
CHARACTERISTICS OF BIRCH SUPPORTERS AND OPPONENTS
IN PER CENT—FEBRUARY, 1962 (GALLUP)

Characteristics	Total Sample	Attitude Groups Pro-Birch	Anti-Birch	Don't Know, Haven't Heard
PARTY				
Democrat	49%	33%	40%	54%
Independent	23	24	30	20
Republican	28	43	30	26
RELIGION				
Protestant	72	66	66	74
Catholic	25	30	27	24
Jewish	3	4	7	2
REGION				
Northeast	28	25	37	25
Midwest	34	32	25	36
South	22	21	16	26
West	16	22	22	13
EDUCATION				
Grade	27	13	13	33
High	55	57	53	57
College	18	30	34	12
INCOME				
Low	32	24	20	37
Medium	38	38	35	39
High	30	38	45	24
SEX				
Men	49	57	57	45
Women	51	43	43	55
OCCUPATION				
Professional	11	20	21	6
Business, executive	11	13	15	10
Clerical, sales	12	17	16	10
Skilled labor	16	16	12	18
Farmer	11	1	6	13
Non-labor force	15	17	13	16
Unskilled, serv.	24	16	17	27
Non-manual	34	50	52	26
Manual	40	32	29	45
AGE				
21–29	15	15	13	15
30–49	45	33	51	44
50 and over	40	52	36	41
	100%	100%	100%	100%
N	(1616)	(76)	(416)	(1124)

the Society. The national Gallup Survey, cited earlier, which was taken at about the same time, indicates that among respondents in the three Pacific Coast states, 79 per cent had heard of the Society as contrasted with 58 per cent in the nation as a whole.[42] The salience of the Birch issue in California in 1962 can hardly be disputed: at the time, two California congressmen were avowed members of the organization; the Attorney General of the State issued a detailed report on the Society that was extensively reported and discussed in the newspapers; the Republican Assembly, meeting to endorse candidates for the 1962 primaries, spent considerable time debating the Party's position with respect to the Society; and both gubernatorial candidates, Governor Edmund Brown and former Vice-President Nixon, vied in attacking the Birchites.[43]

Given the salience of the Birch issue in California politics, and the high degree of public knowledge of the organization, findings for the state of California may be interpreted with somewhat greater confidence than the national data. The January, 1962, California Poll permitted the construction of a measure of Birch support and opposition similar to that used for McCarthy in the I.N.R.A. Survey. The Poll inquired first whether respondents would be more or less likely to vote for a gubernatorial candidate who welcomed Birch Society support, and second whether they would be more or less likely to vote for a candidate who rejected the Society's endorsement. From responses on these two questions, respondents were divided into three groups: those who were sympathetic to the Birch Society on at least one question; those who said that the Birch issue would not affect their vote; and those who were

[42] The wording of the question in the two surveys was similar but not identical, since the California Poll item read: "Have you heard anything about a political group called the John Birch Society?" The Gallup query did not include the word "political."

[43] It should be noted, however, that this does not mean that Californians are more in favor of the Birch Society than those in other parts of the country. Actually, among those with opinions, there are proportionately more pro-Birchers in the Midwest and in the South than in the Far West.

unsympathetic to the Birch Society on one or both questions. A fourth group contained those who did not have an opinion on either question, together with persons who had never heard of the Society. Table 22 gives the distribution among California respondents in these four categories.

TABLE 22
ATTITUDES TOWARD THE BIRCH SOCIETY AMONG
CALIFORNIANS—JANUARY, 1962
(CALIFORNIA POLL)

Favorable	6%
Neutral	15
Unfavorable	41
No Opinion[a]	
Never Heard	38
	100%
N	(1186)

[a] No Opinion includes 2 per cent who gave contradictory responses.

It is clear that in California, as in the nation as a whole, the bulk of those with opinions about the Birchers were hostile. Among the national sample, as we have seen, unfavorable replies outnumbered favorable by a magnitude of five to one (26 per cent to 5 per cent); in California, the negative exceeded the positive by seven to one (41 per cent to 6 per cent). Exact comparisons are, of course, impossible since the questions posed were so different. Moreover, it might be argued that the neutral category in California, those who reported that it made no difference whether a candidate was pro-Birch Society or not—the anti-anti-Birchers, so to speak—were "soft on Birchism." In spite of the propaganda emphasizing the anti-democratic propensities of the Birch Society and its attacks on Eisenhower and other major figures as Communists or dupes, these persons were still willing to say that a candidate's involvement in the Birch Society would not prejudice them against him.

An examination of the data reported in Tables 23 and 24 point up a number of factors associated with Birch support in

TABLE 23
ATTITUDES TOWARD BIRCH SOCIETY BY SELECTED
CHARACTERISTICS IN PER CENT—JANUARY, 1962
(CALIFORNIA POLL)

Characteristics	Pro	Neut	Con	DK/HH	Total	N
PARTY						
Democratic	3%	11	45	41	100%	(673)
Republican	10	21	36	33	100	(468)
RELIGION						
Protestant	6	17	39	38	100	(769)
Catholic	6	11	42	41	100	(273)
Jewish	4	6	63	27	100	(67)
REGION						
No. California	3	13	37	47	100	(499)
So. California	8	17	44	31	100	(687)
EDUCATION						
Grade School	2	15	25	58	100	(127)
High School	4	13	36	47	100	(594)
1–2 Coll./Trade	8	16	50	26	100	(230)
3+ College	11	17	55	17	100	(235)
ECON. LEVEL						
Low	5	11	36	48	100	(306)
Medium	5	17	42	36	100	(639)
High	10	14	47	29	100	(240)
SEX						
Men	7	17	42	34	100	(590)
Women	5	13	40	42	100	(595)
OCCUPATION						
Professional	6	15	53	25	100	(162)
Exec/Mgr	7	18	47	28	100	(71)
Self-empl business	4	20	39	37	100	(67)
Cler/Sales	6	13	47	34	100	(191)
Skilled	4	12	42	42	100	(203)
Unskilled & service	5	12	34	49	100	(258)
Farm	17	29	20	34	100	(35)
Ret'd, etc.	8	17	37	38	100	(174)
Non-manual	6	15	48	31	100	(492)
Manual	5	12	37	46	100	(461)
AGE						
21–29	6	15	39	40	100	(226)
30–49	6	13	47	34	100	(538)
50 and over	6	17	35	42	100	(421)
TOTAL SAMPLE	6	15	41	38	100%	(1186)

Attitudes on Birch Society

TABLE 24
CHARACTERISTICS OF BIRCH SUPPORTERS CONTRASTED
WITH BIRCH OPPONENTS IN PER CENT—JANUARY, 1962
(CALIFORNIA POLL)

Characteristics	Total Sample	Pro-Birch	Neutral	Anti-Birch	DK/HH
PARTY					
Democrat	59%	28%	45%	64%	64%
Republican	41	72	55	36	36
RELIGION					
Protestant	69%	71%	79%	66%	70%
Catholic	25	25	19	25	26
Jewish	6	5	2	9	4
REGION					
No. California	42%	22%	36%	38%	53%
So. California	58	78	64	62	47
EDUCATION					
Grade School	11%	4%	11%.	7%	16%
High School	50	34	46	43	62
1–2 Coll. or Trade	19	26	20	23	14
3+ College	20	36	23	27	8
ECON. LEVEL					
Low	20%	21%	20%	22%	33%
Medium	54	44	61	55	52
High	26	35	19	23	15
SEX					
Men	50%	57%	57%	51%	45%
Women	50	43	43	49	55
OCCUPATION					
Professional	14%	14%	15%	18%	9%
Business	12	11	15	13	10
Cler/sales	17	15	15	19	15
Skilled	17	12	15	17	19
Unskilled & service	22	20	18	18	28
Farm	3	8	6	1	5
Ret'd, etc.	15	20	17	14	15
Non-manual	43%	40%	45%	50%	34%
Manual	39	32	33	35	47
AGE					
21–29	19%	19%	19%	18%	20%
30–49	45	47	39	52	41
50 and over	36	34	42	30	39
	100%	100%	100%	100%	100%
	N (1186)	N (73)	N (176)	N (488)	N (449)

California. A supporter of the Society is more likely to be a Republican than a Democrat, to live in Southern California, to be better educated, and to be in a higher economic category. Occupational variations as such do not seem to be significantly related to attitudes toward the Birchers, with the exception of the fact that the small group of farmers in the sample seem to be the most strongly pro-Birch among the vocational categories. Differences between religious groups are small, although Catholics are somewhat less likely to back the Birch Society than are Protestants.

Since party identification appears so crucial in determining attitude toward the Birch Society, it is possible that some of the above-mentioned relationships are indirectly a consequence of political affiliation. For example, the political commitment of Protestants and Catholics varies greatly. In California, Protestants divide 50–50 in allegiance to the major parties, whereas among Catholics, Democrats outnumber Republicans 4 to 1. These results suggest that the Democratic commitment of Catholics may account for their slightly greater opposition to the Birch Society. And in fact we find that when religious groups are compared *within* party categories Catholics are slightly more likely to favor the Birch Society than are Protestants[44] (Table 25).

TABLE 25
RELATIONSHIP OF PARTY AFFILIATION AND RELIGION TO
ATTITUDE TOWARD JOHN BIRCH SOCIETY IN CALIFORNIA
IN PER CENT—JANUARY, 1962
(CALIFORNIA POLL)

Attitudes toward Birch Society

Party and Religion	Pro	Neutral	Con	Don't Know or Never Heard	Total	N
Democrats						
Protestants	2%	14	41	43	100%	(387)
Catholics	4%	8	44	44	100%	(206)
Republicans						
Protestants	10%	21	37	32	100%	(380)
Catholics	14%	21	32	33	100%	(57)

[44] The same pattern occurs in the national Gallup data.

When the effect of education on attitudes toward the Birch Society is analyzed within party groups, the data suggest little difference among Democrats according to education. If anything, better-educated Democrats are more likely to be more anti-Birch. Among Republicans, however, greater education is associated with being pro-Birch. To a considerable extent these variations would seem to be a product of socio-economic status. That is, with increasing economic level, Republicans are more disposed to support the Birch Society, while Democrats at higher-status levels are somewhat more inclined to oppose the organization than their less-privileged party brethren (Table 26).

TABLE 26

RELATIONSHIP OF PARTY AFFILIATION AND ECONOMIC LEVEL TO ATTITUDES TOWARD THE BIRCH SOCIETY IN CALIFORNIA, IN PER CENT—JANUARY, 1962

(CALIFORNIA POLL)

Party and SES	Pro	Neutral	Con	Attitudes on Birch Society Don't Know or Never Heard	Total	N
Democrats						
High	3%	12	50	35	100%	(109)
Medium	3%	11	49	37	100%	(358)
Low	3%	11	36	50	100%	(218)
Republicans						
High	18%	14	45	23	100%	(126)
Medium	8%	25	33	34	100%	(274)
Low	6%	15	32	47	100%	(68)

The data clearly reflect the strong connection between attitudes toward the Birch Society and basic party commitment—a relationship that is hardly surprising, given the tenor of the organization. Basically, the Birch Society appeals most to well-to-do Republicans, and somewhat more to the Catholics among them than to the Protestants. These findings suggest that the Society's appeal is most effective among those to whom economic conservatism and fear of Communism are crucial issues.

Evidence for this interpretation may be drawn from an analysis of attitudes toward the Birch Society as related to preferences among likely contenders for the G.O.P. Presidential nomination in 1964, and as related to opinions on the importance of the threat of internal Communism. (The first comparison is made only for Republicans.) Among Republicans who supported the Birch Society, almost three-fifths (59 per cent) favored Senator Goldwater for President in 1964 (Table 27). Conversely, while former Vice-President Nixon

TABLE 27

OPINION TOWARD THE BIRCH SOCIETY ACCORDING TO
PREFERRED REPUBLICAN PRESIDENTIAL CHOICE IN 1964
AMONG CALIFORNIA REPUBLICANS
(CALIFORNIA POLL)—JANUARY, 1962

Attitudes on Birch Society

Preferred Candidate	Pro	Neutral	Con	Don't Know or Never Heard	Total Sample
Rockefeller	4%	15%	23%	21%	19%
Nixon	25	38	38	33	35
Romney	8	11	4	7	7
Goldwater	59	22	23	18	25
Don't Know	4	14	12	21	14
	100%	100%	100%	100%	100%
N	(48)	(96)	(170)	(154)	(468)

was the leading candidate among the other categories, Republicans who opposed the Birch Society contained a larger proportion of Rockefeller backers than did any other opinion groups. Examined in terms of the attitudes of the supporters of the different candidates, the data show that 71 per cent of the Rockefeller partisans were anti-Birch, as contrasted with 56 per cent of the Nixon supporters, and 45 per cent of the Goldwater advocates. Clearly, Birchism and general political conservatism were strongly related among California Republicans in 1962.

Among followers of both parties, attitudes toward the Birchers are influenced by views on the importance of internal Communism as a threat to the nation. Three-fourths of Birch supporters see the danger of domestic Communism as great, as contrasted with slightly more than half of the neutral group and a little less than half of the anti-Birch element. Those perceiving minimal threat from internal Communism constitute 4 per cent of the pro-Birchers, 14 per cent of the neutrals, and 20 per cent of the anti-Birchers (Table 28). (The same relationship between Birch opinion and perceived threat holds when Republicans and Democrats are taken separately, although Republicans more often than Democrats perceive the threat as high.)

TABLE 28
BIRCH OPINION RELATED TO PERCEPTION OF DOMESTIC
COMMUNIST THREAT AMONG CALIFORNIANS—
JANUARY, 1962 (CALIFORNIA POLL)

Attitudes on Birch Society

Perception of Communist Threat	Pro	Neutral	Con	Don't Know or Haven't Heard	Total Sample
High	75%	53%	48%	50%	51%
Medium	21	33	32	37	33
Low	4	14	20	13	16
	100%	100%	100%	100%	100%
	N (67)	N (173)	N (471)	N (407)	N (1118)

There is also a difference between supporters and opponents of the Society who agree that the internal Communist threat is great in their opinion of the adequacy of existing agencies dealing with the problem. Approximately three-fifths of the Society's opponents who agree that domestic Communism is a major problem feel that it is not being adequately dealt with, as compared with four-fifths of the Society's supporters. Thus, those who like the Society differ sharply from those who dislike it in their evaluation of the extent of the threat and the way it is being handled. Considering both opinions together, we find that twice the proportion of the former group (60 per cent) feels that the threat is great and that it is being inadequately handled, compared to the latter (30 per cent).

Neither the national Gallup Survey nor the California Poll

included questions concerning attitudes on issues other than
those reported above. However, a questionnaire study conducted in the San Francisco Bay Area in the spring of 1962,
primarily for the purpose of studying opinions on peace issues,
included a question on the John Birch Society and other attitudes relevant to this investigation. Though designed to secure
a representative sample of the Bay Area population, the survey
suffered from defects not uncommon in surveys utilizing self-
administered questionnaires as opposed to interviews—that is,
a heavy bias in the direction of responses by the better educated.[45] Forty-seven per cent of those who answered the questionnaire had at least some college education and two-thirds
were engaged in non-manual occupations. It is impossible,
therefore, to draw any reliable conclusions from this survey
as to the social characteristics of Birch supporters in the San
Francisco region. But since the study did contain a number
of attitude items on a variety of issues, and because the social
characteristics of Birch supporters and opponents corresponded on the whole with the findings of the California Poll,
a brief report on its results seems warranted.[46]

Of particular interest in this survey were a number of questions dealing with attitudes toward minority ethnic and religious
groups. Respondents were asked, "In choosing your friends
and associates, how do you feel about the following types of
people?" Response categories were, "Would rather not deal
with," "Feel some reservations about dealing with," and "Feel
the same about them as others." It was found that those approving the Birch Society (9 per cent) tend to be more
prejudiced against Negroes and Mexicans than those who op-

[45] The questionnaires were left at the homes of those chosen in
the sample, to be filled out by the respondent and picked up the following day.

[46] The survey indicated that Bay Area Birch supporters are more
likely to be Republicans than Democrats, college-educated rather
than less schooled, and white Christians rather than members of
racial or religious minorities. Thus, of the white, Christian, college-
trained Republicans in the sample, 16 per cent reported themselves generally favorable to the Birchers. No Jews or Orientals
and only 4 per cent of the Negroes queried were pro-Birch.

posed the organization.[47] The pro-Birch group is also some-what more hostile to Orientals and Jews than the opposing element, but the differences are relatively minor. The findings hold when respondents of differing educational attainment are treated separately, indicating that, despite the greater prejudice of the less educated generally, Birch supporters tend to show more prejudice than Birch opponents.

TABLE 29

PREJUDICE TOWARD ETHNIC AND RELIGIOUS MINORITIES
ACCORDING TO OPINION ON BIRCH SOCIETY
(WHITE CHRISTIANS ONLY)[a]

| | Proportion Expressing Prejudice Among: | |
Prejudiced Toward:	Pro-Birch Group	Anti-Birch Group
Negroes	53%	37%
Mexicans	38	27
Orientals	22	17
Jews	15	11
Jehovah's Witnesses	44	40
N	(42)	(303)
Catholics[b]	7	8
N	(26)	(193)

a Data presented through the courtesy of Robert Schutz of the Northern California Lobby for Peace and Thomas Tissue, graduate assistant in sociology.
b Only responses by Protestants are presented—N=26 Pro-Birch, N=193 Anti-Birch.

Supporters of the Birch Society are less willing to grant civil liberties to Communists, atheists, and pacifists than those un-favorable to the organization; they are also less likely to feel that search warrants should be required of police entering a house, more likely to favor censorship of "crime comic books," and more likely to deny the right of public meetings to those opposing "our form of government." However, it is important to note that degree of education tends to have a much greater effect on attitude than does opinion of the Birch Society. For example, college-educated Birch *supporters* are

[47] Only white Christians were included in these comparisons, since the findings would presumably have been distorted by the in-clusion of the minorities in ratings of their own groups.

more inclined to allow Communists to speak in their community than are Birch *opponents* who have not attended college (38 per cent versus 28 per cent). Supporters of the Society
also exhibit more prejudice toward Negroes and Mexicans, although they do not register a significantly higher degree of
anti-Semitism than the population at large. In all likelihood,
more refined and comprehensive analysis of various sorts of
ethnic and religious prejudice will be necessary before definitive
conclusions may be reached regarding the relationship, or
relationships, of these phenomena to current forms of right-
wing extremism.

Thus far, I have omitted any discussion of the fact that the
Birch Society is much stronger in Southern than in Northern
California. In fact, the data from the California Poll survey
discussed here and a later one completed in May, 1962 (too
late to be analyzed and reported in detail here) indicate that
California support for the Society is largely a phenomenon
of the south. It has even less backing in Northern California
than in most other sections of the country.

The explanation for the variations between the two sections
would seem to lie largely in certain differences in their community structure. Northern California, centered around San
Francisco, is the old, established part of the State. It was the
original dominant center of population. Los Angeles and
Southern California have emerged as major population centers
only since World War I, and their really rapid mass growth
occurred after 1940. Although Northern California has continued to increase in population, its major center, San Francisco, has grown little for many decades. There are many old
families in the Bay Area who represent four and five generations of wealth, the descendants of those who made their
money in mining, commerce, or railroads in the first decades
after statehood, from 1850–80. Wealth in Los Angeles, on the
other hand, is almost exclusively *nouveaux riches,* and the
well-to-do there possess the attitudes toward politics and economics characteristic of this stratum. They are more likely to
back the rightist groups that oppose the welfare state, the income tax, and trade unions, and, lacking political and cultural

sophistication, are more prone to accept conspiracy interpretations of the strength behind liberal or welfare measures.
There is little that is stabilized or institutionalized in Southern
California. New, rapidly expanding centers of population lack
a traditional leadership structure accustomed to the responsibilities of running community institutions and supportive of
the rights of various groups to share in community decisions
and authority. Ethnic and racial tensions are high in the south,
and whereas in the north community leaders co-operate to
repress any potential conflict, in the south there is little co-
operation to ease such tensions.

Some evidence for the hypothesis that the strength of the
Birch Society in Southern California (and in Arizona, Texas,
and Florida, as well) is related to the tensions of population
growth and community integration may be found in the second (May) California Poll. This survey inquired among those
not native to the state as to when they moved to California.
When respondents are divided between those who have been
in the state more, or less, than 15 years, the data indicate that
a larger proportion of the supporters of the Society (39 per
cent) are among those who migrated to the state since World
War II than is true among opponents (29 per cent). Unfortunately, there are no available data that bear directly on the
political effects of social mobility; that is, the extent to which
the experience of a change in socio-economic position, up or
down the social hierarchy, is related to these political issues.
The California Poll data do clearly suggest, however, that
respondents whose educational and occupational attainments
are not congruent—e.g., manual workers who went to college,
or those in high-status positions with little education—are more
likely to be pro-Birch than others within their strata whose
statuses on these two stratification dimensions are roughly
similar. These findings (based unfortunately on far too few
cases of Birch supporters to be significant) are in line with
the assumption that social mobility and/or status discrepancies
predispose those involved in such experiences to accept extremist forms of politics.

The support the John Birch Society has received is seemingly somewhat different from the radical-rightist movements discussed earlier. As compared to them, it has drawn more heavily from ideological conservatives, those committed to the Republican Party, and, within the ranks of the Republicans, from among the more well-to-do and better educated.[48] Twenty-two per cent of high economic level, college-educated Republicans in the California Poll are favorable to the Birchers, as compared with 6 per cent in the sample as a whole.[49] As a group advocating economic conservatism, the Society naturally has little appeal for the economically deprived. It is

[48] Stories reported in the California press concerning internal conflicts within the Republican Party and the attitudes of wealthy Republicans toward contributing to Nixon's campaign suggest that the Party is troubled by the fact that support for the Birch Society is much greater among Party activists and wealthy contributors than among the Republican electorate. Recent evidence from analysis of national data indicates that local Republican leaders around the country tend to be considerably more conservative than the rank and file of the G.O.P. See Herbert McClosky, Paul J. Hoffman, and Rosemary O'Hara, "Issue Conflict and Consensus Among Party Leaders and Followers," *American Political Science Review,* 54 (1960), pp. 406–27; see, especially, pp. 422–24.

[49] Similar conclusions concerning differences between the support of McCarthy and of the Birch Society drawn from survey data have recently been suggested in a report of a comparative study of mail attacking Senatorial critics of the radical right (Senator Fulbright for his opposition to McCarthy and Senator Kuchel for his attacks on the Birch Society). The report states that "only 15 per cent of the McCarthyite mail could—charitably, at best—be described as reasonable in tone, substance, or literacy." However, the "Birch mail is much more moderate in tone than McCarthy mail, even though it may be as extremist in objective. It is better written and better reasoned. . . . The great bulk of the mail came from people who acknowledge membership in the Birch Society or from sympathizers. . . . Many of the writers seem genuinely concerned over the rise of Communism. . . . But many of them seem more aroused over social-welfare legislation, income taxes, and foreign aid than they are over Communism." (See Herman Edelsberg, "Birchites Make Polite Pen Pals," *The A.D.L. Bulletin,* April, 1962, pp. 7–8.)

Presumably the differences in style and tone of the letters reflected the variation in the class and educational levels of the supporters of both tendencies.

difficult to see a movement with so little popular appeal—and with so conspiratorial a view of the American political process —making headway among the general population. But the considerable progress it has made among well-to-do Republicans who can afford to support their political convictions financially may mean that the Birch Society will be able to maintain the impression of a powerful mass-supported group for some time to come.[50]

IV

Conclusions

In this preliminary report on an analysis of the social bases of the three major "radical-rightist" movements in the thirties, fifties, and sixties, I have deliberately avoided any detailed effort to interpret the data in terms of general sociological theories of political behavior or to analyze them in relation to the larger tensions in American life. This is in large part because I have already written extensively on these matters, both in the original "Radical Right" essay reprinted here, and in the book *Political Man*.[51] The data reported here have been analyzed so as to test the validity of the hypotheses presented in these earlier discussions of the sources of extremist political beliefs. In addition, these quantitative findings represent only the first step in an effort to understand the factors underlying recurrent support for "right-wing radicalism" in this country.

The popular support given to right-wing extremism must be separated into a number of components. Many of those who backed Coughlin, McCarthy, and the Birch Society may have done so in ignorance of their attacks on the democratic proc-

[50] Various journalistic accounts indicate that the Birch Society includes among its members the heads of a number of medium-size corporations, such as independent oil companies, and manufacturing concerns. Such men, as I noted in my original essay, also supported McCarthy, and they are often willing to back up their antagonism to "creeping Socialism" with heavy contributions.

[51] *Op. cit.;* see, especially, Chapters IV and V, those dealing with "Working-Class Authoritarianism" and " 'Fascism'—Left, Right, and Center," pp. 97–176.

ess as such. Conversely, of course, many who are basically intolerant of democratic pluralism and diversity have been hostile to each of these political tendencies. As I have noted elsewhere,[52] prior attachments to specific organizations or values have often led intolerant people to "contradict themselves" and oppose specific forms of intolerant politics. Thus, Southern racial bigots, committed to the Democratic Party and opposed to Catholics, may have opposed Coughlin or McCarthy, as Catholics and opponents of "their party."

Although there may be some individuals and social groups who have been attracted to all three rightist tendencies—Peter Viereck suggests the not unlikely possibility that many Coughlin followers later became McCarthy supporters—and there is some evidence that the more well-to-do, conservative supporters of McCarthy have appeared again as backers of the John Birch Society, the three "movements" do differ considerably in their predominant appeal. Coughlin was primarily successful in attracting a following among Catholics and among the economically deprived. Although he gained much rural support, his main base was among the unemployed and the poor workers. Negroes, though heavily for Roosevelt, were also quite favorable to Coughlin. While Senator McCarthy, too, was supported disproportionately by Catholics and the lower classes as contrasted with Protestants and the urban salaried middle class, the differences were less significant. As contrasted with Coughlin, McCarthy had more success among the traditional sources of Republican and conservative strength, among Protestants, and particularly among the urban and the rural self-employed. Negroes tended to oppose him. As I noted in *Political Man* and have in some part documented here, his following was more comparable to that of the classic European Fascist movements. He appealed to those who were outside the major centers of contemporary power in American life—that is, those opposed to the social and big-business elite *and* to the organized liberal and trade-union forces.

Finally, the Birch Society, with the least popular appeal of

[52] *Ibid.*, pp. 97–131.

the three, has had its primary success with the more well-to-do segments of conservative political opinion. Unlike its two predecessors on the "radical right," the Birch Society does not seem to have any distinct appeal to Catholics as such, although within the ranks of the supporters of each party, Catholics are slightly more likely to favor the Society than are Protestants. This absence of heavy Catholic support may reflect a number of factors, such as the fact that a Catholic Democrat is now in the White House and consequently the current "radical right" is engaged in denouncing the most important Irish Catholic in the country; or the lack of appeal of the Birch Society's conservative program for a Catholic population that as a group must still be counted as among the economically less privileged denominations. The Society is also the only one of the three "movements" not headed by a Catholic, and it has been vigorously denounced by many Catholic leaders and magazines. But whatever the reason, it is certain that in the early 1960s at least, Catholics can no longer be numbered as among the significant backers of rightist extremism. (Parenthetically, it may be noted that many of the groups, other than the Birch Society itself, that have taken the lead on the radical right in the 1960s are led by fundamentalist Protestants.)[53]

Although it is too early to make any definitive statement on the matter, opinion data on these movements suggest that, contrary to the suppositions of many, extreme-rightist tendencies do not seem to be systematically associated with anti-Semitic attitudes. Even Father Coughlin, though as avowedly anti-Semitic as any figure in American political history, does not seem to have been able to unite most anti-Semites behind him or, conversely, to have increased the level of anti-Semitic sentiment in the country. Feeling against Jews, though much stronger in the 1930s than it has been since, does not appear

[53] See David Danzig, "The Radical Right and the Rise of the Fundamentalist Minority," *Commentary*, 33 (1962), pp. 291–98. The John Birch Society does not seem to be particularly fundamentalist in its appeal or its mass base. See also Irwin Suall, *The American Ultras* (New York: New America, 1962), pp. 38–43.

to have been an important influence in popular political alignment. Class position, ideological values, party commitment,
and many other factors have been much more powerful determinants of how people lined up politically. Thus, Coughlin
supporters, who were not anti-Semitic, could be favorably disposed toward the priest because they liked his "leftist" economic program.

As I noted in my original essay, McCarthy's relationship
with Jews was extremely friendly. In his original essay for this
collection, Peter Viereck noted that at one McCarthy mass
meeting, "a rabbi accused the opposition to Roy Cohn of anti-
Semitic intolerance. Next Cohn's was called 'the American
Dreyfus Case' by a representative of a student McCarthyite
organization, Students for America." Viereck went on to suggest a new phenomenon of "transtolerance," a concept that
I think should receive more attention than it has:

> Transtolerance is ready to give all minorities their
> glorious democratic freedom provided they accept Mc-
> Carthyism or some other mob conformism of Right or
> Left. . . . "Right" and "Left" are mere fluctuating pre-
> texts, mere fluid surfaces for the deeper anti-individual-
> ism (anti-aristocracy) of the mass man. . . .
>
> Transtolerance is also a sublimated Jim Crow: against
> "wrong" thinkers, not "wrong" races. . . . It is the Irish-
> man's version of Mick-baiting and a strictly kosher anti-
> Semitism. It very sincerely champions against anti-Semites
> "that American Dreyfus, Roy Cohn"; simultaneously it
> glows with the same mob emotions that in all previous or
> comparable movements have been anti-Semitic.

If I understand Mr. Viereck correctly, he is saying that the
object of intolerance in America has never been as important
as the style, the emotion, the antagonism and envy toward
some specified other who is seen as wealthier, more powerful,
or particularly, as a corrupter of basic values. The Jew, like
the Wall Street banker, has been a symbol on which the intolerant could hang their need to hate what is different, or what
is powerful, more wealthy, or better educated. Basically there

is some undefined segment of the population that responds to the need to hate, not to the specific target. In the American context, anti-Semitism has not been a particularly stable sentiment. European anti-Semitism has had its roots in religious antagonism to the Jew, which was later associated with social conflicts stemming from the special economic position of the Jews in the middleman and money-lending sectors of the economy. Religious and cultural anti-Semitism, however, have never played important roles in the United States. The cultural values have approved of religious pluralism almost since the beginning of the Republic. And while anti-Semitic feelings and stereotypes have existed, it is doubtful that they have ever been as salient for a large part of the population as they have been in most of the European Continent. Hence, it might be argued that a right-wing movement that found other sources of hate and other conspiracies, and that also defined the Jews as among their supporters and leaders, could actually serve to lower the state of anti-Semitism in the country.[54] It is interesting to note that a recent study of the British Fascist movement led by Mosely indicates that as soon as he became openly anti-Semitic, he lost almost all of the significant sources of upper-class support he had obtained when he first started. Apparently, many prominent British conservatives were willing to

[54] A somewhat related set of ideas on the psychological and personality level is presented in Milton Rokeach, *The Open and Closed Mind* (New York: Basic Books, 1960), especially pp. 132–68. As Rokeach states his hypothesis, "The basic principle governing the way in which we organize the world of people is not in terms of abstract ethnic or racial categories as such but in terms of how congruent or incongruent others' belief systems are to our own. The more significance we attach to another's agreement or disagreement with us as grounds for reacting to him, the more the intolerance [or tolerance]. . . . In short, then, we hypothesize that *insofar as psychological processes are involved,* belief is more important than ethnic or racial membership as a determinant of social discrimination. Our theory leads us to propose that what appears at first glance to be discriminations among men on the basis of race or ethnic group may turn out upon closer analysis to be discriminations on the basis of belief congruence over specific issues." Pp. 134–35 (emphasis in original).

support Fascism in the early 1930s but balked at anti-Semitism.[55]

Anti-elitism oriented toward groups that cannot be regarded as oppressed minorities or victims of bigotry, or anti-Communism directed against the agents or dupes of an evil foreign power, can serve as much more palatable outlets for those who require a scapegoat than "un-American" attacks on minorities. To attack Communists in high places, even within the White House or the top circles of the Republican Party, may be nonsense, may be stupid or clever politics, but it cannot be driven beyond the pale of Americanism as racial or religious bigotry.

The current crop of radical rightists seems to understand this difference between religious prejudice, anti-elitism, and anti-Communism. Most of them consciously and explicitly abstain from expressing anti-Jewish prejudice or other traditional forms of bigotry. If they attack a religious group, it is the National Council of Churches and its relatively liberal and high-status Protestant affiliates. To criticize such groups does not lay one open to the charge of prejudice. Robert Welch, the head of the John Birch Society, has followed very clearly in the footsteps of Senator McCarthy in seeking to limit his followers to attacks on Communists and sections of the elite; for Welch, it is the political "power elite," the heads of the Democratic and Republican Parties. He has devoted much of one issue of his *Bulletin,* and parts of others, to bolstering the image of the Birch Society as including many Jews and being opposed to anti-Semitism.

Evidence that Welch's efforts actually coincide with the behavior of his followers may be found in the analysis of mail to senatorial critics of McCarthy and of the Birch Society cited earlier. This study, whose findings coincide with survey data, reports that:

> . . . only a small fraction of the McCarthy mail was anti-Semitic, but the absence of anti-Semitism is even

[55] Colin Cross, *The Fascists in Britain* (London: Barrie and Rockliff, 1961).

more striking in the Birchite mail. Only five pieces [out of 600] revealed anti-Semitic attitudes. . . .

This is, of course, a much lower quotient of anti-Semitism than is to be found in the general population—and particularly among ultra-nationalists and super-patriots. It suggests that the Birch program has the effect —at least for the time being—of discouraging, sublimating, or diverting open anti-Semitism.[56]

All this does not mean, of course, that right-wing anti-Semitism may not arise in the 1960s. There is much journalistic evidence that anti-Semites have tried to attach themselves to the Birch Society. The fundamentalist Protestants do exhibit more religious anti-Semitism than any other segment of American Christendom, and a number of right-wing fundamentalist groups have arisen.[57] But, on the other hand, the dominant leader of the sensible wing of right-wing conservatism, Barry Goldwater, by descent, is half-Jewish, and is the scion on his father's side of a fourth-generation American family of German-Jewish origin, a fact that he emphasizes rather than conceals. Although Goldwater is much too moderate for the Birch Society or other segments of the radical right, he is still the leader of the one major conservative tendency the Birchers see as appropriate to the American tradition and properly anti-Communist.[58] Hence, it is possible that the phenomenon

[56] Edelsberg, *op. cit.*, p. 7.

[57] For a description of one of the most important, see Harold H. Martin, "Doomsday Merchant of the Far, Far Right [Billy Hargis]," *Saturday Evening Post*, 235 (April 28, 1962), pp. 19–24. Hargis, too, tells his followers, "We cannot tolerate anti-Semitic statements, anti-Negro statements. . . ." (p. 22). However, it should be noted that in the past "he has acknowledged he received inspiration from the late Reverend Gerald Winrod, a notorious anti-Semite. In addition, Hargis promoted the *American Mercury* at a time when it was blatantly anti-Semitic." (Arnold Forster, "Clamor from the Far Right," *The A.D.L. Bulletin* [November, 1961], pp. 2, 6.)

[58] The Young Americans for Freedom, which has broader right-wing and conservative support than any other organization, has Jews prominent in its leadership, while the Committee of One Million, established to support Nationalist China, is headed by a Jew.

of "transtolerance" will continue as part of the radical right in the 1960s.

Political intolerance has always been an endemic part of the American political process. From the 1790s to the 1960s, various groups have been attacked as "traitors," "agents of foreign powers," "un-American," and the like. It seems evident that at all times many Americans have been in favor of denying basic civil liberties to beliefs that they find abhorrent. Intolerant movements, while often powerful, have never been able seriously to endanger the normal processes of American democracy. The involved structure of the constitutional system, the division of powers, the juridical protections, the complex and diverse sources of opinion and interest differences, and ultimately the good sense of the large majority have frustrated them. As I wrote in my original essay, it is relatively easy to build a new extremist movement in this country; it is difficult if not impossible to build a party.[59] But if such movements cannot come to power, they can damage the democratic process for short periods of time, and they can and have injured innocent people. Hopefully, a more thorough knowledge of the elements in society responsible for their persistence should contribute to more effective action in restraining them.

[59] The reasons why a new or third party has never been able to succeed in this country are discussed in S. M. Lipset, "Party Systems and the Representation of Social Groups," *European Journal of Sociology*, 1 (1960), pp. 50–85.

Afterword (2001)

FROM CLASS TO CULTURE

Daniel Bell

I appreciate David Plotke's thoughtful and extensive review of the arguments put forth in *The Radical Right*. From a sociological point of view, the most important contribution of the volume, as he points out, is the concept of "status politics" advanced by Richard Hofstadter, S. M. Lipset, and myself.

American history and the analysis of politics was dominated in the first half of the twentieth century by the "progressive historians," in particular Charles A. Beard, who, though not Marxist (Beard was later influenced by Karl Mannheim), had advanced an "economic" interpretation of American history, politics, and literature. In Beard's highly influential volume, the Constitution was less the story of liberty, than a document reflecting the different class interests of merchants and farmers. Later, the populist movement of Tom Watson of Georgia, with the support of William Jennings Bryan, was thought of as movements of dispossessed or threatened farmers reacting against the railroads and money interests, views which were given graphic literary representation in the novels of Frank Norris such as *The Pit* and *The Octopus*. As Hofstadter pointed out, the views of these historians were shaped by the disappearance of the frontier, the great tides of the new immigration, and the fierce labor struggles of the 1890s.[1]

Similar views were held by the "fathers" of American sociology—Lester F. Ward, Albion Small, William Graham

Sumner, and Edward Allsworth Ross. Their views were influenced only indirectly by Marx, but more so by the Austrian sociologist Ludwig Gumplowicz (a sociologist almost completely forgotten today, except by Irving Louis Horowitz)[2]. In his book *Rassenkampf* (1893), Gumplowicz saw society as shaped primarily as a set of race and class conflicts. In the United States, the American sociologists saw these conflicts as derived from the new industrial order, the new immigrants and the sharp labor struggles in the Western mining camps. "The pioneer sociologists," as Charles H. Page has written, "living through those tumultuous years, naturally centered a large share of their attention on the problems of class conflicts." Ward and Ross were part of the intellectual fringe of the populist movement. Sumner, a conservative, but also a determinist, ridiculed socialist doctrine as contrary to evolutionary development, whose first law, he said, "which cannot be abrogated by man," is the survival of the fittest.[3]

This is not to say, of course, that the economic situations and the economic forces at work were not real. But neither did those historians and sociologists write or think of status, and its correlates, culture and ideology, in understanding social attitudes and movements. They did not think of clusters of ideas as sources of social and political cohesion, let alone the autonomy of ideas, or the role of values as prompting individuals to act in the defense of those values. Yet the alarms of the New England Federalist "aristocracy" over their political defeats in the nineteenth century, or the later disdain by Henry Adams and his friends for the plutocracy that flaunted its wealth and power in the gilded age, gain meaning largely in respect to an erosion of status. And the rhetoric of conspiracy and the denunciation of international bankers and Jews expressed by the populists are signifiers less of specific economic realities, than of the deeply rooted and historically widespread fears of dim, inchoate forces that could not be understood (such as the workings of international markets) and to which one responded by demonization, rather than by analysis.

The modern political movement that demonstrates the role

of status politics was the Temperance movement that flourished at the turn of the twentieth century—the Women's Christian Temperance movement and the Anti-Saloon League. By the time of World War I, they had pulled off the remarkable feat of having two-thirds of the States pass a constitutional amendment, the Eighteenth, which created national Prohibition.

Temperance was a movement of moral reform. Drink and drunkenness were forces that shattered the lives of the poor, and the temperance movements sympathetic to their plight sought for other reforms, such as factory reform as well. The Temperance ideals were self-control and industriousness. Sobriety meant virtue and was the basis of self-esteem. In the doctrine of abstinence, the poor and the immigrant would achieve self-respect and the respect of others.

But as Joseph Gusfield writes in his book *Symbolic Crusade*, Temperance was also the exemplar of status politics whereby a cultural group—the small-town and rural Protestant communities, which made up the basis of the movement—could "act to preserve, defend or enhance the dominance and prestige of its own style of living" at a time when that was being threatened by the rising urban and industrial forces in society. In his book, Gusfield distinguished between *class politics* and *status politics*, the two, though analytically separate, comprised the dimensions of symbolic action and social structure. Class politics derived from a common situation in the economic order, sharing common interests. Status politics— which Gusfield derived from the first edition of *The Radical Right*—is based on the evaluation and respect a social group is accorded, or accords to others.[4]

The concept of status politics may be seen, in retrospect, as the "fusion" of two themes of Max Weber and Friedrich Nietzsche. For Weber, a status group is a *communal* group, defined by emotional or traditional ties, such as an ethnic group or religious groups who share common ways of life, and are marked off from other groups by culture and beliefs, as against economically-related groups whose exchange or production relations are defined by the *market*. The status groups are what Weber called *stände*.[5] Such different groups, be they status groups or economically-defined groups, may and do co-exist or even overlap at any point in time. The group with which an individual defines himself often depends upon the *salience* of issues or the kinds of conflicts in the society.

From Nietzsche comes the notion of *ressentiment*, a French term that Nietzsche adopted as there was no exact German equivalent. For Nietzsche, *ressentiment* was a manifestation of repressed envy, which often became expressed as moral indignation. Max Scheler developed the term to argue that bourgeois morality, its crabbed behavior and unctuousness, was a product of *ressentiment* in reaction to the codes of honor of the nobility. In the United States, one could say that the status discontents of small-town Protestant *moralizing* (and moralizing is distinct from morality), was the resentment (and fear) of the freer life-styles of the cosmopolitan urban classes.[6]

Professor Plotke points out that the term "status politics," as used in *The Radical Right*, is somewhat ambiguous; and this is true. The reason, on reflection, arises from the effort to relate a particular set of beliefs to a particular social group in a particular social location. This mode of analysis derives from the "sociology of knowledge," of the late Karl Mannheim. In the early 1920s, Mannheim began a *Habilitationschrift* (a work which qualifies an individual for a university teaching position) on conservative thought in the early nineteenth century. In that essay, published in an abridged form in German in 1927, (and only posthumously in English in 1953) Mannheim sought to show how the old entrenched classes, in particular the Prussian Junkers, sought to combat a utilitarian rationalism which, as a corrosive intellectual force, was undermining the foundations of the old society. The Junkers did so by embracing a form of Romanticism which gave an emotional aura to the feudal past; and as such became established as the German mind.

As Mannheim wrote:

Romanticism took on a feudalistic character; the feudalistic conservatism of the nobility assumed a romantic colouring. From this combination arose the peculiar features which to the present day characterize the 'German' mind . . . . In order to understand this peculiar combination it is necessary to look more closely at the social character of the strata which took part in this ideological struggle . . . . The romantic movement, considered as an *ideological* force, began as a reaction against the Enlightenment. Its *social* basis seems to have been . . . in social strata which stood apart from the general current towards modern capitalism.[7]

The forebear of this analysis is, of course, Marx, with his argument about the bounded class character of social thought. For Marx, classes were rooted in the economic relations of society, even though individuals might not often be aware that their beliefs did not accord with their class position. This was an argument that Marx first laid out in *The German Ideology.* Later Marxists used the phrase "false consciousness" to explain this discordance—even though Marx and Engels never used that term in their published writings. The phrase did occur in a letter from Engels to Marx's epigone, Franz Mehring, in explaining his monograph on Ludwig Feuerbach, and Mehring's use became the source of the later, and widely adopted, usage of the term.[8]

The difficulty with this one-to-one set of imputed relationships is that in a modern society, an individual wears many different hats: age, sex, occupation, religion, language group, class, and color. As Georg Simmel has observed, "The number of different social groups in which the individual participates, is one of the earmarks of culture." One of the definitions of society, then, in Simmel's phrase, would be "the web of group affiliations."[9]

Thus, in any society, every individual has multiple roles, functions, positions, and interests. Moreover, many of these are "cross-cutting." In the Netherlands, a worker can belong to a religious party, the choice depending on his or her sense of identity. In Israel, an individual may be an orthodox Jew, also a Sephardic (of Middle Eastern or Spanish origin), as against an Ashkenazi (or East European background), and a worker. Yet which political tie he chooses may depend on family, friends, or propinquity of neighbors as primary influences. In the United States, an African-American can choose race or class to express a primary identity. In India, an individual can be a Bengali, a Hindu, and a member of a caste, depending on the context; and contexts are not necessarily contradictory to one another.

Since every individual has multiple identities and interests, and multiple group affiliations, the sociological question is which one of these becomes *salient* at particular times. Class conflict may become salient when employers seek to cut wages and workers have to bear the brunt of economic competition. Yet when the government creates privileges and advantage through affirmative action, then gender, race, or language group may become salient. In the United States, for example, the term "Hispanic" largely became relevant when the government included that term as a category for affirmative action.[10]

In Europe, class has been a more salient identity over the past hundred and fifty years because class was not only an economic, but a cultural and social location. Germany before World War I was an enclaved society. A German worker was brought up in a socialist creche, participated in a socialist hiking club or theatrical group, and these were distinct from middle-class and upper-class culture. In the 1920s, Germany saw a large-scale expansion of the salaried workers—"the *neue mittelstand*,"—or the new middle class. For Marxists, these were workers, but not so in their self-conception. During the depression of the 1930s, many such new middle-class lost their jobs (a situation dramatized in the famous novel of Hans Fallada, *Little Man, What Now*). Instead of being radicalized, however, they felt a loss of status and a fear of proletarianization, a fact that led many into the support of the Nazi party. In England, class distinction has been marked, and is quickly evident, by accent; though the society has been remarkably open for talented grammar-school lads to rise into the upper reaches of society, particularly in academe. But English work-

ers, by and large, felt they belonged to the Labour Party because it was a cultural relation as much as a class affiliation.
In the United States, class has not been, by and large, a social
and cultural location. Ethnicity and religion have often been
more important for Irish, Jewish, Polish and Slavic workers.
Education has been available for all, especially the children,
and almost all shared in the popular and Hollywood culture.
There has been no American "working-class culture."[11]

What makes traditional social location more problematic
today is the character of post-industrial society. In the United
States, of a work force of 126 million, almost 30 percent (37.6
million persons) are technicians or in sales and administrative
capacities—the two categories making a total of 60 percent
of the work force. Against this, little more than 10 percent
(13.5 million persons) are skilled workers, and about 15 percent (31 million) are operators and laborers—thus, only 25
percent of the labor force would be classed as working-class.
There is, thus, a new "class structure" of the United States today.[12]

If "social location" in the historical usage has become more
problematic, what can one say of ideas or "styles of thought"
or ideologies? There are values such as "liberty" or "equality" (difficult as they may be to define), which strike individuals as just and retain a permanent appeal as ideals to be realized that transcend history or class. There are moral beliefs,
such as "the right to life" or "the freedom to choose," that derive from religious creeds or from a philosophical liberalism,
yet these cut across different needs. If one is a believer in the
economic freedom of individuals, does this carry over into the
"market freedom" of women for abortion? Clearly these are
different contexts and one does not ask for "logical consistency" as the basis for belief.

What this brief review demonstrates is that the standard
mode of sociological analysis, in which one seeks to relate a
social base or social location to a particular set of beliefs becomes more and more difficult to sustain in a modern complex society today. There is, first, the growing role of the "autonomy of ideas," a problem with which Marx, as I sought to

show in the essay I referred to in Footnote 8, found it difficult to grapple with and which, in fact, he sought to deny.
There is, increasingly, what I once referred to as "discretion-
ary social behavior." In this regard, behavior is not "determined" by, say, religion or class position, but is much more
open, as choice or style by individuals. Who will take drugs,
and of what kind; who pursues a taste for pornography; who
becomes a pedophile or a child abuser; who will divorce and
who will not; who will oppose abortion or who will not, are
not directly related to class, or status positions. There are "clusters" of such groups and, in some instances, such as abortion,
these clusters would be related more directly to religion, than
to any other category. But even on such a relatively "clear-
cut" issue as abortion, different education or cultural beliefs
do create cross-cutting clusters.

In the last forty years, I believe, *culture* and divisions based
on cultural beliefs have become the major source of divergence
and disagreements in society. It is not that status politics, as a
mode of analysis, is wrong. That depends, as I have sought
to show, on the *salience* of issues, and how individuals choose
among their multiple identities, based upon the relative advantages to be gained by competing choices. But on looking at
society from a larger perspective, it is the nature of the culture—and the sets of ideas and beliefs—which becomes central for the analysis of political divisions and social behavior.
And it is to the discussion of culture and ideas that I now wish
to turn.

If we deal with politics and underlying ideas, the starting
point for any discussion of the political "right" is the nature
of *conservatism*. But what is conservatism? Conservatives believe in tradition, but not necessarily in traditionalism. Traditionalism, as Max Weber used the term, means clinging to old
ways of life and giving respect, if not authority, to the elders.
But capitalism, as a social system, tears up the past and is committed to change; its life-blood is innovation. What, then, does
one conserve? And what change does one accept? Can one
have change in the economy but not in morals? For the Catho-

lic Church, taking interest was usury, and imm

talism is dependent necessarily on the interest

crum of capital allocation, as well as a reward

And can one have abstinence and sobriety in work, and hedonism and profligacy in consumption; or is that a necessary
cultural contradiction of capitalism?

It was the protean French writer, the Vicomte de Chateaubriand, who gave the word conservatism its first modern meaning when he called the periodical he issued in 1818–1820 to
propagate the ideas of the Restoration, after the second exile
of Napoleon, *Le Conservateur*. The term entered into general
use in Germany in the early 1830s, and was adopted in England a few years later. Conservatism for Chateaubriand was
intertwined with romanticism, and the organic view of society. In philosophy and literature, Chateaubriand's romanticism
polemicized against reason, espoused mystery and fantasy and
spiritual longing. Yet such is the protean ambiguity of the
word that romanticism is also associated with Rousseau and
Shelley, with sentiment and the unique individual, with a thirst
for liberation and self-expression.

Chateaubriand wrote a book denouncing all revolutions,
and espoused religion (the Catholic faith) as providing the only
answer for the desire for the absolute, which all sentient persons expressed. In politics, continental conservatism set itself
up against liberalism and individualism (which Tocqueville
later wrote of as the "odious individualism") which was held
responsible for the social dislocations of society. Conservatism condemned the contractual theory of society and placed
the community as prior to the individual.

Yet, against Bonald and de Maistre, who wanted to restore
the hierarchical privileges and positions of the *ancien regime*,
conservatives such as Guizot argued that with the march of
civilization, particularly the expansion of commercial life as
the end-product of stages of history, this was no longer possible, and that an effective social bond could only be re-cre-
ated by including all men of property in a new parliamentary
government.[13] Chateaubriand defended the concept of legitimacy (which had first been proposed by Talleyrand at the Con-

gress of Vienna in 1814), but also political liberties (such as had been held by the old communes of France), and the freedom of the press as a matter of public criticism.

Conservatism in England, as a political doctrine, emerged after the Reform Bill of 1832, which enfranchised almost 500,000 middle-class voters (men of property) but which almost destroyed the older Tories, the faction of country gentry that had supported the ecclesiastical authority of the Church of England and the royal prerogatives of the Crown. The term conservative was first used by George Canning, a political disciple of the younger Pitt, and a leader of the anti-Jacobins in England; it was popularized by John Wilson Croker, an editor of Boswell's Life of Johnson, in the *Quarterly Review* of 1830, in an effort to provide a new face for the Tory remnants. But the Conservative Party foundered for years, split by the question of supporting reform, until refashioned by Benjamin Disraeli, who stole a march on the Whigs and Liberals by sponsoring a new political reform act, in 1870, enfranchising the working class.

The philosophical doctrine of conservatism, and the source of its lasting influence, derived from the powerful writings of Edmund Burke, in the latter years of the eighteenth century. Burke had been a member of the Literary Club, whose leading figure was Samuel Johnson, the great raconteur, wit, and a writer of Tory pamphlets. Johnson's conservatism was based on a profound skepticism as to the perfectibility of human nature, and for Johnson, a strict social order was necessary to save man from himself.

Burke, as a liberal, had argued for the value of political parties, rather than family connections and patronage, as the source of parliamentary seats, because he believed that major interests should be represented in the parliament. Yet he attacked the political rationalism and religious skepticism of Bolingbroke, arguing for the wisdom of institutions as the embodiment of historical experience.

But it was the French Revolution that became the fulcrum of political division then, and down to this day. Not only did the French Revolution establish the enduring nomenclature of left and right as political tag lines, but it was its glow for romantics such as the young Wordsworth and the fledgling Shelley, whose poetry proclaimed the bliss and the dawning of a new age.

It was Burke, more than any other writer, who, in his *Reflections* (1827) provided the *vade mecum* for conservatives. His crucial argument was the attack on untrammelled rationalism in setting the course of history as irreversible change. The corollary was the defense of institutions and the continuity of history as providing the experience and wisdom to judge the claims of change. For Burke the emphasis was on the concrete, as against abstract thought. Anticipating Tocqueville, he attacked the "men of letters" who, allied with the "moneyed interest," were undermining religion and authority. ("Writers, especially when they act in a body and with one direction, have great influence on the public mind . . . . A spirit of cabal, intrigue and proselytism pervaded their thoughts, words, and actions . . . . They carefully occupied all the avenues to optimism.") And, praising England, he declares that religion is the basis of civil society. ("We know, and it is our pride to know, we feel inwardly, that religion is the basis of civil society, and the source of all good, and of all comfort.")[14]

A different, more elegant banner of conservatism was unfolded by T. S. Eliot, when he defined himself in 1928 as a "classicist in literature, a royalist in politics, and Anglo-Catholic in religion."[15] To this extent, Eliot was echoing a description of the French writer Charles Maurras, who in 1913 was described as the embodiment of three traditions, "classique, catholique, monarchique." Maurras was an influence on Eliot that lasted for his lifetime, for Maurras, as Eliot said, wrote the most beautiful French prose of any writer he knew.

Maurras, a man of deeply authoritarian temper, was anti-republican and anti-Rousseau, whose romanticism he saw as the source of the corruption of Western culture. But the thought and activities of Maurras summed up so many of the contradictions of conservative thought. Maurras was anti-democratic and rabidly anti-Semitic, whose organization, the Action Française, encouraged student riots and the disruption of classrooms. In 1928, the Vatican condemned the Action Française, and after the war Maurras was incarcerated for his association with the Vichy regime. Eliot did not share Maurras's political views, for they represented a form of populism of which he entirely disapproved, yet he derived much of his distaste for liberalism and modernity from Maurras. As Eliot's biographer, Peter Ackroyd, has stated: Throughout his life, Eliot would continue to support Maurras, and his philosophy was to enter the fabric of Eliot's own concerns.[16]

Given the rich and powerful history of conservative thought in Europe—in many times and places a dominant ideology— is it surprising that there was not a similar set of conservative doctrines in the United States? Not so. The reason is that the United States began in rebellion and revolution, and the foundational themes of the country, as enunciated by Jefferson, were equality and natural universal rights—and even an approval of revolution when necessary to nourish the tree of liberty.

There was Jonathan Edwards, the Puritan president of Princeton (the "highbrow" in the famous distinction of Van Wyck Brooks, against the prodigal Benjamin Franklin, as "lowbrow"), who believed in the depravity of man, which was inevitable because the identity of consciousness made all men one with Adam, yet also in the existence of a privileged elect. The doctrine of original sin, in its strict Calvinist form, could hold small colonies together, but not the larger society. John Adams was conservative, a Federal aristocrat, who, having read Davila on revolution, was aware of its excesses, but his voice had no timbre to stand up against the rhetorical flourishes of Jefferson. Adams' great-grandson, Henry Adams, could chastise "the degradation of the democratic dogma," scorn the grossness of the new plutocracy, and express a disdainful anti-Semitism. And while hailing the wonders of the new technology of the dynamo, this was joined in his mind with the mysteries of Mont Saint-Michel and Chartres. This was a combination of passions that could appeal to intellectuals who despised bourgeois morality, but had little possibility of becoming a popular conservative doctrine. And there were the "Southern agrarians," the movement beginning in the

1920s and '30s, Donald Davidson, Allen Tate, and John Crowe Ransom, who, from George Fitzhugh, denounced the "wage-slavery" of the industrial North and defended the communal life of the ante-bellum South.

This was a romantic image that had its sources in the doctrines of John C. Calhoun and the doctrines of nullification and even secession. But how could this stand against Abraham Lincoln, the iconic founder of the Republican Party, if a national conservative doctrine was to be formulated?

In the opening page of his influential *The Liberal Imagination*, fifty years ago, Lionel Trilling, in a soon to be famous passage, remarked:

> In the United States at this time liberalism is not only the dominant but even the sole intellectual tradition. For it is the plain fact that nowadays there are no conservative or reactionary ideas in general circulation. This does not mean, of course, that there is no impulse to conservatism or to reaction. Such impulses are certainly very strong, perhaps even stronger than most of us know. But the conservative impulse and the reactionary impulse do not, with some isolated and some ecclesiastical exceptions, express themselves in ideas, but only in action or in some irritable mental gestures which seek to resemble ideas.

Trilling did not say this in any triumphal mood. In fact, he went on to say (and this is less often noted by writers who have used the quotation to mock Trilling) that "it is not conducive to the real strength of liberalism that it should occupy the liberal field alone" And he invoked John Stuart Mill, who, though at odds with Samuel Taylor Coleridge, urged all liberals to become acquainted with that powerful intellectual mind.[17]

Curiously, Trilling did not mention Irving Babbitt, who had been T. S. Eliot's mentor at Harvard (and whom Eliot always addressed as "Dear Master"), and Paul Elmer More. Babbitt had argued that "acting out" or expressiveness in the arts (as in life) was destructive of society, saying that Rousseau and romanticism (before Maurras) were the wellsprings of this decadence. Babbitt and More proposed a New Humanism based on moderation and restraint, and a return to the classical norms.[18] Nor did Trilling mention the conservative "new critics"—John Crowe Random or Cleanth Brooks or Yvor Winters—and the plea for a return to religion. The reason, perhaps, is that this would have involved Trilling in a confrontation with the role of religion as the foundation for moral criticism, and this was a course that Trilling may have feared to follow. Yet this course—the path to religion—is the one that was to be the intellectual turn in the past thirty-five years.

In the half-century since Trilling's observation that "there are no conservative or reactionary ideas in general circulation," what an extraordinary change has taken place. A book on "Conservative Intellectuals in the Reagan Era," lists William F. Buckley, Jr., George Will, Irving Kristol, Hilton Kramer, Jeane Kirkpatrick, Robert Nisbet, R. Emmett Tyrell, Jr., and Michael Novak. Given the number of periodicals they edit, the numerous syndicated newspaper columns they write, and the plethora of television programs on which they appear, this becomes an impressive roster of "public intellectuals." Surely there is no comparable list of liberal or left "public intellectuals" on the scene, other than the burgeoning group of Black intellectuals who have come to the fore in the 1990s.[19]

Buckley, who received national attention in 1951 for his book *God and Man at Yale*, launched the *National Review* in 1955 with the help of a core of tough-minded anti-Communist (and largely ex-radical) writers such as James Burnham, Frank Meyer, Whittaker Chambers, and Willmore Kendall, under the initial philosophical aegis of Russell Kirk, the political philosopher, who had launched the interest in Edmund Burke in the U.S. Though focussing strongly on the communist threat, the *National Review*, at its beginning, was opposed to the civil-rights movement and sided with the white South. Were white Southerners justified in resisting civil-rights laws? "The shocking answer is Yes," the editors wrote in 1957, "the white community is so entitled because, for the time being, it is the advanced race."[20] But not so paradoxically, perhaps, in the 1968 school disputes in New York, Buckley argued that the white community should yield to the Blacks control of the largely Black schools, even suspending meritocratic standards, on the ground that local control and policies enhanced a distinct group's cohesiveness.

In the 1960s and 1970s, the lively style of the *National Review* attracted a group of young writers such as Joan Didion, Gary Wills, and John Leonard (later the editor of the *New York Times Book Review*), who later moved to the left—one of the few such instances in American intellectual "discourse" of such a move from right to left, rather than vice-versa. But such is the quixotic nature of the *National Review*.

Irving Kristol, the co-founder of *The Public Interest*, was the creator of neo-conservatism, a movement that gave a large intellectual panache, and public attention, to conservatism. Neo-conservatism has also been identified with Norman Podhoretz, the editor of *Commentary*; and Jeane Kirkpatrick, who became the U.S. ambassador to the United Nations in the Reagan administration.[21]

Though Edmund Burke was the model for Buckley and to some extent of the Old Right, Kristol espoused the ideas of Michael Oakeshott and his strictures on rationalism in politics, and Leo Strauss, the émigré political philosopher who taught for many years at the University of Chicago, and whose disciples included Allan Bloom, Harry V. Jaffa, Walter Berns, Thomas Pangle, and Harvey Mansfield, Jr.

But it is not only the large number of public intellectuals that gave conservatism its firepower, but the large institutional support for hundreds of resident fellows and think tanks, as well as magazines and books, that has made conservatism such a powerful factor on the political scene. This would include the American Enterprise Institute, the Heritage Foundation, the Cato Institute, the Hudson Institute, the Manhattan Institute, as well as grant-giving foundations such as the Olin Foundation, the Bradley Foundation, Smith Richardson, Earhart, and the Carthage Foundation, and the support of such periodicals as *The Weekly Standard,* edited by William Kristol and financed by Rupert Murdoch; *The American Spectator;* the Manhattan *City Journal,* as well as the subvention of books by Charles Murray, Marvin Olasky, Stephan and Abigail Thernstrom, Tamar Jacoby, Dinesh D'Souza, William Bennett, and Francis Fukuyama. The Bradley Foundation, for example, compiled a list of 400 books it had supported in the past fourteen years.

And yet, with all of that, what is most striking is that no coherent conservative philosophy has emerged from all these diverse efforts. What has been true, in fact, have been the many contradictory currents below the large public surface of the conservative presence.

The crux of the problem is the nature of individualism. Individualism has been the most distinctive ethos, if not at one level, of the triumphalist banner of American life. Yet for George Will, one of the most deeply thoughtful of the Reagan intellectuals, conservatism, which he derives from traditionalism, is rooted in the collectivity of the nation and, following Irving Babbitt, he sees individualism as the expression of the unrestrained self that Babbit feared. If conservatism is defined as a community of shared values, as against "an anarchy of self-interestedness" George Will (as David Hoeveler writes) "wanted to extend a protective paternalism to all helpless members of society."

In England, Harold Macmillan, the last great Tory, once described Toryism as paternalistic socialism. But Mrs. Thatcher's "revolution" in English conservative politics was the espousal of laissez-faire in economics, the view she identified with Milton Friedman. For Mrs. Thatcher (like Jeremy Bentham, the great philosophical radical) there was no such entity as "the community," (what Bentham called a "fiction"), but only individuals. Yet Milton Friedman, like the Chicago law professor Richard A. Epstein, and publicist William Safire, is also a libertarian who wants to minimize the role of government not only in economics, but in other areas of life as well, and consistently has argued against the enforcement of some drug laws. It was this argument that led William F.

Buckley to chastise Milton Friedman for his tendency to make laissez-faire a "dogmatic theology."[22]

Most conservatives take as axiomatic the views of Adam Smith on the free market. But Smith, like all other members of the Scottish Enlightenment, believed in a four-stage theory of social development, based on the modes of subsistence—hunting, pastorage, agriculture, and commerce; and to these corresponded different sets of ideas and institutions relating to law, property, and government. In that view, society progressed over time through these consecutive stages. But how many conservatives, with their dour views of human nature, or a belief in the superior views of classical antiquity, would accept the ideas of progress of the Scottish Enlightenment, and the superiority of commerce?

Russell Kirk, the totem of the old conservative right, expresses a distaste for the materialism and vulgarity of bourgeois life, carrying this over, even, to capitalism itself. Kirk's intellectual biography begins with his disgust for what he called the "assembly-line civilization" that Henry Ford was creating in the Michigan of Kirk's youth, and decries the barren spiritual landscape of modern America and the "neat tedium of American middle-class life," revolving as it does around paltry amusements.

Irving Kristol, a believer in the free market in the economic sphere, calls for moral tutelage in cultural life, logically carrying out the case for censorship and the banning of books that are obscene or pornographic. The difficulty, of course, is where does one draw the line. Kristol does so with respect to the *intention* of a work: to degrade a person is to act obscenely. Thus, he says there is no continuum between Fielding's *Tom Jones* and the Marquis de Sade's *Justine*. But evaluations change over time—apart from Simone de Beauvoir's championing of de Sade as an exemplar of freedom. Consider: James Joyce's *Ulysses* (which was barred from the United States until 1933); or D. H. Lawrence's *Lady Chatterly's Lover* (equally barred), which became the occasion of a sensational trial in England, especially when John Sparrow, the Warden of the establishment All Souls, pointed out in his favorable

testimony, that the crucial act in the novel was buggery; or
Henry Miller's *Tropic of Cancer* (also barred), with its relentless exploration of different orifices, a reconnaissance later
repeated by Norman Mailer in his *Ancient Evenings*; or William Burroughs' *Naked Lunch*, with its scenes of ejaculation
during hanging; or Hubert Selby's *Last Exit from Brooklyn,*
with its repeated bangings; or such "high-class" fantasizing
as Jean Genet's homosexual *Our Lady of the Flowers*, or Do-
minique Aury's paean to Jean Paulhan, *L'Histoire d'O*, a novel
of female degradation and sexual abasement that later became
a lurid film as well.

Pointing to difficulty does not lessen the seriousness of the
problem. Kristol, it should be pointed out, has been consistent in his views over time. In 1971, referring to himself then
as a liberal, he wrote an essay entitled "Pornography, Obscen-
ity and the Case for Censorship." Pointing out that bear-baiting and cock-fighting, once permitted in England and the
United States, are now prohibited out of compassion for suffering animals. And Kristol cites the *political* use of obscen-
ity promoted by Abbie Hoffman and Jerry Rubin, and endorsed by Herbert Marcuse, because they are "inherently and
purposefully" subversive, and thus carry the day against authority when students can ascribe to the president of the university a notoriously obscene relation to a mother, or, in the
brilliant quip of Lionel Trilling, their use of the phrase "alma
mater f. . . . ."[23]

Edmund Burke has been the second great avatar of conservative thought. Like many protean thinkers, however, especially one who responds to crucial events of his time, there
is no seamless, logical scheme as, say, in Thomism, that one
can cite as scripture. In the *Reflections on the French Revolution*, Burke writes: "Government is not made in virtue of
natural rights, which may and do exist in total independence
of it . . . *but their abstract perfection is their practical defeat* . . . .[24]

For Burke, the character of his beloved British constitution
embodied three operative principles of monarchy, aristocracy,

and democracy. Monarchy incarnated the "hereditary dignity" of a nation; the natural aristocracy were . . . the virtuous and wise men of the society; and democracy, which Burke distrusted because of the vicissitudes of passions, could constitute a representative body of the people. Yet though all men possessed rights, the right to vote was not one of them. What was crucial was the idea of "prescription," the continuity of durable social arrangements as embodied in the institution of property. Property and prescription gave men a stake in society and its institutions, not the vote.

Given the complex and diffuse character of Burke's thought, how much of it is applicable to the United States, with its belief in the "abstract perfection" of universal suffrage and the principle of equality as the guiding principle of politics and law? Yet Burke is endlessly cited because his fine rhetorical voice is endlessly available for different purposes.

If there is no coherent doctrine in American conservative philosophical and political thought, there has been no single consistency in political practice. Traditional Republican conservatism, as exemplified by Senator Robert A. Taft, was a belief in limited government, economic prudence, balanced budgets, the reduction of the debt, and a rejection of Wilsonian interventionism in the international arena and a limited isolationism in foreign policy.

The change in the character of conservatism came in 1964 with the nomination of Barry Goldwater for President. Goldwater, whose *Conscience of a Conservative* had sold over three million copies, spoke out against the welfare state, forced integration, and for a more aggressive foreign policy against communism. His nomination speech became the ringing tocsin of conservative rhetoric. In a phrase crafted by Harry Jaffa, Goldwater declared: "Extremism in the defense of liberty is no vice. Moderation in the pursuit of justice is no virtue." In policy, Goldwater favored making social security voluntary, a program of selling off the Tennessee Valley Authority, an opposition to the nuclear-test-ban treaty, and allowing NATO commanders to use nuclear weapons against the Soviet Union if they decided that was necessary. Goldwater lost, but the rhetorical echoes persisted.

Paradoxically, under the two Republican administrations that preceded and followed Goldwater, that of Eisenhower and Nixon, the welfare state remained untouched. At one point, uttering the phrase "We are all Keynesians now," Nixon instituted wage and price controls in an effort to curb inflation. And, in foreign affairs, Nixon opened the way for relations with Communist China and a detente with the Soviet Union.

If one thinks of conservative political policy, there were divisions that cut across all positions. In economic questions, there were the divisions between the monetarists of Milton Friedman, and the supply-side fiscal policies of Arthur Laffer. On the role of government, there were the libertarians of Friedman, Richard Epstein, and William Safire. And on cultural matters, the division between fiscal conservatives and social liberals (such as Governors Weld of Massachusetts and Whitman of New Jersey), and fiscal activists (supply-side economics) and cultural conservatives such as Irving Kristol and Ronald Reagan.

What, then, united most conservatives and brought forth a common voice in the political arena? It was the emphasis on the theme of moral decay undermining American society and the role of liberalism in creating, if not permitting, that moral decay. To this was added, as a major political force, the presence of the Christian Coalition, the Radical Right, in the affairs of the Republican Party. That was the turning point in making culture the central focus of American politics in the past thirty-five years.

The attention to the political role of the Fundamentalist evangelical movement obscures the fact, as James Davison Hunter has observed, that "Religiously informed values and the people and organizations that articulate them (conservative *and* progressive) always informed public debate." Martin Luther King, Jr., spoke as a Protestant minister, and the civil-rights movement was supported by the liberal clergy in the North. In fact, until the 1970s, the major voices of the Protestant ministry were concerned with reform and socialism. The Social Gospel movement, which promoted discussions of economic change, was by 1912, as Yehoshua Arieli points out, "the dominant creed of Protestantism." The strength of the Social Gospel movement lay in the fact that it incorporated the views of individuals, such as Richard T. Ely, who had founded the American Economic Association. During the Depression Harry F. Ward, of the Union Theological Seminary, led a large section of the Methodist church to the left, by declaring, "a religion whose function it is to develop the ethic of Jesus remains half bound to and half free from, the living death of this acquisitive society." (But Ward discredited himself later by becoming an active fellow-traveler of the communist movement.)[25]

Protestant evangelism had long been associated with revivalism, holy rollers,speaking with tongues, and similar outbursts of behavior that seemed anathema to more "respectable" brethren. Evangelism was identified with flamboyant preachers such as Aimee Semple McPherson and Billy Sunday, and given a vivid literary image in Sinclair Lewis's hypocritical *Elmer Gantry.*

A 1980 survey classified 25 percent of the American population as evangelical, based on responses to three questions used by evangelicals to define their basic creed: belief that "preaching the Gospel is the way . . . to accept salvation through Jesus Christ;" belief "that the Bible is the actual word of God and is to be taken literally;" and have "personally experienced a religious awakening that can be described as being born again."[26]

The major theological figures of America in the 1970s, Reinhold Niebuhr and Paul Tillich, disparaged the evangelical ministers for their literalness and lack of theological understanding, and for those reasons, they were never regarded as having any intellectual standing. Being evangelical was often thought to be of a lower social status, and Protestant evangelicals who were socially mobile often changed their church affiliation from Baptist to Methodist or Presbyterian.

Yet, in the past thirty years, there has been an extraordinary change in the status and political influence of the fundamentalist movement. One can adduce several reasons. Historically, most evangelicals were Southerners, living in small-town and rural areas and likely to be less educated than the population as a whole. And, like most of the whites in the South, they were Democrats. But after the passage of the Civil Rights and voting legislation, these whites began flocking wholesale into the Republican Party, as did many of the evangelicals, and this gave them a broad respectability.

A secondary and nuanced fact. In the late 1960s, many liberal Protestant theologians became trendy, proclaiming, to wide publicity, "the death of God." Harvey Cox, of the Harvard Divinity School, wrote a book, *The Secular City*, which sold a million copies, a book that derided Reinhold Niebuhr and Paul Tillich as old-fashioned Hegelians, and proclaimed the new "Technopolitan man," principally Albert Camus and John F. Kennedy, as the avatars of a new belief. The quick derision that followed these statements brought about a loss of authority of the liberal-left Protestant ministers.

A new figure, Billy Graham, smoothed the rough edges—the faith healing and flagrant anti-intellectualism of Protestant evangelism, and brought it into the television age. His crusade, staged as a pageant, featured a large and racially integrated cast of singers, musicians and warm-up speakers, and in the large auditoriums, when Graham called for "a decision for Christ" and "to be born again," thousands streamed down the aisles of the large auditoriums, led by coaches, to gather before him to express their emotional fervor. This was no longer "old-time religion," but the new Hollywood image of orchestrated spectacle. The regular appearance of Billy Graham in the White House, beginning with Richard Nixon by almost every President thereafter, gave Protestant evangelicalism an official legitimacy.

Television became the substitute for the camp-fire meetings, and through television preachers like Jerry Falwell and Jimmy Swaggert (before his Gantryesque disgrace) and Pat Robertson, reached millions of persons each week and proclaimed "a moral majority" in the nation.

More directly, politics became the modus operandi for the Christian Right. Pat Robertson's Christian Coalition, which became the major right-wing religious group after Jerry Falwell disbanded his Moral Majority (because of sex scandals involving two leading figures in the movement), emphasized that evangelical had become a political, rather than theological, designation. This was described by those involved as a "grassroots coalition of pro-family, pro-life, Evangelicals, conservative Catholics and their allies formed to make government and the media responsive to our concerns [by] mobilizing and training Christians for effective political action. It is our purpose to reverse the moral decline and encroaching secularism in this country, and reaffirm our godly heritage."[27]

From the 1930s to the mid-1960s, liberalism had dominated the political and intellectual scene. It was Harry Truman who had confronted Stalin, had helped turn back Communist aggressiveness in Greece, and had proclaimed the Marshall Plan, which led the way to the recovery of Western Europe. George Kennan had planned the doctrine of containment and proposed the cultural counter-attack, which took form in the Congress for Cultural Freedom. Truman had initiated a security program that led to the hearings against communists in government. The C.I.O. had expelled the communist-dominated unions, while former communist trade-union leaders such as Michael Quill of the Transport workers and Joseph Curran of the Seamens union had abandoned the Party. The American Veterans Committee and the Americans for Democratic Action had swept communists from those fields. In fact, communist influence was at its nadir and the Party itself had gone underground, resulting in a further disillusionment among a number of its leaders who then left the Party.

And yet, it was at this point that Senator McCarthy had opened his malevolent publicity campaign against communists in government and communist influence in U.S. government cultural programs abroad. What we witnessed, in fact, was what may be called the reverse Tocqueville effect. In *The Old*

Regime, Tocqueville had noted that it was not when things went from bad to worse but when things went from worse to better that protest movements took heart and began expressing their views. The reverse effect, one might say, is that when the influence of a group goes from strength to weakness that opponents can speak out more harshly, and exaggerate that influence in order to gain advantage.

But the question remains: Why is it that liberalism faltered in the late sixties and the seventies, and gave the political and intellectual right the issues they have used so effectively? What changes took place in social behavior that divided the counter and gave rise to the theme of "two cultures" in the society? Some facts are clear, and a scenario can quickly be sketched.

First was the rise of a youth culture which, in the phrase of some promoters, was dubbed "a counter-culture." The emphasis on the sixties, however, and proclaiming this as a "revolution," misses the historical roots of such behavior. In the period before World War I there had been Greenwich Village and the poetry of Edna St. Vincent Millay announcing free love, and with that the multiplicity of Greenwich Villages in many cities across the country (such as Louise Bryant in Seattle becoming enamored of John Reed, and in Warren Beatty's mythmaking film *Reds* joining him across the snows of Russia). In the 1920s there was the jazz age, the flappers, and the speakeasies (the unforeseen consequences of the Prohibition act) and the widespread drinking of bootleg liquor. The spread of the automobile, as Robert Lynd remarked in *Middletown,* brought necking out of the parlor into the back seat of the roadster, which became the "cabinet particulier" of the teen-age lotharios. The movies became so wild as to lead finally to the adoption of censorship by the Hays office, acting under the influence of the Catholic Church.

What was distinctive of the 1960s was a demographic "bulge." From 1940 to 1950 there had been no increase in the size of the coming-of-age youth cohort in the society. From 1950 to 1960 there had been no increase. But from 1960 to 1968, reflecting the return of soldiers from the army and early marriage, the youth cohort had jumped 54 percent, and had become a phenomenon reported on by the media, as well as a large market for commercial products, in particular music. In the late 1950s, the Beats had been an enclaved circle of drop-out poets, homosexuals, and acid freaks in San Francisco, such as Allen Ginsberg, Jack Kerouac, and Ken Kesey. In the 1960s they were featured in *Life* magazine and taken up by radical-chic circles, becoming "role models," as the jargon puts it, for the "flower children" who congregated in the Haight-Ashbury section of San Francisco. There was the new rock music, the flaunting of sexual gyrations (initiated by Elvis Presley and made flamboyant by Mick Jagger and the Rolling Stones), and the use of hallucinogenic drugs such as LSD. For some writers such as Charles Reich, of the Yale Law School, this was the "Greening of America," and for liberal sociologists such as Philip Slater, Kenneth Keniston and Amitai Etzioni, the youth movement was the leading edge of an emergent "new culture," a shift in the temper of society stressing autonomy, intimacy, and pleasure.

In and of itself, this might have passed more quickly than it has. But other factors conjoined:

The assassination of John F. Kennedy had punctured the bubble of rhetoric and idealism and the strident claims about a new young generation coming to power. The Great Society of Lyndon Johnson (a phrase created initially by the British political scientist Graham Wallas in 1914 to decry the notions of Adam Smith as to the tasks of "a great society") sought to fulfill the promises of Franklin D. Roosevelt for the aged and Medicaid for the poor, but failed in the effort to institute a comprehensive health-care program.

The stone of stumbling was the Vietnam War. It was "the liberals' war" fashioned by the "best and the brightest"— McNamara, Rostow, Bundy in the Kennedy and Johnson administrations. The step up in combat troops and the virtual takeover of the war in South Vietnam, plus the bombing of the north, was initiated by President Kennedy (with the advice of the liberal general Maxwell Taylor) and extended by Lyndon Johnson. Johnson further created havoc by hiding the expansion of the troop call-up and refusing to increase taxes to pay for the war. He did not tell Gardner Ackley, the chairman of his Council of Economic Advisers, of this prepared step, and the Council therefore issued false estimates of the next year's economic estimates, thus misleading many corporations and the capital markets about the level of spending. The war was financed by printing money, thus initiating an inflation that took a long time to be wrung out of the American economy. It was an instance of lying which became so characteristic of the presidency in these decades.

The Vietnam War radicalized the student movement, especially as the college generation realized the threat of the draft after graduation—leading to refusals, flight, or stratagems of evasion, including service in the National Guard, as featured in the careers of Quayle, Gingrich, and Clinton.

The Port Huron statement of the Students for Democratic Society in 1962 had turned its back on the working class in an emphasis on community and participatory democracy. "The young radicals of the 'New Left,'" writes Howard Brick, "shared in the idea of postindustrial society . . . .the premise was that the university was a new strategic locus of contemporary society tied to centers of political power and social action . . . .SDS leader Greg Calvert and Carol Neiman [described] a body of 'Scientific, technical, and professional workers' who displaced the 'old working class' and Marx's proletarian strategy."[28] C. Wright Mills, always alert to "historic" turning points, hailed the students as a new revolutionary force in society in place of the tired working class.

But the Vietnam War shattered these utopian fantasies. Students and academics began long and disruptive marches on Washington (reported in stunning prose by Norman Mailer) and began occupying and trashing universities such as Columbia and Harvard, as being complicit in the war, as well as doing sporadic bombings of research sites.

As the war wound down in the 1970s, the young radicals began their long march through the cultural institutions, occupying tenured places in the universities, especially in the humanities and social-science departments of the elite universities, as well as the entertainment industries and Hollywood.

Together with the rise of the popular rock-music concerts, initiated by Elvis Presley (later an icon for Reagan's America) and expanded by the highly lucrative record and MTV businesses, a transformation began to take place in the cultural landscape, featuring open sex and drugs, and the scorn of authority.

But it was a political victory by the New Left that for twenty years changed the character of the Democratic Party. In 1968, a weary Lyndon Johnson had decided not to stand for re-election and somewhat reluctantly chose his vice-president, Hubert Humphrey, the most certified liberal of his generation, to run instead (though hog-tying Humphrey, by refusing him the freedom of a more independent position on the Vietnam War,). In August 1968, the Democratic Party met in Chicago. A National Mobilization Committee, an umbrella body of anti-war groups, planned a large but peaceful demonstration. But on the opening of the convention, the pacifist leader David Dellinger was thrust aside by Tom Hayden, the radical leader of the SDS, who organized a charge on the Democratic Party hotel headquarters. Mayor Richard Daley responded in full force. (12,000 of the city police, 6000 National Guardsmen, and 7500 regular Army troops had been assembled.) As the scene unfolded, the National Guardsmen began clubbing and using mace gas on the thousands of demonstrators in front of the Hilton Hotel, where the only live camera in town beamed the violence to the entire nation for a full seventeen minutes. From the podium of the convention amphitheater, Connecticut Senator Abraham Ribicoff accused the police of using "Gestapo tactics," and Mayor Daley roared back: "Fuck you, you Jew son of a bitch, you lousy motherfucker, go home." (Fortunately for the Mayor, no microphone was close enough to pick up his words. Later, lip-readers used news footage to decipher them.)[29]

Humphrey lost the election of 1968 to Richard Nixon by a thin amount. The Democratic Party became splintered, with the Humphrey wing beginning to disintegrate. A commission under the direction of Senator George McGovern was set up to reform the election of convention delegates, requiring their number to be "in reasonable relationship to [the group's] presence in the population of the State." In 1972 the number of women and minority delegates tripled from 1968, the number of delegates under the age of thirty increased ten fold. George McGovern secured the Party's designation for President in 1972. It was the beginning of "identity politics," in which race, gender and same-sex issues replaced economics as the center of affiliation. It signaled the shift from class to culture on the Democratic side as the ground for political conflict.

Race has become a major focus in American politics, changing the political landscape in the past thirty years. The early sit-downs and civil disobedience actions of Martin Luther King, Jr., and the sickening responses of the Southern police, such as in Selma, Alabama in September 1965, had led directly to the Voting Rights act of the Johnson administration. Inevitably, the passage of such legislation led to the classic "revolution of rising expectations." Strong black nationalist movements arose, led by Ron Karenga, and at the extreme, the Black Panther movement of Huey Newton and Bobby Seale (which had been fashioned, ironically enough, when the two men were on the Federal government community-action programs in Oakland, California). The Black Panthers, with their emphasis on macho appearance—the talismanic picture of Huey Newton sitting in a large wicker chair with spear and gun—soon gathered wide media coverage and the financial support of upper-class liberal circles—leading to the famous article by Tom Wolfe about a fund-raising party at the home of composer Leonard Bernstein, which Wolfe tagged with the indelible phrase "radical chic."

But like all such "revolutionary" movements, the Black Panthers came to an impasse. They could either "come into the system" and seek office, or attempt some more violent actions—but of what kind? The major difficulty was that too many of the Black Panthers, harassed as they were by the FBI, had committed crimes and were on the run. Or, one of their leaders, Eldridge Cleaver, whose *Soul on Ice*, the confessions of a black rapist (but ghosted by a white female lover) had

become a best-seller (in particular for the harsh portrait of
Jimmy Baldwin as a homosexual), had fled abroad. After wan-
dering for years in Cuba, Algeria, and other places, Cleaver
returned, disillusioned, to become a born-again Christian.

The overwhelming number of activist Blacks moved into
the political system, becoming a major presence in the Democratic Party, especially in the South, electing a large contin-
gent in the House of Representatives, and winning the may-
oralty in New York, Chicago, Detroit, Los Angeles, Philadelphia, Cleveland, Atlanta, and dozens of other cities across the
country. It was a stunning illustration of the viability of the
American political system. But it could not change, substantially, the underlying economic poverty rates of the broken
Black families, though a substantial Black middle class did
emerge. The other, "unintended" consequence, which I had
mentioned, was that the white voters in the South left the
Democratic Party in droves and joined the Republican Party,
especially the Christian evangelicals, thus creating a new force
in American electoral politics and the basis for the sometime
Republican majority, especially in the Congress.

The seventies, eighties, and nineties were decades of
marked political contradictions, which polarized the society
along different political lines and created large political confusions and angers.

The election of Richard Nixon as president in 1968 and
1972, ironically, could have created a new, unique two-party
system in which the Republicans would have had a modest
platform on domestic policy (as indicated by the roles of
Moynihan and Erlichman) and an activist foreign policy
(Kissinger), while the Democrats would be left with a concentration on identity issues (but losing much of their trade-
union support) and a neoisolationist foreign policy. But it was
not to be, in great measure owing to the personality of Richard Nixon and the displacement (as Harold Lasswell might
have put it) of personal insecurity onto the political stage.

What all this led to was the erosion of trust in government,
as symbolized by Watergate. For some persons, particularly

many abroad, it is puzzling why a failed "third-rate burglary"
of Democratic Party headquarters in the Watergate building
complex, by a group of White House "plumbers," should have
been the occasion of a national scandal and the ultimate resignation, under the tangible threat of impeachment, of Richard Nixon. But "Watergate" was more, far more, than a "third-
rate burglary." It was the climax of Richard Nixon's hardball
politics, politics by any means, illegal and unethical, and his
paranoia. Paranoids do have enemies, Freud once insisted, and
Nixon had his and more.

"Watergate" resulted in the conviction for lying of *two* At-
torneys General, John Mitchell (who went to jail) and Richard Kleindienst (his successor, who was fined and put on pro-
bation); the two chief White House deputies, H. R. Haldemann
and John Erlichman; as well as half a dozen other White House
aides and Republican officials who also went to jail. And the
resignation—and pardon—of Richard Nixon.

The Reagan years were the apogee of American conservatism. The victory of Jimmy Carter over Gerald Ford in 1976
was but an interlude in which the Democratic Party had been
unable to consolidate its victory. In part this was because
Carter himself had been an outsider who could not pull together the diverse elements in the Party. In part because Carter,
immersed as he was in details, had never been able to become
a major symbolic figure, as a president needs to be, for the
country. In fact, given the sorry state of the economy, he
blamed the American people for the "malaise" of the country—a strange claim for an American President to make. Inevitably the people rejected the burden of that charge The one
major achievement of the Carter administration—recognized
only grudgingly at the time—was the declaration of human
rights as a commitment of government, as a constitutive obligation of foreign policy, an accomplishment that has come to
be recognized as one of the high marks of morality at the end
of the twentieth century.

The American political system, as has been evident from
the start, is a two-tiered structure: the President represents the
passions; the Congress, the interests. Being the head of state,

the President is a symbolic figure, speaking for all the nation, as well as the executive of the administration. The Congress, rooted in particular localities, is necessarily responsive to the concentration of interests—rural, ethnic, labor, small business—in these locales. It is no accident, so to speak, that so many Presidents of the United States have been generals, usually after military victories, from Washington to Jackson to Grant to Eisenhower. As heroes, they demonstrate the radiance of the country and carry the nimbus of monarchy. After a dozen years of gray clouds, Ronald Reagan could stir the emotions of the American people.

Ronald Reagan was an actor, with the gift of playing affable roles, thus allowing people to project onto him their varied yearnings, hopes, and identifications. Among intellectuals he may have invoked contempt, but for the large majority of ordinary Americans, he invited warmth and friendship. He had simple prejudices—I do not use the word invidiously, but to designate deep-engrained and simple beliefs, which reject complicated interpretations and analyses of events. There were good guys and bad guys, and any American knew immediately who they were. And drawing from these prejudices, Reagan reiterated strongly a love of country and patriotism which touched a deep chord in the American people. In that respect, and crucially, he largely erased the stain of Vietnam and the sense of guilt—for the role we had played and the dismay at the defeat we had suffered—that had pervaded the country. The Vietnam "grunt," once an object of derision, was now regarded as an honorable person to be respected and rewarded—an emotional decision that was given marbled embodiment in the remarkable memorial by Maya Lin, which quickly became the singular tombstone for the nation.[30]

But there was also the cultural side. In an article in *Commentary*, January 1981, Norman Podhoretz wrote that the election of Ronald Reagan was due to a "wave of cultural disgust" at the "new culture" typified by "Gay Lib and abortion," and that Mr. Reagan was "perfect" to "reconstitute the new majority that Nixon had coaxed into emerging and that he never had a chance to consolidate."

But Reagan—or the shrewd advisers behind him, such as Michael Deaver—were cautious about any cultural crusade. Though Reagan gave lip-service to the cause of abortion (he was always a great lip man), the Reagan political team thought that it would risk destruction if the "social issues" became paramount. They decided to trump the Democrats by emphasizing tax cuts and supply-side economics; by concentrating on foreign-policy issues, such as pressure on the Soviet Union; by proposing a missile defense through Star Wars; and, responding initially to the pleas of Helmut Schmidt, placing intermediate-range missiles in central Europe, panicking the Russians in the consequence, and bringing Gorbachev to Helsinki. But, the administration also engaged secretly in the Intra-Contra affair to provide arms to Iran in exchange for hostages and to use the proceeds (plus secret sums from the Sultan of Brunei, which went awry when he was given the wrong Swiss bank-account number!) to finance the contras in Nicaragua, in violation of Congressional bans on such efforts.

Seeking to capitalize on an anti-Washington mood, Mr. Reagan took the extraordinary step of telling the American people "not to trust government"—not bad government, but "government." It was the first time in American democracy that a President had given its people such astonishing advice. Yet, Mr. Reagan took the extraordinary steps of fully legitimating the Radical Right. In 1980, during the Republican national convention in Detroit, Reagan met with Jerry Falwell, who then gave one of the invocations at the nominating convention, and helped fashion the convention platform, which called for a constitutional ban on abortion—a plank that remains there to this day.

When Falwell retreated from open political activity, he was succeeded by Pat Robertson, who built his influence with the Christian Broadcasting Network, and whose flagship show, the 700 Club, was available twice daily on 10,000 cable systems with a reported national audience of 58 million homes, and the organization, the Christian Coalition.[31]

But it is not as a political activist that Pat Robertson is troublesome. It is the character of his fundamental world outlook. In his 1991 book, *The New World Order*, Robertson sketched a conspiracy theory tying together Federal Reserve Board, the Rockefellers, the Council on Foreign Relations, Henry Kissinger, the Trilateral Commission, and European bankers, to steer the United States to "one clear goal—world government." And drawing from the Elders of Zion sources about secret societies, these threads were traced back to a demonic plot in 1776, of a Masonic society known as the Order of the Illuminati, founded by one Adam Weisshaupt, which then came under the control of the Rothschild Jewish banking family.[32] Robertson has never repudiated these views.

For Robertson, America is a "Christian nation," a nation that is threatened by secular humanists. "The centers of power in our culture—government, education, media, business and philanthropy are firmly in the hands of secular humanists who are exerting every effort to debase and eliminate Bible-based Christianity from our society." The litany of names is a tired and familiar one—the American Civil Liberties Union, the National Organization of Women, the Planned Parenthood organizations, the United Nations, most members of the Supreme Court, etc. etc.

To combat that pernicious influence, says Robertson, religion must be made integral to the public schools. By that he meant the introduction of daily school prayer (which the Supreme Court decided in 1962, in *Engel* vs. *Vitale*, was unconstitutional), of mandatory Bible readings, and the daily recital of the Lord's Prayer (which the Court, a year later, in the *Schempp* and *Murray* cases, also declared unconstitutional, and, the teaching of Creationism, and the like. In all this, the radical right has gone far beyond the introduction of cultural and moral issues onto the political scene, but religious matters as well, religious themes with distinct tones of divisiveness and dark incitements of conspiracy.

In the nineteen-nineties, two new men came to the center of the political stage, Bill Clinton and Newt Gingrich, and their actions—and combat—shaped one of the most turbulent domestic decades in a half century of U.S. political history.

Newt Gingrich, with the force of his personality, swept the Republican Party into control of the House of Representatives, and for the first time in forty years, there was a Republican majority in both houses of Congress. As speaker of the House, he promised a "Contract with America," that would be enacted within the first one hundred days of the session of Congress. More than that, he said boldly he would "rethink the entire structure of American society and the entire structure of American government."

His guru was Alvin Toffler, whose book, *The Third Wave*, provided the "theoretical" license for his "cyber-speak." In the flashcube prose that has been his medium, Toffler beamed out his apocalypse: "A powerful tide is surging across much of the world today . . . . Value systems splinter and crash, while the lifeboats of family, church, and state are hurled about . . . . Humanity faces a quantum leap forward. It faces the deepest social upheaval and creative restructuring of all time . . . ."

The existing political institutions, said Toffler and George Gilder, who joined him as an adviser to Mr. Gingrich, were products of an agrarian age. These were now outmoded by the battering forces of technology, which made majority rule obsolete in the face of a new electronic democracy. How one squared this with the idea of "traditional values" was never explained. After all, the founders of American democracy rightly understood, and feared, instant democracy because of the volatility of instant democracy and the dangers of demagoguery. But Gingrich was never one to let any stumbling cultural contradictions stop his glib tongue. His intention, always, was to make a dazzling impression, and he always did.

In an effort to demonstrate his mastery of the Congress, Gingrich entered into a shoot-out with President Clinton on the Federal budget. When Mr. Clinton threatened to veto the several appropriations bills, which Gingrich had proposed to cut several government departments, Gingrich quite literally shut down those departments, since monies were not available to pay salaries, and employees were sent home. But the public outcry led to Gingrich backing down and a loss of face for him. It was also a black mark for conservatism in the demonstration of his ludicrous cyber-language and reckless behavior.

More troublesome during this time was the spread of conspiracy theories and the rise of militia groups that called for outright resistance to government. In 1995, a bomb made from fertilizer chemicals destroyed a federal building, killing hundreds. A shadowy group called The Organization had launched its first attacks to bring down The System. But that was not fact but fiction, a tract called " The Turner Diaries," written in 1978 by William Pierce, a 63–year-old physicist who had quit academe to begin a crusade against Jews and Blacks. The tract sold some 200,000 copies outside the mainstream book stores. It was also the scripture of the Militia of Montana, a paramilitary group headed by one John Trochman, who issued a call to arms on the basis that the President was planning to impose martial law and proclaim a world government through the United Nations. He warned that the "One World Government" would track people's activities by implanting electrical transponders the size of a rice grain under the skins of individuals.

Literary coincidences, fact and fiction, paranoid fantasies, militia organizing in a dozen states—all these apparitions became a dreadful reality in April 1995 when Timothy McVeigh set off a bomb, made from chemical fertilizers, that destroyed the federal building in Oklahoma City and killed one hundred and sixty-eight persons. Fiction was now fact.

One cannot, and should not, hold vociferous politicians responsible for the actions of radical fringes, left or right: neither a George McGovern for the actions of left-wing crazies who bombed universities and held up banks (and one forgets how extensive this was), or a Ronald Reagan or a Newt Gingrich for the manic right who literally have sniped at federal officials when enforcing the laws against grazing on federal lands as an infringement of their "freedom." Yet one cannot discount, either, the atmosphere generated by ideologues who voice distrust of government, and thus become the screen for those who act out their wrath.

By the end of the decade, at the end of Mr. Clinton's two terms in office, the political spectrum, as David Plotke has pointed out, had shifted to the right. If a Great Society liberal toted up the economic record of the Clinton administration, he would have to reckon on the fiscal discipline, the balanced budget, and the reduction of the national debt as its achievements—the most traditional of all Republican platforms, which none of the Republicans had been able to achieve in fifty years.

When Mr. Clinton assumed office in 1992, during a period of depression inherited from the Bush administration, the new President convened an economic-strategy conference in Little Rock. Prompted by his adviser Robert Reich, it called for increased government spending, and large public investment, the macro-Keynesian nostrums that had been embraced even by Richard Nixon. But Mr. Clinton never went ahead with these proposals. Influenced by Robert Rubin, first as head of the national economic council, and then as Secretary of the Treasury, the administration embarked on a course of assuaging the capital markets by promising stability, low inflation, and low interest rates, in order to encourage private investment. And that happened. During the Clinton administration, federal spending fell from about 22 per cent of gross domestic product to 19 percent in 1999, the lowest share in thirty years. And as against a $455 billion deficit projected in 1992, there was a projected surplus of several hundred billion dollars in the year 2000. The federal welfare program was ended, and welfare returned to the states with the proviso that any welfare recipients had to go to work after three years. Crime went down steadily for seven years, whether because of more community policing financed by the Clinton administration, the incarceration of two million persons in prison (half of these young Blacks), or the aging of the population, and the availability of jobs for those who wanted one—or a combination of all these factors.

The Presidential campaign in the year 2000 marked the new sea-change in the American political scene—namely, the competition for the center. Neither party now wanted to end the role of the state. Indeed, Republicans and Democrats vied for the role of the position of saving social security, Medicare, and Medicaid; they differed largely on how much the projected surpluses would go for these programs. The Democratic administration took the first tangible steps to buy back the federal debt, reducing the figures that had been flashing on Republican billboards for forty years. The reform of health care and education had become the major domestic issue between the Presidential candidates in the year 2000. Ideological conflicts?

In the Presidential primaries in the year 2000, George W. Bush proclaimed himself to be a born-again Protestant, whose life had been changed directly by Jesus Christ. John McCain described himself as a born-again Protestant, who testified that his faith had helped him survive in the prisoner-of-war camp. Al Gore asserted that he was a born-again Protestant who, he said, frequently asked himself "W.W.J.D." [What Would Jesus Do?]. And Bill Bradley, who, though refusing to discuss his faith, indicated that he had belonged to the Fellowship of Christian Athletes, who had evangelized his basketball teammates. Nothing like this had ever been seen before in an American presidential political campaign.

The Christian Radical Right became an issue in the Republican primaries. In South Carolina, in early February, George W. Bush made fervent appeals to the Christian right and went to Bob Jones University, a fundamentalist institution that is anti-Catholic and had opposed interracial dating. And later that month, in the Michigan primary, supporters of Senator John McCain received automated telephone calls in which the recorded voice of the evangelist Pat Robertson urged them "to protect unborn babies and restore religious freedom: by opposing Mr. McCain." And, as he had on his cable-television program, Mr. Robertson accused Mr. McCain of having chosen as his national chairman, "a vicious bigot who wrote that conservative Christians in politics are anti-abortion zealots, homophobes, and would-be censors." The reference was to former Senator Warren Rudman, a Jew, who had used those phrases in his autobiography to describe some in the Christian right, although he also said there were "some fine, sincere people in its ranks." Mr. Robertson's remarks dismayed a number of Jewish conservatives who had been ardent defenders of the Christian right. William Kristol, the editor of

The Weekly Standard, called Reverend Robertson's words "appalling." And Elliott Abrams, who had been assistant secretary of state in the Reagan administration and had called for an alliance of Jewish and Christian conservatives against "secular humanism," condemned the attack on former Senator Rudman, stating, "Here you have someone invoking religion on behalf of a candidate, as if Pat Robertson knows what God wants in terms of a candidate."[33]

The names of Pat Robertson and Jerry Falwell were featured in a major speech of Senator McCain on February 29th, in Virginia, a few miles from the headquarters of the Christian Coalition. Here he delivered a harsh attack on "self-appointed leaders" of the religious right, naming the two men as "agents of intolerance," and declaring that "The politics of division and slander are not our values . . . . They are corrupting influences on religion and politics, and those who practice them in the name of religion or in the name of the Republican Party or in the name of America shame our faith, our party, and our country."[34]

Can one exempt religion from American political life? No. Religion is an indelible component of American society. It is bound up with the Declaration of Independence and the founding of the republic—though a number of the founders, such as Jefferson, were Deists. The Establishment clause of the Constitution was not a denial of religion—"Congress shall make no law respecting an establishment of religion"—but the effort to keep the nation apart from the *wars of religion* that had wracked Europe in the 17th and 18th centuries.

And it is that intention which needs to be emphasized today. What is troublesome is the politicization of moral and cultural issues, for by their very nature they are *non-negotiable* and serve to polarize a society. The saving grace of American society is that it has sought to avoid or deflect such polarization. For almost eighty years, from 1870 to 1950, the country was threatened with "class war," as labor disputes violently divided the society. (One can cite a dozen indicators, such as the number of times troops were called out, the num-

ber of individuals killed, in instances such as the railroad
strikes, Homestead, the automobile sit-downs, and the like.)
Labor had long lived in the tension of being a social movement and a trade union. But what had been an *ideology* became an *interest*, and the emphasis on being a trade union won
out. And as interest it became negotiable, as a collective bargaining between private parties under the law.

If the issues are non-negotiable, as the issue of abortion
may be, the only answer may be to "privatize" them, just as
one seeks to privatize the economic activities of government.[35]
If such moral and cultural questions cannot then be privatized,
then the country may remain in trouble as new wars of religion take hold. That is the prospect of the continuing involvement of the radical right in politics. The conventional wisdom
of American politics is that candidates appeal to the extremes
in the primaries and to the center in the general election. If
that is true, the question, then, is whether the center can hold.

Coda

In the year 2000 election, Al Gore won the popular vote
by more than five hundred thousand votes, out of more than
a hundred million votes cast. George W. Bush was elected
president by one electoral vote, the margin supplied by a disputed vote count in Florida.

The puzzling question is why did Vice President Gore do
relatively poorly, or George W. Bush relatively well, when the
administration of which Mr. Gore was the second most prominent member had held office during the time when the
economy recovered, a thirty-year budget deficit had become
a surplus, and unemployment had almost cleared all markets.
One consideration may have been that a smaller proportion
of the electorate had voted than in 1992, when Bill Clinton
had won against George Bush, Sr. A second factor was the
vote for Ralph Nader, which, while less than the coveted five
percent, surely was decisive in Florida. But the more unusual
fact, perhaps, was the character and appeal of the two men.

As I had noted earlier in this essay, the American political
system is two-tiered, what I have called "the passions and the

interests," the passions centering on the presidency and the interests tied closely to the Congress. Few persons felt passionate about Al Gore. He seems to have had, as Jacob Weisberg noted (in *Slate* on Nov. 8, 2000), a disdain for the vote-grubbing necessary in politics, "a sentiment manifested in his...almost mannered speaking style and his failure to create a human connection with his listeners." George W. Bush, on the other hand, was relaxed, affable, and folksy, a man with whom one could spend time in a bar or a locker room.

But beyond these personal elements, this was an election almost entirely different in issues and outcomes from almost any in American politics of the past fifty years. It has long been observed that candidates, in seeking a nomination, appeal to the activists: in the Republican party to the Christian right; in the Democratic Party to the trade union officials and vocalists of the black minority. In the election, the appeal is to the center.

What was extraordinary, this time, was the broad agreement of both men on the centrality of socioeconomic issues: prescription drugs for the elderly, extending Medicare, and saving Social Security. Each man contended that he could do better than the other in providing solutions for these problems— which they both agreed were real. Twelve years before, Ronald Reagan had proposed to abolish the federal Department of Education. George W. Bush declared that extending the federal role in education would be his priority.

There were differences between the two men, but these were principally on *cultural* issues: gay and lesbian rights, abortion, affirmative action, the role of faith-based organizations (i.e., religious groups) in receiving government monies, and-the environment. But these questions rarely surfaced during the campaign. Nor was there any discussion of foreign policy or globalization and trade. Few passions were aroused in the campaign, other than by Ralph Nader, while Pat Buchanan had disappeared under the radar screen. Was it no accident, therefore, that character and personality (Gore the character, Bush the personality) were the main staples of media concentration. (In American life, as David Riesman observed long ago, character had evaporated in America's other-directed consumer society.)

And yet, the very role of culture indicates that a radical change has taken place in American politics in the past twenty-five years. The politics established by the New Deal was largely *class politics*, represented by functional groups—business, farmers, and workers. The cultural politics is principally *identity politics* in which race, gender, and ethnicity dominate the activist scene.

Does the new cultural politics mean, then, a different divided nation, as functional group politics once differentiated the society? The noted conservative historian Gertrude Himmelfarb, in a thoughtful work, has argued (as in the title of her book) that we have become *One Nation, Two Cultures*. Ms. Himmelfarb opens with the piquant observation of Adam Smith that "in every civilized society" there have been two different modes of morality, one he called "liberal or loose," the other, "strict or austere." The loose is the world of fashion, the libertine or Bohemian. In England, quite often, an upper-class morality. The strict, of thrift, diligence and self-reliance, was characteristic of the Wesley Methodist working class and middle class. Outside the two were the dissolute poor of the slums and the waterfront.

How this distinction, a provocative one, applies to American society is less clear. There are the small-town religious groups proclaiming family values, and the swinging sets of Hollywood and the Upper East Side of New York. But these are more media definitions than bounded worlds. More broadly there are the religious and the secular, the frugal and the hedonist. But any effort to define these as "cultures"—that is, as ways of life—runs into the difficulty of establishing social locations for such lifestyles. The crucial point is that hedonism is intrinsic to the very nature of twentieth-century capitalism, with its imperatives to stimulate wants and demands. And if David Brooks' new book, *Bobos in Paradise*, is to be believed, the new economy has given rise to the Bourgeois

Bohemians (Bobos) where, as one of his chapter headings has it, "The Cultural Contradictions of Capitalism [are] Resolved."

The essence of Ms. Himmelfarb's charge is directed against what Lionel Trilling in 1965 had called "the adversary culture," the modernist attack against bourgeois society and bourgeois morality. By the end of the decade this had spilled over into the youth culture, the counter-culture, the sexual "revolution" abetted by the birth-control pill, the rise of a militant feminism, all under the banner of "liberation" flaunted as the attack on authority.

That these large cultural changes have taken place goes without saying. What is less clear are the consequences. To identify all this with liberalism surely goes too far. It is true that George McGovern was able to change the rules of the Democratic Party so as to enlarge and even stipulate the role of women and minorities (especially blacks) in the Democratic convention. But the Democratic Party has moved away from McGovern (who is now almost a forgotten name in political history). What one can say is that liberalism failed to establish limits against the excesses of the movements proclaiming "liberation."

Equally it is much too simple to attribute the rise in divorce or the break-up of the family to the "cultural revolutions" of the sixties. The change in the nature of the family'' and the new role of women in the workplace (now almost half of the labor force) are one of the most fundamental changes in Western society in the millennium. But this is due, principally, to what I have called the onset of post-industrial society.

A vast social change of this kind is an intersect of two forces: one of values and ideals, the other the ability to institutionalize these in market terms. The cultural force here is the ideal of equality (in the privilege of voting, control of property, the choice of work, etc.). which goes back already a hundred years, while the vote itself was established in the 1920s. But the ability to institutionalize those cultural ideals goes back only more recently, to the change in the nature of work in modern society.

Industrial society, so to speak, was "man's work." In 1950,

seventy percent of the labor force was a man at work, with a wife and two children at home. (In the middle class, it was shameful for the man to have his wife go to work after marriage.) Today that figure is fifteen percent.

Post-industrial employments—health, education, social services, research, professional services, business services—can be done, and are more often done, by women. In that respect, the role of women, as an economic and political force, is a product of a *structural* change in society. As for divorce, one can point out that as of 1950, uncontested divorce was possible in only one state in the U.S., Nevada, which required a six-weeks' residence. Desertion, therefore, was quite frequent. The rise of no-fault divorce laws, now common in almost every state of the union, facilitated legal divorce.

What does remain of the "adversary culture" is the extent of "post-modernist" thought in the humanities and history departments of leading universities, and the undermining of a canon, or the idea of an authoritative body of works, in those fields. Literary and cultural studies have become pop sociology (and sociology itself has become narrow and technical) and one reads Shakespeare as much to discuss cross-dressing as for the language and poetry. And yet while this has dominated an "elite culture," it may be tendentious to see this as a major player in the polity, or to ignore the fact that such beliefs are ebbing, both because of the exhaustion of the doctrines and the aging of the baby boomers of the sixties, many of whom are now entering their retirement age.

This is a nation of 276 million people, and inevitably there are bound to be diverse communities, diverse values, and different moral codes. As Ms. Himmelfarb herself points out, "The 'two cultures' are neither monolithic nor static. Nor are they totally separate or distinct." Individuals are not usually rigidly consistent in attitudes being more tolerant, say, of premarital sex (which most young people in the country now engage in) than adultery or sexual promiscuity.

There is, then, the larger question as to whether there may be a "third culture," the sizable "middle majority" of the center whose voice is rarely heard often because those individuals are not interested in giving "voice" to their views. We may see this in the distinction, arbitrary to be sure, between the *polity* and the *society*. The polity is the world of the politically activist, an arena that has expanded hugely in the past forty years because government has become the expanded source of rights and entitlements, or contracts and regulations, as well as a large military and foreign-aid sector.

The society is the quotidian world, of family, schools, jobs and neighborhoods. Divorces may have increased, but the greater majority of the divorced remarry. Most social life consists of members of families visiting their families on weekends, of individuals in jobs and businesses socializing with each other.

This is the picture of "Middletown," the prototypical city of Muncie, Indiana, first visited by Robert and Helen Lynd in 1929 and 1937, but re-visited in 1982 by Theodore Caplow and his associates. In the concluding chapter of *Middletown Families*, entitled "The Myth of the Declining Family," Caplow writes that kinship ties permeate Middletown. "No other affiliative bond directly links as many of the city's people to one another as the extended family...we discovered increased family solidarity, a smaller generation gap, more religion and less mobility." And, contrary to the media image, "Middletown families are reasonably similar to American families in general."

Almost twenty years later, in a further replication of the Middletown study, Caplow found roughly the same picture. One striking finding, for example, was that the time and attention that American parents devote to their children increased significantly. "In the 1999 survey, 83 percent of fathers reported spending an hour or more each day with their children, up from 60 percent" in the original 1924 survey. This was equally true of mothers, despite the increased employment of women. The simple explanation is that both men and women spend fewer hours on the job and much less time doing housework, as well as the significant fact that the "generation gap" between parents and children had narrowed considerably: "[M]ost parents in 1999 had the same urban back-ground and outlook as their children. They watched many of the same television programs and followed the same sports."

The society then remains relatively strong, and people have more of a stake in that stability. In 1999, 52 percent of Americans owned shares in public companies or equity mutual funds, either directly or through retirement accounts, a percentage four times higher than in 1980, when only 13 percent of Americans owned stock. If some variant of the Bush proposals is enacted for individuals to privatize some portion of their social-security accounts, that figure will increase significantly.

And the society has become more liberal in its social attitudes. Years back, a majority believed that one's creed held a monopoly of religious truth. That has given way to a majority view—62 percent of Protestants and 74 percent of Catholics in a 1996 survey—that all religions are equally good. More to the point, as Caplow writes in his 1999 account in *The Measured Century*: "American religion [has] lost much of its authoritative character. The mainline Protestant churches no longer [apply] their traditional sanctions against fornication, illegitimacy, divorce, homosexuality, and blasphemy. The majority of Catholics favor and practice birth control contrary to church doctrine."

The major societal change in the postwar years has been the expansion of education. At the turn of the century, fewer than seven percent of young people had finished high school, and only one in fifty had completed college; by 1998, eighty-eight percent of young persons had graduated from high school, and twenty-eight percent had completed four or more years of college. And what every sociological study has shown is that higher education is associated with greater liberalism, especially on the level of personal values, if not politics.

In the election 2000, while Gore won most of the urban coastal areas by large margins, and Bush scored in the South, the Great Plains, and the Rockies, the vote in the heartland states of Pennsylvania, Michigan, Missouri, Wisconsin, Iowa and Ohio, and of course Florida, were extraordinarily close, divided often by less than two or three percentage points. In other words, apart from Republican and Democratic concentrations (reflecting the two cultures?), there was a third America that was balanced in the middle.

But beyond the one or two or three cultures is at the forefront of political debate, a more dramatic change in American society has been taking place: the fact that because of the new immigration, and the differential birth rates between "whites" and other groups in the society, by the year 2050, the "minorities"—Hispanic, Black and Asian—may become the majority population in the United States.

America has always been—apart from the native American Indians—an immigrant society. Historically, the overwhelming majority have been from Europe. Blacks were never "immigrants," but were brought in as slaves, though import was halted after 1808, and the population increase was a natural one. By 1924, when immigration was virtually halted by an act of Congress, nearly fifteen percent of the population were foreign-born. Blacks were then about ten percent of the population.

In 1965, the new Immigration Act eliminated ethnic and racial restrictions, and a major change in the U.S. population followed. The new immigrants have been of two kinds: "Hispanic" from Mexico, the Caribbean, and Central America; and "Asian" from Korea, Vietnam, the Philippines, and China. And, for the first time since the end of the slave trade, a sizable number from sub-Saharan Africa.

Equally, there has been a geographical redistribution of minorities in the United States. In 1900, about 90 percent of the Black population lived in the rural areas of the South. But after World War II there were large migrations to the north. The major reason, curiously, was the consequence of a "technological revolution"—the introduction of chemical fertilizers on the farms. From 1900 to 1940, agricultural productivity had been a stagnant one to two percent a year. But because of the wartime introduction of chemical fertilizers, agricultural productivity rose to about eight to ten percent a year. Blacks in the South had been sharecroppers, or tenants who lived on the farms and received a share of the crops. But blacks were now no longer needed and thus were forced off the farms—moving to Watts in Los Angeles, Bronzeville in Chicago, the inner city of Detroit, and Harlem in New York, and entering the labor market in those cities. Previously, they were not counted as "unemployed" since they were simply extra mouths on hand to feed. But now, in the labor markets, they were counted, and unemployment became visible.

In the North, the Blacks also became a political force. Given the new geography and immigration, in the ten largest cities of the United States, the "white" population today constitutes only 38 percent of the inhabitants; Blacks are 31 percent, and Hispanic and Asian the remaining 31 percent. In Los Angeles and New York, the combined minority population was 64 percent and 61 percent respectively. Blacks have been mayors of almost every major city in the United States—New York, Los Angeles, Chicago, Cleveland, Detroit, Atlanta, New Orleans, Baltimore—with the exception of Boston.

From 1950 to 2000, the Asian proportion of the American population rose about twenty-fold, that of the Hispanic about ten-fold. In all, minorities in the U.S. today make up about 30 percent of the total population. And given the different fertility rates, this may rise to 50 percent by the year 2050, according to some estimates.

In the United States today, if one were to draw a shaded map of the country, there would be a "minorities" strip along the East Coast from Boston to Miami, a band running across southern Alabama, Louisiana, Texas, and Arizona, and a belt up the coast of California to San Francisco. There is no necessary single political conclusion to be drawn from this. Although ninety percent of the black vote went to Gore, and this weighting may continue, the Hispanic and Asian populations may shift their allegiances, depending upon the political policies and climate of the Bush administration. And the latter may meld into the third culture.

In his inaugural address on January 20, 2001, George W.

Bush affirmed a "commitment to live out our nation's promise through civility." We are, he said, " a civil society which demands from each of us good will and respect, fair dealing and forgiveness." Yet as Gertrude Himmelfarb wryly remarked in her *One Nation, Two Cultures,* " 'Civil society' has become the mantra of our time." Liberals and conservatives, Democrats-and Republicans, religious and secular thinkers agree that "civil society is the key to our redemption." And as she concludes: "There is something suspect about a message that appeals to so many people of such different persuasions" (p. 30).

President Bush's words may only have been rhetoric, yet rhetoric often binds a speaker, and may be compelling, especially if the people believe that *he* believes those words. This was true of the rhetoric of Goldwater and Reagan. But the consequence of Mr. Bush's "compassionate" rhetoric may be that the Goldwater "extremism in the defense of liberty" and the Reagan "populism" of "don't trust government" are gone. Mr. Bush is stating that government is no longer the problem, but has a moral obligation to find solutions—especially if those solutions lead to the use of market mechanisms and privatization of government programs.

Just as the compulsions of the primaries and the dynamics of the election campaign have different logics, so the problems of governing—of taking responsibility for legislations and administration—have different programmatic outcomes. In his first months, President Bush brought back what *The Economist* has called "Main Street Republicanism." Alongside with Vice President Cheney, the heart of his cabinet is made up of a corporate and managerial group sophisticated about its role in being capitalist. The religious and environmental right were given their due (John Ashcroft at the Justice Department and Gayle Norton at Interior). Yet in a deft political grace note, he appointed two African-Americans to-highly visible posts (General Powell at the State Department and Roderick Paige at Education), two East Asians to other posts, and one Hispanic, as well as three women—in all, what Hendrik Hertzberg at *The New Yorker* has nicely called "the routinization of diversity."

In his first executive order, Mr. Bush rescinded the use of government monies to international agencies that counsel abortion, thus reverting to the status quo ante of twelve years before. But in his first legislative initiative, he proposed an increased role for the federal government in education, an action applauded by the Republican Congress (with the exception of Tom DeLay) which, until 1994 had been committed to the abolition of that role.

Though tacking initially between 'left' and 'right in the consequent areas of environment, energy, judicial appointments and tax cuts, the conservative imprint was clear. The stamp of the new administration was laid down in Mr. Bush's proposal for a 1.6 trillion dollar tax cut to be paid out over a ten year period. Though the proposal was designed to give back some monies to all who paid income taxes, what was clear was that the overwhelming benefits would go to the rich. The rationale for this, which was never publicly stated, was two-fold: one, that since 20 percent of the taxpayers pay 80 percent of the taxes as a matter of "fairness" they should get the larger portion of the money; the second was the argument that if the rich received the benefits, they would invest those sums and thus stimulate the economy. But as matters of moral and political theory, or economic analysis, those rationales were never defended.

The ongoing agenda of the Bush administration however received a jolt after the first hundred days (and the passage of the tax bill largely congruent with Mr. Bush's wishes) with the defection from the Republican party of the three-term Vermont senator Jim Jeffords, who stated that he could no longer support the "conservative" proposals of the Bush administration.[36] The defection tipped the 50/50 balance in the Senate to give the Democrats control of the chamber. While not changing the ideological divisions in the Senate, it did mean that the Democrats would assume the chairmanship of all the committees and control the calendar of the legislative agenda. They would have the power to initiate public hearings on issues they would wish to spotlight, to hold up judicial nominations, and to give priority to their own agenda such as guaranteed rights to managed-care patients, prescription drugs for the elderly, a halt to environmental oil drilling and different incentives for the energy problems. None of this guaranteed the enactment of such proposals, for the ideological complexities of the Senate remained, but it did put awry the Bush agenda, and probably gave the Democrats some advantage, in publicity, if nothing else, for the Congressional 2002 year elections.

Given all these maneuverings, what is striking is that these divisions go back to the "traditional" liberal-conservative domestic divergences of the Eisenhower era. Eisenhower did not dismantle "the welfare state" (neither did Nixon), and Bill Clinton, despite the visceral rage inspired among the Republicans by his personal conduct and mendacity, left a record that historians can only count as Republican (fiscal discipline, welfare reform, the Defense of Marriage act, an increase in the number of federal death penalty offenses, a capital-gains cut, etc.). Rhetoric aside, the political arena has been redefined as an ambiguous center. On the "left," class and identity politics (in its strident senses) have been reduced; on the "right," the Christian and evangelical coalitions have been enfolded into the administration coalition. What has remained, however, is the cultural unease, the legacy of the cultural wars of the 1970s which have been detailed on these pages. That unease colors so much of the political discourse still.

Two new issues have emerged, with extraordinary consequences perhaps, for the character of American politics. One is the proposal of the Bush administration for government monetary support of "faith-based organizations." This is a "code" word for religion. It is a practical move however for the support of the black churches. The black community is increasingly a divided one: there is a large, and growing black middle class, many of whom seek to move to the suburbs and escape the stigma of being black; the other is the black community of the urban ghettoes, with a heavy crime rate among the young, broken by the lack of stable families, a fact underscored by the large unemployment. The black churches are one of the few institutions that provide stability in the urban areas, and some source of job training and social services. The Bush administration proposes to support those black churches.

The words "faith-based," raise the question of "separation" of church and state, and a dilemma for liberals, especially for the Jewish organizations who, paradoxically, provided the financial support for the poor Jewish youth fifty years ago, and provided the means for their rise out of the ghetto and into the professional and business classes, one of the most extraordinary sociological transformations of society that we know. And the proposal has incurred the opposition of the Christian evangelicals who fear the scrutiny by government of their operations or the competitive role of government organization. Yet, if family stability is a necessary condition of societal stability, then the issue has to be directly confronted and answered, I believe, in support of the Bush proposals.

The second issue is foreign policy. The break-up of the Soviet Union has meant the end of the bi-polar world and the ways in which regions such as in the Middle East and Africa were pulled into the competitive orbits of the two powers. Yet the new world order, such as it is, is one of economic integration and political fragmentation, of globalization replacing the older international economy with a single world market for capital, currencies, goods and services. The national states are being fragmented by ethnic, religious, cultural or linguistic entities who seek to assert their homogeneous identities, as in the former Soviet Union. In Europe they are being fragmented by the demands for cultural autonomy, as in the breakup of the United Kingdom, Belgium, and Spain.[37]

What role, then, will the United States as the major, if not the sole military and technological hegemon, play? One course would be greater participation in the United Nations, or some such cooperative alliance, as with the nascent European Union. The other would be a unilateralism, in which the United States defines its policies primarily by national interest and power (as in withdrawing from the Kyoto global warming treaty) or creating a missile shield and jettisoning the Anti-Ballistic Military treaty with Russia. Though in the first hundred days of the Bush administration no clear policy has been enunciated, the indications are that the United States will favor a unilateral stance.

All of these are tentative judgments from the signs and portents of the first hundred days. Two conditions can change these. One, a set of contingencies, is the possibility of military conflicts and confrontations in different parts of the world, especially the Middle East and Asia. The second is the state of the economy. The balloon of the euphoric New Economy and the stock market for the dot.coms has been punctured. The onset of a recession, and the question of who is hurt most badly, would change the nature of domestic politics and with it the return to a class politics of a new kind. The trade union movement, concentrated as it is in manufacturing, transportation, government and low-paying services, is weak. The newer areas have been in Silicon Valley and the new technology, with its spirited individuals and high-paying jobs. If those are the areas of new depression, then there might be a second coming, and a different political story would begin to unfold.

JUNE 2001

Notes

1. Richard Hofstadter, *The Progressive Historians* (New York: Knopf, 1968), p. 42.

2. Horowitz has written a long, monographic 85-page survey of Gumplowicz's work and thought in his Introduction to Ludwig Gumplowicz's *Outlines of Sociology* (New York: Paine-Whitman publishers, 1963).

3. Charles H. Page, *Class and American Sociology: From Ward to Ross* (New York: The Dial Press, 1940), pp. 6–7, 103.

4. Joseph R. Gusfield, *Symbolic Crusade: Status Politics and the American Temperance Movement* (Urbana: University of Illinois Press, 1961), esp. pp. 16–17.

5. Since for Weber the *market* defines the economically-related groups, these are of several kinds: debtors/creditors; tenant/landlords; workers, selling their labor power, and employers. Class conflicts will vary in accordance with the centrality of the economic relations. In ancient Greece, for example, the main conflicts were between debtors on the land and creditors, resulting, until its abolition by Solon, in debt slavery. In the U.S. debtor/creditors have been the major source of agrarian conflicts. With the rise of the industrial societies, the worker/employer relation became central.

One needs, too, to clarify a confusion in using Weber's concepts of *stände* and *class*. In standard German usage, class was restricted to employers and workers only, while white-collar workers, or craftsmen, or peasants, or even the older nobility, would never be referred to in terms of class, but as *stände*. Thus, the growth of the white-collar and salaried class in Germany, in the nineteen twenties, was referred to (by Lederer and Marshak, among others) as the "*neue mittelstand*." For a relevant discussion, see Ralf Dahrendorf, *Class and Class Conflict in an Industrial Society* (Stanford University Press, 1959), pp. 6–7.

6. Max Weber, *Economy and Society* (Bedminster Press, 1968), Vol. I, Chapter IV, "Status Groups and Classes," pp. 302–309.

Nietzsche's use of the notion of *ressentiment* is found most directly in *The Genealogy of Morals,* First Essays, sections 8, 10, 14. The sociological use of the term was expanded by Max Scheler, in *Ressentiment,* translated by Wolfgang Holdheim, ed., with an introduction by Lewis A. Coser (New York: The Free Press), 1961.

There is a knotted effort to apply the concept to various religious and social groups by Svend Ranulf, in *Moral Indignation and Middle Class Psychology,* first printed in Denmark in 1938, and reprinted in 1964, with a preface by Harold Lasswell, by Shocken Books.

7. Karl Mannheim, "Essays on Sociology and Social Psychology," edited by Paul Kecskemeti (London: Routledge & Kegan Paul, 1953), pp. 122–123; italics in the original. This essay was the forerunner of Mannheim's famous *Ideology and Utopia,* itself a collection of disparate essays (New York: Harcourt,Brace, 1936). For a discussion of the "development of the Sociology of knowledge," see the comprehensive essay by Paul Kecskemeti, in the introduction to the volume, Karl Mannheim, *Essays on the Sociology of Knowledge* (London: Routledge & Kegan Paul, 1952).

8. For a history of this complicated intellectual set of digressions, see my essay "The Misreading of Ideology: The Social Determination of ideas in Marx's Thought," in the *Berkeley Journal of Sociology,* 1990.

9. Georg Simmel, "The Web of Group Affiliations," in the volume containing his two long essays, *Conflict/ The Web of Group Affiliations* (The Free Press, 1955), p. 138. See also my discussion of The Macrosocial Units of Society, in my essay "Ethnicity and Social Change" in *The Winding Passage* (Transaction Publishers, 1991), pp. 193–198.

10. At one point, a group of Sephardic Jews in Brooklyn claimed such entitlement on the ground that they spoke Ladino, which is of Spanish origin. The government denied the claim, stating that they were primarily Jews, and not eligible for those considerations.

11. For an extended development of this argument, see my Afterword to the re-issue of *Marxian Socialism in the United States* (Cornell University Press, 1996).

12. These figures are from the Statistical Abstract of 1997, and reported in the Foreword 1999 of my book, *The Coming of Post-Industrial Society* (New York: Basic Books, pp. xv–xvi.

13. I have written of Guizot and the debates about the restoration of the old order, and the effect of these debates on Alexis de Tocqueville, in my essay, "Tocqueville at the Crossroads of History," in *The Tocqueville Review* (Winter, 2000).

14. Edmund Burke, *Reflections on the Revolution in France,* in *Burke's Politics,* edited by Ross J. S. Hoffman & Paul Levack (New York: Knopf, 1949), pp. 324–325 on the "men of letters" and p. 313 on "Religion as the basis of-civil society." The most comprehensive edition of the *Reflections* is *The Writings and Speeches of Edmund Burke,* Volume VIII, "The French Revolution 1790–1794," edited by L. G. Mitchell, Clarendon Press, Oxford, 1989.

15. The phrase appears in the preface of *For Lancelot Andrewes* (1928). A year before, Eliot had been received into the Church of England, and the homage to Lancelot Andrewes, a bishop who had been eminent in the formation of the Church, expressed Eliot's interest in Christian orthodoxy. Eliot expresses his preference for Andrewes, as against John Donne, "because he is the more pure, and because his bond was with the Church and tradition." See the essay on Lancelot Andrewes in Eliot's *Selected Essays* (New York: Harcourt Brace & World, 1964).

16. Peter Ackroyd, *T. S. Eliot, A Life* (New York: Simon & Schuster, 1984), p. 42. Interestingly, Ackroyd observes that Eliot's respect for communism was far greater than for fascism, and in his commentaries in his magazine *The Criterion,* he suggested that it might be the only practicable alternative to the Christian faith. As Ackroyd further writes: " . . . fascism offered a temporary emotional stimulus, especially for someone of Eliot's temperament, but unlike communism, it could not provide any objective set of values or principles. In distinction to [Wyndham] Lewis and [Ezra] Pound, whose aesthetic view of politics was such that they embraced the discipline and authority of fascism without properly understanding its implications, Eliot recognized very well that the reliance upon order and 'the state' alone was a form of escapism, a cover for unprincipled militarisms and nationalism. He was as skeptical of 'order' as he was of 'liberty.'" Ibid., p. 171.

On the relations between Eliot and Maurras, see also the discussion by Stephen Spender in *T. S. Eliot* (New York: Viking Press, Modern Masters series, 1975), pp. 226–228.

17. Lionel Trilling, *The Liberal Imagination* (New York: The Viking Press, 1950), pp. ix–x.

18. For a succinct but useful discussion of "New Humanism" see the essay by Stephen C. Brennan, in *The Johns Hopkins Guide to Literary Theory and Criticism,* edited by Michael Grodin and Charles Kreiswirth (Johns Hopkins Press, 1994), pp. 540–549.

19. See J. David Hoeveler, Jr., *Watch on the Right: Conservative Intellectuals in the Reagan Era* (University of Wisconsin Press, 1991). A more extensive volume is George Nash's *The Conservative Intellectual Movement in America* (Basic Books, 1976); a new edition with an added preface was published by the Intercollegiate Studies Institute in 1996.

For a discussion of the broad intellectual scene of the past thirty years, see my essay, "America's Cultural Wars," in *The Wilson Quarterly* (Summer, 1992).

The one new major liberal magazine to appear in recent years is *The American Prospect*, edited by Robert Kutner and Paul Starr. Originally a quarterly, it now appears as a handsome bi-weekly, subsidized by a foundation headed by Bill Moyers.

20. Quoted in Maurice Isserman and Michael Kazin, *America Divided, The Civil War of the 1960s* (New York: Oxford University Press, 2000). Isserman and Kazin cite as their source Paul Gottfried and Thomas Fleming, *The Conservative Movement* (Boston: Twayne, 1988), p. 10. Though Isserman and Kazin are of the Left, Gottfried and Fleming, it may be pointed out, have impeccable conservative, even reactionary credentials.

21. The confusion about the term "neo-conservative" was initiated by Peter Steinfels in his misleading book, *The Neo-Conservatives: The Men Who Are Changing American Politics*, who used the designation to characterize *The Public Interest* and its influence.

I was the co-founder with Irving Kristol of *The Public Interest*. It began in 1965 as a liberal periodical dealing entirely with domestic social policy. It was skeptical of the claims of the Great Society, not because of lack of sympathy with those aims, but out of the realization that these programs lacked grounding in social science data, and hard-headed analysis, and therefore needed criticism from that standpoint. It quickly attracted a number of like-minded individuals, such as Senator Daniel Patrick Moynihan, Nathan Glazer, James Q. Wilson, and Roger Starr. Its early contributors on economic policy included Robert M. Solow, Robert Heilbroner, Thomas Schelling, and the late Edward Kuh of M.I.T., who first proposed the "demo-grant" program in its pages that was taken over by George McGovern in his campaign proposals in 1972. It was so detailed in such policy proposals that Norman Podhoret, then a radical, in his autobiography *Making It* (1967) mocked *The Public Interest* "as a suggestion box for the capitalist class."

Podhoretz became a conservative initially on the issue of foreign policy, in particular because of his support of the right-wing Likud party in Israel. Jeane Kirkpatrick, who had been a staunch liberal, turned to the right on foreign policy, writing in a famous article in *Commentary* that authoritarian regimes could change their stripe, but totalitarian regimes could not, an article that prompted President Reagan to appoint Ms. Kirkpatrick as ambassador to the United Nations.

In his point of view and political choices, Kristol by 1972 had turned to the Republican Party. Respecting these differences, I found it difficult to continue editing the journal with him, and resigned as co-editor, stating that I regarded friendship as more important than ideology. Nathan Glazer, who succeeded me as co-editor, did not share Kristol's (or Podhoretz's) point of view on foreign policy. And Daniel P. Moynihan, of course, remained in the Democratic Party. But the journalistic prominence of Kristol, Podhoretz and

Kirkpatrick, and their active public presence, led to the use of the term "neoconservative" as a "movement" headed by these three. History is often defeated by publicity.

22. For a discussion of some of these disputes, see George H. Nash, *The Conservative Intellectual Movement in America* (1996, ibid.) Chapter ll. For the citation of Buckley, see p. 321.

23. Kristol's essay is reprinted in the anthology *Conservatism . . . from David Hume to the Present*, edited by Jerry Z. Muller (Princeton University Press, 1997), pp. 361–371

24. In Hoffman and Levack, (op. cit.) p. 304. First italics added, the second in the text.

25. For the relevant citations, see James Davison Hunter, *Before the Shooting Wars: Searching for Democracy in America's Culture Wars* (New York: The Free Press, 1994) p. 82; Yehoshua Arieli, *Individualism and Nationalism in American Democracy* (Harvard University Press, 1964) pp. 339-340; Arthur A. Ekirch, Jr., *Ideologies and Utopias: The Impact of the New Deal on American Thought* (Chicago: Quadrangle Books) pp. 58-59.

26. The figures are cited by S. M. Lipset, *Conflict and Consensus* (Transaction Books, 1985) p. 279.

27. I have drawn here from Maurice Isserman and Michael Kazin, *America Divided* (op. cit.) p. 243 and James Hunter Davison, *Before the Shooting Begins* (op. cit.) pp. 182–183.

28. Howard Brick, *Age of Contradiction* (New York: Twayne Publishers, 1998), p. 55.

29. I have taken this account from Isserman and Kazin (op. cit..) pp. 230–234. However the two authors do not mention the action of Tom Hayden, which I have added from my own reading of the events.

30. With all this, one forgets the darker side of the behavior of some of the troops in Vietnam: the derogatory term "geeks" used about the natives; the massacre of some villages, such as My Lai; the extraordinary acts of "fragging" in which exposed combat soldiers killed their own officers in order to retreat from combat—one of the first such episodes in the history of the American military—and the fact that much of the widespread drug use later in the United States came from American soldiers in Vietnam who could obtain cheap hash from Montagnard tribesmen, who grew the opium to raise money for the C.I.A.—all of these sober indications of the anger and fear of so many workingmen and Black soldiers pressed into combat while so many more middle-class individuals escaped those risks.

31. According to the Anti-Defamation League: The Christian Coalition is the most influential religious right organization of the 1990s, and is considered one of the best-organized political groups in the country. The Coalition claims 900,000 members . . . . It lists an additional 350,000 grassroots activists on its mailing rolls, volunteers in 50,000 precincts, full-time staff in 19 states, and a 'pro-family' database of 1.6 million. [*The Religious Right*, a publication of the Anti-Defamation League', 1994].

32. The "uncovering" of the Illuminati as the source of the world conspiracy was first raised by the John Birch Society in the 1950s, which also named Dwight Eisenhower as a member of the conspiracy.

33. The comments of Mr. Kristol and Mr. Abrams are reported in the Jewish newspaper *The Forward*, March 3, 2000.

34. *The New York Times*, February 29, 2000.

35. To declare a personal view: in respect to my faith, I am opposed to abortion (and the death penalty), as I believe in the sanctity of life. But recognizing also the consequences of a polarization that can inflame a society, I also believe therefore that abortion should be a private matter, so long as it is private and involves no public monies, monies taxed from individuals who find abortion morally abhorrent.

36. The Jeffords statement is printed in *The New York Times*. May 25, 2001.

37. I have elaborated these sets of issues in my essay, "The Resumption of History," the new Introduction to the re-publication of my book, *The End of Ideology* (Harvard University Press, 2000).

ACKNOWLEDGMENTS

Of the essays in the 1955 edition of this volume, "The Pseudo-Conservative Revolt," by Richard Hofstadter, was given as a lecture at Barnard College and printed in *The American Scholar,* Winter, 1954–55; "The Intellectuals and the Discontented Classes," by David Riesman and Nathan Glazer, appeared in *Partisan Review,* Winter, 1955; "The Revolt Against the Elite," by Peter Viereck, was given originally before the American Historical Association in December, 1954; and "Social Strains in America," by Talcott Parsons, appeared in the *Yale Review,* Winter, 1955.

Of the essays written in 1962, those by Daniel Bell, Richard Hofstadter, David Riesman, Talcott Parsons, and S. M. Lipset were written for this volume. Herbert Hyman's essay was adapted from a longer report on the climate of intolerance in England, based on a Guggenheim Foundation fellowship, and is published here for the first time. Alan Westin's essay is a revised version of two earlier essays, "The John Birch Society" and "The Radical Right and the Radical Left," which appeared in *Commentary,* August, 1961, and *Harper's,* April, 1962.

The editor wishes to thank Nathan Glazer and Seymour Martin Lipset for the discussions that led to the original volume; to William Phillips for aiding in the original publication; Mrs. Iris Lewin who provided secretarial help on the 1962 essays; and his wife, Pearl Kazin Bell who gave the manuscript her expert editorial scrutiny.

INDEX

Abrams, Mark, 269n., 302n.
Academic Mind, The, 152n., 273n.
Acheson, Dean, 106, 157, 162, 180, 222
Adams, Henry, 182, 190
Adams, John, 52, 187, 196, 200
Adams, John Quincy, 187, 196
Adenauer, Konrad, 187, 357n.
A.D.L. Bulletin, 438n., 445n.
Adorno, Theodore W., 77n., 91n., 358n., 411n.
Age of Reform, 312n.
Agrarian League, 53
Agrarian Socialism, 49n.
Aldrich, Winthrop W., 330n.
Alger, Jr., Frederick M., 329n.
Alien and Sedition Acts, 281, 315n.
Allen Bradley Co., 31n.
Alliance, Inc., 333n.
Almond, Edward M., 40
Almond, Gabriel, 280n., 299n., 306n., 318n.
Alsop brothers, 60, 122
America (magazine), 250n.
America First, 163, 167, 334
American Bar Assn., 264
American Civil Liberties Union, 304n.
American Coalition of Patriotic Soc., 250
American Council of Christian Laymen, 250
American Diplomacy, 1900–1950, 318n.
American Dreams, 282n.
American Enterprise Assn., 266
American Farm Bureau Fed., 264

American Fed. of Labor (AFL), 335n.
American Inquisitors, 25, 25n.
American Jewish League . . . , 256
American Jewish Yearbook, 59n.
American Journal of Sociology, 91n., 313n., 342n., 411n.
American Legion, 24, 166, 264, 337n.
American Medical Assn., 245, 264
American Mercury, 255, 445n.
American Opinion, 243, 250, 265
American Party, 310
American People and Foreign Policy, 318n.
American Political Science Review, 52n., 346n., 349n., 438n.
American Protective Assn., 310–11, 314, 311n.
American Retail Foundation, 252
American Scholar, 137n., 152n.
American Scientists . . . , 36n.
American Security Council, 4, 40
American Strategy, Inc., 40
American Strategy for the Nuclear Age, 6
American Style, 18n.
American Telephone & Telegraph, 249n.
American Ultras, 441n.
American Voter, 302n.
Americanism, 320–21. *See also* Fundamentalism; Loyalty; Nationalism